ADA Guide to

Dental Therapeutics

Second Edition

PUBLISHING ®

A Division of ADA Business Enterprises, Inc.

A Division of ADA Business Enterprises, Inc.

ADA Publishing
211 East Chicago Avenue
Chicago, Illinois 60611-2678

e-mail: adapub@ada.org
World Wide Web: http://www.ada.org

Chief Operating Officer and Publisher: Laura A. Kosden
Associate Publisher, Editorial: James H. Berry
Associate Publisher, Marketing and Operations: Gabriela Radulescu
Editorial Director: Lisbeth Maxwell
Director of Production: Beth Cox
Assistant Editors: Carol Dikelsky, Janyce Hamilton

The editor, authors and publisher of the ADA Guide to Dental Therapeutics have used care to confirm that the drugs and treatment schedules set forth in this book are in accordance with current recommendations and practice at the time of publication. As the science of dental therapeutics evolves, changes in drug treatment and use become necessary. The reader is advised to consult the package insert for each drug to consider and adopt all safety precautions before use, particularly with new and infrequently used drugs. The reader is responsible for ascertaining the U.S. Food and Drug Administration clearance of each drug and device used in his or her practice.

The editor, authors and publisher disclaim all responsibility for any liability, loss, injury or damage resulting directly or indirectly from the reader's use and application of the information in this book and make no representations or warranties with respect to such information, including the products described herein.

The editor, authors and publisher have produced this book in their individual capacities and not on behalf or in the interest of any pharmaceutical companies or state or federal agencies.

Many of the proprietary names of the products listed in this book are trademarked and registered in the U.S. Patent Office.

Printed by R.R. Donnelley & Sons Company, Chicago, Illinois 60610

Design and composition by Perolio, Inc.

ISBN 1-891748-01-7

Introduction

Dentists are prescribing more medications today than ever before. Patients seeking dental care are using a wide range of medications for medical problems. And both dentists and patients have choices to make about the variety of nonprescription products available for treating various disorders of the mouth.

Dentists are vocal about their need for a quick and accurate drug reference that is more than a dictionary and yet not a textbook of pharmacology. In response, the ADA published the first edition of the ADA Guide to Dental Therapeutics in 1998. The Guide was based on what dentists told us they needed to make their practices complete: concise and accurate information about the medications they use, information based on the science of pharmacology and organized by drug category in an easy-to-use tabular format. This second edition of the ADA Guide to Dental Therapeutics is expanded and updated and is the most comprehensive dental drug reference of its kind—the only one complete enough to bear the ADA name.

Every chapter in this new edition has been updated, and some have been completely rewritten. New authors have made significant contributions and revisions, especially in the areas of antibiotics and glucocorticoids. There are more than 30 new tables and two important new appendixes: one on the increasingly popular herbs and dietary supplements and another on drugs that cause photosensitivity.

As a practical chairside resource, the Guide offers easy access to crucial information about the drugs prescribed for and taken by dental patients—more than 800 generic drugs and more than 2,200 brand-name drugs in all. Every practicing dentist, dental educator, dental student and member of the dental team can profit from using this book. In addition, it serves as a useful resource in preparing for various board examinations.

A major strength of this book is that it was written by both academicians and clinicians in a team approach. Writers were selected because of their expertise and reputations in dental therapeutics. The content is as up to the minute as possible and is scheduled to be updated every two years. Readers and reviewers of the first edition gave us their comments, many of which were incorporated into this second edition. I encourage you to send us your comments so that the third edition can grow even more than the second.

The ADA Council on Scientific Affairs has reviewed all the material in this book, which is the only one of its kind that identifies medications—both prescription and nonprescription—that carry the ADA Seal of Acceptance. This Seal is designed to help the public and dental professionals make informed decisions about dental products. Backed by the knowledge of the Council, it provides an assurance that all products have met the ADA's standards of efficacy, safety and truth in advertising. Knowing which products carry the ADA Seal will enable all members of the dental team to select professional products knowledgeably and to discuss various toothpastes, mouthrinses and other nonprescription medications with their patients.

Key Features of the Book

The Guide is unlike any other drug book available, offering a host of benefits to the practicing dentist:

- clear, well-organized tables that offer rapid access to information on more than 900 drugs used in dentistry, including therapeutic products that carry the ADA Seal of Acceptance;
- crucial data on dosage, interactions, precautions and adverse effects at the reader's fingertips;
- brief but informative descriptions of drug categories that bridge the gap between drug handbooks and pharmacology texts;
- information on more than 1,100 drugs used in medicine, enabling dentists to communicate knowledgeably with other medical professionals about patients' medications and their dental side effects;
- a new, evidence-based overview of herbs and dietary supplements;
- a one-of-a-kind chapter on oral manifestations of systemic agents;
- an appendix on drugs that cause photosensitivity;
- a special section on drug-related issues that affect dental practice: substance abuse, tobacco-use cessation, infection control.

Drugs Used in Dentistry

This book is arranged in three sections. The first focuses on drugs prescribed primarily by dentists, so that the practitioner can readily prescribe them with a full understanding of their actions, adverse effects and interactions. It contains drug information essential to solving patients' dental problems. Dentists will be able to quickly locate dosages and, in italics, information of clinical significance (interactions, adverse effects, precautions and contraindications). Drugs and products that have received the ADA Seal of Acceptance are identified with a green star ⋆. The names of drugs available only in Canada are followed by the designation [CAN].

In Section I, each chapter is organized by

- description of the general category of drugs and the accepted indications;
- listings of specific drugs by generic and brand name—including adult and child dosages, forms and strengths;
- special dental considerations—drug interactions, pertinent laboratory value alterations, drug cross-sensitivities and effects on pregnant and nursing women, children, elderly patients and other patients with special needs;
- adverse effects and precautions, arranged by body systems;
- pharmacology;
- information for patient/family consultation.

If any of these categories or subcategories does not appear (for instance, laboratory value alterations), it is because it did not pertain to the particular type of drug or because there was no such information available.

In each chapter in Section I, the dosage information table (usually the first in the chapter) is based on the assumption that the dentist has determined—through taking a health history and interviewing the patient—that the patient is in general good health and is not taking any medications that may interact with the drug in question. Adverse effects and precautions/contraindications, which are listed under the heading "General," are arranged according to body systems and abbreviated as follows:

CV	cardiovascular
CNS	central nervous system
Endoc	endocrine
EENT	eye/ear/nose/throat
GI	gastrointestinal
GU	genitourinary
HB	hepatobiliary
Hema	hematologic
Integ	integumentary
Musc	musculoskeletal

Oral	oral
Renal	renal
Resp	respiratory

This book includes all ADA-accepted products in the various categories discussed. However, in some cases we have included only a representative sampling of products in a category—ADA-accepted or not. Inclusion of a particular product in no way indicates that it is superior to others.

Drugs Used in Medicine

Increasingly, dental patients are taking one or more prescription drugs. To assist the dentist, the second section of the book focuses on drugs prescribed primarily by physicians. It presents drug information in a more abbreviated form, emphasizing each drug's effect on dental diagnosis and treatment planning. The information here will help the dentist interact effectively with the patient's physician about the patient's medications, particularly when a modification of drug therapy is in question. Helpful dosage ranges enable dentists to anticipate potential side effects in patients at the upper end of the dosage range.

Drug Issues in Dental Practice

The book's third section focuses on issues related to dental pharmacology that affect the dentist's practice: patients with addictions, cessation of tobacco use, infection control, legal considerations in using drugs in dentistry. As part of the community of practitioners interested in patients as people and not just as "teeth and gums," dentists can use the information discussed here as building blocks for a successful and expanding practice. A highlight of this section is the chapter on oral manifestations of systemic medications. The topics presented in Section III are not addressed in most dental drug handbooks.

Appendixes and Index

The book features several appendixes, including new additions covering herbs and dietary supplements and drugs that cause photosensitivity.

An expanded index—which includes generic and brand-name drugs and highlights dental indications in bold—makes it even easier to find information quickly.

Acknowledgments

I wish to acknowledge the pioneering efforts of contributors to the ADA's Accepted Dental Therapeutics (which ceased publication in 1984), who laid the foundation for this book. I also wish to thank the authors, who applied their time and their broad talents generously to this task. I am grateful to my dean, Louis Goldberg, D.D.S., Ph.D., and to my wife, Marilyn, both of whom gave me the time and support I needed to serve as editor. The authors and I thank the following people, who lent us their editorial or administrative assistance: my son, Sebastian J. Ciancio, M.D.; Barbara Collier; Harold L. Crossley, D.D.S., Ph.D.; Hazel Dean; Judy Dorsheimer; Richard Hall, D.D.S., M.D., Ph.D.; Michael Lynch, D.M.D., Ph.D.; Mary E. Martin, D.D.S., M.Ed.; Matshediso Matome, Ph.D.; Santos Robles; Victor Sandoval, D.D.S., M.P.H.; Christine Ulrich, B.S. The talents and commitment of copyeditor Helen Walker, typesetter/ designer Kelly Mahoney and indexer Lillian Rodberg enhanced the quality of our finished product. Finally, a special thanks is due to the staff of ADA Publishing: to Publisher Laura Kosden for her visionary approach to this book; to Associate Publisher, Editorial, James Berry for his tireless support; to the staff for helping me through the months of preparation; and especially to Editorial Director Lisbeth Maxwell for her patience, persistence and devotion to excellence, and to her assistant editors, Carol Dikelsky and Janyce Hamilton, whose abilities and dedication helped make this a dental therapeutics book of true distinction.

Sebastian G. Ciancio, D.D.S.
State University of New York at Buffalo

Editorial Board

Editor

Sebastian G. Ciancio, D.D.S.
Professor and Chair
Department of Periodontics and Endodontics
Adjunct Professor of Pharmacology
Director, Center for Dental Studies
State University of New York at Buffalo
Buffalo, New York

Authors

Kenneth H. Burrell, D.D.S., S.M.
Senior Director
Council on Scientific Affairs
American Dental Association
Chicago, Illinois

B. Ellen Byrne, R.Ph., D.D.S., Ph.D.
Associate Professor
Department of Endodontics
School of Dentistry
Medical College of Virginia
Virginia Commonwealth University
Richmond, Virginia

Jarvis T. Chan, D.D.S., Ph.D.
Professor of Pharmacology
Vice Chair, Department of Basic Sciences
University of Texas Dental Branch
Houston, Texas

Adriane Fugh-Berman, M.D.
Assistant Clinical Professor
Department of Health Care Sciences
George Washington University School
    of Medicine and Health Sciences
Washington, D.C.

Steven Ganzberg, D.M.D., M.S.
Assistant Professor of Anesthesiology
College of Dentistry
College of Medicine and Public Health
Director, Pain Management Program
College of Dentistry
The Ohio State University
Columbus, Ohio

Michael Glick, D.M.D.
Professor of Oral Medicine
Director, Programs for Medically
    Complex Patients
University of Pennsylvania School
    of Dental Medicine
Philadelphia, Pennsylvania

Martin S. Greenberg, D.D.S.
Professor and Chair, Oral Medicine
Associate Dean, Hospital Affairs
University of Pennsylvania School
    of Dental Medicine
Philadelphia, Pennsylvania

Margaret M. Grisius, D.D.S.
Assistant Professor of Oral Medicine
University of Pennsylvania School
    of Dental Medicine
Philadelphia, Pennsylvania

Continued on next page

Authors (cont.)

Jed Jacobson, D.D.S., M.S., M.P.H.
Assistant Dean for Community and
    Outreach Programs
Associate Professor of Oral Medicine
School of Dentistry
University of Michigan
Ann Arbor, Michigan

Linda Kittelson, M.S., R.N., C.S.A.D.C.
Manager
Dentist Well-Being Programs
American Dental Association
Chicago, Illinois

Alan M. Kramer, M.D.
Clinical Assistant Professor of Medicine
University of California, San Francisco
San Francisco, California

Stanley F. Malamed, D.D.S.
Professor of Anesthesia and Medicine
School of Dentistry
University of Southern California
Los Angeles, California

Angelo J. Mariotti, D.D.S., Ph.D.
Chair
Section of Periodontology
College of Dentistry
The Ohio State University
Columbus, Ohio

Robert E. Mecklenburg, D.D.S., M.P.H.
Coordinator
Tobacco and Oral Health Initiatives
Tobacco Control Research Branch
National Cancer Institute
Bethesda, Maryland

Chris H. Miller, Ph.D.
Professor of Oral Microbiology
Director of Infection Control Research
    and Services
Associate Dean for Research and
    Graduate Education
School of Dentistry
Indiana University
Indianapolis, Indiana

Brian C. Muzyka, D.M.D.
Associate Professor of Oral Medicine
Louisiana State University School of Dentistry
Director, Oral Medicine Residency Program
Louisiana State University Health Science Center
New Orleans, Louisiana

Sol Silverman Jr., M.A., D.D.S.
Professor of Oral Medicine
School of Dentistry
University of California, San Francisco
San Francisco, California

Martha Somerman, D.D.S., Ph.D.
William K. and Mary Anne Najjar
    Endowed Professor
Professor and Chair
Department of Periodontics/Prevention/Geriatrics
School of Dentistry
Professor of Pharmacology
School of Medicine
University of Michigan
Ann Arbor, Michigan

Leonard S. Tibbetts, D.D.S., M.S.D.
Private Practitioner
Arlington, Texas
Visiting Assistant Professor of Periodontics
University of Washington
Seattle, Washington

Kathleen M. Todd, J.D.
Associate General Counsel
Division of Legal Affairs
American Dental Association
Chicago, Illinois

Clay Walker, Ph.D.
Professor of Oral Biology
Periodontal Disease Research Center
Health Science Center
College of Dentistry
University of Florida
Gainesville, Florida

Jill Wolowitz, J.D., LL.M.
Chicago, Illinois

John A. Yagiela, D.D.S., Ph.D.
Professor and Chair
Division of Diagnostic and Surgical Sciences
School of Dentistry
Professor
Department of Anesthesiology
School of Medicine
University of California, Los Angeles
Los Angeles, California

Table of Contents

Section I. Drugs Used in Dentistry (cont.)

Section II. Drugs Used in Medicine: Treatment and Pharmacological Considerations for Dental Patients Receiving Medical Care

Section III. Drug Issues in Dental Practice

Appendixes and Index

Appendixes and Index (cont.)

Section I.

Drugs Used in Dentistry

Chapter 1.

Injectable and Topical Local Anesthetics

John A. Yagiela, D.D.S., Ph.D.

Injectable Local Anesthetics

Local anesthetics reversibly block neural transmission when applied to a circumscribed area of the body. Cocaine, the first local anesthetic (introduced in 1884), remains an effective topical agent, but it proved too toxic for parenteral use. Procaine, introduced in 1904, was the first practical local anesthetic for injection and contributed greatly to breaking the historic connection between dentistry and pain.

Vasoconstrictors are agents used in local anesthetic solutions to retard systemic absorption of the local anesthetic from the injection site. Although not active themselves in preventing neural transmission, vasoconstrictors such as epinephrine and related adrenergic amines can significantly increase the duration and even the depth of anesthesia. The vasoconstriction they produce also may be useful in reducing bleeding during intraoral procedures.

Chemistry and classification. Injectable local anesthetics consist of amphiphilic molecules; that is, they can dissolve in both aqueous and lipid environments. A lipophilic ring structure on one end of the molecule confers fat solubility, and a secondary or tertiary amino group on the other permits water solubility. Local anesthetics intended for injection are prepared commercially as the hydrochloride salt.

Two major classes of injectable local anesthetics are recognized: esters and amides. They are distinguished by the type of chemical bond joining the two ends of the drug molecules.

Early local anesthetics, such as cocaine and procaine, were esters. Most local anesthetics introduced since 1940 have been amides.

The use of injectable local anesthetics in dentistry is almost exclusively limited to amide-type drugs. In fact, no ester agent is currently being marketed in dental cartridge form in the United States. Given the number of local anesthetic injections administered in dentistry (conservatively estimated at more than 300 million in the United States annually), a drug with a minimal risk of allergy is desirable. Amide anesthetics offer a significantly lower risk of allergy than ester anesthetics. Conversely, amides also have a somewhat greater risk of systemic toxicity than do esters. However, as toxic reactions usually are dose-related, adherence to proper injection techniques—including the use of minimal volumes of anesthetic—minimizes this risk. Amide formulations have also proved more effective than esters for achieving intraoral anesthesia. Thus, amide local anesthetics, as used in dentistry, offer the fewest overall risks and the greatest clinical benefits.

Selecting a local anesthetic. The selection of a local anesthetic for use in a dental procedure is based on four criteria:

- duration of the dental procedure;
- requirement for hemostasis;
- requirement for postsurgical pain control;
- contraindication(s) to specific anesthetic drugs or vasoconstrictors.

Duration. Local anesthetic formulations intended for use in dentistry are categorized by their expected duration of pulpal anesthesia as short-, intermediate- and long-acting drugs.

- Short-acting drugs, which typically provide pulpal and hard tissue anesthesia for up to 30 min after submucosal infiltration: 2% lidocaine, 3% mepivacaine and 4% prilocaine.
- Intermediate-acting agents, which provide up to 60 min of pulpal anesthesia: 4% articaine with 1:100,000 or 1:200,000 epinephrine, 2% lidocaine with 1:50,000 or 1:100,000 epinephrine, 2% mepivacaine with 1:20,000 levonordefrin and 4% prilocaine with 1:200,000 epinephrine.
- Long-acting drugs, which last up to 8 h after nerve block anesthesia: 0.5% bupivacaine with 1:200,000 epinephrine and 1.5% etidocaine with 1:200,000 epinephrine.

For most clinical situations, an intermediate-acting formulation is appropriate. These agents are highly effective and have durations of action that can accommodate most intraoral procedures. The 4% prilocaine and 3% mepivacaine solutions, however, may be preferred for maxillary supraperiosteal injections when there is a need for pulpal anesthesia of only short duration. (The 2% lidocaine plain formulation cannot be recommended because pulpal anesthesia is not consistently achieved.) Long-acting local anesthetics are helpful for providing anesthesia of extended duration. Unfortunately, pulpal anesthesia after supraperiosteal injection is less reliable than with the intermediate-acting drugs, because the highly lipophilic long-acting drugs do not readily reach the superior dental nerve plexus.

Hemostasis. Lidocaine with epinephrine is the formulation usually administered to achieve temporary hemostasis in tissues undergoing treatment. Although the 1:50,000 strength of epinephrine provides little benefit over the 1:100,000 concentration with regard to the duration of local anesthesia, it can significantly decrease bleeding associated with periodontal tissue when given by local infiltration.

Postsurgical pain control. The bupivacaine and etidocaine formulations can help the sur-

gical patient remain pain-free for up to 8 h after treatment. These agents may be administered before the procedure to provide local anesthesia intraoperatively or afterward to maximize the duration of postsurgical pain relief.

Contraindications. True allergy is the only absolute contraindication to the use of any local anesthetic formulation. Although there is little evidence of cross-allergenicity among the amides, it is probably prudent to avoid amides with the greatest molecular similarity to the putative allergen. Lidocaine is most similar to prilocaine and etidocaine in structure, whereas mepivacaine is most similar to bupivacaine. If a sulfite preservative is the allergen, then the 3% mepivacaine and 4% prilocaine solutions without vasoconstrictor are the formulations of choice because they are free of sulfites.

These plain solutions also are indicated when the use of epinephrine and levonordefrin is not recommended. However, formulations containing 1:200,000 epinephrine may be considered when modest doses of vasoconstrictor are permissible and when the plain solutions might not provide anesthesia of sufficient depth or duration. (Specific contraindications and restrictions to vasoconstrictors are reviewed later in this chapter.)

Accepted Indications

Injectable local anesthetics are used to provide local or regional analgesia for surgical and other dental procedures.

They are also used for diagnostic or other therapeutic purposes via routes of administration specified in product labeling.

General Dosing Information

General dosing information is provided in Table 1.1. In addition, standard textbooks provide information on the appropriate dosage (both concentration and injection volume) of local anesthetic to be used for specific injection techniques and dental procedures.

Table 1.1

Injectable Local Anesthetics: Dosage and Prescribing Information*

Generic name	Brand name(s)	Max adult dosage	Max child dosage	PRC	Content/form
Articaine hydrochloride with epinephrine	Septocaine; Septanest N [CAN], Septanest SP [CAN], Ultracaine [CAN], Ultracaine Forte [CAN]	(7 mg/kg)	**Age < 4 y:** NE **Age 4-12 y:** 5 mg/kg)	B (estimated)	Articaine HCl, 40 mg/mL; epinephrine, 5, 10 µg/mL
Bupivacaine hydrochloride with epinephrine	Marcaine with Epinephrine ★	90 mg†	**Age < 12 y:** NE	C	Bupivacaine HCl, 5 mg/mL; epinephrine, 5 µg/mL
Etidocaine hydrochloride with epinephrine	Duranest with Epinephrine ★	8 (5.5) mg/kg up to 400 mg	NE	B	Etidocaine HCl, 15 mg/mL; epinephrine, 5 µg/mL
Lidocaine hydrochloride	Alphacaine, Xylocaine ★	4.5 mg/kg up to 300 mg	Same as adult (5 mg/kg)	B	20 mg/mL
Lidocaine hydrochloride with epinephrine	Alphacaine with Epinephrine, Lignospan Standard ★, Lignospan Forte ★, Octocaine with Epinephrine, Xylocaine with Epinephrine ★; Octocaine-100 [CAN], Octocaine-50 [CAN]	7 mg/kg up to 500 mg	Same as adult (4-5 mg/kg up to a maximum of 100-150 mg)	B	Lidocaine HCl, 20 mg/mL; epinephrine, 10, 20 µg/mL
Mepivacaine hydrochloride	Arestocaine, Carbocaine ★, Isocaine, Polocaine ★, Scandonest ★	6.6 mg/kg up to 400 mg	Same as adult (5-6 mg/kg up to a maximum of 270 mg)	C	30 mg/mL
Mepivacaine hydrochloride with levonordefrin	Arestocaine with Levonordefrin, Carbocaine with Neo-Cobefrin ★, Isocaine with Levonordefrin ★, Polocaine with Levonordefrin ★, Scandonest with Levonordefrin ★	6.6 mg/kg up to 400 mg	Same as adult (6.6 mg/kg up to a maximum of 180 mg)	C	Mepivacaine HCl, 20 mg/mL; levonordefrin, 50 µg/mL
Prilocaine hydrochloride	Citanest ★	8 mg/kg up to 600 mg	Same as adult	B	40 mg/mL
Prilocaine hydrochloride with epinephrine	Citanest Forte ★	8 mg/kg up to 600 (400) mg	Same as adult	B	Prilocaine HCl, 40 mg/mL; epinephrine, 5 µg/mL

★ indicates a drug bearing the ADA Seal of Acceptance.
[CAN] indicates a drug available only in Canada.
PRC: Pregnancy risk category.
NE: Not established.
*Dosages are the maximum recommended doses approved by the U.S. Food and Drug Administration. Dosages in parentheses are the generally more restrictive usual prescribing limits listed in the U.S. Pharmacopeia Dispensing Information. For conversion purposes, one cartridge delivers 1.8 mL of anesthetic solution (1.7 mL for articaine).
† The maximum dose for other (nondental) indications is 225 mg.

The dosage depends on
- the specific anesthetic technique and operative procedure;
- tissue vascularity in the area of injection;
- individual patient response.

In general, the dentist should administer the lowest concentration and volume of anesthetic solution that provide adequate anesthesia.

Maximum Recommended Doses

Table 1.1 lists the maximum recommended doses for local anesthetic formulations per procedure or appointment, as approved by the U.S. Food and Drug Administration (FDA). Additional anesthetic may be administered only after sufficient time is allowed for elimination of the initial dose.

Dosage Adjustments

The actual maximum dose for each patient must be individualized depending on his or her size, age and physical status; other drugs he or she may be taking; and the anticipated rate of absorption of the local anesthetic from the injected tissues. Reduced maximum doses are often indicated for pediatric and geriatric patients, patients who have serious illness or disability and patients who have medical conditions or are taking drugs that alter responses to local anesthetics or vasoconstrictors.

Table 1.1 presents specific limits for local anesthetic doses in pediatric patients.

Vasoconstrictors

A vasoconstrictor added to a local anesthetic may significantly prolong the anesthetic's duration of action by reducing blood flow around the injection site. This, in turn, may reduce the local anesthetic's peak plasma concentration and the risk of adverse systemic reactions.

Repeated injection of vasoconstrictors in local anesthetics also may decrease blood flow sufficiently to cause anoxic injury in the local tissue, leading to delayed wound healing, edema or necrosis. The use of local anesthetic solutions containing vasoconstrictors may be restricted or contraindicated in patients who have advanced cardiovascular disease or

who are taking medications that increase the activity of the vasoconstrictor.

Although there are no officially recognized maximum doses for vasoconstrictors when administered with local anesthesia, it is widely accepted that vasoconstrictor usage be minimized in patients with increased risk of vasoconstrictor toxicity. Because plasma concentrations of epinephrine measured in standing subjects are comparable to those achieved by the intraoral injection of two cartridges of lidocaine with 1:100,000 epinephrine (about 0.04 mg epinephrine) in reclining subjects, it is assumed that this dosage should be safe in the ambulatory patient with cardiovascular disease. Slow, careful injection with frequent aspiration attempts and avoidance of the 1:50,000 epinephrine formulation are additional precautions to take with the patient with reduced vasoconstrictor tolerance.

Special Dental Considerations

Drug Interactions of Dental Interest

Drug interactions and related problems involving local anesthetics (Table 1.2) and vasoconstrictors (Table 1.3) are potentially of clinical significance in dentistry.

Cross-Sensitivity

Table 1.4 describes potential cross-sensitivity considerations.

Special Patients

Pregnant and nursing women

Local anesthetics readily cross the placenta and enter the fetal circulation. Although retrospective investigations of pregnant women receiving local anesthesia during the first trimester of pregnancy have found no evidence of fetal toxicity, animal investigations indicate a potential for birth defects—albeit at enormous doses—with some local anesthetics.

Considerations of risk/benefit suggest that purely elective treatment be delayed until after delivery and that other dental care be performed, if possible, during the second trimester. Lidocaine and, probably, other

Table 1.2

Local Anesthetics: Possible Interactions With Other Drugs*

Drug taken by patient	Interaction with local anesthetics	Dentist's action
Amiodarone, cimetidine, β-adrenergic blocking agents (propranolol, metoprolol)	Hepatic metabolism of lidocaine and probably other amide local anesthetics may be depressed by competition for hepatic enzymes and possibly by decreased liver blood flow	Use local anesthetics cautiously, especially with regard to repeated dosing
Antidysrhythmic drugs, Class I (mexiletine, tocainide)	Additive CNS and cardiovascular depression	Use local anesthetics cautiously— as low a dose as possible to achieve anesthesia
CNS depressants: alcohols, antidepressants, antihistamines, antipsychotics, barbiturates, benzodiazepines, centrally acting antihypertensives and muscle relaxants, general anesthetics, other local anesthetics, opioids, parenteral magnesium sulfate	*Possible additive or supraadditive CNS and respiratory depression*	Consider limiting the maximum dose of local anesthetics, especially with opioids
Cholinesterase inhibitors: antimyasthenics, muscle paralysis reversal drugs, antiglaucoma agents, organophosphate insecticides	Antimyasthenic dosage may require adjustment because local anesthetic inhibits neuromuscular transmission May inhibit metabolism of ester local anesthetics	Consult with physician (dose reduction may be necessary) Use ester agents cautiously
Dapsone	May produce additive methemoglobinemia with prilocaine	Use prilocaine cautiously—as low a dose as possible to achieve anesthesia
Sulfonamides	Therapeutic effect may be blocked by ester local anesthetics that release para-aminobenzoic acid on hydrolysis	Avoid concurrent use of sulfonamides and ester local anesthetics

Italics indicate information of major clinical significance.
Avoid storing anesthetic cartridges in disinfectant solutions because leakage into anesthetic cartridge and injection into tissue may cause severe local tissue damage.

local anesthetics are distributed into breast milk; again, however, no problems with injected local anesthetics have been documented in humans.

Table 1.1 lists the FDA pregnancy category classifications for injectable local anesthetics used in dentistry.

Pediatric, geriatric and other special patients
Although there are some data to suggest that adverse reactions to local anesthetics may be more prevalent in pediatric and geriatric populations, studies involving mepivacaine and other local anesthetics have found no age-specific problem that would limit use. However, overdosage is more likely to occur in young children because of their small size and the commensurately low margin for error. Increased variability of response to the local anesthetic or vasoconstrictor is likely to be encountered in elderly patients and in those with significant medical problems. Lower maximum doses in these patients provide an extra margin of safety.

Table 1.3

Vasoconstrictors: Possible Interactions With Other Drugs

Drug taken by patient	Interaction with vasoconstrictors	Dentist's action
α-adrenergic blockers (phenoxybenzamine, prazosin), antipsychotic drugs (haloperidol, thioridazine)	Blockade of α-adrenergic receptors may lead to hypotensive responses to large doses of epinephrine	Use vasoconstrictors cautiously—as low a dose as feasible for the procedure
Cocaine	*Increases effects of vasoconstrictor; can result in cardiac arrest*	Avoid using vasoconstrictors in patient under the influence of cocaine
Digitalis glycosides (digoxin, digitoxin)	*Increase risk of cardiac dysrhythmias*	Use in consultation with physician
Hydrocarbon inhalation anesthetics (halothane, enflurane)	*Sensitization of the heart may lead to cardiac dysrhythmias*	Inform anesthesiologist of intended use of vasoconstrictors
Levodopa, thyroid hormones (levothyroxine, liothyronine)	Large doses of levodopa or thyroid hormone (beyond replacement amounts) may increase risk of cardiac toxicity	Use vasoconstrictors cautiously—as low a dose as feasible for the procedure
Maprotiline, tricyclic antidepressants (amitriptyline, doxepin, imipramine)	*May enhance the systemic effects of vasoconstrictor*	Avoid the use of levonordefrin or norepinephrine; use epinephrine cautiously—as low a dose as feasible for the procedure
Methyldopa, adrenergic neuronal blocking drugs (guanadrel, guanethidine, reserpine)	May enhance systemic responses to the vasoconstrictor	Use vasoconstrictors cautiously—as low a dose as feasible for the procedure
Nonselective β-adrenergic blockers (propranolol, nadolol)	*Blockade of β-adrenergic receptors in skeletal muscle may lead to hypertensive responses to the vasoconstrictor, especially epinephrine*	Monitor blood pressure after initial local anesthetic injection

Italics indicate information of major clinical significance.

Local anesthetics are less effective than normal in the presence of inflammation or infection. Strategies that may assist the clinician in achieving pain control include the use of nerve block techniques proximal to the affected tissue and intraosseous anesthesia.

Patient Monitoring: Aspects to Watch

- State of consciousness
- Respiratory status
- Cardiovascular status

Adverse Effects and Precautions

The incidence of adverse reactions to local anesthetic agents is low. Many reactions (headache, palpitation, tremor, nausea, dyspnea, hyperventilation syndrome, syncope) result from the perceived stress of injection and are not caused by the agents themselves. Toxic systemic reactions generally are associated with high plasma concentrations of the local anesthetic or vasoconstrictor, or both, after an accidental intravascular injection,

Table 1.4

Local Anesthetics: Potential Cross-Sensitivity With Other Drugs

A person with a sensitivity to	May also have a sensitivity to
Para-aminobenzoic acid (PABA) or paraben preservative	Procaine, chloroprocaine, benzocaine, butamben, tetracaine, other local anesthetic solutions containing paraben preservatives (as in multidose vials)
Any ester local anesthetic	Other ester local anesthetics
Any amide local anesthetic	Other amide local anesthetics (rarely)
Sulfites	Any local anesthetic with an adrenergic vasoconstrictor (sulfites are included with vasoconstrictors as antioxidants)

administration of drug in a manner that causes rapid absorption, administration of a true overdosage or selection of a drug formulation inappropriate for the specific patient. Idiosyncratic and allergic reactions account for a small minority of adverse responses. In addition, a small subset of asthmatic patients intolerant of inhaled or dietary sulfites may develop bronchospasm after injection of local anesthetic solutions containing sulfite antioxidants.

Systemic reactions to local anesthetics may occur immediately on administration or may be delayed for up to 30 min or more. Oxygen, resuscitative equipment and drugs necessary to treat systemic emergencies must be immediately available whenever a local anesthetic is administered. The adverse effects listed in Tables 1.5 and 1.6 apply to all routes of administration.

Pharmacology

Local Anesthetics

Local anesthetics bind to sodium channels in the nerve membrane and prevent the entry of sodium ions in response to the membrane's depolarization. Propagation of the action potential is inhibited in the area of injection, and nerve conduction fails when an adequate length of nerve is exposed to a sufficient concentration of local anesthetic. Nerve conduc-

tion is restored as the anesthetic diffuses away from the injection site and is absorbed into the systemic circulation. Systemic effects, should they occur, are largely the result of the local anesthetic's inhibiting other excitable tissues. Systemic reactions are minimized when metabolism of the local anesthetic is able to inactivate the drug as it is absorbed into the bloodstream.

The rate of absorption of a local anesthetic is governed by several factors, including the drug, its concentration and dose, the vascularity of the injection site and the presence of a vasoconstrictor. Generally, peak concentrations are achieved in 10 to 30 min.

Most amide anesthetics are metabolized in the liver. Prilocaine is unusual in that it is metabolized in the kidneys to some extent.

Most esters are hydrolyzed by plasma esterase to inactive products; some metabolism also occurs in the liver. Although classified as an amide local anesthetic, articaine is inactivated by plasma esterase, which cleaves a vital side chain from the drug.

Small amounts of local anesthetics (2%-20%) and the various metabolites eventually are excreted into the urine.

Vasoconstrictors

Epinephrine, levonordefrin and other adrenergic amine vasoconstrictors help retard absorption of the local anesthetic by stimulat-

Table 1.5

Local Anesthetics: Adverse Effects, Precautions and Contraindications

Body system	Adverse effects	Precautions/contraindications
General	Allergic reactions, including contact dermatitis, skin rash, urticaria, erythema, itching, swelling of injection site, lips, tongue, eyelids and throat; may be accompanied by nausea with or without vomiting; much more likely to occur with esters than with amides Serious anaphylactoid reactions, including shock (rare) Numbness and tingling possible in area affected by injection; long-lasting or permanent paresthesia (rare)	*Inflammation or infection in the region of injection or in the area to be anesthetized may decrease or eliminate anesthetic effect* *Contraindicated in patients who have history of drug sensitivity to the anesthetic being considered for use, to any preservative or other component of the anesthetic solution and to chemically related agents; it is not known whether a small test dose can predict the risk of allergic reaction*
CV	Cardiovascular depression may be caused by excessive doses of local anesthetics, especially bupivacaine and etidocaine, but is usually secondary to respiratory depression; if not treated promptly, may cause or worsen hypoxia and acidosis and may lead to heart block and cardiac arrest	*Cardiovascular disease or impairment, especially serious forms of heart block and hypotension, may increase responsiveness to the cardiovascular depressant effects of local anesthetics*
CNS	Stimulation, including anxiety, minor twitching and tonic-clonic convulsions *(especially in children)*; may be transient after intravascular injection or administration of large toxic doses Depression, including drowsiness, unconsciousness and respiratory depression; may follow initial stimulant phase or occur by itself *(especially in children* and with lidocaine)	None of significance to dentistry
GI	Nausea, vomiting	None of significance to dentistry
GU	None of significance to dentistry	Local anesthetic metabolites may accumulate in patients with renal disease
Hema	Methemoglobinemia, *common with prilocaine overdose*, but rarely observed with other local anesthetics; cyanosis, symptomless with mild reactions, possibly accompanied by respiratory distress, tachycardia, headache, fatigue, dizziness and cardiopulmonary collapse	*Methemoglobinemia, congenital or acquired, contraindicates the use of prilocaine*
HB	None of significance to dentistry	Any condition that involves decreased hepatic blood flow or function (congestive heart failure, cirrhosis, other hepatic disorders) may impair amide metabolism in the liver Decreased synthesis of plasma cholinesterase may reduce ester metabolism
Oral	Trismus after nerve block injection (inferior alveolar, posterior superior alveolar nerves)	None of significance to dentistry

Italics indicate information of major clinical significance.

Table 1.6

Vasoconstrictors: Adverse Effects, Precautions and Contraindications

Body system	Adverse effects	Precautions/contraindications
General	Asthma and other allergiclike reactions may be caused by the sulfite antioxidant used to prevent oxidation of the vasoconstrictor Local tissue damage; ischemia from decreased blood flow and increased oxygen demand may lead to delayed healing, edema or necrosis of injected tissue	History of nonallergic sulfite sensitivity, especially in systemic corticosteroid-dependent patient, may increase risk of asthmatic reaction Multiple injections at the same tissue site increase likelihood of local tissue damage *Contraindicated in patients with history of true allergic reaction to sulfites*
CV	Cardiac stimulation; may result in increased blood pressure, headache, palpitation, tachycardia, dysrhythmias, angina pectoris and heart attack Peripheral vasoconstriction; may result in acute hypertension and reflex bradycardia, dysrhythmias, angina pectoris, heart attack and stroke	Vasoconstrictor may acutely lower plasma potassium concentration in hypokalemic patient, increasing potential for dysrhythmias *Cardiac defects (aortic stenosis, septal hypertrophy), disease (coronary atherosclerosis) or dysrhythmias (atrial fibrillation, ventricular dysrhythmias) increase potential for cardiac toxicity* *Cardiovascular toxicity is more likely in patients with poorly controlled hypertensive disease, pheochromocytoma or uncontrolled hyperthyroidism, or from interaction with antihypertensive medications* Exaggerated vascular responsiveness in patients with peripheral vascular disease may lead to hypertension or hypoxic injury to local tissues
CNS	CNS stimulation, including anxiety, nervousness, restlessness, tremor	None of significance to dentistry
GI	Nausea, vomiting	None of significance to dentistry
Resp	Dyspnea, pulmonary edema	None of significance to dentistry

Italics indicate information of major clinical significance.

ing α-adrenergic receptors in the local vasculature. The resultant reduction in tissue blood flow gives the local anesthetic more time to reach its site of action in the nerve membrane.

Systemic effects of vasoconstrictors are associated with stimulation of both α- and β-adrenergic receptors. The intensity and duration of these effects parallel the rate of absorption of the vasoconstrictor from the injection site. Stimulation of β receptors results in cardiac stimulation and vasodilation in skeletal muscle (β$_2$ receptors only). Stimulation of α receptors causes constriction of resistance arterioles throughout the body as well as capacitance veins in the legs and abdomen, which increases peripheral vascular resistance and venous return to the heart. Both α- and β-receptor effects contribute to the potential for cardiac dysrhythmias.

The adrenergic vasoconstrictors used in dentistry are quickly inactivated (plasma half-life of 1-2 min) by the enzyme catechol-O-methyltransferase. Additional metabolism of epinephrine by monoamine oxidase may occur, and the products are then excreted in the urine.

Patient Advice

- Injury to the anesthetized tissues may occur without any resulting sensation.
- To prevent injury, patients should not test for anesthesia by biting the lip or tongue, nor should they eat or chew anything until the anesthetic effect has dissipated.
- Children should be warned not to bite their lip or tongue and be monitored by their parents to prevent injury.

Suggested Readings

Daublander M, Muller R, Lipp MD. The incidence of complications associated with local anesthesia in dentistry. Anesth Prog 1997;44(4):132-41.

Jastak JT, Yagiela JA, Donaldson D. Local anesthesia of the oral cavity. Philadelphia: Saunders; 1995.

Malamed SF. Handbook of local anesthesia. 4th ed. St. Louis: Mosby–Year Book; 1996.

Moore PA. Adverse drug interactions associated with local anesthetics, sedatives and anxiolytics. JADA 1999;130(4):541-54.

Yagiela JA. Adverse drug interactions in dental practice: interactions associated with vasoconstrictors. JADA 1999;130(5):701-9.

Topical Local Anesthetics

Topical local anesthetic preparations used on oral mucosa differ in several respects from injectable preparations. Topical agents are selected for their ability to penetrate the oral mucosa and depend on diffusion to reach their site of action. Many of the anesthetics effective for nerve block or infiltration do not cross the mucosa adequately and, therefore, are not used for topical anesthesia.

In contrast to their injectable counterparts, topical ester-type agents are important for producing anesthesia, and some drugs used for mucosal anesthesia are neither esters nor amides. Life-threatening allergic reactions are extremely unlikely with topical anesthetics, regardless of type, and the inclusion of paraben preservatives in some topical amide formulations reduces the disparity in risk of allergy among these preparations.

Topical anesthetics are manufactured in a variety of forms. Gels, viscous gels and ointments are best used to limit the area of coverage of the topical anesthetic; aerosol sprays and solution rinses are best used for widespread application; lozenges, pastes and film-forming gels are specifically formulated to provide prolonged pain relief.

Several drugs used as topical anesthetics are so insoluble in water that they cannot be prepared in aqueous solutions. They are soluble in alcohol, propylene glycol, polyethylene glycol, volatile oils and other vehicles suitable for surface application. Included in this group of anesthetics are benzocaine and lidocaine base. The poor water solubility of benzocaine in particular makes it safe for topical use on abraded or lacerated tissue.

To facilitate diffusion, the concentration of anesthetic used for surface application usually is much higher than that of injectable preparations. As a consequence, the potential toxicity of these preparations can be significant if large quantities are absorbed or even ingested. Systemic absorption of some topical anesthetics applied to the mucosa can be rapid, and blood concentrations approaching those with intravenous infusion may be achieved with tetracaine, depending on the area of coverage and method of application.

The rate of onset for topical anesthesia varies from 30 s to 5 min, depending on the

Table 1.7

Topical Anesthetics: Duration of Action

Drug	Duration of anesthetic action
Benzocaine	10-20 min
Cocaine	20-40 min
Dyclonine	20-40 min
Lidocaine	10-20 min*
Tetracaine	20-60 min

*Duration can be extended up to 45 min if lidocaine transoral delivery patch is applied for 15 min.

anesthetic agent. Optimum effectiveness may be delayed, depending on the preparation. The mucosa should be dried before application to improve local uptake. The duration of topical anesthesia is generally shorter than with injected anesthesia. Table 1.7 indicates the approximate durations of action of the various topical anesthetics for mucosal anesthesia.

An occlusive dressing preventing the loss of agent can extend the duration; removing the residual agent and rinsing the mouth can shorten it. Topical preparations do not contain adrenergic vasoconstrictors.

Generally, mucosal anesthesia is only about 2 mm deep and is poor or nonexistent in the hard palate. Lidocaine and prilocaine prepared together in a eutectic mixture have been shown to improve anesthetic depth; however, no preparation for intraoral use has been marketed at this time. A mucoadhesive patch containing lidocaine—DentiPatch Lidocaine Transoral Delivery System—also has shown increased efficacy. It is applied directly to the mucosa in the area where anesthesia is desired so that the lidocaine's effect is maximized and the flow and dilution of the medication are limited. Anesthesia begins in 2.5 min, but the patch can be left in place for up to 15 min to increase the effect. Site-specific topical anesthesia additionally can be obtained with the use of a solid gel patch containing 18% benzocaine (Topicale GelPatch). The patch can be trimmed and shaped to fit the intended target. Anesthesia begins in about 30 sec and is maintained as the patch dissolves during the next 20 min.

Accepted Indications

Topical local anesthetics are used to provide mucosal analgesia before local anesthetic injection; to facilitate dental examination, the taking of radiographs and other relatively noninvasive dental procedures by minimizing pain and the gag reflex; and to provide temporary symptomatic relief of toothache, oral lesions and wounds, as well as irritation caused by dentures and other appliances.

Additional uses for diagnostic and therapeutic purposes are described in product labeling.

General Dosing Information

The dosage of topical anesthetics depends on the anesthetic preparation selected, the area to be anesthetized, the ability to maintain the anesthetic agent on the area of application, the vascularity of the administration site and the patient's age, size and health status. Physical removal of the anesthetic and rinsing of the mouth once the need for topical anesthesia has passed preclude further absorption of the drug.

Maximum Recommended Doses

Table 1.8 lists the usual dose and the maximum recommended dose for topical anesthetic formulations per application and, where appropriate or available, the application interval.

Dosage Adjustments

The actual maximum dose for each patient must be individualized depending on his or her size, age and physical status; other drugs he or she may be taking; and the anticipated rate of absorption of the topical anesthetic from the application site. Reduced maximum doses are often indicated for pediatric and geriatric patients, people who have serious illness or disability and patients who have medical conditions or are taking drugs that alter responses to topical anesthetics.

Specific limits for topical anesthetic use in pediatric patients appear in Table 1.8.

Special Dental Considerations

Drug Interactions of Dental Interest

Drug interactions and related problems involving topical anesthetics are in general the same as those listed in Table 1.2. Interactions specific to cocaine (rarely used in dentistry) are listed in Table 1.9.

Cross-Sensitivity

The potential for cross-sensitivity of topical local anesthetics is addressed in Table 1.4.

Table 1.8

Topical Anesthetics: Dosage and Prescribing Information*

Generic name	Brand name(s)	Adult dosage	Max adult dosage	Child dosage	PRC	Content/form
Benzocaine	**Aerosol:** Americaine, Hurricane ★, Super-Dent ★, Topex ★ **Film-forming gel:** Oratect, Zilactin-B **Gel:** Americaine Anesthetic Lubricant, Anbesol (several forms), Anbocaine, Baby Orabase, ComfortCaine, Gingicaine ★, Hurricaine ★, Numzident, Num-Zit, Orajel (several forms), Rid-A-Pain Dental, SensoGARD Canker Sore Relief, Super-Dent ★, Topex ★, Topicale ★, Xylonor, Zilactin-Baby; Topicaine [CAN] **Gel patch:** Topicale GelPatch **Lozenges:** Children's Chloraseptic, Spec-T Sore Throat Anesthetic **Ointment:** Benzodent ★, Cora-Caine ★, Dentapaine, Topicale ★ **Paste:** Orabase-B with Benzocaine ★ **Solution:** Anbesol Maximum Strength, Dent-Zel-Ite, Gingicaine ★, Hurricaine ★, Kank-a ★, Num-Zit Lotion, Topex ★, Topicale ★; Baby Oragel [CAN], Dentocaine [CAN], Oragel [CAN]	**Aerosol:** 1-s spray **Lozenges:** 10-mg lozenge q 2 h or 5-mg lozenge q h **Other forms:** Amount needed to cover area to be anesthetized, up to qid	NE	**Most forms:** Dosage must be individualized up to 2 y of age (6 y for paste) **Lozenges:** 5-mg lozenge q 2 h for ages ≥ 2 y **Ointment:** Dosage not established	C	**Aerosol:** 200 mg/mL **Film-forming gel:** 100, 150 mg/mL **Gel:** 63, 75, 100, 150, 180, 200 mg/mL **Gel patch (2 cm long × 1 cm wide × 1 mm thick):** 36 mg/patch **Lozenges:** 5, 10 mg **Ointment:** 161, 200 mg/mL **Paste:** 200 mg/mL **Solution:** 2, 50, 200 mg/mL; 65 [CAN], 75 [CAN] mg/mL
Benzocaine and menthol	**Lozenges:** Chloraseptic	1 lozenge q 2 h	U	**Age ≤ 2 y:** Dosage must be individualized	C	Benzocaine, 6 mg; menthol, 10 mg
Benzocaine and phenol	**Gel:** Anbesol Regular Strength; Anbesol [CAN] **Solution:** Anbesol Regular Strength; Anbesol Maximum Strength [CAN], Anbesol [CAN]	Amount needed to cover area to be anesthetized, up to qid	U	**Age ≤ 2 y:** Dosage must be individualized	C	**Gel:** benzocaine, 63 mg/mL, 64 [CAN] mg/mL; phenol, 0.5% **Solution:** benzocaine, 63 mg/kg, 65 [CAN] mg/kg; 200 [CAN] mg/kg; phenol, 0.5%, 0.45% [CAN]

Drug	Product/Brand	Usual Dosage	Maximum Dose	Child/Special Dosage	PRC	Available Forms
Benzocaine, butamben and tetracaine hydrochloride	**Aerosol, gel, ointment and solution:** Cetacaine ★	**Aerosol:** 1-s spray **Other forms:** Amount needed to cover area to be anesthetized	**Aerosol:** 2-s spray **Other forms:** 1 mL (20 mg tetracaine)	NE	C	Benzocaine, 140 mg/mL; butamben, 20 mg/mL; tetracaine HCl, 20 mg/mL
Cocaine hydrochloride†	**Powder, solution and tablets:** (generic)	**Solution:** 1% to 4% given by spray, instillation or topical application	400 mg	**Age < 6 y:** NE **Age ≥ 6 y:** Dosage must be individualized	C	**Powder:** bulk chemical **Solution:** 40, 100 mg/mL **Tablets:** 135 mg
Dyclonine hydrochloride‡	**Lozenges:** Sucrets	**Lozenges:** 1 lozenge q 2 h	NE	NE (exception: 1.2-mg lozenge for ages ≥ 2 y)	C	**Lozenges:** 1.2, 2, 3 mg
Lidocaine	**Aerosol:** Xylocaine **Ointment:** Xylocaine ★ **Patch:** DentiPatch **Solution:** Xylocaine ★	**Aerosol:** 2 sprays (20 mg) per quadrant **Ointment:** Amount to cover area to be anesthetized **Patch:** 1 application **Solution:** 1 application, 50-200 mg	**Aerosol:** 3 sprays (30 mg) per quadrant q 30 min **Ointment:** 5 g (250 mg lidocaine base)/dose or 20 g/day **Solution:** Up to 250 mg q 3 h	**Aerosol:** 3 mg/kg **Patch:** Safety and effectiveness NE for ages < 12 y **Other forms:** 4.5 mg/kg	B	**Aerosol:** 10 mg/metered spray **Ointment:** 50 mg/mL **Patch (2 cm long × 1 cm wide × 2 mm thick):** 46.1 mg/patch **Solution:** 25, 50 mg/mL
Lidocaine hydrochloride	**Oral topical solution:** Xylocaine Viscous ★ **Solution:** Xylocaine ★	**Oral topical solution:** q 3 h **Solution:** 1 application, 40-200 mg	4.5 mg/kg up to 300 mg q 3 h	**Oral topical solution:** 25 mg up to age 3 y; 4.5 mg/kg for ages ≥ 3 y **Solution:** Dosage must be individualized	B	**Oral topical solution:** 20 mg/mL **Solution:** 40 mg/mL
Tetracaine [CAN]	**Aerosol:** Supracaine	2 sprays (1.4 mg) per site	20 mg (~28 sprays)	NE	C	**Aerosol:** 0.7 mg/metered spray

★ indicates a drug bearing the ADA Seal of Acceptance.
[CAN] indicates a drug available only in Canada.
PRC: Pregnancy risk category.
NE: Not established.
U: Unavailable.
* Dosages are the maximum recommended doses approved by the U.S. Food and Drug Administration or listed in the USPDI.
† Cocaine is a Schedule II drug and rarely used in dentistry because there are safer alternatives.
‡ The solution form of dyclonine hydrochloride is no longer marketed in the United States.

Table 1.9

Cocaine: Possible Interactions With Other Drugs

Drug taken by patient	Interaction with cocaine	Dentist's action
Monoamine oxidase inhibitors (furazolidone, phenelzine)	*May increase stimulant effects of cocaine*	Avoid use of cocaine within 2 w of last use of monoamine oxidase inhibitor
Sympathomimetic drugs (epinephrine, levonordefrin, dopamine)	*Effects of the sympathomimetic drug are increased*	Avoid concurrent use of cocaine and sympathomimetic drugs
Digitalis glycosides (digoxin, digitoxin), tricyclic antidepressants (amitriptyline, doxepin, imipramine), nitrates (nitroglycerin, isosorbide dinitrate)	Risk of cardiac toxicity is increased	Use cautiously and in restricted doses
Hydrocarbon inhalation anesthetics (halothane, enflurane)	*Sensitization of the heart by anesthetic may lead to cardiac dysrhythmias*	Inform anesthesiologist of intended use
Levodopa, methyldopa, thyroid hormones (levothyroxine, liothyronine)	*Risk of cardiac toxicity may be increased in patients taking large doses of these agents*	Use cautiously and in restricted doses
CNS stimulants (amphetamine, methylphenidate)	*Additive CNS stimulation possible*	Avoid concurrent use of cocaine and CNS stimulants
Adrenergic neuronal blocking drugs (guanadrel, guanethidine, reserpine)	*May enhance systemic responses to cocaine; therapeutic effects of the blocking drugs may be reduced*	Use cautiously
β-adrenergic blockers (propranolol, nadolol)	*β-blocking effects on the heart may be attenuated by cocaine; blockade of β-adrenergic receptors in skeletal muscle by nonspecific β-adrenergic blockers may lead to hypertensive responses*	Use cautiously and in restricted doses

Italics indicate information of major clinical significance.

Special Patients

Pregnant and nursing women

Once absorbed into the systemic circulation, topical anesthetics can cross the placenta to enter the fetal circulation. Table 1.8 includes the FDA pregnancy category classifications for topical anesthetics used in dentistry. Considerations of risk/benefit suggest that purely elective treatment should be delayed until after delivery and that other dental care should be performed, if possible, during the second trimester. Lidocaine and probably other topical anesthetics are distributed into breast milk, but no problems have been documented in humans, except with cocaine. Cocaine intake by infants during nursing has led to overt toxicity, including convulsions and cardiovascular derangements.

Pediatric, geriatric and other special patients

Adverse reactions to topical anesthetics are rare in dentistry but may be more prevalent in pediatric and geriatric populations. Overdosage is more likely to occur in young children because of their small size and the commensurately low margin of error. Methemoglobinemia with use of benzocaine is largely limited to young children. Increased variability of response to local anesthetics is likely to be encountered in elderly patients and in those with significant medical problems. Lower maximum doses in these patients provides an extra margin of safety.

Patient Monitoring: Aspects to Watch

- State of consciousness
- Respiratory status
- Cardiovascular status

Adverse Effects and Precautions

Systemic reactions may occur when local anesthetics are applied topically. Systemic absorption of these agents should be minimized by limiting the concentration of the drug, the area of application, the total amount of agent applied and the time of exposure for drugs that can be removed once the effect has been achieved. To minimize absorption, special caution is needed when applying topical agents to severely traumatized mucosa or to areas of sepsis.

Several topical anesthetic preparations are marketed in pressurized spray containers.

It is difficult to control the amount of drug expelled with unmetered spray devices and to confine the agent to the desired site. Thus, a patient inadvertently may inhale sufficient quantities of the aerosol spray to provoke an adverse reaction. Therefore, caution is advised when using any spray device, and metered spray devices are preferred because they dispense a set amount of drug.

Adverse effects and precautions in addition to those included in Table 1.5 are listed in Table 1.10.

Pharmacology

Topical local anesthetics provide anesthesia by anesthetizing the free nerve endings in the mucosa. The mechanism of action is identical to that described in the previous section for injectable local anesthetics. Cocaine, however, has a distinct pharmacology. In addition to its local anesthetic action, cocaine blocks the reuptake of released adrenergic neurotransmitters (norepinephrine, dopamine) back into the nerve terminal. This action gives cocaine its vasoconstrictor and CNS stimulant

Table 1.10

Topical Anesthetics: Adverse Effects, Precautions and Contraindications

Body system	Adverse effects	Precautions/contraindications
CV	*Stimulation with cocaine; may cause hypertension and dysrhythmias*	*Cocaine should be used cautiously in patients with cardiovascular disease, hyperthyroidism, cerebrovascular disease*
CNS	*Stimulation with cocaine; may cause excitement, hallucinations and confusion*	*Cocaine should be used cautiously in patients with Tourette's syndrome or seizure history* Cocaine use contraindicated in patients with history of cocaine abuse
Hema	Methemoglobinemia, rare but occasionally observed with benzocaine in small children	Benzocaine should be used cautiously in patients with congenital or acquired methemoglobinemia
Oral	Numbness of throat; may impair swallowing and increase risk of aspiration; slight irritation at application site (rarely)	None pertinent to dentistry

Italics indicate information of major clinical significance.

properties, as well as its addictive potential and increased risk of cardiovascular toxicity.

The rate of absorption of a topical anesthetic depends on the dose administered, the duration of exposure, the area of coverage, the mucosa's permeability, the mucosa's intactness and the vascularity of the tissue. Benzocaine is unique in its poor solubility in water and is the least absorbed into the bloodstream.

A considerable portion of topical anesthetics administered intraorally is swallowed. Although absorption from the gastrointestinal tract occurs, extensive metabolism of the drug in the hepatic-portal system prevents toxic blood concentrations except with excessive doses. The metabolic fate and excretion of these drugs is covered in the first part of this chapter, in the section on injectable local anesthetics.

Patient Advice

- Injury to the anesthetized tissues may occur without any resulting sensation.
- To prevent pulmonary aspiration, patients who have undergone topical anesthesia of the pharynx should use caution when eating or drinking until normal sensation has returned.
- To prevent injury, patients should not test for anesthesia by biting the lip or tongue, nor should they eat or chew anything until the anesthetic effect has dissipated.
- Children should be warned not to bite their lips or tongue and be monitored by their parents to prevent injury.
- Patients using topical anesthetics to manage toothache, intraoral conditions or ill-fitting dental appliances should seek professional dental care for definitive treatment.

Suggested Readings

Hersh EV, Houpt MI, Cooper SA, et al. Analgesic efficacy and safety of an intraoral lidocaine patch. JADA 1996;127(11):1626-34.

Jastak JT, Yagiela JA, Donaldson D. Local anesthesia of the oral cavity. Philadelphia: Saunders; 1995.

Malamed SF. Handbook of local anesthesia. 4th ed. St. Louis: Mosby–Year Book; 1997.

Middleton RM, Kirkpatrick MB. Clinical use of cocaine. A review of the risks and benefits. Drug Safety 1993;9(3):212-7.

Chapter 2.

Conscious Sedation and Agents for the Control of Anxiety

B. Ellen Byrne, R.Ph., D.D.S., Ph.D.; Leonard S. Tibbetts, D.D.S., M.S.D.

All types of dental care—from that rendered with no anesthesia to that rendered under general anesthesia—require accurate diagnosis, proper treatment and effective patient monitoring. This involves obtaining a complete medical history, performing a comprehensive examination and doing a thorough pretreatment evaluation.

Providing care and ensuring the well-being of patients in the dental office is based on a continuum of techniques that are available for the management of anxiety and pain (Figure 2.1). This chapter focuses on the calming of apprehensive and/or nervous patients through the use of drugs, without causing the loss of consciousness.

Using various techniques to control anxiety and pain has been an integral part of the practice of dentistry since the profession's early years. Today, the term "conscious sedation" is used to describe the amelioration of patient anxiety, the blunting of the stress

---

Figure 2.1

The Spectrum of Pain and Anxiety Control

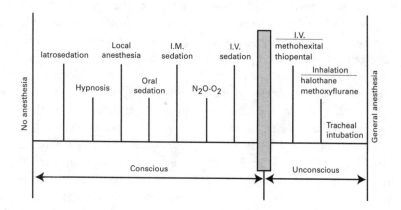

The continuum of techniques for the management of patients' pain and anxiety, ranging from no anesthesia to general anesthesia. The vertical bar represents the loss of consciousness.

---

response and often some degree of amnesia produced by a combination of psychological techniques and drugs. Unfortunately, the term "intravenous sedation" means general anesthesia to much of the public and to many medical and dental professionals. When properly understood, the term "conscious sedation," coined by dentist/anesthesiologist Richard Bennett in the 1970s, does much to alleviate this misconception. Conscious sedation is a minimally depressed level of consciousness in which the patient retains the ability to independently and continuously maintain an airway—as well as to respond appropriately to physical stimulation or verbal command—that can be produced by a pharmacological or nonpharmacological method or both.

Examples of nonpharmacological methods used for anxiety and pain management are hypnosis, acupuncture, acupressure, audioanalgesia, biofeedback, electroanesthesia (transcutaneous electrical nerve stimulation) and electrosedation.

Appropriately trained dentists may use any of a number of preoperative and operative pharmacological conscious sedation techniques to achieve the goals of anxiety reduction and pain control. Such techniques may include sedation by enteral (absorption by way of the alimentary canal), inhalation (absorption into the lungs) and parenteral (introduction via subcutaneous, intramuscular, intraorbital or intravenous routes) means.

Each category of pharmacological conscious sedation has specific educational and monitoring requirements for safe and effective patient usage, as well as specific licensing requirements mandated by regulatory agencies. The use of conscious sedation techniques in the various categories by appropriately trained dentists has a remarkable safety record. (For further information, consult the American Dental Association's Policy Statement "The Use of Conscious Sedation, Deep Sedation and General Anesthesia in Dentistry," as adopted by the ADA House of Delegates in October 1999, and the "Guidelines for Teaching the Comprehensive Control of Anxiety and Pain in Dentistry," as adopted by the ADA Council on Dental Education and Licensure in October 1999.)

Whatever the methods of conscious sedation in which dentists strive to be educationally and professionally competent, the use of a wide array of drugs for various types of conscious sedation is contraindicated without an adequately detailed working knowledge about them. In fact, using as few drugs as possible to appropriately and adequately sedate patients is advised as the dentist can become intimately familiar with a limited number of drugs, their pharmacological actions, indications, contraindications, precautions and drug interactions.

Intravenous conscious sedation induced in the dental office, for example, can be handled almost entirely by a combination of the following five drugs, which fall into these three classes:

- benzodiazepines—diazepam, midazolam;
- sedatives—pentobarbital;
- narcotic analgesics—morphine, meperidine.

Today, the most common pharmacological method of controlling anxiety with intravenous sedation is through the use of one of the benzodiazepines in combination with a narcotic analgesic. The benzodiazepines are used to reduce the apprehension and fear, as well as to provide an amnesia effect, while the narcotics produce analgesia and euphoria. The sedative pentobarbital, in combination with meperidine, can be used when there are contraindications to the use of the benzodiazepines.

Administration routes. Of the various administration routes for conscious sedation drugs, each has advantages and disadvantages.

The oral route is most commonly used, and it has the advantages of almost universal acceptance by patients, ease of administration and relative safety. Its disadvantages include its requirement of a bolus dosage of medication, based on the patient's weight and age; its long latent period; its unreliable absorption; its inability to be titrated; and its prolonged duration of action.

The rectal route of administration is used in dentistry only occasionally, when patients are either unwilling or unable to take the drugs by mouth. This route's advantages and disadvantages are similar to those of oral administration.

Another option is the combined inhalation-enteral route of conscious sedation. The advantages of using this combination include greater patient acceptance and a higher degree of effectiveness than either technique offers individually. The disadvantage is that the dentist must be proficient in the pharmacology of agents used in the management of both inhalation and enteral sedation—drug interactions and incompatibilities, problems and complications—as well as in making the distinction between the conscious and unconscious state and in clinical airway management.

All other routes of drug administration bypass the gastrointestinal system. In these routes, the drugs are absorbed directly by the body from the site of administration into the cardiovascular system. This includes inhalation and parenteral routes of administration. In dentistry, nitrous oxide and oxygen sedation are synonymous with inhalation sedation. The advantages of inhalation conscious sedation with nitrous oxide and oxygen are that the observed latent period is short, the administrator can titrate the agent appropriately, actions of the agent can be quickly adjusted to decrease or increase the depth of sedation, and recovery is rapid. The disadvantage is that the nitrous oxide–oxygen combination, with no less than a 70:30 ratio, is not a very potent agent, and a certain proportion of patients will not experience the desired effect.

The subcutaneous (SC) route of administration is used primarily in pediatric dentistry. It offers advantages and disadvantages similar to those of intramuscular (IM) administration as compared with enteral administration. Compared with enteral administration, both SC and IM administrations offer more rapid onset of action, as well as a more pronounced clinical effect with the same dosage. The SC route is useful for injecting nonvolatile, water- and fat-soluble hypnotic and narcotic drugs. The relatively poor blood supply of subcutaneous tissues, however, limits the effectiveness of this technique. For the uncooperative pediatric patient, both SC and IM techniques require a short period of restraint during administration. The major disadvantage of both techniques is the inability to titrate the medications accurately, so typically a bolus dosage is administered based on the patient's age and size. It is also impossible to retrieve the dosage should overdosage occur. For this reason, proper patient monitoring is extremely important, so complications can be intercepted early.

Intravenous (IV) conscious sedation represents the most effective method of acquiring adequate and predictable sedation in virtually all patients, with the exception of disruptive patients, whose cooperation is needed for successful venipuncture. IV conscious sedation allows effective blood levels of drugs to be achieved rapidly with titration (the incremental administration of small drug dosages over appropriate time intervals until the desired level of sedation is achieved) and rapidly enhances the action of a drug. For many IV-administered drugs, the desired and maximum clinical sedative effects are reached within 2 to 8 min. Some of the currently available drugs for anxiety reduction are capable of producing an amnesia effect in 80% to 90% of patients for 20 to 40 min after administration.

While it is possible with the use of specific antagonists to reverse the actions of some medications in conscious sedation, it is not possible to reverse the action of all drugs after they have been injected. The rapid onset of action and the pronounced clinical actions of intravenously injected drugs will result in exaggerated problems with overdosage. This means the entire dental office staff must be well-trained in the recognition and management of adverse reactions and emergencies that may accompany the drugs used so that patient safety and quality dental care are never compromised.

Records and monitoring. Written, advised, informed consent for all forms of conscious sedation is essential. The standard of care for physiological and vital-sign monitoring for the various types of conscious sedation is well-established, as is that for documentation of drugs used, dosage, adverse reactions to medications and recovery from the anesthetic.

State-of-the-art monitoring of patients' vital signs has improved dramatically in the past several years. Pulse rate, blood pressure and respiration now can be monitored either physically or electronically. Today, pulse oximetry offers a rapid and effective means of monitoring the blood oxygen saturation and pulse rate. These methods, in combination with the old standbys of close patient observation and conversation, are the current standards of monitoring care for patients in ASA Class I and II (healthy or with mild-to-moderate systemic disease) who are undergoing any type of parenteral conscious sedation or inhalation-enteral conscious sedation. In the treatment of patients of ASA Class III (with severe systemic disease that limits activity) or higher (ranging from IV, with severe life-threatening systemic disease, to VI, clinically dead but being maintained for harvesting of organs), electrocardiogram monitoring also becomes the standard of care, in addition to the other means of monitoring.

This chapter covers the drugs most frequently used in dental conscious sedation (benzodiazepines and their antagonist flumazenil, barbiturates, opioids and their antagonist naloxone). It also addresses older, less frequently used drugs: chloral hydrate, ethchlorvynol and meprobamate.

Benzodiazepines

The benzodiazepines are among the most popular classes of drugs available today, having been used since the late 1950s for effective and safe treatment of a variety of anxiety states, as well as for epilepsy (diazepam, clonazepam) and sleep disorders (flurazepam, temazepam, triazolam). In addition to their use in anxiety, the benzodiazepines have extensive clinical applications in anesthesia procedures (diazepam, midazolam) and as muscle relaxants (diazepam).

Although the benzodiazepines have a wide margin of safety, they are not without adverse effects. Their time course of action is variable among patients as well as among various agents. Although all benzodiazepines are effective, there are significant differences among them. When used enterally, diazepam and flurazepam are among the most rapidly absorbed, whereas oxazepam is one of the most slowly absorbed. Use of IM routes of administration for benzodiazepines often results in erratic and poor absorption. Most of the benzodiazepines are poorly soluble in water and are not available for IV use. Diazepam and midazolam, however, are the two agents most commonly used for IV conscious sedation, and an anterograde amnesia is strongly associated with this class of drugs. The level of amnesia varies with agent and route of administration.

All benzodiazepines in use are bound 50% or more to plasma proteins. Their distribution to tissue depends on their lipid solubility.

The metabolism and excretion of the benzodiazepines are complex. Clorazepate is a pro-drug converted by metabolism to the active form; others are inactivated by metabolism; still others are biotransferred to metabolites that retain activity. Many of the metabolites of benzodiazepines have longer half-lives than the parent compound and so accumulate to a greater extent. It is important to recognize that some of these compounds have the potential for extremely long durations of action. Thus, benzodiazepine half-lives vary from a few hours to as long as a week.

The imidazopyridine sedative hypnotic zolpidem is included in this section of the chapter because, although it is structurally dissimilar to the benzodiazepines, many of its actions are explained by its action on the benzodiazepine receptor.

Antagonist. The benzodiazepines have a specific antagonist, flumazenil, that is administered intravenously. It reverses the CNS effects of benzodiazepines, including respiratory depression. Its duration of action may be as brief as 30 minutes, so treatment with it requires continuous monitoring of the patient and possibly repeated administration.

Accepted Indications

Benzodiazepines are used for the treatment of anxiety, insomnia, epilepsy, panic disorders and alcohol withdrawal. As adjuncts in anesthesia, they are used as a preanesthetic medication to produce sedation, relieve anxiety and produce anterograde amnesia.

General Dosing Information

All benzodiazepines have similar pharmacologic actions. Their different clinical uses are often based on pharmacokinetic differences and availability of clinical use data. Optimal dosage of benzodiazepines varies with diagnosis, method of administration and patient response. The minimum effective dose should be used for the shortest period of time. Prolonged enteral use (for weeks or months) may result in psychological or physical dependence. After prolonged administration, benzodiazepines should be withdrawn gradually to prevent withdrawal symptoms.

For parenteral dosing, after administration of the drug, patients should be kept under observation until they have recovered sufficiently to return home. Bolus doses and rapidly administered IV doses may result in respiratory depression, apnea, hypotension, bradycardia and cardiac arrest. When parenteral benzodiazepines are administered intravenously, equipment necessary to secure and maintain an airway should be immediately available.

Table 2.1 provides benzodiazepine dosing information.

Dosage Adjustments

Geriatric or debilitated patients, children and patients with hepatic or renal function impairment should receive a lower initial dosage, as elimination of benzodiazepines may be slower in these patients, resulting in impaired coordination, dizziness and excessive sedation.

Special Dental Considerations

Drug Interactions of Dental Interest

Table 2.2 lists possible interactions of the benzodiazepines and zolpidem with other drugs.

Cross–Sensitivity

There may be cross-sensitivity between benzodiazepines.

Special Patients

Pregnant and nursing women

See Table 2.1 for pregnancy risk categories.

Benzodiazepines are reported to increase the risk of congenital malformations when used during the first trimester; chronic use may cause physical dependence in the neonate, resulting in withdrawal symptoms and CNS depression.

Benzodiazepines and their metabolites may distribute into breast milk, thus creating feeding difficulties and weight loss in the infant.

Pediatric, geriatric and other special patients

Children (especially the very young) and geriatric patients are usually more sensitive to the CNS effects of benzodiazepines. In the neonate, prolonged CNS depression may be produced because of the newborn's inability to metabolize the benzodiazepine into inactive products. In the geriatric patient, the dosage should be limited to the smallest effective dose and increased gradually to minimize ataxia, dizziness and oversedation.

Patient Monitoring: Aspects to Watch

- Respiratory status
- Patient requests for benzodiazepines (all of which are Schedule IV controlled substances in the United States)
- Possible abuse and dependence

Table 2.1

Benzodiazepines: Dosage and Prescribing Information

Generic name	Brand name(s)	Adult dosage	Max adult dosage	Child dosage	Max child dosage	PRC	Content/form
Alprazolam	**Solution:** Alprazolam Intensol **Tablets:** Xanax; Apo-Alpraz [CAN], Novo-Alprazol [CAN], Nu-Alpraz [CAN], Xanax [CAN]	**Antianxiety:** 0.25-0.5 mg tid	4 mg/day	NE	NE	D	**Tablets:** 0.25, 0.5, 1, 2 mg **Oral solution:** 1 mg/1 mL; 0.1 mg/1 mL
Bromazepam	Lectopam [CAN]	6-30 mg q day in divided doses	Up to 60 mg/day	NE	NE	NE	**Tablets:** 1.5, 3 mg; 6 mg [CAN]
Chlordiazepoxide	Libritabs, Librium; Apo-Chlordiazepoxide [CAN], Novopoxide [CAN], Solium [CAN]	**Antianxiety—oral:** 5-25 mg tid or qid **Sedative-hypnotic:** 50-100 mg **Elderly patients:** 5 mg bid-qid **Antianxiety—IM or IV:** 50-100 mg initially, then 25-50 mg tid-qid **Preoperative—IM:** 50-100 mg 1 h before surgery	Up to 300 mg/day **In alcohol withdrawal:** Up to 400 mg/day, then reduce to maintenance level	**Age < 6 y:** Safety and efficacy not established **Age ≥ 6 y:** 5 mg bid or qid	NE	D	**Tablets:** 5, 10, 25 mg **Capsules:** 5, 10, 25 mg; 10, 25 mg [CAN] **Solution:** Sterile chlordiazepoxide HCl, 100 mg with 2 mL special IM diluent

Generic name	Brand names	Usual adult dose	Maximum adult dose	Usual pediatric dose	Maximum pediatric dose	PRC	Dosage forms
Clonazepam	Klonopin; Rivotril [CAN], Syn-Clonazepam [CAN]	**Antianxiety:** 0.5 mg tid **Anticonvulsant:** 0.5 mg tid	Up to 20 mg q day	**Antianxiety:** 0.01-0.03 mg/kg in 2-3 divided doses **Anticonvulsant:** 0.01-0.03 mg/kg in 2-3 divided doses	0.05 mg/kg in 2-3 divided doses	C	**Tablets:** 0.5, 1, 2 mg; 0.5, 2 mg [CAN]
Clorazepate	Gen-XENE, Tranxene-T-Tabs, Tranxene-SD, generic; Apo-Clorazepate [CAN], Novo-Clopate [CAN], Tranxene [CAN]	**Antianxiety:** 7.5-15 mg bid-qid **Sedative-hypnotic:** 30 mg initially, then 15 mg bid-qid, then tapering off **Anticonvulsant:** 7.5 mg tid	90 mg q day	NE	NE	NE	**Capsules:** 3.75, 7.5, 15 mg **Tablets:** 3.75, 7.5, 11.25, 15, 22.5 mg
Diazepam	Valium, generic; Apo-Diazepam [CAN], Novodipam [CAN], Valium [CAN], Vivol [CAN]	**Anxiety/sedation/skeletal-muscle relaxation—oral:** 2-10 mg bid-qid **IM, IV:** 2-10 mg; may repeat in 3-4 h if needed **Status epilepticus—IV:** 5-10 mg every 10-20 min, up to 30 mg in an 8-h period; may repeat in 2-4 h if necessary *Continued on next page*	NE	**Conscious sedation for procedures—oral:** 0.2-0.3 mg/kg (maximum: 10 mg) 45-60 min before procedure **Sedation, muscle relaxation or anxiety—oral:** 0.12-0.8 mg/kg/day in divided doses q 6-8 h *Continued on next page*	NE	D	**Tablets:** 2, 5, 10 mg

Continued on next page

[CAN] indicates a drug available only in Canada.
PRC: Pregnancy risk category.
NE: Not established.

Table 2.1 (cont.)

Benzodiazepines: Dosage and Prescribing Information

Generic name	Brand name(s)	Adult dosage	Max adult dosage	Child dosage	Max child dosage	PRC	Content/form
Diazepam (cont.)		**Elderly, for anxiety— oral:** 1-2 mg 1-2 times/day, initially; increase gradually as needed (rarely need to use > 10 mg/day) **Skeletal-muscle relaxant:** 2-5 mg bid-qid		**IM, IV:** 0.04-0.3 mg/kg/dose every 2-4 h to a maximum of 0.6 mg/kg within an 8-h period **Adolescents: Conscious sedation for procedures —oral:** 10 mg **IV:** 5 mg, may repeat with 1/2 dose if needed			
Diazepam, extended-release capsule	Valrelease	Oral: 15 or 30 mg once a day	NE	NE	NE	NE	**Extended-release capsules:** 15 mg **Tablets:** 2, 5, 10 mg
Diazepam, oral solution	Diazepam Intensol, generic; PMS-Diazepam [CAN]	2-10 mg bid-qid	NE	**Age ≤ 6 mo:** NR **Age > 6 mo:** 1-2.5 mg, 0.04-0.2 mg/kg tid-qid	**Age ≤ 6 mo:** NR **Age > 6 mo:** 1-2.5 mg, 0.04-0.2 mg/kg tid-qid	D	**Intensol oral solution:** 5 mg/mL **Generic oral solution:** 5 mg/5 mL **PMS-Diazepam oral solution:** 1 mg/mL
Diazepam, injection	D-Val, Valium, Zetran, generic; Valium [CAN]	**Antianxiety:** 5-10 mg	NE	NE	NE	D	5 mg/mL
Diazepam, sterile emulsion	Diazemuls [CAN]	**Antianxiety:** 10 mg 1-2 h before surgery	NE	NE	NE	D	5 mg/mL

Estazolam	ProSom	Sedative-hypnotic—oral: 1 mg (2 mg may be necessary in some patients)	NE	NE	NE	X	**Tablets:** 1, 2 mg
Flurazepam	Dalmane, generic; Apo-Flurazepam [CAN], Novoflupam [CAN]	Sedative-hypnotic—oral: 15-30 mg	NE	NE	NE	X	**Capsules:** 15, 30 mg
Halazepam	Paxipam	Antianxiety—oral: 20-40 mg tid or qid	NE	NE	NE	NE	**Tablets:** 20, 40 mg
Ketazolam	Loftran [CAN]	Antianxiety—oral: 15 mg 1-2 times a day	NE	NE	NE	NE	**Capsules:** 15, 30 mg
Lorazepam	Ativan, Lorazepam Intensol Concentrated Solution, generic; Apo-Lorazepam [CAN], Ativan [CAN], Novo-Lorazem [CAN], Nu-Loraz [CAN]	Antianxiety—oral: 1 to 3 mg bid-tid Sedation, hypnotic—oral: 2-4 mg at bedtime Antianxiety—IM: 50 µg per kg, maximum 4 mg Antianxiety—IV: 44 µg per kg, maximum 2 mg Antianxiety—sublingual: 2-3 mg/day in divided doses Sedation, hypnotic—oral: 5-10 mg at bedtime	NE	**Age < 18 y—injection:** NE **Age < 12 y—oral, solution:** NE **Age < 6 y—oral, sublingual tablets:** NR **Age 6-18 y—oral, sublingual tablets:** NE	**Age < 12 y:** NE	D	**Injection:** 2 mg/mL, 4 mg/mL, 4 mg/mL [CAN] **Oral solution:** 2 mg/mL **Sublingual tablets:** 0.5, 1, 2 mg **Tablets:** 0.5, 1, 2 mg

Continued on next page

[CAN] indicates a drug available only in Canada.
PRC: Pregnancy risk category.
NE: Not established.
NR: Not recommended.

Table 2.1 (cont.)

Benzodiazepines: Dosage and Prescribing Information

Generic name	Brand name(s)	Adult dosage	Max adult dosage	Child dosage	Max child dosage	PRC	Content/form
Midazolam*	Versed	**Age < 60 y, ASA† I or II, preoperative sedation and amnesia—IM:** 70-80 µg/kg (0.07-0.08 mg/kg body weight), approximately 30-60 min before surgery **Age < 60 y, ASA III or IV, or aged > 60 y, preoperative sedation and amnesia—IM:** 20-50 µg/kg (0.02-0.05 mg/kg body weight), approximately 30-60 min before surgery **Age < 60 y, unpremedicated, conscious sedation—IV:** Initially no more than 2.5 mg administered slowly over at least 2 min immediately before procedure	**Age < 60 y, ASA I or II, preoperative sedation and amnesia—IM:** NE **Age < 60 y, ASA III or IV, preoperative sedation and amnesia—IM:** NE **Age < 60 y, unpremedicated, conscious sedation—IV:** 5 mg	**Age ≤ 6 mo, preoperative sedation and amnesia or conscious sedation:** NE **Age ≥ 6 mo, preoperative sedation and amnesia or conscious sedation—oral:** 0.25-0.5 mg/kg body weight 30-45 min before procedure **Age 6 mo-5 y, preoperative sedation and amnesia or conscious sedation—IV:** 50-100 µg (0.05-0.1 mg/kg body weight) by intermittent injection **Age 6 mo-5 y, preoperative sedation and amnesia or conscious sedation—IM:** 100-150 µg (0.1-0.15 mg/kg body weight)	**Age ≤ 6 mo, preoperative sedation and amnesia or conscious sedation:** NE **Age ≥ 6 mo, preoperative sedation and amnesia or conscious sedation—oral:** 20 mg **Age 6 mo-5 y, preoperative sedation and amnesia or conscious sedation—IV:** 6 mg **Age 6 mo-5 y, preoperative sedation and amnesia or conscious sedation—IM:** NE	D	Solution: 1, 5 mg/mL Syrup: 2 mg/mL

Midazolam (*cont.*)	**Age ≥ 60 y or debilitated/chronically ill, unpremedicated, conscious sedation—IV:** Initially no more than 1.5 mg administered slowly over at least 2 min immediately before procedure **Healthy adults < 60 y:** May respond to doses as low as 1 mg; administer no more than 2.5 mg within 2 min; dentist may administer additional doses after waiting 2 min and evaluating sedation after each dose; total dose > 5 mg generally not needed; reduce dose by 30% if narcotics or other CNS depressants administered concomitantly	**Age ≥ 60 y or debilitated/chronically ill, unpremedicated, conscious sedation—IV:** 3.5 mg	**Age 6-12 y, preoperative sedation and amnesia or conscious sedation—IM:** 100-150 µg (0.1-0.15 mg/kg body weight) **Age 6-12 y, preoperative sedation and amnesia or conscious sedation—IV:** 25-50 µg (0.025-0.05 mg/kg body weight) by intermittent injection	**Age 6-12 y, preoperative sedation and amnesia or conscious sedation—IM:** NE **Age 6-12 y, preoperative sedation and amnesia or conscious sedation—IV:** 10 mg	NE	**Tablets:** 5, 10 mg
Nitrazepam	**Sedative-hypnotic—oral:** 5-10 mg at bedtime	NE	NE	NE	NE	
Mogadon [CAN]						

Continued on next page

[CAN] indicates a drug available only in Canada.
PRC: Pregnancy risk category.
NE: Not established.
* Midazolam should be used only in a hospital or ambulatory care setting (including physicians' and dentists' offices) that is equipped to provide continuous monitoring of respiratory and cardiac function.
† American Society of Anesthesiologists classification (see p. 20).

Table 2.1 (cont.)

Benzodiazepines: Dosage and Prescribing Information

Generic name	Brand name(s)	Adult dosage	Max adult dosage	Child dosage	Max child dosage	PRC	Content/form
Oxazepam	Serax, generic; Apo-Oxazepam [CAN], Novoxapam [CAN]	**Antianxiety—oral:** 10-30 mg tid or qid **Sedative-hypnotic—oral:** 15-30 mg tid or qid	NE	NE	NE	C	**Tablets and capsules:** 10, 15, 30 mg
Prazepam	Centrax, generic	**Antianxiety—oral:** 10 mg tid	NE	NE	NE	C	**Capsules:** 5, 10, 20 mg **Tablets:** 5, 10 mg
Quazepam	Doral	**Sedative-hypnotic—oral:** 15 mg initially, then reduce to 7.5 if needed	NE	NE	NE	X	**Tablets:** 7.5, 15 mg
Temazepam	Restoril, generic	**Sedative-hypnotic—oral:** 15 mg	NE	NE	NE	X	**Capsules:** 7.5, 15, 30 mg **Tablets:** 15, 30 mg
Triazolam	Halcion; Apo-Triazo [CAN], Gen-Triazolam [CAN], NovoTriolam [CAN], Nu-Triazo [CAN], generic [CAN]	**Sedative-hypnotic—oral:** 125-250 µg	NE	NE	NE	X	**Tablets:** 125, 250 µg (0.125, 0.250 mg)
Zolpidem (IV)	Ambien	10 mg at bedtime; limit use to 7-10 days	20 mg/day	NE	NE	B	**Tablets:** 5, 10 mg

[CAN] indicates a drug available only in Canada.
PRC: Pregnancy risk category.
NE: Not established.

Table 2.2

Benzodiazepines and Zolpidem: Possible Interactions With Other Drugs

Drug taken by patient	Interaction with benzodiazepines	Dentist's action
Alcohol or CNS depressants	*Concurrent use may increase CNS depressant effects of either medication*	Watch for increased response to CNS depression; decrease dose of benzodiazepine if necessary
Chlorpromazine	**With zolpidem:** Concurrent use may prolong elimination half-life of chlorpromazine	
Cimetidine	Inhibition of hepatic metabolism may increase serum levels of some benzodiazepines; may enhance certain actions, especially sedation	Monitor for enhanced response to benzodiazepine
Disulfiram	May inhibit hepatic metabolism of benzodiazepines that undergo oxidation, increasing the benzodiazepine's CNS depressant effect	Monitor for enhanced benzodiazepine response
Erythromycin, troleandomycin, clarithromycin	May decrease the metabolism of certain benzodiazepines, increasing the benzodiazepines' CNS depressant effect	Watch for increased response to benzodiazepines
Imipramine	**With zolpidem:** Concurrent use may increase drowsiness and risk of anterograde amnesia; may also decrease peak concentrations of imipramine	
Omeprazole	Inhibits the oxidative metabolism of benzodiazepines, thus increasing or prolonging the benzodiazepines' CNS depressant effects	Monitor for enhanced benzodiazepine response
Oral contraceptives	May inhibit metabolism of benzodiazepines that undergo oxidation	Watch for evidence of increased response to benzodiazepines that undergo oxidative metabolism
Theophyllines	May antagonize sedative effects of benzodiazepines	Monitor for decreased benzodiazepine response

Italics indicate information of major clinical significance.

Table 2.3

Benzodiazepines: Adverse Effects, Precautions and Contraindications

Body system	Adverse effects	Precautions/contraindications
General	Variable per patient medication	Low serum albumin predisposes patients to a higher incidence of side effects
CV	Cardiac arrest, hypotension, tachycardia, local phlebitis, pain with injection, venous thrombosis	None of significance to dentistry
CNS	*Drowsiness, ataxia, amnesia, confusion, slurred speech, paradoxical excitement, fatigue, lightheadedness, insomnia, headache, anxiety, depression, hallucinations*	*Should be used with caution in patients using other CNS depressants or who have a history of drug abuse or dependence* *Pre-existing mental depression: suicidal tendencies may be present* *May exacerbate sleep apnea*
Endoc	Decreased libido, menstrual irregularities	None of significance to dentistry
EENT	*Blurred vision, diplopia*	*Narrow-angle glaucoma (benzodiazepines have an anticholinergic effect)*
GI	Constipation, nausea, vomiting, diarrhea, abdominal or stomach cramps	None of significance to dentistry
HB	Hepatic dysfunction	None of significance to dentistry
Integ	Allergic reaction or rash	None of significance to dentistry
Musc	Impaired coordination, rigidity, tremor, muscle cramps	*May exacerbate myasthenia gravis* Long-acting benzodiazepines have been associated with falls in elderly patients
Oral	Dry mouth, increased thirst	None of significance to dentistry
Resp	*Decrease in respiratory rate, apnea, laryngospasm, nasal congestion, hyperventilation*	*Severe chronic obstructive pulmonary disease*

Italics indicate information of major clinical significance.

Adverse Effects and Precautions

Table 2.3 lists adverse effects, precautions and contraindications related to benzodiazepines.

Pharmacology

Benzodiazepines depress all levels of the CNS, resulting in mild sedation, hypnosis or coma, depending on the dose. It is believed that benzodiazepines enhance or facilitate the inhibitory neurotransmitter action of γ-aminobutyric acid (GABA). After oral administration, benzodiazepines are absorbed well from the gastrointestinal tract. After IM injection, absorption of lorazepam and midazolam is rapid and complete, whereas that of chlordiazepoxide and diazepam may be slow and erratic. Rectal absorption of diazepam is rapid. The benzodiazepines are metabolized by the liver to inactive or other active metabolites. During repeated dosing with long–half-life benzodiazepines, there is accumulation of the parent compound and/or active metabolites. During repeated dosing with short– to intermediate–half-life benzodiazepines, accumulation is minimal.

Patient Advice

- Avoid concurrent use of alcohol and other CNS depressants.
- Until CNS effects are known, avoid activities needing good psychomotor skills.
- A responsible adult should drive the patient to and from dental appointments.
- Recurrent use of these drugs may cause physical or psychological dependence.
- Benzodiazepines may cause xerostomia, which can be countered using sugarless candy, sugarless gum or a commercially available saliva substitute.

Benzodiazepine Antagonist: Flumazenil

Accepted Indications

Flumazenil is used to reverse the pharmacological effects of benzodiazepines used in anesthesia and to manage benzodiazepine overdose.

General Dosing Information

Flumazenil selectively reverses the pharmacologic effects of benzodiazepines used in anesthesia and is used to manage benzodiazepine overdose. Flumazenil does not antagonize other CNS depressants except for zolpidem. See Table 2.4.

Special Dental Considerations

Drug Interactions of Dental Interest

Table 2.5 lists the possible interactions of flumazenil with other drugs.

Cross-Sensitivity

There may be cross-sensitivity to benzodiazepines.

Special Patients

Pregnant and nursing women

Caution should be used in administering flumazenil to a nursing woman because it is not known whether flumazenil is excreted in human milk.

Pediatric, geriatric and other special patients

Flumazenil is not recommended for use in children, either for the reversal of sedation, the management of overdose or resuscitation of newborns. Pulmonary management is advised as the treatment of choice.

The pharmacokinectics of flumazenil have been studied in elderly people and are not significantly different from those in younger patients.

Patient Monitoring: Aspects to Watch

- Respiratory status
- Patient alertness
- Possible resedation
- Possible seizure activity

Adverse Effects and Precautions

Table 2.6 lists adverse effects, precautions and contraindications related to flumazenil.

Pharmacology

Flumazenil, an imidazobenzodiazepine derivative, antagonizes the actions of benzodiazepines on the CNS. Flumazenil competitively inhibits the activity at the benzodiazepine recognition site on the benzodiazepine-GABA receptor-chloride ionophore complex. Flumazenil is a weak partial agonist in some animal models of activity, but has little or no agonist activity in humans.

The onset of reversal is usually evident 1 to 2 min after the injection is completed. Eighty percent response will be reached within 3 min, with peak effect occurring at 6 to 10 min. The duration and degree of reversal are related to the plasma concentration of the sedating benzodiazepine as well as the dose of flumazenil given. Resedation is possible if a large single or cumulative dose of benzodiazepine has been given in the course of a

Table 2.4

Flumazenil: Dosage and Prescribing Information

Generic name	Brand name(s)	Adult dosage	Max adult dosage	Child dosage	PRC	Content/form
Flumazenil	Romazicon	**For reversal of conscious sedation, initial dose—IV:** 0.2 mg over 15 s; if desired level of consciousness is not obtained, 0.2-mg dose may be repeated at 1-min intervals; most patients respond to dose of 0.6-1 mg **For suspected benzodiazepine overdose—IV:** 0.2 mg over 30 s initially, then 0.5 mg over 30 s, repeated at 1-min intervals	**For reversal of conscious sedation:** Up to 1 mg at any one time or 3 mg/h **For suspected benzodiazepine overdose:** Maximum total cumulative dose 5 mg	Not established, but may be used in ranges from 0.01 mg/kg for reversing sedation to 0.1 mg/kg for life-threatening overdose up to maximum cumulative dose of 1 mg	C	**Injection:** 0.1 mg/mL

PRC: Pregnancy risk category.

Table 2.5

Flumazenil: Possible Interactions With Other Drugs

Drug taken by patient	Interaction with flumazenil	Dentist's action
Benzodiazepines taken chronically, especially with tricyclic or tetracyclic antidepressants	Effect is reversed by flumazenil; this may cause excitatory effects such as convulsions	Monitor patient for seizure activity

long procedure and is least likely in cases where flumazenil is administered to reverse a low dose of a short-acting benzodiazepine.

Suggested Readings

American Dental Association. The use of conscious sedation, deep sedation and general anesthesia in dentistry. Adopted by the ADA House of Delegates, October 1996.

American Dental Association. Guidelines for the use of conscious sedation, deep sedation and general anesthesia for dentists. Chicago: ADA; 1999.

American Dental Association Council on Dental Education and Licensure. Guidelines for teaching the comprehensive control of anxiety and pain in dentistry. Chicago: ADA; 1999.

Giangrego E. Conscious sedation: benefits and risks. JADA 1984;109:546-57.

Kallar SK, Dunwiddie WC. In: Wetchler BV, ed. Problems in anesthesia. Philadelphia: JB Lippincott Co.; 1988:93-100.

Malamed SF. Sedation: A guide to patient management. 3rd ed., St. Louis: Mosby; 1995.

Miller RD. Clinical Therapeutics 1992;14(Special Supplemental Section): 861-995.

Table 2.6

Flumazenil: Adverse Effects, Precautions and Contraindications

Body system	Adverse effects	Precautions/contraindications
CV	Cutaneous vasodilation (sweating, flushing, hot flashes) Dysrhythmias (atrial, nodal, ventricular extrasystoles), bradycardia, tachycardia, hypertension, chest pain	Should be used cautiously with patients who have increased left ventricular end-diastolic pressure
CNS	Confusion (difficulty in concentrating), delirium, convulsions, somnolence (stupor), agitation, anxiety, dizziness, emotional lability (crying, euphoria, depression, paranoia)	Should not be used in cases of suspected heterocyclic antidepressant overdose, with patients physically dependent on benzodiazepines or with patients maintained on benzodiazepines for control of potentially life-threatening situations (for example, seizure disorder) Whether for reversal or conscious sedation or for suspected benzodiazepine overdose, administer through a freely running IV infusion into a large vein to minimize pain at the injection site
EENT	Abnormal vision, diplopia	None significant to dentistry
GI	Nausea, vomiting, hiccups	None significant to dentistry
Oral	Dry mouth	None significant to dentistry
Resp	Dyspnea, hyperventilation	None significant to dentistry

Barbiturates

The barbiturates were the first drugs truly effective for the management of anxiety. The barbiturates are generalized CNS depressants, depressing the cerebral cortex, the limbic system, and the reticular activating system. These actions produce reduction in anxiety level, decreased mental acuity and a state of drowsiness. Barbiturates are capable of producing any level of CNS depression, ranging from light sedation through hypnosis, general anesthesia, coma and death. IV barbiturate compounds can be infused in subhypnotic doses to produce sedation.

The barbiturates used for conscious sedation are classified as sedative hypnotics and are categorized by their duration of clinical action following an average oral dose.

Short-acting barbiturates (with 3 to 4 h duration of action), most notably pentobarbital and secobarbital, are the barbiturates best suited for dental situations. The ultra–short-acting barbiturates are classified as general anesthetics and are contraindicated for conscious sedation. They are described in Chapter 3. The long-acting (16- to 24-h duration of action) and the intermediate-acting (6- to 8-h duration of action) barbiturates produce clinical levels of sedation for a period exceeding that required for the usual dental or surgical appointment. The long-acting barbiturates, such as phenobarbital, are commonly used as anticonvulsants or when long-term sedation is necessary. The intermediate-acting barbiturates occasionally are used as "sleeping pills" for some types of insomnia.

Accepted Indications

Barbiturates have been used in routine cases requiring conscious sedation to relieve anxiety, tension and apprehension; however, these agents have generally been replaced with the benzodiazepines for these treatments. Barbiturates are used as adjuncts in anesthesia to reduce anxiety and facilitate induction of anesthesia. They are also used in the treatment of epilepsy and insomnia.

General Dosing Information

IV dosage of the barbiturates must be titrated individually in all patients, particularly for patients with impaired hepatic function; a low dose should be used initially. Tolerance and physical dependence occurs with repeated administration. These agents are controlled substances in the United States and Canada. See Table 2.7.

Special Dental Considerations

Drug Interactions of Dental Interest

Possible drug interactions and/or related problems of clinical significance in dentistry are shown in Table 2.8.

Special Patients

Pregnant and nursing women

Barbiturates readily cross the placenta and increase the risk of fetal abnormalities. Use during the third trimester may result in physical dependence and respiratory depression in newborns.

Barbiturates distribute into the breast milk and may cause CNS depression in the infant.

Patient Monitoring: Aspects to Watch

- Respiratory status

Adverse Effects and Precautions

Adverse effects and precautions related to barbiturates are listed in Table 2.9.

Pharmacology

Barbiturates can produce all levels of CNS mood alteration, from excitation to sedation, hypnosis and coma. In sufficient therapeutic doses, barbiturates induce anesthesia, and overdose can produce death. These agents depress the sensory cortex, decrease motor activity, alter cerebellar function and produce drowsiness, sedation and hypnosis. Barbiturates are respiratory depressants and the degree of respiratory depression is dose-dependent. All barbiturates exhibit anticonvulsant activity.

Barbiturates are enzyme-inducing drugs. This class of drugs can enhance the metabolism of other agents. The onset of this enzyme induction is gradual and depends on the accumulation of the barbiturate and the synthesis of the new enzyme, while offset depends on elimination of the barbiturate and decay of the increased enzyme stores.

Absorption varies depending on the route of administration: oral or rectal, 20 to 60 min; IM, slightly faster than oral or rectal routes; IV, immediate to 5 min. The sodium salts of the barbiturates are more rapidly absorbed than the free acids because they dissolve rapidly. The rate of absorption is increased if the agents are taken on an empty stomach. The barbiturates are weak acids and distribute rapidly to all tissues, with high concentrations initially in the brain, liver, lungs, heart and kidneys. The more lipid-soluble the drug, the more rapidly it penetrates all tissues of the body. The barbiturates are metabolized by the liver; phenobarbital is partially excreted unchanged in the urine.

Table 2.7
Barbiturates: Dosing and Prescribing Information

Generic name	Brand name(s)	Adult dosage	Max adult dosage	Child dosage	Max child dosage	PRC	Content/form
Amobarbital (II*; C†)	Amytal sterile solution	**Sedative—IV/IM:** 30-50 mg bid-tid **Hypnotic—IV/IM:** 65-200 mg	**Oral:** Not available **IM:** 500 mg/dose **IV:** 1 g/dose	**Age < 6 y, hypnotic—IM:** 2-3 mg/kg **Age ≥ 6 y, hypnotic—IM:** 2-3 mg/kg **Age ≥ 6 y, hypnotic—IV:** 65-500 mg/dose **Age ≥ 6 y, sedative, preoperative—IV:** 65-500 mg or 3-5 mg/kg/dose	NE	D	**Sterile solution:** 500 mg
	Amytal, generic	**Hypnotic—oral:** 65-200 mg **Sedative, daytime—oral:** 50-300 mg/day divided doses **Preoperative:** 200 mg 1-2 h before procedure	NE	NE	NE	NE	**Capsules:** 200 mg
	Amytal [CAN]	**Hypnotic:** 65-200 mg at bedtime **Preoperative:** 2-6 mg/kg 1-2 h before procedure **Sedative:** 50-300 mg a day in divided doses	NE	**Hypnotic:** NE **Sedative:** 2 mg/kg **Preoperative—oral:** 100 mg/dose	NE	NE	**Tablets:** 100 mg [CAN]
Aprobarbital (III*)	Alurate	**Hypnotic—oral:** 40-160 mg at bedtime **Sedative—oral:** 40 mg tid	NE	NE	NE	D	**Elixir:** 40 mg/5 mL

Continued on next page

[CAN] indicates a drug available only in Canada.
PRC: Pregnancy risk category.
NE: Not established.
* Controlled substance in the United States; see Appendix A for complete description of schedule.
† Controlled substance in Canada; see Appendix A for complete description of schedule.

Table 2.7 (cont.)
Barbiturates: Dosing and Prescribing Information

Generic name	Brand name(s)	Adult dosage	Max adult dosage	Child dosage	Max child dosage	PRC	Content/form
Butabarbital (III*; C†)	**Elixir:** Busodium, Butalan, Butisol, generic **Tablets:** Busodium, Butisol, generic	**Hypnotic:** 50-100 mg at bedtime **Sedative—oral:** 15-30 mg tid-qid **Preoperative—oral:** 50-100 mg 60-90 min before surgery	NE	**Sedative—oral:** 2-6 mg per kg of body weight per day **Preoperative—oral:** 2-6 mg/kg, 100 mg/dose	NE	D	**Elixir:** 30 mg/5 mL **Tablets:** 15, 30, 50, 100 mg; 15, 30, 100 mg [CAN]
Mephobarbital (IV*; C†)	Mebaral	**Anticonvulsant—oral:** 200 mg at bedtime to 600 mg/day in divided doses **Sedative-hypnotic, daytime—oral:** 32-100 mg tid-qid	NE	**Anticonvulsant:** up to age 5 y, 16-32 mg tid-qid **Sedative-hypnotic—daytime:** 16-32 mg tid-qid	NE	D	**Tablets:** 30, 100 mg; 32, 50, 100 [CAN]
Pentobarbital (II*; C†)	**Capsules:** Nembutal, generic; Novopentobarb [CAN] **Elixir:** Nembutal **Parenteral:** Nembutal	**Hypnotic:** 100 mg at bedtime **Sedative, oral elixir:** 20 mg tid-qid **Sedative, preoperative, capsules:** 100 mg **Hypnotic—IM:** 150-200 mg **Hypnotic—IV:** Must be titrated to effect, 5 mg initially to check for sensitivity to drug, followed by 10 mg/30 s; may require 30-300 mg in repeated titrations; usual dose for adequate sedation in adults: 125-175 mg	**Hypnotic—IV:** 50 mg total	**Sedative—oral:** 2-6 mg/kg **Preoperative—oral:** 2-6 mg/kg, up to maximum of 100 mg/dose **Hypnotic—IM:** 2-6 mg per kg up to 100 mg maximum **Hypnotic—IV:** 50 mg initially, then small doses after 1 min	**Sedative—oral:** 2-6 mg/kg **Preoperative—oral:** 2-6 mg/kg, up to maximum of 100 mg/dose **Hypnotic—IM:** 2-6 mg/kg up to 100 mg maximum **Hypnotic—IV:** 50 mg initially, then small doses after 1 min **Age 1-4 y, preoperative—rectal:** 30 or 60 mg **Age 5-12 y, preoperative—rectal:** 60 mg **Age 12-14 y, preoperative—rectal:** 60 or 120 mg	D	**Capsules:** 50, 100 mg; 100 mg [CAN] **Elixir:** 20 mg/5 mL pentobarbital sodium (18.2 mg pentobarbital) **Injection:** 50 mg/mL **Suppositories:** 30, 60, 120, 200 mg; 25, 50 mg [CAN]

Drug	Available as	Adult dosage		Child dosage		PRC	Dosage forms
Pentobarbital (II*; C†) (cont.)	NovaRectal [CAN]	**Preoperative—IM:** 150-200 mg **Hypnotic—rectal:** 120-200 mg at bedtime **Sedative—rectal:** 30 mg bid-qid	NE	**Age 1-4 y, preoperative—rectal:** 30 or 60 mg **Age 5-12 y, preoperative—rectal:** 60 mg **Age 12-14 y, preoperative—rectal:** 60 or 120 mg	NE	NE	**Sterile solution:** 500 mg **Suppositories:** 25, 50 mg
Phenobarbital (IV*; C†)	**Capsules:** Barbita, Solfoton **Tablets:** Barbita, Solfoton, generic **Injection:** Luminal, generic **Sterile solution:** generic	**Hypnotic—oral:** 100-320 mg at bedtime **Sedative—oral:** 30-120 mg in 2 or 3 divided doses/day **Preoperative—IM:** 120-200 mg 60-90 min before surgery	U	**Preoperative—oral:** 1-3 mg/kg **Preoperative—IM or IV:** 1-3 mg/kg 60-90 min before surgery	NE	D	**Tablets:** 8, 15, 30, 60, 100 mg; 15, 30, 60, 100 mg [CAN] **Capsules:** 15 mg **Elixir:** 20 mg/5 mL **Phenobarbital sodium injection USP:** 30, 60, 65, 130 mg/mL; 30, 120 mg/mL [CAN] **Sterile phenobarbital sodium USP:** 120 mg

Continued on next page

[CAN] indicates a drug available only in Canada.
PRC: Pregnancy risk category.
NE: Not established.
U: Unavailable.
* Controlled substance in the United States; see Appendix A for complete description of schedule.
† Controlled substance in Canada; see Appendix A for complete description of schedule.

Table 2.7 (cont.)

Barbiturates: Dosing and Prescribing Information

Generic name	Brand name(s)	Adult dosage	Max adult dosage	Child dosage	Max child dosage	PRC	Content/form
Secobarbital (II*, oral, C†)	Seconal; Novosecobarb [CAN]	**Preoperative—oral:** 200-300 mg 1-2 h before surgery **Hypnotic—oral:** 100 mg at bedtime **Sedative—oral:** 30-50 mg tid-qid	U	**Preoperative—oral:** 2-6 mg/kg, up to maximum of 100 mg/dose 1-2 h before surgery **Sedative—oral:** 2 mg/kg tid **Preoperative—IM:** 4-5 mg/kg	U	D	**Capsules:** 100 mg; 50, 100 mg [CAN] **Injection:** 50 mg/mL
Secobarbital and amobarbital (II*; C†)	Tuinal	1 capsule at bedtime or preoperatively	U	NE	NE	D	**Capsules:** 50 mg secobarbital and 50 mg amobarbital; 100 mg secobarbital and 100 mg amobarbital

[CAN] indicates a drug available only in Canada.

PRC: Pregnancy risk category.

NE: Not established.

U: Unavailable.

* Controlled substance in the United States; see Appendix A for complete description of schedule.

† Controlled substance in Canada; see Appendix A for complete description of schedule.

Table 2.8
Barbiturates: Possible Interactions With Other Drugs

Drug taken by patient	Interaction with barbiturates	Dentist's action
Acetaminophen	Risk of increased hepatotoxicity may exist with large or chronic barbiturate doses	Monitor liver enzymes Avoid prolonged high dosage use
Alcohol	*Concurrent use may increase the CNS depressant effects of either agent*	Patients receiving a barbiturate and another CNS depressant should be monitored for additive effects
Anticoagulants: coumarin oral anticoagulants	*Barbiturates can increase metabolism of anticoagulants, resulting in a decreased response*	No barbiturate therapy should be started or stopped without considering the possibility of readjustment to the anticoagulant dose
Carbamazepine	*Plasma concentrations may decrease owing to increased metabolism that results from induction of hepatic enzymes*	No special precautions appear necessary, but be aware that carbamazepine plasma concentrations may be lower
Charcoal	Charcoal reduces the absorption of barbiturates	Advise patient to avoid large amounts of food cooked over charcoal
Chloramphenicol	Chloramphenicol may inhibit phenobarbital metabolism; barbiturates may enhance chloramphenicol metabolism	Advise patient that sedative effect of phenobarbital may be prolonged Limit use of barbiturates and be aware that anticonvulsant effect of clonazepam may be reduced
Clonazepam	Increased clonazepam clearance may occur, which can lead to lower steady-state levels and less efficacy	
Contraceptives, oral	*Reliability may be reduced because of accelerated estrogen metabolism caused by barbiturates' induction of hepatic enzymes*	Suggest alternate form of birth control
Corticosteroids	Barbiturates may enhance corticosteroid metabolism through induction of hepatic microsomal enzymes	
Doxycycline	Phenobarbital decreases doxycycline's half-life and serum levels	Dose of doxycycline may have to be increased
Griseofulvin	Phenobarbital appears to interfere with the absorption of oral griseofulvin	Dose of griseofulvin may have to be increased
Hydantoins	Effect of barbiturates on metabolism of hydantoins is unpredictable	Advise patient that anticonvulsant effect may be reduced

Italics indicate information of major clinical significance.

Continued on next page

Table 2.8 (cont.)
Barbiturates: Possible Interactions With Other Drugs

Drug taken by patient	Interaction with barbiturates	Dentist's action
MAO-I	MAO-I may enhance the sedative effects of barbiturates	Reduced dosage of barbiturate should be considered
Methoxyflurane	Enhanced renal toxicity may occur	
Metronidazole	Antimicrobial effectiveness of metronidazole may be decreased	Dose of metronidazole may have to be increased
Narcotics	May increase the toxicity of meperidine and reduce the effect of methadone	Monitor for excessive meperidine effect; dose of methadone may have to be increased
Phenylbutazone	Elimination half-life of phenylbutazone may be reduced	Consultation with patient's physician may be needed
Quinidine	Phenobarbital may significantly reduce serum levels and half-life of quinidine	Dose of phenobarbital may have to be reduced
Rifampin	Rifampin induces hepatic microsomal enzymes and may decrease the effectiveness of barbiturates	Increased dose of barbiturates may be necessary
Theophylline	Barbiturates decrease theophylline levels, possibly resulting in decreased effects	Consultation with patient's physician may be needed
Valproic acid	*Concurrent use may decrease the metabolism of barbiturates, resulting in increased plasma concentrations*	Monitor for excessive phenobarbital effect
Verapamil	Clearance of verapamil may be increased and its bioavailability decreased	

Italics indicate information of major clinical significance.

Table 2.9

Barbiturates: Adverse Effects, Precautions and Contraindications

Body system	Adverse effects	Precautions/contraindications
General	Local pain on IM injection	None significant to dentistry
CV	Hypotension, cardiac dysrhythmias, bradycardia, gangrene with inadvertent intra-arterial injection, thrombophlebitis with IV use	Should be used cautiously in patients with congestive heart failure
CNS	Dizziness, lightheadedness, "hangover" effect, drowsiness, lethargy, CNS excitation or depression, impaired judgment, confusion, depression, insomnia, nightmares	Should be used cautiously with patients who have history of drug abuse, suicidal tendencies Use caution when administering to patients with acute or chronic pain, because of paradoxical excitement Contraindicated in patients with pre-existing CNS depression
GI	Nausea, vomiting, constipation	None significant to dentistry
Hema	Agranulocytosis, megaloblastic anemia, thrombocytopenia, porphyria	Should be used cautiously in patients with anemia
Integ	Exfoliative dermatitis, Stevens-Johnson syndrome, rash	None significant to dentistry
Resp	Apnea (especially with rapid IV use), respiratory depression, laryngospasm	Should be used cautiously in patients with asthma Contraindicated in patients with severe respiratory disease involving dyspnea or obstruction

Opioids

The term "opioid" is used in a broad sense to include both opioid agonists and opioid agonists/antagonists. The opioids are administered from their analgesic properties and are considered excellent drugs for the relief of moderate to severe pain. The parenteral dosage forms of this class of drugs are also used as general anesthesia adjuncts in conjunction with other drugs, such as the benzodiazepines, neuromuscular blocking agents and nitrous oxide for the maintenance of "balanced" anesthesia. Sufentanil, alfentanil and remifentanil are discussed in Chapter 3, as they are used most often in dentistry for deep sedation and general anesthesia. All opioid narcotic agents are classified as controlled substances in the U.S. and Canada. Opioids are classified into 3 types: agonists, antagonists and mixed agents. Agonists include codeine, fentanyl, hydrocodone, hydromorphone, levorphanol, meperidine, methadone, morphine, oxycodone and oxymorphone. Antagonists are naloxone and naltrexone. Mixed agents are buprenorphine, butorphanol, nalbuphine and pentazocine.

General Dosing Information

Narcotic drugs are used to produce mood changes, provide analgesia and elevate the pain threshold. Opioid analgesics may not provide sufficient analgesia when used with nitrous oxide for the maintenance of balance anesthesia. Narcotic agents can be used in combination with other agents such as benzodiazepines, antihistamines, ultrashort-acting barbiturates and a potent hydrocarbon inhalation anesthetic. Dosage and dosing intervals should be individualized for the patient based on duration of action of the specific drug, other medications the patient is currently taking, the patient's condition and the patient's response. See Table 2.10.

Special Dental Considerations

Drug Interactions of Dental Interest

Possible drug interactions of clinical significance in dentistry are shown in Table 2.11.

Laboratory Value Alterations

- Opioids delay gastric emptying, thereby invalidating gastric emptying studies.
- In hepatobiliary imaging, delivery of technetium Tc99m disofenin to the small bowel may be prevented because opioids may constrict sphincter of Oddi; this results in delayed visualization and resembles an obstruction in the common bile duct.
- Cerebrospinal fluid may be increased secondary to respiratory-depression–induced carbon dioxide retention.
- Plasma amylase activity may be increased.
- Plasma lipase activity may be increased.
- Serum alanine aminotransferase may be increased.
- Serum alkaline phosphatase may be increased.
- Serum aspartate aminotransferase may be increased.
- Serum bilirubin may be increased.
- Serum lactate dehydrogenase may be increased.

Cross-Sensitivity

Patients hypersensitive to fentanyl may be hypersensitive to the chemically related alfentanil or sufentanil.

Special Patients

Pregnant and nursing women
Risk-benefit must be considered because opioid analgesics cross the placenta.

Pediatric, geriatric and other special patients
Geriatric patients are more susceptible to the effects of opioids, especially respiratory depression. Clearance of opioid analgesics can be reduced in the geriatric patient, which leads to a delayed postoperative recovery. Children aged up to 2 y may be more susceptible to opioids' effects, especially respiratory depression. Paradoxical excitation is especially likely to occur in the pediatric population.

Patient Monitoring: Aspects to Watch

- Respiratory status
- State of consciousness
- Heart rate
- Blood pressure

Adverse Effects and Precautions

Table 2.12 lists adverse effects, precautions and contraindications related to opioids.

Pharmacology

Opioid analgesics bind to receptors within the central nervous system and peripheral nervous system. This interaction affects both the perception of pain and the emotional response to pain. There are at least five types of opioid receptors—mu (μ), kappa (K), sigma (σ), delta (Δ) and epsilon (ϵ)—located throughout the body that may be activated by exogenous or endogenous opioid-like substances (endorphins). The action of various opioids at the various receptors determine the agents' specific actions and side effects (Table 2.13). Based on their actions at these receptors, the commercially available opioids may be divided into three groups: pure agonists,

Table 2.10

Opioids: Dosage and Prescribing Information

Generic name	Brand name(s)	Adult dosage	Max adult dosage	Child dosage	Max child dosage	PRC	Content/form
Butorphanol	Stadol	**Preoperative—IV:** usually 2 mg 60-90 min before surgery	NE	NE	NE	C	**With preservative:** 2 mg/mL **Without preservative:** 1 mg/mL, 2 mg/mL
Fentanyl	Sublimaze, generic	**Sedation for local anesthesia adjunct:** 0.07-1.14 µg/kg **Sedation for minor procedures:** 2 µg/kg	NE	**Age 2-12 y—IV:** 2-3 µg/kg	NE	C	**Without preservative:** 50 µg/mL
Meperidine	Demerol, generic	**Preoperative—IM or SC:** 50-100 mg 30-90 min before anesthesia **IV:** repeated slow injection of fractional doses of a solution diluted to 10 mg/mL **IV:** infusion, as a solution diluted to 1 mg/mL	NE	**Preoperative—IM or SC:** 1-2.2 mg/kg q 3-4 h	Not to exceed 100 mg	NE	**Solution with preservative:** 25, 50, 75, 100-mg/mL solution; 50, 100 mg/mL [CAN] **Solution without preservative:** 10, 25, 50, 75, 100 mg/mL; 10, 25, 50, 75, 100 mg/mL [CAN]
Morphine	Astramorph PF, Duramorph, generic; Epimorph [CAN], Morphine Forte [CAN], Morphine Extra Forte [CAN], Morphine HP [CAN]	**Analgesic—IM or SC:** 5-20 mg q 4 h **Analgesic—IV:** 4-10 mg in 4-5 mL water, administered slowly	NE	**Preoperative—IM:** 0.05-1 mg/kg	Not to exceed 10 mg/dose	C	**Injection with preservative:** 1, 2, 4, 5, 8, 10, 15 mg/mL; 1, 2, 5, 10, 15 mg/mL [CAN] **Injection without preservative:** 0.5, 1, 25 50 mg/mL; 0.5, 1, 25, 50 mg/mL [CAN]
Nalbuphine	Nubain	**Balanced anesthesia—IV:** 300 µg-3 mg/kg administered over 10-15 min period **Supplemental—IV:** 250-500 µg/kg as required	20-mg single dose; 160 mg/day	NE	NE	C	**Solution with preservative:** 10, 20 mg/mL; 10, 20 mg/mL [CAN]
Pentazocine lactate	Talwin	**Analgesic—IM, IV, SC:** 30 mg q 3-4 h	Up to 360 mg/day	NE	NE	C	**Injection:** 30 mg/mL

[CAN] indicates a drug available only in Canada.
PRC: Pregnancy risk category.
NE: Not established.

Table 2.11

Opioids: Possible Interactions With Other Drugs

Drug taken by patient	Interaction with opioids	Dentist's action
Barbiturate anesthetics (methohexital, thiamylal, thiopental)	Dose of thiopental required to induce anesthesia may be reduced in presence of narcotic analgesics Apnea may occur	No additional precautions other than those routinely used in anesthesia appear necessary
Benzodiazepines	*Increased respiratory depression* *Increased recovery time* *Increased risk of hypotension*	Titrate dosages and monitor for excess sedation
Cimetidine	Actions of narcotic analgesics may be enhanced, resulting in toxicity	If significant CNS depression occurs, withdraw the drugs; if warranted, administer a narcotic antagonist such as naloxone
CNS depressants	*Increased CNS depression*	Monitor for excess sedation
Diuretics/antihypertensives	Hypotensive effects increased by opioids	Monitor blood pressure
MAO inhibitors	*With meperidine: agitation, seizures, fever, coma, apnea, death*	Avoid this combination
Phenothiazines	Increased or decreased effects of opioid analgesic supplements Hypotension may occur when phenothiazine is administered with meperidine	Avoid concurrent use of meperidine and phenothiazines

Italics indicate information of major clinical significance.

Table 2.12

Opioids: Adverse Effects, Precautions and Contraindications

Body system	Adverse effects	Precautions/contraindications
General	Bradycardia; physical dependence, with or without psychological dependence, may occur with chronic administration	Emotional instability, suicide attempts
CV	Hypotension, peripheral circulatory collapse, cardiac arrest	Cardiac dysrythmias
CNS	Weakness, tiredness, drowsiness, dizziness, confusion, nervousness, headache, restlessness, malaise, increased intracranial pressure, paradoxical CNS stimulation	History of convulsions, head injury, increased intracranial pressure, intracranial lesions

Continued on next page

Table 2.12 (cont.)

Opioids: Adverse Effects, Precautions and Contraindications

Body system	Adverse effects	Precautions/contraindications
EENT	Miosis	None of significance to dentistry
GI	*Nausea, vomiting, constipation, xerostomia, biliary spasm, paralytic ileus*	*Diarrhea associated with pseudomembranous colitis, poisoning* *In inflammatory bowel disease: risk of toxic megacolon may be increased*
GU	Ureteral spasms, decreased urination	Renal function impairment—risk of convulsions because opioids and/or their metabolites are excreted via the kidney Prostatic hypertrophy
HB	None of significance to dentistry	Hepatic function impairment (opioids metabolized by the liver)
Oral	All opioids may cause xerostomia, which can lead to caries, periodontal disease, oral candidiasis and discomfort with prolonged use	None of significance to dentistry
Resp	*Shortness of breath, troubled breathing, rigid chest syndrome*	*Respiratory depression, chronic respiratory disease, acute asthma attack*

Italics indicate information of major clinical significance.

Table 2.13

Opioids: Effect on Types of Nerve Receptors

Receptor	Effect
$mu_1 (\mu_1)$	Supraspinal analgesia
$mu_2 (\mu_2)$	Respiratory depression, bradycardia, hypothermia, euphoria, moderate sedation, physical dependence, miosis
kappa (K)	Spinal analgesia, heavy sedation, miosis
sigma (σ)	Dysphoria, tachycardia, tachypnea, mydriasis
delta (Δ)	Modulation of μ receptor
epsilon (ε)	Altered neurohumoral functions

pure antagonists and mixed agents (agonists/antagonists or partial agonists).

All opioids are respiratory depressants. By exerting a depressant action on respiratory center neurons in the medulla, they decrease respiratory rate, tidal volume and minute ventilation. They may increase arterial CO_2 tensions. All opioids affect the cardiovascular system by their actions on the autonomic nervous system. Hypotension may result from arteriolar and venous dilation as a result of either histamine release or decreased sympathetic nervous system tone. Bradycardia results from vagal stimulation. Finally, all opioids disorganize GI function, causing increased tone and muscle spasm but delayed emptying and decreased motility and secretions.

Opioid (Narcotic) Antagonist: Naloxone

Like the benzodiazepines, the opioids have a specific antagonist that reverses the pharmacologic effects caused by the opioid drugs.

Accepted Indications

Naloxone is used for the complete or partial reversal of narcotic depression, such as respiratory depression induced by opioids (including both natural and synthetic narcotics). Naloxone is also used for the diagnosis of suspected acute opioid overdose.

General Dosing Information

Varying amounts of naloxone may be needed to antagonize the effects of different agents. Lack of significant improvement of CNS depression and/or respiration after administration of an adequate dose (10 mg) of naloxone may indicate that the condition is due to a nonopioid CNS depressant. Naloxone reverses the analgesic effects of the opioid and may precipitate withdrawal symptoms in physically dependent patients. See Table 2.14. for dosage and prescribing information for naloxone.

Dosage Adjustments

Repeat dosing may be required within 1- or 2-h intervals depending on the amount and type (short- or long-acting) of narcotic and the interval since the last administration of the narcotic. Supplemental IM doses can produce a long-lasting effect.

Special Dental Considerations

Drug Interactions of Dental Interest

A possible drug interaction of clinical significance in dentistry is shown in Table 2.15.

Special Patients

Pregnant and nursing women
Naloxone crosses the placenta and may precipitate withdrawal in the fetus as well as the mother. Breast-feeding problems in humans have not been documented.

Pediatric, geriatric and other special patients
Studies performed in pediatrics have not shown problems that would limit the usefulness of naloxone in children. Geriatric-specific problems do not seem to limit the usefulness of this medication in elderly patients.

Patient Monitoring: Aspects to Watch

- Cardiac status
- State of consciousness
- Respiratory status, oxygen saturation

Adverse Effects and Precautions

Adverse effects, precautions and contraindications related to naloxone are listed in Table 2.16.

Pharmacology

Naloxone reverses the CNS and respiratory depression associated with narcotic overdose. It also reverses postoperative opioid depression. Naloxone competes with and displaces narcotics at narcotic receptor sites.

Because of naloxone's short half-life, a continuous infusion may be required to maintain alertness. A patient should never be released soon after receiving naloxone because the ingested narcotic may have a longer half-life than naloxone, and its toxic

Table 2.14

Naloxone: Dosage and Prescribing Information

Generic name	Brand name(s)	Adult dosage	Child dosage	PRC	Content/form
Naloxone	Narcan ★	Dose must be individualized **Opioid toxicity—IV, IM or SC:** 0.4-2 mg in a single dose; repeat at 2- to 3-min intervals **Postoperative opioid depression—IV:** 0.1-0.2 mg q 2-3 min until adequate ventilation and alertness without pain are obtained	**Opioid toxicity—IV, IM or SC:** 0.01 mg/kg, repeated every 2-3 min for 1 or 2 additional doses **Postoperative opioid depression—IV:** 0.005 to 0.01 mg q 2-3 min until adequate ventilation and alertness without pain are obtained	B	**Solution with preservative:** 20 µg/mL, 400 µg/mL, 1 mg/mL **Solution without preservative:** 20 µg/mL, 400 µg/mL, 1 mg/mL; 20 µg/mL, 400 µg/mL [CAN]

★ indicates a drug bearing the ADA Seal of Acceptance.
[CAN] indicates a drug available only in Canada.
PRC: Pregnancy risk category.

Table 2.15

Naloxone: Possible Interactions With Other Drugs

Drug taken by patient	Interaction with naloxone	Dentist's action
Narcotic analgesics	*Effect decreased by naloxone*	Monitor patient for withdrawal

Italics indicate information of major clinical significance.

Table 2.16

Naloxone: Adverse Effects, Precautions and Contraindications

Body system	Adverse effects	Precautions/contraindications
CV	Sweating, hypertension, hypotension, tachycardia, ventricular arrhythmias	Contraindicated in patients with hypersensitivity to naloxone
CNS	Insomnia, irritability, anxiety, convulsions	None significant to dentistry
EENT	Blurred vision	None significant to dentistry
GI	Nausea and vomiting	None significant to dentistry

effects—such as respiratory depression—may break through.

Chloral Hydrate

Chloral hydrate is an oral sedative-hypnotic that is used when providing dental treatment to the uncooperative preschool child.

Accepted Indications

Accepted indications for chloral hydrate are nocturnal sedation; preoperative sedation to lessen anxiety; in postoperative care and control of pain as an adjunct to opiates and analgesics.

General Dosing Information

Deaths have been associated with the use of chloral hydrate, especially in children. Repetitive dosing of chloral hydrate is not recommended owing to the accumulation of the active metabolite trichloroethylene. As with any sedation procedure, this sedative should be administered where there can be proper monitoring. Practitioners must know how to properly calculate and administer the appropriate dose. See Table 2.17.

Special Dental Considerations

Drug Interactions of Dental Interest

Drug interactions between chloral hydrate and other drugs are listed in Table 2.18.

Laboratory Value Alterations

- Chloral hydrate may interfere with the copper sulfate test for glucosuria (confirm suspected glucosuria by glucose oxidase test) and with fluorometric tests for urine catecholamines (do not administer chloral hydrate for 48 h preceding the test).

Special Patients

Pregnant and nursing women

Chloral hydrate crosses the placenta, and chronic use of chloral hydrate during pregnancy may cause withdrawal symptoms in the neonate. In addition, chloral hydrate is distributed into breast milk; its use by nursing mothers may cause sedation in the infant.

Pediatric, geriatric and other special patients

Chloral hydrate is not recommended for use in infants and children in cases in which repeated dosing would be necessary. With repeated dosing, accumulation of trichloroethanol and trichloroacetic acid metabolites may increase the potential for excessive CNS depression.

No information is available on the relationship of age to the effects of chloral hydrate in geriatric patients. Elderly patients are more likely to have age-related hepatic function impairment and renal function impairment. Dose reduction may be required.

Patient Monitoring: Aspects to Watch

- Respiratory status
- Possible abuse and dependence
- Blood pressure

Adverse Effects and Precautions

Table 2.19 lists adverse effects, precautions and contraindications related to chloral hydrate.

Pharmacology

The mechanism of action of chloral hydrate is unknown; however, it is believed that the CNS depressant effects are due to its active metabolite, trichloroethanol. It is rapidly absorbed from the gastrointestinal tract after oral administration and is metabolized in red blood cells in the liver to the active metabolite. Its onset of action is usually within 30 min and its duration of action is 4-8 h.

Patient Advice

- Swallow the capsule whole; do not chew because of unpleasant taste.
- Take with a full glass of water or juice to reduce gastric irritation.
- For syrup dose: Mix with glassful of juice or water to improve flavor and reduce gastric irritation.
- For suppository form: If too soft for insertion, chill suppository in refrigerator for 30 min before removing foil wrapper.

Table 2.17
Chloral Hydrate: Dosage and Prescribing Information

Generic name	Brand name(s)	Adult dosage	Max adult dosage	Child dosage	Max child dosage	PRC	Content/form
Chloral hydrate	**Capsules:** generic; Novo-Chlorhydrate [CAN] **Suppositories:** Aquachloral Supprettes, generic **Syrup:** generic; PMS–Chloral Hydrate [CAN], generic [CAN]	**Preoperative— oral:** 500 mg-1 g 30 min before surgery **Sedative, day-time—oral:** 250 mg tid after meals **Sedative hyp-notic—oral:** 500 mg-1 g 15-30 min before bedtime	2 g/day	**Sedative-hypnotic premedication before proce-dure:** 50 mg/kg, up to maximum of 1 g per single dose; doses of 25-100 mg/kg may be used in individual patients; total dose should not exceed 100 mg/kg or 2 g	100 mg/kg or 2 g	C	**Capsules:** 250, 500 mg; 500 mg [CAN] **Suppositories:** 325, 500, 650 mg **Syrup:** 250, 500 mg/5 mL; 500 mg/5 mL [CAN]

[CAN] indicates a drug available only in Canada
PRC: Pregnancy risk category.

Table 2.18
Chloral Hydrate: Possible Interactions With Other Drugs

Drug taken by patient	Interaction with chloral hydrate	Dentist's action
Alcohol or other CNS depressants	*Concurrent use may increase CNS depressant effects of either medication*	Monitor for excessive CNS depression
Anticoagulants, coumarin or indandione-derivative	*Displacement of the anticoagulant from its plasma protein increases the anticoag-ulant effect*	Avoid use
Catecholamine	Large doses of chloral hydrate may sensitize cardiac tissues to cate-cholamine	Avoid treating chloral hydrate over-dose with adrenergic vasoconstrictor
Furosemide (IV)	Flushing, diaphoresis and blood pressure changes	Avoid use

Italics indicate information of major clinical significance.

Table 2.19

Chloral Hydrate: Adverse Effects, Precautions and Contraindications

Body system	Adverse effects	Precautions/contraindications
General	None of significance to dentistry	Should be used with caution in patients with history of drug or alcohol abuse Contraindicated for patients with hypersensitivity to chloral hydrate or any component
CV	None of significance to dentistry	Contraindicated for patients with severe cardiac disease
CNS	Clumsiness, hallucinations, drowsiness, "hangover" effect, disorientation, sedation ataxia, paradoxical excitement, dizziness, fever, confusion	None of significance to dentistry
GI	Gastric irritation, flatulence, nausea and vomiting, diarrhea	Contraindicated for patients with gastritis or ulcers
Hema	Leukopenia, eosinophilia	None of significance to dentistry
HB	None of significance to dentistry	Contraindicated for patients with hepatic or renal impairment Should be used with caution in patients who have porphyria

Ethchlorvynol

Ethchlorvynol is a sedative hypnotic used for the short-term management of insomnia. This medication has been replaced with other safer sedative-hypnotic agents (listed earlier in this chapter). Remember the following principles when using sedative-hypnotics such as ethchlorvynol:

- never sedate any patient with any technique of sedation without an assistant present in the room;
- reposition supine patient slowly to avoid orthostatic hypotension;
- provide escort assistance to departing patient owing to possibility of dizziness.

Accepted Indications

Ethchlorvynol is used as a sedative and a hypnotic.

General Dosing Information

Give the smallest effective dose to elderly and debilitated patients. Do not prescribe for longer than 1 w. See Table 2.20.

Special Dental Considerations

Drug Interactions of Dental Interest

Possible drug interactions with ethchlorvynol are listed in Table 2.21.

Special Patients

Pregnant and nursing women
Ethchlorvynol crosses the placenta and produces CNS depression in the neonate. It is not known if ethchlorvynol is excreted in breast milk.

Pediatric, geriatric and other special patients
Safety and efficacy have not been established in the pediatric population. Elderly patients are more sensitive to the effects of ethchlorvynol.

Table 2.20

Ethchlorvynol: Dosage and Prescribing Information

Generic name	Brand name(s)	Adult dosage	Max adult dosage	Child dosage	PRC	Content/form
Ethchlorvynol	Placidyl, generic	500 mg-1 g at bedtime	1 g	NE	C	**Capsules:** 200, 500, 750 mg

PRC: Pregnancy risk category.
NE: Not established.

Table 2.21

Ethchlorvynol: Possible Interactions With Other Drugs

Drug taken by patient	Interaction with ethchlorvynol	Dentist's action
Alcohol or CNS depressant medications	Increased CNS depressant effects	Dosage of one or both medications should be reduced
Anticoagulants	Decreased effect due to ethchlorvynol's increased metabolism of anticoagulant (through enzyme induction in the liver)	Anticoagulant dosage adjustments may be necessary
Antidepressants	Transient delirium	

Table 2.22

Ethchlorvynol: Adverse Effects

Body system	Adverse effects
CV	Bradycardia
CNS	Dizziness, weakness, clumsiness, confusion, daytime drowsiness, excitement
GI	Indigestion, nausea, stomach pain, unpleasant aftertaste
HB	Cholestatic jaundice
Musc	Trembling

Adverse Effects

Adverse effects related to ethchlorvynol are listed in Table 2.22.

Pharmacology

The mechanism of action of ethchlorvynol is unknown. Absorption is rapid from the gastrointestinal tract, with onset of action in 15-60 min and a duration of action of 5 h.

Meprobamate

Meprobamate is an antianxiety agent used for the management of anxiety disorders. It is not indicated for the treatment of anxiety or tension associated with everyday life. Prolonged use of meprobamate may decrease or inhibit salivary flow, thus contributing to the development of caries, periodontal disease, oral candidiasis and oral discomfort.

Accepted Indications

Meprobamate is used for management of anxiety disorders.

General Dosing Information

Dosing information for meprobamate is listed in Table 2.23.

Special Dental Considerations

Drug Interactions of Dental Interest

Drug interactions with meprobamate are listed in Table 2.24.

Cross-Sensitivity

Patients sensitive to other carbamate derivatives (carbromal, carisoprodol, mebutamate or tybamate) may be sensitive to this medication.

Special Patients

Pregnant and nursing women

Meprobamate crosses the placenta and has been associated with congenital malformations. It is excreted in the breast milk in a concentration of 2 to 4 times maternal plasma concentration and may cause sedation in the infant.

Pediatric, geriatric and other special patients

No pediatric-specific problems have been documented. Elderly patients are more sensitive to the effects of meprobamate.

Adverse Effects and Precautions

Adverse effects and precautions related to meprobamate are listed in Table 2.25.

Pharmacology

Mechanism of action of meprobamate is unknown. It is well absorbed from the gastrointestinal tract, with an onset of action within 1 h.

Suggested Readings

Briggs GG, Freeman RK, Vaffe SJ. Drugs in pregnancy and lactation. 4th ed. Baltimore: Williams & Wilkins; 1994.

Jastak JT, Donaldson D. Nitrous oxide. Anesth Prog 1991;38:142-53.

Kallar SK, Dunwiddie WC. Problems in anesthesia: outpatient anesthesia. In: Wetchler BV, ed. Conscious sedation. Philadelphia: JB Lippincott Co.; 1988:93-100.

Malamed SF. Sedation: a guide to patient management. 3rd ed. St. Louis: Mosby; 1995.

Roberge RJ, Maciera-Rodriguez L. Seizure-related oral lacerations: incidence and distribution. JADA 1985; 111:279.

Thompson PL, Lown B. Nitrous oxide as an analgesic in acute myocardial infarction. JAMA 1976;235:924.

Table 2.23

Meprobamate: Dosage and Prescribing Information

Generic name	Brand name(s)	Adult dosage	Max adult dosage	Child dosage	PRC	Content/ form
Meprobamate	**Tablets:** Equanil, Miltown, Trancot; Apo-Meprobamate [CAN], Equanil [CAN], Miltown [CAN] **Extended-release capsules:** Meprospan 200, Meprospan 400; Meprospan 400 [CAN]	**Tablets:** 400 mg tid-qid or 600 mg bid **Capsules:** 400-800 mg tid	2.4 g/day	**Age < 6 y:** Dosage not established **Age 6-12 y—oral:** 100-200 mg bid-tid	D	**Tablets:** 200, 400, 600 mg; 400 mg [CAN] **Extended-release capsules:** 200, 400 mg; 400 mg [CAN]

[CAN] indicates a drug available only in Canada.
PRC: Pregnancy risk category.

Table 2.24

Meprobamate: Possible Interactions With Other Drugs

Drug taken by patient	Interaction with meprobamate
Alcohol or CNS-depression–producing medication	Increased CNS depressant effects

Table 2.25

Meprobamate: Adverse Effects, Precautions and Contraindications

Body system	Adverse effects	Precautions/contraindications
General	None of significance to dentistry	Physical and psychological dependence may occur
CNS	Drowsiness, ataxia, clumsiness, dizziness, paradoxical excitement, confusion, slurred speech, headache, chills	None of significance to dentistry
EENT	Blurred vision	None of significance to dentistry
GI	Nausea and vomiting, stomatitis	None of significance to dentistry
HB	None of significance to dentistry	Should be used cautiously for patients with hepatic impairment
Renal	None of significance to dentistry	Should be used cautiously for patients with renal impairment
Resp	Wheezing	None of significance to dentistry

Chapter 3

General Anesthetics

John A. Yagiela, D.D.S., Ph.D.

General Anesthetics

General anesthesia can be defined as an induced state of unconsciousness accompanied by loss, partial or complete, of protective reflexes—among them the ability to independently maintain an airway and respond purposefully to physical stimulation or verbal command. General anesthesia has been an integral part of dental practice since 1844, when Dr. Horace Wells first used nitrous oxide to induce the loss of consciousness in patients. General anesthesia was, for many years, a major part of the pain control armamentarium of dentists, primarily because other pain control techniques were less well-developed. The introduction of local anesthetics in the clinical setting in 1884 and their steady improvement throughout the 20th century, however, has decreased the need for general anesthesia as a primary means of achieving pain control in dentistry. Furthermore, the introduction of sedation techniques has lessened the need for general anesthesia in managing patients' fear and apprehension. Despite dentists' decreasing need to rely on general anesthesia, its use may be indicated for patients who

- are extremely anxious and fearful;
- are mentally or physically challenged, or both;
- are too young to cooperate with the dentist;
- fail to respond to local anesthesia; or
- are undergoing stressful, traumatic procedures.

Inhalation anesthetics provided the first reliable means of producing controlled unconsciousness. Originally including only nitrous oxide and ether, inhalation anesthetics now comprise a number of easily volatilized halogenated hydrocarbons.

Various injectable agents, including the ultrashort-acting barbiturates, several opioid and benzodiazepine anesthetics and miscellaneous drugs, also are available. Injectable anesthetics have been used alone, in combination with each other and in conjunction with inhalation anesthetics for inducing and maintaining general anesthesia. As used in total intravenous anesthesia (TIVA), some of these drugs can provide the same control of anesthetic depth normally associated with inhalation agents and are especially suited for in-office anesthesia.

Dentists administer anesthetic drugs in lower doses to produce deep sedation, an induced state of depressed consciousness accompanied by a partial loss of protective reflexes such as those mentioned earlier.

The techniques of general anesthesia and deep sedation cannot be taught in a short course. Dentists who are contemplating using any anesthetic technique in which the patient's airway or protective reflexes could be impaired should have extensive training; this training is outlined in Part 2 of the *Guidelines for Teaching the Comprehensive Control of Pain and Anxiety in Dentistry*, published by the ADA Council on Dental Education and Licensure. All states and Canada now regulate dentists' use of general anesthesia and deep sedation.

This section includes a discussion of the following drugs: the inhalation anesthetics, the ultrashort-acting barbiturates methohexital and thiopental, etomidate, propofol, ketamine, droperidol/fentanyl and the opioids alfentanil, remifentanil and sufentanil. With the notable exception of nitrous oxide, these drugs are not generally recommended for use in conscious sedation in dentistry because they do not have a margin of safety wide enough to render unintended loss of consciousness unlikely. However, the benzodiazepines, fentanyl and several other opioids used for general anesthesia and deep sedation also can be used to produce conscious sedation. These drugs are discussed in Chapter 2, and opioids are discussed further in Chapter 4.

Accepted Indications

Inhalation and injectable anesthetics are used to induce and maintain general anesthesia. Selected agents such as nitrous oxide, methoxyflurane, enflurane, droperidol/fentanyl, sufentanil, remifentanil, thiopental and propofol have also been approved for use in providing sedation and analgesia for specific procedures that do not require general anesthesia. The product literature describes additional indications for specific agents.

General Dosing Information

General anesthetics have a narrow margin of safety, and their administration must be individualized (titrated) according to the desired depth of anesthesia, the concomitant use of other medications and the patient's physical condition, age, size and body temperature. Table 3.1 provides general dosing guidelines for inducing and maintaining anesthesia.

Maximum Recommended Doses

Because of the inherent danger of general anesthetics and significant variations in patients' responsiveness, maximum recommended doses do not guarantee a safe upper limit and have not been identified for most drugs. The risk of hypoxia limits the maximum concentration of nitrous oxide to 70%. Excitation of the CNS restricts the amount of enflurane that can be used to a maximum final induction dose of 4.5% and a maintenance dose of 3%. The following usual maximum doses apply to injectable anesthetics: 4 g of thiopental (rectal), 4.5 mg/kg IV and 13 mg/kg IM of ketamine and 0.05 (children) and 0.1 mL/kg (adults) IV of droperidol/fentanyl.

Dosage Adjustments

The patient's size and physical status and the procedure being performed determine the actual dose. Infants, geriatric patients and people with medical conditions or who are on drug therapy that can alter responses to general anesthetics often require reduced doses, even after correcting for the usual variables of size and physical status. Conversely, children and adolescents are resistant to most CNS depressants and require increased doses of inhalation anesthetics and, corrected for body weight, propofol.

Special Dental Considerations

Drug Interactions of Dental Interest

Table 3.2 lists the drug interactions and related problems involving general anesthetics that are potentially of clinical significance in dentistry.

See Chapter 2 (Table 2.11) for drug interactions specific to the fentanyl component of droperidol/fentanyl and the opioid anesthetics.

Laboratory Value Alterations

- Liver function tests (aminotransferases, lactate dehydrogenase) are abnormal with volatile anesthetics.
- Blood glucose is increased with desflurane and sevoflurane.
- Blood urea nitrogen and serum creatinine are increased with sevoflurane.
- Leukocyte count is increased with desflurane and sevoflurane.
- Serum fluoride is increased with methoxyflurane, enflurane and sevoflurane.
- Cerebrospinal fluid and intraocular pressures may be increased with ketamine.
- Thyroid uptake tests may be abnormal with the barbiturates.

Table 3.1

General Anesthetics: Dosage and Prescribing Information

Generic name	Brand name(s)	Adult dosage	Child dosage	PRC	Content/form
		Inhalation			
Desflurane	Suprane	**Inhalation:** Must be individualized—0.5-3% initially, to be increased by 0.5-1% every 2-3 breaths or as tolerated until onset of anesthesia **Maintenance:** 2.5-8.5%	**Induction:** Use not recommended **Maintenance:** Individualized, usually 5.2-10%	B	**Liquid:** 240-mL bottles
Enflurane	Ethrane	**Inhalation:** Must be individualized **Maintenance:** 0.5-3%	Must be individualized	B	**Liquid:** 125-, 250-mL bottles
Halothane	Fluothane, Somnothane [CAN]	**Induction:** Must be individualized (usually 0.5-3%) **Maintenance:** 0.5-1.5%	Must be individualized	C	**Liquid:** 125-, 250-mL bottles
Isoflurane	Forane	**Inhalation:** 1.5-3% **Maintenance:** 1-3.5%	Must be individualized	B	**Liquid:** 100-mL bottles
Methoxyflurane	Penthrane	**Induction:** Up to 2% with ≥ 50% nitrous oxide and oxygen **Maintenance:** Not to exceed 4 h of 0.25% or 2 h of 0.5% **Analgesia:** Intermittent inhalation of 0.3-0.8%	Must be individualized	C	**Liquid:** 15-, 125-mL bottles
Nitrous oxide	(generic)	**Induction:** 70% with 30% oxygen **Maintenance:** 30-70% with oxygen **Sedation/analgesia:** 25-50% with oxygen	Must be individualized	NC	**Pressurized liquid:** Steel cylinders

		IM/IV			
Sevoflurane	Ultane, Sevorane [CAN]	**Inhalation:** Must be individualized **Maintenance:** 0.5-3%	Same as adult	B	**Liquid:** 250-mL bottles
Alfentanil hydrochloride (II, N)*	Alfenta	**Induction—IV:** 0.13-0.245 µg/kg (for procedures ≥ 45 min) **Maintenance for procedures ≤ 30 min—IV:** 8-20 µg/kg initially, followed by increments of 3-5 µg/kg or continuous infusion of 0.5-1 µg/kg/min **Maintenance for procedures > 30 min—IV:** 20-75 µg/kg initially, followed by increments of 5-15 µg/kg or continuous infusion of 0.5-4 µg/kg/min	**Maintenance —IV:** 30-50 µg/kg initially, followed by increments of 10-15 µg/kg or continuous infusion of 0.5-1.5 µg/kg/min	C	**Injection (500 µg/mL):** 2, 5, 10-, 20-mL ampules
Droperidol/fentanyl citrate (II, N)*	Innovar	**Induction:** 0.1 mL/kg slowly or rapid drip of 10 mL in 250 mL 5% dextrose solution until somnolence **Premedication—IM:** 0.5-2 mL 45-60 min before procedure	**Induction and maintenance:** Up to 0.05 mL/kg (not established for children aged < 2 y) **Premedication—IM:** 0.025 mL/kg 45-60 min before procedure	C	**Injection (2.5 mg/mL droperidol and 0.05 mg/mL fentanyl citrate):** 2, 5-mL ampules
Etomidate	Amidate	**Induction—IV:** 0.2-0.6 mg/kg **Maintenance—IV:** Smaller increments with doses individualized	Same as adult (not established for children aged < 10 y)	C	**Injection (2 mg/mL):** 10, 20-mL ampules and 20-mL syringes
Ketamine hydrochloride (III)*	Ketalar	**Induction—IV:** 1-4.5 mg/kg **Induction—IM:** 6.5-13 mg/kg **Maintenance:** Increments are one-half to full dose	Same as adult	NC	**Injection (10 mg/mL):** 20-, 25-, 50-mL vials **Injection (50 mg/mL):** 10-mL vials **Injection (100 mg/mL):** 5-mL vials

Continued on next page

[CAN] indicates a drug available only in Canada.
PRC: Pregnancy risk category.
NC: Not classified.
* Controlled substances (United States, Canadian classifications).

Table 3.1 (cont.)

General Anesthetics: Dosage and Prescribing Information

Generic name	Brand name(s)	Adult dosage	Child dosage	PRC	Content/form
		IM/IV (cont.)			
Methohexital Na (IV, F)*	Brevital, Brietal [CAN]	**Induction—IV:** 1-2.0 mg/kg **Induction—IM:** 5-10 mg/kg **Maintenance—IV:** 0.25-1 mg/kg increments or continuous drip of 0.2% solution with flow rate individualized	**Induction:** NE **Maintenance:** NE **Rectal basal anesthesia:** 15-30 mg/kg as a 5-10% solution	B	**Powder:** 500-mg, 2.5-, 5-g vials
Propofol	Diprivan	**Adults ≤ age 55 y, induction—IV:** 2-2.5 mg/kg **Adults > age 55 y, induction—IV:** 1-1.5 mg/kg **Adults ≤ age 55 y, maintenance—IV:** Increments of 25-50 mg or continuous infusion of 100-200 µg/kg/min, beginning in upper range and decreasing to lower range during next 30 min **Adults > age 55 y, maintenance—IV:** Increments of 25-50 mg or continuous infusion of 50-100 µg/kg/min, beginning in upper range and decreasing to lower range during next 30 min **Adults ≤ age 55 y, conscious sedation—IV:** 0.5 mg/kg over 3-5 min followed by continuous infusion of 25-75 µg/kg/min **Adults > age 55 y, conscious sedation—IV:** Same as for adults ≤ age 55 y, with 20% lower infusion rates	**Induction:** 2.5-3.5 mg/kg (not established for children under age 3 y) **Maintenance—IV:** Continuous infusion of 125-300 µg/kg/min, beginning in upper range and decreasing to lower range during next 30 min	B	**Injection (10 mg/mL):** 50-, 100-mL vials and 20-mL ampules

Remifentanil hydrochloride (II, N)*	Ultiva	**Induction—IV:** 0.5-1 µg/kg/min with inhalation or intravenous anesthetic **Maintenance —IV:** 0.05-0.2 µg/kg/min with inhalation or intravenous anesthetic **Postoperative analgesia—IV:** 0.1 µg/kg/min initially, adjusted as needed q 5 min in 0.025 µg/kg/min increments **Analgesic supplement—IV:** 1 µg/kg over 30-60 s, followed 60-90 s later by local anesthetic injection; or 0.1 µg/kg/min beginning 5 min before local anesthetic injection, followed by 0.05 µg/kg/min, adjusted as needed q 5 min in 0.025 µg/kg/min increments; initial doses should be reduced 50% when coadministered with benzodiazepine sedation	Same as adult (NE for children aged < 2 y)	C	**Powder:** 1-, 2-, 5-mg vials
Sufentanil citrate (II, N)*	Sufenta	**Induction—IV:** 8-30 µg/kg **Maintenance—IV:** 25-50 µg as needed **Anesthesia adjunct—IV:** Low dose: 0.5-1 µg/kg initially, followed by increments of 10-25 µg as needed; moderate dose: 2-8 µg/kg initially, followed by increments of 10-50 µg as needed	**Induction—IV:** 10-25 µg/kg **Maintenance—IV:** up to 25-50 µg as needed	C	**Injection (50 µg/mL):** 1-, 2-, 5-mL ampules
Thiopental Na (III, F)*	Pentothal	**Induction—IV:** 3-5 mg/kg **Maintenance —IV:** 25-100 mg increments or continuous drip of 0.2-0.4% solution **Rectal sedation:** 30 mg/kg **Rectal narcosis:** 9 mg/kg	**Induction—IV:** Same as adult **Maintenance—IV:** 1 mg/kg increments **Rectal sedation/narcosis:** Same as adult	C	**Powder:** 250-, 400-, 500-mg vials and syringes; 0.5-, 1-, 2.5-, 5-, 10-g kits **Suspension (400 mg/g):** 2-g rectal syringes

[CAN] indicates a drug available only in Canada.
PRC: Pregnancy risk category.
NE: Not established.
* Controlled substances (United States, Canadian classifications).

Table 3.2

General Anesthetics: Possible Interactions With Other Drugs

Drug taken by patient	Interaction with general anesthetics	Dentist's action
Adrenergic amines, cocaine, doxapram, *levodopa,* methylxanthines	Coadministration of volatile anesthetics, especially *halothane,* potentiates dysrhythmogenic action of these drugs	Limit concurrent use, especially with halothane anesthesia
Aminoglycosides, capreomycin, clindamycin, neuromuscular blockers, polymyxins, tetracyclines	Increased skeletal muscle weakness with volatile anesthetics	Monitor neuromuscular function and respiratory status
Antimyasthenic cholinesterase inhibitors: ambenonium, neostigmine, pyridostigmine	Volatile anesthetics may antagonize antimyasthenic effects postoperatively	Monitor neuromuscular function and respiratory status
CNS depressants: alcohols, antidepressants, antihistamines, antipsychotics, barbiturates, benzodiazepines, centrally acting antihypertensives and muscle relaxants, local anesthetics, opioids, parenteral magnesium sulfate	*Summation of drug effects may lead to increased CNS depression, respiratory depression or cardiovascular depression; anesthetic dosage requirements may be decreased significantly and recovery times prolonged*	Avoid overmedicating patient by carefully titrating inhalation and IV agents to the desired effect and by reducing dosages of drugs administered IM or rectally
Hepatic enzyme inducers: alcohol, barbiturates, carbamazepine, glutethimide, griseofulvin, isoniazid, phenytoin, rifampin	Increased metabolism of volatile anesthetics may increase the risk of hepatitis (halothane, enflurane, methoxyflurane) or renal toxicity (methoxyflurane, enflurane, sevoflurane)	Use cautiously
Hypotension-producing drugs: adrenergic neuron blockers, α- and β-adrenergic blockers, amiodarone, angiotensin-converting enzyme inhibitors, centrally acting antihypertensives, calcium channel blockers, diuretics, ganglionic blockers, levodopa, vasodilators	Summation of drug effects may lead to significant hypotension	Monitor patient's blood pressure at regular intervals; ensure proper hydration and adjust anesthetic dosage as necessary
Hypothermia-producing drugs: CNS depressants, α- and β-adrenergic blockers, insulin, vasodilators	Increased tendency toward hypothermia	Monitor core temperature during general anesthesia for other than brief cases
Nephrotoxic drugs: aminoglycosides, nonsteroidal anti-inflammatory drugs, cyclosporine	*With methoxyflurane, increased risk of renal toxicity*	Avoid concurrent or sequential use
Thyroid hormones	Increased cardiovascular stimulation with ketamine	Recognize minimal risk with replacement therapy only; otherwise avoid concurrent use
Volatile anesthetics	Decreased elimination of ketamine	Use cautiously

Italics indicate information of major clinical significance.

Table 3.3

General Anesthetics: Potential Cross-Sensitivity With Other Substances

A person with a sensitivity to	May also have a sensitivity to
Barbiturates	Thiopental or methohexital
Droperidol	Droperidol/fentanyl
Fentanyl-type opioids	Droperidol/fentanyl, alfentanil, remifentanil or sufentanil
Egg phosphatide (lecithin), soybean oil	Propofol (its emulsion vehicle)
Volatile anesthetics or other halogenated hydrocarbons	Other volatile anesthetics

Laboratory value alterations involving the opioids are listed in Chapter 2.

Cross-Sensitivity

Table 3.3 lists the potential cross-sensitivities between general anesthetics and other substances.

Special Patients

Pregnant and nursing women

General anesthetics cross the placenta and enter the fetal circulation. Although retrospective investigations of pregnant women receiving general anesthetics during pregnancy have found no evidence of fetal toxicity, investigations using animals indicate that with some agents—namely, nitrous oxide, halothane, alfentanil, etomidate, ketamine, propofol and sufentanil (although at greater than usual doses or exposure times or both)—can pose the risk of fetal death or birth defects. Table 3.1 lists the U.S. Food and Drug Administration pregnancy category classifications for general anesthetics. Considerations of the risks versus the benefits suggest that purely elective treatment be delayed until after delivery and that other dental care be delayed, if possible, until the second trimester. Halothane, thiopental, methohexital, propofol, alfentanil and, it is presumed, other general anesthetics are distributed into breast milk, although no

problems associated with general anesthetics have been documented in humans.

Of special concern to the dental profession is the link between occupational exposure to nitrous oxide and reproductive toxicity in exposed females and spontaneous abortion in the spouses of exposed males. Because no health risks were observed when scavenging inhalation circuits were used to minimize nitrous oxide pollution, it is believed that existing technologies, when used appropriately, permit nitrous oxide to be administered with minimal risk to both the patient and the dental team.

Pediatric, geriatric and other special patients

Pediatric patients. Specific approved dosage recommendations for pediatric patients are not available either for inhalation anesthetics or for the following injectable drugs: etomidate (in children < age 10 y), propofol (in children < age 3 y), droperidol/fentanyl (in children < age 2 y) and remifentanil (in children < age 2 y). Although children > age 1 y tend to be relatively resistant to drugs administered on the basis of weight—because of higher clearance rates, more active homeostatic mechanisms and other variables—differences in metabolic rates, oxygen consumption and cardiovascular responses can complicate the treatment of reactions to an overdose. Qualitative differences in responses to general anesthetics also can occur. Excitement is more likely to occur in response to subanesthetic doses of these agents; however, disturbing hallucinations with ketamine are less problematic. Because of their behavior, young children and mentally challenged patients may cause difficulties when the dentist is trying to induce anesthesia with inhalation or an IV injection. In these cases, alternative methods of drug delivery, such as IM injection or rectal suppositories, should be considered.

Geriatric patients. Separate geriatric dosage guidelines for most general anesthetics have not been published. Age-related limitations of respiratory function may slow the onset of and recovery from inhalation anesthesia.

Recovery from IV anesthesia is also commonly delayed due to a decreased total body clearance and altered volume of distribution in these patients. Lower induction doses and a reduced maintenance schedule for many injectable agents should be used with geriatric patients. Elderly patients are more susceptible to cardiovascular instability, such as orthostatic hypotension, during and after general anesthesia.

Other special patients. IV drugs that pose the potential for abuse may be inappropriate for certain patients, such as those who have a history of drug abuse. Mentally challenged patients are more likely than other patients to exhibit excitement reactions.

Table 3.4
Inhalation General Anesthetics: Adverse Effects, Precautions and Contraindications

Body system	Adverse effects	Precautions/contraindications
General	*Malignant hyperthermia*	*Personal or family history of malignant hyperthermia contraindicates use of inhalation agents other than nitrous oxide*
		Muscular dystrophy is associated with increased risk of malignant hyperthermia
		Nitrous oxide increases pressures of enclosed air spaces, as with pneumothorax, acute intestinal obstruction, middle ear infections, air-containing cysts, air emboli and pneumoencephalography
		History of drug sensitivity to the volatile anesthetic contraindicates its use
CV	Cardiac arrhythmias (fast, slow or irregular heartbeat)	Preexisting cardiovascular disease or pheochromocytoma predisposes patient to cardiovascular effects, *especially with halothane and desflurane*
	Hypotension from myocardial depression and/or peripheral vasodilatation (minimal with nitrous oxide)	Ensure proper fluid replacement before anesthesia in patients who are dehydrated or have had a blood loss
CNS	Increased intracranial pressure	*Patients with head injuries, increased intracranial pressure or intracranial tumors are at increased risk of intracranial hypertension; barbiturates help reduce intracranial pressure*
	Excitatory effects during induction; electrical convulsive activity with enflurane	Hyperventilation may increase the risk of excitatory effects with enflurane

Italics indicate information of major clinical significance.

Continued on next page

Table 3.4 (cont.)

Inhalation General Anesthetics: Adverse Effects, Precautions and Contraindications

Body system	Adverse effects	Precautions/contraindications
GI	Nausea and vomiting	Employ dietary restrictions and consider use of antiemetic agents to minimize risk of nausea and vomiting
GU	Decreased renal blood flow, glomerular filtration and urine production	Risk of renal toxicity is increased in patients with preexisting renal disease or impairment Ensure proper hydration before anesthesia *Methoxyflurane is contraindicated in patients with renal disease*
HB	Hepatitis, both reversible and fulminant (most common with halothane)	Preexisting hepatic disease increases risk of hepatotoxicity *Repeated use of halothane in adults is contraindicated*
Musc	None of significance to dentistry	Postoperative weakness is possible with volatile anesthetics in patients with myasthenia gravis, muscular dystrophy or related disorders
Resp	*Respiratory depression, hypoxemia and hypercarbia* Increased secretions, coughing, breath-holding, laryngospasm, bronchospasm Pulmonary aspiration Loss of airway patency	*Maintain inspired oxygen tension ≥ 30% and use nitrous oxide or inhalation anesthesia delivery systems equipped with fail-safe and minimum oxygen flow devices* *Avoid very light anesthesia and the use of desflurane for mask induction* *Use dietary restrictions to minimize risk of aspiration, which increases with a full stomach, obesity, alcohol intake and gastric reflux disorders*

Italics indicate information of major clinical significance.

Patient Monitoring: Aspects to Watch

- Cardiovascular status: arterial blood pressure, heart rate, electrocardiogram
- Respiratory status: oxygenation and ventilation
- Core body temperature

Adverse Effects and Precautions

General anesthetics differ from each other in the incidence and severity of their adverse effects. Most adverse effects are dose-related and are extensions of the normal pharmacology of the drug—for example, exaggerated CNS responses or cardiovascular depression.

Idiosyncratic and allergic reactions account for a small minority of adverse responses to general anesthetics. Appropriate resuscitative and endotracheal intubation equipment, oxygen and medications for preventing and treating anesthetic emergencies must be immediately available.

The adverse effects and precautions/contraindications listed in Tables 3.4 and 3.5 apply to all routes of administration. See Chapter 2 (Table 2.12) for adverse effects and precautions/contraindications specific to the opioids.

Table 3.5

Injectable General Anesthetics: Adverse Effects, Precautions and Contraindications

Body system	Adverse effects	Precautions/contraindications
General	Allergic reactions, including anaphylaxis *Infection, sometimes fatal, after injection of contaminated propofol solution*	*Use proper aseptic technique in the handling and administration of propofol, including individual patient use of unit doses and discarding unused drug after 12 h (6 h if not in original container)* *Contraindicated in patients with history of drug sensitivity to the injectable anesthetic being considered for use or to any component of the selected preparation*
CV	Cardiac dysrhythmias (fast, slow, or irregular heartbeat); tachycardia more likely to occur with barbiturates and ketamine; bradycardia with propofol and droperidol/fentanyl Hypotension from myocardial depression and/or peripheral vasodilatation; more likely to occur with barbiturates and propofol Hypertension from ketamine Vascular irritation, including pain on injection, phlebitis and thrombophlebitis; pain most likely with etomidate, propofol and methohexital	Hypotension and dysrhythmias are more likely to occur in patients with preexisting cardiovascular disease Ensure proper fluid replacement before anesthesia in patients with dehydration or blood loss *Avoid intra-arterial injection;* venous sequelae less likely when drugs are infused slowly into large vein with rapid IV drip *Ketamine is contraindicated in patients with severe hypertension or cardiovascular disease, or a recent (within last 6 mo) stroke or heart attack*
CNS	Excessive CNS depression Postoperative drowsiness, confusion, depression CNS excitation, hyperactivity, anxiety, hallucinations, dysphoria Extrapyramidal signs and symptoms (dystonia, akathisia) with droperidol/fentanyl Increased intracranial pressure with ketamine	Avoid too-rapid IV injection Avoid multiple repeated injections or prolonged infusion leading to drug accumulation (exception: propofol) Excitatory reactions are more likely with ketamine and in patients with psychiatric disorders Ensure adequate anesthesia intraoperatively; minimize aversive, intensive stimuli in the recovery period *Ketamine is contraindicated in patients with head injuries, increased intracranial pressure, intracranial tumors or history of stroke or intracranial hemorrhage*
EENT	Elevation of intraocular pressure, diplopia and nystagmus with ketamine	Ketamine increases risk of eye injury in patients with open eye wound, increased intraocular pressure
GI	Nausea and vomiting	*Employ dietary restrictions* and consider the use of antiemetic agents with ketamine or etomidate to minimize risk of nausea and vomiting
GU	None of significance to dentistry	CNS depressant effects may be prolonged in patients with renal function impairment

Italics indicate information of major clinical significance.

Continued on next page

Table 3.5 (cont.)

Injectable General Anesthetics: Adverse Effects, Precautions and Contraindications

Body system	Adverse effects	Precautions/contraindications
HB	Porphyria after repeated doses of barbiturates	Prolonged CNS depressant effects of barbiturates and fentanyl/droperidol may occur in patients with impaired hepatic function Barbiturates are contraindicated with history of acute intermittent porphyria, hereditary coproporphy or porphyria variegata
Musc	Skeletal muscle movements; unilateral movements may occur in response to noxious stimuli; bilateral movements, possibly a manifestation of disinhibition of cortical activity, may include tonic and clonic movements resembling seizure activity Muscle rigidity with ketamine	None of significance to dentistry
Resp	*Respiratory depression, hypoxemia and hypercarbia* Increased secretions, coughing, breath-holding, laryngospasm (especially with ketamine), bronchospasm, pulmonary aspiration, loss of airway patency	*Avoid manipulation of the airway in the lightly anesthetized patient* Consider administering an antisialogogue when using ketamine *Use dietary restrictions to minimize risk of aspiration, which increases with a full stomach, obesity, alcohol intake and gastric reflux disorders*

Italics indicate information of major clinical significance.

Pharmacology

General anesthetics produce their effects through a variety of actions, some of which may be unique to individual drugs. Because of their respective routes of administration, inhalation and injectable anesthetics should be considered separately. Within each group there are also some important similarities, as well as differences, with respect to the mechanism of action and pharmacologic profile.

Inhalation anesthetics. Inhalation anesthetics are believed to produce general anesthesia by interacting with the nerve cell membrane. The anesthetic potency of these agents increases in direct correlation with the oil:gas partition coefficient, a measure of hydrophobicity. Recent findings suggest that inhalation agents interact directly with membrane proteins to cause general anesthesia. Postsynaptic inhibition of the brain stem and midbrain is believed to account for most anesthetic actions. With drugs such as nitrous oxide and enflurane, certain areas of the brain may become disinhibited and demonstrate increased electrical activity.

Some inhalation anesthetics have specific analgesic actions; in the case of nitrous oxide, an interaction with the endogenous opioid system has been proposed. Respiratory depression is a common feature of all inhalation anesthetics; it is often moderated when a reduced dose of volatile anesthetic is administered with nitrous oxide. Cardiovascular depression is an effect shared by all volatile inhalation agents in common use but not by nitrous oxide. Some drugs, most notably halothane, reduce blood pressure by direct myocardial depression, whereas some (such as isoflurane) induce peripheral vascular relaxation and still others (such as enflurane) produce both effects. Volatile agents produce

Table 3.6

Inhalation General Anesthetics: Pharmacokinetic Parameters

Drug	Blood:gas partition coefficient	Onset of action	Recovery time	Metabolism (%)
Desflurane	0.42	Very rapid*	Very rapid	0.02
Enflurane	1.91	Rapid*	Rapid	2.4
Halothane	2.3	Rapid	Rapid	up to 20
Isoflurane	1.43	Rapid*	Rapid	0.17
Methoxyflurane	13	Slow	Slow	65
Nitrous oxide	0.47	Very rapid	Very rapid	0
Sevoflurane	0.69	Rapid	Rapid	5

The pungent odor of these drugs, especially desflurane, may cause breath-holding and laryngospasm and limit the onset of anesthesia.

varying degrees of muscle relaxation; nitrous oxide tends to increase muscle tone in anesthetic concentrations.

The pharmacokinetics of inhalation anesthetics are strongly governed by the blood:gas partition coefficient. As indicated in Table 3.6, drugs with a low partition coefficient equilibrate very quickly between the inspired tension and the brain concentration. The irritating odor of desflurane, the least soluble inhalation anesthetic, negates much of the drug's potential benefit, especially in children, because of breathing disturbances (such as breath-holding, coughing and laryngospasm) that limit ventilation. Metabolism plays a minor role in the pharmacokinetics of all the inhalation agents except methoxyflurane. However, the metabolism of halothane helps speed recovery, as does (in short cases) the redistribution of volatile agents from the brain to other tissues. The metabolic release of fluoride and other potentially toxic metabolites has severely limited the use of methoxyflurane and is of potential concern with the use of sevoflurane and enflurane.

Injectable anesthetics. Injectable anesthetics also depress CNS function by binding to specific membrane receptors. Ultrashort-acting barbiturates bind to receptor sites on the γ-aminobutyric acid (GABA)–activated chloride channel to enhance responsiveness to GABA, increase membrane conductance of chloride and hyperpolarize the cell. Inhibition of certain glutamate receptor responses may be a secondary mechanism. The ultrashort-acting agents etomidate and propofol appear to exert similar effects. Other receptors are involved in the actions of ketamine and droperidol-fentanyl. The binding of opioid anesthetics to endogenous opioid receptors is reviewed in Chapter 2.

The pharmacology of the ultrashort-acting barbiturates, etomidate and propofol share important similarities. They produce unconsciousness and decrease cerebral blood flow but cause no specific analgesia or muscle relaxation. They are rapidly redistributed from the brain and other highly perfused organs (liver, kidneys, heart) to muscle and later to fatty tissues. Induction doses depress laryngeal reflexes and often cause brief periods of apnea (shortest with etomidate, longest with propofol). Etomidate also produces minimal changes in cardiovascular

Table 3.7

Injectable General Anesthetics: Pharmacokinetic Parameters

Drug	Elimination half-life (h)	Onset of action	Duration of action (min)	Plasma protein binding (%)
Alfentanil	1-2.1	< 60 s	5-10	92
Droperidol	1.7-2.2	3-10 min	120-240	Not available
Etomidate	1.25	< 60 s	3-5	76
Ketamine	2-3	30 s	5-10	12
Methohexital	1.5-5	< 60 s	5-7	73
Propofol	24-72	< 40 s	3-5	95-99
Remifentanil	3-10 min	< 60 s	5-10	70
Sufentanil	2.7	< 60 s	5-180*	93
Thiopental	10-12	30-60 s	10-30	72-86

* The duration of action varies with the dose and duration of administration.

status, whereas propofol generally depresses myocardial contractility and arterial blood pressure. Thiopental and methohexital each reduce myocardial contractility, but arterial pressures are usually well maintained unless the patient is hypovolemic or the drug is used in combination with opioids. Decreases in renal and cerebral blood flow commonly occur with all four induction anesthetics. Pain on injection is common with etomidate and propofol, less so with methohexital and infrequent with thiopental. Involuntary movements follow a similar pattern of incidence.

Ketamine and droperidol/fentanyl are not simple CNS depressants. The "dissociative" anesthetic state produced by ketamine is notable for its profound analgesia, nystagmus, increased muscle tone, relative lack of respiratory depression, maintenance of laryngeal reflexes and cardiovascular stimulation. Excitatory reactions are made manifest by involuntary motor movements, vivid dreams or frank hallucinations and emergence delirium. The adverse excitatory effects of ketamine can be minimized by coadministration

of diazepam or midazolam; glycopyrrolate is useful in blunting the secretory stimulation caused by ketamine. Ketamine acts rapidly after IV injection and is one of the fastest agents for inducing anesthesia after IM injection. Droperidol/fentanyl produces a quiescent state known as "neuroleptanalgesia." As with ketamine, there is indifference to the environment and analgesia. Droperidol reduces peripheral vascular tone by blocking α-adrenergic receptors; fentanyl tends to lower the heart rate. In contrast to ketamine, droperidol produces an antiemetic effect and reduces motor activity.

The intravenous opioids are not true anesthetics because they cannot reliably produce total unconsciousness even in enormous doses. However, they are powerful analgesics, produce modest cardiovascular depression and can obtund autonomic arousal responses to noxious surgical stimuli. For these reasons, opioids are often used as adjuncts to other anesthetic drugs. Opioids are also strong respiratory depressants and likely to cause nausea and vomiting in the postoperative period. These dose-dependent adverse effects weigh against the administration of large amounts of opioids in the outpatient setting. Pharmacokinetic differences play a prominent role in drug selection. Although all of the intravenous opioid anesthetics enjoy a fast onset of action, remifentanil is an ideal opioid for total intravenous anesthesia because it is so short-acting that the intensity of drug action can be easily reduced or increased. Sufentanil, on the other hand, produces a much longer-lasting effect when used in high doses for cardiac surgery.

All of the injectable anesthetics are metabolized to inactive products, and the liver plays the predominant role. However, Table 3.7 illustrates the independence between the elimination half-life and the duration of action of these drugs. After multiple injections or continuous infusion, the redistribution sites become saturated with the drug, and the duration of action becomes progressively longer. Propofol, which has an enormous capacity for redistribution, and remifentanil, which is rapidly hydrolyzed in the plasma, are important exceptions. Because of the extended duration of droperidol, attributed to that drug's tight binding to its receptor, repeated injections are rarely administered. Pharmacokinetic aspects of fentanyl are discussed in the opioid section of Chapter 2.

Patient Advice

- Because of the possibility of psychomotor impairment after the use of anesthetics, driving or other tasks requiring alertness and coordination should be avoided or performed with added caution, as appropriate, for the first 24 h after anesthesia.
- Use of alcohol or other CNS depressants should be avoided during the first 24 h after anesthesia except as directed by the dentist or physician.
- Patients should be aware of the potential for delayed side effects, especially mood or mental changes, nightmares or unusual dreams and blurred vision.

Suggested Readings

American Dental Association. Guidelines for the use of conscious sedation, deep sedation and general anesthesia for dentists. Chicago: American Dental Association; 1999.

American Dental Association Council on Dental Education and Licensure. Guidelines for teaching the comprehensive control of anxiety and pain in dentistry. Chicago: American Dental Association; 1999.

Little HJ. How has molecular pharmacology contributed to our understanding of the mechanism(s) of general anesthesia? Pharmacol Ther 1996;69(1):37-58.

Longnecker DE, Murphy FL, eds. Dripps/Eckenhoff/Vandam introduction to anesthesia. 9th ed. Philadelphia: Saunders; 1997.

McGlothlin JD, Crouch KG, Mickelsen RL. Control of nitrous oxide in dental operatories. Cincinnati: U.S. Department of Health and Human Services, Public Health Service, Centers for Disease Control and Prevention, National Institute for Occupational Safety and Health, 1994; DHEW publication no. 94-129.

Stoelting RK. Pharmacology and physiology in anesthetic practice. 3rd ed. Philadelphia: Lippincott-Raven; 1999.

Neuromuscular Blocking Drugs

Muscle relaxation during general anesthesia is often desirable and sometimes required for surgical procedures. Endotracheal intubation is also greatly facilitated by paralysis of the vocal cords. Although varying degrees of muscle relaxation can be produced by the volatile general anesthetics, the dosages required are generally excessive compared to those needed to produce unconsciousness and unresponsiveness to noxious stimuli. Neuromuscular blocking drugs, beginning with the clinical introduction of tubocurarine in 1942, are commonly used whenever flaccidity of skeletal muscle is sought, and are among the most important adjuncts in general anesthesia.

With the exception of succinylcholine, which is a classified as a "depolarizing" blocker because it acts like acetylcholine in stimulating muscle nicotinic receptors, the neuromuscular blocking drugs competitively inhibit the binding of acetylcholine to its receptor on the motor endplate and are thus characterized as "competitive" or "nondepolarizing" blockers.

Table 3.8

Neuromuscular Blocking Drugs: Dosage and Prescribing Information*

Generic name	Brand name(s)	Adult dosage	Child dosage	PRC	Content/form
Atracurium besylate	Tracrium	0.4-0.5 mg/kg initially and 0.08-0.1 mg/kg as needed	Age > 2 y: Same as adult dose	C	Injection, 10 mg/mL: 5-, 10-mL vials
Cisatracurium besylate	Nimbex	0.15-0.20 mg/kg initially and 0.03 mg/kg as needed or infusion of 1-3 µg/kg/min as needed	Age > 2 y: 0.1 mg/kg initially and then same as adult dose	B	Injection, 2 mg/mL: 5-, 10-mL vials Injection, 10 mg/mL: 20-mL vials
Doxacurium chloride	Nuromax	50 µg/kg initially and 5-10 µg/kg as needed	Age > 2 y: Same as adult dose	C	Injection, 1 mg/mL: 5-mL vials
Gallamine triethiodide	Flaxedil	1 mg/kg initially and 0.5-1 mg/kg as needed, not to exceed 100 mg per dose †	Same as adult dose	NC	Injection, 20 mg/mL: 10-mL vials
Metocurine iodide	Metubine Iodide	0.2-0.4 mg/kg initially and 0.5-1 mg as needed	NE	C	Injection, 2 mg/mL: 20-mL vials
Mivacurium chloride	Mivacron	0.15 mg/kg initially and 0.10 mg/kg as needed	Age 2-12 y: 0.2 mg/kg initially and 0.1 mg/kg as needed	C	Infusion, 0.5 mg/mL: 50-mL containers Injection, 2 mg/mL: 5-, 10-mL vials
Pancuronium bromide	Pavulon	40-100 µg/kg initially and 10 µg/kg as needed	Age ≥ 1 mo: Same as adult dose	C	Injection, 1 mg/mL: 10-mL vials Injection, 2 mg/mL: 2-, 5-mL ampules, syringes, vials

Continued on next page

PRC: Pregnancy risk category
NC: Not classified.
NE: Not established.
* All medications are given IV.
† Intubation doses (4-6 mg/kg) for gallamine are generally not used. Strong vagolytic activity of gallamine restricts normal initial dose to 1 mg/kg.

Table 3.8 (cont.)

Neuromuscular Blocking Drugs: Dosage and Prescribing Information*

Generic name	Brand name(s)	Adult dosage	Child dosage	PRC	Content/form
Pipecuronium bromide	Arduan	70-85 µg/kg initially and 10-15 µg/kg as needed	**Age ≥ 1 mo:** Same as adult dose †	C	**Powder, 10 mg:** 10-mL vials
Rapacuronium bromide	Raplon	1.5 mg/kg initially and up to 3 doses of 0.5 mg/kg as needed	**Age 1 mo-12 y:** 2 mg/kg as a single dose	C	**Powder:** 100-, 200-mg vials
Rocuronium bromide	Zemuron	0.6 mg/kg initially and 0.1-0.2 mg/kg as needed	Same as adult dose †	B	**Injection, 10 mg/mL:** 5-, 10-mL vials
Succinylcholine chloride	Anectine, Quelicin, Sucostrin	0.3-1.1 mg/kg initially and 0.04-0.07 mg/kg as needed or infusion of 0.5-1.0 mg/min as needed ‡	**Infants and small children:** 2 mg/kg ‡ **Older children and adolescents:** 1 mg/kg‡	C	**Injection, 20 mg/mL:** 10-mL vials **Injection, 50 mg/mL:** 10-mL ampules **Injection, 100 mg/mL:** 10-mL vials **Powder, 100 mg/mL:** 5-mL vials **Powder:** 500-mg, 1-g vials
Tubocurarine chloride	(generic); Tubarine [CAN]	0.5-0.6 mg/kg initially and 3 mg as needed §	**Age > 1 mo:** 0.5-0.6 mg/kg initially and 0.1 mg/kg as needed	C	**Injection, 3 mg/mL:** 5-mL syringes and 10-, 20-mL vials
Vecuronium bromide	Norcuron	80-100 µg/kg initially and 10-15 µg/kg as needed	**Age > 1 y:** Same as adult dose †	C	**Powder:** 10-, 20-mg vials

[CAN] indicates a drug available only in Canada.
PRC: Pregnancy risk category.
NC: Not classified.
NE: Not established.
* All medications are given IV.
† Children aged 1 y to puberty may be less sensitive to neuromuscular blockade and need increased dosage and/or more frequent administration.
‡ May also be given IM (2.5-4 mg/kg; not to exceed 150 mg). The routine use of succinylcholine in children, particularly by continuous infusion, is considered unsafe because of sudden death linked to ventricular dysrhythmia and malignant hyperthermia.
§ Histamine release is prominent with tubocurarine, and doses such as 0.16 mg/kg are generally recommended.

Accepted Indications

Neuromuscular blocking drugs are used for the induction and maintenance of skeletal muscle relaxation during general anesthesia and to facilitate the management of patients receiving mechanical ventilation. The product literature describes additional indications for specific agents.

General Dosing Information

Table 3.8 lists the usual IV doses for induction of paralysis (intubation) and for maintenance of neuromuscular blockade. The clinician should individualize the actual maintenance dosage, using a peripheral nerve stimulator to monitor motor responsiveness.

Dosage Adjustments

When nondepolarizing neuromuscular blocking agents are administered concurrently with inhalation general anesthetics other than nitrous oxide, the dosage of the neuromuscular blocker should be reduced by up to 50%, as determined with a peripheral nerve stimulator. A reduced dosage may also be indicated for patients with neuromuscular disorders and severe electrolyte disturbances.

Table 3.9

Neuromuscular Blocking Drugs: Possible Interactions With Other Drugs

Drug taken by patient	Interaction with neuromuscular blocking drugs	Dentist's action
Anticholinesterases, including antimyasthenics, organophosphate insecticides, nerve gases and eye drops and hexafluorenium, phenelzine, thiotepa, cyclophosphamide	*Antimyasthenic agents and edrophonium antagonize effect of competitive blockers and vice versa; duration of action of succinylcholine and mivacurium may be prolonged by anticholinesterases* and other drugs *that reduce cholinesterase activity*	Avoid concurrent use in myasthenic patients if possible; otherwise, use a short-acting agent such as cisatracurium or rocuronium that is not metabolized by esterases and monitor patient carefully Anticholinesterases such as edrophonium and neostigmine are used to reverse the action of competitive blockers Hexaflurenium has been used to prolong the action of succinylcholine Avoid concurrent use of other agents with succinylcholine and mivacurium
Digitalis glycosides	*May increase cardiac effects when used concurrently with succinylcholine and, to a lesser extent, with pancuronium, possibly resulting in cardiac dysrhythmias*	Avoid concurrent use
Local anesthetics (large doses), aminoglycosides, clindamycin, lincomycin, capreomycin, polymyxins, procainamide, quinidine, lithium, β-adrenergic blockers, magnesium salts (parenteral), calcium channel blockers	*May increase respiratory depression or paralysis (apnea); incomplete reversal of neuromuscular blockade at the end of surgery may significantly increase possibility of inadequate ventilation*	Carefully monitor patient and reduce dosage of neuromuscular blocker in accordance with clinical response
Methotrimeprazine	May stimulate CNS, evoke extrapyramidal reactions and cause hypotension with tachycardia when used with succinylcholine	Avoid concurrent use

Italics indicate information of major clinical significance.

Continued on next page

Table 3.9 (cont.)

Neuromuscular Blocking Drugs: Possible Interactions With Other Drugs

Drug taken by patient	Interaction with neuromuscular blocking drugs	Dentist's action
Neuromuscular blockers	Competitive blockers produce additive effects when used with each other; prior administration of a competitive blocker reduces activity of succinylcholine initially but may prolong effect of repeated administrations; prior administration of succinylcholine may increase duration of competitive blocker	Adjust dosage in accordance with actual or predicted clinical response
Opioid analgesics	CNS depressant effects may increase respiratory depressant effects of neuromuscular blockers; hypotension also more likely, except with vagolytic drugs such as gallamine and pancuronium, which may cause tachycardia and hypertension Histamine release by meperidine or morphine-like opioids may add to effects of histamine-releasing neuromuscular blockers (tubocurarine, atracurium, metocurine, rapacuronium, succinylcholine)	Carefully monitor patient; consider use of antihistamines to prevent or treat histamine responses
Potassium-depleting drugs such as thiazide and high-efficacy diuretics, corticosteroids, carbonic anhydrase inhibitors, amphotericin B	Enhances blockade produced by nondepolarizing neuromuscular blocking agents	Reduce dosage of neuromuscular blocker in accordance with clinical response
Volatile inhalation anesthetics	Enhances neuromuscular blockade, especially with nondepolarizing neuromuscular blocking agents	Reduce dosage of neuromuscular blocker in accordance with clinical response

Table 3.10

Neuromuscular Blocking Drugs: Potential Cross-Sensitivity With Other Substances

A person with a sensitivity to	May also have a sensitivity to
Bromides	Bromide salts of pancuronium, pipecuronium, rapacuronium, rocuronium or vecuronium
Iodine or iodides	Iodide salts of gallamine or metocurine
Para-aminobenzoic acid (PABA) or paraben preservative	Neuromuscular blocker preparations containing paraben preservatives
Sulfites	Neuromuscular blocker preparations containing sulfite antioxidants

Special Dental Considerations

Drug Interactions of Dental Interest
The following drug interactions and related problems involving neuromuscular blocking agents (Table 3.9) are potentially of clinical significance in dentistry.

Laboratory Value Alterations
- Serum potassium concentrations: May be temporarily increased by succinylcholine

Cross-Sensitivity
Table 3.10 lists potential cross-sensitivities between neuromuscular blocking drugs and other substances.

Special Patients
Pregnant and nursing women
Neuromuscular blocking agents cross the placenta in small amounts to enter the fetal circulation. Table 3.8 lists the FDA pregnancy risk category classifications for neuromuscular blocking agents. Considerations of risk/benefit suggest that purely elective treatment should be delayed until after delivery and that other dental care be performed, if possible, during the second trimester. Problems related to breast-feeding have not been reported in humans.

Pediatric, geriatric and other special patients
Pediatric patients. Many side effects of succinylcholine are noted in children. Of major concern is an increased sensitivity to the vagal effects of succinylcholine, with profound bradycardia and asystole, which occasionally occur after a standard dose. Administration of atropine often is recommended before administration of succinylcholine to prevent vagally induced dysrhythmias. Cardiac arrest associated with acute muscle destruction (rhabdomyolysis) and hyperkalemia has occurred in children with undiagnosed skeletal muscle disorders. Malignant hyperthermia may be a related condition. For these reasons, succinylcholine is no longer recommended for routine use in children.

Geriatric patients. Neuromuscular blocking agents, except for doxacurium, have shown no significant differences in effectiveness, safety or dosage requirements when given to healthy elderly and younger patients. With doxacurium, the neuromuscular blockade has a slower onset, is more intense and has a longer but more variable duration in older patients. Elderly patients are more likely to have impaired renal function, however, which may decrease the clearance of doxacurium, gallamine, metocurine, mivacurium, pancuronium, pipecuronium or tubocurarine from the body and prolong their effects.

Patient Monitoring: Aspects to Watch
- Cardiovascular status (arterial blood pressure, heart rate, electrocardiogram)
- Core body temperature
- Neuromuscular responsiveness (peripheral nerve stimulator)
- Respiratory status (oxygenation and ventilation)

Adverse Effects and Precautions

Adverse effects, precautions and contraindications related to the use of neuromuscular blocking agents are presented in Table 3.11.

Neuromuscular blocking agents do not alter consciousness or the perception of pain; therefore, adequate general anesthesia must be ensured when these drugs are used during surgery. Since neuromuscular blocking agents commonly induce respiratory depression or respiratory arrest, they should be used only by dentists experienced in the techniques of tracheal intubation, artificial respiration and the administration of oxygen under positive pressure; in addition, facilities for these procedures should be immediately available.

Succinylcholine, the only depolarizing neuromuscular blocker in clinical use, is associated with a unique set of side effects. Myalgia, malignant hyperthermia, hyperkalemia and profound bradycardia are related to succinylcholine's ability to excite acetylcholine receptors in skeletal muscle and the heart. The likelihood of each of these effects is increased in special groups of patients with the following disorders:

Table 3.11

Neuromuscular Blocking Drugs: Adverse Effects, Precautions and Contraindications

Body system	Adverse effects	Precautions/contraindications
General	*Malignant hyperthermia after succinylcholine* Allergy-induced hypotension, bronchospasm, edema, erythema, skin rash and hives—all are rarely noted; similar reactions are more common with drugs (tubocurarine, metocurine, mivacurium, succinylcholine, rapacuronium and atracurium) that cause histamine release	*Personal or family history of malignant hyperthermia contraindicates use of succinylcholine* *Muscular dystrophy is associated with increased risk of malignant hyperthermia* Premedication with antihistamine may blunt or eliminate allergiclike responses in patients with increased sensitivity to histamine *Contraindicated in patients with history of drug sensitivity to the neuromuscular blocker considered for use*
CV	Hypotension, especially after large doses of tubocurarine, metocurine or atracurium; hypertension with gallamine Tachycardia with gallamine, pancuronium or rocuronium Bradycardia, dysrhythmias, cardiac arrest with succinylcholine, *especially in children and after second dose*	Cardiovascular reactions are more likely in patients with preexisting cardiovascular disease *Hyperkalemia, severe trauma or burns, spinal cord injury or neuromuscular disease increases the risk of cardiac reaction to succinylcholine* *Atropine should be administered before second dose of succinylcholine*
EENT	Increased intraocular pressure immediately after injection of succinylcholine	*Succinylcholine contraindicated in patients with open eye injury*
GU	Myoglobinuria after succinylcholine, especially in children	Renal function impairment may lead to prolonged neuromuscular blockade; *absolute contraindication for gallamine* and relative contraindication for other competitive blockers excreted renally
HB	None of significance to dentistry	Effect of vecuronium and rocuronium may be increased in patients with decreased hepatic function Decreased cholinesterase synthesis may prolong action of succinylcholine and mivacurium
Musc	Persisting muscle weakness Fasciculation and postoperative myalgia with succinylcholine	Prolonged muscle weakness may follow administration of succinylcholine or mivacurium in patients with acquired pseudocholinesterase deficiency (as from severe hepatic disease, anemia, dehydration or malnutrition) *Myasthenia gravis*, electrolyte disturbances, hypotension and hyperthermia increase risk of postoperative weakness Muscle fasciculation may worsen tissue damage associated with fractures *Continued on next page*

Italics indicate information of major clinical significance.

Continued on next page

Table 3.11 (cont.)

Neuromuscular Blocking Drugs: Adverse Effects, Precautions and Contraindications

Body system	Adverse effects	Precautions/contraindications
Musc (cont.)		Myalgia, likely in ambulatory patients, may be prevented by a defasciculating dose of nondepolarizing blocker *Succinylcholine and mivacurium are contraindicated in patients with congenital pseudocholinesterase deficiency*
Resp	*Respiratory depression and arrest* Excessive salivation with succinylcholine or pancuronium	Decreased pulmonary function, bronchogenic carcinoma or *myasthenia gravis* increases risk of postoperative respiratory complications

Italics indicate information of major clinical significance.

Table 3.12

Neuromuscular Blocking Drugs: Pharmacokinetic Properties

Drug	Onset time (min)*	Time to peak effect (min)	Duration of peak effect (min)	Time to recovery (min)	Primary route of elimination
Atracurium	2-2.5	3-5	35-45	60-70	Plasma†
Cisatracurium	1.5-2	4-6	55-60	75-100	†
Doxacurium	4-5	2.5-13	40-230	90-280	Kidneys
Gallamine ‡	1-2	3-5	90-120	Not available	Kidneys
Metocurine	1-4	3-5	60-120	> 360	Kidneys
Mivacurium	2-2.5	2.5-3.5	15-20	25-30	Plasma
Pancuronium	2-3	3-5	60-120	100-160	Kidneys/liver
Pipecuronium	2.5-3	3-5	60-120	90-150	Kidneys
Rapacuronium	1	1-2	15-20	25-50	Kidneys/liver
Rocuronium	1-1.5	2-3	20-30	60	Kidneys/liver
Succinylcholine	0.5-1	1-2	4-10	12-15	Plasma
Tubocurarine ‡	1-2	2-5	60-100	Not available	Kidneys/liver
Vecuronium	2.5-3	3-5	25-40	45-65	Kidneys/liver

* Time required for muscle relaxation to become sufficient to permit endotracheal intubation.
† Cisatracurium, one of the isomers in atracurium, undergoes spontaneous inactivation (Hofmann elimination).
‡ Intubation doses generally are not used.

- myalgia in ambulatory patients;
- malignant hyperthermia in patients with a family history of malignant hyperthermia or young males with dystrophic muscle disorders;
- hyperkalemia in patients with neurologic disorders or recent history of severe trauma or burns;
- bradycardia in patients with increased vagal sensitivity, including young children and patients receiving a second dose of succinylcholine.

Pharmacology

Nondepolarizing neuromuscular blocking drugs cause muscle relaxation by blocking the ability of acetylcholine to activate its receptors at the motor endplate. In order of increasing resistance to blockade are the levator muscles of the eyelids, muscles of mastication, limb muscles, trunk muscles, muscles of the glottis, intercostal muscles and the diaphragm. Doses that cause paralysis of the respiratory muscles are commonly used, and mechanical ventilation of the patient is necessary. Reversal of paralysis can be achieved by administration of a suitable anticholinesterase, such as edrophonium or neostigmine, which increases the amount of acetylcholine at the neuromuscular junction. Atropine or glycopyrrolate is also administered to block the unwanted muscarinic side effects of acetylcholine.

Succinylcholine produces a prolonged activation of acetylcholine receptors. A short period of uncoordinated muscle contraction, evident by the fasciculation of surface muscles of the neck and shoulders, is followed by muscle relaxation, in which the cell membrane becomes refractory to the continued depolarization of the motor endplate. Administration of anticholinesterase potentiates the depolarizing block. With repeated administration or continuous infusion of succinylcholine, the motor endplate repolarizes gradually, probably as a result of receptor inactivation, and the blockade takes on some characteristics of a competitive block.

Cardiovascular responses to neuromuscular blocking drugs are common but are usually of minor consequence. Mild hypotension may follow muscle flaccidity and mechanical ventilation. Contributing to the pharmacology of some neuromuscular blockers is their propensity to release histamine from storage cells. The release of histamine is most prominent with tubocurarine but also occurs clinically with succinylcholine, metocurine, atracurium, rapacuronium and mivacurium. Hypotension and skin erythema are the most common responses. Large doses of tubocurarine may also reduce blood pressure by blocking autonomic ganglia. Conversely, the vagolytic effects of rocuronium, pancuronium and, especially, gallamine may increase the heart rate.

The muscle depolarization caused by succinylcholine results in significant potassium efflux and even hyperkalemia in burn patients and patients with recent traumatic injuries, especially those involving the spinal cord.

Neuromuscular blocking drugs are selected according to their freedom from side effects, their route of elimination and their pharmacokinetic properties. Table 3.12 reviews some of the salient pharmacokinetic characteristics of these drugs. The duration of effect and the recovery time after a single administration strongly depend on the dose. Recovery after repeated doses with some agents, such as tubocurarine, metocurine, gallamine, rocuronium and succinylcholine, may be prolonged.

Suggested Readings

Booij LH. Neuromuscular transmission and its pharmacological blockade. Part 1: Neuromuscular transmission and general aspects of its blockade. Pharm World Sci 1997;19(1):1-12.

Booij LH. Neuromuscular transmission and its pharmacological blockade. Part 2: Pharmacology of neuromuscular blocking agents. Pharm World Sci 1997;19(1):13-34.

Savarese JJ, Caldwell JE, Lien CA, Miller RD. Pharmacology of muscle relaxants and their antagonists. In: Miller RD, ed. Anesthesia. 5th ed. New York: Churchill Livingstone; 2000:412-9.

Stoelting RK. Pharmacology and physiology in anesthetic practice. 3rd ed. Philadelphia: Lippincott-Raven; 1999.

Chapter 4.

Analgesics: Opioids and Nonopioids

Steven Ganzberg, D.M.D., M.S.

The use of systemically acting medications to reduce pain perception is an integral part of dental practice. Analgesic medications in dentistry are indicated for the relief of acute pain, postoperative pain and chronic pain, as well as for adjunctive intraoperative pain control. In addition, these medications can be given preoperatively to decrease expected postoperative pain. There are two general categories of analgesic medications: opioid and nonopioid.

Opioid Analgesics

Accepted Indications

Moderate-to-Severe Pain
Opioid medications are generally reserved for moderate-to-severe pain. Codeine, hydrocodone, dihydrocodeine and oxycodone, in combination preparations that contain aspirin, acetaminophen or ibuprofen, are commonly prescribed to manage acute orodental and postoperative pain in dental practice. This type of pain is generally considered to be moderate to severe in intensity. Based on the amount of drug needed to produce a specific analgesic effect, oxycodone is a more potent analgesic than these other medications, but an equianalgesic dose can be found with any of the other agents. At an equianalgesic dose, opioid side effects of sedation, nausea, vomiting, constipation, respiratory depression and pupillary constriction are relatively similar. Table 4.1 lists the commonly prescribed combination opioids, along with oral dosages and schedule of dosing. For severe pain,

opioids such as morphine and methadone are available without a nonsteroidal anti-inflammatory drug (NSAID) or acetaminophen.

Other accepted indications for opioids include treatment of diarrhea, cough and some types of acute pulmonary edema; as an adjunct to anesthesia and sedation; and detoxification from opioids.

Table 4.2 lists commonly prescribed opioids not in combination with other analgesics, along with oral dosages and schedule of dosing.

Cancer and Chronic Nonmalignant Pain
Long-acting opioid analgesics, such as MS Contin, Oramorph, Oxycontin, methadone, levorphanol and fentanyl patches, are available for treating cancer pain and selected cases of chronic nonmalignant pain. These agents are not indicated for acute pain relief and should be prescribed only for people who can tolerate short-acting opioids. Only practitioners who are skilled in the management of chronic pain should prescribe these agents.

Another potentially useful agent for chronic pain management is tramadol (Ultram), which acts as a mu (μ) agonist and a serotonin reuptake blocker. The latter effect, which would be expected to be helpful for chronic pain conditions, may also produce analgesia. The intravenous use of opioid medications for intraoperative sedation is discussed in Chapters 2 and 3.

General Dosing Information
Analgesic medications should be prescribed in a manner that affords the patient the

greatest degree of comfort within a high margin of safety. If the dentist suspects that a patient will have pain for 24-48 h after a dental or surgical procedure, it is prudent to prescribe either opioid or NSAID analgesics on a regularly scheduled basis for at least 24-36 h rather than on an as-needed or prn basis. The rationale for this approach is to provide as continuous a plasma level of medication as possible. If a patient waits until an analgesic medication loses effect and then takes another dose, he or she will be in pain for an additional 30-60 min. Furthermore, it requires more analgesic medication to overcome pain than to maintain pain relief once it has been established. Therefore, the clinician needs knowledge of a specific analgesic's duration of action to prescribe appropriately.

Likewise, it is well-established that if an NSAID or an opioid is given preoperatively, pain relief can be more easily achieved with postoperative analgesics. Similarly, analgesic medication should be started before cessation of local anesthetic activity to achieve a sufficient plasma level of medication before the onset of pain perception.

All opioid medications can cause tolerance, a reduced drug effect that results from continued use and the need for higher doses to produce the same effect. These medications also can cause physical dependence, the physiological state associated with discontinuation of the drug after prolonged use (withdrawal), and psychological dependence, which is an intense craving for the drug and compulsive drug-seeking behavior. Because the pain commonly encountered in dental practice is of the acute type, tolerance of and physical and psychological dependence on opioids are so rare as to be of little concern, because such drugs are used only over the short term. The dentist should use opioid medications in sufficiently large doses for high-quality management of acute pain without fear that patients will develop dependence. The one exception may be patients with a history of drug abuse. For these patients, nonopioid analgesics should be prescribed initially. The majority of important drug interactions involve the possibility of sedative and gastrointestinal side effects, among others. A complete listing of these is provided in Table 4.3.

Maximum Recommended Doses
Adult
Recommended doses for the combination products are listed in Table 4.1. The combination opioid products are generally limited by the dosage of the nonopioid product (for example, 4,000 mg per day for acetaminophen or aspirin). In general, there is no maximum dose of an opioid alone if proper titration has occurred other than the dose at which side effects are not tolerated. The use of noncombination opioids in this way is generally reserved for the management of severe acute pain and selected chronic pains.

Pediatric
Generally, in pediatric patients, codeine and acetaminophen would be used for pain not responsive to acetaminophen alone. The maximum dosages for codeine with acetaminophen are shown in Table 4.1.

Geriatric
Geriatric patients may develop exaggerated sedative effects with opioid medications. Postural hypotension may occur. Consider starting at lower dose ranges.

Dosage Adjustments
Adjust dosage based on patient response. If duration of analgesia is insufficient, a shorter period between doses (for example, q 3 h vs. q 4 h) or a higher dosage (for example, 7.5 mg vs. 5 mg of hydrocodone) is appropriate. If analgesia itself is insufficient, a higher dosage of pain medication is appropriate. For short-term acute pain conditions, dependence on opioids is generally not of concern and efforts should be made to provide adequate postoperative analgesia.

Table 4.1

Opioid Combination Analgesics for Moderate-to-Severe Pain: Dosage and Prescribing Information

Generic name	Brand name(s)	Narcotic component	Non-narcotic component	Adult dosage	Child dosage	PRC
			Codeine combinations			
Codeine with acetaminophen (III*; N†)	Capital with Codeine, Tylenol with Codeine Elixir; PMS-Acetaminophen with Codeine [CAN]	Codeine 12 mg	Acetaminophen 120 mg	**Elixir/solution:** 15 mL q 4 h	Must adjust according to codeine content **Age 2-6 y:** 2.5-5 mg q 4-6 h, maximum 60 mg/24 h **Age 6-12 y:** 5-10 mg q 4-6 h, maximum 60 mg/24 h	C
	Phenaphen w/codeine #2	Codeine 15 mg	Acetaminophen 325 mg	1-2 capsule(s) q 4 h	See note above	C
	Phenaphen w/codeine #3	Codeine 30 mg	Acetaminophen 325 mg	1-2 capsule(s) q 4 h	See note above	C
	Phenaphen w/codeine #4	Codeine 60 mg	Acetaminophen 325 mg	1 capsule q 4 h	See note above	C
	Tylenol #1	Codeine 7.5 mg	Acetaminophen 300 mg	1-2 tablet(s) q 4 h	See note above	C
	Tylenol #2	Codeine 15 mg	Acetaminophen 300 mg	1-2 tablet(s) q 4 h	See note above	C
	Tylenol #3	Codeine 30 mg	Acetaminophen 300 mg	1-2 tablet(s) q 4 h	See note above	C
	Tylenol #4	Codeine 60 mg (MDD 360 mg)	Acetaminophen 300 mg (MDD 4,000 mg)	1 tablet q 4 h	See note above	C

Continued on next page

PRC: Pregnancy risk category.
MDD: Maximum daily dose.
† Controlled substance in Canada; see Appendix A for complete description of schedule.
* Controlled substance in the United States; see Appendix A for complete description of schedule.

Table 4.1 (cont.)

Opioid Combination Analgesics for Moderate-to-Severe Pain: Dosage and Prescribing Information

Generic name	Brand name(s)	Narcotic component	Non-narcotic component	Adult dosage	Child dosage	PRC
Codeine combinations (cont.)						
Codeine with acetaminophen, caffeine and butalbital ‡ (II*; N†)	Fioricet #3	Codeine 30 mg	Acetaminophen 325 mg, butalbital† 50 mg, caffeine 40 mg	1-2 tablet(s) q 4 h (MDD 6 tablets)	NE	C
Codeine with aspirin (III*; N†)	Empirin #2	Codeine 15 mg	Aspirin 325 mg	1-2 tablet(s) q 4 h	NE	C
	Empirin #3	Codeine 30 mg	Aspirin 325 mg	1-2 tablet(s) q 4 h	NE	C
	Empirin #4	Codeine 60 mg (MDD 360 mg)	Aspirin 325 mg (MDD 4,000 mg)	1 tablet q 4 h	NE	C
Codeine with aspirin, caffeine and butalbital § (III*; N†)	Ascomp with codeine, butalbital compound with codeine, Butinal with codeine, Fiorinol #3, Idenal with codeine, Isolly1 with codeine; Fiorinal-C1/2 or C1/4 [CAN], Tecnal-C1/2 or C1/4 [CAN]	Codeine 30 mg	Aspirin 325 mg, butalbital§ 50 mg, caffeine 40 mg	1-2 tablet(s) q 4 h (MDD 6 tablets)	NE	C
Dihydrocodeine combinations						
Dihydrocodeine bitar-trate with acetamino-phen and caffeine (III*)	DHC Plus	Dihydrocodeine 16 mg	Acetaminophen 356.4 mg (MDD 4,000 mg), caffeine 30 mg	2 capsules q 4 h (MDD 6 capsules)	NE	NC

Dihydrocodeine bitartrate with aspirin and caffeine (III*)	Synalgos DC	Dihydrocodeine 16 mg	Aspirin 356.4 mg (MDD 4,000 mg), caffeine 30 mg	2 capsules q 4 h (MDD 6 capsules)	NE	NC
Hydrocodone combinations						
Hydrocodone bitartrate with acetaminophen (III*; N†)	Lortab 2.5/500	Hydrocodone 2.5 mg	Acetaminophen 500 mg	1-2 tablet(s) q 4-6 h (MDD 8 tablets)	NE	C
	Capsules: Allay, Anolar DH5, Bancap-HC, Dolacet, Dolagesic, Hycomed, Hyco-pap, Hydroset, Hydrogesic, Lorcet-HD, Margesic-H, Panlor, Polygesic, Stagesic, T-Gesic, Ugesic, Vendone, Zydone, generic **Tablets:** Anexsia 5/500, Co-gesic, Duocet, Hy-phen, Lortab 5/500, Oncet, Panacet 5/500, Vanacet, Vicodin ★, generic	Hydrocodone 5 mg	Acetaminophen 500 mg	1-2 tablets or capsules q 4-6 h, 2 q 6 h (MDD 8 tablets or capsules)	NE	C

Continued on next page

[CAN] indicates a drug available only in Canada.
PRC: Pregnancy risk category.
MDD: Maximum daily dose.
NE: Not established.
NC: Not classified.
* Controlled substance in the United States; see Appendix A for complete description of schedule.
† Controlled substance in Canada; see Appendix A for complete description of schedule.
‡ Butalbital is a barbiturate. This medication may be more sedating than other combination products. Barbiturate drug interactions and contraindications should be observed.

Table 4.1 (cont.)

Opioid Combination Analgesics for Moderate-to-Severe Pain: Dosage and Prescribing Information

Generic name	Brand name(s)	Narcotic component	Non-narcotic component	Adult dosage	Child dosage	PRC
Hydrocodone combinations (cont.)						
Hydrocodone bitartrate with acetaminophen (III*; N†) *(cont.)*	Lortab 7.5/500, generic	Hydrocodone 7.5 mg	Acetaminophen 500 mg	1 tablet q 4-6 h, 2 q 6 h	NE	C
	Anexsia 7.5/650, Lorcet Plus	Hydrocodone 7.5 mg	Acetaminophen 650 mg	1 tablet q 4-6 h, 2 q 6 h	NE	C
	Vicodin ES	Hydrocodone 7.5 mg	Acetaminophen 750 mg	1 tablet q 4-6 h	NE	C
	Lortab 10/500, Lorcet 10/650	Hydrocodone 10 mg	Acetaminophen 500/650 mg (MDD 4,000 mg)	1 tablet q 4-6 h (MDD 6 tablets)	NE	C
	Lortab	Hydrocodone 2.5 mg/5 mL	Acetaminophen 167 mg/5 mL	**Elixir/solution:** 5-15 mL q 4-6 h	NE	C
Hydrocodone bitartrate with ibuprofen	Vicoprofen	Hydrocodone 7.5 mg	Ibuprofen 200 mg	1 tablet q 4-6 h (MDD 5 tablets)	NE	C
Oxycodone combinations						
Oxycodone with acetaminophen (II*; N†)	**Tablets:** Endocet, Percocet ★, Roxicet, generic **Oral solution:** Roxicet	**Tablets:** Oxycodone 5 mg **Oral solution:** Oxycodone 5 mg/mL	**Tablets:** Acetaminophen 325 mg **Oral solution:** Acetaminophen 325 mg/ 5 mL	**Tablets:** 1 q 4-6 h **Oral solution:** 5-10 mL q 4-6 h	NE	C

					PRC	
	Capsules: Roxilox, Tylox **Tablets:** Roxicet 5/500, generic	**Capsules:** Oxycodone 5 mg **Tablets:** Oxycodone 5 mg	**Capsules:** Acetaminophen 500 mg (MDD 4,000 mg) **Tablets:** Acetaminophen 500 mg (MDD 4,000 mg)	**Capsules:** 1 capsule q 4-6 h **Tablets:** 1 tablet q 4-6 h	NE	C
Oxycodone with aspirin (II*; N†)	Percocet-Demi [CAN]	2.5 mg oxycodone	325 mg acetaminophen	NE; do not use in children	NE	C
	Percodan-Demi ★	Oxycodone 2.5 mg	Aspirin 325 mg	1-2 tablet(s) q 4-6 h	NE	NC
	Percodan ★, Roxiprin	Oxycodone 5 mg	Aspirin 325 mg (MDD 4,000 mg)	1 tablet q 4-6 h	NE	NC
Pentazocine ‡ combinations						
Pentazocine with acetaminophen (IV*; N†)	Talacen	Pentazocine 25 mg	Acetaminophen 650 mg (MDD 4,000 mg)	1 tablet q 4 h (MDD 6 tablets)	NE	C
Pentazocine with aspirin (IV*; N†)	Talwin Compound	Pentazocine 12.5 mg	Aspirin 325 mg (MDD 4,000 mg)	2 tablets tid/qid	NE	NC

Continued on next page

★ indicates a drug bearing the ADA Seal of Acceptance.
[CAN] indicates a drug available only in Canada.
PRC: Pregnancy risk category.
MDD: Maximum daily dose.
NE: Not established.
NC: Not classified.
* Controlled substance in the United States; see Appendix A for complete description of schedule.
† Controlled substance in Canada; see Appendix A for complete description of schedule.
‡ Agonist-antagonist opioid.

Table 4.1 (cont.)

Opioid Combination Analgesics for Moderate-to-Severe Pain: Dosage and Prescribing Information

Generic name	Brand name(s)	Narcotic component	Non-narcotic component	Adult dosage	Child dosage	PRC
			Propoxyphene combinations			
Propoxyphene HCl or napsylate with acetaminophen (IV*; N†)	E-Lor, Wygesic	Propoxyphene HCl 65 mg	Acetaminophen 650 mg	1 tablet q 4 h	NE	NC
	Darvocet N-50 ★	Propoxyphene napsylate 50 mg	Acetaminophen 325 mg	1-2 tablet(s) q 4 h	NE	NC
	Darvocet N-100 ★	Propoxyphene napsylate 100 mg	Acetaminophen 650 mg (MDD 4,000 mg)	1 tablet q 4 h	NE	NC
Propoxyphene HCl with aspirin and caffeine (IV*; N†)	Darvon Compound-65, PC-Cap, Propoxyphene Compound-65, generic; 692 [CAN]	Propoxyphene 65 mg (MDD 390 mg)	Aspirin 389 mg (MDD 4,000 mg), caffeine 32.4 mg	**Capsules:** 1 q 4 h **Tablets [CAN]:** 1 q 4 h	NE	NC
Propoxyphene napsylate w/ aspirin	Darvon-P with ASA [CAN]	Propoxyphene napsylate 100 mg	Aspirin 325 mg	1 tablet q 4 h (MDD 6 tablets)	NE	NC

★ indicates a drug bearing the ADA Seal of Acceptance.
[CAN] indicates a drug available only in Canada.
PRC: Pregnancy risk category.
MDD: Maximum daily dose.
NE: Not established.
NC: Not classified.
* Controlled substance in the United States; see Appendix A for complete description of schedule.
† Controlled substance in Canada; see Appendix A for complete description of schedule.

Dosage Forms

Opioid medications are available for oral, intravenous, intramuscular, transnasal or transdermal use. The dentist will likely use oral forms (capsule, tablet or elixir—see Tables 4.1 and 4.2) or perhaps butorphanol, which is available in a nasal spray form.

Special Dental Considerations

Opioids may decrease salivary flow. Consider opioid use in the differential diagnosis of caries, periodontal disease or oral candidiasis.

Drug Interactions of Dental Interest

The most common drug interactions of concern for dentistry involve the potential sedative side effects, which are exaggerated in patients taking other CNS depressants (see Table 4.3).

Cross-Sensitivity

Possible cross-sensitivity is possible with opioids. It is important for the dentist to distinguish whether a true allergic reaction occurred, as most opioids can produce nausea and/or vomiting and release histamine. These reactions are typically referred to as "allergic" by patients. Consider using a nonopioid analgesic in these patients. Switching to a different opioid may produce fewer side effects.

Special Patients

Opioids should be used with extreme caution in patients with chronic obstructive pulmonary disease, such as emphysema or chronic bronchitis, owing to possible respiratory compromise. Opioids may precipitate an asthmatic episode because of their potential for histamine release. This is considerably more likely with parenteral vs. oral administration of opioids. Asthmatic patients should be warned to discontinue use of oral opioids if they experience asthmatic attacks during therapy. Combination opioid products that contain aspirin should not be prescribed to asthmatic patients. Likewise, patients with severe cardiac disease, such as advanced congestive heart failure, may not tolerate hypotensive side effects. Owing to constipating effects, opioids should be used with caution in patients with severe inflammatory bowel disease. If mentally challenged patients are prescribed opioids, they should be closely monitored by an appropriate caregiver. Opioids should be prescribed cautiously for a patient with emotional instability, suicidal ideation or attempts, or a history of substance abuse.

Pregnant and nursing women
Opioids should not be prescribed for a pregnant or nursing patient without consultation with the patient's physician.

Pediatric, geriatric and other special patients
Pediatric and geriatric patients should be considered for lower opioid dosages.

Patient Monitoring: Aspects to Watch

- Respiratory depression and sedation: the patient should contact the dentist if these side effects are observed.

Adverse Effects and Precautions

The majority of important drug interactions involve the possibility of sedative and gastrointestinal side effects; a more complete listing is provided in Tables 4.3 and 4.4.

Pharmacology

Opioid medications produce analgesia by interaction at specific receptors in the central nervous system, mimicking the effect of endogenous pain-relieving neurochemicals (for example, dynorphin, enkephalin and β-endorphin). These receptors are present in higher brain centers such as the hypothalamus and periaqueductal gray regions, as well as in the spinal cord and trigeminal nucleus. The result of this interaction is a decrease in pain transmission to higher thalamocortical centers and a corresponding decrease in pain perception. Recent evidence suggests a possible peripheral effect of opioid analgesics.

Opioids undergo hepatic transformation generally to inactive metabolites, which are excreted in the urine and/or bile. These

Table 4.2

Opioid Noncombination Analgesics: Dosage and Prescribing Information

Generic name	Brand name(s)	Narcotic component	Adult dosage	Max child dosage	PRC
Butorphanol (agonist-antagonist) (IV*)	Stadol	Butorphanol 1, 2 mg/mL; 1 mg/dose	**IM:** 1-4 mg q 3-4 h **IV:** 0.5-2 mg q 3-4 h **Nasal spray:** 1-2 doses q 4-6 h	NE	C
Codeine phosphate (II*; C†)	generic	30, 60 mg; 15, 30 mg [CAN]	**Tablets:** 15-60 mg (usually 30 mg) q 3-6 h up to 120 mg/day maximum	**Premature infants:** NR **Newborn infants and children:** NE	C
	generic	30, 60 mg; 30, 60 [CAN]	**Injection:** 15-60 mg (usually 30 mg) q 4-6 h	**Premature infants:** NR **Newborn infants and children:** NE	C
	generic	30, 60 mg	**Soluble tablets:** 15-60 mg (usually 30) q 4-6 h	**Premature infants:** NR **Newborn infants and children:** NE	C
Codeine sulfate (II*; C†)	generic	15, 30, 60 mg	**Tablets:** 15-60 mg (usually 30 mg) q 3-6 h up to 120 mg/day	**Premature infants:** NR **Newborn infants and children:** NE	C

	Brand names	Dosage forms	Dosage	PRC
Hydromorphone HCl (II*, C†)	generic	30, 60 mg	**Soluble tablets:** 15-60 mg (usually 30 mg) q 4-6 h	**Premature infants:** NR **Newborn infants and children:** NE	C
	Dilaudid, Hydrostat IR; PMS Hydromorphone [CAN], generic	**Dilaudid:** 2, 4, 8 mg; 1, 2, 4, 8 mg [CAN] **Hydrostat IR:** 1, 2, 3, 4 mg **PMS Hydromorphone [CAN]:** 1, 2, 4, 8 mg **Generic:** 2, 4 mg; 2, 4 mg [CAN]	**Tablets:** 2 mg q 3-6 h	U	C
	Dilaudid-5, Dilaudid; PMS-Hydromorphone Syrup [CAN]	5 mg/mL	**Oral solution:** 2.5-10 mg q 3-6 h	U	C
	Dilaudid, generic	**Dilaudid with preservatives:** 2 mg/mL; 2 mg/mL [CAN] **Generic with preservatives:** 1, 2, 3, 4 mg/mL **Dilaudid without preservatives:** 1, 2, 4 mg/mL; 2 mg/mL [CAN] **Dilaudid-HP without preservatives:** 10 mg/mL; 10 mg/mL [CAN]	**Injection:** 1-2 mg q 3-6 h; if severe, 3-4 mg q 4-6 h	U	C

Continued on next page

[CAN] indicates a drug available only in Canada.
PRC: Pregnancy risk category.
NE: Not established.
NR: Not recommended.
U: Unavailable.
* Controlled substance in the United States; see Appendix A for complete description of schedule.
† Controlled substance in Canada; see Appendix A for complete description of schedule.

Table 4.2 (cont.)

Opioid Noncombination Analgesics: Dosage and Prescribing Information

Generic name	Brand name(s)	Narcotic component	Adult dosage	Max child dosage	PRC
Meperidine (II*; C†)	Demerol, generic	**Tablets:** 50, 100 mg **Syrup:** 50 mg/mL **Solution for injection:** 25, 50, 75, 100 mg/mL; 100 mg/mL [CAN]	**Tablets, syrup:** 50-150 mg q 3-4 h **Analgesic, solution—IM or SC:** 50-150 mg q 3-4 h **Analgesic, solution—IV infusion:** 15-35 mg/h as required **Anesthesia adjunct, preoperative, solution—IM or SC:** 50-100 mg 30-90 min prn to anesthesia **Anesthesia adjunct, preoperative, solution—IV:** By repeated slow injection of fractional doses of a solution diluted to 10/mg/mL **Anesthesia adjunct, preoperative, solution—IV infusion:** As a solution diluted to 1 mg/mL	**Tablets, syrup:** 1.1-1.76 mg/kg, not to exceed 100 mg q 3-4 h as needed **Analgesic, solution—IM or SC:** 1.1-1.76 mg/kg, not to exceed 100 mg q 3-4 h **Analgesic, solution, preoperative—IM or SC:** 1-2.2 mg/kg, not to exceed 100 mg, 30-90 min prior to anesthesia	NC
Morphine HCl (II*; C†)	**Syrup:** Morphitec; M.O.S. [CAN] **Tablets:** M.O.S. [CAN] **Extended-release tablets:** M.O.S.-S.R. [CAN] **Suppositories:** M.O.S. [CAN]	**Syrup:** 1, 5, 10, 20, 50 mg/mL **Tablets:** 10, 20, 40, 60 mg **Extended-release tablets:** 30, 60 mg **Suppositories:** 10, 20, 30 mg	**Syrup:** 10-30 mg q 4 h **Tablets:** 10-30 mg q 4 h **Extended-release tablets:** Established by physician **Suppositories:** 20-30 mg q 4-6 h	**Syrup:** U **Tablets:** U **Extended-release tablets:** U **Suppositories:** U	C

Drug	Product forms	Dosing		
Morphine sulfate (II*; C†)	**Capsules:** MSIR	**Capsules:** 10–30 mg q 4 h	NE	C
	Extended-release capsules: M-Eslon [CAN]	**Extended-release capsules:** Initially, 30 mg q 12 h		
		Capsules: 15, 30 mg		
	Extended-release capsules: 10, 30, 60, 100 mg	**Extended-release capsules:** Initially, 30 mg q 12 h		
	Oral solution: Rescudose, Roxanol UD, MSIR, MS/L, MS/L Concentrate, OMS Concentrate, Roxanol, Roxanol 100, generic; Statex drops [CAN]	**Oral solution:** 10 mg/2.5 mL, 10 mg/5mL, 20 mg/5 mL, 20 mg/mL, 30 mg/1.5 mL, 100 mg/5 mL; 2, 4, 50 mg/mL [CAN]		
		Oral solution: Initially, 30 mg q 12 h		
	Syrup: Statex [CAN]	**Syrup:** 1, 5, 10 mg/mL		
		Syrup: Initially, 30 mg q 12 h		
	Tablets: MSIR, MSIR [CAN], Statex [CAN], generic	**Tablets:** 15, 30 mg; 5, 10, 20, 25, 50 mg [CAN]		
		Tablets: Initially, 30 mg q 12 h		
	Injection: Astramorph PF, Duramorph, generic; Epimorph [CAN], Morphine Extra-Forte [CAN], Morphine Forte [CAN], Morphine H.P. [CAN]	**Injection:** 0.5, 1, 2, 4, 5, 8, 10, 15, 25, 50 mg/mL	**Injection, IM or SC:** 5–20 mg initially, then q 4 h		
	Soluble tablets: generic	**Soluble tablets:** 10, 15, 30 mg	**Soluble tablets:** 5–20 mg initially, then q 4 h		
	Suppositories: MS/S, RMS Inserts, Roxanol, generic; MSIR [CAN], Statex [CAN]	**Suppositories:** 5, 10, 20, 30 mg	**Suppositories:** 10–30 mg q 4 h		
Oxycodone HCl (II*; C†)	**Oral solution:** Roxicodone, Roxicodone Intensol	**Oral solution:** 5 mg/5 mL, 20 mg/mL	**Oral solution:** 5 mg q 3–6 h; may be increased if severe pain is present	U	NC
	Tablets: Roxicodone; Supeudol [CAN]	**Tablets:** 5 mg; 10 mg [CAN]	**Tablets:** 5 mg q 3–6 h or 10 mg q 6–8 h; may be increased if severe pain is present		
	Extended-release tablets: OxyContin	**Extended-release tablets:** 10, 20, 40, 80 mg	**Extended-release tablets:** 1 tablet q 12 h		
	Suppositories: Supeudol [CAN]	**Suppositories:** 10 mg; 20 mg [CAN]	**Suppositories:** 10–40 mg tid-qid		

[CAN] indicates a drug available only in Canada.
PRC: Pregnancy risk category.
NC: Not classified.
NE: Not established.
U: Unavailable.
* Controlled substance in the United States; see Appendix A for complete description of schedule.
† Controlled substance in Canada; see Appendix A for complete description of schedule.

drugs are subdivided into agonist, agonist-antagonist or antagonist compounds based on their receptor effects.

Agonists

The opioid medications typified by morphine act primarily in the CNS through varied activity on specific opioid receptor subgroups. Although there is activity at all opioid receptors, morphine and related agents—such as codeine, hydrocodone, dihydrocodeine and oxycodone, as well as meperidine and the fentanyl derivatives—provide analgesia chiefly through agonist activity at the μ receptor.

Agonist-Antagonists

Another group of opioid analgesics, the agonist-antagonists—including pentazocine, nalbuphine and butorphanol—are agonists at the kappa (κ) receptor, and antagonists at the μ receptor.

Antagonists

Specific competitive opioid antagonist medications—namely, naloxone and naltrexone—have also been developed. Naloxone's main use in dentistry is reversal of excessive opioid IV sedation. Naltrexone is used to treat former opioid abusers and recently has been used for patients with certain CNS disorders.

Table 4.3
Standard Opioids: Possible Interactions With Other Drugs

Drug taken by patient	Interaction with standard opioids	Dentist's action
Agonist-antagonist drugs (nalbuphine, butorphanol, pentazocine)	Can lead to withdrawal syndrome or loss of analgesia with hypertension, tachycardia	Never prescribe agonist-antagonist opioids with conventional agonist opioids
Alcohol	Sedative side effects	Advise patients to never drink alcohol when taking opioids
Amphetamines	With meperidine: hypotension, respiratory collapse	Do not prescribe meperidine to a patient taking amphetamines
Anticholinergics	Constipation	Prescribe opioids only for short periods of time; consider physician consultation
Antidiarrheals	Constipation	Prescribe opioids only for short periods of time; consider physician consultation
Antihypertensives and vasodilators	Potentiation of hypotensive effects	Advise patients to notify dentist if postural hypotension or dizziness occurs
Barbiturates	Sedative side effects	Alert patient to possible additive side effects and to notify dentist if not tolerated
Carbamazepine	With propoxyphene: Increased carbamazepine levels	Do not prescribe propoxyphene to patients taking carbamazepine
CNS depressants	Sedative side effects	Alert patient to possible additive side effects and to notify dentist if not tolerated

Continued on next page

Table 4.3 (cont.)

Standard Opioids: Possible Interactions With Other Drugs

Drug taken by patient	Interaction with standard opioids	Dentist's action
Coumarin anticoagulants	With propoxyphene: Increased anticoagulant effects	Avoid prescribing propoxyphene to patients taking coumarin anticoagulants
Hydroxyzine	Sedative side effects	Alert patient to possible additive side effects and to notify dentist if not tolerated
Hypnotics (sedative)	Sedative side effects	Alert patient to possible additive side effects and to notify dentist if not tolerated
MAO inhibitors	With meperidine: severe hypertension	Avoid prescribing meperidine to a patient taking MAO inhibitors
Metoclopramide	Can antagonize metoclopramide	Prescribe opioids only for short periods of time; consider physician consultation
Other opioids	Sedative side effects	Avoid prescribing two opioids at one time unless for chronic pain
Tobacco	With propoxyphene: May decrease the effect of propoxyphene	Advise patient to stop smoking; do not prescribe propoxyphene to tobacco users

Patient Advice

- Avoid use of alcohol or other CNS depressant medications unless physician or dentist gives approval.
- Inform dentist if nausea, vomiting, excessive dry mouth, dizziness or lightheadedness, itching, hives or difficulty in breathing occurs.
- Exercise caution when getting up suddenly from a lying or sitting position.
- Avoid driving a motor vehicle or operating heavy machinery, especially if sedative side effects are present.

Suggested Readings

Dionne RA, Snyder J, Hargreaves KM. Analgesic efficacy of flurbiprofen in comparison with acetaminophen, acetaminophen plus codeine, and placebo after impacted third molar removal. J Oral Maxillofac Surg 1994;52(9):919-24.

Forbes JA, Bates JA, Edquist IA, et al. Evaluation of two opioid-acetaminophen combinations and placebo in post-operative oral surgery pain. Pharmacotherapy 1994;14(2):139-46.

Hargreaves KM, Troullos ES, Dionne RA. Pharmacologic rationale for the treatment of acute pain. Dent Clin North Am 1987;31(4):675-94.

Neidle EA, Yagiela JA, eds. Pharmacology and therapeutics for dentistry. St. Louis: Mosby; 1989.

The United States Pharmacopeial Convention, Inc. USP Dispensing Information. Drug information for the health care professional. Vol. I. 17th ed. Rockville, Md.: The United States Pharmacopeial Convention, Inc.; 1997.

Nonopioid Analgesics

This group of analgesics includes the nonsteroidal anti-inflammatory drugs and acetaminophen. The site of action of these drugs is primarily peripheral, although recent evidence suggests an important role for CNS activity as well.

Nonsteroidal Anti-inflammatory Drugs

Although NSAIDs influence a number of systems, a primary effect is the inhibition of the synthesis of prostaglandins, which are potent

Table 4.4

Opioids: Adverse Effects, Precautions and Contraindications

Body system	Adverse effects	Precautions/contraindications
General	Possible allergic reaction	Contraindicated in those with a history of allergy to agent
CV	Hypotension	Can cause postural hypotension, especially in elderly
CNS	Cough suppression, pupillary constriction, sedation, mental clouding, hallucinations, dependence with chronic use	History of or current drug abuse or dependence, intracranial conditions Emotional instability, suicidal ideation
GI	Constipation, increased biliary duct pressure, hepatic toxicity, xerostomia	Chronic GI disease in which constipation would not be desirable Gallbladder disease Contraindicated in patients with diarrhea secondary to colitis Contraindicated with use of toxic materials Contraindicated in some acute GI conditions
GU	Urine retention	Prostatic hypertrophy Renal function impairment
Hema	Histamine release or itching, or both; true allergic reaction	None of significance to dentistry
Integ	Itching, hives	None of significance to dentistry
Oral	Xerostomia	None of significance to dentistry
Resp	Respiratory depression, asthma attack	Asthma, especially when opioids are given through the IV route with histamine-releasing opioids Contraindicated in patients with chronic respiratory impairment, such as chronic obstructive pulmonary disease and acute respiratory depression

vasodilators and mediators of the inflammatory response at the site of injury. These compounds also decrease the threshold needed for nerves conducting pain information to signal the CNS. By decreasing the production of prostaglandins, NSAIDs depress the inflammatory response. This decrease in prostaglandin concentration also raises the threshold for pain-conducting nerves to discharge, thus providing an analgesic effect. NSAIDs also reduce fever by decreasing the concentration of prostaglandins in the hypothalamus, a brain center regulating body temperature. A CNS role for prostaglandin inhibition in pain modulation also has been postulated.

The NSAIDs consist of several basic

groups of drugs with different structures but similar actions. They are primarily indicated for the relief of mild-to-moderate pain. Although no individual NSAID has been found to be significantly superior for pain relief in all patients, NSAIDs do differ in duration of action and side-effect profile. If one NSAID is ineffective for pain control, the dentist should keep in mind that another from a different structural group may be effective. Many NSAIDs have a ceiling dose for analgesia and require a higher dose for the anti-inflammatory effect. For instance, ibuprofen, at 400 mg taken qid, provides close to a maximum analgesic effect, but a dose of 2,400-3,200 mg per day may be required for the anti-inflammatory effect. NSAIDs with an easier dosing schedule, such as bid or tid, may provide better patient compliance and result in a more pain-free patient. Some NSAIDs may be better analgesics while others are better anti-inflammatories. Table 4.5 lists acetaminophen and NSAIDs by structural group, indicating dosing schedule, maximum daily dose and drugs that may be more analgesic than others.

Acetaminophen

Acetaminophen's mechanism of action is poorly understood. Its analgesic and antipyretic properties are similar to those of aspirin, but acetaminophen has poor anti-inflammatory action.

Accepted Indications

NSAIDs are indicated for use as analgesics for mild to moderate pain, including pain of acute dental origin or for postoperative dental pain. These drugs are also indicated for pain of inflammatory origin, especially for rheumatic conditions and primary non-rheumatic inflammatory conditions. These drugs may also be used as antipyretics (ibuprofen and naproxen) and for treatment of primary dysmenorrhea.

NSAIDs may be indicated for longer-term use in patients with chronic orofacial pain, especially pain with an inflammatory compo-nent such as temporomandibular joint synovitis. If these medications are prescribed for a longer term, appropriate laboratory studies—including CBC, renal function tests and liver function tests—should be considered. Recent studies indicate that specific subtypes of the cyclooxygenase enzyme may lead to the development of NSAIDs with considerably less prominent side effects (see Pharmacology section). Regardless, the long-term use of these agents should be undertaken only by those skilled in chronic pain management.

General Dosing Information

It appears that many NSAIDs have a ceiling effect for analgesia. For instance, lower doses of ibuprofen may provide maximum analgesic efficacy, while higher doses are required for an anti-inflammatory effect. Depending on the condition being treated, the dentist may consider higher or lower dosages. For chronic conditions, one NSAID may be ineffective while another provides excellent pain relief. The dentist may consider switching NSAIDs, perhaps to one from a different structural category, to obtain desired results.

As a general rule, analgesic medications should be prescribed in a manner that affords the patient the greatest degree of comfort within a high margin of safety. If the dentist suspects that a patient will have pain for 24-48 h after a surgical procedure, it is prudent to prescribe either opioid or NSAID analgesics on a regularly scheduled basis for at least 24-36 h rather than on an as-needed basis. The rationale for this approach is to provide as continuous a plasma level of medication as possible. If a patient waits until an analgesic medication loses effect and then takes another dose, the patient will be in pain for an additional 30-60 min. Further, it requires more analgesic medication to overcome pain than to maintain pain relief once it has been established. Therefore, the clinician needs knowledge of a specific analgesic's duration of action to prescribe appropriately.

Likewise, it is well-established that if an NSAID is given preoperatively, pain relief can be more easily achieved with postoperative analgesics. Similarly, analgesic medication should be started before cessation of local anesthetic activity to allow a sufficient plasma level of medication to be achieved before the onset of pain perception.

Owing to the possible gastrointestinal side effects, NSAIDs should be prescribed with meals and/or taken with a full glass of water.

Maximum Recommended Doses

Adults
See Table 4.5.

Pregnant women
NSAIDs are generally contraindicated during pregnancy. Some NSAIDs do carry Pregnancy Category B classification during the first trimester of pregnancy. Regardless, the use of NSAIDs should be considered contraindicated in dental practice for all pregnant patients, unless prescribed in consultation with the patient's obstetrician. Acetaminophen, although generally acceptable, should be prescribed in consultation with the patient's obstetrician if there are any questions about the appropriateness of its use in an individual case.

Pediatric and geriatric patients
As with most medications, dosages should be reduced for children and elderly patients. Owing to their possible gastrointestinal side effects, NSAIDs should be prescribed with meals.

Dosage Forms
NSAIDs and acetaminophen are available for oral use except for ketorolac tromethamine, which is also available in an IV/IM preparation. Elixir, liquid and rectal preparations are available for aspirin and acetaminophen. Liquid forms of ibuprofen are also available.

Special Dental Considerations
In the differential diagnosis of appropriate conditions, dentists should take into consideration that NSAIDs may cause soreness or irritation of the oral mucosa. Although rare, some NSAIDs may cause leukopenia and/or thrombocyopenia.

Drug Interactions of Dental Interest
Major drug interactions with NSAIDs stem from the effect of these drugs on platelet, gastrointestinal and renal function.

Laboratory Value Alterations
* There are no laboratory tests whose results are specifically altered by NSAIDs and acetaminophen.
* The effect of these drugs on platelet function will likely increase bleeding times.
* There may also be changes in renal and hepatic function, especially with long-term NSAID use.

Cross-Sensitivity
All NSAIDs and aspirin may exhibit cross-sensitivity. Any of these drugs should be used with extreme caution, if at all, in patients who have developed signs and symptoms of allergic reaction to any NSAID, including aspirin. It should also be noted that patients with a history of nasal polyps and asthma have an increased risk of sensitivity, including allergic reactions, to aspirin, particularly, but also to other NSAIDs.

Special Patients

Pregnant and nursing women
NSAIDs should not be prescribed by dentists for pregnant or nursing women. Acetaminophen may be prescribed in consultation with the patient's physician.

Pediatric, geriatric and other special patients
Only acetaminophen, aspirin and ibuprofen are approved for pediatric use. Aspirin may cause Reye's syndrome in children infected with influenza virus. Reye's syndrome is a serious medical condition that can lead to severe hepatic and CNS disease, as well as death. Because other drugs are available that do not manifest this concern, the dentist should consider avoiding use of aspirin in all children with fever.

Geriatric patients may be more susceptible

Table 4.5

NSAIDs and Acetaminophen: Dosage and Prescribing Information

Generic name	Brand name(s)	Adult dosage	Max adult dosage	Max child dosage	PRC	Content/form
			Aminophenol			
Acetamino-phen	Tylenol (various brand names)	325-500 mg q 4-6 h	4,000 mg q day short-term; 2,600 mg q day long-term unless monitored	**Age < 6 mo/1 y:** 15-60 mg/dose q 4-6 h; do not exceed 65 mg/kg/day **Age 1-2 y:** 120 mg/dose q 4 h **Age 2-3 y:** 160 mg/dose q 4 h **Age 3-4 y:** 180 mg/dose q 4 h **Age 4-5 y:** 240 mg/dose q 4 h **Age 5-10 y:** 325 mg/dose q 4 h **Age 6-11 y:** Not to exceed 1,625 mg in 24 h **Age > 12 y:** Not to exceed 4,000 mg in 24 h	B	**Capsules:** 325, 500 mg **Elixir:** 120, 160, 325 mg/5mL **Granules:** 80, 120, 160 mg **Solution:** 100 mg/mL, 80 mg/5 mL, 120 mg/5 mL, 130 mg/5 mL **Suspension:** 48 mg/mL, 160 mg/5 mL, 100 mg/mL; 80 mg/mL [CAN], 80 mg/5 mL [CAN] **SOC (infant drops):** 100 mg/1 mL, 120 mg/2.5 mL **Suppositories:** 120, 125, 325, 650 mg **Tablets, chewable:** 80, 160 mg
			Fenamates			
Meclofen-amate sodium*	Meclomen	50-100 mg tid-qid	400 mg	NE	NE	**Capsules:** 10, 20 mg
Mefenamic acid	Ponstan, Ponstel	500 mg initially, then 250 mg qid	1,500 mg (max 7 days)	NE	C	**Capsules:** 250 mg
			Furanone			
Rofecoxib	Vioxx	12.5-50 mg q day	50 mg	NE	C	**Oral suspension:** 12.5, 25 mg/cc **Tablets:** 12.5, 25 mg
			Indoles			
Indometh-acin	Indocid, Indocin; Apo-Indometha-cin [CAN], Novo-Methacin [CAN], Nu-Indo [CAN]	25-50 mg tid	200 mg	1.5-2.5 mg/kg/day in 3-4 doses, up to maximum of 4 mg/kg/day or 150-200 mg/day, whichever is less	NE	**Capsules:** 25, 50 mg **Oral suspension:** 25 mg/5 mL **Suppositories:** 50 mg

[CAN] indicates a drug available only in Canada.
PRC: Pregnancy risk category.
NE: Not established.
* indicates a medication possessing good analgesic properties.

Continued on next page

Table 4.5 (cont.)

NSAIDs and Acetaminophen: Dosage and Prescribing Information

Generic name	Brand name(s)	Adult dosage	Max adult dosage	Max child dosage	PRC	Content/form
Indoles (cont.)						
Indometh-acin, sustained release	Indocin SR	75 mg q day or bid	150 mg	NE	NE	**Capsules:** 75 mg
Ketorolac trometha-mine*	Toradol	**Oral:** 20 mg initially, then 10 mg qid **IM:** 30 mg q 6 h **IV:** 30 mg q 6 h OR loading dose 15-30 mg IV/IM, then 10 mg qid oral	**Oral:** Not to exceed 40 mg/day, max 5 days **IM:** 20 doses over 5 days (120 mg/day) **IV:** 20 doses over 5 days (120 mg)	NE	C	**Tablets:** 10 mg **Parenteral:** 15 mg/mL, 30 mg/mL
Tolmetin sodium	Tolectin	200-600 mg tid	2,000 mg	15-30 mg/kg/ day in divided doses	C	**Capsules:** 400 mg **Tablets:** 200, 600 mg
Naphthylalkanone						
Nabumetone	Relafen	1,000 mg q day-bid	2,000 mg	NE	C	**Tablets:** 500, 750 mg
Oxicams						
Piroxicam	Feldene; Apo-Piroxicam [CAN], Novo-Pirocam [CAN], Nu-Pirox [CAN], PMS-Piroxicam [CAN]	20 mg q day or 10 mg bid	20 mg	NE	C	**Capsules:** 10, 20 mg
Phenylacetic acids						
Diclofenac potassium*	Cataflam; Voltaren Rapide [CAN]	50 mg tid	150 mg	NE	B	**Tablets:** 25, 50 mg
Diclofenac sodium*	Voltaren (delayed release), Voltaren SR; Apo-Diclo [CAN], Novo-Difenac [CAN], Novo-Difenac SR [CAN], Nu-Diclo [CAN]	50 mg tid-qid; 75 mg bid; 100 mg q day	150 mg	NE	B	**Tablets:** 25, 50, 75 mg

[CAN] indicates a drug available only in Canada.
PRC: Pregnancy risk category.
NE: Not established.
* indicates a medication possessing good analgesic properties.

Continued on next page

Table 4.5 (cont.)

NSAIDs and Acetaminophen: Dosage and Prescribing Information

Generic name	Brand name(s)	Adult dosage	Max adult dosage	Max child dosage	PRC	Content/form
Propionic acids						
Fenoprofen	Nalfon, Nalfon 200	300-600 mg tid-qid	3,200 mg	NE	NE	**Capsules:** 200, 300 mg **Tablets:** 600 mg
Flurbiprofen*	Ansaid, Froben; Apo-Flurbiprofen [CAN], Novo-Flurprofen [CAN], Nu-Flurbiprofen [CAN]	50-100 mg bid-tid	300 mg	NE	B	**Tablets:** 50, 100 mg
Ibuprofen*	Dolgesic, Ibu, Ibu-4, Ibuprohm, Ibu-Tab, Motrin, Rufen; Apo-Ibuprofen [CAN], Novo-Profen [CAN], Nu-Ibuprofen [CAN] OTC 200 mg: Advil★, Bayer Select Ibuprofen, Cramp End, Excedrin IB, Genpril, Haltran, Ibu-200, Ibuprin, Ibuprohm, Ibu-Tab, Medipren, Midol, Motrin, Nuprin, Pamprin, Q-profen, Trendar	200, 400, 600, 800 mg tid-qid	3,600 mg	**Age 6 mo-12 y, usual dose:** 5-10 mg/kg q 4-6 h **Max pediatric dose:** 40-50 mg/kg/day	NE	**Oral suspension:** 40 mg/mL, 100 mg/5 mL **Tablets:** 100, 200, 300, 400, 600, 800 mg **Tablets, chewable:** 50, 100 mg
Ketoprofen*	Orudis, Rhodis; Apo-Keto [CAN] OTC 12.5 mg: Actron, Orudis KT	25, 50, 75 mg tid/qid	300 mg	NE	B	**Capsules:** 25, 50, 75 mg **Tablets:** 12.5 mg
Ketoprofen, sustained relief	Orudis-E, Oruvail, Rhodis-EC; Apo-Keto-E [CAN], Novo-Keto-EC [CAN]	100, 150, 200 mg q day	200 mg	NE	B	**Capsules:** 100, 150, 200 mg

★ *indicates a product bearing the ADA Seal of Acceptance.*
[CAN] *indicates a drug available only in Canada.*
PRC: Pregnancy risk category.
NE: Not established.
* *indicates a medication possessing good analgesic properties.*

Continued on next page

Table 4.5 (cont.)

NSAIDs and Acetaminophen: Dosage and Prescribing Information

Generic name	Brand name(s)	Adult dosage	Max adult dosage	Max child dosage	PRC	Content/form
Propionic acids (cont.)						
Naproxen*	Naprosyn, Naxen; Apo-Naproxen [CAN], Novo-Naprox Sodium [CAN], Nu-Naprox [CAN]	**Tablets:** 250, 375 q 6-8 h; 500 mg bid **Elixir:** 125 mg/5 mL	1,250 mg	10 mg/kg/day in 2 doses	B	**Tablets:** 250, 375, 500 mg **Oral suspension:** 125 mg/5 mL
Naproxen sodium*	Anaprox, Anaprox DS, Synflex; Apo-Napro-Na [CAN], Novo-Naprox Sodium [CAN] OTC 220 mg: Aleve	275 q 8 h, 550 mg q 12 h	1,375 mg	NR	B	**Tablets:** 220, 275, 550 mg
Oxaprozin	Daypro	600 mg bid or 1,200 mg q day	1,800 mg or 26 mg/kg, whichever is lower	NE	C	**Tablets:** 600 mg
Pyranoindole acetic acid						
Etodolac	Lodine ★	200-400 mg tid	1,200 mg	NE	C	**Capsules:** 200, 300 mg **Tablets:** 400 mg
Pyrazole						
Celecoxib	Celebrex	100-200 mg q 12 h	400 mg	NR	C	**Tablets:** 100, 200 mg
Phenylbutazone	Apo-phenylbutazone [CAN], Butazolidin [CAN]	100 mg q 4 h	600 mg	NR	C	**Capsules:** 100 mg **Tablets:** 100 mg
Pyroleacetic acid						
Sulindac	Clinoril; Apo-Sulin [CAN]	150-200 mg bid	400 mg	NE	NE	**Tablets:** 150, 200 mg

★ *indicates a product bearing the ADA Seal of Acceptance.*
[CAN] indicates a drug available only in Canada.
PRC: Pregnancy risk category.
NE: Not established.
NR: Not recommended.
* indicates a medication possessing good analgesic properties.

Continued on next page

Table 4.5 (cont.)

NSAIDs and Acetaminophen: Dosage and Prescribing Information

Generic name	Brand name(s)	Adult dosage	Max adult dosage	Max child dosage	PRC	Content/form
Salicylates						
Aspirin	(generic)	325-500 mg q 4-6 h	4,000 mg	40-100 mg/ kg/day in divided doses q 4-6 h prn	D	**Capsules:** 325, 500 mg **Cream; gum:** 227.5 mg **Suppositories:** 60, 120, 125, 130, 195, 200, 300, 325, 600, 650 mg, 1.2 g **Tablets:** 65, 81, 325, 500, 690, 975 mg **Tablets, chewable:** 81 mg **Tablets, time-release:** 650 mg
Choline and magnesium trisalicylate	Trilisate	500, 750, 1,000 mg tid	4,000 mg	**Weight ≤ 37 kg:** 50 mg/kg/day in 2 doses **Weight > 37 kg:** 2,250 mg/day in 2 doses	C	**Liquid:** 500 mg/5 mL **Tablets:** 500, 750, 1,000 mg
Diflunisal*	Dolobid	1 g initially, then 250, 500 mg q 8-12 h	1,500 mg	NE	C	**Tablets:** 250, 500 mg
Salsalate	Disalcid	500, 750 mg tid	3,000 mg	NE	C	**Capsules/tablets:** 500, 750 mg

PRC: Pregnancy risk category.
NE: Not established.
* indicates a medication possessing good analgesic properties.

to the gastrointestinal and renal side effects of NSAIDs. Start at lower dosages and avoid longer-acting agents that may accumulate.

Patient Monitoring: Aspects to Watch

- Short-term NSAID therapy: no laboratory monitoring generally necessary, but patient should notify dentist of symptoms of dyspepsia or fluid retention
- Long-term NSAID therapy: hematologic parameters, renal and hepatic function require periodic evaluation

Adverse Effects and Precautions

These drugs have numerous drug interactions (Table 4.6) and side effects (Table 4.7). For short-term use, gastrointestinal side effects such as dyspepsia, diarrhea and abdominal pain are the most common. Longer-term use can lead to gastrointestinal ulceration, bleeding or perforation. As a precaution, NSAIDs should be taken with meals and/or a full glass of water. Various drugs have been developed to counteract some of the gastrointestinal side effects of NSAIDs, and NSAIDs that have fewer gastrointestinal side effects are listed later in this section. NSAIDs are contraindicated in patients who have active peptic ulcer disease and should be prescribed with extreme caution to patients who have a history of peptic ulcer disease or a history of long-term corticosteroid use.

Renal complications can also occur as idiosyncratic reactions with short-term use or as renal failure with long-term use. These medications are metabolized by the liver and should be prescribed cautiously to people who have liver disease.

It is important to note that NSAIDs can increase bleeding through their reversible inhibition of platelet aggregation by their effect on a platelet aggregating agent, thromboxane A_2. This is the case with all NSAIDs except aspirin, which irreversibly inhibits platelet aggregation for the entire life of the platelet (11 days). If major oral surgery is planned,

- discontinue aspirin use for 4-5 days before surgery;
- for NSAIDs that require dosing of 4-6 times per day, stop NSAID use 1-2 days before surgery;
- for NSAIDs that require bid-tid dosing, stop NSAID use 2-3 days before surgery;
- for q day NSAIDs, stop NSAID use 3-4 days before surgery to avoid excessive bleeding.

Drug interactions are presented in Table 4.6. An important contraindication involves the use of aspirin in children, which can lead to Reye's syndrome. Hypersensitivity reactions, such as anaphylactoid reactions, also have occurred with NSAIDs, especially aspirin. Patients with a history of bronchospastic disease and/or nasal polyps have an increased risk of having hypersensitivity reactions. If a patient's medical history indicates that this type of reaction could be encountered, it is prudent not to prescribe another NSAID. Some patients may exhibit minor hypersensitivity reactions to one NSAID but not another. If a patient tolerates a specific NSAID without difficulty, it seems reasonable to allow him or her to continue using that agent. Medical consultation may be appropriate. A history of anaphylactoid/anaphylactic reaction to any NSAID precludes use of another NSAID.

Some NSAIDs have potentially fewer gastrointestinal complications. The following drugs may cause less gastrointestinal irritation in a patient who, for instance, has a history of peptic ulcer disease and no longer requires ulcer medication but for whom an NSAID is indicated:

- choline magnesium trisalicylate;
- diflunisal;
- Iodine;
- nabumetone;
- salsalate;
- sulindac.

Pharmacology

Although NSAIDs influence a number of systems, a primary effect is the inhibition of the breakdown of arachidonic acid by the enzyme cyclooxygenase. One of the by-products of this breakdown is prostaglandins, which are potent vasodilators and mediators of the inflammatory response. These compounds also decrease the threshold needed for nerves conducting pain information to signal the CNS. By decreasing the production of prostaglandins, NSAIDs depress the inflammatory response. This decrease in prostaglandin concentration also raises the threshold for pain-conducting nerves to discharge, thus providing an analgesic effect. NSAIDs also reduce fever, in part by decreasing the concentration of prostaglandins in the hypothalamus, a brain center regulating body temperature.

Two forms of cyclooxygenase have now been identified and are designated COX I and COX II. COX I is a constitutive form of the enzyme producing "protective" prostaglandins that, for example, serve to promote renal blood flow and decrease gastric acid secretion. COX II is an inducible form of the enzyme whose concentration significantly increases during inflammation. Specific agents are now being developed that are more specific to the COX II isoform. Theoretically, this should lead to safer NSAIDs, which have less

Table 4.6

NSAIDs: Possible Interactions With Other Drugs

Drug taken by patient	Interaction with NSAIDs	Dentist's action
Alcohol	Increased risk of ulceration	Advise patient to avoid if possible
Anticoagulants (oral)	Increased risk of bleeding	Advise patient that concurrent use is contraindicated
Antihypertensives	Effect decreased by NSAIDs	Monitor blood pressure
Aspirin	Increased risk of ulceration and bleeding	Advise patient that concurrent use is contraindicated
NSAIDs other than aspirin	Increased risk of ulceration and bleeding	Avoid this combination
Colchicine	Increased risk of bleeding	Advise patient that concurrent use is contraindicated
Corticosteroids	Increased risk of ulceration	Avoid combination if possible
Cyclosporine	Can cause nephrotoxicity	Avoid combination if possible
Digitalis	Increased digitalis levels	Avoid combination if possible
Diuretics (especially triamterene)	Effect decreased by NSAIDs	Monitor blood pressure/excessive fluid retention
Heparin	Increased risk of bleeding	Advise patient that concurrent use is contraindicated
Hypoglycemics (oral)	Effect increased by NSAIDs	Advise patient to monitor blood glucose carefully
Lithium	Concentration increased by NSAIDs	Contraindicated unless approved by physician, so avoid concurrent use
Methotrexate (when plasma level is increased)	Increased risk of bleeding	Advise patient that concurrent use is contraindicated
Potassium supplements	Increased risk of ulceration	Avoid combination if possible
Valproic acid	Increased risk of ulceration and bleeding	Avoid combination if possible

deleterious effects on renal, gastric and other systems. Celecoxib (Celebrex) and rofecoxib (Vioxx) are the first of the new generation of COX II inhibitors to receive FDA approval. It should be noted that celecoxib has a sulfonamide structure and should not be prescribed to patients with a history of sulfonamide ("sulfa") allergy.

It is important to realize that some older NSAIDs (such as etodolac and nabumetone), although not specifically designed as COX II inhibitors, have favorable COX I/COX II activity ratios with better side-effect profiles than those of other older NSAIDs.

It is expected that short-term use of NSAIDs, such as for three or four days of acute pain management after dental surgery, is unlikely to lead to serious sequelae in most healthy patients. It should be noted that idiosyncratic reactions (primarily manifesting as renal complications) can occur, and gastric mucosal irritation has been reported even with very brief use of NSAIDs.

Cyclooxygenase metabolism of arachidonic acid also produces thromboxane A_2, which increases platelet aggregability. NSAIDs

Table 4.7
NSAIDs: Adverse Effects, Precautions and Contraindications

Body system	Adverse effects	Precautions/contraindications
General	Drowsiness, angioedema, weight loss (long-term use), fever	None of significance to dentistry
CV	May cause fluid retention, tachycardia; may exacerbate hypertension	Severe cardiac disease Patients taking diuretics Phenylbutazone is contraindicated in patients with severe cardiac disease
CNS	Dizziness, headache, sedation, tinnitus, photophobia, decreased hearing	May have additive effects with other CNS depressants; may indicate NSAID overdose
GI	Abdominal pain, diarrhea, dyspepsia, peptic ulcer, ulcerated bowel, diarrhea, nausea, vomiting, constipation	History of GI disease History of chronic alcohol abuse History of tobacco use Patients with diabetes Contraindicated in patients with active peptic ulcer disease Contraindicated in patients with inflammatory bowel disease
GU	Impaired renal function, renal disease, dysuria, polyuria, cystitis	Patient taking diuretics Contraindicated in severe renal disease
Hema	Increased bleeding time, blood dyscrasia (rare), petechia, anemia	*Stop NSAID use for at least 3-4 half-lives and aspirin for 4-5 days before procedures that may involve significant bleeding if possible* Contraindicated in patients receiving anticoagulation therapy

Italics indicate information of major clinical significance.

Continued on next page

Table 4.7 (cont.)
NSAIDs: Adverse Effects, Precautions and Contraindications

Body system	Adverse effects	Precautions/contraindications
HB	Elevated enzyme activity	Severe hepatic disease Phenylbutazone is contraindicated in patients with severe hepatic disease Children with certain viral infections may develop Reye's syndrome precipitated by use of aspirin
Integ	Dermatitis, Stevens-Johnson syndrome, stomatitis, petechia, alopecia	*Unusual hypersensitivity reactions*
Musc	*Muscle weakness*	None of significance to dentistry
Oral	Stomatitis, glossitis, gingival ulceration	None of significance to dentistry
Resp	Anaphylaxis, angioedema, bronchospasm	Relatively contraindicated in patients with history of bronchospasm, nasal polyps and asthma Contraindicated in patients with allergic reaction to aspirin or other NSAIDs

Italics indicate information of major clinical significance.

decrease the production of thromboxane A_2; this decreases platelet aggregation and causes an increased tendency toward bleeding. NSAID inactivation of cyclooxygenase, and thus increased bleeding tendency, is reversible for all drugs except aspirin, which binds cyclooxygenase irreversibly.

Patient Advice

- Patients should be cautioned regarding the gastrointestinal side effects of these medications.
- These medications preferably should be taken with or after meals with a full glass of water to prevent lodging of the capsule or tablet in the esophagus.
- The patient should notify the dentist of any side effects that occur after starting use of the medication.

Suggested Readings

Brandt KD. The mechanism of action of non-steroidal antiinflammatory drugs. J Rheumatol 1991;27(Supplement): 120-1.

Dionne RA, Gordon SM. Nonsteroidal anti-inflammatory drugs for acute pain control. Dent Clin North Am 1994;38(4):645-67.

Joris J. Efficacy of nonsteroidal antiinflammatory drugs in post-operative pain. Acta Anaesthesiol Belg 1996; 47(3):115-23.

Lawton GM, Chapman PJ. Diflunisal—a long acting non-steroidal anti-inflammatory drug. A review of its pharmacology and effectiveness in management of dental pain. Aust Dent J 1993;38(4):265-71.

Neidle EA, Yagiela JA, eds. Pharmacology and therapeutics for dentistry. St. Louis: Mosby; 1989.

The United States Pharmacopeial Convention, Inc. USP Dispensing Information. Drug information for the health care professional. Vol. I. 17th ed. Rockville, Md.: The United States Pharmacopeial Convention, Inc.; 1997.

Woolf CJ, Chong MS. Preemptive analgesia—treating postoperative pain by preventing the establishment of central sensitization. Anesth Analg 1993;77(2)362-79.

Chapter 5

Hemostatics, Astringents and Gingival Retraction Cords

Kenneth H. Burrell, D.D.S., S.M.; Michael Glick, D.M.D.

Hemostatics

An understanding of hemostasis, identification of patients with excessive bleeding tendencies, and interventions to stop abnormal bleeding is essential to the provision of safe and appropriate dental care.

Hemostasis can be divided arbitrarily into four phases: a vascular phase and a platelet phase, also referred to as "primary hemostasis"; and a coagulation phase and a fibrinolytic phase, also referred to as "secondary hemostasis."

Defects in any phase of normal hemostasis have characteristic signs and symptoms. Most commonly, dental health care providers will be faced with patients who have defects of the platelet and coagulation phases.

People with quantitative or qualitative platelet disorders usually have superficial signs such as petechiae and ecchymosis on the mucosa and skin. Furthermore, patients may report spontaneous gingival bleeding, epistaxis, prolonged postextraction bleeding or prolonged bleeding after minor trauma. Spontaneous clinical hemorrhage is usually present when the platelet count drops below 15,000-20,000/mm^3. (For normal laboratory values, see Appendix H.)

The clinical value of a bleeding time for dental procedures has been challenged. However, significant prolonged bleeding times beyond 15-20 min may suggest significant hemorrhage after dental surgery.

Causes of defects of primary hemostasis include congenital as well as acquired disorders. The most common inherited bleeding disorder in the United States is von Willebrand's disease. This disorder is characterized by various degrees of deficiency of the von Willebrand factor, which is needed primarily for platelet adhesion. In severe cases of von Willebrand's disease, spontaneous bleeding may occur. However, mild cases may be associated with prolonged bleeding only after major trauma. Common acquired dysfunctions of primary hemostasis include idiopathic thrombocytopenia purpura, liver disease and drug-induced platelet disorders. Also, both acute and chronic leukemia are associated with thrombocytopenia. Some medications are used intentionally to decrease platelet functions, such as aspirin-containing medications and ticlopidine, in patients with disorders such as coronary artery disease.

Disorders of secondary hemostasis include hemophilia, vitamin K deficiency and liver disease. Hemophilia is usually classified according to the specific factor deficiency, such as hemophilia A for factor VIII deficiency and hemophilia B for factor IX deficiency. Patients with hemophilia lack the ability to form fibrin and have bleeding episodes particularly within stress-bearing joints (deep-seated bleeding). This eventually can cause destruction of these joints.

General dentistry can be performed in patients with > 50% factor activity, but 100% activity is recommended for surgical procedures. In a 60-kg patient with hemophilia A, a 100% plasma level equals 6,000 units of factor VIII.

Vitamin K deficiency causes decreased activation and production of factors II, VII, IX and X, resulting in a defective coagulation cascade and consequent decreased fibrin production. Virtually all coagulation factors are produced in the liver, and vitamin K is stored in the liver. Thus, liver disease may result in increased bleeding tendencies. Medications such as warfarin, an anticoagulant that impairs the action of vitamin K, is used to prevent thrombosis in patients with such disorders as atrial fibrillation, deep venous thrombosis, ischemic cardiovascular disease and stroke.

A thorough medical history, examination and laboratory evaluation will identify most patients who have increased bleeding tendencies. Included in the patient assessment should be questions addressing whether the patient has relatives with bleeding problems, has experienced prolonged bleeding after trauma, or takes medications or has diseases associated with increased bleeding tendencies. Examination should focus on signs of bruising, jaundice, hyperplastic gingival tissue, spontaneous gingival bleeding and hemarthrosis. Screening tests for impaired hemostasis include platelet count and bleeding time for primary hemostasis, as well as prothrombin time, international normalization ratio, activated partial thromboplastin time and thrombin time for secondary hemostasis. (See Appendix H for normal values.)

Dental treatment of patients with impaired hemostasis includes the use of both local and systemic measures. The use of the appropriate technique or agent depends on the patient's underlying condition and specific hemostatic impairment.

Accepted Indications

If blood flow is profuse, mechanical aids such as a compress, hemostatic forceps, a modeling compound splint or hemostatic ligatures can be used. Mechanical obliteration with cryosurgery, electrocauterization and laser also can be used. Although these thermal methods are effective, they may be associated with impaired healing. A third kind of mechanically aided hemostasis is the use of chemical glues, such as n-butyl cyanoacrylate and bone wax. These compounds have a mechanical effect without directly affecting the coagulation process.

For slow blood flow and oozing, a combination of hemostatics can be used. The three kinds of hemostatics to be noted here are absorbable hemostatic agents, agents that modify blood coagulation and vasoconstrictors. Vasoconstrictors act by constricting or closing blood vessels. They are used to a limited extent to control capillary bleeding. Vasoconstrictors are described in detail in Chapter 1 (Tables 1.3, 1.6). See Table 5.1 for a comparison of various hemostatics useful in dentistry.

Absorbable Gelatin Sponge
The absorbable gelatin sponge consists of a tough, porous matrix prepared from purified pork skin gelatin, granules and water that is indicated as a hemostatic device for control of capillary, venous or arteriolar bleeding when pressure, ligature or other conventional procedures are either ineffective or impractical. It can be used in extraction sites and is absorbed in 4-6 w.

Oxidized Cellulose
Oxidized cellulose is a chemically modified form of surgical gauze or cotton that is used to control moderate bleeding by forming an artificial clot when suturing or ligation is impractical and ineffective. Because it is friable, oxidized cellulose is difficult to place and retain in extraction sockets, but can be used as a sutured implant or temporary pack-

Table 5.1

Hemostatics: Dosage and Prescribing Information

Generic name	Brand name(s)	PRC	Dosage	Form
Local agents that modify coagulation				
Absorbable gelatin sponge	Gelfoam	U	Absorbable gelatin sponge may be cut; may be applied to bleeding surfaces to cover area	**Dental packing blocks:** $20 \times 20 \times 7$ mm **Powder:** 1 g
Oxidized cellulose	Oxycel	U	Hemostatic effect is greater when material is applied dry as opposed to moistened with water or saline	**Pad:** 3×3 in **Pledget:** $2 \times 1 \times 1$ in **Strip:** 18×2, $5 \times \frac{1}{2}$, $36 \times \frac{1}{2}$ in
Oxidized regenerated cellulose	Surgicel Absorbable Hemostat *, Surgicel Nu-Knit Absorbable Hemostat	U	Can be laid over extraction socket for control of bleeding; minimal amounts of the material should be placed on bleeding site; may be held firmly against tissue	**Surgicel sheets:** 2×14, 4×8, 2×3, $\frac{1}{2} \times 2$ in **Surgicel Nu-Knit sheets:** 1×1, 3×4, 6×9 in
Microfibrillar collagen hemostat	Avitene, Collacote *, Collaplug, Collatape *, Instat MCH	U	Is applied topically and adheres firmly to bleeding surfaces	**Avitene Flour:** $\frac{1}{2}$-, 1-, 5-g syringes **Avitene Sheets:** 35×35, 70×35, 70×70 mm **Collacote, Collaplug, Collatape:** 1×3, $\frac{3}{4} \times 1\frac{1}{2}$, $\frac{3}{8} \times \frac{3}{4}$ in **Instat MCH:** Coherent fibers packaged in 0.5- and 1.0-g containers
Collagen hemostat	Instat	U	Should be applied directly to bleeding surface with pressure; is more effective when applied dry, or may be moistened with sterile saline or thrombin solution; may be left in place as necessary; is absorbed 8-10 w after placement	**Pads:** 1×2, 3×4 in

Systemic agents that modify blood coagulation

		PRC		
Aminocaproic acid	Amicar	C	**Adult—IV:** 16-20 mL in 250 mL of diluent IV first h, followed by 4 mL/h in 50 mL diluent for up to 8 h or until hemostasis has been achieved; MDD 30 g **Adult—oral, syrup:** 4 teaspoons first h followed by 1 teaspoon/h; MDD 30 g **Adult—oral, tablets:** 10 tablets first h followed by 2 tablets/h; MDD 30 g **Child—oral:** 100 mg/kg for first h, followed by 33.3 mg/kg for 24 h or until appropriate response is achieved; MDD 18 g	**Solution:** 250 mg/mL in 20-, 96-mL vials **Syrup:** 250 mg/mL. **Tablets:** 500 mg
Desmopressin acetate	DDAVP	B	**Adult and child—IV:** 0.3 µg/kg over 20 min	**Solution:** 4 µg/mL, 15 µg/mL in cartons of 10 1-mL single-dose ampules or 10-mL multiple-dose vials
Tranexamic acid	Cyklokapron	B	**Adult and child:** immediately before surgery, 10 mg/kg IV; after surgery, 25 mg/kg orally tid or qid for 2-8 days	**Solution:** 100 mg/mL in 10-mL vials **Tablets:** 500 mg
Vitamin K₁ or phytonadione	AquaMephyton, Konakion, Mephyton	C	**Anticoagulant-induced prothrombin deficiency (except heparin)—oral:** 2.5-10 mg or up to 25 mg (rarely 50 mg) **Anticoagulant-induced prothrombin deficiency (except heparin)—IM, aqueous dispersion:** 5-10 mg initially, up to 20 mg **Anticoagulant-induced prothrombin deficiency (except heparin)—SC or IM, aqueous colloidal solution:** 2.5-10 mg or up to 25 mg (rarely 50 mg) *(continued on next page)*	**Aqueous colloidal solution (AquaMephyton):** 2, 10 mg/mL **Aqueous dispersion (Konakion):** 2, 10 mg/mL **Tablets (Mephyton):** 5 mg

Continued on next page

PRC: Pregnancy risk category.
★ indicates a product bearing the ADA Seal of Acceptance.
MDD: Maximum daily dose.
U: Unavailable.

Table 5.1 (cont.)

Hemostatics: Dosage and Prescribing Information

Generic name	Brand name(s)	Dosage	PRC	Form
Systemic agents that modify blood coagulation (cont.)				
Vitamin K$_1$ or phytonadione (cont.)		**Hypoprothrombinemia owing to other causes and factors limiting absorption or synthesis—SC or IM, aqueous colloidal solution:** 2.5-25 mg or more (rarely up to 50 mg) **Hypoprothrombinemia owing to other causes and factors limiting absorption or synthesis—IM, aqueous dispersion:** 2-20 mg **Hypoprothrombinemia owing to other causes and factors limiting absorption or synthesis—oral:** 0.5-25 mg or more (rarely up to 50 mg)		
Vitamin K$_3$ or menadione	generic	2-10 mg/day, 4-7 days before surgery	U	**Powder**
Vitamin K$_4$ or menadiol sodium diphosphate	Synkayvite	**Injection:** 5-10 mg q day, 4-7 days **Oral:** 5 mg q day, 4-7 days	U	**Injection:** 5, 10, 37.5 mg/mL **Tablets:** 5 mg
Thrombin (topical agent)				
Thrombin	Thrombin-JMI, Thrombinar, Thrombogen, Thrombostat	For profuse bleeding—solution: 1,000-2,000 units/mL For bleeding from skin or mucosa—solution: 100 units/mL	C	**Powder:** 1,000, 5,000, 10,000, 20,000 units; 50,000 units (Thrombinar only) **Powder with isotonic saline diluent:** 5,000-, 10,000- and 20,000-unit containers with 5-, 10-, and 20-mL of isotonic saline **Thrombostat:** Also contains 0.02 mg/mL phemerol as a preservative

PRC: Pregnancy risk category.
U: Unavailable.

ing. The cotton or gauze can be removed before dissolution is complete by irrigation with saline or a mildly alkaline solution.

Absorption of oxidized cellulose ordinarily occurs between the second and seventh day after implantation of material, but complete absorption of large amounts of blood-soaked material may take six weeks or longer.

Oxidized Regenerated Cellulose

Oxidized regenerated cellulose is prepared from alpha-cellulose by reaction with alkali to form viscose, which is then spun into filaments and oxidized. This process results in greater chemical purity and uniformity of physical structure than oxidized cellulose. It is a sterile, absorbable, knitted fabric that is strong enough to be sutured or cut. It has less tendency to stick to instruments and gloves and is less friable than oxidized cellulose.

Oxidized regenerated cellulose is used to control capillary, venous and small arterial hemorrhage when ligature, pressure, or other conventional methods of control are impractical or ineffective. The product can be used as a surface dressing because it does not retard epithelialization. It is bactericidal against numerous gram-negative and gram-positive microorganisms, both aerobic and anaerobic.

It can be placed over extraction sites.

Microfibrillar Collagen Hemostat

Microfibrillar collagen hemostat is a hemostatically active agent prepared from bovine deep flexor tendon (Achilles tendon) as a water-soluble, partial-acid salt of natural collagen. It reduces bleeding from surgical sites such as those involving cancellous bone and gingival graft donor sites. It should not be left in infected or contaminated spaces because it may prolong or promote infection and delay healing.

Collagen Hemostat

Collagen hemostat is absorbable and composed of purified and lyophilized bovine dermal collagen. Used as an adjunct to hemostasis, collagen absorbable hemostat can be sutured into place. It reduces bleeding when ligation

and other conventional methods are ineffective or impractical. Excess material should be removed before the wound is closed.

Aminocaproic Acid

Aminocaproic acid, or ε-aminocaproic acid, is used in patients with excessive bleeding due to underlying conditions such as systemic hyperfibrinolysis and coagulopathies stemming from promyelocytic leukemia. This medication is seldom used for elective oral surgery procedures, but rather during emergency situations in combination with transfusion of fresh frozen blood and fibrinogen.

Desmopressin Acetate

Desmopressin acetate is used primarily to reduce spontaneous bleeding in patients with von Willebrand's disease and in patients with moderate-to-mild hemophilia A (factor VIII levels above 5%). It also is used prophylactically during procedures to reduce the incidence of bleeding, as well as after procedures to achieve better hemostasis in these patient populations.

Tranexamic Acid

Tranexamic acid is used primarily to reduce the amount of factor replacement necessary after dental extractions in hemophiliac patients. It is indicated for only 2-8 days during and after the dental procedure. It also is used for other patient populations with impaired secondary hemostasis, including patients who are receiving anticoagulation therapy.

Vitamin K

Vitamin K therapy is required when hypoprothrombinemia results from inadequately available vitamins K_1 and K_2. This occurs when there is decreased synthesis by intestinal bacteria, inadequate absorption from the intestinal tract or increased requirement by the liver for normal synthesis of prothrombin.

Vitamin K, in its various forms, is an essential component of blood coagulation. Vitamins K_1, K_2 or menadione (vitamin K_3) are required for the production of the functional forms of six coagulation proteins: prothrombin, factors VII, IX and X and proteins C and S.

Phytonadione (vitamin K₁)

Phytonadione (vitamin K$_1$)

Phytonadione—known as vitamin K$_1$—is used for

- anticoagulant–induced prothrombin deficiency;
- prophylaxis and therapy of hemorrhagic disease of the newborn;
- hypoprothrombinemia resulting from oral antibacterial therapy;
- hypoprothrombinemia secondary to factors limiting absorption or synthesis of vitamin K such as obstructive jaundice, biliary fistula, sprue, ulcerative colitis, celiac disease, intestinal resection, cystic fibrosis of the pancreas and regional enteritis;
- other drug-induced hypoprothrombinemia such as that which results from salicylate use.

Menadione (vitamin K$_3$)

Menadione is a synthetic form of vitamin K, which is sometimes referred to as vitamin K$_3$.

Menadiol sodium diphosphate (vitamin K$_4$)

Menadiol sodium diphosphate is effective as a hemostatic agent only when bleeding results from prothrombin deficiency.

Thrombin

Thrombin is useful as a topical local hemostatic agent when blood is oozing from accessible capillaries or venules. In certain kinds of hemorrhage, it can be used to wet pledgets of absorbable gelatin sponge and placed on bleeding tissue or in extraction sockets with or without sutures. It is particularly useful whenever blood is flowing from accessible capillaries and small venules.

General Dosing Information

Table 5.1 lists the general dosing information for specific hemostatics.

Dosage Adjustments

The actual dose for each patient must be individualized according to factors such as his or her size, age and physical status. Reduced doses of vitamin K may be indicated for patients who are taking anticoagulants as opposed to those who have malabsorption problems. The other hemostatic agents should be used as needed.

Special Dental Considerations

Cross-Sensitivity

Patients may experience delayed healing using the gelatin, cellulose and collagen hemostatics. This is more often observed when the surgical site is infected.

Patient Monitoring: Aspects to Watch

Patients receiving vitamin K, especially parenterally, may experience allergic reactions such as rash, urticaria and anaphylaxis.

Adverse Effects and Precautions

The incidence of adverse reactions to hemostatic agents is relatively low. Many reactions are temporary. Idiosyncratic and allergic reactions account for a small minority of adverse responses. See Table 5.2.

Pharmacology

Absorbable Gelatin Sponge

The absorbable gelatin sponge promotes the disruption of platelets and acts as a framework for fibrin, probably because of its physical effect rather than the result of its alteration of the blood clotting mechanism. It can be placed in dry form or may be moistened with sterile saline or thrombin solution and used in extraction sites.

Oxidized Cellulose

Oxidized cellulose is a chemically modified form of surgical gauze or cotton. Its hemostatic action depends on the formation of an artificial clot by cellulosic acid, which has a marked affinity for hemoglobin.

Oxidized Regenerated Cellulose

Oxidized regenerated cellulose probably serves as a hemostatic by providing a physi-

Table 5.2

Hemostatics: Adverse Effects, Precautions and Contraindications

Agent	Adverse effects	Precautions/contraindications
Absorbable hemostatic agents		
Oxidized cellulose	May lead to a foreign-body reaction	Extremely friable and difficult to place
		Should not be used at fracture sites because it interferes with bone regeneration
		Should not be used as a surface dressing except for the immediate control of hemorrhage, as cellulosic acid inhibits epithelialization
		Should not be used in combination with thrombin because the hemostatic action of either alone is greater than that of the combination
Oxidized regenerated cellulose	NS	Placement in extraction sites may delay healing; it should not be placed in fracture sites because it may interfere with callus formation and may cause cyst formation
		Encapsulation of fluid and foreign bodies possible
Collagen hemostat	Incidence of pain has been reported to increase when this material is placed in extraction sockets	Should not be used in mucous membrane closure because it may interfere with healing due to mechanical interposition
	Allergic reactions can occur in patients with known sensitivity to bovine material	Should not be left in infected or contaminated space because of possible delay in healing and increased likelihood of abscess formation
		Should not be used in patients with a known sensitivity to bovine material
		Should not be overpacked because collagen absorbable hemostat absorbs water and can expand to impinge on neighboring structures
		Should not be used in cases where point of hemorrhage is submerged, because collagen must be in direct contact with bleeding site to achieve desired effect
Microfibrillar collagen hemostat	May potentiate abscess formation, hematoma and wound dehiscence	Is not intended to treat systemic coagulation disorders
		Placement in extraction sites has been reported to increase pain
		Should not be left in infected or contaminated spaces because of possible adhesion formation, allergic reaction, foreign body reaction
		Interferes with wound margins
Absorbable gelatin sponge	May form a nidus for infection or abscess formation	Should not be overpacked in extraction sites or surgical defects because it may expand to impinge on neighboring structures

NS: None of significance to dentistry.

Continued on next page

Table 5.2 (cont.)

Hemostatics: Adverse Effects, Precautions and Contraindications

Agent	Adverse effects	Precautions/contraindications
Systemic agents that modify blood coagulation		
Aminocaproic acid	Headache, dizziness, convulsions, weakness, psychosis, dysrhythmias, orthostatic hypotension, thrombosis, renal failure, ejaculatory failure, tinnitis, nasal congestion, rash	Use with caution in patients with mild-to-moderate renal failure, hepatic disease, thombosis, cardiac disease or hypertension, as well as in lactating women *Contraindicated in patients with abnormal bleeding, postpartum bleeding, new burns, nephrogenic diabetes insipidus*
Desmopressin acetate	Headache, drowsiness, lethargy, flushing, increased blood pressure, nausea, heartburn, vulval pain	See note above
Tranexamic acid	Giddiness, nausea, vomiting, diarrhea, blurred vision; hypotension with IV dose	Dose should be reduced for patients with renal impairment *Contraindicated in patients with acquired defective color vision and subarachnoid hemorrhage*
Vitamin K_1 or phytonadione	Parenteral administration can cause transient "flushing sensations" and "peculiar sensations" of taste; also (rarely) dizziness, rapid and weak pulse, profuse sweating, brief hypotension, dyspnea and cyanosis; allergic sensitivity, including an anaphylactoid reaction, has been reported	Patient undergoing prothrombin reduction therapy should not receive vitamin K preparations except under a physician's supervision Determine if patient is taking anticoagulants, as the drug can decrease effect of anticoagulant Contraindicated in patients with known sensitivity to the drug
Vitamin K_3 or menadione	Adverse reactions are similar to those produced by phytonadione, but incidence is low	Requires normal flow of bile or administration of bile salts Patient undergoing prothrombin reduction therapy should not receive vitamin K preparations except under physician supervision
Vitamin K_4 or menadiol sodium diphosphate	See note above	Before administering drug, determine if patient is receiving anticoagulant therapy; a patient undergoing prothrombin reduction therapy should not receive vitamin K preparations except under physician supervision If patient is taking anticoagulants, this agent may decrease their effectiveness
Thrombin (topical)		
Thrombin	Allergic reactions can occur in patients with known sensitivity to bovine material	Thrombin must not be injected into blood vessels because it might cause serious or even fatal embolism from extensive intravascular thrombosis; instead, should be applied to surface of bleeding tissue as solution or powder

Italics indicate information of major clinical significance.

cal effect rather than altering the normal physiological clotting mechanism.

Microfibrillar Collagen Hemostat

This hemostatic agent is used topically to trigger the adhesiveness of platelets and stimulate the release phenomenon to produce aggregation of platelets leading to their disintegration and to release coagulation factors that, together with plasma factors, enable fibrin to form. The physical structure of microfibrillar collagen hemostat adds strength to the clot.

Collagen Hemostat

When collagen comes into contact with blood, platelets aggregate and release coagulation factors, which together with plasma factors, cause the formation of fibrin and a clot.

Aminocaproic Acid

Aminocaproic acid is an antifibrinolytic agent that slows or stops fibrinolysis by inhibiting the action of plasminogen. Consequently, it delays the breakdown of the hemostatic plug. This medication is administered both intravenously and orally in the form of tablets and syrup. Concurrent use of other hemostatic agents in patients with significant bleeding tendencies is recommended.

Desmopressin Acetate

Desamino-*D*-arginine vasopressin is a synthetic analogue of the natural pituitary hormone 1-8-D-arginine vasopressin. This medication increases plasma levels of von Willebrand factor-VIII complex and factor VIII levels. It is administered 30 min before the dental appointment. It facilitates outpatient care for patients with hemophilia, but should always be used in conjunction with other hemostatic agents.

Tranexamic Acid

Tranexamic acid is an antithrombolytic hemostatic agent that acts by decreasing conversion of plasminogen to plasmin. At much higher doses, it acts as a noncompetitive inhibitor of plasmin. It is indicated for pro-

phylaxis and treatment of patients with hemophilia, to prevent or reduce hemorrhage during and after tooth extraction. Unlabeled uses include topical use as a mouthwash, along with systemic therapy to reduce bleeding after oral surgery. It is contraindicated for use in patients receiving anticoagulant therapy. This medication is administered both intravenously and orally.

Vitamin K

Two forms of naturally occurring vitamin K have been isolated and prepared synthetically. The naturally occurring forms are designated vitamins K_1 and K_2. Vitamin K_1 is present in most vegetables, particularly in their green leaves. Vitamin K_2 is produced by intestinal bacteria. Menadione has vitamin K activity and is derived from a breakdown of the vitamin K molecule by intestinal bacteria and is sometimes referred to as vitamin K_3. Menadiol sodium diphosphate, or vitamin K_4, is a water-soluble derivative that is converted to menadione in the liver.

Hypoprothrombinemia may result from inadequately available vitamins K_1 and K_2 because of decreased synthesis by intestinal bacteria, inadequate absorption from the intestinal tract or increased requirement by the liver for normal synthesis of prothrombin. Liver dysfunction may also decrease the production of prothrombin, but the hypoprothrombinemia from hepatic cell injury may not respond to the administration of vitamin K as many coagulation proteins are produced in hepatocytes.

Insufficient vitamin K in ingested foods becomes significant only when the synthesis of the vitamin by intestinal bacteria is markedly reduced by the oral administration of antibacterial agents. Biliary obstructions or intestinal disorders may result in an inadequate rate of absorption of vitamin K.

Phytonadione (vitamin K_1)

Vitamin K_1 is required for the production of the functional forms of six coagulation proteins: prothrombin, factors VII, IX and X and proteins C and S.

Menadione (vitamin K_3)

Although it is readily absorbed from the intestine, menadione must be converted to vitamin K_2 by the liver. Therefore, it requires a normal flow of bile into the intestine or the concomitant administration of bile salts.

Menadiol sodium diphosphate (vitamin K_4)

Vitamin K_4, because of its water solubility, is absorbed from the intestinal tract even in the absence of bile salts.

Thrombin

Thrombin is a sterile protein substance that is an essential component of blood coagulation. It combines with fibrinogen to form fibrin.

Patient Advice

- Let the patient know that a hemostatic has been used, what kind of hemostatic it is and why it was used.
- Advise the patient to let you know if bleeding continues from the surgical site.

Astringents

Astringents cause contraction of tissues. They accomplish this by constricting small blood vessels, extracting water from tissue or precipitating protein.

Accepted Indications

Dentists can apply astringents to gingival tissues before taking impressions or placing Class V or root-surface restorations. They can be used alone or in combination with retraction cords. Aluminum and iron salts are the compounds used as astringents in dentistry.

Aluminum Chloride

Aluminum chloride causes contraction or shrinking of tissue, making it useful in retracting gingival tissue. It also reduces secretions and minor hemorrhage.

Aluminum Potassium Sulfate

Aluminum potassium sulfate, or alum, is not widely used even though it is relatively innocuous, because its tissue retraction and hemostatic properties are limited.

Aluminum Sulfate

Aluminum sulfate, as with other aluminum salts, serves as an effective astringent for gingival retraction and hemostatic action.

Ferric Sulfate

Ferric sulfate is an effective and safe astringent and hemostatic for use in gingival retraction. It also can be used in vital pulpotomies.

General Dosing Information

Table 5.3 lists the general dosing and administration information for specific astringents.

Adverse Effects

The incidence of adverse reactions to astringents is relatively low. Most reactions (presented in Table 5.4) are temporary. The adverse effects listed in Table 5.4 apply to all major types of astringents.

Pharmacology

The ability of any astringent to contract or shrink mucous membrane or skin tissue is related to its mode of action involving protein precipitation and water absorption.

Gingival Retraction Cords

Gingival retraction cords can be used alone or in combination with astringents or vasoconstrictors. They are usually made of cotton and are woven in various ways to suit the practitioner's preference. They are also available in a variety of diameters to accommodate the variation in gingival sulcus width and depth.

These cords can be impregnated with astringents or vasoconstrictors either by the manufacturer or at chairside. Aluminum chloride, aluminum sulfate and ferric sulfate

Table 5.3

Astringents: Dosage and Prescribing Information

Generic name	Brand name(s)	Adult dosage	Content/form
Aluminum chloride	Gingi-Aid, Hemodent ★, Hemodettes, Hemogin-L, Rastringent, Styptin, Ultradent	Apply product directly to tissues using a cotton pledget or apply to gingival retraction cords	**Gel:** 20% (Hemodettes) **Solution:** 20% (Hemodent, Styptin), 25% (Gingi-Aid, Rastringent, Ultradent) **Ointment:** 25% (Hemogin-L) **Retraction cords:** Average concentration of 0.915, 3.5 mg/in
Aluminum potassium sulfate	generic	Any concentration, including 100% powder, can be used	**Powder:** 100% Various concentrations, all available and prepared by chemical supply houses
Aluminum sulfate	Gel-Cord	Apply product directly to tissues using a cotton pledget or apply to gingival retraction cords	**Gel:** In unit-dose cartridge **Impregnated retraction cord:** Average concentration of 0.48, 0.85, 1.45 mg/in **Topical solution:** 25%
Ferric sulfate	Astringedent ★, Hemodent-FS, Stasis, ViscoStat	Apply product directly to tissues using a cotton pledget or apply to gingival retraction cords	**Solution:** 13.3% (Astringedent), 15.5 (Hemodent-FS), 20% (ViscoStat—for use in infuser kit), 21% (Stasis)

★ *indicates a product bearing the ADA Seal of Acceptance.*

are used as the astringents, while racemic epinephrine is used as the vasoconstrictor.

Although epinephrine cord is used by a majority of practitioners rather than an astringent cord for gingival retraction and hemostasis, epinephrine cord is contraindicated in patients with a history of cardiovascular diseases, diabetes and hyperthyroidism and in those taking monoamine oxidase inhibitors, rauwolfias and ganglionic blocking agents.

Some practitioners and educators believe that epinephrine-containing retraction cord and solutions should not be used in dentistry. However, plasma epinephrine concentration increased significantly only after 60 min in a study of healthy subjects without a history of high blood pressure. In spite of the elevated plasma epinephrine levels, the subjects' heart rates, mean arterial pressures and pulse pres-

sure products were not significantly different when the same subjects were exposed to a potassium aluminum sulfate (alum) impregnated cord. The gingival tissues of the subjects were intact, however. Therefore, the patient's medical history, oral health, type of procedure to be done, amount and length of retraction, and exposure of the vascular bed should be considered before deciding to use epinephrine-containing retraction cords. Table 5.5 provides gingival retraction cord information; Table 5.6 shows the adverse effects, precautions and contraindications of a variety of commercially available retraction cords.

Accepted Indications

Gingival retraction cord is used for all kinds of gingival retraction before taking impressions or placing restorations.

Table 5.4

Astringents: Adverse Effects

Agent	Adverse effects
Aluminum chloride	Concentrated solutions of aluminum chloride are acidic and may have an irritating and even caustic effect on tissues
Aluminum potassium sulfate	May have an irritating effect
Aluminum sulfate	May have an irritating and even caustic effect
Ferric sulfate	Compound may cause tissue irritation to a greater degree than aluminum compounds

Table 5.5

Gingival Retraction Cords: Usage Information*

Generic name	Brand name(s)	Content/form
Retraction cord, plain	Gingi-Plain, Gingi-Plain Z-Twist, Hemodent, Retrax, Sil-Trax Plain, Ultrapak	**Gingi-Plain Firm Cord:** #1 (thin); #2 (medium); #3 (thick) **Gingi-Plain Z-Twist Braided Cord:** #00 (very thin); #1 (thin); #2 (medium); #3 (thick) **Hemodent:** #9 (medium thin); #3 (medium heavy) **Retrax Twisted Cord:** #7 (thin); #8 (small); #9 (medium); #10 (large) **Sil-Trax Plain Braided Cord:** #7 (thin); #8 (small); #9 (medium); #10 (large) **Ultrapak:** Ultrapak #000 (ultra thin); #00 (very thin); #0 (thin); #1 (medium); #2 (thick); #3 (ultra thick)
Retraction cord with aluminum chloride	Hemodent ★, Retreat	**Hemodent:** #9 (medium thin); #3 (medium heavy), 0.915 mg/in **Retreat:** #1 (thin); #2 (medium); #3 (thick)

★ indicates a product bearing the ADA Seal of Acceptance.
* A number of retraction cords are available with racemic epinephrine in concentrations ranging from 0.3-1.45 mg/in and varying concentrations of zinc phenylsulfonate.

Continued on next page

Table 5.5 (cont.)

Gingival Retraction Cords: Usage Information*

Generic name	Brand name(s)	Content/form
Retraction cord with aluminum sulfate	Gingi-Aid Z-Twist, Pascord, R-Cord, Sil-Trax AS	**Gingi-Aid Z-Twist Braided Cord:** #00 (very thin); #1 (thin); #2 (medium); #3 (thick); 0.5 mg/in **Pascord Twisted Cord:** #7 (thin), 0.48 mg/in; #8 (small), 0.48 mg/in; #9 (medium), 0.85 mg/in; #10 (large), 1.45 mg/in **R-Cord:** Braided cord with or without epinephrine **Sil-Trax AS Braided Cord:** #7 (thin), 0.48 mg/in; #8 (small), 0.48 mg/in; #9 (medium), 0.85 mg/in; #10 (large), 1.45 mg/in
Retraction cord with potassium aluminum sulfate	GingiBraid, GingiKnit, Gingi-Tract, Sulpak, Sultan Ultra, UniBraid	**GingiBraid:** 0 (fine); 1 (small); 2 (medium); 3 (large); also available plain **GingiKnit:** 000 (very fine); 00 (fine); 0 (small); 1 (medium); 2 (large); 3 (extra large) **Gingi-Tract:** Thin, medium, thick **Sulpak:** Braided cord in thin, medium, large **Sultan:** Braided cord in thin, medium, large; available with either aluminum potassium sulfate or racemic epinephrine **UniBraid:** 0 (fine); 1 (small); 2 (medium); 3 (large); also available plain
Retraction cord with epinephrine	Gingi-Pak	#1 (thin); #2 (medium); #3 (thick); 0.5 mg/in
Retraction cord with racemic epinephrine	R-Cord, Racord, Sil-Trax EPI, Sultan	**Racord Twisted Cord:** #7 (thin), 0.50 mg/in.; #8 (small), 0.50 mg/in.; #9 (medium), 0.85 mg/in.; #10 (large), 1.15 mg/in **Sil-Trax EPI Braided Cord:** #7 (thin), 0.50 mg/in; #8 (small), 0.50 mg/in; #9 (medium), 0.85 mg/in; #10 (large), 1.15 mg/in **Sultan:** 0.108-0.48 mg/in
Retraction cord with zinc chloride	Sultan	0.06-0.218 mg/in

A number of retraction cords are available with racemic epinephrine in concentrations ranging from 0.3-1.45 mg/in and varying concentrations of zinc phenylsulfonate.

Table 5.6

Gingival Retraction Cords: Adverse Effects, Precautions and Contraindications

Type of cord	Adverse effects	Precautions/contraindications
Retraction cord, plain	NS	NS
Retraction cord with aluminum chloride	May cause irritation or tissue destruction	Contraindicated in those with a history of allergy
Retraction cord with aluminum sulfate	See note above	NS
Retraction cord with potassium aluminum sulfate	See note above	NS
Retraction cord with epinephrine	See note above	Patient's medical history and oral health, type of procedure to be done, amount and length of retraction, and exposure of the vascular bed should be considered before epinephrine-containing retraction cords are used Contraindicated in patients with a history of cardiovascular diseases, diabetes, hyperthyroidism, hypertension or arteriosclerosis and in patients taking tricyclic antidepressants, monoamine oxidase inhibitors, rauwolfias, or ganglionic blocking agents
Retraction cord with racemic epinephrine	See note above	See note above

NS: None of significance to dentistry.

General Dosing Information

Dosage Adjustments

The actual maximum dose for each patient must be individualized depending on factors such as oral health and sensitivity.

Adverse Effects and Precautions

The incidence of adverse reactions to gingival retraction cords is relatively low. Most reactions are temporary, but gingival tissue destruction may permanently alter gingival architecture, especially after vigorous cord placement.

Pharmacology

Gingival retraction cords work mechanically to widen the gingival sulcus. With the addition of astringents or vasoconstrictors, the gingival tissue is retracted further. The astringents act by constricting blood vessels, extracting water from tissue or precipitating proteins.

Suggested Readings

American Medical Association. AMA drug evaluations annual 1992. Chicago: American Medical Association; 1992.

Colman RW, Hirsch J, Marder VJ, Salzman EW, eds. Hemostatics and thrombosis: basic principles and clinical practice. 3rd ed. Philadelphia: Lippincott; 1994.

Garfunkel AA, Galili D, Findler M, Lubliner J. Bleeding tendency: a practical approach to dentistry. Compend Contin Educ Dent 1999;20:836-52.

Rossman JA, Rees TD. The use of hemostatic agents in dentistry. Postgrad Dent 1996;3:3-12.

Vitamin K. In: Kastrup EK, Olin BR, Connell SI. Facts and comparisons 1987. St. Louis: Facts and Comparisons; 1987:83-84a.

Wahl MJ. Myths of dental surgery in patients receiving anticoagulant therapy. JADA 2000;131:77-81.

Chapter 6.

Glucocorticoids

Michael Glick, D.M.D.; Martha Somerman, D.D.S., Ph.D.

Glucocorticoids are hormones secreted by the adrenal gland in response to ultradian and circadian rhythms and to stress. These hormones affect cardiovascular functions, metabolism, and inflammatory and immune responses. Glucocorticoids are different hormones than mineralcorticoids and anabolic steroids and are the only type of steroids discussed in this chapter.

The immune suppressive and anti-inflammatory properties of glucocorticoids have been used in medicine and dentistry for more than four decades. However, glucocorticoids have been proven to be a double-edged sword, as their beneficial effects often are accompanied by multiple side effects.

Glucocorticoids influence many metabolic pathways and all organ systems, and they are essential for survival. The major effects of glucocorticoids can broadly be defined as influencing the metabolism of carbohydrates, protein and fat metabolism, as well as water and electrolyte balance. Consequently, glucocorticoids are involved in the deposition of glucose as glycogen and the conversion of glycogen and protein into glucose when needed; the stimulation of protein loss from specific organs; the redistribution of fatty tissue in facial, abdominal and shoulder regions; and alterations of the filtration rate of specific electrolytes that cause water retention.

Glucocorticoids mainly regulate the metabolic pathways, while mineralcorticoids are involved with electrolyte and water balance. The secretion of glucocorticoids from the adrenal glands is controlled by hormones, such as corticotropin-releasing factor, produced by the hypothalamus, and adrenocorticotropic hormone (ACTH), produced by the anterior pituitary gland. This pathway is often referred to as the hypothalamic-pituitary-adrenal (HPA) axis. Glucocorticoid secretion from the adrenal glands is regulated by a negative feedback mechanism; that is, the adrenal glands will diminish glucocorticoid secretion when excess plasma levels of steroids are present. However, the glands cannot distinguish between endogenously and exogenously supplied glucocorticoids. Consequently, administration of supraphysiological levels of exogenous glucocorticoids for long periods may result in secondary adrenal insufficiency.

Glucocorticoids are, among other things, essential for a person's ability to adapt to stressful situations. Adrenal insufficiency or dysfunction, therefore, may predispose a person to inadequate physiological response to stress. Severe adrenal suppression and accompanied diminished stress response may have clinical significance after 7-10 days of steroid administration. In stressful situations, cardiovascular collapse may ensue and, if not treated appropriately, can result in a high degree of morbidity and even death. Dentists need to be able to assess the level of patients' adrenal suppression and provide patients with glucocorticoid replacement therapy when necessary.

Assessment of adrenal suppression. Many different factors play a role in assessing the diminished output of glucocorticoids from the adrenal glands in patients who are prescribed glucocorticoids. These factors include, but are not limited to, the type of glucocorticoids the patient is prescribed, the route of administration, the dosing schedule, the duration of taking the steroids, concomitant systemic disorders and drug interactions.

Each type and formulation of glucocorticoids has been assigned a specific level of potency that is compared to the potency of hydrocortisone (Table 6.1). Thus, prednisone is four times more potent than hydrocortisone, while betamethasone is 25 times more potent. The more potent the drug, the higher the risk of causing adrenal suppression. The most common modes of long-term steroid administration are topical application or systemic administration by mouth.

Except for the high-potency topical glucocorticoids, topically applied glucocorticoids—including those used intraorally—have not been associated with adrenal suppression. However, systemically administered glucocorticoids have been associated with adrenal suppression and diminished stress response in patients.

Physiological secretion of glucocorticoids is highest in the morning and lowest in the evening. Thus, giving an entire dose of glucocorticoids in the morning causes less adrenal suppression than giving the same amount equally divided throughout the day. There is a disassociation between plasma levels and biological half-life of glucocorticoids. Consequently, the effect of a glucocorticoid is determined by its binding to intracellular receptors rather than its presence in the circulation. Thus, lengthening the intervals between administration may allow the drug to have the same beneficial effect while at the same time cause fewer side effects. For patients receiving chronic glucocorticoid therapy who require more than 1 mo of therapy, this concept has resulted in alternate-day therapy to reduce potential side effects.

The normal output of glucocorticoids from the adrenal glands is in the range of 20-30 mg of hydrocortisone equivalent per day.

This value is a function of the size of the person and is usually calculated according to a person's body surface, which is approximately 2 square meters for an average adult. During short periods of stress, the adrenal glands can produce up to 300 mg of hydrocortisone-equivalent glucocorticoids. Any exogenous dosage above the physiological level of 30 mg of hydrocortisone equivalent will affect the adrenal glands. The higher the dosage, the greater the effect that can be anticipated. Adrenal suppression occurs rapidly and may be present for up to 2 y, even after as little as 2 w of glucocorticoid therapy. However, although the adrenal function is suppressed, the stress response returns after approximately 11-14 days. For the purpose of not causing stress-related adverse events, the return of the stress response is of the essence.

The risk of experiencing adverse effects from glucocorticoid administration usually increases with duration of therapy and frequency of administration.

Accepted Indications

Glucocorticoid therapy, when used appropriately and for the right patient, can ameliorate both systemic and oral conditions that are associated with severe morbidity, and it can greatly improve patients' quality of life. Oral health care providers need to be aware of both the value and the detrimental effect of glucocorticoids.

Glucocorticoids are used to induce immune suppression in patients with a variety of conditions. Patients who have undergone organ transplantations, for example, often are prescribed high doses of glucocorticoids to prevent organ rejection. Although other conditions—such as autoimmune diseases, respiratory diseases, dermatologic diseases and some hematologic disorders—also require long-term glucocorticoid therapy, there is usually no need for such high doses as used with transplant patients.

Glucocorticoids are also used in dental settings. Various oral conditions—such as lichen planus, aphthous ulcers, benign mucous membrane pemphigoid, pemphigus, postherpetic neuralgia, and temporomandibular joint disorders—benefit from glucocorticoid therapy. Furthermore, glucocorticoids also are used to reduce swelling after major oral-maxillofacial surgical procedures.

General Dosing Information

Table 6.1 provides dosage and prescribing information for systemic glucocorticoids, separated into low-, intermediate- and high-potency categories. Table 6.2 provides dosage and prescribing information for topical glucocorticoids, separated into low-, intermediate-, high- and very high-potency categories. Table 6.3 provides dosage and prescribing information for inhaled glucocorticoids.

When administering glucocorticoids, dentists may use topical formulations, intralesional and intra-articular injections or systemic forms. Topical agents are the ones most commonly used by dentists and, if employed for less than 1 mo, usually will not cause significant detrimental effects. However, very high-potency topical glucocorticoids used to treat oral lesions can cause adrenal suppression and should not be used for more than 2 w without a thorough medical evaluation of the patient. Creams, ointments and gels all can be used intraorally and are applied to lesions 2-4 times daily. Gels adhere fairly well to the oral mucosa and are applied directly to lesions. To increase penetration and time in contact with lesions, gel formulations also can be placed inside a mouthguard covering the affected area. Ointments usually are mixed with equal amounts of Orabase, a compound that adheres to the oral mucosa, and is placed directly on lesions. Ointments also can be placed inside mouthguards. Although creams can be used for oral lesions, these formulations are not commonly used for this purpose. Dexamethasone elixir and prednisolone syrup are the oral rinses commonly used for topical purposes. The patient is instructed to rinse for 30 s with these med-ications, and then to expectorate them, 2-4 times daily.

Intralesional injections commonly are used only intermittently; when used for soft-tissue pathologies, they have not been associated with systemic complications. Triamcinolone hexacetonide is the most frequently used medication for this purpose.

Intra-articular injections, also predominantly performed with triamcinolone hexacetonide, should be performed only in 3-w intervals to diminish bone pathology.

Systemic glucocorticoid therapy is used in the short term before, during and after oral surgery to reduce postoperative edema. Oral lesions associated with very high morbidity sometimes are treated with systemic glucocorticoid therapy. High doses of prednisone, up to 60-80 mg per day for 7-10 days, can be used for treatment of lichen planus, major aphthous ulcerations, oral pemphigoid and oral pemphigus. Treatment beyond 2 w should be coordinated with the patient's physician.

Dentists need to be aware of the complications associated with long-term use of systemic glucocorticoid therapy. The potential harmful effects of these medications always must be carefully weighed against the benefit.

Maximum Recommended Doses

The maximum recommended doses for systemic glucocorticoid formulations per procedure or appointment are 5-20 mg of prednisone for a maintenance dose and 5-60 mg for continuous or alternate-day therapy, but doses depend on the patient's condition. Dosing schedules and maximum doses are based on the assumption that the dentist has determined (through taking a health history and interviewing the patient) that the patient is in general good health and is not taking any medications that can interact with the glucocorticoid agent. The main concerns are patients with hyperglycemic conditions and patients who cannot tolerate immunosuppressive therapy.

Table 6.1

Systemic Glucocorticoids: Dosage and Prescribing Information*

Generic name	Brand name(s)	REP	Adult dosage	Max adult dosage	Child dosage	Content/form
Low potency						
Cortisone	Cortisone Acetate, Cortone Acetate; Cortone [CAN]	0.8	**IM:** 20-300 mg/day **Oral:** 25-300 mg/day, single or divided dose	300 mg/day	**IM:** 1-5 mg/kg/day q 12-24 h **Oral:** 2.5-10 mg/kg q 6-8 h	**Injection (acetate):** 50 mg/mL in 10-mL vials **Tablets:** 5, 10, 25 mg; 5, 25 mg [CAN]
Hydro-cortisone	Cortef, Hydrocortisone, Hydrocortone, Solu-Cortef	1	**Intra-articular, intralesional (acetate):** 5-75 mg q 2-3 weeks **IM, IV, SC (sodium phosphate):** 15-240 mg/day **IM, IV (succinate):** 100-500 mg q 2-10 h **IM, IV, SC (sodium phosphate):** 15-240 mg/day **Oral suspension (cypionate):** 20-240 mg/day in 2-4 divided doses **Oral, tablets:** 20-240 mg/day, single or divided dose	300 mg/day	**IM:** 1-5 mg/kg/day q 12-24 h **Oral:** 2.5-10 mg/kg q 6-8 h	**Injection (acetate):** 25, 50 mg/mL in 5-, 10-mL vials **Injection (sodium phosphate):** 50 mg/mL in 2-, 10-mL vials **Injection (succinate):** 100, 200 mg in 2-mL vials; 500 mg in 4-mL vials; 1,000 mg in 8-mL vials **Oral suspension:** 10 mg/5 mL in 120-mL bottles **Tablets:** 5, 10, 20 mg; 25 mg [CAN]
Intermediate potency						
Prednisone	Deltasone, Liquid Pred, Meticorten, Orasone, Panasol-S, Prednicen-M, Prednisone, Prednisone Intensol Concentrate, Strerapred; Apo-Prednisone [CAN], Jaa-Prednisone [CAN], Novo-Prednisone [CAN], Wimpred [CAN]	4	**Oral:** 5-60 mg/day, single or divided dose	250 mg/day	**Oral:** 0.05-2 mg/kg/day	**Oral solution (5% alcohol):** 5 mg/5 mL in 5-, 500-mL vials **Oral solution (30% alcohol):** 5 mg/mL in 30-mL vials **Syrup (5% alcohol):** 5 mg/5 mL in 120, 240-mL vials **Tablets:** 1, 2.5, 5, 10, 20, 50 mg

[CAN] indicates a drug available only in Canada.
REP: Relative equivalent potency.
* All systemic glucocorticoids are categorized as pregnancy risk factor C.

Continued on next page

Table 6.1 (cont.)

Systemic Glucocorticoids: Dosage and Prescribing Information*

Generic name	Brand name(s)	REP	Adult dosage	Max adult dosage	Child dosage	Content/form
			Intermediate potency (cont.)			
Prednisolone	Delta-Cortef, Hydeltrasol, Key-Pred 25, Key-Pred 50, Key-Pred-SP, Pediapred, Predalone 50, Predcor-50, Prednisol TBA, Prednisolone, Prednisolone Tebutate, Prelone	4	**Intra-articular, intralesional (acetate):** 4-100 mg/day **IM (acetate):** 4-60 mg/day **Intra-articular, intralesional (sodium phosphate):** 4-30 mg **IM, IV (sodium phosphate):** 4-60 mg/day **Intra-articular, intralesional (tebutate):** 4-20 mg **Oral, syrup or tablets:** 5-60 mg/day, single or divided dose	200 mg/day Do not exceed 40 mg	**Tablets or syrup:** 5-60 mg/day	**Injection (acetate):** 25, 50 mg/mL in 10-, 30-mL vials **Injection (sodium phosphate):** 20 mg/mL in 2-, 5-, 10-mL vials **Injection (tebutate):** 20 mg/mL in 10-mL vials **Syrup (0.4% alcohol):** 5 mg/5 mL in 120-mL bottles **Syrup (5% alcohol):** 15 mg/5 mL in 240-mL bottles **Syrup (Pediaprep):** 5 mg/5 mL in 120-mL bottles **Tablets:** 5 mg
Methyl-prednisolone	A-methaPred, depMedalone 40, depMedalone 80, Depoject, Depo-Medrol, Depopred-40, Depopred-80, Duralone-40, Duralone-80, M-Prednisol-40, M-Prednisol-80, Medralone 40, Medralone 80, Medrol, Methyl-prednisolone, Methyl-prednisolone Acetate, Methyl-prednisolone Sodium Succinate, Solu-Medrol	5	**Intra-articular, intralesional, IM (acetate):** 4-120 mg q 1-2 w **IM, IV (succinate):** 10-40 mg/day in 1 dose **Oral, tablets:** 4-48 mg/day in 1-4 divided doses	Do not use for more than 48-72 h	**IM, IV, oral:** 0.12-0.17 mg/kg/day q 6-12 h (not less than 0.5 mg/kg/24 h)	**Injection (acetate):** 20 mg/mL in 5-, 10-mL vials; 40 mg/mL in 1-, 5-, 10-mL vials; 80 mg/mL in 1-, 5-mL vials **Injection (succinate):** 40 mg/vial in 1-, 3-mL vials; 125 mg/vial in 2-, 5-mL vials; 500 mg/vial in 1-, 4-, 8-, 20-mL vials; 1 g/vial in 1-, 8-, 50-mL vials; 1 g/vial in 1-, 8-, 50-mL vials; 2 g/vial in 30.6-mL vials **Act-O-Vial System (Single-Dose Vial) for Solu-Medrol:** 40 mg/1 mL, 125 mg/2 mL, 500 mg/4 mL, 1,000 mg/8 mL **Tablets:** 2, 4, 8, 16, 24, 32 mg; dosepack (4 mg) with 21 tablets

REP: *Relative equivalent potency.*
* *All systemic glucocorticoids are categorized as pregnancy risk factor C.*

Continued on next page

Table 6.1 (cont.)

Systemic Glucocorticoids: Dosage and Prescribing Information*

Generic name	Brand name(s)	REP	Adult dosage	Max adult dosage	Child dosage	Content/form
Intermediate potency (cont.)						
Triam-cinolone	Amcort, Aristocort, Aristocort Forte, Aristocort Intralesional, Aristospan Intra-articular, Aristospan Intralesional, Atolone, Clinacort, Kenacort, Kenaject-40, Kenalog-10, Kenalog-40, Tac-3, Tac-40, Triam Forte, Triam-A, Triamcinolone, Triamcinolone Acetonide, Triamolone, Triamonide 40, Tri-Kort, Trilog, Trilone, Tristoject	5	**Intra-articular, intralesional (acetonide), IM:** 2.5-60 mg/day **Intra-articular, intralesional, intrasynovial (diacetate):** 5-48 mg q 4-7 days, up to 3-4 w **Intra-articular, intralesional (hexacetonide):** 2-20 mg q 3-4 w **Oral:** 4-60 mg/day	**Intra-articular:** 40 mg at one time **Intralesional:** 30 mg at one time	**Intra-articular (hexacetonide):** 2.5-15 mg, repeated as needed **Aged 6-12 y—IM (acetonide or hexacetonide):** 0.03-0.2 mg/kg at 1-7 day intervals	**Injection (acetonide):** 3, 10 mg/mL in 5-mL vials; 40 mg/mL in 1-, 5-, 10-mL vials **Injection (diacetate):** 25 mg/mL in 5-mL vials; 40 mg/mL in 1-, 5-mL vials **Injection (hexace-tonide):** 5 mg/mL in 5-mL vials; 20 mg/mL in 1-, 5-mL vials **Syrup (diacetonide):** 4 mg/5 mL in 120-mL bottles **Tablets:** 4, 8 mg
High potency						
Beta-methasone	Betamethasone Sodium Phosphate, Betamethasone Sodium Phosphate/ Betamethasone Acetate, Celestone, Celestone Phosphate, Cel-U-Jec; Betnelan [CAN], Celestone [CAN]	30	**Intra-articular, intralesional (acetate, sodium phosphate):** 0.5-9 mg/day **IM, IV (sodium phosphate):** 0.6-9 mg/day **Oral:** 0.6-7.2 mg/day in single or divided dose	9 mg/day	**IM:** 0.0175-0.25 mg/kg/day or 0.5-7.5 mg/m²/day **Oral:** 0.0175-0.25 mg/kg/day or 0.5-7.5 mg/m²/day	**Injection (acetate and sodium phos-phate):** 3 mg sodium phosphate and 3 mg acetate/mL in 5-mL vials **Injection (sodium phosphate):** 4 mg/mL in 5-mL vials **Syrup (< 1% alcohol):** 0.6 mg/5 mL in 118-mL vials **Tablets:** 0.6 mg

[CAN] indicates a drug available only in Canada.
REP: Relative equivalent potency.
* All systemic glucocorticoids are categorized as pregnancy risk factor C.

Continued on next page

Table 6.1 (cont.)

Systemic Glucocorticoids: Dosage and Prescribing Information*

Generic name	Brand name(s)	REP	Adult dosage	Max adult dosage	Child dosage	Content/form
High potency (cont.)						
Dexa-methasone	Cortastat L.A., Dalalone, Dalalone D.P., Decadron, Decadron L.A., Decadron Phosphate, Decadron with xylocaine, Decaject, Decaject L.A., Dexamethasone, Dexamethasone Acetate, Dexamethasone Intensol, Dexamethasone Sodium Phosphate, Dexasone, Dexasone L.A., Dexone, Dexone L.A., Hexadrol, Hexadrol Phosphate, Solurex, Solurex L.A.	30-40	**Intra-articular (acetate):** 4-16 mg; repeat at 1-3–w intervals **Intra-articular, intralesional (sodium phosphate):** 0.8-6 mg; repeat at 1-3–w intervals **Intralesional (acetate):** 0.8-1.6 mg; repeat at 1-3–w intervals **Intralesional (Decadron with xylocaine):** 0.1-0.75 mg/day **IM (acetate):** 8-16 mg; repeat at 1-3–w intervals **Oral:** 0.75-9 mg/day, in divided doses, q 6-12 h	U	**IM, IV, oral (sodium phosphate):** 0.08-0.3 mg/kg/day, in divided doses, q 6-12 h	**Elixir (5% alcohol):** 0.5 mg/5 mL in 100-, 120-, 237-, 240-, 500-mL bottles **Injection (acetate):** 8, 16 mg/mL, in 1-, 5-mL vials **Injection (Decadron with xylocaine):** 4 mg dexamethasone with 10 mg lidocaine/mL in 5-mL vials **Injection (sodium phosphate):** 4, 10, 20 mg/mL in 1-, 5-, 10-, 25-, 30- mL vials **Oral solution (with or without 30% alcohol):** 0.5 mg/0.5 mL in 30-mL bottles **Tablets:** 0.25, 0.5, 0.75, 1, 1.5, 2, 4, 6 mg; therapeutic pack (6 1.5-mg tablets and 8 0.75-mg tablets)

REP: *Relative equivalent potency.*
U: *Unavailable.*
* *All systemic glucocorticoids are categorized as pregnancy risk factor C.*

Dosage Adjustments

The actual maximum dose for each patient must be individualized depending on his or her size, age and physical status; other drugs he or she may be taking; and duration of existing glucocorticoid therapy (long-term use considerations). Reduced maximum doses may be indicated for pediatric and geriatric patients, patients with serious illness or disability, and patients with medical conditions or who are taking drugs that alter responses to glucocorticoids.

Special Dental Considerations

The effect of glucocorticoids can be divided arbitrarily into two categories that have significance for dentists:

- dental patients taking glucocorticoids may need modifications and alterations of routine dental therapy, for purposes such as reducing patients' stress response and glucocorticoid replacement;
- glucocorticoid users may exhibit intraoral manifestations.

Table 6.2

Topical Glucocorticoids: Dosage and Prescribing Information

Generic name	Brand name(s)	Adult dosage	Max adult dosage*	Child dosage*	Content/form
Low potency					
Aclometasone diproprionate	Aclovate	2-4 applications/day	U	NE, but use least amount that yields effect	**Cream:** 0.05% in 15-, 45-g tubes **Ointment:** 0.05% in 15-, 45-g tubes
Betamethasone valerate	Psorion, Valisone Reduced Strength	See note above	U	See note above	**Cream:** 0.01%, 0.05% in 15-, 45-, 60-g tubes
Desonide	Desonide, DesOwen, Tridesilon	See note above	U	See note above	**Cream:** 0.05% in 15-, 60-g tubes **Ointment:** 0.05% in 15-, 60-g tubes
Dexamethasone sodium phosphate	Decadron Phosphate	See note above	U	See note above	**Cream:** 0.1% in 15-, 30-g tubes
Fluocinolone acetonide	Fluocinolone, Flurosyn, Synalar	See note above	U	See note above	**Cream:** 0.01% in 15-, 30-, 60-, 425-g tubes
Hydrocortisone	Ala-Cort, Anusol-HC 2.5%, Cort-Dome, Delcort, Dermacort, Eldecort, Hi-Cor 1.0, Hi-Cor 2.5, Hydrocort, Hydrocortizone, Hycort, Hytone, Nutracort, 1% HC, Penecort, Synacort	See note above	U	See note above	**Cream:** 0.5%, 1%, 2.5% in 15-, 20-, 30-, 45-, 60-, 120-, 240-g tubes **Ointment:** 0.5%, 1%, 2.5% in 15-, 20-, 30-, 45-, 60-, 120-, 240-g tubes
Medium potency					
Betamethasone valerate	Betamethasone Valerate, Betatrex, Beta-Val, Valisone	1-3 applications/day	U	NE, but use least amount that yields effect	**Cream:** 0.1% in 15-, 45-, 110-, 430-g tubes
Clocortolone pivalate	Cloderm	See note above	U	See note above	**Cream:** 0.1% in 15-, 45-g tubes
Desoximetasone	Topicort-LP	See note above	U	See note above	**Cream:** 0.05% in 15-, 60-, 120-g tubes

NE: Not established.
U: Unavailable.
* Do not exceed 50 g/w for adults or 15 g/w for children.

Continued on next page

Table 6.2 (cont.)

Topical Glucocorticoids: Dosage and Prescribing Information

Generic name	Brand name(s)	Adult dosage	Max adult dosage*	Child dosage*	Content/form
Medium potency (cont.)					
Fluocinolone acetonide	Fluocinolone, Flurosyn, Synalar	1-3 applications/day	U	NE, but use least amount that yields effect	**Cream:** 0.025% in 15-, 60-, 425-g tubes **Ointment:** 0.025% in 15-, 30-, 60-, 425-g tubes
Fluticasone proprionate	Cutivate	See note above	U	See note above	**Cream:** 0.05% in 15-, 30-, 60-g tubes **Ointment:** 0.005% in 15-, 30-, 60-g tubes
Halcinonide	Halog	See note above	U	See note above	**Cream:** 0.025% in 15-, 60-g tubes
Hydrocortisone butyrate	Locoid	See note above	U	See note above	**Cream:** 0.1% in 15-, 45-g tubes **Ointment:** 0.1% in 15-, 45-g tubes
Hydrocortisone valerate	Hydrocortisone Valerate, Westcort	See note above	U	See note above	**Cream:** 0.2% in 15-, 45-, 60-g tubes **Ointment:** 0.2% in 15-, 45-, 60-g tubes
Mometasone furoate	Elocon	See note above	U	See note above	**Cream:** 0.1% in 15-, 45-g tubes **Ointment:** 0.1% in 15-, 45-g tubes
Triamcinolone acetonide	Aristocort, Aristocort A, Delta-Tritex, Flutex, Kenalog, Kenalog-H, Kenonel, Triacet, Triderm	See note above	U	See note above	**Cream:** 0.025%, 0.1% in 15-, 20-, 30-, 60-, 80-, 90-, 120-, 240-, 454-g tubes **Ointment:** 0.025%, 0.1% in 15-, 20-, 28-, 57-, 80-, 113-, 240-, 454-g tubes
High potency					
Amcinonide	Cyclocort	1-3 applications/day	U	NE, but use least amount that yields effect	**Cream:** 0.1% in 15-, 30-, 60-g tubes **Ointment:** 0.1% in 15-, 30-, 60-g tubes

NE: Not established.
U: Unavailable.
* Do not exceed 50 g/w for adults or 15 g/w for children.

Continued on next page

Table 6.2 (cont.)

Topical Glucocorticoids: Dosage and Prescribing Information

Generic name	Brand name(s)	Adult dosage	Max adult dosage*	Child dosage*	Content/form
			High potency (cont.)		
Augmented betamethasone diproprionate	Diprolene, Diprolene AF	1-3 applications/day	U	NE, but use least amount that yields effect	**Cream:** 0.05% in 15-, 45-g tubes **Gel:** 0.05% in 15-, 45-g tubes
Betamethasone diproprionate	Alphatrex, Betamethasone Diproprionate, Diprosone, Maxivate, Teladar	See note above	U	See note above	**Cream:** 0.05% in 15-, 45-g tubes **Ointment:** 0.05% in 15-, 45-g tubes
Betamethasone valerate	Betamethasone Valerate, Betatrex, Valisone	See note above	U	See note above	**Ointment:** 0.1% in 15-, 45-g tubes
Desoximetasone	Topicort	See note above	U	See note above	**Cream:** 0.25% in 15-, 60-, 120-g tubes **Gel:** 0.05% in 15-, 60-g tubes **Ointment:** 0.25% in 15-, 60-g tubes
Diflorasone diacetate	Florone, Maxiflor, Psorcon	See note above	U	See note above	**Cream:** 0.05% in 15-, 30-, 60-g tubes **Ointment:** 0.05% in 15, 30-, 60-g tubes
Fluocinolone acetonide	Synalar-HP	See note above	U	See note above	**Cream:** 0.2% in 12-g tubes
Fluocinonide	Fluocinonide, Fluocinonide "E" Cream, Fluonex, Lidex, Lidex-E	See note above	U	See note above	**Cream:** 0.05% in 15-, 30-, 60-, 120-g tubes **Gel:** 0.05% in 15-, 30-, 60-, 120-g tubes **Ointment:** 0.05% in 15-, 30-, 60-, 120-g tubes
Halcinonide	Halog, Halog-E	See note above	U	See note above	**Cream:** 0.1% in 15-, 30-, 60-, 240-g tubes **Ointment:** 0.1% in 15-, 30-, 60-, 240-g tubes

NE: Not established.
U: Unavailable.
* Do not exceed 50 g/w for adults or 15 g/w for children.

Continued on next page

Table 6.2 (cont.)

Topical Glucocorticoids: Dosage and Prescribing Information

Generic name	Brand name(s)	Adult dosage	Max adult dosage*	Child dosage*	Content/form
High potency (cont.)					
Triamcinolone acetonide	Aristocort, Aristocort A, Flutex, Kenalog, Triamcinolone Acetonide	1-3 applications/day	U	NE, but use least amount that yields effect	**Cream:** 0.5% in 15-, 30-, 60-, 120-, 240-g tubes **Ointment:** 0.5% in 15-, 20-, 28-, 57-, 113-, 240-g tubes
Very high potency					
Augmented betamethasone diproprionate	Diprolene	1-2 applications/day divided into morning and afternoon doses	45 g/w	Not to be used in children < age 12 y	**Ointment:** 0.05% in 15-, 45-g tubes
Clobetasol propionate	Clobetasol Propionate, Cormax, Embeline E 0.05%, Temovate, Temovate Emollient	See note above	50 g/w for 2 consecutive w	Not to be used in children < age 12 y	**Cream:** 0.05% in 15-, 30-, 45-, 60-g tubes **Ointment:** 0.05% in 15-, 30-, 45-g tubes
Diflorasone diacetate	Psorcon	See note above	See note above	Not to be used in children < age 12 y	**Ointment:** 0.05% in 15-, 30-, 60-g tubes
Halobetasol propionate	Ultravate	See note above	See note above	Not to be used in children < age 12 y	**Cream:** 0.05% in 15-, 45-g tubes **Ointment:** 0.05% in 15-, 45-g tubes

NE: Not established.
U: Unavailable.
* Do not exceed 50 g/w for adults or 15 g/w for children.

Modifications of routine dental therapy. There are no definitive data regarding the need for patients taking glucocorticoids to receive antibiotic prophylaxis before undergoing dental therapy. However, it is prudent for dental providers to consider antibiotic prophylaxis in patients taking a combined dose of more than 700 mg of prednisone. No antibiotic prophylaxis is recommended if a patient takes less than 10 mg of prednisone per day. Dentists should routinely use the same protocol for antibiotic prophylaxis as that put forth by the American Heart Association for prevention of subacute bacterial endocarditis (see Appendix D).

There are two situations in which dentists need to provide patients with extra glucocorticoids. First, patients with dysfunctional adrenal glands may not be able to produce enough glucocorticoids to respond to the stress associated with dental therapy. The most common condition associated with primary adrenal destruction is Addison's disease, an autoimmune destruction of the

Table 6.3

Inhaled Glucocorticoids: Dosage and Prescribing Information

Generic name	Brand name(s)	REP	Adult dosage	Max adult dosage	Child dosage	Content/form
Beclomethasone diproprionate	Beclovent, Vanceril, Vanceril Double Strength; Beclo-forte [CAN]	U	168-840 µg, 2-20 puffs	> 840 µg, > 20 puffs	**Age 6-12 y:** 84-672 µg, 2-16 puffs	**Inhaler:** 6.7-, 16.8-g canisters delivering 42 µg/puff; 5.4-, 12.2-g canisters delivering 84 µg/puff
Budesonide	Pulmicort Turbuhaler	U	200-600 µg, 1-3 puffs	> 600 µg, > 3 puffs	**Age ≥ 6 y:** 200-400 µg, 1-2 puffs	**Inhaler:** Turbuhaler delivering 200 µg/puff
Flunisolide	AeroBid, AeroBid-M; Bronalide [CAN]	U	500-2000 µg, 2-8 puffs	> 2000 µg, > 8 puffs	**Age 6-15 y:** 500-1250 µg, 2-5 puffs	**Inhaler:** Canister delivering 250 µg/puff
Fluticasone MDI (metered dose inhaler)	Flovent	U	88-660 µg, 2-6 puffs	> 660 µg, > 6 puffs (110 µg) or > 3 puffs (220 µg)	**Age > 12 y:** 88-440 µg, 4-10 puffs (44 µg) or 2-4 puffs (110 µg)	**Inhaler:** 7.9-, 13-g canister delivering 44, 110, 220 µg/puff
Fluticasone DPI (dry powder inhaler)	Flovent Rotadisk	U	88-660 µg, 2-6 inhalations	> 660 µg, > 6 inhalations (100 µg)	**Age ≥ 12 y:** 88-440 µg, 2-4 inhalations (100 µg)	**Inhaler:** Rotodisk delivering 50, 100 µg/inhalation
Triamcinolone acetonide	Azmacort	U	400-2000 µg, 4-20 puffs	> 2000 µg, > 20 puffs	**Age 6-12 y:** 400-1200 µg, 4-12 puffs	**Inhaler:** 100 µg/puff

[CAN] indicates a drug available only in Canada.
REP: Relative equivalent potency.
U: Unavailable.

adrenal glands. Patients with inadequately functioning adrenal glands will need prophylactic glucocorticoid therapy before undergoing dental procedures. Second, patients who have been taking glucocorticoids for a long period may have iatrogenic adrenal suppression and will need glucocorticoid replacement therapy before undergoing dental procedures.

As the stress response returns within 11-14 days after cessation of glucocorticoid therapy, patients do not need replacement therapy after a 2-4-w period of not having taken glucocorticoids. Furthermore, patients being switched from daily therapy to alternate-day therapy can be treated without glucocorticoid replacement therapy on the nonglucocorticoid day. As a rule, patients needing replacement therapy should receive the equivalent of up to 300 mg of hydrocortisone or 60-75 mg of prednisone the morning of a dental appointment.

The amount of glucocorticoid replacement should be gauged according to the anticipated level of stress. Accordingly, depending on the patient's level of fear and anxiety, oral examinations generally require no replacement therapy, while any procedure requiring local anesthetics warrants additional glucocorticoid coverage.

Oral health care providers should follow this protocol for the management of patients who are receiving glucocorticoid therapy:

- Schedule elective procedures in the morning.
- Use mild sedatives for apprehensive patients.
- Use glucocorticoid replacement therapy when indicated.
- Always use long-acting local anesthetics.
- Monitor blood pressure during the procedure.
- Use medications to alleviate postoperative pain.

As a rule, replacement therapy is indicated for patients who presently are taking more than 30 mg of hydrocortisone equivalent of glucocorticoids for more than 2 w. It also is indicated for patients seeking dental care within the first 2-4 w after having stopped glucocorticoid therapy subsequent to having taken at least 30 mg of hydrocortisone equivalent of glucocorticoids for more than 2 w.

Intraoral manifestations. Of all the intraoral manifestations caused by glucocorticoids, the most common is oral candidiasis. It has been estimated that up to 75% of people using inhalers that contain glucocorticoids may develop intraoral candidiasis (Table 6.3). These inhalers are used mainly by patients with asthma, but they also can be prescribed for patients with allergies and other respiratory conditions. To diminish the occurrence of candidiasis, dentists should properly instruct patients in the use of spacer devices and to rinse their mouths with water after using the inhalers. Resolution of intraoral candidiasis can be accomplished effectively with antifungal troches, lozenges or oral solutions (see Chapter 8).

Long-term systemic administration of glucocorticoids may impair wound healing. This may be the result of the catabolic effect and the reduced inflammatory response induced by these compounds.

The anti-inflammatory property of glucocorticoids may mask a chronic infection. Glucocorticoids will prevent accumulation of neutrophils and monocytes at sites of inflammation (impaired chemotaxis) and further suppress the phagocytic abilities of cells. Thus, the classic clinical inflammatory response may be greatly blunted.

Intraoral dryness has also been reported in patients taking glucocorticoids, both systemically and in the form of inhalers. An increased caries rate can be anticipated, and patients should be instructed about improved oral hygiene procedures and use of topical fluorides, as well as in-office fluoride therapy.

Drug Interactions of Dental Interest

Table 6.4 lists drug interactions with glucocorticoids and related problems of potential clinical significance in dentistry.

Laboratory Value Alterations

- Low serum cortisol levels, < 5-10 µg/dL in a specimen obtained between 8 and 10 a.m., and increased serum ACTH, 200-1,600 µg/dL, are diagnostic for adrenal insufficiency. Dentists may want to request a complete blood count, as neutropenia and lymphocytosis may be present.

Special Patients

Pregnant and nursing women

All systemic glucocorticoid preparations are classified in pregnancy risk category C and may cause birth defects such as cleft lip and palate. Consequently, glucocorticoid administration during pregnancy and during breast feeding should be avoided.

Pediatric, geriatric and other special patients

Administration of as little as 5 mg of prednisone may cause growth retardation in children. However, if glucocorticoid therapy ceases before the epiphyses close, catch-up growth may take place.

Pediatric patients may have a greater susceptibility to topical glucocorticoid–induced adrenal suppression than adults have, because children have thinner skin and their ratio of skin surface area to body weight is larger than that of adults. Topical glucocorticoids should be used with caution in children.

Geriatric patients exhibit a propensity to

develop hypertension, as well as osteoporosis, while receiving glucocorticoid therapy. Glucocorticoid dosage also needs to be adjusted in younger and older patients to minimize damage to kidney and liver functions.

Patient Monitoring: Aspects to Watch

- Symptoms of blood dyscrasias (such as infection, bleeding and poor healing): for patients with these symptoms, the dentist should request a medical consultation for blood studies and postpone dental treatment until normal values are re-established
- Vital signs, at every appointment: necessary to monitor possible cardiovascular side effects
- Salivary flow: as a factor in caries, periodontal disease and candidiasis
- Dose and duration of glucocorticoid therapy: to assess stress tolerance and risk of immunosuppression
- Need for medical consultation: to assess disease control and patient's stress tolerance

Adverse Effects and Precautions

The multitude of potential side effects of systemic glucocorticoids necessitates complete disclosure of the risks to patients (Table 6.4). Withdrawal of glucocorticoids after patients are treated for more than 10 consecutive days needs to be accomplished gradually to diminish side effects. Patients taking daily doses of 60 mg of prednisone should reduce their daily intake by 10 mg every day before completely stopping therapy. Too-quick withdrawal of glucocorticoid therapy may result in flare-up of the underlying condition or even adrenal crisis. If it is necessary that a patient continue to receive glucocorticoid therapy for longer than 2 w, a consultation with a physician is appropriate.

Severe hepatic disease may prevent prednisone metabolism; when treating such patients, the dentist may have to administer the active form of the medication, prednisolone, to achieve a clinical effect. Furthermore, patients with severe liver disease may not be able to take glucocorticoids with acetaminophen, as acetaminophen toxicity may ensue.

Concurrent administration of other medications such as barbiturates, phenytoin and rifampin may double the clearance of prednisolone. Interactions also may occur with other medications and need to be considered when prescribing glucocorticoids (Table 6.4).

The most common adverse signs of glucocorticoid therapy include changes in skin (such as acne, ecchymosis, thinning, violaceous abdominal striae), weight gain, truncal obesity, "buffalo hump" (adipose tissue accumulation on the back of the neck), thin extremities, decreased muscle mass and "moon face." These features appear in 13% of patients after as little as 60 days of glucocorticoid use and in up to 50% of patients treated for 5-8 y. Patients with these signs need to be encouraged to keep a low-fat, low-calorie diet and to exercise.

Skeletal fractures may occur in 11-20% of patients treated with daily doses of 7.5-10 mg of prednisone for more than 1 y. The major underlying cause of these osteoporotic changes may be decreased osteoblastic activity and maturation. The most rapid loss of trabecular bone loss occurs within the first 2 mo of high-dose glucocorticoid therapy, with an average of 5% bone mass loss within the first year. It is prudent to give calcium and vitamin D supplements and hormone replacements and to initiate weight-bearing exercise programs for patients receiving long-term glucocorticoid therapy. Another complication, more commonly found with patients taking long-term glucocorticoids, is osteonecrosis, which specifically affects the hip joint.

Patients taking a total dose of more than 1,000 mg of prednisone are more predisposed than patients taking lesser doses to develop peptic ulcers. This side effect is aggravated in patients already taking other potentially ulcerogenic medications. Administration of an H_2-antagonist may be beneficial as a prophylactic measure to reduce the incidence of peptic ulcerations.

Table 6.4

Glucocorticoids: Possible Interactions With Other Drugs

Drug taken by patient	Interaction with glucocorticoids	Dentist's action
Acetaminophen	May enhance hepatic toxicity of acetaminophen	Use caution in patients with hepatic disorders
Amphotericin B, carbonic anhydrase inhibitors	Hypokalemia, edema, heart disease	Use caution with concomitant use
Antidiabetic agents	Increased blood glucose	Adjust antidiabetic drugs
Antacids	Decreased absorption of glucocorticoid	Adjust glucocorticoid dosage
Barbiturates	Increased glucocorticoid metabolism and decreased effect of glucocorticoid	See note above
β_2 adrenergic agonists	May cause pulmonary edema	Discontinue glucocorticoid use if edema occurs
Digitalis glycosides	Increased risk of dysrhythmias	Use caution with concomitant use
Ketoconazole	Increased glucocorticoid metabolism and decreased effect of glucocorticoid	Adjust glucocorticoid dosage
Nonsteroidal anti-inflammatory drugs	Increased gastrointestinal side effects	Avoid concomitant use
Oral contraceptives	Increased half-life and decreased elimination of glucocorticoid	Adjust glucocorticoid dosage
Phenytoin	Increased glucocorticoid metabolism and decreased effect of glucocorticoid	See note above
Rifampicin	See note above	See note above

Glucocorticoids initially may induce a psychological state of well-being, which subsequently may become a state of glucocorticoid-induced depression when the glucocorticoids are withdrawn.

Increased incidence of accelerated atherosclerosis has been noted in patients with systemic lupus erythematosus or rheumatoid arthritis who are treated with long-term glucocorticoids. Furthermore, patients with preexisting hypertension may experience a worsening of their hypertensive control when treated with glucocorticoids.

Glucocorticoid-induced glucose intolerance is not associated with serious complications, but caution should be heeded when treating diabetic patients.

Progression of carcinoma of the breast and Kaposi's sarcoma has been reported in patients receiving glucocorticoid therapy. Although renewed development of Kaposi's sarcoma may occur, this lesion usually disappears after cessation of glucocorticoid therapy.

Pharmacology

Mechanism of action/effect. The effectiveness of glucocorticoid hormones is based on their ability to bind to cytosolic receptors in target tissues and subsequently enter the nucleus, where the glucocorticoid-receptor complex interacts with nuclear chromatin. This results in a cascade of events including the expression of hormone-specific ribonucleic acids, or RNAs, which in turn increases synthesis of specific proteins that mediate distinct physiological functions. The glucocorticoid cortisol is a normal circulating hormone secreted by the adrenal gland that functions in regulating normal metabolism and providing resistance to stress. In addition, at high levels—whether the result of disease or drug intake—glucocorticoids can have one or more physiological effects. These include

- altering levels of blood cells in the plasma (that is, decreasing eosinophils, basophils, monocytes and lymphocytes and increasing levels of hemoglobin, erythrocytes and polymorphonuclear leukocytes), which decreases circulating levels of cells involved in fighting off infections and results in increased susceptibility to infections;
- reducing the inflammatory response as a result of a decrease in lymphocytes as well as altering lymphocytes' ability to inhibit the enzyme-phospholipase A2, which is required for production of prostaglandins and leukotrienes;
- suppressing the hypothalmic-pituitary-adrenal (HPA) axis, thus inhibiting further synthesis of glucocorticoids.

Therefore, patients taking glucocorticoids warrant special attention as discussed in the introduction to this chapter.

Absorption. Systemically, most glucocorticoids are rapidly and readily absorbed from the GI tract because of their lipophilic character. Also, absorption occurs via synovial and conjunctival spaces.

Topically, absorption through the skin is very slow. However, chronic use in a nasal spray, for example, for use in seasonal rhinitis, can lead to pulmonary epithelial atrophy. Furthermore, excessive or prolonged use of topical glucocorticoids can result in sufficient absorption to cause systemic effects.

Both cortisone and prednisone contain a keto group at position II that must be hydroxylated in the liver to become activated. Thus, these drugs should be avoided in patients with abnormal liver function. Also, topical application of position II ketocorticoids is ineffective as a result of inactivity of this form of the glucocorticoid.

Distribution. In general, circulating cortisol is bound to plasma proteins: about 80-90% bound to transcortin—a cortisol-binding globulin with high affinity—while about 5-10% binds loosely to albumin. About 3-10% remains in the free (bioactive) form. Transcortin can bind to most synthetic glucocorticoids as well. However, some glucocorticoids, such as dexamethasone, do not bind to transcortin and, thus, are almost 100% in free form.

Biotransformation. Inactivation occurs primarily in the liver and also in the kidney, mostly to inactive metabolites. However, cortisone and prednisone are activated only after being metabolized to hydrocortisone and prednisolone, respectively. Fluorinated glucocorticoids are metabolized more slowly than the other members of this group.

Elimination. About 30% of inactive metabolite is metabolized further and then excreted in the urine.

Patient Advice

- Emphasize the importance of good oral hygiene to prevent soft-tissue inflammation.
- Caution the patient to prevent injury when using oral hygiene aids; he or she should use a soft toothbrush and have the dentist or hygienist evaluate his or her brushing and flossing techniques.
- Suggest the use of daily home fluoride preparations if chronic xerostomia occurs.
- Suggest the use of sugarless gum, frequent

sips of water or artificial saliva substitutes if chronic xerostomia occurs.

- Caution against using mouthrinses with high alcohol content, as they have drying effects on the oral mucosa.
- The patient should use a topical glucocorticoid after brushing and eating and at bedtime for optimal effect.
- Use of topical glucocorticoids on oral herpetic ulcerations is contraindicated.
- The patient should apply the agent with a cotton-tipped applicator by pressing, not rubbing, the paste on the lesion.
- When a topical glucocorticoid is used to treat oral lesions, a tissue response should be noted within 7-14 days. If not, the patient should return for oral evaluation. If glucocorticoids are used chronically, the patient should return for frequent recall visits.
- If irritation, infection or sensitization occurs at site, the patient should discontinue use and return for evaluation.
- The patient should avoid exposing the affected area to sunlight; burns may occur.

- Topical glucocorticoids are for external use only.
- The patient should prevent the topical glucocorticoid from coming in contact with his or her eyes.
- The patient should not bandage or wrap the affected area unless directed to do so.
- The patient should report adverse reactions.
- The patient should avoid taking anything by mouth for ½ h and 1 h after topical use in the mouth (as a mouthrinse or an ointment, respectively).

Suggested Readings

Effect of corticosteroids for fetal maturation on perinatal outcomes. NIH Consensus Statement 1994;12(2):1-24.

Glick M. Glucocorticosteroid replacement therapy: a literature review and suggested replacement therapy. Oral Surg Oral Med Oral Pathol 1989;67:614-20.

Lester RS, Knowles SR, Shear NH. The risks of systemic corticosteroid use. Dermatol Clin 1998;16(2):277-86.

Little JW, Falace DA, Miller CS, Rhodus NL, eds. Dental management of the medically compromised patient. 5th ed. St. Louis: Mosby-Year Book; 1997:410-8.

Rosenberg SW, Arm RN, eds. Clinician's guide to treatment of common oral lesions. 4th ed. Baltimore: American Academy of Oral Medicine; 1997.

Chapter 7

Antibiotics

Jed J. Jacobson, D.D.S, M.S., M.P.H.; Clay Walker, Ph.D.

The term "antibiotic" initially was used to refer to any compound produced by a microorganism that inhibited another microorganism. Through common usage, this definition has evolved to include any natural, semisynthetic or, in some cases, totally manmade antimicrobial agent that inhibits bacterial growth. An antibiotic can be classified as either bactericidal or bacteriostatic. Bactericidal drugs, such as penicillins, directly kill an infecting organism; bacteriostatic drugs, such as tetracyclines and erythromycin, inhibit the proliferation of bacteria by interfering with an essential metabolic process, resulting in the elimination of bacteria by the host's immune defense system.

Antibiotics are used commonly in dentistry for both therapeutic and preventive measures involving oral bacterial infections. Oral infections can occur for a number of reasons and primarily involve pulpal and periodontal tissues. Secondary infections of the soft tissues pose special therapeutic challenges. The drugs of choice in treating most oral infections are used because they provide adequate blood levels for delivery to the oral tissues and because of their proven ability to resolve oral infections.

Regardless of the oral infection being treated, monitoring the course of the infection with observation of the patient between 24 and 72 hours is recommended to ensure efficacy of the drug selected. Although culturing oral infections is not always possible or necessary, consideration of this procedure followed by antibiotic sensitivity testing should be included in the treatment of patients who do not respond to the antibiotic used initially.

Before undertaking the therapeutic use of

any antibiotic, the clinician should determine an established need for antibiotic therapy, take a careful history to determine if the patient has experienced any previous adverse reactions or developed a sensitivity to a specific antibiotic, determine which antibiotic is or is most likely to be effective against a bacterium or bacteria, and ensure that he or she has a thorough knowledge of the side effects and drug interactions.

Penicillin is still the drug of choice for treatment of infections in and around the oral cavity. In patients allergic to penicillin, erythromycin may be an appropriate alternative. Also, clindamycin may be an appropriate alternative to either penicillin or erythromycin. Finally, if there is no response to penicillin V, then amoxicillin with clavulanic acid may be a good alternative in patients not allergic to penicillin, as the spectrum of sensitivity is altered.

Prophylactic use of antibiotics is recommended before the performance of invasive dental procedures on patients who are at risk of developing bacterial endocarditis (Appendix D) and late prosthetic joint infections (those occurring 6 or more months after placement of the prosthesis) (Appendix E). Injudicious use of antibiotics can have dire consequences, and the clinician must carefully consider, and discuss with the patient, the advantages and disadvantages of prescribing an antibiotic (Appendix F).

In general, there is no advantage in selecting a bactericidal rather than a bacteriostatic antibiotic for the treatment of healthy people. However, if the patient is immunocompromised either by concurrent treatment (such as cancer chemotherapy or drugs associated with a bone-marrow transplant) or by a pre-existing disease (such as HIV infection), a bactericidal antibiotic would be indicated.

For an antimicrobial agent to be useful in the treatment of pathogenic microorganisms, the following criteria should be met:

- the microorganism must be susceptible to the agent;
- the agent must be capable of penetrating to the site of the infection;
- adequate concentrations of the agent must be achieved and maintained at the site of the infection;
- the agent should be low in toxicity to the host but should exhibit selective toxicity to the microorganisms;
- the agent should not readily promote resistance or create a serious imbalance in the normal flora of the host.

This chapter focuses on the compounds that are clinically applicable for treating dental-related bacterial infections and diseases; it also describes agents that dental patients may be receiving as concurrent therapy for medical conditions. Comprehensive coverage of all available antimicrobial agents, and every potential adverse effect that may have been directly or indirectly associated with the use of different antimicrobial agents is not attempted.

The chapter is organized as follows:

- penicillins and cephalosporins;
- macrolides;
- tetracyclines;
- locally delivered antibiotics;
- clindamycin;
- metronidazole;
- quinolones;
- sulfonamides.

Penicillins and Cephalosporins

Antibiotics belonging to these two classes are referred to as "β-lactam antibiotics" owing to the presence of the β-lactam ring common to all drugs in these classes. These drugs are considered bactericidal because they directly result in the death of bacteria by inhibiting specific bacterial enzymes required for the assembly of the bacterial cell wall. Many of the β-lactam antibiotics are rendered inactive by the bacterial production of β-lactamase, an enzyme that hydrolyzes the β-lactam ring and renders the antibiotic inactive. The bacterial production of β-lactamase is the primary reason that treatment with penicillins or cephalosporins can fail.

The cephalosporins and the closely related cephamycins normally are listed together as a single related group and are similar to the penicillins in structure and action. Although penicillins are usually superior for treating dental-related infections, the cephalosporins/cephamycins are included in this chapter because they are used frequently in medical practice and may be encountered in patients seeking dental treatment. Additionally, they may be indicated in the prevention of infections arising from bacteremias of an oral nidus, as in prophylaxis against late prosthetic joint infections.

Accepted Indications

Table 7.1 lists penicillins and cephalosporins and common indications for their use.

General Dosing Information

Table 7.2 provides dosage and prescribing information for oral administration only. These are the dosages more frequently recommended for the treatment of dental-related infections. Higher and more frequent oral dosages may be indicated for severe or life-threatening infections. Other semisynthetic penicillins (azlocillin, mezlocillin, piperacillin, ticarcillin, methicillin) as well as most of the cephalosporins/cephamycins (cephalothin, cephapirin, cefazolin, cefamandole, cefoxitin, cefonicid, cefotaxime, ceftizoxime, ceftazidime, cefoperazone) are available only for intramuscular or intravenous injection owing to poor oral absorption and instability in the presence of gastric acids. These are generally reserved for the treatment of severe infections and diseases that require hospitalization.

Dosage Adjustments

Under normal circumstances, penicillins and cephalosporins are rapidly eliminated from the body primarily through the kidneys and, partly, in the bile and by other routes. In the case of patients with reduced renal function, dosages should be adjusted downward relative to creatinine clearance rates in consultation with the patient's physician. In patients undergoing peritoneal dialysis, an alternative antibiotic should be considered because most penicillins and cephalosporins are effectively removed from the bloodstream by hemodialysis.

Special Dental Considerations

Drug Interactions of Dental Interest

Probenecid, when used concurrently with penicillins and cephalosporins, may decrease renal tubular secretion of these drugs; this may result in increased and prolonged antibiotic blood levels.

The concurrent use of allopurinol with ampicillin, amoxicillin or amoxicillin/clavulanic acid substantially increases the incidence of rashes in patients receiving both drugs relative to that in patients receiving the antibiotic alone.

Table 7.1

Penicillins and Cephalosporins: Characteristics and Common Indications for Use

Generic name	Characteristics	Common indications for use
Penicillins		
Amoxicillin	Similar to ampicillin but yields higher serum levels More rapidly and completely absorbed from stomach than ampicillin Penetrates gingival crevicular fluid well but is hydrolyzed rapidly if significant levels of β-lactamases are present	Has same uses as ampicillin Designed specifically for oral administration Recommended as a prophylactic antibiotic to prevent bacterial endocarditis and late prosthetic joint infections following invasive dental procedures in at-risk patients
Amoxicillin/ clavulanic acid	Has same properties as amoxicillin but is resistant to wide range of β-lactamases Penetrates gingival crevicular fluid well Resistant to most β-lactamases produced by oral bacteria	Broad-spectrum antibiotic with excellent activity against many β-lactamase-producing oral and nonoral bacteria Recommended as a prophylactic antibiotic to prevent late prosthetic joint infections following invasive dental procedures in at-risk patients
Ampicillin	Provides broad-spectrum activity against both gram-negative and gram-positive bacteria Stable to stomach acids and readily absorbed from the stomach Susceptible to β-lactamases	Broad-spectrum penicillin for use against a variety of bacteria that do not produce β-lactamase (for example, *Escherichia coli,* as well as *Neisseria, Haemophilus* and *Proteus* species) For dental patients at risk for bacterial endocarditis and unable to take oral medication, the IM or IV route is recommended

Continued on next page

Table 7.1 (cont.)

Penicillins and Cephalosporins: Characteristics and Common Indications for Use

Generic name	Characteristics	Common indications for use
Penicillins (cont.)		
Carbenicillin indanyl	Stable to gastric acids Relatively resistant to certain β-lactamases produced by gram-negative bacteria	Indicated in the treatment of penicillin-resistant *Proteus* and *Pseudomonas* species
Cloxacillin	Relatively resistant to β-lactamases produced by *Staphylococcus aureus* but not to other bacterial β-lactamases	Use is generally limited to treatment of infections involving β-lactamase-producing staphylococcal microorganisms such as *Staphylococcus aureus*
Dicloxacillin	Same as for cloxacillin	Same as for cloxacillin
Nafcillin	Relatively stable to β-lactamase produced by *Staphylococcus aureus* Inactivated to varying degree by gastric acids Irregular absorption following oral dosage	Primarily used for treatment of infections due to *Staphylococcus aureus*
Oxacillin	Same as for cloxacillin	Same as for cloxacillin
Penicillin G benzathine suspension	Active against most gram-positive but not gram-negative bacteria Unstable to gastric acid Susceptible to β-lactamases Poor and unpredictable absorption after an oral dose, so usually given IM	Drug of choice for wide variety of serious infections, such as pneumococci, meningococcal meningitis, gonorrhea, syphilis, hemolytic streptococci, actinomycosis
Phenoxymethyl-penicillin (Penicillin V)	Activity primarily limited to gram-positive bacteria Stable to stomach acids Susceptive to β-lactamases Readily absorbed from the stomach	Use is limited to treatment of minor infections such as ulcerative gingivostomatitis, and the prophylaxis and continued treatment of streptococcal infections Initial drug of choice for most odontogenic infections
Cephalosporins		
Cefaclor Cefadroxil Cefixime Cefuroxime Cephalexin Cephradine	All can be given orally Primarily excreted through the kidneys	Primary use is the treatment of urinary tract infections Most dental-related infections can be better treated with a penicillin Indicated as a prophylactic antibiotic in dental patients at risk of late prosthetic joint infections and is an alternative in dental patients at risk for bacterial endocarditis with an allergy to penicillin

Table 7.2

Penicillins and Cephalosporins: Oral Dosage and Prescribing Information

Generic name	Brand name(s)	Adult dosage	Max adult dosage	Max child dosage	PRC	Content/form	Oral dosage suggestions
				Penicillins			
Amoxicillin	Amoxil, Polymox, Trimox	250-500 mg q 8 h	4 g/day	**Weight < 20 kg:** 20-40 mg/kg in divided doses tid	B	**Tablets and capsules:** 125, 250, 500 mg **Oral suspension:** 125, 250 mg/5 mL	Given without regard to meals
Amoxicillin/clavulanic acid	Augmentin	250-500 mg q 8 h; 500 mg q 12 h; 875 mg q 12 h*	4.5 g/day	**Weight < 20 kg:** 20-40 mg/kg in divided doses tid	B	**Tablets:** 250, 500, 875 mg **Oral suspension:** 125, 250, 400 mg/5 mL	Given without regard to meals
Ampicillin	Amcill, Omnipen, Polycillin, Principen	250-500 mg q 6 h	4 g/day	**Weight < 20 kg:** 100-200 mg/kg in divided doses qid	B	**Capsules:** 50, 500 mg **Oral suspension:** 125, 500 mg/5 mL	Given 1 h before or 2 h after meal
Bacampicillin	Spectrobid	400-800 mg q 12 h	3.2 g/day	25-50 mg/kg in 2 divided doses	U	**Tablets:** 400 mg **Oral suspension:** 125 mg/5 mL	Given without regard to meals
Carbenicillin	Geocillin	500-1,000 mg q 6 h	**Solution:** 4 g/day **Tablets:** Not listed	NR	U	**Tablets:** 500 mg **Pediatric solution:** not available	Given without regard to meals
Cloxacillin	Cloxapen, Tegopen	250-500 mg q 6 h	6 g/day	**Weight < 20 kg:** 50-100 mg/kg in 4 divided doses qid	B	**Capsules:** 250, 500 mg **Oral suspension:** 125 mg/5 mL	Given 1 h before or 2 h after meal

					PRC		
Dicloxacillin	Dynapen, Dycill, Pathocil	250-500 mg q 6 h	6 g/day	**Weight < 40 kg:** 25 mg/kg as 4 divided doses qid	B	**Capsules:** 125, 250, 500 mg **Oral suspension:** 62.5 mg/5 mL	Given 1-2 h before meal
Nafcillin	Unipen	250-500 mg q 6 h	6 g/day	100-200 mg/kg in divided doses given q 4-6 h	U	**Capsules and tablets:** 100, 250, 500 mg	Given 1 h before or 2 h after meal
Oxacillin	Bactocill, Prostaphlin	500-1,000 mg q 6 h	6 g/day	**Weight < 20 kg:** 50-100 mg/kg administered in a single dose	B	**Capsules:** 50 or 500 mg **Oral suspension:** 250 mg/5 mL	Given 1 h before or 2 h after meal
Penicillin G benzathine suspension†	Penicillin-G, Benzylpenicillin	200,000-800,000 units q 6 h	2,000,000 units/day (1,248 mg/day)	50,000-100,000 units/kg as 2 divided doses	B	**Tablets:** 200,000-800,000 units each	Given 1 h before or 2 h after meal
Phenoxymethyl-penicillin (Penicillin V-potassium)	Betapen-K, Pen-Vee K, Phenoxymethyl-penicillin, V-Cillin K, Veetids	250-500 mg q 6 h	7.2 g/day	**Weight < 20 kg:** 50-100 mg/kg in 4 divided doses qid	B	**Tablets:** 125, 250, 500 mg **Oral suspension:** 125, 250 mg/5 mL	Given without regard to meals
Cephalosporins							
Cefaclor	Ceclor	250 mg q 8 h	4 g/day	**Weight < 20 kg:** 20 mg/kg in divided doses tid	B	**Capsules:** 250, 500 mg **Oral suspension:** 125, 375 mg/5 mL	Given without regard to meals
Cefadroxil	Duricef, Ultracef	500 mg q 12 h or 1,000 mg/day	4 g/day	**Weight < 40 kg:** 30 mg/kg in divided doses bid	B	**Capsules:** 500 mg **Oral suspension:** 125, 500 mg/5 mL	Given without regard to meals

Continued on next page

PRC: Pregnancy risk category.
NR: Not recommended.
U: Unavailable.
* For severe infections.
† Also available as salt of potassium or sodium or in combination with procaine (parenteral only).

Table 7.2 (cont.)
Penicillins and Cephalosporins: Oral Dosage and Prescribing Information

Generic name	Brand name(s)	Adult dosage	Max adult dosage	Max child dosage	PRC	Content/form	Oral dosage suggestions
		Cephalosporins (cont.)					
Cefixime	Suprax	200 mg q 12 h or 400 mg q day	U	**Weight < 40 kg:** 8 mg/kg in single dose or divided doses bid	B	**Tablets:** 200, 400 mg **Oral suspension:** 100 mg/5 mL	Given without regard to meals
Cefuroxime	Ceftin	250 mg q 12 h	U	**Age < 12 y:** 125 mg bid for child under 12 years of age	B	**Tablets:** 125, 250, 500 mg	Given without regard to meals
Cephalexin	Biocef, Cefanex, Keftab, Keflex	250 mg q 6 h or 500 mg q 12 h	4 g/day	**Weight < 40 kg:** 25-50 mg/kg in divided doses bid	B	**Tablets:** 250, 500 mg **Oral suspension:** 125, 250 mg/5mL	Given without regard to meals
Cephradine	Anspor, Velosef	250 or 500 mg q 6 h	4 g/day	**Weight < 40 kg:** 25-50 mg/kg in divided doses bid	B	**Capsules:** 250, 500 mg **Oral suspension:** 125, 250 mg/5mL	Given without regard to meals

PRC: Pregnancy risk category.
U: Unavailable.

Amoxicillin/clavulanic acid should not be coadministered with the antiabuse drug disulfiram.

Table 7.3 lists possible interactions between penicillins and cephalosporins and other drugs.

Laboratory Value Alterations
- High urine concentrations of a penicillin or cephalosporin may result in false-positive reactions when the urine is tested for the presence of glucose using certain commercially available test kits.

Cross-Sensitivity
Before initiating therapy with any penicillin or cephalosporin, careful inquiry should be made concerning previous hypersensitivity reactions to any penicillin, cephalosporin, or other allergens. Serious and occasionally fatal hypersensitivity (anaphylactoid) reactions have been reported in patients receiving penicillin or cephalosporin therapy. These reactions are more apt to occur in people with a history of penicillin and/or cephalosporin hypersensitivity and/or a history of sensitivity to multiple allergens. Penicillins and cephalosporins should be used with caution in patients who have a history of significant allergies and/or asthma. Because of the similarity in the structure of the penicillins and cephalosporins, patients allergic to one class may manifest cross-reactivity to members of the other class. Cross-reactivity to cephalosporins may occur in as many as 20% of the patients who are allergic to penicillins.

Special Patients
Pregnant and nursing women
Penicillins and cephalosporins are secreted in human breast milk, and caution should be exercised when a drug from either group is administered to nursing women. Clinical experience with the penicillins and cephalosporins during pregnancy has not shown any evidence of adverse effects on the fetus. However, there have been no adequate and well-controlled studies in pregnant women that show conclusively that harmful effects of these drugs on the fetus can be ruled out.

Table 7.3

Penicillins and Cephalosporins: Possible Interactions With Other Drugs

Drug taken by patient	Interaction with penicillins and cephalosporins	Dentist's action
Allopurinol	Concurrent use with ampicillin, amoxicillin or amoxicillin with clavulanic acid increases incidence of rashes	Monitor for signs of rash and any need for switching to another antibiotic
Oral contraceptives, combined estrogen and progestin	There have been sporadic reports of reduced oral contraceptive effectiveness in women taking ampicillin, amoxicillin and penicillin, resulting in unplanned pregnancy; antibiotics may significantly alter the gut flora, thereby possibly interfering with the enterohepatic recycling of the estrogen component of the oral contraceptive and leading to subtherapeutic blood levels and ovulation	Patients should be advised of the possible reduction in effectiveness and encouraged to use an alternate or additional method of contraception while taking these penicillins
Probenecid	May reduce renal tubular secretion of penicillin and cephalosporins, resulting in increased and prolonged antibiotic blood levels	Monitor patient and any need for adjustment of antibiotic dose

Therefore, penicillins and cephalosporins should be used during pregnancy only if clearly needed.

Patient Monitoring: Aspects to Watch

• Patients with a history or suspected history of hypersensitivity to a penicillin or cephalosporin: if given any antibiotic in this class, should be observed for any difficulty in breathing or other sign of allergic reaction for a minimum of 1 h before being released

Adverse Effects and Precautions

Adverse effects, precautions and contraindications related to penicillins and cephalosporins are listed in Table 7.4.

Pharmacology

Penicillins

Because penicillin absorption after oral administration is influenced by the presence of food in the stomach, more predictable blood levels can be obtained if it is given on an empty stomach. Alternatively, predictable blood levels are also seen when penicillin is given parenterally.

Once absorbed, penicillin is widely distributed throughout the body, including the saliva and gingival crevicular fluid. It does not pass the blood-brain barrier in healthy patients, but in patients with meningitis it does pass through and may be clinically effective. Penicillin is rapidly eliminated from plasma

Table 7.4

Penicillins and Cephalosporins: Adverse Effects, Precautions and Contraindications

Body system	Adverse effects	Precautions/contraindications
General	Hypersensitivity	Up to 10% of all patients may have some sensitivity or allergy
		Mild reactions are often limited to rash or skin lesions of head and neck, but may include facial swelling
		More severe reactions may involve swelling and tenderness of joints
		Hypersensitivity reactions occur more frequently in patients with infectious mononucleosis after they have been treated with ampicillin or amoxicillin
	Superinfection	Superinfection, or overgrowth by resistant bacteria or *Candida*, can occur after prolonged use or high dosage
	Direct toxicity	Rare; most likely to occur in patients who have impaired renal function or in elderly people
CNS	Varied	Reversible hyperactivity, agitation, anxiety, insomnia, confusion and/or dizziness have been reported
GI	Gastric upset	Can range from mild to severe and can include nausea, vomiting, diarrhea, gastritis, stomatitis and enterocolitis; more common with amoxicillin/clavulanic acid and the cephalosporins than with other penicillins
Resp	Anaphylactic or anaphylactoid reactions	Can cause death in highly sensitized subjects; reactions occur after administration by injection more often than by oral route

by the kidneys, crosses the placenta and has been found in cord blood and amniotic fluid.

Penicillins are excreted in breast milk in low concentrations. Although significant problems in humans have not been documented, risk-benefit must be considered, as penicillin use by nursing mothers may lead to sensitization, diarrhea and candidiasis.

Cephalosporins

The cephalosporins pass into most body fluids and tissues in adequate levels to allow their use in the treatment of most infections. They can also pass through the placenta and occur in small amounts in the milk of lactating mothers. Most cephalosporins are excreted unchanged in the urine.

Patient Advice

- In case of the development of any adverse effect (rash; nausea; vomiting; diarrhea; swelling of lips, tongue or face; fever and so forth), the patient should be advised to stop taking the medication and promptly inform the dentist.
- Encourage compliance with the full course of therapy despite improvement in clinical signs and symptoms of an infection.
- There have been reports of reduced oral contraceptive effectiveness in women taking ampicillin, amoxicillin and penicillin, resulting in unplanned pregnancy. Although the association is weak, advise patients of this information and encourage them to use an alternate or additional method of contraception while taking any of these penicillins.

Macrolides

The macrolide group of antibiotics contains approximately 40 compounds, but only a limited few have clinical use. Erythromycin has generally been the most effective and is widely used as an alternative to penicillins for the treatment and prevention of infections caused by gram-positive microorganisms.

Clarithromycin, a semisynthetic macrolide antibiotic, is similar to erythromycin, but has a broader spectrum of activity. Both antibiotics have good activity against most gram-positive bacteria associated with the mouth. Unlike erythromycin, clarithromycin has relatively good activity against a number of gram-negative bacteria.

In recent years, a novel class of antibiotics called the azalides has surfaced. These new macrolide derivatives appear superior to erythromycin and clarithromycin in that they offer better pharmacokinetic properties, excellent tissue distribution, longer therapeutic half-life and activity against many gram-negative and gram-positive bacteria. Of the azalides, azithromycin has received extensive clinical use.

Accepted Indications

Erythromycin, clarithromycin and azithromycin are indicated in the treatment of mild-to-moderate infections involving the upper and lower respiratory tract and for uncomplicated skin and skin structure infections due to susceptible strains of *Staphylococcus aureus*, *Streptococcus pyogenes*, or *Streptococcus agalactiae* (see Table 7.5). These drugs are indicated as an alternate in patients with hypersensitivity to penicillins. Azithromycin is not indicated for use in individuals under 16 years of age or in the treatment of patients with pneumonia who are judged to be inappropriate for outpatient oral therapy.

General Dosing Information

See Table 7.6 for dosage and prescribing information.

Dosage Adjustments

Erythromycin and azithromycin are principally eliminated from the body via the liver. Therefore, dosages and/or the dosage interval should be adjusted when these drugs are administered to a patient with impaired hepatic function. Clarithromycin is eliminated via the liver and kidney and may be administered

Table 7.5

Macrolides: Characteristics and Common Indications for Use

Generic name	Characteristics	Common indications for use
Azithromycin	Broad spectrum of activity for both gram-positive and gram-negative bacteria Given once daily	Indicated in the treatment of patients ≥ age 16 y who have mild-to-moderate infections Alternative prophylactic antibiotic for dental patients at risk of bacterial endocarditis and allergic to penicillin Alternative to penicillin G and other penicillins for treatment of gram-positive coccoid infections in patients with hypersensitivity to penicillins
Clarithromycin	Active against gram-positive and many gram-negative bacteria	Treatment of mild-to-moderate respiratory infections and uncomplicated skin infections Alternative prophylactic antibiotic for dental patients at risk of bacterial endocarditis and allergic to penicillin Alternative to penicillin G and other penicillins for treatment of gram-positive coccoid infections in patients with hypersensitivity to penicillins
Erythromycin base	Active against gram-positive bacteria, particularly gram-positive cocci Provides only limited activity against gram-negative bacteria Yields irregular and unpredictable serum levels Given during a fasting state	Treatment of upper and lower respiratory tract, skin and soft tissue infections of mild-to-moderate severity Alternative to penicillin G and other penicillins for treatment of gram-positive coccoid infections in patients with hypersensitivity to penicillins
Erythromycin ethylsuccinate	Activity same as for erythromycin base	Uses same as for erythromycin base
Erythromycin stearate	Activity same as for erythromycin base Less subject to gastric acids than erythromycin base Yields more predictable serum levels	Uses same as for erythromycin base

without dosage adjustment in patients with hepatic impairment and normal renal function. However, in the presence of severe renal impairment with or without coexisting hepatic impairment, decreased dosage or prolonged dosage intervals may be appropriate. Hepatotoxicity has been associated rarely with all erythromycin salts, but more frequently with erythromycin estolate.

Special Dental Considerations

Drug Interactions of Dental Interest
Concurrent use of theophylline, digoxin, astemizole, terfenadine, cisapride or pimozide and erythromycin or clarithromycin is contraindicated because it can result in cardiotoxicity and death. Although a new form of erythromycin, azithromycin, has not been

Table 7.6

Macrolides: Oral Dosage and Prescribing Information

Generic name	Brand name(s)	Adult dosage	Max adult dosage	Max child dosage	PRC	Content/form	Oral dosage suggestions
Azithromycin	Zithromax	500 mg initial loading dose, followed by single dose of 250 mg/day	U	**Age < 16 y:** Safety not clearly established for children	B	**Capsules:** 250 mg	Given 1 h before or 2 h after meal
Clarithromycin	Biaxin	250-500 mg q 12 h	U	**Age < 12 y:** Safety not established	C	**Tablets:** 250, 500 mg	May be given without regard to meals
Erythromycin base	E-Mycin, Ery-Tab, Erythromycin Base Filmtab	250 mg q 6 h	4 g/day	30-50 mg/kg in divided doses qid	B	**Tablets:** 250, 500 mg	Given 1 h before or 2 h after meal
Erythromycin ethylsuccinate	E.E.S., Pediamycin, Eryped, Erythro	400 mg q 6 h	4 g/day	30-50 mg/kg in divided doses qid	B	**Tablets:** 400 mg **Oral suspension:** 200, 400 mg/ 5 mL	May be given without regard to meals
Erythromycin stearate	Erypar, Erythrocin, Erythrocot	250 mg q 6 h	4 g/day	30-50 mg/kg in divided doses qid	B	**Tablets:** 250, 500 mg	Given 1 h before or 2 h after meal

PRC: Pregnancy risk category.
U: Unavailable.

reported to be implicated in this drug interaction, patients receiving concurrent therapy with any of the above medications should be carefully monitored for signs of cardiotoxicity.

The use of erythromycin in patients receiving carbamazepine, cyclosporine, hexobarbital or phenytoin may result in elevated serum levels. Additionally, erythromycin may inhibit the metabolism of carbamazepine and valproic acid, resulting in increased levels of anticonvulsant as well as in toxicity. Erythromycin should be used with caution, if at all, in patients taking carbamazepine or valproic acid. The concurrent use of erythromycin and

ergotamine or dihydroergotamine has been associated with acute ergot toxicity in some patients. Erythromycin has been reported to decrease the clearance rate of triazolam and may increase the pharmacological effect of this drug. Many of the adverse drug interactions that have been reported for erythromycin are being reported for clarithromycin. Drug interaction studies have shown that azithromycin does not share the interactions seen with erythromycin or clarithromycin.

Use of erythromycin in patients receiving warfarin therapy may result in prolongation of prothrombin time and increased risk of

Table 7.7
Macrolides: Possible Interactions With Other Drugs

Drug taken by patient	Interaction with macrolides	Dentist's action
Alfentanil	Enhanced and/or prolonged respiratory depression with concurrent use of erythromycin	Chronic preoperative or perioperative use of erythromycin contraindicated
Astemizole, cisapride, pimozide or terfenadine	Life-threatening ventricular dysrhythmias have been reported with concurrent use of erythromycin or clarithromycin	*Concurrent use of these drugs is contraindicated*
Bromocriptine	Increased risk of adverse CNS effects, dyskinesias and hypotension with concurrent use of erythromycin	*Concurrent use of these drugs is contraindicated*
Carbamazepine	Increased risk of ataxia, vertigo, drowsiness and confusion with concurrent use of erythromycin or clarithromycin	If used concurrently, must be done with great caution
Cyclosporine	Enhanced immunosuppression and nephrotoxicity with concurrent use of erythromycin or clarithromycin	*Concurrent use of these drugs is contraindicated*
Digoxin	Erythromycin can reduce gut flora, in particular *Eubacterium lentum*, which metabolizes a significant amount of oral digoxin in 10% of patients taking digoxin; elevated levels of digoxin may occur, leading to digitalis toxicity with resulting cardiac dysrhythmias Clarithromycin has also been reported to result in elevated levels of digoxin, yet the mechanism is not clear	*Concurrent use of these drugs is contraindicated*
Felodipine	Increased risk of hypotension, tachycardia and edema with concurrent use of erythromycin	*Concurrent use of these drugs is contraindicated*
Lovastatin	Muscle pain and skeletal muscle lysis with concurrent use of erythromycin	*Concurrent use of these drugs is contraindicated*
Oral contraceptives, estrogen and progestin combined	There have been sporadic reports of reduced oral contraceptive effectiveness in women taking erythromycin and clarithromycin, resulting in unplanned pregnancy; antibiotics may significantly alter the gut flora, thereby possibly interfering with the enterohepatic recycling of the estrogen component of the oral contraceptive and leading to subtherapeutic blood levels and ovulation	Patients should be advised of possible reduction in effectiveness and encouraged to use an alternate or additional method of contraception while taking these macrolides
Theophylline	Increased risk of tachycardia, cardiac dysrhythmias, tremors and seizures has been reported with concurrent use of erythromycin or clarithromycin	*Concurrent use of these drugs is contraindicated*

Italics indicate information of major clinical significance.

Continued on next page

Table 7.7 (cont.)
Macrolides: Possible Interactions With Other Drugs

Drug taken by patient	Interaction with macrolides	Dentist's action
Triazolam or midazolam	Marked increases in blood levels of both benzodiazepines leading to increases in sedative depth and duration are reported with concurrent use of erythromycin	*Concurrent use of these drugs is contraindicated*
Warfarin	Erythromycin and clarithromycin decrease the metabolism of warfarin and may significantly increase prothrombin and/or INR times and increase the risk of serious bleeding in patients receiving anticoagulation therapy	Warfarin dosage adjustments may be necessary during and after therapy and prothrombin or INR times should be monitored closely

Italics indicate information of major clinical significance.

hemorrhage, especially in elderly people. Prothrombin times should be monitored closely.

Aluminum- and magnesium-containing antacids reduce the peak serum levels obtained with azithromycin.

Concurrent use with ampicillin, gentamicin and cefamanadole can antagonize the action of these drugs. Concurrent use with clindamycin is contraindicated because of similar modes of action.

Table 7.7 lists possible interactions between macrolides and other drugs.

Laboratory Value Alterations
- There are no reported laboratory test alterations for azithromycin or clarithromycin.
- Erythromycin interferes with the fluorometric determination of urinary catecholamines.

Cross-Sensitivity
Erythromycin, azithromycin or clarithromycin are contraindicated in patients with known hypersensitivity to any of the macrolide antibiotics.

Special Patients
Pregnant and nursing women
Clarithromycin should not be used in pregnant women except in clinical circumstances in which no alternative therapy is appropriate. If pregnancy occurs while taking the

drug, the patient should be advised that clarithromycin has demonstrated teratogenicity in animals, but as of yet not in humans. Although no evidence of impaired fertility or harm to the fetus has been found with either erythromycin or azithromycin, these drugs should be used during pregnancy only if needed.

Erythromycin and clarithromycin are secreted in human breast milk and should be used with caution in nursing mothers. As it is not known if azithromycin is secreted in human breast milk, the same cautions should be applied to this drug as well.

Pediatric, geriatric and other special patients
The safety of clarithromycin has not been established for children aged < 12 y, and the safety of azithromycin has not been established for children and youths aged < 16 y.

Dosage adjustment does not appear to be necessary in elderly patients who have normal renal and hepatic function.

Adverse Effects and Precautions
Serious adverse effects are rarely encountered with these drugs. The majority of the side-effects associated with erythromycin, azithromycin and clarithromycin have been of a mild and transient nature. The most frequently reported events have been diarrhea, nausea, abnormal taste, dyspepsia, abdominal pain/discomfort and headache (see Table 7.8).

Table 7.8

Macrolides: Adverse Effects, Precautions and Contraindications

Body system	Adverse effects	Precautions/contraindications
General	Shifts in oral flora and possible colonization by exogenous organisms may occur during oral therapy Allergic reactions are rare, but can be manifested as skin rashes Epigastric distress most common side effect	Erythromycin, azithromycin and clarithromycin cross the placenta, and erythromycin and azithromycin should be given during pregnancy with caution; clarithromycin should not be given during pregnancy due to potential adverse effects to fetus Erythromycin and, most likely, azithromycin and clarithromycin are secreted in human breast milk and should be given to nursing mothers with caution Azithromycin is not approved for youths under 16 years and clarithromycin is not approved for children under 12 years
CV	Heart palpitations, chest pain (both extremely rare)	Use with caution in patients with history of cardiac arrhythmias; consider alternate antibiotic
CNS	Dizziness, headache, vertigo (extremely rare)	Transient hearing loss has been associated with large doses of erythromycin in patients with renal impairment
GI	Nausea, vomiting, abdominal pain and diarrhea (all relatively common but rarely severe)	Dose-related, more common in children and young adults
GU	Vaginitis (extremely rare)	More common in patients with history of antibiotic-associated vaginitis
HB	Hepatotoxicity Nephritis (extremely rare)	Caution should be exercised if administrated to patients with impaired hepatic function Cholestatic hepatitis may occur with erythromycin estolate but rarely with other forms

Pharmacology

The macrolides inhibit bacterial protein synthesis by binding reversibly to the 50S ribosomal subunits of sensitive bacteria. Erythromycin base is incompletely absorbed from the upper part of the small intestine. The drug is inactivated by gastric acid and is thus administered as protected tablets or capsules that dissolve in the duodenum. Food in the stomach delays the drug's ultimate absorption. The esters of erythromycin, erythromycin stearate and ethylsuccinate provide greater stability and facilitate absorption. Both clarithromycin and azithromycin are better absorbed than erythromycin and yield higher serum levels.

The macrolides diffuse readily into intracellular fluids, and antibacterial activity can be achieved at essentially all body sites with the exception of the brain and cerebrospinal fluid.

Patient Advice

• Any of these drugs may cause gastric discomfort and may result in diarrhea, abdominal cramping, nausea, unpleasant taste and/or headache.

- Clarithromycin may have adverse effects on fetal development and should not be taken by pregnant patients; use of this drug should be immediately stopped if pregnancy occurs.

Tetracyclines

The tetracyclines, which include tetracycline, doxycycline and minocycline, all have essentially the same spectrum of activity. They are considered to be bacteriostatic at normal dosages and inhibit bacterial protein synthesis in sensitive bacteria by binding to the 30S ribosomal subunits and preventing the addition of amino acids to the growing peptide chain. At high concentrations, the tetracyclines are bactericidal and may inhibit protein synthesis in mammalian cells.

The advantage of using either doxycycline or minocycline, rather than tetracycline, is that the former two antibiotics are absorbed better after oral administration. This greater absorption results in higher serum levels and a lesser need for frequent dosing. Unfortunately, resistance to one tetracycline often indicates resistance to all tetracyclines.

Accepted Indications

The tetracyclines are broad-spectrum antibiotics and as such are frequently indicated in the treatment of gram-positive and gram-negative bacterial infections of the head and neck as well as other regions of the body (see Table 7.9). Dental applications include the adjunctive treatment of refractory periodontitis and juvenile periodontitis, dental abscesses, soft tissue abscesses, and as an alternative when penicillins are contraindicated or when β-lactamase-producing microorganisms are involved. Due to bacterial resistance, the tetra-

Table 7.9

Tetracyclines: Characteristics and Common Indications for Use

Generic name	Characteristics	Common indications for use
Doxycycline hyclate	Has the same characteristics as tetracycline except that it is absorbed more completely following oral administration and yields higher serum levels	Uses same as for tetracycline (below)
Minocycline hydrochloride	Has the same characteristics as tetracycline except that it is absorbed more completely following oral administration and yields higher serum levels More lipophilic than doxycycline and provides better tissue penetration	Uses same as for tetracycline (below)
Tetracycline hydrochloride	Broad-spectrum antibiotic with activity against gram-positive and gram-negative bacteria, mycoplasmas, rickettsial and chlamydial infections	Adjunctive treatment of adult periodontitis and juvenile periodontitis Treatment of acute necrotizing ulcerative gingivitis and dental abscesses Alternative to penicillins for treatment of actinomycosis and other oral infections

cyclines are not indicated in the treatment of streptococcal or staphylococcal infections.

Resistance to tetracycline-HCl has become so widespread that this drug is rarely used in clinical medicine. However, the drug still appears to be beneficial in the treatment of certain dental infections, including periodontitis, that do not respond favorably to conventional periodontal therapy.

Subantimicrobial-Dose Doxycycline

The U.S. Food and Drug Administration has approved the use of a subantimicrobial dose (20 mg bid, or q 12 h) of doxycycline hyclate as an adjunctive periodontal therapy. Although this drug is classified as an antibiotic, the mechanism of action is suppression of collagenase, particularly that which is produced by polymorphonuclear leukocytes, and so the drug is not necessarily antimicrobial. As the dose is too low to affect bacteria, resistance to this medication should not develop. The therapeutic objective is to modulate the inflammatory host response, not necessarily kill bacteria. Since a subantimicrobial dose of doxycycline hyclate has no antibacterial properties, it is important that it be used as an adjunct to mechanical therapy.

Treatment with a subantimicrobial dose of doxycycline hyclate, 20 mg q 12 h, in conjunction with either dental prophylaxis or scaling and root planing, significantly and consistently improved clinical signs of periodontal disease in clinical trials. A subantimicrobial dose of doxycycline hyclate represents the application of the concept of host modulation to the treatment of periodontal disease.

Clinical studies suggest that in patients with adult periodontitis, continuous therapy may not be necessary after completion of definitive periodontal care. Rather, a cyclical therapy—which can range from 2 months of dosing followed by 2 months of cessation of therapy to 9 months of dosing followed by 3 months of cessation of therapy—has been shown to be effective. Each patient must be monitored to determine the appropriate therapeutic cycle and redosing time. In a study of daily therapy with a subantimicrobial dose of doxycycline hyclate (20 mg bid), periodontal parameters remained stable 3 months after cessation of 9 months of therapy.

Safety studies showed that use of a subantimicrobial dose of doxycycline hyclate twice daily was well-tolerated, and that the rates and types of adverse events were not different than those associated with placebos. Furthermore, the dose demonstrated neither an antimicrobial effect on the periodontal microflora nor a shift in normal flora. Lastly, there was no evidence of the development of multiantibiotic resistance.

General Dosing Information

See Table 7.10 for dosage and prescribing information.

Dosage Adjustments

Because tetracyclines have been shown to depress plasma prothrombin activity, patients receiving anticoagulant therapy may require downward adjustment of the anticoagulant dosage.

If renal impairment exists, the recommended doses for any tetracycline may lead to excessive systemic accumulation of the antibiotic and, possibly, liver toxicity. The antianabolic action of the tetracyclines may cause an increase in blood urea nitrogen. In patients with significant renal insufficiency, this may lead to azotemia, hyperphosphatemia and acidosis. Total dosages of any tetracycline should therefore be decreased in patients with renal impairment by reduction of recommended individual doses and/or by extending the time between doses.

Special Dental Considerations

Drug Interactions of Dental Interest

Table 7.11 lists possible interactions between the tetracyclines and other drugs.

As described above, the tetracyclines may depress plasma prothrombin activity and should be used with caution in patients receiving anticoagulant therapy.

Table 7.10

Tetracyclines: Oral Dosage and Prescribing Information

Generic name	Brand name(s)	Adult dosage	Max adult dosage	Max child dosage	PRC	Content/form	Dosage suggestions
Doxycycline	Doryx, Doxycin, Doxylin, Monodox, Vibramycin, Vibra-tabs	100 mg q 12 h on 1st day, followed by 100 mg/day as either single dose or 50 mg q 12 h	300 mg/day	**Age > 8 y:** 4 mg/kg divided into equal doses bid on 1st day, followed by 2 mg/kg as single dose or divided into equal doses bid	D	**Capsules:** 50, 100 mg **Oral suspension:** 25 or 50 mg/5 mL	Given 1 h before or 2 h after meal
	Atridox ★ *	Single injection of gel into periodontal pocket; repeat at 4 mo	One injection/pocket/7 days	NR	D	**Gel syringe:** 10%	One dose delivers local antibacterial concentrations for 7 days
	Periostat†	20 mg q 12 h	20 mg q 12 h	NR	D	**Capsules:** 20 mg	Given 1 h before or 2 h after meal
Minocycline hydrochloride	Dynacin, Minocin	200 mg loading dose, followed by 100 mg q 12 h	350 mg on 1st day, then 200 mg/day	**Age > 8 y:** 4 mg/kg initially, followed by 2 mg/kg bid	D	**Capsules:** 50, 100 mg **Oral suspension:** 50 mg/5 mL	Given 1 h before or 2 h after meal
Tetracycline hydrochloride	Achromycin, Achromycin V, Sumycin	250 mg q 6 h	4 g/day	**Age > 8 y:** 25-50 mg/kg in equal doses bid	D	**Capsules:** 250, 500 mg **Oral suspension:** 125 mg/5 mL	Given 1 h before or 2 h after meal
	Actisite*	Place one fiber into periodontal pocket for 7-10 days	One fiber/pocket/7-10 days	NR	D	**Fiber:** 12.7 mg/23 cm	Remove fiber in 7-10 days

★ *indicates a drug bearing the ADA Seal of Acceptance.*

PRC: *Pregnancy risk category.*

NR: *Not recommended.*

* *Locally delivered sustained-release system.*

† *At this dose, not antibacterial, but modulates the inflammatory host response.*

Table 7.11

Tetracyclines: Possible Interactions With Other Drugs

Drug taken by patient	Interaction with tetracyclines	Dentist's action
Combinations containing any of the following: antacids, calcium, magnesium, aluminum, iron supplements, sodium bicarbonate	Tetracycline molecules chelate divalent and trivalent cations, impairing absorption	Patients should be advised not to take these medications within 1-3 h of taking oral tetracycline
Cholestyramine or cholestipol	Concurrent use may result in binding of oral tetracycline, thus impairing their absorption	Patient should be advised not to take these medications within 1-3 h of taking oral tetracycline
Digoxin	Tetracycline can reduce gut flora, in particular *Eubacterium lentum*, which metabolizes a significant amount of oral digoxin in 10% of patients taking digoxin; elevated levels of digoxin may occur, leading to digitalis toxicity with resulting cardiac dysrhythmias Clarithromycin also has been reported to result in elevated levels of digoxin, yet the mechanism is not clear	*Concurrent use of these drugs is contraindicated*
Methoxyflurane	Concurrent use may increase the potential for nephrotoxicity	*Concurrent use of these drugs is contraindicated*
Oral contraceptives, estrogen and progestin combined	There have been sporadic reports of reduced oral contraceptive effectiveness in women taking tetracyclines, resulting in unplanned pregnancy; antibiotics may significantly alter the gut flora, thereby possibly interfering with the enterohepatic recycling of the estrogen component of the oral contraceptive and leading to subtherapeutic blood levels and ovulation; the clinical significance of this interaction is under review	Patients should be advised of the possible reduction in the effectiveness and encouraged to use an alternate or additional method of contraception while taking these tetracyclines until this issue is clarified
Warfarin	Tetracycline may decrease the metabolism of warfarin and may significantly increase prothrombin and/or INR times and increase the risk of serious bleeding in patients receiving anticoagulation therapy	Warfarin dosage adjustments may be necessary during and after therapy, and prothrombin or INR times should be monitored closely

Italics indicate information of major clinical significance.

The concurrent use of tetracycline and methoxyflurane has been reported to result in fatal renal toxicity.

Because bacteriostatic antibiotics such as the tetracyclines may interfere with the bactericidal action of penicillins and cephalosporins, it is not advisable to administer these antibiotics concomitantly.

Concurrent use of tetracyclines with oral contraceptives may render the contraceptives less effective.

Divalent cations bind the tetracyclines to varying degrees. Therefore, bismuth subsalicylate and antacids containing aluminum, calcium or magnesium interfere with the absorption of these antibiotics and should not be ingested at the same time as a tetracycline.

Laboratory Value Alterations

- False elevations of urinary catecholamine levels may occur due to interference with the fluorescence test.

Cross-Sensitivity

A hypersensitivity or allergic reaction to one tetracycline is indicative of hypersensitivity to all other tetracyclines.

Special Patients

Pregnant and nursing women

All tetracyclines cross the placenta and form a stable calcium complex in bone-forming tissue. Consequently, use of tetracyclines is not recommended during the last half of pregnancy, as the drugs may cause permanent discoloration of teeth, enamel hypoplasia and inhibition of skeletal growth in the fetus.

Although previous recommendations advised against prescribing tetracycline in nursing mothers, the latest statement of the American Academy of Pediatrics considers tetracycline safe in nursing mothers.

Pediatric, geriatric and other special patients

Tetracycline drugs should not be used in children aged ≤ 8 y because these drugs may cause permanent discoloration of the teeth.

Concurrent, long-term use of tetracyclines with estrogen-containing oral contraceptives may result in reduced contraceptive reliability. Patients should be advised of this information and encouraged to use an alternative or additional method of contraception while taking any tetracycline.

Adverse Effects and Precautions

The adverse effects of and precautions and contraindications related to the tetracyclines are listed in Table 7.12.

Pharmacology

The tetracyclines are readily absorbed from the gastrointestinal tract after oral administration. Most of the absorption takes place in the stomach and upper small intestine and is greater in the fasting state. The tetracyclines are distributed throughout the body and readily penetrate soft tissues, the CNS and the brain. The drugs readily cross the placenta and enter the fetal circulation and amniotic fluid. Relatively high concentrations are also present in breast milk. The drugs are stored in the reticuloendothelial cells of the liver, spleen and bone marrow, and in the bone, dentin and enamel of unerupted teeth.

Excretion is via the urine and feces; the primary route is the kidneys. However, renal clearance of minocycline is much lower than tetracycline and persists in the body long after administration is stopped. Doxycycline is not eliminated by the same pathways as are the other tetracyclines and does not accumulate significantly in the blood of patients with renal failure.

Patient Advice

- Photosensitivity manifested by an exaggerated sunburn may occur in patients taking tetracyclines. Patients apt to be exposed to direct light or ultraviolet light should be advised that this reaction can occur and that the dosage should be discontinued at the first evidence of skin erythema. This reaction is relatively rare with minocycline.
- Patients who experience central nervous system symptoms should be cautioned against driving vehicles or operating hazardous machinery while taking minocyclines.
- Concurrent use of tetracyclines may render oral contraceptives less effective. Patients should be informed about the risks of becoming pregnant during the time they are taking tetracyclines and encouraged to use alternative or additional methods of contraception.
- If patients are taking calcium-containing products, iron or antacids, they should not be given tetracyclines, with the exception of doxycycline.

Table 7.12

Tetracyclines: Adverse Effects, Precautions and Contraindications

Body system	Adverse effects	Precautions/contraindications
General	Benign intracranial hypertension	Manifested as headache and blurred vision
CNS	Dizziness, vertigo and tinnitus may occur with minocycline	Avoid operating vehicles or hazardous machinery
GI	Nausea, heartburn, epigastric pain, vomiting and diarrhea relatively common with oral administration Superinfection or overgrowth of intestinal flora by tetracycline-resistant organisms	Avoid taking medication immediately before bedtime to help alleviate symptoms of epigastric distress and heartburn
HB	Mild leukopenia	Should not be used when patients are taking anticoagulants such as coumarin, heparin and protoamine because of depressed plasma prothrombin; use with these anticoagulants could require downward adjustment of the anticoagulant
Integ	Maculopapular and erythematous rashes Photosensitivity	Avoid direct sunlight if possible; use of sunscreen may be recommended Stop dosage if skin erythema occurs
Oral	Deposits in the calcifying areas of the bones and teeth and permanent discoloration when administered to children < age 8 y Superinfection or overgrowth of oral flora by tetracycline-resistant organisms	Do not administer to children < age 8 y or to pregnant women Minocycline may produce a grayish pigmentation in gingiva and may discolor permanent, erupted teeth
Renal	Increase in blood urea nitrogen	Adjusted dosages required if renal impairment exists

Locally Delivered Antibiotics

There is evidence that locally delivered, sustained-release antimicrobial agents—such as doxycycline hyclate gel (10%), tetracycline ethylene/vinyl acetate copolymer fiber (12.7 mg/9 in) and minocycline hydrochloride gel (2%)—are effective in the treatment of periodontal pockets that do not respond to scaling and root planing. The general benefit of locally delivered, sustained-release antibiotics is the achievement of high site concentrations of antibiotic with low systemic drug levels. Accordingly, one is able to reduce the putative pathogenic bacteria while minimizing the risk of adverse systemic side effects.

Accepted Indications

Ethylene/vinyl acetate copolymer fiber containing tetracycline 12.7 mg/9 in. (Actisite) is packed into a periodontal pocket. It is well-tolerated by oral tissues, and for 10 days it maintains tetracycline levels necessary to inhibit growth of pathogens in the periodontal pocket. It is "sealed" in the pocket with cyanoacrylate. Thus, controlled, site-specific delivery of antibacterial agents can be achieved at approximately 1/1,000th of the systemic dose. Tetracycline fibers used in conjunction with scaling and root planing have been shown to be more effective than scaling and root planing alone.

Clinical studies suggest that subgingival delivery of doxycycline hyclate 10% has a potential periodontal benefit. Doxycycline gel injected into a periodontal pocket through a syringe system is intended to deliver an antibacterial concentration for 7-14 days. The effects of doxycycline on attachment level gain and probing depth reduction were equivalent to those of scaling and root planing. After placement, the material is sealed into a pocket with either a periodontal dressing or cyanoacrylate. In clinical studies, a second placement occurred 4 months after the initial treatment. Only the tetracycline fiber and doxycycline hyclate gel are discussed in Table 7.10, because as of this writing they alone have been cleared by the FDA for use in humans. A chip containing chlorhexidine (PerioChip) is discussed under chlorhexidine in Chapter 11.

General Dosing Information

Table 7.10 provides dosage and prescribing information for doxycycline hyclate gel and tetracycline fiber.

Adverse Effects and Precautions

The most common side effect of sustained-release antibiotic agents is localized erythema and rare occurrences of localized candidiasis. The clinician should keep in mind the potential side effects of antibiotics described earlier such as development of resistant strains or increased growth of opportunistic organisms—when considering prescription of local sustained-release antibiotics for periodontal pocket delivery.

Patient Advice

- Until more evidence becomes available, the clinician would be prudent to advise patients receiving locally delivered antibiotics in the same manner as he or she would those taking the antibiotic in its oral form. Please refer to the section on Patient Advice for each antibiotic.
- Inform the patient that 7-10 days after placement of the tetracycline-impregnated fiber, he or she will have to return for removal of the fiber.

Clindamycin

Clindamycin is a semisynthetic derivative of lincomycin. Although not structurally related to erythromycin, it shares the same primary mode of action in that it binds to the 50S ribosomal subunits and inhibits bacterial protein synthesis in sensitive organisms (bacteriostatic). At higher concentrations, clindamycin can be bacteriocidal. Clindamycin is relatively active against gram-positive and gram-negative anaerobic bacteria, including most of those associated with the mouth. Essentially, all gram-negative aerobic bacteria are resistant.

Accepted Indications

Clindamycin is generally reserved for the treatment of serious infections of the respiratory tract, skin and soft tissue, female genital tract, intra-abdominal infections and abscesses, and septicemia involving gram-positive and/or gram-negative anaerobes, streptococci, staphylococci, and mixed infections involving anaerobes and facultative gram-positive bacteria.

However, clindamycin is indicated as a prophylactic antibiotic for dental patients at risk of developing bacterial endocarditis and who are allergic to penicillin and unable to take oral medications. Additionally, clindamycin is effective as adjunctive treatment of chronic and acute osteomyelitis caused by staphylococcus and is an alternative to penicillin V and erythromycin for treatment of orofacial infections. See Table 7.13.

Table 7.13

Clindamycin: Characteristics and Common Indications for Use

Generic name	Characteristics	Common indications for use
Clindamycin hydrochloride	Active against most gram-positive bacteria, including many staphylococcal and streptococcal species Excellent activity against both gram-positive and gram-negative anaerobic bacteria	Treatment of severe infections caused by anaerobic bacteria Adjunct to treatment of adult refractory periodontitis Adjunct to treatment of chronic and acute osteomyelitis caused by staphylococcus Alternative to penicillin and erythromycin for treating orofacial infections Alternative prophylactic antibiotic for dental patients allergic to penicillin and unable to take oral medication

Table 7.14

Clindamycin: Oral Dosage and Prescribing Information

Generic name	Brand name(s)	Adult dosage	Max adult dosage	Max child dosage	PRC	Content/ form	Oral dosage suggestions
Clindamycin hydrochloride	Cleocin HCl, Cleocin Pediatric	150-300 mg q 6 h	1.8 g/24 h	8-12 mg/ kg/day in 3-4 equally divided doses	B	**Capsules:** 75, 150, 300 mg **Oral suspension:** 75 mg/ 5 mL	Given with full glass of water or with meals to avoid esophageal ulceration

PRC: Pregnancy risk category.

General Dosing Information

See Table 7.14 for dosage and prescribing information.

Dosage Adjustments

In patients with severe renal and/or hepatic impairment, clindamycin should be administered only for very severe infections, with the dosages and dosage intervals adjusted accordingly.

Special Dental Considerations

Drug Interactions of Dental Interest

Table 7.15 lists possible interactions between clindamycin and other drugs.

Clindamycin has been shown to have neuromuscular blocking properties that may enhance the action of other neuromuscular blocking agents and should be used with caution in patients receiving such agents.

Cross-Sensitivity

There are no cross-sensitivities reported between clindamycin and any other antibiotic group. However, the 75- and 150-mg capsules of clindamycin hydrochloride contain FD&C Yellow no. 5 (tartrazine), which may cause allergic reactions in some patients with hypersensitivity to aspirin.

Special Patients

Pregnant and nursing women

Clindamycin is secreted in breast milk in sufficient concentrations to cause disturbances of the intestinal flora of infants and should not be administered to nursing mothers

Table 7.15

Clindamycin: Possible Interactions With Other Drugs

Drug taken by patient	Interaction with clindamycin	Dentist's action
Antidiarrheals	Concurrent use of clindamycin and anti-diarrheals containing kaolin or attapulgite may delay the absorption of oral clindamycin	Concurrent use is contraindicated; otherwise, patients should be advised to take absorbent antidiarrheals not less than 2 h before or 3-4 h after taking oral clindamycin
Narcotic analgesics	Concurrent use with clindamycin may possibly lead to increased or prolonged respiratory depression or paralysis (apnea)	If concurrent use of these drugs is necessary, caution and careful monitoring of the patient's respiration are recommended
Neuromuscular blocking agents	Concurrent use with clindamycin may enhance the blockade, resulting in skeletal muscle weakness and respiratory depression or paralysis	Avoid concurrent use; if such use is necessary, patient should be carefully monitored for muscle weakness or respiratory depression as a result of concurrent use

unless warranted by clinical circumstances. Jaundice and abnormalities in liver function tests also may occur.

The safety of clindamycin for use during pregnancy has not been established.

Pediatric, geriatric and other special patients Clindamycin should not be administered to older patients who have an associated severe illness that may render them more susceptible to diarrhea.

The drug should be administered with caution to any patient with a history of gastrointestinal disease, particularly colitis, or to a patient with severe renal disease and/or severe hepatic disease.

Adverse Effects and Precautions

Any broad-spectrum antibiotic therapy may result in the disturbance of the normal intestinal flora and lead to colonization by the opportunistic pathogen *Clostridium difficile*. This may result in a severe form of colitis, referred to as "pseudomembraneous colitis," which can be fatal. The disease may begin during therapy, or it may be delayed for several weeks after the cessation of therapy. Although the disease can occur after therapy with a number of antibiotics, its incidence has

been higher after the use of the intravenous form of clindamycin (clindamycin phosphate). However, it has been reported to occur after the use of oral clindamycin hydrochloride as well. Therefore, the drug always should be used with caution and reserved for severe infections that are not amenable to other therapy. See Table 7.16.

Pharmacology

Clindamycin is nearly completely absorbed from the stomach after oral administration and the absorption is not appreciably influenced by the presence of food. The drug is widely distributed to many fluids and tissues, including bone. However, significant concentrations are not obtained in the cerebrospinal fluid even if the meninges are inflamed. The drug readily crosses the placental barrier and enters the fetal circulation. Clindamycin concentrates in the polymorphonuclear leukocytes and alveolar macrophages and in soft-tissue abscesses.

The drug is excreted in the urine and the feces. Antimicrobial activity may persist in the colonic contents for up to 1 w after therapy is stopped, and the growth of sensitive microorganisms in the colon may be suppressed for up to 2 w.

Table 7.16

Clindamycin: Adverse Effects, Precautions and Contraindications

Body system	Adverse effects	Precautions/contraindications
General	Generalized mild-to-moderate skin rashes due to hypersensitivity to clindamycin (appear in up to 10% of patients) Hypersensitivity reactions to tartrazine, yellow dye present in some clindamycin capsules (can occur in patients who are allergic to aspirin)	Should be discontinued if hypersensitivity reaction occurs Should be used with caution in patients with aspirin hypersensitivity
GI	Diarrhea, abdominal pain, esophagitis and stomach irritation are relatively common Pseudomembranous colitis (PMC) has been associated with parenteral administration of clindamycin and other antibiotics, but rarely with oral administration (incidence of PMC varies from 0.01-10.00% and appears more frequently in elderly people and patients with history of colitis)	Oral dosages should be taken with food and a full glass of water to help prevent stomach irritation Drug should be discontinued if diarrhea persists and patient immediately referred to a physician
HB	Jaundice and abnormalities in liver function tests have occurred	Use with caution in patients with history of liver disorders; for long-term therapy, monitor liver function tests

Patient Advice

- Dosage should be stopped in the case of persistent diarrhea or severe abdominal pain, or if blood appears in the stool.
- Dosage should be stopped in the event of a skin rash, as this may indicate hypersensitivity to the drug.

Metronidazole

Metronidazole was initially introduced in the 1960s as a treatment for trichomonal vaginitis. The observation that the drug also had a beneficial effect on acute ulcerative gingivitis led to studies culminating in its use in the treatment of anaerobic bacterial infections. Indeed, the drug is still used in the treatment of infections caused by anaerobic protozoa. However, its primary use is in the (bactericidal) treatment of obligate anaerobic bacteria associated with the mouth, the intestinal tract and the female genital tract.

Metronidazole has been used with considerable success as an adjunct to the treatment of periodontitis; this probably is related to its high activity against the gram-negative anaerobic bacilli that are often associated with the disease. The concurrent oral administration of metronidazole with either amoxicillin or amoxicillin/clavulanic acid has been used with some success in the treatment of both juvenile and adult forms of periodontitis. The combination of metronidazole and amoxicillin has been reported to be particularly effective in the treatment of *Actinobacillus actinomycetemcomitans*-associated periodontitis. Additionally, the use of metronidazole and penicillin V for severe mixed odontogenic infections has been a successful adjunct in clinically resolving these infections.

Metronidazole has been used in combination with both amoxicillin and amoxicillin/clavulanic acid for the adjunctive treatment of juvenile periodontitis in those in their late teens and young adults and in the treatment of refractory periodontitis that has not responded favorably to other forms of periodontal therapy. The dosages used for these combination therapies have usually consisted of 250 mg of metronidazole and 250 mg of amoxicillin or amoxicillin/clavulanic acid given concurrently at 8-h intervals (tid) for a period of 7 to 10 days.

Note: The combined use of metronidazole with amoxicillin or amoxicillin/clavulanic acid has not been approved by the U.S. Food and Drug Administration.

Accepted Indications

Metronidazole is generally reserved for the treatment of serious infections of the lower respiratory tract, skin and soft tissue, female genital tract, intra-abdominal infections and abscesses, bones and joints, and bacterial septicemia involving obligate gram-positive anaerobic cocci, gram-negative anaerobic bacilli and *Clostridium* species.

The drug is indicated in the treatment of symptomatic and asymptomatic trichomoniasis in both females and males and in the treatment of amebic dysentery.

Metronidazole is indicated in the treatment of antibiotic-associated colitis and in pseudomembraneous colitis due to infection by *Clostridium difficile* (see Table 7.17).

General Dosing Information

See Table 7.18 for dosage and prescribing information.

Dosage Adjustments

Patients with severe hepatic disease or impairment metabolize metronidazole slowly, with a resultant accumulation in the plasma. For such patients, the drug should be given with caution and the dosages adjusted downward from those normally given. However, for patients receiving renal dialysis, adjustment is not necessary because metronidazole is rapidly removed by dialysis.

Table 7.17
Metronidazole: Characteristics and Common Indications for Use

Generic name	Characteristics	Common indications for use
Metronidazole	Antibacterial activity against all anaerobic cocci and both gram-negative bacilli and gram-positive spore-forming bacilli	Indicated in treatment of trichomoniasis, amebiasis and giardiasis as well as a variety of infections caused by obligate anaerobic bacteria
	Nonsporulating gram-positive bacilli are often resistant as are most facultative bacteria	Indicated in treatment of obligate anaerobic bacterial infections associated with mouth, intestinal tract and female genital tract
		Has been used as adjunct in treatment of periodontitis

Table 7.18
Metronidazole: Oral Dosage and Prescribing Information

Generic name	Brand name(s)	Adult dosage	Max adult dosage	Max child dosage	PRC	Content/form	Oral dosage suggestions
Metronidazole	Flagyl, Protostat	250 mg q 6 h or q 8 h	4 g/day	NR	B	**Tablets:** 250, 500 mg **Oral suspension:** Not available	Given without regard to meals

PRC: Pregnancy risk category.
NR: Not recommended.

In elderly patients, the pharmacokinetics of the drug may be altered and monitoring of serum levels may be necessary to adjust the dosage.

Special Dental Considerations

Drug Interactions of Dental Interest

Metronidazole has been reported to potentiate the anticoagulant effect of warfarin and other oral coumarin anticoagulants, resulting in a prolongation of prothrombin time. Increased blood levels of the gastroesophageal reflux agent cisapride have been demonstrated with concurrent use of metronidazole, possibly leading to serious cardiac dysrhythmias.

The simultaneous administration of drugs that induce microsomal liver enzymes or enzyme activity—such as phenytoin, phenobarbital, or cimetidine—may affect the clearance rate of metronidazole.

In patients stabilized on relatively high doses of lithium, short-term metronidazole therapy has been associated with the elevation of serum lithium and, in some cases, with signs of lithium toxicity.

Abdominal cramping, nausea, vomiting, headache and flushing may occur if alcoholic beverages are consumed during the period of metronidazole administration.

Metronidazole should not be given to patients who are presently taking or have taken in the past 2 w the antiabuse drug disulfiram, since psychotic reactions have been reported when the two drugs are taken concurrently.

Table 7.19 lists possible interactions between metronidazole and other drugs.

Laboratory Value Alterations

- Metronidazole may interfere with certain types of determination of serum chemistry values, and values of 0 may be obtained for aspartate transaminase (AST), serum glutamic-oxaloacetic transaminase (SGOT), alanine amino transferase (ALT), serum glutamate pyruvate transaminase (SGPT), lactic dehydrogenase (LDH), triglycerides and/or hexokinase glucose.

Cross-Sensitivity

Metronidazole is contraindicated in patients with a history of hypersensitivity to metronidazole or any other nitroimidazole derivative.

Special Patients

Pregnant and nursing women

Metronidazole should be used with caution

Table 7.19

Metronidazole: Possible Interactions With Other Drugs

Drug taken by patient	Interaction with metronidazole	Dentist's action
Alcohol	Metronidazole produces a disulfiram effect by allowing accumulation of acetaldehyde, leading to facial flushing, headache, palpitations and nausea	Concurrent use is contraindicated, and use should be delayed at least 1 day after ingestion of alcohol
Anticoagulants	Coumarin or indandione-derived anticoagulants may be potentiated by metronidazole, resulting in increased prothrombin or INR times	Anticoagulant adjustments may be necessary in consultation with the appropriate medical professional
Cimetidine, phenobarbitol, phenytoin	Hepatic clearance rates may be affected by concurrent use of metronidazole	*Concurrent use of these drugs is contraindicated*
Disulfiram	In alcoholic patients, psychotic reactions have been reported in concurrent use or within 2 weeks of use of disulfiram	*Concurrent use of these drugs is contraindicated*

Italics indicate information of major clinical significance.

in pregnant women. Animal reproduction studies have failed to demonstrate teratogenic effects on the fetus, and there are no adequate, well-controlled studies in pregnant women. Metronidazole is distributed in breast milk and has been shown in some animal studies to have a carcinogenic effect and possibly adverse effects in infants. Therefore, its use is not recommended in nursing mothers.

Pediatric, geriatric and other special patients
As the pharmacokinetics of metronidazole may be altered in elderly patients, the drug should be given with caution and only when an alternative antibiotic is not available.

The safety and effectiveness of metronidazole has not been established in children except for the treatment of amebiasis.

Patients with Crohn's disease should not be treated with metronidazole, as the drug may potentiate the tendency for the formation of gastrointestinal and certain extraintestinal cancers.

Patient Monitoring: Aspects to Watch

- In elderly patients or patients with severe hepatic disease or impairment: drug serum levels (to avoid toxicity)

Adverse Effects and Precautions

Several serious adverse reactions have been associated with the use of metronidazole (see Table 7.20). The most serious have been convulsive seizures and peripheral neuropathy, the latter being characterized by numbness or paresthesia of an extremity. Patients should be specifically warned about these reactions and told to stop taking the drug if any neurological symptoms should occur.

The most common adverse effects involve the gastrointestinal tract. Nausea has been reported in approximately 12% of the patients receiving the drug. This may be accompanied by headache, anorexia and, occasionally, vomiting, diarrhea, epigastric distress and abdominal cramping.

Table 7.20
Metronidazole: Adverse Effects, Precautions and Contraindications

Body system	Adverse effects	Precautions/contraindications
General	Nasal congestion, fever, decrease of libido, fleeting joint pains	None of significance to dentistry
CNS	Convulsive seizures, peripheral neuropathy, dizziness, vertigo, ataxia, confusion, irritability, depression, weakness and insomnia	Dosage should be stopped immediately if any neurological symptoms occur
GI	Nausea possibly accompanied by headache, anorexia, vomiting, diarrhea and abdominal cramps (experienced by approximately 12% of patients)	Symptoms of nausea are common and may be lessened if medication is taken at meals
GU	Dysuria, cystitis, polyuria, incontinence and sense of pelvic pressure Urine may be darkened	Use with caution in patients with history of kidney disorders
Oral	Sharp, unpleasant metallic taste is not uncommon Furry tongue, glossitis and stomatitis may occur and are associated with sudden overgrowth of *Candida* Xerostomia	Unpleasant taste may be lessened somewhat if medication is taken with food

Pharmacology

Metronidazole is usually completely and promptly absorbed after oral administration and achieves therapeutic levels in the serum about 1 h after the first dosage. The drug is readily distributed throughout the body and penetrates well into body tissues and fluids, including vaginal secretions, saliva, breast milk and cerebrospinal fluid. In pregnancy, the drug passes the placental barrier and enters the fetal circulation.

The liver is the site for the metabolism of metronidazole and accounts for more than 50% of the systemic clearance. However, unchanged metronidazole and its metabolites are excreted in various proportions in the urine.

Patient Advice

- Patients should be informed of the adverse effects that have been associated with taking metronidazole. Approximately 12% of patients probably will experience nausea with or without an accompanying headache and possibly other gastrointestinal symptoms. A sharp, unpleasant, metallic taste also may occur.
- The use of alcoholic beverages while taking the drug or within a day of cessation of the drug may result in abdominal distress, nausea, vomiting and/or headache.
- As convulsive seizures and peripheral neuropathy have occurred in patients treated with metronidazole, patients should be instructed to immediately stop taking the drug and contact the dentist if any neurological symptoms such as dizziness, vertigo, ataxia, confusion, depression, weakness or insomnia occur.

Quinolones

The quinolones are a group of 1,8-naphthyridine derivatives that are not chemically related to any other antibacterial agents. These are synthetically produced bactericidal drugs and therefore are not true antibiotics, because they

are not the by-product of microorganisms. Nalidixic acid, which was introduced into clinical use in 1964, is the prototype of the quinolone drugs. A number of other drugs, chemically similar to nalidixic acid but with an improved antibacterial spectrum, have been synthesized. These can be divided into the older quinolones, such as nalidixic acid, which have limited antibacterial activity, and the newer second-generation quinolones. The latter have a much broader spectrum of activity and only recently have become clinically available.

Ciprofloxacin, a fluorinated quinolone carboxylic derivative, is an example of the newer drugs and is currently the most frequently used quinolone. This antimicrobial agent has excellent activity against a wide range of gram-negative organisms, including many that are resistant to third-generation cephalosporins, broad-spectrum penicillins and the newer semisynthetic aminoglycosides. It also produces good activity against gram-positive bacteria and is particularly useful for managing mixed infections. However, most anaerobic bacteria, including those of the mouth, are resistant to the drug. It is very likely that a number of patients coming for dental treatment will be taking ciprofloxacin; fortunately, this drug reportedly does not cross-react with most antibiotics. In fact, it has been reported to have an additive effect with antibiotics such as the β-lactams, aminoglycosides, clindamycin and metronidazole.

Accepted Indications

Ciprofloxacin is indicated in the treatment of infections caused by aerobic or facultative gram-negative rods or by *Staphylococcus aureus, Staphylococcus epidermidis, Streptococcus pyogenes* or *Streptococcus faecalis* that involve the lower respiratory tract, the skin and skin structures, the bones and joints and the urinary tract. The drug is also indicated in the treatment of infectious diarrhea caused by enterotoxigenic strains of *Escherichia coli,* or by *Campylobacter jejuni* or *Shigella*

Table 7.21

Ciprofloxacin: Characteristics and Common Indications for Use

Generic name	Characteristics	Common indications for use
Ciprofloxacin	Bactericidal Broad spectrum of activity against both gram-positive and gram-negative bacteria Inactive against most anaerobic bacteria	Indicated in treatment of infections of the lower respiratory tract, skin, bone and joints, and urinary tract and for the treatment of infectious diarrhea As a single agent or in combination with metronidazole in the treatment of periodontitis associated with *Actinobacillus actinomycetemcomitans*

Table 7.22

Ciprofloxacin: Oral Dosage and Prescribing Information

Generic name	Brand name(s)	Adult dosage	Max adult dosage	Max child dosage	PRC	Content/form	Oral dosage suggestions
Ciprofloxacin	Cipro	250 or 500 mg q 12 h	1.5 g/day	**Age < 18 y:** Safety and effectiveness not established	C	**Tablets:** 250, 500, 750 mg **Oral suspension:** Not available	Given without regard to meals

PRC: Pregnancy risk category.

species. The drug is not indicated in the treatment of infections caused by obligate anaerobic bacteria. See Table 7.21.

General Dosing Information

See Table 7.22 for dosage and prescribing information.

Dosage Adjustments

In patients who have impaired renal clearance and are not undergoing renal dialysis, dosage intervals should be adjusted based on serum creatinine levels. For patients who are undergoing renal dialysis, dosages of 250-500 mg should be given either q day or should be based on serum creatinine levels.

For patients with changing renal function or for patients with both renal and hepatic insufficiency, adjusted dosages should be based on serum concentrations of ciprofloxacin.

Special Dental Considerations

Drug Interactions of Dental Interest

Concurrent administration of ciprofloxacin with theophylline may lead to elevated serum concentrations of theophylline and substantially increase the risk of theophylline-associated adverse reactions. Serious and fatal reactions have occurred in patients receiving these two drugs together.

Ciprofloxacin has been shown to interfere with the metabolism of caffeine. This may lead to reduced clearance of caffeine and the prolongation of its effects, particularly in people sensitive to caffeine.

Concurrent administration with antacids containing magnesium, aluminum or calcium or with divalent and trivalent cations such as iron may substantially interfere with the absorption of ciprofloxacin. To a lesser extent, this effect is observed with multivitamins containing zinc.

Ciprofloxacin has been reported to enhance the effects of the anticoagulant warfarin and its derivatives. If it is necessary to administer these drugs concomitantly, prothrombin time should be monitored.

In patients receiving cyclosporine, ciprofloxacin may result in transient elevations of serum creatinine.

Due to the risk of seizures and convulsions, ciprofloxacin should be used with extreme caution in patients with known or suspected CNS disorders, such as severe cerebral arteriosclerosis, epilepsy or other factors that predispose people to seizures.

Table 7.23 lists possible interactions between ciprofloxacin and other drugs.

Cross-Sensitivity
A history of hypersensitivity to ciprofloxacin or to any other quinolone is a contraindication to its use.

Special Patients
Pregnant and nursing women
The safety and effectiveness of ciprofloxacin in pregnant or lactating women has not been established. The drug should be used during pregnancy only if the potential benefit justifies the potential risk to the fetus.

Table 7.23
Ciprofloxacin: Possible Interactions With Other Drugs

Drug taken by patient	Interaction with ciprofloxacin	Dentist's action
Aminophylline, oxtriphylline or theophylline	Concurrent use of these drugs and ciprofloxacin may result in increased risk of theophylline-related toxicity with serious, life-threatening reactions	*Concurrent use of these drugs is contraindicated*
Antacids containing aluminum, calcium or magnesium; laxatives containing magnesium	Absorption of ciprofloxacin may be reduced through chelation by these drugs	*Concurrent use of these drugs is contraindicated*
Caffeine	Concurrent use of caffeine and ciprofloxacin may reduce the metabolism of caffeine, resulting in a CNS stimulation	*Concurrent use of these drugs is contraindicated;* all others need to be warned and monitored
Cyclosporine	Concurrent use of ciprofloxacin has been reported to elevate serum creatinine and serum cyclosporine concentrations	Cyclosporine concentrations should be monitored and dosage adjustments may be required
Sucralfate	Absorption of ciprofloxacin may be reduced through chelation by this drug	*Concurrent use of this drug is contraindicated*
Vitamin or mineral supplements containing ferrous sulfate or zinc	Absorption of ciprofloxacin may be reduced through chelation by these agents	*Concurrent use of these agents is contraindicated*
Warfarin	Concurrent use of warfarin with ciprofloxacin has been reported to increase the anticoagulant effect of warfarin, increasing the risk of bleeding	The prothrombin time or INR of patients receiving warfarin and ciprofloxacin should be carefully monitored

Italics indicate information of major clinical significance.

Ciprofloxacin is excreted in human milk. Owing to the potential for serious adverse reactions in nursing infants, nursing should be discontinued if it is necessary to administer ciprofloxacin to the mother.

Pediatric, geriatric and other special patients
The safety and effectiveness of ciprofloxacin in children and adolescents aged < 18 y has not been established.

Patient Monitoring: Aspects to Watch

Serum creatinine levels should be monitored in patients receiving ciprofloxacin who have severe renal impairment.

Owing to the potential for serious adverse reactions, serum levels of theophylline should be monitored closely if it is necessary to administer ciprofloxacin to patients receiving theophylline.

Adverse Effects and Precautions

Adverse effects that were thought to be probably or possibly related to ciprofloxacin therapy have been reported in 16% of the patients treated. The most frequent reported adverse effects, in order of occurrence, have been nausea, diarrhea, vomiting, abdominal pain/discomfort, headache, restlessness and rash (see Table 7.24). Each of these has been reported in 1% to 5% of patients receiving the drug.

Pharmacology

Ciprofloxacin is rapidly absorbed from the stomach after oral administration. Serum concentrations increase proportionately with dosage, and maximum serum concentrations are obtained 1-2 h after oral administration. After absorption, the drug is widely distributed throughout the body. Tissue concentrations often exceed serum concentrations in both men and women, particularly in the genital tissue. The drug is present in antibacterial concentrations in saliva, nasal and bronchial secretions, sputum, breast milk, skin blister fluid, lymph, peritoneal fluid and prostatic secretions. Ciprofloxacin is also present in lung, skin, fat, muscle, cartilage and bone. The drug diffuses across the placenta to enter the fetal circulation.

When ciprofloxacin is given concomitantly with food, there is delay in its absorption with a corresponding delay in peak serum levels; however, overall absorption is not substantially affected.

Concomitant administration of ciprofloxacin with theophylline decreases the clearance of theophylline and results in an increased risk of a patient's developing CNS or other adverse reactions.

In patients with reduced renal function, the half-life of the drug is slightly prolonged and dosage adjustments may be required.

Patient Advice

- Ciprofloxacin can be taken with or without a meal. The preferred time of dosing is 2 h after a meal. Patients should drink fluids liberally and should not take antacids containing magnesium, aluminum, or calcium; products containing iron; or multivitamins containing zinc.
- Moderate to severe photosensitivity may occur and be manifested as exaggerated sunburn; excessive sunlight should be avoided.
- The drug may cause dizziness and lightheadedness; therefore, patients should know how they react to the drug before they operate an automobile or machinery or engage in activities requiring mental alertness or coordination.
- There is a possibility of caffeine accumulation when coffee, tea or other caffeine-containing products are consumed while taking the drug.

Sulfonamides

The sulfonamides, or "sulfa drugs," are antimetabolites that competitively inhibit the synthesis of folic acid and folic acid derivatives in bacterial cells. Folic acid derivatives are

Table 7.24

Ciprofloxacin: Adverse Effects, Precautions and Contraindications

Body system	Adverse effects	Precautions/contraindications
General	Photosensitivity, flushing, fever, edema of face, neck, lips, or hands (these occur in about 1% of patients) Allergic reactions ranging from urticaria to anaphylactic reactions have been reported but are rare	Stop therapy if signs of allergic reactions observed; patients allergic to one quinolone may be allergic to others
CV	Palpitation, atrial flutter, hypertension, angina pectoris, myocardial infarction (relatively rare)	None of significance to dentistry
CNS	Dizziness, lightheadedness, insomnia, hallucinations, manic reaction, irritability, convulsive seizures, depression, drowsiness, weakness and malaise (incidence relatively high in patients receiving theophylline and ciprofloxacin concurrently)	Caution advised in prescribing for patients with CNS disorders
EENT	Blurred vision, disturbed vision, decreased visual acuity, diplopia, tinnitus, hearing loss (effects may be CNS-related; incidence higher in patients receiving theophylline concomitantly)	Avoid concomitant usage with theophylline
GI	Nausea (most common side effect and may occur in 5% of patients; effect may be lessened by taking medication with food); also diarrhea, vomiting, abdominal discomfort, dysphagia, gastrointestinal bleeding	Use of drug may have to be discontinued if GI problems persist
GU	Urine retention, vaginitis	None of significance to dentistry
Musc	Joint or back pain, tendonitis, tendon rupture, joint stiffness, neck or chest pain, flare-up of gout (first two are reported in about 1% of patients)	Use of drug may have to be discontinued in patients with gout
Oral	Painful oral mucosa and oral candidiasis; bad taste in mouth (more likely to occur with high or prolonged dosage)	Patient should be monitored for signs of oral candidiasis
Renal	Nephritis (reported in about 1% of patients), renal failure	Reduced dose recommended in patients with renal impairment
Resp	Epistaxis, laryngeal or pulmonary edema, dyspnea, bronchospasm (all relatively rare)	Use of drug may have to be discontinued if respiratory problems persist

essential for the synthesis of DNA precursors in both mammalian and bacterial cells. Unlike mammalian cells, bacterial cells are unable to absorb folic acid across the cell membrane and must synthesize it within the cell.

The sulfonamides competitively compete with para-aminobenzoic acid (PABA), which is required by bacteria in the metabolic pathway for the synthesis of folic acid. When a sulfonamide is substituted in place of PABA, the pathway cannot proceed any further and the bacterium is unable to synthesize the purine moieties needed for DNA synthesis. However, because inhibition by sulfonamides is competitive, the continued inhibition of growth depends on high concentrations of the drug. If the drug concentration falls below the competitive level, the synthesis of folic acid continues.

Most bacteria readily develop or acquire resistance to the sulfonamides through genetic transfer. This has been partially overcome by the use of a drug combination consisting of trimethoprim (also a competitive inhibitor of folic acid synthesis, but at a different point in the metabolic pathway) and sulfamethoxazole, a sulfonamide. The combination has been given the name "co-trimoxazole." Trimethoprim acts synergistically with sulfamethoxazole because both drugs inhibit sequential steps in the folic acid pathway. Although each of the drugs is bacteriostatic when used alone, the combination appears to be bactericidal. Use of co-trimoxazole is limited primarily to the treatment of urinary infections, chronic bronchitis and acute otitis media infections in children, and as a prophylaxis for traveler's diarrhea. Dental infections usually are better treated with a more appropriate antibiotic.

Accepted Indications

Sulfonamides are indicated in the treatment of urinary tract infections due to *Escherichia coli*, *Klebsiella*, *Enterobacter* or *Proteus* species.

They are used in the treatment of acute otitis media in children aged > 2 y or of chronic bronchitis in adults caused by susceptible strains of *Streptococcus pneumoniae* or *Haemophilus influenzae*. However, these drugs are not indicated for prophylactic or prolonged administration for patients with otitis media at any age.

Sulfonamides can be useful in the treatment of *Shigella* enteritis when antimicrobial therapy is indicated.

Finally, these agents frequently are used prophylactically for people traveling to countries in which the water and food may be contaminated with fecal organisms such as *Escherichia coli*, *Klebsiella* or *Enterobacter*. See Table 7.25.

General Dosing Information

See Table 7.26 for dosage and prescribing information.

Dosage Adjustments

Trimethoprim and sulfamethoxazole should be given with caution to patients with impaired renal or hepatic function, to those with possible folate deficiency (for example, elderly people, chronic alcoholics, patients receiving anticonvulsant therapy or patients with malabsorption syndrome or in malnutrition states), and to those with severe allergy or bronchial asthma. In such patients, lower dosages or a prolonged interval between doses may be indicated.

Table 7.25

Trimethoprim and Sulfamethoxazole: Characteristics and Common Indications for Use

Generic name	Characteristics	Common indications for use
Trimethoprim and sulfamethoxazole	Spectrum of activity limited to gram-negative aerobic or facultative bacteria and to a few streptococcal species; little activity against most gram-positive bacteria or anaerobic bacteria	Preventive prophylaxis for traveler's diarrhea Treatment of acute otitis media in children, chronic bronchitis in adults, urinary tract infections and *Shigella*-associated enteritis

Table 7.26

Trimethoprim and Sulfamethoxazole: Oral Dosage and Prescribing Information

Generic name	Brand name(s)	Adult dosage	Max adult dosage	Max child dosage	PRC	Content/ form	Oral dosage suggestions
Trimethoprim and sulfamethoxazole	Bactrim, Septra	**Oral suspension:** 20 mL q 12 h **Tablets, double-strength:** 1 tablet q 12 h **Tablets, regular:** 2 tablets q 12 h	U	8 mg/kg trimethoprim and 40 mg/kg sulfamethox-azole given in 2 equal doses q 12 h	C	**Tablets, double-strength:** 160 mg trimethoprim/ 800 mg sulfa-methoxazole **Tablets, regular:** 80 mg trimetho-prim/400 mg sulfa-methoxazole **Oral suspension:** 40 mg trimetho-prim/200 mg sulfamethoxazole/ 5 mL	Given without regard to meals

PRC: Pregnancy risk category.
U: Unavailable.

Special Dental Considerations

Drug Interactions of Dental Interest

Trimethoprim and sulfamethoxazole may prolong the prothrombin time in patients receiving the anticoagulant warfarin or its derivatives. The drug combination may inhibit the hepatic metabolism of phenytoin and result in excessive phenytoin serum levels.

In patients receiving thiazide diuretics, particularly elderly patients, an increased incidence of thrombocytopenia with purpura has been reported when trimethoprim and sulfamethoxazole are given concomitantly with the diuretic.

Table 7.27 lists possible interactions between trimethoprim and sulfamethoxazole and other drugs.

Laboratory Value Alterations

- The trimethoprim component may interfere with serum methotrexate assay when a bacterial dihydrofolate reductase is used as the binding protein.

Cross-Sensitivity

Trimethoprim and sulfamethoxazole use is contraindicated in patients with hypersensitivity to trimethoprim or any sulfonamide.

Special Patients

Pregnant and nursing women

A trimethoprim-and-sulfamethoxazole combination is not indicated for use in either pregnant or lactating women. Sulfonamides, including the sulfamethoxazole component, pass the placenta and enter the fetal circulation. Sulfa drugs are also excreted in breast milk.

Pediatric, geriatric and other special patients

There may be an increased risk of severe adverse reactions in elderly patients, particularly in the presence of complicating conditions—for example, impaired kidney and/or liver function—or when the patients are concomitantly using other drugs (see Drug Interactions). Severe skin reactions, generalized bone marrow depression or a specific decrease in platelets are frequently reported adverse effects in elderly patients.

Table 7.27

Trimethoprim and Sulfamethoazole: Possible Interactions With Other Drugs

Drug taken by patient	Interaction with trimethoprim and sulfamethoxazole	Dentist's action
Coumarin or indandione-derived anticoagulants	Concurrent use may prolong the patient's prothrombin time or INR and lead to bleeding	The prothrombin time or INR of patients concurrently taking these drugs should be monitored carefully
Hydantoin anticonvulsants	Concurrent use may lead to excessive phenytoin serum levels	*Concurrent use of these drugs is contraindicated*
Thiazide diuretics	Elderly patients taking thiazide diuretics have an increased risk of thrombocytopenia if these drugs are taken concurrently	If these drugs are taken concurrently, platelet counts and clinical signs of purpura should be carefully monitored

Italics indicate information of major clinical significance.

Table 7.28

Trimethoprim and Sulfamethoxazole: Adverse Effects, Precautions and Contraindications

Body system	Adverse effects	Precautions/contraindications
General	Hypersensitivity manifested as skin rash most common, anaphylactic reactions, serum sicknesslike syndrome, photosensitivity, allergic myocarditis Weakness, fatigue, insomnia	Dosage should be immediately stopped if skin rash develops
CNS	Convulsions, ataxia, vertigo, tinnitus, headache, depression, nervousness, apathy, hallucinations	If convulsions occur, use of drug should be discontinued; use of drug may have to be discontinued if other CNS symptoms persist
GI	Nausea, vomiting, anorexia, glossitis, stomatitis (all relatively common) Diarrhea (rare)	Medical attention is necessary if GI symptoms persist
Hema	Agranulocytosis, thrombocytopenia, leukopenia, neutropenia, eosinophilia	Not recommended for patients with hepatic impairment If blood dyscrasia is suspected, appropriate laboratory tests should be ordered
Musc	Arthralgia, myalgia	None of significance to dentistry
Renal	None of significance to dentistry	Not recommended for patients with renal impairment

Trimethoprim and sulfamethoxazole should not be given to infants aged < 2 mo except in unusual clinical circumstances in which another antimicrobial agent cannot be used.

Trimethoprim and sulfamethoxazole should not be given to patients receiving a thiazide diuretic because an increased incidence of thrombocytopenia has been reported when the two drugs are given concomitantly.

Patient Monitoring: Aspects to Watch

Hypersensitivity to sulfa drugs is relatively common and is usually manifested as rash and urticaria.

Adverse Effects and Precautions

The adverse effects associated with the sulfonamides are numerous and varied (Table 7.28), with an overall incidence of about 5%. The most common adverse reactions are gastrointestinal disturbances, which may include nausea, vomiting and/or anorexia, and allergic skin reactions such as rash and urticaria.

Pharmacology

The trimethoprim-and-sulfamethoxazole combination is rapidly absorbed after oral administration, with peak serum levels for the individual components occurring 1 to 4 h after dosage. The trimethoprim component is widely distributed, is concentrated in the tissues and readily enters cerebrospinal fluid and sputum. The sulfamethoxazole component is widely distributed through the body fluids and crosses the placenta to enter the fetal circulation. Both components are secreted in human breast milk.

About 60% of trimethoprim and 25% to 50% of sulfamethoxazole are excreted in the urine within 24 h of dosage.

Patient Advice

- Trimethoprim and sulfamethoxazole should be discontinued at the first appearance of skin rash or any sign of an adverse reaction. Clinical signs of a rash, sore throat, fever, cough, shortness of breath, pallor, purpura or jaundice may be early indications of serious reactions.

Suggested Readings

American Academy of Pediatrics Committee on Drugs. The transfer of drugs and other chemicals into human milk. Pediatrics 1994;93(1):137-50.

Consensus reports from the 1996 World Workshop in Periodontics. JADA 1998;29(supple):1S-69S.

United States Pharmacopeial Convention, Inc. Drug information for the health care professional. 18th ed. Rockville, Md.: United States Pharmacopeial Convention, Inc.; 1998.

Walker CB. Antimicrobial agents and chemotherapy. In: Slots J, Taubman M, eds. Contemporary oral microbiology and immunology. St. Louis: Mosby; 1992:242-64.

Walker CB. Selected antimicrobial agents: Mechanisms of action, side effects, and drug interactions. In: Slots J, Rams T, eds. Periodontology 2000. Vol. 10: Systemic and topical antimicrobial therapy in periodontics. Copenhagen: Munksgaard; 1996:12-28.

Chapter 8.

Antifungal and Antiviral Agents

Brian C. Muzyka, D.M.D.; Martha Somerman, D.D.S., Ph.D.

Antifungal Agents

Oral fungal infections are being seen in increasing numbers in the dental office. The most common oral fungal infection is caused by *Candida* species; up to 60% of healthy non-hospitalized patients may harbor this organism in the oropharyngeal region. *Candida* is an obligate organism in humans and is found as a normal constituent of the digestive and vaginal tract. Usually, *Candida* causes a localized superficial infection; however, in certain rare cases, it may be disseminated. This disseminated disease state is usually associated with immunosuppressive medications or immunosuppressive diseases.

Oral *Candida* infections may have four clinical presentations. Pseudomembranous candidiasis (thrush) appears as white or yellow plaque on mucosal surfaces that may be wiped away easily. Erythematous (atrophic) candidiasis appears as red patches on any mucosal surface. When found on the tongue, it may cause depapillation. Hyperplastic (chronic) candidiasis is similar to the pseudomembranous variant, but the plaques cannot readily be removed. Angular chelitis (perleche), the last variant of oral *Candida* infection, is a mixed *Candida* and bacterial infection. Angular chelitis appears as red radiating fissures from the corners of the mouth and is often accompanied by a pseudomembranous covering.

Candida infections may be diagnosed empirically or through oral cultures or cytological smears. As *Candida* is a normal constituent of the oral cavity, care should be used to interpret findings of oral *Candida* species.

Other, more rare fungal infections also can infect the oral cavity. These infections are considered to be deep-seated fungal infections and are a sign of disseminated disease. These rare oral infections usually present as ulcerations, nodules or granulomas or may typically have a thrushlike appearance. A diagnosis is made by use of special histological staining procedures on formalin-fixed biopsy tissue samples. Dentists should refer patients with deep-seated fungal infections to an appropriate medical specialist for further work-up to rule out an underlying cause of immunodeficiency or involvement of the central nervous or pulmonary system. Deep-seated fungal infections include aspergillosis, blastomycosis, geotrichosis, histoplasmosis, mucormycosis and cryptococcosis.

Pharmacological treatment for oral fungal infections is limited to two classes of drugs: azoles and polyene antibiotic antifungals. The azole group is further subdivided into imidazole and triazole groups.

Table 8.1 provides dosage and prescribing information on antifungal drugs.

Accepted Indications

Superficial oral fungal infections are most commonly treated with topical antifungal agents. These agents are available in several forms such as rinses, troches and creams. Systemic fungal infections with an oral presentation are treated with systemic medications.

Drug Categories

Azole antifungal agents

These drugs are divided into the following subgroups:

- imidazoles: clotrimazole, miconazole and ketoconazole;
- triazoles: fluconazole and itraconazole.

Many of the azoles are used to treat oropharyngeal candidiasis. They are also used for other fungal infections, such as aspergillosis, blastomycosis, chromomycosis, coccidioidomycosis, cryptococcosis and histoplasmosis.

Polyene antifungal agents

Polyenes are amphotericin B and nystatin. Polyenes are used for local treatment of fungal infections of the mouth caused by *Candida albicans* and other *Candida* species. Intravenous formulations of amphotericin B are used for treatment of severe systemic fungal infections.

Table 8.1

Antifungal Agents: Dosage and Prescribing Information

Generic name	Brand name(s)	Adult dosage	Child dosage	PRC	Content/form
		Azoles			
Clotrimazole	Fungold Creme, Gyne-Lotrimin, Lotrimin, Mycelex, Mycelex Troche; Myclo [CAN]	**Oral troche:** Dissolve 10-mg troche in mouth 5 times a day for 14 days **Topical cream, lotion:** Rub into affected area bid for 1-8 w **Topical solution:** Soak dental prosthesis daily during treatment period	**Oral troche:** Not recommended in children < age 3 y **Topical cream, lotion:** Not recommended in children < age 2 y	Oral troche: C Topical cream, lotion: B Topical solution: B	**Oral troche:** 10 mg **Topical cream:** 1% in 15-, 30-, 45- and 60-g tubes **Topical lotion:** 1% in 10-mL bottles **Topical solution:** 1% in 10-and 30-mL bottles
Fluconazole	Diflucan	**Oral suspension:** 200-400 mg/day **Tablets:** 200 mg immediately, then 100 mg daily for 7-14 days	3-12 mg/kg daily for 14 days, not to exceed 600 mg daily	C	**Oral suspension:** 300 or 1,400 mg/24 mL **Tablets:** 50, 100, 150, 200 mg
Itraconazole	Sporanox	**Capsules:** 200-400 mg/day **Solution:** Swish 10 mL vigorously and swallow bid for 1-2 w	NE	C	**Capsules:** 100 mg in packs of 28 **Solution:** 10 mg/mL
Ketoconazole	Nizoral; Akorazol [CAN]	**Cream:** Rub into affected area 1-2 times daily **Tablets:** 200-400 mg daily for 1-4 w	**Cream:** NE **Age > 2 y, oral—tablets:** 3.3-6.6 mg/kg daily as a single dose	C	**Cream:** 2% in 15-, 30-, 60-g tubes **Tablets:** 200 mg in bottles of 100

[CAN] indicates a drug available only in Canada.
PRC: Pregnancy risk category.
NE: Not established.

Continued on next page

Table 8.1 (cont.)

Antifungal Agents: Dosage and Prescribing Information

Generic name	Brand name(s)	Adult dosage	Child dosage	PRC	Content/form
Polyenes					
Amphotericin B	Fungizone Oral Suspension	**Oral suspension:** 1 mL swished in mouth qid for 2 w	**Oral suspension:** 1 mL swished in mouth qid for 2 w	B	**Oral suspension:** 100 mg/mL in 20-mL vial
Nystatin	Mycostatin, Nilstat, Nystex; Nadostine [CAN], Nyaderm [CAN]	**Oral suspension:** Swish and swallow 400,000-600,000 units qid **Powder/cream/ointment:** Rub into affected area bid or tid **Troche:** 200,000-400,000 units 4-5 times/day, dissolved slowly and completely in mouth	**Oral suspension:** Swish and swallow 400,000-600,000 units qid **Powder/cream/ointment:** Rub into affected area bid or tid **Troche:** 200,000-400,000 units 4-5 times/day, dissolved slowly and completely in mouth; use oral suspension in children ≤ age 5 y	Oral suspension: C Troche: B	**Oral suspension:** 100,000 units/mL in 60-mL vial **Powder/cream/ointment:** 100,000 units/g **Troche:** 200,000 units in packages of 30
Nystatin with triamcinolone	Mycogen, Mycolog II, Myco-Triacet, Mytrex, N.T.A., Tri-Statin II	**Cream/ointment:** Rub into affected area bid-tid	**Cream/ointment:** Rub into affected area bid-tid	C	**Cream/ointment:** With 0.1% triamcinolone in 15- and 30-g tubes (cream also in 60-g tubes)

[CAN] indicates a drug available only in Canada.
PRC: Pregnancy risk category.
NE: Not established.

General Dosing Information

General dosing information is provided in Table 8.1. The selection of agent and dosage depends on the extent of the oral fungal infection. Topical forms of treatment are recommended for superficial infections in patients who are immunocompetent, and systemic medications are recommended for deep fungal infections or for the treatment of patients who are immunocompromised.

Special Dental Considerations

General Considerations

- The oral mucosa should be examined for signs of fungal infection such as white plaque, erythematous areas, ulcerations, nodules or granulomas.
- Laboratory confirmation should be considered for deep fungal or superficial fungal disease in patients who are immunocompromised.
- Removable dental prosthetics and oral

appliances should be disinfected with a 1:1 solution of hydrogen peroxide and water during the treatment period for superficial disease.

- Toothbrushes, denture brushes and other oral hygiene devices that may be contaminated with fungal organisms should be replaced.
- Systemic formulations of antifungal medications should be considered for use with dentate patients who have poor oral hygiene or a high caries index, as the troche formulations have a high sugar content.
- Topical solutions, topical creams or systemic treatment should be considered for use with patients with xerostomia who may have difficulty using troches.

Drug Interactions of Dental Interest

Table 8.2 lists interactions of potential concern to clinicians administering antifungal drugs.

Azoles

- Absorption of itraconazole and ketoconazole can be affected by concomitant use of antacids. If concomitant administration of sulcralfate or of drugs that affect gastric acidity is necessary, it is recommended that these drugs should be given at least 2 h after or 1 h before ketoconazole or itraconazole administration.
- Other drug classes that may affect absorption of itraconazole and fluconazole include anticholinergics, antispasmodics, antimuscarinics, H_2-histamine receptor agonists, omeprazole and sulcralfate.
- Increased anticoagulant effects may occur in patients who are taking antifungal agents in conjunction with coumadin. Anticoagulation levels should be closely monitored and anticoagulation medication dosage adjusted accordingly.
- Concomitant use of antihistamines (such as terfenadine and astemizole) with itraconazole and ketoconazole has led to cardiac arrythmias and is contraindicated.
- Concomitant use of cisapride and ketoconazole is contraindicated and has result-

ed in serious cardiovascular effects.

- Concomitant use of ketoconazole and rifampin has resulted in decreased serum concentrations of ketoconazole. These drugs should not be administered concomitantly.
- Concomitant use of ketoconazole with cyclosporine or phenytoin may increase plasma levels of cyclosporine and phenytoin. Patients taking these drugs should be monitored closely.
- Concomitant administration of ketoconazole and the steroid drugs methylprednisone or prednisolone may result in increased plasma levels of the steroids.
- Concomitant use of alcohol and antifungal drugs may increase liver damage. Patients should be counseled not to drink alcohol while taking antifungal medications. Additionally, a disulfiram-type reaction (such as flushing, rash, peripheral edema, nausea or headache) has occurred in patients ingesting alcohol while receiving ketoconazole therapy.
- Concomitant use of ketoconazole and the benzodiazepines midazolam or triazolam may result in increased plasma concentration of the benzodiazepine agents. Because of the potentiated hypnotic and sedative effects, these agents should not be used concomitantly with ketoconazole.
- Itraconazole and ketoconazole may increase serum digoxin levels; therefore, digoxin levels should be closely monitored when administered with itraconazole or ketoconazole.

Polyenes

- Nephrotoxic effects of certain drugs (such as aminoglycosides, capreomycin, cisplatin, colistin, cyclosporine, methoxyflurane, pentamidine, polymixin B, vancomycin) may be additive with the concurrent or sequential use of IV amphotericin B and should be avoided. Intensive monitoring of renal function is recommended if amphotericin B is used in conjunction with any nephrotoxic agent.
- Serum potassium concentrations should

Table 8.2

Antifungal Agents: Possible Interactions With Other Drugs

Drug taken by patient	Interaction with antifungal agents	Dentist's action
Alcohol	May increase risk of liver damage	Counsel patient to discontinue alcohol use during antifungal treatment
Aminoglycosides, cyclosporine, vancomycin	IV amphotericin B increases risk of nephrotoxic effects	Do not prescribe concomitantly
Antacids	Decrease absorption of itraconazole and ketoconazole	Advise patient to take antifungal agent 1 h prior to or 2 h after taking antacids
Anticholinergics, antimuscarinics, antispasmodics, H_2-histamine receptor agonists, omeprazole, sulcralfate	Affect absorption of itraconazole and ketoconazole	Advise patient to take antifungal agent 1 h before or 2 h after taking drugs affecting gastric acidity
Antihistamines: Astemizole and terfenadine	May lead to cardiac dysrhythmias if taken concomitantly with itraconazole and ketoconazole	Do not prescribe concomitantly
Benzodiazepines: Midazolam, triazolam	Ketoconazole increases benzodiazepine plasma levels	Do not prescribe concomitantly
Cardiac glycosides	IV amphotericin B may alter serum potassium levels	Monitor serum potassium levels Do not prescribe concomitantly
Cisapride	Has serious cardiovascular effects if taken concomitantly with ketoconazole	Do not prescribe concomitantly
Cyclosporine and phenytoin	Ketoconazole increases levels of these drugs	Monitor drug levels carefully
Digoxin	Itraconazole and ketoconazole may increase digoxin levels	Closely monitor digoxin levels
Glucocorticoids	IV amphotericin B may alter serum potassium levels	Monitor serum potassium levels Do not prescribe concomitantly
Methylprednisone, prednisolone	Ketoconazole increases plasma levels of these steroid drugs	Monitor patient's plasma steroid levels
Rifampin	Decreases efficacy of ketoconazole	Do not prescribe concomitantly
Skeletal muscle relaxants	IV amphotericin B may alter serum potassium levels	Monitor serum potassium levels Do not prescribe concomitantly
Warfarin	All antifungal agents may increase anticoagulation effects	Monitor anticoagulation levels and adjust warfarin accordingly

be monitored closely in patients receiving any amphotericin B formulation concomitantly with a cardiac glycoside or skeletal muscle relaxant.

- Corticosteroids may enhance potassium depletion caused by amphotericin B and should not be used concomitantly.

Special Patients

Pregnant and nursing women

Most antifungal drugs are classified in pregnancy risk category B or C. Caution should be taken in prescribing these agents to pregnant women. As some antifungal agents may enter breast milk, the clinician should use caution in prescribing these agents to women who are nursing.

Pediatric, geriatric and other special patients

Many antifungal agents can alter kidney and liver function, which may be severely damaging to older and younger patients. Therefore, dentists may need to adjust doses of antifungal agents accordingly.

Adverse Effects and Precautions

Table 8.3 lists adverse effects and precautions related to antifungal agents.

Pharmacology

The azole antifungal agents interfere with cytochrome P-450 activity, which is necessary for the demethylation of 14-α methylsterol to ergosterol. Ergosterol is the major sterol associated with fungal cell membranes. This interference in ergosterol causes changes in the cell membrane permeability and allows fungal cell elements to escape from the cell.

The polyenes inhibit fungal growth by binding with sterol in the fungal cell wall to interfere with cell membrane permeability, resulting in cell lysis.

Patient Advice

The following advice can be given to all patients diagnosed with oral fungal infections.

- Long-term therapy may be indicated to clear the infection and prevent relapse.

- Patients should take the medication as prescribed and should complete the course of the medication.
- Patients should not use commercial alcohol-based mouthrinses during treatment unless they are prescribed by the dentist.
- Removable oral appliances and dental prosthetics should be treated daily with a 1:1 disinfection solution of hydrogen peroxide and water during the treatment period for superficial disease.
- Oral hygiene devices (such as toothbrushes and denture brushes) that may be contaminated should be replaced.

Antiviral Agents

Viruses are subcellular agents containing a nucleic acid core (either DNA or RNA) that is surrounded by a protein coat. They are among the simplest and smallest forms of life and must use a living host to replicate. Human viral infections have a wide spectrum of presentation, from subclinical infection to lethal infection. Viruses that affect the oral cavity, however, usually are self-limiting and heal spontaneously in a host with an intact immune system. Some viral infections that affect the oral cavity also cause a generalized systemic reaction (such as fever, myalgia, general malaise and anorexia).

Oral viral infections encountered in dental practice are usually limited to Coxsackie-type viruses (such as herpangina, acute lympho-nodular pharyngitis and hand-foot-and-mouth disease), herpes-type viruses (herpes labialis, chicken pox and shingles) and human papilloma viruses (HPV). Diagnosis and treatment considerations for these viral diseases are addressed below. Other viral diseases that affect the delivery of dental care include all forms of viral hepatitis and human immunodeficiency virus (HIV) disease. As a description of these disease processes would be lengthy, the reader may learn more about these diseases by reviewing the suggested readings.

Table 8.3

Antifungal Agents: Adverse Effects, Precautions and Contraindications

Agent	Adverse effects	Precautions/contraindications
	Azoles	
Clotrimazole	**GI:** Nausea and vomiting *HB: Abnormal liver function tests* **Integ:** Rash, urticaria, stinging, burning, peeling, blistering	Should not be used for treatment of systemic fungal infection Sugar content of lozenge preparations warrants use of other options in caries-prone patients
Fluconazole	**GI:** Nausea, vomiting, diarrhea, cramping, flatus **HB:** Hepatotoxicity, hepatitis, jaundice **Integ:** Skin rash, exfoliative skin disorders such as Stevens-Johnson syndrome (rare), photosensitivity **Renal:** Renal disease	Renal dysfunction Hepatic dysfunction
Itraconazole	**CV:** Hypertension, edema, hypokalemia, malaise **CNS:** Headache, dizziness, anorexia, fatigue, fever **GI:** Nausea, vomiting, diarrhea, abdominal pain, hepatitis, hepatic dysfunction **GU:** Impotence **HB:** Hepatotoxicity **Integ:** Rash, pruritus	Other drugs that interfere with the P-450 system may be influenced by or may influence itraconazole in terms of plasma levels, so precautions are warranted when using such drugs in combination with itraconazole; examples of these drugs include but are not limited to astemizole, carbamazepine, cisapride, cyclosporine, diazepam, digoxin, indinivar, isoniazid, lovastatin, methylprednisolone, midazolam, phenobarbital, phenytoin, quinidine, rifabutin, rifampin, ritonavir, simvastatin, triazolam, warfarin
Ketoconazole	**CNS:** Headache, dizziness, lethargy, anxiety, insomnia, dreams, paresthesia **Endoc:** Gynecomastia, depressed adrenocortical function **GI:** Nausea, vomiting, anorexia, diarrhea, cramps, abdominal pain, constipation, flatulence, GI bleeding **GU:** Impotence **HB:** Hepatotoxicity **Integ:** Pruritus (cream and oral), severe irritation and stinging (cream), fever, chills, photophobia, rash, dermatitis, purpura, urticaria	Renal disease Hepatic disease (periodic liver function tests are recommended) Drug-induced achlorhydria Other drugs that interfere with the P-450 system may be influenced by or may influence ketoconazole in terms of plasma levels, so precautions are warranted when using such drugs in combination with ketoconazole; examples of these drugs include but are not limited to astemizole, carbamazepine, cisapride, cyclosporine, diazepam, digoxin, indinivar, isoniazid, lovastatin, methylprednisolone, midazolam, phenobarbital, phenytoin, quinidine, rifabutin, rifampin, ritonavir, simvastatin, triazolam, warfarin

Italics indicate information of major clinical significance.

Continued on next page

Table 8.3 (cont.)

Antifungal Agents: Adverse Effects, Precautions and Contraindications

Agent	Adverse effects	Precautions/contraindications
Polyenes		
Amphotericin B	**CV:** Hypotension, hypertension **CNS:** *Fever, chills,* delirium, convulsions **Endoc:** *Hypokalemia, hypomagnesemia* **GI:** *GI disturbance* **GU:** Urinary retention **Hema:** *Phlebitis, anemia,* leukocytosis, leukopenia **HB:** Acute liver failure **Integ:** Hypersensitivity, burning, itching, redness at site **Renal:** *Nephrotoxicity*	Contraindicated in patients with sensitivity to amphotericin B
Nystatin	**GI:** *Nausea, vomiting, anorexia, diarrhea, abdominal pain* **Integ:** Hypersensitivity reaction, rash, urticaria (rare) **Oral:** Bad taste with oral suspension and lozenges	Sugar content of some lozenge preparations may warrant use of other options in caries-prone patients
Nystatin with triamcinolone acetonide	**Integ:** Dryness, acne, allergic dermatitis, skin maceration and atrophy, burning, irritation	Avoid use of occlusive dressings

Italics indicate information of major clinical significance.

Coxsackie virus infection. Coxsackie viruses are a group of RNA viruses responsible for herpangina, acute lymphonodular pharyngitis and hand-foot-and-mouth disease. Herpangina occurs in epidemics with symptoms a bit milder than those of herpetic infections. These epidemics are most frequent in the months of June through October, and the majority of cases affect young children. Macules (well-circumscribed flat lesions) quickly progress into vesicles on the posterior pharynx, tonsils, faucial pillars and soft palate. Less frequently, lesions are found on the hard palate and buccal mucosa. The vesicles rupture quickly, leaving 1- to 2-millimeter ulcers that will heal spontaneously, usually within 1 w. Acute lymphonodular pharyngitis is a variant of herpangina in which yellowish-white nodules appear but do not progress into vesicles. Treatment for herpangina and acute lymphonodular pharyngitis is usually supportive.

Herpesvirus infection. A crucial factor for the transmission of herpesvirus is intimate contact between an infected shedding host and another susceptible host. With inoculation into the epidermis or mucous membranes, an incubation period of 4-6 days is followed by the appearance of vesicles (elevated blisters less than 1 centimeter in diameter containing a clear fluid on an erythematous base). The virus generally ascends to the peripheral nerves and then to the dorsal root ganglia, where the virus can establish a latent infection and be reactivated in the future. Clinical signs of herpes-type viruses often are preceded by a prodromal period in which a sharp burning or shooting pain occurs along the affected nerve distribution. Vesicles appear and rupture, leaving a raw ulcerated hemorrhagic surface that is quite painful. Multiple intraoral lesions may interfere with the ability to maintain an adequate nutritional status, and supportive therapy will be required. Diagnosis of herpetic infections can be difficult, and a cytological smear or biopsy of the affected site may be necessary to rule out other disease processes such as aphthous ulcerations, pemphigus, pemphigoid or lichen planus. This is especially true in a patient who has a fulminant manifestation of disease or in a patient whose immune system is compromised.

Oral herpetic infections usually are self-limiting, and treatment consists mainly of nutritional support and pain palliation. Patients with compromised immune function are at increased risk of reactivation of viral disease, and often the reactivated disease will be more involved and more difficult to control. Patients with HIV may develop severe herpes simplex virus (HSV) infections that affect the oral cavity. These infections can be life-threatening, and appropriate diagnosis and treatment are crucial. Patients who are immunocompromised may be treated with antiviral agents to hasten the rate of healing. Acyclovir is most commonly used for the treatment of HSV infection in this population.

Aphthous ulcers. Quite often, recurrent aphthous ulcers are misdiagnosed as herpes. Recurrent aphthous ulcers (RAUs) are characterized by periodic ulcerations confined to the oral mucosa. No single etiologic agent has been implicated for RAUs; however, many theories have been put forward, suggesting multifactorial causes including stress, vitamin deficiency, diet, hormonal changes, allergies, trauma and immune dysfunction. Use of different medications, including dideoxycytidine (ddC) in patients who are HIV-seropositive, also has been implicated in the progression and periodic exacerbation of oral ulcerations.

Minor aphthous ulcers (ulcers less than 1 cm in diameter) usually are found on the less keratinized tissues in the oral cavity such as the buccal mucosa, the floor of the mouth and the ventral surface of the tongue. These aphthous ulcerations heal spontaneously without scarring in 7 to 10 days. RAUs are diagnosed by history and clinical presentation and by exclusion of known etiologic pathogens. A simple cytological smear from the area surrounding the ulcer may be used in determining etiologic agents.

A prescription drug, amlexanox (Aphthasol), is approved for the treatment of aphthous ulcerations. Amlexanox is a potent inhibitor of the formation and release of inflammatory mediators from mast cells. A number of nonprescription products also are available for treatment of aphthous ulcers. They exert their major effect by providing a protective coating over the ulcer to decrease pain and promote healing. Also, the use of dentifrices formulated without sodium lauryl sulfate may decrease the incidence of aphthous ulcers.

Human papilloma virus (HPV). Presently, 17 different subtypes of HPV have been isolated from oral mucosa. HPV lesions in the oral cavity may present as verrucous, hyperplastic or papillomatous growths that are asymptomatic. Various modalities of treatment for HPV have been employed with limited success. These treatments include excision, laser ablation, cryotherapy, application of keratinolytic agents and injection of antiviral agents.

Accepted Indications

Because of substantial toxicity and side effects, antiviral agents usually are reserved for immunocompromised patients with mucocutaneous HSV-associated lesions. It has been demonstrated in immunocompromised patients that the use of topical acyclovir for treatment of herpes labialis has decreased the duration of both pain and viral shedding. Conversely, studies in immunocompetent patients have shown no clinical benefit of using topical acyclovir in treatment of herpes labialis. Anecdotal reports, however, do exist in which patients claim to prevent recurrent herpes labialis themselves by immediately applying topical acyclovir upon development of the prodromal symptom of tingling.

Initial clinical trials evaluating penciclovir for the treatment of herpes labialis included only immunocompetent patients. Application of penciclovir to herpes labialis lesions decreased the duration of pain, viral shedding and time required for healing. The clinical benefit of penciclovir is modest, however; on average, it shortens the duration of pain and viral shedding by less than one day.

General Dosing Information

Dosage and prescribing information for antiviral agents can be found in Table 8.4 and for amlexanox in Table 8.5. (It should be noted that while the etiology of aphthous ulcers is unclear in terms of viral origin, the prescribing information for amlexanox is included here in hopes that it will be useful to clinicians.)

Special Dental Considerations

Drug Interactions of Dental Interest

Table 8.6 presents information regarding drug interactions with antiviral agents.
- Systemic acyclovir and ganciclovir are nephrotoxic and should be used with caution in patients who have renal disease or in patients who are receiving other nephrotoxic medications.
- Concomitant administration of acyclovir and probenecid may delay the urinary excretion and renal clearance of acyclovir. Probenecid also may interfere with the renal clearance and urinary excretion of ganciclovir.
- Concomitant use of acyclovir and zidovudine (AZT) may increase CNS symptoms such as drowsiness or lethargy; therefore, patients should be monitored closely.
- Famciclovir is eliminated by the kidneys.

Its dosage should be adjusted accordingly for patients with renal impairment.
- Foscarnet has a high toxic profile and should be used with care, especially in patients with a history of renal impairment.

Adjunctive Therapy

For relief of pain associated with viral lesions and aphthous ulcers, typical anesthetic agents bring temporary relief. Lidocaine viscous, 2%, can be of value. Diphenhydramine elixir, an antihistamine containing 12.5 milligrams of diphenhydramine per mL, also can be used for its topical anesthetic properties. Lidocaine viscous sometimes is mixed with equal parts of antacids and diphenhydramine elixir to improve adherence to the oral mucosa.

If patients are experiencing difficulty in eating, liquid dietary supplements may be recommended.

Adverse Effects and Precautions

Table 8.7 lists adverse effects, precautions and contraindications associated with antiviral agents.

Pharmacology

Viral resistance to antiviral agents has become an increasing problem. Drug resistance has many causes and, depending on the specific drug, can have many mechanisms. With acyclovir, it is believed that resistant herpes simplex viruses have developed because of alterations in either the viral thymidine kinase or the viral DNA polymerase. Viral thymidine kinase starts the process through which acyclovir is transformed to its active derivative, acyclovir triphosphate. This process does not occur in uninfected cells to any great extent, and because acyclovir is taken up selectively by infected cells, the concentration of acyclovir triphosphate in infected cells is 40-100 times greater than in uninfected cells. Clinically, acyclovir-resistant HSV infections are seen in patients whose

Table 8.4
Antiviral Agents: Dosage and Prescribing Information

Generic name	Brand name(s)	Adult dosage	Child dosage	PRC	Content/form
Acyclovir	Zovirax; Avirax [CAN]	**Immunocompetent, for herpes labialis—topical:** No clinical benefit **Immunocompromised, for herpes labialis—topical:** Apply to lesions q 3 h 6 times/day for 7 days **Immunocompetent, for herpes simplex—oral:** 400 mg q 4 h 5 times/day **Immunocompromised, for herpes simplex—oral:** 200-800 mg 5 times/day **HIV-positive, for herpes simplex, suppression/prophylaxis—oral:** 200 mg tid or 400 mg bid **Immunocompetent, for herpes zoster—oral:** 800 mg q 4 h 5 times/day for 5-10 days **Immunocompetent, weight > 40 kg, for varicella—oral:** 800 mg qid for 5 days	**For herpes labialis—topical:** NE **Immunocompetent, for herpes simplex—oral:** Unknown in children < 2 y **Immunocompromised, for herpes simplex—oral:** 1 g in 3-5 divided doses/day for 7-14 days **HIV-positive, for herpes simplex, suppression/prophylaxis—oral:** 600-1,000 mg in 3-5 doses/day **Age ≤ 2 y, immunocompetent, for varicella—oral:** 20 mg/kg qid for 5 days (max daily dose 80 mg/kg) **Weight ≤ 40 kg, immunocompetent, for varicella—oral:** 800 mg qid for 5 days **Immunocompromised, age < 12 y, for herpes zoster—IV:** 20 mg/kg q 8 h for 7 days	C	**Capsules:** 200 mg **Oral suspension:** 200 mg/5 mL **Tablets:** 400, 800 mg **Topical ointment:** 50 mg in 3- and 15-g tubes
Famciclovir	Famvir	**Immunocompetent, for herpes zoster:** 500 mg q 8 h for 7 days within 72 h of onset of rash	NE	B	**Tablets:** 125, 250, 500 mg
Foscarnet	Foscavir	**For cytomegalovirus (CMV) retinitis—IV induction:** 60 mg/kg q 8 h for 14-21 days **Acyclovir-resistant, for mucocutaneous herpes simplex—IV:** 40 mg/kg q 8-12 h for 14-21 days until clinical resolution	NE	C	**Parenteral for IV infusion:** 24 mg/mL
Ganciclovir	Cytovene	**For CMV retinitis:** IV induction 5 mg/kg q 12 h; oral maintenance 1 g tid; IV maintenance 5 mg/kg/day **For extraocular CMV infections—IV:** 5 mg/kg q 12 h for 14-21 days	**IV:** NE **Oral:** NE	C	**Capsules:** 250, 500 mg **IV:** 500 mg

[CAN] indicates a drug available only in Canada.
PRC: Pregnancy risk category.
NE: Not established.

Continued on next page

Table 8.4 (cont.)

Antiviral Agents: Dosage and Prescribing Information

Generic name	Brand name(s)	Adult dosage	Child dosage	PRC	Content/form
Interferon alfa	Alferon-N, Intron, Roferon-A	**For human papilloma virus:** Intralesional injections of 1,000,000 IU per cm² 1-2 times/w; SC injections of 3,000,000 IU 2-3 times/w	NE	C	**Injection:** Alferon-N, 1-mL vial containing 5 million units; Intron, 1-mL vial containing 3 million units; Roferon-A, 1-mL vial containing 3, 6 or 9 million units
Penciclovir, topical	Denavir	**For herpes labialis:** Rub into area q 2 h 9 times/day	NE	B	**Topical cream:** 1% in 2-g tubes
Valacyclovir	Valtrex	**Immunocompetent, for herpes zoster:** 1 g q 8 h for 7 days	NE	B	**Tablets:** 500 mg, 1 g

PRC: Pregnancy risk category.
NE: Not established.

Table 8.5

Amlexanox: Dosage and Prescribing Information

Generic name	Brand name(s)	Adult dosage	Child dosage	PRC	Content/form
Amlexanox	Aphthasol	Apply ¼-in. ribbon of paste to ulcers qid	NE	B	5% oral paste in 5-g tubes

PRC: Pregnancy risk category.
NE: Not established.

immunodeficiency is increasing. Other antiviral medications, such as foscarnet, must be used to treat such acyclovir-resistant patients.

Patient Advice

- Topical acyclovir and penciclovir should be applied using a finger cot or some type of protective covering.
- Patients who have oral viral disease should avoid using mouthrinses with a high alcohol content.
- Patients who have oral viral disease should dispose of toothbrushes used during periods of infection.
- Amlexanox paste should be applied using a finger cot. If a protective finger covering is not used, the hands should be washed immediately after applying the medication.

Table 8.6

Antiviral Agents: Possible Interactions With Other Drugs

Drug taken by patient	Interaction with antiviral agents	Dentist's action
Antacids	May cause decreased renal clearance of valacyclovir's active agent (acyclovir) in patients with renal disease	Use with caution in patients with renal disease
Antibiotics: Dapsone, pentamidine, sulfamethoxazole, trimethoprim	May cause additive toxicity when used with ganciclovir or foscarnet	Use with caution
Antidysrhythmic agent: Digoxin	May cause additive toxicity when used with ganciclovir or foscarnet May cause decreased renal clearance of valacyclovir's active agent (acyclovir) in patients with renal disease	Use with caution in patients with renal disease
Antifungal agents: Amphotericin B, flucytosine	May cause additive toxicity when used with ganciclovir or foscarnet	Use with caution
Antineoplastic agents: Adriamycin, vinblastine, vincristine	May cause additive toxicity when used with ganciclovir or foscarnet	Use with caution
Cimetidine	May cause decreased renal clearance of valacyclovir's active agent (acyclovir) in patients with renal disease	Use with caution in patients with renal disease
Imipenem/cilastatin	May cause seizures when administered with ganciclovir	Do not prescribe concomitantly
Nucleoside analogs	May cause additive toxicity when used with ganciclovir or foscarnet	Use with caution
Probenecid	Delay in urinary excretion and delay in renal excretion of acyclovir and ganciclovir Increase in plasma concentration of famciclovir	Both systemic acyclovir and systemic gancyclovir are nephrotoxic and should be used with caution
Ritonavir and saquinavir	May cause abnormal renal function when administered with foscarnet	Use with caution
Thiazide diuretics	May cause decreased renal clearance of valacyclovir's active agent (acyclovir) in patients with renal disease	Use with caution in patients with renal disease
Zidovudine	May increase chance of neutropenia when administered with ganciclovir	Use with caution

Table 8.7

Antiviral Agents: Adverse Effects, Precautions and Contraindications

Body system	Adverse effects	Precautions/contraindications
Systemic acyclovir		
General	None significant to dentistry	Contraindicated in patients with hypersensitivity to acyclovir
CNS	Neuropsychiatric toxicity (may be more common in immunocompromised and geriatric patients) Light-headedness, dizziness	*Contraindicated in patients who have neurologic abnormalities or abnormal neurologic reactions to cytotoxic medications*
GI	GI disturbances; anorexia	None significant to dentistry
HB	None significant to dentistry	Patients with serious hepatic abnormalities, because of difficulties with biotransformation
Musc	Tremors	None significant to dentistry
Oral	Taste disturbances	None significant to dentistry
Renal	*Acute renal insufficiency due to precipitation of acyclovir in renal tubes has been reported*	Maintain adequate hydration to prevent precipitation of acyclovir in the renal tubules Adults with chronic renal impairment require reduced dose Patients who have serious electrolyte abnormalities
Topical acyclovir and penciclovir		
General	Hypersensitivity at the local site Mild pain, burning, stinging	Effects of penciclovir have not been established in immunocompromised patients Avoid contact with eye
Oral	Taste disturbances	None significant to dentistry

Italics indicate information of major clinical significance.

Suggested Readings

Balfour HH Jr. Antiviral drugs. N Engl J Med 1999; 340:1255-68.

Cottone JA, Puttaiah R. Hepatitis B virus infection: current status in dentistry. Den Clin North Am 1996; 40:293-308.

Miller CS, Danaher RJ, Jacob RJ. Molecular aspects of herpes simplex virus I latency, reactivation, and recurrence. Crit Rev Oral Biol Med 1998;9:541-62.

Muzyka BC, Glick M. A review of oral fungal infections and appropriate therapy. JADA 1995;126:63-72.

Samaranayake LP. Oral mycoses in HIV infection. Oral Surg Oral Med Oral Pathol 1992;73:171-80.

Scully C, de Almeida OP. Orofacial manifestations of the systemic mycoses. J Oral Pathol Med 1992;21:289-94.

Chapter 9.

Topical Antiseptics

Chris H. Miller, Ph.D.; B. Ellen Byrne, R.Ph., D.D.S., Ph.D.

An antiseptic is a broad-spectrum antimicrobial chemical solution that is applied topically to body surfaces to reduce the microbial flora in preparation for surgery or at an injection site. In contrast, antibiotics (see Chapter 7) are organic chemical substances originally produced by microorganisms and used systemically or topically to treat infectious diseases in humans, animals and plants. Disinfectants (see Chapter 29) are antimicrobial chemical solutions used on inanimate surfaces. Sterilants are agents that, when used properly, can kill all microbes. Germicides (see Chapter 29) are agents that can kill at least some microbes; sporocides, fungicides, virucides, bacteriocides and tuberculocides are agents that can kill specific types of microbes.

The antimicrobial activity of antiseptics usually is weaker than that of disinfectants and sterilants because less harsh, or weaker, chemicals usually must be applied to body surfaces to avoid irritating the tissues. However, the antimicrobial activity of antiseptics can be lethal to the microbes on the body surfaces (the word "bactericidal" contains the stem "-cidal," derived from the Latin root meaning "destroy"), or the activity may merely inhibit the growth of microbes (the word "bacteriostatic" contains "-static," derived from the Latin root meaning "inhibit"). The specific activity depends on the nature of the antiseptic chemical and the microbes involved.

In general, antiseptics have a broad spectrum of activity in killing a wide variety of microbes. However, they are not considered to be sterilants, although they may kill all the microbes on a particular surface at a given time. Some antiseptics have substantivity, also known as residual, long-lasting or persistent activity. These agents adhere to tissue surfaces and may remain active for a period of a few hours after their application.

In dentistry, antiseptics are grouped into three classes: handwashing agents, skin and mucosal antiseptics and root canal and cavity preparations.

Handwashing Agents

There are two types of microbial flora on the skin: resident flora and transient flora. The resident flora, also referred to as the "colonizing flora," consist of microbes that colonize the skin; in other words, they attach to, multiply on and are considered permanent residents of the skin. Prominent members of the resident flora include *Staphylococcus epidermidis* and several species of *Corynebacterium*, *Acinetobacter*, *Propionibacterium* and *Peptococcus*. Members of the resident flora are not readily removed from the skin by mechanical friction.

The transient flora, also referred to as the "contaminating flora," comprise microbes that are not consistently found on the skin and that, after being acquired, exist for a relatively short time (usually until the next handwashing). They are acquired by contact with contaminated surfaces and can include any known microbe. Because members of the transient flora do not colonize the skin, they are readily removed by mechanical friction, such as that in handwashing. This is fortunate, because the transient flora are those most involved in spreading diseases by contaminating people's hands.

Accepted Indications

Handwashing with a detergent solution facilitates the suspension of most of the transient microbes and a few of the resident microbes from the surface of the skin; subsequent rinsing removes the microbes from the hands. Thus, both mechanical friction and rinsing are crucial for effective handwashing. The addition of an antimicrobial agent to the handwashing detergent adds another important component to the process—that of destroying most of the remaining transient microbes and even some, but not all, of the resident flora.

Handwashing products include
- antimicrobial soap, which contains an ingredient with in vitro and in vivo activity against skin flora;
- healthcare personnel handwash, a broad-spectrum antimicrobial preparation that reduces the number of transient flora on intact skin to a baseline level (it is fast-acting, nonirritating and designed for frequent use);
- surgical hand scrub, a broad-spectrum, fast-acting, persistent and nonirritating preparation that contains an antimicrobial ingredient designed to significantly reduce the number of microorganisms on intact skin.

The antimicrobial agents in handwashing agents include chlorhexidine gluconate, *para*-chloro-*meta*-xylenol, iodophors (which contain iodine) and triclosan (Table 9.1).

Chlorhexidine gluconate. Chlorhexidine gluconate, or CHG, is a fairly broad-spectrum antimicrobial agent that is intermediate in its speed of action. It has a high affinity for skin, and it continues to be effective for at least 6 h. There have been relatively few reports of adverse reactions (Table 9.2) to chlorhexidine, although a few allergic reactions have been noted.

Iodophors. Iodophors are complexes of iodine and an organic carrier that increase the solubility of iodine and provide a reservoir of iodine. An example is the complex of iodine with polyvinylpyrrolidone (povidone-iodine). With iodophors, the presence of free iodine (the antimicrobial component) is increased during dilution; the recommended levels for free iodine in antiseptics are 1 to 2 mg per L (1-2 parts per million). Iodophors have an intermediate speed of action and a low level of persistence. Table 9.1 lists some iodophor products, their forms and their uses.

Para-chloro-meta-xylenol. *Para*-chloro-*meta*-xylenol also is known as PCMX or chloroxylenol. It is intermediate in its speed of action and exhibits some persistence in its activity. The incidence of adverse reactions to PCMX is low. Preparations with lower concentrations of PCMX are more appropriate for routine handwashing than as surgical scrubs. Some PCMX products are shown in Table 9.1.

Triclosan/irgasan. Triclosan, or irgasan, is 2,4,4'-trichloro-2'-hydroxydiphenolchlorophenol. Its speed of action is intermediate and it does have some persistence on the skin. At lower concentrations, it is bacteriostatic. This antiseptic agent is the common active ingredient in household liquid antibacterial soaps, deodorant soaps and underarm deodorants and is present in similar concentrations in products marketed to healthcare professionals. These preparations, some of which are listed in Table 9.1, are more appropriate for routine handwashing than as surgical scrubs.

General Usage Information

See Table 9.1.

Adverse Effects and Precautions

See Table 9.2.

Table 9.1

Handwashing Agents: Usage Information

Generic name	Brand name(s)	Content/form	Actions/uses
4% chlorhexidine gluconate solution	BrianCare Antimicrobial Skin Cleanser, Dencide Antimicrobial Solution, Dial Surgical Hand Scrub, Dyna-Hex 4% Antimicrobial Skin Cleanser, Excell Antimicrobial Skin Cleanser, Hibiclens Antiseptic Antimicrobial Skin Cleanser ★, Luroscrub Antimicrobial Skin Cleanser ★, Maxiclens, MetriCare Surgical Hand Scrub, Novoclens Topical Solution, Scrub-Stat IV Antimicrobial Solution ★	4% chlorhexidine gluconate, 4% isopropyl alcohol	Very effective against gram-positive bacteria, moderately effective against gram-negative bacteria, bacteriostatic only against mycobacteria According to laboratory studies, can eliminate infectivity of lipophilic viruses such as HIV, influenza and herpes simplex but is not very effective against hydrophilic viruses such as poliovirus and some enteric viruses
2% chlorhexidine gluconate solution	Chlorostat Antimicrobial Skin Cleanser ★, Cida-Stat Antimicrobial Solution, Dyna-Hex 2% Antimicrobial Skin Cleanser	2% chlorhexidine gluconate, 4% isopropyl alcohol	Not as effective as the 4% solution but has similar spectrum of activity
0.75% chlorhexidine gluconate solution	Perfect Care	0.75% chlorhexidine gluconate	Not as effective as the 4% solution; best for nonsurgical routine handwashing
Iodophors	Betadine Surgical Scrub (1% available iodine), Sana Scrub Surgical Scrub (0.75% available iodine)	0.75%, 1% available iodine	Very effective against gram-positive bacteria and moderately effective against gram-negative bacteria, the tubercle bacillus, fungi and many viruses
Para-chloro-*meta*-xylenol (PCMX) (chloroxylenol)	DermAseptic (3% PCMX), DisAseptic (4% PCMX), Lurosep Antimicrobial Lotion Soap (0.5% PCMX), PCMX Scrub (3% PCMX), Vionex (0.5% PCMX), Vionex (0.5% PCMX with Nonoxynol-9)	0.5%, 3%, 4% PCMX, 0.5% PCMX with Nonoxynol-9	Although some studies have shown CHG and iodophors to be more active than PCMX against skin flora, PCMX is a fairly broad-spectrum antimicrobial agent that is moderately effective against gram-positive bacteria and somewhat effective against gram-negative bacteria, the tubercle bacillus and some fungi and viruses
Triclosan or irgasan	Dial Liquid Antimicrobial Soap (0.2% triclosan), Bacti-Stat (0.3% triclosan), Lysol I.C. Antimicrobial Soap (0.3% triclosan), SaniSept (0.3% triclosan), Septisol Solution (0.25% irgasan)	0.2%, 0.3% triclosan, 0.25% irgasan	Moderately effective against gram-positive bacteria and most gram-negative bacteria, but it may be less effective against *Pseudomonas aeruginosa*; somewhat effective against the tubercle bacillus; level of its effectiveness against viruses is unknown

★ *indicates a product bearing the ADA Seal of Acceptance.*
The products listed here might not include all of those that are available. Also, the listing of a product does not denote its superiority to any other product that is either listed or not listed, nor does it guarantee its availability or quality.

Table 9.2

Handwashing Agents: Adverse Effects, Precautions and Contraindications

Body system	Adverse effects	Precautions/contraindications
General	Allergic reaction in sensitive persons (may occur with any product)	Avoid contact with agent if sensitive
EENT	Eye damage (with chlorhexidine gluconate)* Damage to the middle ear (with chlorhexidine gluconate)*	Avoid placing chlorhexidine gluconate in eyes and ears
Endoc	Induction of hyperthyroidism in infants by iodine	Do not use iodophors on infants
Integ	Skin irritation (with iodophor products)	Rinse off iodophors after handwashing

* Chlorhexidine is nontoxic on the skin but may cause damage if placed directly into the eye or ear.

Suggested Readings

Aly R, Maibach HI. Comparative antibacterial efficacy of a 2-minute surgical scrub with chlorhexidine gluconate, povidone-iodine, and chloroxylenol sponge brushes. Am J Infect Control 1988;16:173-7.

Denton GW. Chlorhexidine. In: Block SS, ed. Disinfection, sterilization, and preservation. Philadelphia: Lea and Febiger; 1991:274-89.

Gottardi W. Iodine and iodine compound. In: Block SS, ed. Disinfection, sterilization, and preservation. Philadelphia: Lea and Febiger; 1991:152-66.

Larson E, Mayur K, Laughon BA. Influence of two handwashing frequencies on reduction of colonizing flora with three handwashing agents used by health care personnel. Am J Infect Control 1989;17:83-8.

Larson E, Talbot GH. An approach for selection of health care personnel handwashing agents. Infect Control 1986;7:419-24.

Skin and Mucosal Antiseptics

In dentistry, antiseptics may be used on the skin or the oral mucosa to reduce the microbial load before injections, incisions, or other invasive procedures. Such agents should be fast-acting and nonirritating. Both alcohols and iodine preparations used separately or in combination have been shown to reduce the microbial load on body surfaces.

Alcohols. Isopropyl (2-propanol, isopropanol) and ethyl (ethanol) alcohols are used as skin antiseptics, but because of the burning or stinging sensations they cause, they are not recommended for use on mucosal tissues. Although there are some differences in the antiseptic activity of ethyl and isopropyl alcohols, their concentration is more important in determining their overall effectiveness. Because some water must be present to enhance the denaturation of microbial proteins (which is the mechanism of antimicrobial action), effective concentrations range from 60% to 90% aqueous solutions. Usually, however, to reduce chances of skin irritation and drying, an amount of alcohol no higher than 70% by weight is used.

Iodophors. As mentioned above, presurgical preparation of the skin may involve an alcohol treatment followed by application of an iodophor. The antimicrobial activity of iodophor preparations involves the binding of iodine to amino acids, thus causing changes in protein structure and functioning. Iodine binds to the S-H group of cysteine, which interferes with the bridging of peptides during protein synthesis. Also under alkaline conditions, iodine can bind to the N-H group of several amino acids interfering with peptide bond formation. Iodine solutions stain and may irritate the skin, whereas iodophors have reduced staining properties and are less irritating.

Accepted Indications

See Table 9.3.

General Usage Information

See Table 9.3.

Adverse Effects and Precautions

See Table 9.4.

Suggested Readings

Brenman HS, Randell E. Local degerming with povidone-iodine. II. Prior to gingivectomy. J Periodontol 1974;45: 870-2.

Groschel DHM, Pruett TL. Surgical antisepsis. In: Block SS, ed. Disinfection, sterilization, and preservation. Philadelphia: Lea and Febiger; 1991:642-54.

Larson EI, Morton HE. Alcohols. In: Block SS, ed. Disinfection, sterilization, and preservation. Philadelphia: Lea and Febiger; 1991:191-203.

Randell E, Brenman HS. Local degerming with

Table 9.3

Skin and Mucosal Antiseptics: Usage Information

Generic name	Brand name(s)	Content/form	Actions/uses
Ethyl alcohol	(generic)	70% ethyl alcohol	Very effective; gives rapid protection against most vegetative gram-positive and gram-negative bacteria; has good activity against the tubercle bacillus, most fungi and many viruses
Iodophors	Betadine Solution (1% available iodine), Sana Prep Solution (0.75% available iodine)	0.75%, 1% available iodine	May be applied to oral mucosa to reduce bacteremias during treatment of patients who are at increased risk of developing endocarditis (as indicated by American Heart Association) or who may be immunocompromised and have a neutropenia; antiseptic mouthrinses containing chlorhexidine or phenolic compounds also may be used in these instances (see Chapter 11); aqueous iodine preparations or a tincture of iodine (iodine in alcohol) also may be used for skin antisepsis
Isopropyl alcohol	(generic)	70% isopropyl alcohol	Alcohols are very effective and give rapid protection against most vegetative gram-positive and gram-negative bacteria; have good activity against the tubercle bacillus, most fungi and many viruses

The products listed here might not include all of those that are available. Also, the listing of a product does not denote its superiority to any other product that is either listed or not listed, nor does it guarantee its availability or quality.

Table 9.4

Skin and Mucosal Antiseptics: Adverse Effects, Precautions and Contraindications

Body system	Adverse effects	Precautions/contraindications
General	Defatting of skin and enhanced exposure of bacteria in hair follicles (alcohols) Painful stinging and burning when applied directly to mucosa and wounds (alcohols) Possible irritation (iodophors) Possible induction of hyperthyroidism in infants by iodine	Do not use alcohols or alcohol-based products on mucous membranes Do not use iodophors on infants

povidone-iodine. Part I. Prior to dental prophylaxis. J Periodontol 1974;45:866-9.

Zinner DD, Jablon JM, Saslaw MS. Bacteriocidal properties of povidone-iodine and its effectiveness as an oral antiseptic. Oral Surg 1961;14:1377-82.

Root Canal Medications/ Periodontal Dressings

Irrigants. Irrigants are used during root canal therapy to flush debris from the canal, lubricate the canal, disinfect the canal, and act as a tissue or debris solvent. The three preparations most commonly used as irrigants are sodium hypochlorite, ethylenediamine-tetra-acetic acid and hydrogen peroxide.

Intracanal medications. The primary purpose of intracanal medications is to reduce microflora in the root canal after canal débridement while producing a minimal effect on normal host tissue. A secondary reason is to reduce postinstrumentation pain. The medications most commonly used for this purpose are calcium hydroxide, phenolic compounds, and the aldehyde formocresol (formaldehyde 48.5%, cresol 48.5%).

Accepted Indications

Irrigants
Sodium hypochlorite (NaOCl)
See Table 9.5.

Ethylenediamine-tetra-acetic acid (EDTA)
EDTA is a chelator, an organic substance that removes metal ions such as calcium by binding them chemically. This action aids in removal of calcified tissue. See Table 9.5.

Hydrogen peroxide 3% (H_2O_2)
Hydrogen peroxide should not be sealed into a canal because of the danger of forcing infected material beyond the apex. In pulp canals, hydrogen peroxide should be used carefully to avoid emphysema of the adjacent soft tissue. See Table 9.5.

Intracanal medications
Calcium hydroxide (Ca[OH]$_2$)
See Table 9.5.

Phenolic compounds
Phenolic compounds such as camphorated parachlorophenol, which are considered protoplasmic poisons, are potent antimicrobial agents. They are capable of destroying tissue cells by binding cell membrane lipids and proteins. See Table 9.5.

Eugenol
Eugenol, which is an antiseptic and anodyne, is the essential chemical in clove oil and has similar uses. It is used in protective packs after excision of gingival tissues and is found in some temporary cements. Eugenol can also be used as an antiseptic in root canal therapy and for temporary relief of toothache.

Aldehydes
Formocresol is used routinely in pulpotomy procedures in primary teeth and as a temporary intracanal medicament.

Zinc oxide and zinc oxide-eugenol preparations
Zinc oxide is slightly antiseptic and weakly astringent and is used in combination with eugenol in many dental preparations. Some preparations use oils other than eugenol. Zinc oxide-eugenol preparations are used as therapeutic bases, temporary fillings, inlay and crown cements, periodontal surgical dressings and root canal sealers. The therapeutic value of zinc oxide-eugenol preparations is based on their compatibility with both hard and soft tissues of the mouth as well as their analgesic and topical local anesthetic effects. Zinc oxide-eugenol cements are recognized particularly for their sedative effect on pulpal tissue, especially in the restoration of teeth with deep carious lesions. Additionally, zinc oxide-eugenol cements are mildly antiseptic and provide a good marginal seal and good thermal insulation.

Zinc oxide-eugenol mixtures set into a hardened mass when mixed; the setting process involves both chemical and physical processes. Dressings containing zinc oxide and eugenol can be applied to the gingiva after surgical periodontal procedures. These dressings usually contain other ingredients such as tannic acid, rosin and oils such as mineral, peanut or vegetable oils. In some zinc oxide preparations, eugenol is completely replaced by other oils. These products are marketed as two components that must be combined and mixed to a paste or a putty-like consistency before being applied as a dressing to the tissue. One component is generally a powder consisting of zinc oxide, rosin, tannic acid, binders and soluble salts; the other component is a liquid consisting of eugenol, other oils or both.

General Usage Information

See Table 9.5.

Adverse Effects and Precautions

See Table 9.6.

Suggested Readings

Ingle JI, Bakland LF. Endodontics. 4th ed. Baltimore: Williams & Wilkins; 1994.

Walton RE, Torabinejad M. Principles and practice of endodontics. 2nd ed. Philadelphia: WB Saunders; 1996.

Table 9.5
Root Canal Medications and Periodontal Dressings: Usage Information

Generic name	Brand name(s)	Content/form	Actions/uses
Aldehydes			
Formocresol	Buckley's Formo Cresol ★	**Liquid:** 35% cresol, 19% formaldehyde, 17.5% glycerine, 28.5% water	Vital pulp therapy in primary teeth
	Formo Cresol ★	**Liquid:** 48.5% cresol, 48.5% formaldehyde, 3% glycerine	Vital pulp therapy in primary teeth
Intracanal medications			
Calcium hydroxide (Ca[OH]₂)	Calcium hydroxide powder (generic) ★	Calcium hydroxide, USP, powder	Used to create an environment for healing pulpal and periapical tissues, to produce antimicrobial effects, to aid in elimination of apical seepage, to induce formation of calcified tissue, and to prevent inflammatory resorption after trauma
	Pulpdent Temp Canal ★	Calcium hydroxide in aqueous methylcellulose	Used to create an environment for healing pulpal and periapical tissues, to produce antimicrobial effects, to aid in elimination of apical seepage, to induce formation of calcified tissue, and to prevent inflammatory resorption after trauma

★ *indicates a product bearing the ADA Seal of Acceptance.*
The products listed here might not include all of those that are available. Also, the listing of a product does not denote its superiority to any other product that is either listed or not listed, nor does it guarantee its availability or quality.

Continued on next page

Table 9.5 (cont.)

Root Canal Medications and Periodontal Dressings: Usage Information

Generic name	Brand name(s)	Content/form	Actions/uses
		Irrigants	
Ethylenediamine-tetra-acetic acid (EDTA)	EDTA (generic)	17% in aqueous solution, pH 8.0	In combination with sodium hypochlorite, EDTA removes smear layer; alone, aids in removal of calcified tissue by chelating metal ions
	EDTAC	EDTA with Centrimide	In combination with sodium hypochlorite, EDTA removes smear layer; alone, aids in removal of calcified tissue by chelating metal ions
	File-EZE	EDTA in an aqueous solution	In combination with sodium hypochlorite, EDTA removes smear layer; alone, aids in removal of calcified tissue by chelating metal ions
	RC Prep ★	Urea peroxide 10%, EDTA 15% in a special water soluble base	In combination with sodium hypochlorite, EDTA removes smear layer; alone, aids in removal of calcified tissue by chelating metal ions
	REDTA	EDTA 17% in an aqueous solution, pH of 8.0	In combination with sodium hypochlorite, EDTA removes smear layer; alone, aids in removal of calcified tissue by chelating metal ions
Hydrogen peroxide 3% (H_2O_2)	generic	Aqueous solution	Oxidizing power of hydrogen peroxide kills certain anaerobic bacteria in cultures; in contact with tissues, its germicidal power is very limited because it is readily decomposed by organic matter and antimicrobial effect lasts only as long as oxygen is being released; can be used to cleanse and treat infected pulp canals
Sodium hypochlorite (NaOCl)	Chlorox	5.25% sodium hypochlorite	Has a solvent action on pulp tissue and organic debris, is used for irrigation of root canals, and is useful for cleaning dentures; aqueous solutions of 2.5% and 5% sodium hypochlorite are reported to be equally effective in dissolving pulpal debris when used as root canal irrigants

★ indicates a product bearing the ADA Seal of Acceptance.
The products listed here might not include all of those that are available. Also, the listing of a product does not denote its superiority to any other product that is either listed or not listed, nor does it guarantee its availability or quality.

Continued on next page

Table 9.5 (cont.)

Root Canal Medications and and Periodontal Dressings: Usage Information

Generic name	Brand name(s)	Content/form	Actions/uses
Irrigants (cont.)			
	Hypogen	5.25% sodium hypochlorite	Has a solvent action on pulp tissue and organic debris, is used for irrigation of root canals, and is useful for cleaning dentures; aqueous solutions of 2.5% and 5% sodium hypochlorite are reported to be equally effective in dissolving pulpal debris when used as root canal irrigants
Miscellaneous preparations			
Zinc oxides	COE-Pak ★	**Paste 1:** 45% zinc oxide, 37% magnesium oxide, 11% peanut oil, 6% mineral oil, 1% chloroxylenol, chlorothymol and coumarin, 0.02% Toluidine-Red pigment **Paste 2:** 43% polymerized rosin, 24% coconut fatty acid, 10% ethyl alcohol, 9% petroleum jelly, 4% gum elemi, 4% lanolin, 3% ethyl cellulose, 1.5% chlorothymol, 1% carnauba, 0.2% zinc acetate, 0.1% spearmint oil	Periodontal dressing
	Perio-Care Periodontal Dressing ★	**Paste:** 38.5% magnesium oxide, 29.8% vegetable oils, 19.2% zinc oxide, 12.5% calcium hydroxide, 0.2% coloring **Gel:** 63.2% resins, 29.8% fatty acids, 3.5% ethyl cellulose, 3.5% lanolin	Periodontal dressing
	Perio-Putty	**Base:** 3.1% polyvinylpyrrolidone-iodine complex, 9% polymer, 5% benzocaine, 82.9% fillers **Catalyst:** 19.9% zinc oxide, 10.3% magnesium oxide, 12.3% mineral and vegetable oils, 58% inert fillers **Skin lubricant:** 95% silicone oils, 5% inert fillers	Periodontal dressing with skin lubricant

★ *indicates a product bearing the ADA Seal of Acceptance.*
The products listed here might not include all of those that are available. Also, the listing of a product does not denote its superiority to any other product that is either listed or not listed, nor does it guarantee its availability or quality.

Continued on next page

Table 9.5 (cont.)

Root Canal Medications and Periodontal Dressings: Usage Information

Generic name	Brand name(s)	Content/form	Actions/uses
Miscellaneous preparations (cont.)			
	Zinc Oxide, U.S.P. ★	Zinc oxide powder	Periodontal dressing
	Zone Periodontal Pack	**Base:** 3.1% polyvinylpyrroli-done-iodine complex, 38.3% rosin, 2% chlorobutanol, 10% mineral oil, 9.3% isopropyl myristate, 37.3% propylene glycol monoisostearate	Periodontal dressing
Zinc oxide-eugenol	Kirkland Periodontal Pack ★	**Powder:** 40% zinc oxide, 40% rosin, 20% tannic acid **Liquid:** 46.5% eugenol, 46.5% peanut oil, 7.5% rosin	Periodontal dressing
	Peridres	**Powder:** 49% rosin, 46% zinc oxide, 3% tannic acid, 3% kaolin **Liquid:** 98% eugenol, 2% thymol	Periodontal dressing
Phenolic compounds			
Parachlorophenol (PCP)	Cresanol Root Canal Dressing	**Liquid:** 25% parachlorophe-nol, 25% metacresyl acetate, 50% camphor	Intracanal medicament
	M.C.P. Root Canal Dressing ★	**Liquid:** 25% metacresyl-acetate, 25% parachlorophenol, 50% camphor	Intracanal medicament
	Parachlorophenol Liquefied	**Liquid:** 98% parachlorophe-nol, 2% glycerin	Intracanal medicament
Camphorated parachlorophenol (CPC)	Camphorated Parachlorophenol, U.S.P. ★	**Liquid:** 35% parachlorophe-nol and 65% camphor	Intracanal medicament
Eugenol	Eugenol U.S.P. ★	**Liquid:** 100% eugenol	Anodyne/oral tissues, teeth

★ indicates a product bearing the ADA Seal of Acceptance.
The products listed here might not include all of those that are available. Also, the listing of a product does not denote
its superiority to any other product that is either listed or not listed, nor does it guarantee its availability or quality.

Table 9.6

Root Canal Medications: Adverse Effects, Precautions and Contraindications

Body system	Adverse effects	Precautions/contraindications
General	Sodium hypochlorite is caustic and not suitable for application to wounds or areas of infection in soft tissues	Minimize soft-tissue contact
	Hydrogen peroxide should be used carefully to avoid emphysema of adjacent soft tissue	
	Phenolic compounds can destroy tissue cells by binding cell membrane lipids and proteins	
	Combined action of cresol, a protein-coagulating phenolic compound, and formaldehyde, an alkylating agent, make formocresol extremely cytotoxic and capable of causing widespread necrosis of vital tissue in the mouth or elsewhere	

Chapter 10

Agents Affecting Salivation

John A. Yagiela, D.D.S., Ph.D.

Anticholinergic Drugs

Saliva plays a vital role in protecting the health of soft and hard tissues of the mouth and in such functions as taste, mastication and deglutition. Excessive salivation, however, can complicate the performance of dental procedures such as the taking of impressions and the placement of restorations.

A number of anticholinergic drugs—otherwise referred to as cholinergic antagonists, antimuscarinic agents or parasympatholytics—are effective antisialogogues and are used by dentists and physicians for treating inappropriate salivary secretions and for reducing normal salivation to facilitate the performance of intraoral procedures. Because none of these agents is selective in its action, they all have a tendency to produce side effects, and this must be considered before proceeding with antisialogogue therapy. The anticholinergic drugs included in this chapter are limited to agents that have been approved for use to control salivation or that are used in dentistry for that purpose.

Accepted Indications

The control of salivation for dental procedures is a generally recognized but not officially accepted indication for these drugs. Atropine, glycopyrrolate, methantheline, propantheline and scopolamine are the most commonly used agents. These drugs also have several medical indications. For example, parenteral atropine has been approved

- for the control of bradycardia and first-degree heart block associated with excessive vagal activity or administration of succinylcholine;
- to inhibit salivation and respiratory tract secretions during general anesthesia;
- to minimize the muscarinic side effects of cholinesterase inhibitors used to reverse the action of neuromuscular blocking drugs.

Parenteral glycopyrrolate has been approved for the same purposes, except for the prophylaxis of succinylcholine-induced bradyarrhythmias. It also is indicated before general anesthesia to reduce secretion of gastric acid and to minimize the danger of pulmonary aspiration. Parenteral scopolamine has been approved for the control of secretions during general anesthesia and as a preanesthetic sedative and anesthetic adjunct in conjunction with opioid analgesics.

Anticholinergic drugs also have been approved for the management of peptic ulcers and various gastrointestinal, biliary and genitourinary disorders. For most drugs and conditions, these indications are considered obsolete. Selected anticholinergic drugs also are used to treat parkinsonism and as mydriatics and cycloplegics in ophthalmology. Atropine is a recognized antidote for the muscarinic toxicity of mushrooms, parasympathomimetic agonists and anticholinesterase drugs, insecticides and nerve gases.

Atropine usually is the anticholinergic of choice for most uses in dentistry. Oral dosage forms of atropine are not widely available in neighborhood pharmacies, however, so the dentist should be familiar with the use of other antisialogogues. By parenteral injection, glycopyrrolate is excellent for the control of salivation; scopolamine is a suitable parenteral choice when its sedative, amnestic and antiemetic effects are desired.

General Dosing Information

Low doses of the anticholinergic drugs described in this chapter for blocking excessive salivary secretion, properly adjusted for route of administration, are relatively selective in effect. Larger doses, such as those required to treat vagally induced bradydysrhythmias, uniformly produce side effects, including pronounced dryness of the mouth. General dosing guidelines for the control of salivation and uses associated with general anesthesia are provided in Table 10.1.

Maximum Recommended Doses

Maximum recommended doses have not been established for single administrations of anticholinergics beyond the usual doses indicated in Table 10.1.

Dosage Adjustments

Within the recommended range, the dose of an anticholinergic drug may be adjusted according to need. For control of salivation, a low dose may be adequate when only moderation of salivation is required, whereas a larger dose may be necessary if secretions are preventing the successful accomplishment of a procedure, such as an impression. Reduced doses should be considered for infants, geriatric patients and those with medical conditions that alter their responses to anticholinergic drugs.

Special Dental Considerations

Drug Interactions of Dental Interest

Drug interactions and related problems involving anticholinergic antisialogogues listed in Table 10.2 are potentially of clinical significance in dentistry.

Laboratory Value Alterations

- Gastric acid secretion tests are impaired by anticholinergic drugs because they decrease stimulation of gastric acids.
- Radionuclide gastric emptying tests are impaired by anticholinergic drugs because of delayed gastric emptying.
- Phenolsulfonphthalein excretion tests are impaired by atropine because the two agents compete for the same transport mechanism.
- Serum uric acid is decreased in patients with hyperuricemia or gout who are receiving glycopyrrolate.

Cross-Sensitivity

Table 10.3 lists potential cross-sensitivities between anticholinergic agents and other drugs.

Special Patients

Pregnant and nursing women

Atropine and scopolamine cross the placenta. Although there is no evidence of teratogenic effects, intravenous atropine can cause tachycardia in the fetus, and parenteral scopolamine given during labor may adversely affect the neonate by depressing the CNS and reducing vitamin K-dependent clotting factors. Glycopyrrolate, methantheline and propantheline are quaternary ammonium compounds, and it is unlikely that they reach the fetal circulation in large amounts.

All anticholinergic drugs may inhibit lactation. In addition, atropine and scopolamine are distributed into breast milk. Although single doses to control salivation have not been associated with any health problem, it may be advisable for nursing mothers to collect sufficient milk to cover the 8-h period after taking an anticholinergic drug.

Pediatric, geriatric and other special patients

Pediatric patients. Infants and small children are especially sensitive to the toxic effects of anticholinergic drugs, even when the dose is corrected for body size. Because of their high metabolic rate, children generate relatively large amounts of heat and must dissipate that heat in a warm environment by sweating. Blockade of acetylcholine-mediated perspiration by these agents can quickly lead to grossly

Table 10.1

Anticholinergic Drugs: Dosage and Prescribing Information

Generic name	Brand name(s)	Adult dosage	Child dosage	PRC	Content/form
Atropine sulfate	Sal-Tropine ★	**To control salivation—oral:** 0.3-1.2 mg **In anesthesia:** 2 mg orally or 0.2-0.6 mg IM ½-1 h before induction for prophylaxis of excessive secretions, 0.4-1 mg IV (up to 2 mg total) for dysrhythmia, 0.3-1.2 mg for use with anticholinesterase in reversal of neuromuscular blockade	**To control salivation—oral:** 0.01 mg/kg up to 0.4 mg, not to exceed 0.4 mg q 4-6 h **In anesthesia—IV:** 0.01-0.03 mg/kg IV for dysrhythmia, 0.01-0.02 mg/kg for use with anticholinesterase in reversal of neuromuscular blockade	C	**Injection, 0.05 mg/mL:** in 5-mL syringes **Injection, 0.1 mg/mL:** in 5-, 10-mL syringes **Injection, 0.3 mg/mL:** in 1-, 30-mL vials **Injection, 0.4 mg/mL:** in 1-mL ampules and 1-, 10-, 30-mL vials **Injection, 0.5 mg/mL:** in 1-, 30-mL vials and 5-mL syringes **Injection, 0.6 mg/mL [CAN]:** in 1-mL ampules **Injection, 0.8 mg/mL:** in 0.5-, 1-mL ampules and 0.5-mL syringes **Injection, 1 mg/mL:** in 1-mL ampules and 10-mL syringes **Tablets:** 0.4 mg **Tablets, soluble:** 0.4, 0.6 mg
Glycopyrrolate	Robinul, Robinul Forte	**To control salivation—oral:** 1-2 mg **In anesthesia:** 4.4 µg/kg IM ½-1 h before induction for prophylaxis of excessive secretions (including gastric), 0.1 mg IV q 2-3 min for dysrhythmia, 0.2 mg/1 mg neostigmine or 5 mg pyridostigmine for reversal of neuromuscular blockade	**To control salivation:** NE **In anesthesia:** 4.4-8.8 µg/kg IM ½-1 h before induction for prophylaxis of excessive secretions (including gastric), 4.4 µg/kg up to 0.1 mg q 2-3 min for dysrhythmia; 0.2 mg/ 1 mg neostigmine or 5 mg pyridostigmine for reversal of neuromuscular blockade	B	**Injection, 0.2 mg/mL:** in 1-, 2-, 5-, 20-mL vials **Tablets:** 1, 2 mg

Generic name	Brand name(s)	Adult dosage	Pediatric dosage	PRC	How supplied
Methantheline bromide	Banthine	To control salivation—oral: 50-100 mg	To control salivation: 12.5-50 mg	C	Tablets: 50 mg
Propantheline bromide	Pro-Banthine	To control salivation—oral: 15-30 mg	To control salivation: 0.375 mg/kg up to adult dose	C	Tablets: 7.5, 15 mg
Scopolamine butylbromide [CAN]	Buscopan [CAN]	To control salivation—oral: 10-20 mg	NE	C	Injection, 20 mg/mL: in 1-mL ampules; Suppositories: 10 mg; Tablets: 10 mg
Scopolamine hydrobromide	Scopace	To control salivation—oral: 0.4-0.8 mg; In anesthesia: 0.2-0.6 mg IM for prophylaxis of excessive secretions; 0.3-0.6 mg IV, IM or SC for prophylaxis of emesis and for anticholinergic effects; As an anesthetic adjunct—IV, IM, SC: 0.32-0.65 mg	To control salivation: NE; Age 4-7 mo, in anesthesia—IM: 0.1 mg (for prophylaxis of excessive secretions); Age 7 mo-3 y, in anesthesia—IM: 0.15 mg (for prophylaxis of excessive secretions); Age 3-8 y, in anesthesia—IM: 0.2 mg (for prophylaxis of excessive secretions); Age 8-12 y, in anesthesia—IM: 0.3 mg (for prophylaxis of excessive secretions); In anesthesia: 6 µg/kg IV, IM or SC for prophylaxis of emesis and for anticholinergic effects	C	Injection, 0.3 mg/mL: in 1-mL vials; Injection, 0.4 mg/mL: in 0.5-mL ampules and 1-mL vials; Injection, 0.86 mg/mL: in 0.5-mL ampules; Injection, 1 mg/mL: in 1-mL vials; Tablets, soluble: 0.4 mg

★ indicates a drug that has the ADA Seal of Acceptance.
[CAN] indicates a drug that is available only in Canada.
PRC: Pregnancy risk category.
NE: Not established.

Table 10.2

Anticholinergic Drugs: Possible Interactions With Other Drugs

Drug taken by patient	Interaction with anticholinergic drugs	Dentist's action
Antacids or absorbent antidiarrheal drugs	*May impair absorption of anticholinergic drug*	Avoid administration of an anticholinergic drug within 2-3 h of ingestion of the interacting drug
Antimyasthenics	Muscarinic effects are blocked by anticholinergic drugs, possibly obscuring early signs of an antimyasthenic overdose	Use cautiously
CNS depressants	Summation of CNS depression with scopolamine; hallucination and behavioral disturbances have been reported with parenteral lorazepam and scopolamine	Use cautiously
Drugs with anticholinergic side effects: antiparkinsonism drugs, antipsychotic agents, carbamazepine, digoxin, dronabinol, orphenadrine, procainamide, quinidine, sedative antihistamines, tricyclic antidepressants	*Additive anticholinergic effects*	Use cautiously
Ketoconazole	*Absorption may be impaired by increased gastric pH caused by anticholinergic drugs*	Have the patient take ketoconazole at least 2 h before the anticholinergic drug
Metoclopramide	Effect of hastening gastric emptying may be blocked by anticholinergic drugs	Use cautiously
Opioid analgesics	Summation of constipating effects	Use cautiously
Potassium chloride	*Delayed absorption may increase gastrointestinal toxicity of potassium chloride*	Avoid concurrent use

Italics indicate information of major clinical significance.

Table 10.3

Anticholinergic Drugs: Potential Cross-Sensitivity With Other Drugs

A person with a sensitivity to	May also have a sensitivity to
Any belladonna alkaloid	Atropine or scopolamine
Methantheline	Propantheline (and vice versa)

elevated temperatures. Flushing of the skin is an important early visual cue that steps must be taken to improve heat loss. Young children may also be especially sensitive to the CNS effects of atropine and scopolamine.

Geriatric patients. Geriatric patients are particularly susceptible to the parasympatholytic effects of anticholinergic drugs on visceral smooth muscle. Although single doses, as used in dentistry for control of salivation, are generally well tolerated by elderly people, large doses of atropine and scopolamine have been associated with excessive depressant and excitatory CNS reactions. Repeated doses can cause constipation and, especially in men, urinary retention. Xerostomia and associated increased dental caries and fungal infections are dental concerns

linked to chronic use of these drugs in elderly patients. In addition, patients aged > 40 y are at increased risk of an acute attack of previously undiagnosed angle-closure glaucoma.

Patients with medical problems. Patients with certain medical problems are especially susceptible to the adverse effects of anticholinergic drugs. These include patients with obstructive or paralytic gastrointestinal and urinary tract disorders, cardiac disease and angle-closure glaucoma. Specific recommendations regarding these patients are listed in Table 10.4.

Patient Monitoring: Aspects to Watch

- Cardiovascular status (arterial blood pressure, heart rate, electrocardiogram) with parenteral anticholinergic drugs

Table 10.4

Anticholinergic Drugs: Adverse Effects, Precautions and Contraindications

Body system	Adverse effects	Precautions/contraindications
General	Decreased sweating, hyperthermia *(mainly in small children)* Skin rash, urticaria	Monitor temperature in patients with fever *Contraindicated in patients with history of drug sensitivity to the anticholinergic drug considered for use*
CV	*Tachycardia*, hypertension Orthostatic hypotension (with large doses of quaternary ammonium derivatives)	*Avoid large doses or parenteral administration in patients with cardiac disease, tachycardia or acute hypovolemia* Use cautiously in patients with Down's syndrome, hyperthyroidism, hypertension or pregnancy toxemia
CNS	CNS depression, drowsiness, dizziness, tiredness, anterograde amnesia, confusion with *scopolamine* or atropine CNS excitation, headache, hallucination, seizures with *scopolamine* or atropine	Children with brain damage are more likely to develop CNS effects
EENT	*Mydriasis, cycloplegia, blurred vision and increased intraocular pressure, especially with scopolamine or atropine*	Use cautiously with patients who have open-angle glaucoma Increased mydriatic effect is likely in patients with Down's syndrome *Contraindicated in patients with history of angle-closure glaucoma*

Italics indicate information of major clinical significance.

Continued on next page

Table 10.4 (cont.)

Anticholinergic Drugs: Adverse Effects, Precautions and Contraindications

Body system	Adverse effects	Precautions/contraindications
GI	Constipation, obstruction, gastric reflux, nausea and vomiting *(mainly with chronic use)*	*Patients with obstructive or paralytic GI disease, intestinal atony, hiatal hernia, reflux esophagitis or ulcerative colitis are at risk of exacerbating their existing disorder* Patients with reflux esophagitis or obstructive GI disease have an increased risk of emesis during anesthesia when an anticholinergic drug is used preoperatively
GU	Urinary retention *(mainly with chronic use)*	*History of obstructive or paralytic uropathy, prostatic hypertrophy or urinary retention increases risk of urinary retention* Renal function impairment may prolong anticholinergic effects
HB		Hepatic function impairment may prolong anticholinergic effects
Musc	Muscle weakness (large doses of quaternary ammonium derivatives)	*Myasthenia gravis increases risk of muscle weakness*
Oral	*Xerostomia*, difficulty in swallowing Increased incidence/severity of dental caries, periodontal disease and candidiasis *(with chronic use)*	Patients with xerostomia are likely to experience increased inhibition of salivation
Resp	Dryness of respiratory tree Decreased ventilation from muscle weakness (large doses of quaternary ammonium derivatives)	Pulmonary problems from obstruction of bronchial passages by thickened secretions are more likely with patients—especially young children and bedridden patients—who have chronic pulmonary disease *Myasthenia gravis increases risk of impaired ventilation*

Italics indicate information of major clinical significance.

Adverse Effects and Precautions

The adverse effects of the anticholinergic drugs are the predictable consequences of the inhibition of various physiological actions of acetylcholine. Single oral doses of agents used to control salivation are usually well-tolerated, but large parenteral doses invariably induce a host of side effects. Although these effects may be unpleasant, they are virtually never life-threatening except in small children and medically compromised patients. The adverse effects and precautions and contraindications listed in Table 10.4 apply to all routes of administration.

Pharmacology

Anticholinergic drugs competitively block the effects of acetylcholine and cholinergic drugs at muscarinic receptor sites. Muscarinic receptors mediate tissue responses to parasympathetic nervous system stimulation and cholinergic-induced sweating and vasodilation. Tertiary amines, such as atropine and especially scopolamine, may produce CNS effects because of their ability to cross the blood-brain barrier. Quaternary amines, such as glycopyrrolate, methantheline and propantheline, are largely excluded from the brain and do not act directly on the CNS. The existence of muscarinic receptor subtypes (designated M_1 through M_5) also accounts for some of the differences in peripheral effects among the anticholinergic drugs because of different relative affinities of the drugs for these subtypes. It has been determined that the M_3 receptor supports serous salivary gland secretion and the M_2 receptor is responsible for parasympathomimetic cardiac effects. In tissues where acetylcholine release at muscarinic receptors is chronically active, anticholinergic drugs will exert pronounced antimuscarinic effects. If acetylcholine or other cholinergic drugs are absent, anticholinergic drugs will elicit little or no observable effect.

Atropine and scopolamine, two naturally occurring belladonna alkaloids, are well-absorbed from the gastrointestinal tract; however, absorption is less complete with the synthetic quaternary ammonium drugs. Atropine is partially metabolized in the liver and excreted in the urine as both the parent compound and metabolite. A similar fate presumably occurs with the other anticholinergic agents. Table 10.5 lists the time to effect and duration of effect of anticholinergic drugs used orally for control of salivation.

Patient Advice

- Patients should be aware of the potential common side effects, such as dryness of the mouth, nose and throat; difficulty in swallowing; and inhibition of sweating.
- Parents should be warned of the potential for hyperthermia in small children, especially when the children are overdressed, physically active or in a warm environment.
- Because of the possibility of psychomotor impairment after use of scopolamine, driving or other tasks requiring alertness and coordination should be avoided or performed with added caution, as appropriate, on the day of treatment. It is also desirable to avoid the use of alcohol or other CNS depressants during this time.

Suggested Readings

Brown JH, Taylor P. Muscarinic receptor agonists and antagonists. In: Hardman JG, Limbird LE, eds. Goodman & Gilman's the pharmacological basis of therapeutics. 9th ed. New York: McGraw-Hill; 1996:141-60.

Mandel ID. The role of saliva in maintaining oral homeostasis. JADA 1989;119:298-304.

Voltz-Zang C, Waldhauser T, Schulte B, Palm D. Comparison of the effects of atropine in vivo and ex vivo (radioceptor assay) after oral and intramuscular administration to man. Eur J Clin Pharmacol 1995;49(1-2):45-9.

Table 10.5

Anticholinergic Drugs: Pharmacokinetic Parameters

Drug	Time of onset (min)	Duration of effect (h)	Amine structure
Atropine	60-120	4-6	Tertiary
Scopolamine	30-60	4-6	Tertiary
Glycopyrrolate	30-45	6-8	Quaternary
Methantheline	30-45	6	Quaternary
Propantheline	30-45	6	Quaternary

Cholinergic Drug: Pilocarpine

In contrast to the anticholinergic agents, cholinergic drugs produce effects that mimic those of acetylcholine, the natural ligand for cholinergic receptors. Additional terms used to identify cholinergic drugs include cholinergic agonists, cholinomimetics, parasympathomimetics and muscarinic agonists. Pilocarpine, a naturally occurring cholinergic agonist, is the only drug currently approved for the treatment of xerostomia. Diseases or conditions that cause xerostomia commonly result in opportunistic infection, increased caries and difficulty in speaking and in maintaining normal dietary intake. Although pilocarpine has been used as a sialogogue for nearly a century to treat such diverse conditions as Sjögren's syndrome and postradiation xerostomia, it was approved for the latter purpose by the U.S. Food and Drug Administration only in 1994, after being developed under the provisions of the Orphan Drug Act of 1983.

Successful stimulation of salivary secretion by pilocarpine requires the presence of intact salivary gland tissue and nerve supply. In the case of radiation therapy, this requirement may be met by residual active tissue in the irradiated field or healthy tissue outside the field.

Accepted Indications

Pilocarpine has been approved for the relief of xerostomia caused by radiation therapy of the head and neck. In its topical forms, pilocarpine has also been approved for treating various types of glaucoma and producing pupillary constriction (miosis) after surgery or ocular examination.

General Dosing Information

As shown in Table 10.6, the usual adult daily dose of pilocarpine is 5 mg tid, usually 30 min before meals. A dose of 10 mg tid may be tried in refractory cases; however, the incidence of dose-related side effects increases at this dosage and, as a general rule, the dentist should use the lowest effective dose that is tolerated by the patient. Pilocarpine has not been tested in children.

Special Dental Considerations

Drug Interactions of Dental Interest

Table 10.7 lists possible drug interactions and related problems involving pilocarpine that are potentially of clinical significance in dentistry.

Cross-Sensitivity

Patients sensitive to other forms of pilocarpine dosage (that is, ophthalmic) should be considered sensitive to oral pilocarpine.

Special Patients

Pregnant and nursing women

There are no data regarding the influence of pilocarpine on reproduction and fetal development. Pilocarpine has been designated as FDA pregnancy category C. It has not been determined if pilocarpine is distributed into breast milk, and there are no reports of related problems in humans.

Table 10.6

Pilocarpine: Dosage and Prescribing Information

Generic name	Brand name(s)	Adult dosage	Child dosage	PRC	Content/form
Pilocarpine hydrochloride	Salagen	5 mg tid **In refractory cases:** 10 mg tid	NE	C	**Tablets:** 5 mg

PRC: Pregnancy risk category.
NE: Not established.

Pediatric, geriatric and other special patients
Pilocarpine has not been tested for, nor is it indicated for, use in children.

There appears to be no special concern regarding pilocarpine and the geriatric population, although elderly people are more likely to have specific medical problems, such as angle-closure glaucoma, pulmonary disease or cardiovascular disease, that may complicate pilocarpine therapy.

Adverse Effects and Precautions

Most of the adverse effects observed with pilocarpine (Table 10.8) are dose-dependent extensions of the drug's ability to stimulate cholinergic muscarinic receptors. Hypertension may be an important exception to this generalization. Excessive secretions (sweating, bronchial secretions, rhinitis) are the most common side effects associated with oral pilocarpine.

Pharmacology

Pilocarpine stimulates muscarinic receptors to elicit most of its effects. Muscarinic receptors are linked to specific G proteins that mediate intracellular signaling in response to drug-receptor binding. For the M_3 receptor involved in salivary secretion, stimulation of its G protein causes the intracellular formation of inositol 1,4,5-trisphosphate and diacylglycerol, which promote secretion and smooth muscle contraction. Anomalous hypertensive responses to pilocarpine may be due to ganglionic or adrenal medullary stimulation. Pilocarpine, which is a tertiary amine, gains access to the CNS and can produce excitatory reactions.

Pilocarpine is readily absorbed from the gastrointestinal tract. Peak drug effects occur within 1 h and last 3-5 h. Pilocarpine is partially metabolized, possibly in the plasma or at neuronal synapses, and is then excreted in the urine.

Patient Advice

- Because adverse effects are dose-dependent, patients should be cautioned to take the medication as directed.
- If dizziness, lightheadedness or blurred vision occurs, patients should refrain from driving or other tasks requiring alertness, coordination and visual acuity until the problem is resolved.

Table 10.7

Pilocarpine: Possible Interactions With Other Drugs

Drug taken by patient	Interaction with pilocarpine	Dentist's action
Drugs with anticholinergic activity: anticholinergics, antiparkinson drugs, antipsychotic agents, carbamazepine, digoxin, dronabinol, orphenadrine, procainamide, quinidine, sedative antihistamines, tricyclic antidepressants	*Antagonistic drug effects*	Use cautiously when the anticholinergic effect of the interacting drug is not the goal of therapy; otherwise consult with a physician to optimize drug treatment
Drugs with cholinergic activity: cholinergic antiglaucoma drugs, antimyasthenic agents, bethanechol	Summation of drug effects	Use cautiously
β-adrenergic blocking drugs	*Summation of drug effects on cardiac automaticity and conduction*	Use cautiously

Italics indicate information of major clinical significance.

Table 10.8
Pilocarpine: Adverse Effects, Precautions and Contraindications

Body system	Adverse effects	Precautions/contraindications
General	Sweating, chills, flushing	*Contraindicated in patients with history of drug sensitivity to pilocarpine*
CV	Bradycardia, *tachycardia*, atrioventricular heart block *Hypertension*, transient hypotension	*Patients with cardiovascular disease have increased risk of cardiovascular instability*
CNS	Confusion, headache	Psychiatric disorders increase risk of CNS disturbances
EENT	Increased intraocular pressure, blurred vision, eye pain, lacrimation	*Patients with angle-closure glaucoma or acute iritis have an increased risk of acute attack of glaucoma* History of or predisposition for retinal detachment may increase risk of detachment
GI	Nausea and vomiting, diarrhea	
GU	Frequent urination	Use in patients with nephrolithiasis may lead to renal colic
HB	None of significance to dentistry	Patients with cholelithiasis have increased risk of acute biliary disorder
Musc	Tremors	
Resp	Bronchoconstriction, increased mucous secretions, wheezing, pulmonary edema Rhinitis, nose bleed	*History of asthma, chronic bronchitis or chronic obstructive pulmonary disease increases risk of respiratory distress*

Italics indicate information of major clinical significance.

Suggested Readings

Davies AN, Daniels C, Pugh R, Sharma K. A comparison of artificial saliva and pilocarpine in the management of xerostomia in patients with advanced cancer. Palliative Med 1998;12(2):105-11.

Niedermeier W, Matthaeus C, Meyer C, et al. Radiation-induced hyposalivation and its treatment with oral pilocarpine. Oral Surg Oral Med Oral Pathol Oral Radiol Endod 1998;86(5):541-9.

Vivino FB, Al-Hashimi I, Khan Z, et al. Pilocarpine tablets for the treatment of dry mouth and dry eye symptoms in patients with Sjögren syndrome: a randomized, placebo-controlled, fixed-dose, multicenter trial. Arch Intern Med 1999;159(2):174-81.

Wiseman LR, Faulds D. Oral pilocarpine: a review of its pharmacological properties and clinical potential in xerostomia. Drugs 1995;49(1):143-55.

Saliva Substitutes

When salivary function is absent or minimal, cholinergic drug therapy with pilocarpine or related agents is ineffective. Replacement of missing saliva is a natural therapeutic alternative. Water is most commonly used by patients afflicted with chronic xerostomia because of its unique advantages of availability and low cost. Water is a poor substitute for saliva, however, because it lacks necessary ions, buffering capacity, lubricating mucins and protective proteins. Saliva substitutes, or artificial salivas, are designed to more closely match the chemical and physical characteristics of saliva. These preparations often contain complex mixtures of salts, with cellulose derivatives or animal mucins added to increase viscosity (often a viscosity greater than that of natural saliva, in an attempt to improve retention within the mouth). Flavoring agents, usually sorbitol or xylitol, generally are added to improve taste, and parabens are sometimes included to inhibit bacterial growth. A deficiency of all artificial salivas to date is their complete lack of anti-infective proteins, such as immunoglobulin A, histatins and lysozyme. A saliva substitute in the form of a long-lasting moisturizing gel (Oral*balance*; see Table 10.9), however, contains various ingredients that are claimed to be biologically active, but clinical data are minimal.

Accepted Indications

Saliva substitutes are indicated for the symptomatic relief of dry mouth and dry throat in patients with xerostomia.

Table 10.9

Saliva Substitutes: Product Information

Brand name(s)	Content/form
Entertainer's Secret	**Solution:** sodium carboxymethylcellulose, dibasic sodium phosphate, potassium chloride, parabens, aloe vera gel, glycerin in 60-mL spray
Moi-Stir, Moi-Stir Swabsticks	**Solution:** sodium carboxymethylcellulose, dibasic sodium phosphate, calcium, magnesium, potassium and sodium chlorides, parabens, sorbitol in 120-mL pump spray and 3-stick packets
MouthKote	**Solution:** mucoprotective factor, yerba santa, saccharin, sorbitol, xylitol in 60- and 240-mL spray
Optimoist	**Solution:** hydroxyethyl cellulose, acesulfame potassium, calcium phosphate monobasic, citric acid, sodium benzoate, sodium hydroxide, sodium monofluorophosphate in 60- and 355-mL spray
Oral*balance*	**Gel:** hydroxyethyl cellulose, hydrogenated starch, glycerate polyhydrate, potassium thiocyanate, glucose oxidase, lactoperoxidase, lysozyme, lactoferrin, aloe vera, xylitol
Saliva Substitute ★	**Solution:** sodium carboxymethylcellulose, sorbitol in 5- and 120-mL vials
Salivart ★	**Solution:** sodium carboxymethylcellulose, dibasic potassium phosphate, calcium, magnesium, potassium and sodium chlorides, sorbitol, nitrogen propellant in 25- and 75-mL spray cans
Salix	**Lozenges:** hydroxypropyl methylcellulose, carboxymethylcellulose, dicalcium phosphate, malic acid, hydrogenated cottonseed oil, sodium citrate, citric acid, silicon dioxide, sorbitol
Xero-Lube	**Solution:** hydroxyethylcellulose, dibasic and monobasic potassium phosphates, calcium, magnesium and potassium chlorides, sodium fluoride, methylparaben, flavor, xylitol in 6-oz spray

★ *indicates a product bearing the ADA Seal of Acceptance.*

General Dosing Information

Saliva substitutes are meant to be taken ad libitum throughout the day, usually in the form of sprays, to keep the oral mucosa moist. There are no specific dosing guidelines, nor are there specific recommendations for special patients. Table 10.9 lists, by manufacturer's brand name, the ingredients of some commercially available preparations.

Special Dental Considerations

Patients with severe xerostomia who use a saliva substitute containing sorbitol on a regular basis may be at increased risk of caries associated with a very limited fermentation of sorbitol. A proper professionally designed topical fluoride treatment program undertaken to protect the teeth of the patient with xerostomia from caries should also overcome any problem posed by sorbitol.

Use of sugarless chewing gum, some of which may contain a remineralizing agent, and sugarless citrus-flavored lozenges may increase salivary flow. Some patients have claimed benefits from use of Biotène products (Oral*balance*), but there are no controlled studies published in peer-reviewed journals to substantiate these claims.

There are no known drug interactions involving saliva substitutes, nor any need for patient monitoring pertaining to these products. Laboratory tests are likewise unaffected.

Cross-Sensitivity

Saliva substitutes containing parabens pose a risk of cross-sensitivity in patients allergic to parabens, para-aminobenzoic acid or its derivatives, such as ester local anesthetics. Some products contain other ingredients that pose additional risks of allergic cross-reactions.

Adverse Effects and Precautions

Aside from the allergic potential of parabens or other components of selected preparations and the possibility of increased caries inci-

dence with sorbitol, there are few potential adverse effects or precautions associated with saliva substitutes. Microbial contamination is a possibility with multiple dose formulations, but this risk is partially offset by the inclusion of paraben preservatives.

Pharmacology

Saliva substitutes are physically active agents. When used regularly, they help minimize the sequelae of xerostomia by keeping the oral mucosa moist and lubricated. Surface abrasion is reduced, and patients are more able to perform the everyday activities of speaking, eating and sleeping. Long-term compliance, however, is a problem with these products because of their perceived inconvenience and relatively high cost.

Because saliva substitutes are quickly swallowed and their activity is of limited duration, they must be administered repeatedly. The components of the ingested solution undoubtedly undergo gastrointestinal absorption; however, there is no information on the pharmacokinetics of the currently available saliva substitutes.

Patient Advice

- Patients should be informed of the necessity of the continual use of saliva substitutes.
- Patients with chronic xerostomia should be educated on the need for regular professional care and for a high degree of compliance with the dental professional's recommendations for minimizing caries and soft-tissue pathology.

Suggested Readings

Fox PC. Management of dry mouth. Dent Clin North Am 1997;41(4):863-75.

Levine MJ. Development of artificial salivas. Crit Rev Oral Biol Med 1993;4:279-86.

Levine MJ, Aguirre A, Hatton MN, Tabak LA. Artificial salivas: present and future. J Dent Res 1987;66(Special Issue):693-8.

Chapter 11.

Mouthrinses and Dentifrices

Angelo J. Mariotti, D.D.S., Ph.D.; Kenneth H. Burrell, D.D.S., S.M.

Mouthrinses

Mouthrinses are solutions formulated to control or reduce halitosis through topical deoxidization, to act as antibacterial agents to reduce and prevent gingivitis, to interact with saliva and mucosal proteins, or to help prevent caries. The major components of mouthrinses are water, flavoring, humectant, surfactant, alcohol and the active ingredients.

Water is the major vehicle used to solubilize the ingredients. The flavor is designed to make the mouthrinse pleasant to use. The humectant adds substance or "body" to the product and inhibits crystallization around the opening of the container. The surfactant is used to solubilize the flavoring agent and provide foaming action. In addition, the surfactant helps remove oral debris and has some limited antimicrobial properties. If the formulation requires an antimicrobial agent, the surfactant must be compatible with it. Alcohol also helps solubilize some of the ingredients present in the formulation. There has been some concern about the association between mouthrinses containing alcohol and oral cancers, but current findings do not establish a causal relationship.

Active ingredients vary considerably within the product category, but they can be placed into four general groups: antimicrobial agents, fluoride, astringent salts and chlorophyllins.

Antimicrobial agents can be useful in reducing plaque formation, decreasing the severity of gingivitis and controlling halitosis. Chlorhexidine rinses are available by prescription only, while all others are available over the counter. Mouthrinses containing chlorhexidine are the only products that have received FDA approval for efficacy in reducing plaque and gingival inflammation. Numerous antibacterial agents have been used as subgingival irrigants in patients with gingivitis and periodontitis. In general, both home-applied and professionally applied subgingival antimicrobial agents have been shown to reduce gingivitis; however, subgingival irrigation as an adjunct to conventional periodontal therapy has produced equivocal results. Moreover, subgingival irrigation with antimicrobial agents does not appear to have significantly greater benefits than irrigation with water alone.

Fluoride rinses will reduce carious lesions substantially. However, these agents have little or no effect in reducing supragingival plaque.

Oxygenating compounds with concentrations of 3% or greater of hydrogen peroxide should not be considered for frequent and extended use, as such use can result in damage to oral tissues. In solutions containing carbamide peroxide, one-third of the carbamide peroxide is converted to hydrogen peroxide, which has the potential to damage oral tissue if the dose exceeds 3% hydrogen peroxide. A solution of 10% carbamide peroxide releases approximately 3% hydrogen peroxide when introduced into the mouth.

Since the introduction of the first prebrushing rinse, the marketing of similar generic products has proliferated. Although some studies have reported plaque reductions in patients using these agents, a large number of studies found no advantage to using prebrushing rinses for the purpose of reducing plaque levels. Thus, the recommendation of prebrushing rinses is questionable.

The reasons for halitosis are complex, and dentists recognize that a mouthrinse may treat the symptoms and not the causes of halitosis. Astringent salts present in mouthwashes can interact with salivary and mucosal proteins to control halitosis, and chlorophyllins can serve as topical deodorizers to mask halitosis. The effect of using mouthrinses to disguise malodor is transitory and ineffective. To diagnose and treat the cause of halitosis effectively, the dentist must perform a thorough examination.

Accepted Indications

Mouthrinses are used in dentistry for a variety of reasons: to freshen breath (reduce halitosis), to prevent or control dental caries, to reduce plaque formation on teeth and gingiva, to prevent or reduce gingivitis or to produce a combination of these effects.

Gingivitis

To receive the ADA Seal of Acceptance, a mouthrinse used for the control of gingival inflammation must demonstrate a statistically significant reduction in gingival inflammation that represents a proportionate reduction of at least 15% in favor of the mouthrinse in any one study and an average of 20% reduction in two studies.

Halitosis

Mouthrinses used to mask oral odor pose several problems. Breath odors can result for a myriad of reasons, including poor oral hygiene, oral or systemic disease, types of food eaten and bacterial flora in the alimentary canal and on the tongue. Furthermore, the duration of action of mouthrinses in masking halitosis is quite variable, but these agents generally have a short duration of action because of poor substantivity.

Mouthrinses thought to be useful in the control of halitosis either contain agents that limit the growth of bacteria responsible for common mouth odors or inactivate the malodorous volatile sulfur-containing compounds that are present owing to amino acid degradation. The antimicrobial agents include chlorhexidine, chlorine dioxide, cetylpyridium chloride and oral rinses based on a mixture of the volatile oil constituents (such as eucalyptol, menthol, thymol and methyl salicylate). Examples of agents that inhibit odor-causing compounds are zinc salts, ketone terpene and ionone, a compound found in tomato juice.

At press time, there were no ADA-accepted mouthrinses for the control of halitosis. Although several ADA-accepted mouthrinses and toothpastes can substantiate their claims using criteria that are currently used by the oral care industry, these criteria may not be sufficient to support the claims once the ADA has established guidelines for evaluating products' effectiveness against oral malodor. Mouthrinses containing chlorine dioxide are available, but there are no adequate controlled trials of their efficacy to control sulfide-associated odors from bacteria or oral mucosa, and these rinses have not been compared to mechanical débridement of oral mucosal surfaces.

General Dosing Information

The usual adult dosage (and often the geriatric dosage) for mouthrinses (see Table 11.1) is 10-20 mL for therapeutic rinses; it is not established for cosmetic and prebrushing rinses and so can be dictated by individual choice. For oxygenating agents, dosage regimens are more restrictive in terms of frequency and duration of usage. Duration of rinsing varies by the type of agent used. Safety and efficacy typically have not been established for antigingivitis mouthrinse use by pediatric patients.

Maximum Recommended Doses

Maximum recommended doses for mouthrinses are typically what can be held in the mouth comfortably (10-20 mL). The exception is an oxygenating agent of 1.5% hydrogen peroxide (Peroxyl), which is used in smaller quantities. Depending on whether the formulations are purchased over the counter (with directions on packaging) or are prescribed (with directions on the label), additional mouthrinse should be taken only after sufficient time has been allowed for the therapeutic effect of the previous dose to need augmentation.

Dosage Adjustments

The actual maximum dose for each patient must be individualized depending on factors such as his or her size, age and physical status; ability to effectively rinse and expectorate; oral health; and sensitivity. Mouthrinses are not often prescribed for pediatric patients. As patients often swallow some of the product, reduced maximum doses may be indicated for geriatric patients, patients with serious illness or disability and patients with medical conditions who are taking drugs that alter oral responses to mouthrinses.

Special Dental Considerations

Drug Interactions of Dental Interest

Concurrent use of agents that contain either calcium hydroxide or aluminum hydroxide may form a complex with fluoride ions and reduce a rinse's effectiveness in the mouth. Concomitant use of chlorhexidine and stannous fluoride mouthrinses may reduce the efficacy of each agent.

Cross-Sensitivity

Some patients can develop allergic reactions (such as skin rash, hives and facial swelling) to rinses. If this occurs, treatment should be discontinued immediately.

Special Patients

Problems in women who are pregnant or breast feeding have not been documented with normal daily use of oral rinses containing fluorides.

Patient Monitoring: Aspects to Watch

- Extrinsic staining and increased calculus buildup: possible in some instances (see Table 11.2)
- Sanguinarine rinses: have been implicated in epithelial dysplasia, although there are no data to support a cause-and-effect relationship
- Patients in recovery from alcoholism: caution should be used in prescribing mouthrinses containing alcohol to these patients
- Rinsing with water or drinking anything after using the mouthrinse: should be avoided for at least 30 min to prevent clearance of the drug from the mouth and reduction in effectiveness of the mouthrinse

Adverse Effects and Precautions

The incidence of adverse reactions to mouthrinses is relatively low. Many reactions (burning, taste alterations, tooth staining) are temporary. Idiosyncratic and allergic reactions account for a small minority of adverse responses. Preliminary data have suggested that chronic use of sanguinarine may be associated with oral leukoplakias; however, further information must be gathered before a link between sanguinarine and oral lesions is firmly established. The adverse effects listed in Table 11.2 apply to all major types of mouthrinses.

Pharmacology

Chlorhexidine

Chlorhexidine is a bisbiguanide with broad-spectrum antibacterial activity. It is a symmetrical, cationic molecule that binds strongly to hydroxylapatite, the organic pellicle of the tooth, oral mucosa, salivary proteins and bacteria. As a result of the binding of chlorhexidine to oral structures, the drug exhibits substantivity (for example, 30% of the drug is retained after rinsing, with subsequent slow release over time). Chlorhexidine is poorly absorbed from the gastrointestinal tract, and whatever

Table 11.1

Mouthrinses: Dosage and Prescribing Information

Generic name/ active ingredient	Brand name(s)	Adult dosage*	Child dosage†	Indications	Content
Anesthetic mouthrinse	Chloraseptic Mouthwash	10 mL prn (no more often than q 3 h)	NI	Topical anesthesia	1.4% phenol, 12.5% alcohol
Antitartar mouthrinse	Tartar Control Listerine ★	Rinse with 20 mL for 30 s	NE	To prevent tartar buildup, help prevent and reduce plaque and gingivitis	Active ingredients for plaque control include thymol (0.064%), eucalyptol (0.092%), methyl salicylate (0.060%) and menthol (0.042%), alcohol (21.6%), zinc chloride (0.09%), miscellaneous ingredients
Chlorhexidine ‡	Peridex ★, PerioGard	15 mL swished for 30 s and expectorated; use bid	NE	Antibacterial	**Peridex ★:** 0.12% chlorhexidine, 11.6% alcohol **PerioGard:** 0.12% chlorhexidine, 11.6% alcohol
Cosmetic mouthrinses	Rembrandt Age Defying Mouthrinse, Rembrandt Dazzling Fresh Mouthrinse	Amount, duration, and frequency of use depend on individual choice	NR	Tooth whitening	**Rembrandt Age Defying Mouthrinse:** Sodium fluoride 0.05% wt/vol, 1.5% hydrogen peroxide solution, miscellaneous agents **Rembrandt Dazzling Fresh Mouthrinse:** Methylparaben, sodium citrate, sodium lauryl sulfate, miscellaneous ingredients
	Targon	Before brushing, rinse with 20 mL for 30 s	NE	To reduce tar stains on teeth from smoking	Principal ingredients by volume include alcohol (15.6%), PEG-40, hydrogenated castor oil, sodium lauryl sulfate, disodium phosphate, miscellaneous ingredients

Essential oils	Listerine ★ §	20 mL swished full strength for 30 s and expectorated bid or prn dentist	NE	Antibacterial	Listerine ★ §: 0.092% eucalyptol, 0.062% thymol, 0.06% methyl salicylate, 0.042% menthol, ranging from 21.6 (Cool Mint, Fresh Burst) to 26.9% (Original) alcohol
Fluorides	Act Anti-Cavity Fluoride Rinse ★, Act for Kids Anti-Cavity Fluoride Treatment ★, Dentinbloc Dentin Desensitizer, Fluorigard Anti-Cavity Dental Rinse, Phos-Flur Daily Oral Rinse ★, PreviDent Dental Rinse, Reach Fluoride Dental Rinse, NaF rinse Acidulated Oral Rinse ★, Oral-B Rinse Therapy Anti-Cavity Treatment ★, Pro-Dent$_x$ 0.2% Neutral Sodium Fluoride Rinse ★	10 mL of sodium fluoride swished for 60 s and expectorated q day; patient should not eat or drink for 30 min after rinsing	Age < 6 y: NR Age ≥ 6 y: Children can rinse with 10 mL of 0.05% sodium fluoride for 60 s and expectorate q day and should not eat or drink for 30 min after rinsing	Prevention or remineralization of carious lesions	Act Anti-Cavity Fluoride Rinse: 0.05% sodium fluoride, 7% alcohol Act for Kids Anti-Cavity Fluoride Treatment ★: 0.05% sodium fluoride Dentinbloc Dentin Desensitizer: 1.09% sodium fluoride, 0.4% stannous fluoride, 0.14% hydrogen fluoride Fluorigard Anti-Cavity Dental Rinse, Phos-Flur Daily Oral Rinse ★: 0.02% fluoride PreviDent Dental Rinse ★: 0.2% sodium fluoride, 6% alcohol Reach Fluoride Dental Rinse, NaF rinse Acidulated Oral Rinse ★, Oral-B Rinse Therapy Anti-Cavity Treatment ★: 0.05% sodium fluoride Pro-Dent$_x$ 0.2% Neutral Sodium Fluoride Rinse ★

Continued on next page

★ indicates a product bearing the ADA Seal of Acceptance.
NE: Not established.
NI: Not indicated.
NR: Not recommended.
* Geriatric dosage is same as usual adult dosage.
† Pediatric safety and efficacy have not been established except with fluoride rinses in children aged 6 y and older.
‡ Pregnancy risk category B. Pregnancy risk categories have not been established for other products in this table.
§ Although Listerine was the first antiseptic oral rinse formulated, today there are a significant number of generic compounds with similar antibacterial properties. See footnote on page 218 for examples.

Table 11.1 (cont.)

Mouthrinses: Dosage and Prescribing Information

Generic name/ active ingredient	Brand name(s)	Adult dosage*	Child dosage†	Indications	Content
Mouthrinses for halitosis	Astring-O-Sol, Cepacol, Lavoris Crystal Fresh, Lavoris Mint, Lavoris Original, Lavoris Original Cinnamon, Lavoris Peppermint, Listermint Mint, Oxyfresh Natural Mouthrinse, Platinum, Rembrandt Mouth Refreshing Rinse, Retardex Oral Rinse, Scope Mouthwash and Gargle, Scope Mouthwash and Gargle with Baking Soda, Signal Mouthwash, Therasol Mouthwash, Tom's of Maine Natural Mouthwash, Viadent Advanced Care Oral Rinse	Amount, duration and frequency depend on individual choice	NR	Masking of odors in mouth	**Astring-O-Sol (concentrate):** SD alcohol 38-B, 75.6% methyl salicylate, miscellaneous ingredients **Cepacol:** 14.5% alcohol, cetylpyridinium chloride 0.05%, miscellaneous ingredients **Lavoris Crystal Fresh, Original, Peppermint:** alcohol, citric acid, sodium hydroxide, zinc oxide, miscellaneous ingredients **Lavoris Mint, Cinnamon:** alcohol, aromatic oils, zinc chloride and/or zinc oxide **Listermint Mint (alcohol-free):** zinc chloride, sodium benzoate, sodium lauryl sulfate, miscellaneous ingredients **Oxyfresh Natural Mouthrinse (alcohol-free):** oxygene (contains chlorine dioxide), miscellaneous ingredients **Platinum:** monofluorophosphate, tetrapotassium pyrophosphate, miscellaneous ingredients **Rembrandt Mouth Refreshing Rinse (alcohol-free):** sodium benzoate, methyl paraben, miscellaneous ingredients **Retardex Oral Rinse (alcohol-free):** Ciosysii (contains chlorine dioxide), miscellaneous ingredients **Scope Mouthwash and Gargle:** 18.9% alcohol, sodium benzoate, cetylpyridinium chloride, benzoic acid, domiphen bromide, miscellaneous ingredients **Scope Mouthwash and Gargle with Baking Soda:** 9.9% alcohol, cetylpyridinium chloride, domiphen bromide, miscellaneous ingredients

					Signal Mouthwash: 14.5% alcohol, sodium lauryl sulfate, miscellaneous ingredients **Therasol Mouthwash:** 8% alcohol, 0.3% C31G (alkyl dimethyl amine oxide and alkyl dimethyl glycine), miscellaneous ingredients **Tom's of Maine Natural Mouthwash:** Menthol **Viadent Advanced Care Oral Rinse:** 10% alcohol, cetylpyridinium chloride 0.05%, miscellaneous ingredients
Oxygenating agents	Gly-Oxide, Orajel Rinse, Perimax Hygenic Perio Rinse, Peroxyl Mouthrinse	Regimens used for rinses containing oxygenating agents will vary depending on formulation: e.g., recommendation for Gly-Oxide is that several drops be applied to affected areas, followed by a 2-3-min rinsing; the recommendation for Peroxyl Mouthrinse is that 10 mL of it be used, followed by a 60-s rinsing	NE	Cleansing suppurating wounds and inflamed mucous membranes	**Gly-Oxide:** 10% carbamide peroxide **Orajel Rinse:** 4% alcohol, 1.5% hydrogen peroxide **Perimax Hygenic Perio Rinse:** 1.5% hydrogen peroxide **Peroxyl Mouthrinse:** 1.5% hydrogen peroxide, 6% alcohol

NE: Not established.
NR: Not recommended.
** Geriatric dosage is same as usual adult dosage.*
† Pediatric safety and efficacy have not been established except with fluoride rinses in children aged 6 y and older.

Continued on next page

Table 11.1 (cont.)

Mouthrinses: Dosage and Prescribing Information

Generic name/active ingredient	Brand name(s)	Adult dosage*	Child dosage†	Indications	Content
Prebrushing rinse	Advanced Formula Plax	Efficacy has not been established for adult or geriatric population	NE	Impairing attachment of plaque to tooth and therefore aiding in mechanical removal of plaque	Advanced Formula Plax: Principal ingredients by volume include water, glycerin, 8.5% alcohol, tetrasodium pyrophosphate, benzoic acid, sodium lauryl sulfate, sodium benzoate (original flavor, peppermint, soft mint)
Sanguinarine	Viadent Oral Rinse	Swish 10 mL for 60 s and expectorate prn dentist	NE	Antibacterial	0.03% sanguinaria extract, 10% alcohol

NE: Not established.

* Geriatric dosage is same as usual adult dosage.

† Pediatric safety and efficacy have not been established except with fluoride rinses in children aged 6 y and older.

Essential Oils: Various essential oil compound mouthrinses are available generically as store brands. The following generic products carry the ADA Seal of Acceptance: Albertson's Antiseptic Mouth Rinse; Ames Blue Mint Antiseptic Mouth Rinse; Arbor Antiseptic Mouth Rinse; Arbor Antiseptic Mouth Rinse, blue mint; Bi-Mart Blue Mint Antiseptic Mouth Rinse; Brite-Life Antiseptic Mouth Rinse; Brooks Antiseptic Mouth Rinse; Brooks Blue Mint Antiseptic Mouth Rinse; Chateau Antiseptic Mouth Rinse; Chateau Blue Mint Antiseptic Mouth Rinse; Cool Mint Listerine Antiseptic; CVS Antiseptic Mouth Rinse; CVS Antiseptic Mouth Rinse, Blue Mint; Diamond Products Original Flavor Antiseptic Mouth Rinse; Discount Drug Mart Food Fair Blue Mint Antiseptic Mouth Rinse; Drug Emporium Antiseptic Mouth Rinse; Drug Emporium Blue Mint Antiseptic Mouth Rinse; Drug Guild Antiseptic Mouth Rinse; Equate Antiseptic Mouth Rinse; Fame Antiseptic Blue Mint Mouth Rinse; Family Pharmacy Antiseptic Mouth Rinse; FDC Antiseptic Mouth Rinse; Food Lion Antiseptic Mouth Rinse; Fred Myer Antiseptic Mouth Rinse; Fred's Antiseptic Mouth Rinse; Fred's Blue Mint Antiseptic Mouth Rinse; FreshBurst Listerine Antiseptic; Full Value Antiseptic Mouth Rinse; Full Value Blue Mint Antiseptic Mouth Rinse; Furr's Antiseptic Mouth Rinse; Giant Eagle Antiseptic Mouth Rinse; Giant Eagle Blue Mint Antiseptic Mouth Rinse; Goldline Antiseptic Mouth Rinse; Good Neighbor Pharmacy Antiseptic Mouth Rinse; Good Neighbor Pharmacy Blue Mint Antiseptic Mouth Rinse; Good Sense Antiseptic Mouth Rinse; Good Sense Blue Mint Antiseptic Mouth Rinse; Hannaford Antiseptic Mouth Rinse; Hannaford Blue Mint Antiseptic Mouth Rinse; Happy Harry's Antiseptic Mouth Rinse; Harmon Antiseptic Mouth Rinse; Harmon Blue Mint Antiseptic Mouth Rinse; Harris Teeter Antiseptic Mouth Rinse; Health Mart Antiseptic Mouth Rinse; Hills Antiseptic Mouth Rinse, blue mint; Hills Antiseptic Mouth Rinse; Homebest Antiseptic Mouth Rinse; Homebest Blue Mint Antiseptic Mouth Rinse; Hy-Vee Antiseptic Mouth Rinse; Hy-Vee Blue Mint Antiseptic Mouth Rinse; K&B Antiseptic Mouth Rinse; K&B Blue Mint Antiseptic Mouth Rinse; Kroger Antiseptic Mouth Rinse; Kroger Blue Mint Antiseptic Mouth Rinse; Lander Mouthrinse and Gargle, green; Leader Antiseptic Mouth Rinse; Legend Antiseptic Mouth Rinse; Longs Antiseptic Mouth Rinse; Longs Blue Mint Antiseptic Mouth Rinse; Marquee Antiseptic Mouth Rinse; May's Antiseptic Mouth Rinse; May's Blue Mint Antiseptic Mouth Rinse; Medalist Antiseptic Mouth Rinse; Meijer Antiseptic Mouth Rinse; Meijer Blue Mint Antiseptic Mouth Rinse; Money Supply Antiseptic Mouth Rinse; Navarro Antiseptic Mouth Rinse; Navarro Blue Mint Antiseptic Mouth Rinse; Oral Pure Antiseptic Mouth Rinse; Oral Pure Blue Mint Antiseptic Mouth Rinse; Osco Antiseptic Mouth Rinse; Osco Blue Mint Antiseptic Mouth Rinse; Our Family Antiseptic Mouth Rinse; Our Family Blue Mint Antiseptic Mouth Rinse, blue mint; Perfect Choice Blue Mint Antiseptic Mouth Rinse; Perfect Choice Mouth Rinse; Perrigo Antiseptic Mouth Rinse; Perrigo Blue Mint Mouth Rinse; Phar-Mor Antiseptic Mouth Rinse; Phar-Mor Blue Mint Antiseptic Mouth Rinse; Price Chopper Antiseptic Mouth Rinse; Price Chopper Blue Mint Antiseptic Mouth Rinse; Publix Antiseptic Mouth Rinse; Publix Blue Mint Antiseptic Mouth Rinse; Quality Choice Blue Mint Antiseptic Mouth Rinse; Raley's Antiseptic Mouth Rinse; Safeway Antiseptic Mouth Rinse; Sav-On Antiseptic Mouth Rinse; Sav-On Blue Mint Antiseptic Mouth Rinse; Schnucks Antiseptic Mouth Rinse; Shaw's Antiseptic Mouth Rinse; Shurfine Antiseptic Mouth Rinse; Smith's Antiseptic Mouth Rinse; Smith's Blue Mint Antiseptic Mouth Rinse; Smitty's Antiseptic Mouth Rinse; Spartan Antiseptic Mouth Rinse; Spartan Blue Mint Antiseptic Mouth Rinse; Stater Bros. Antiseptic Mouth Rinse; Stater Bros. Markets Antiseptic Mouth Rinse; Stater Bros. Markets Blue Mint Antiseptic Mouth Rinse; Super G Antiseptic Mouth Rinse; Swan Antiseptic Mouth Rinse; Swan Blue Mint Antiseptic Mouth Rinse; Target Antiseptic Mouth Rinse; Target Blue Mint Antiseptic Mouth Rinse; The Pharm Antiseptic Mouth Rinse; The Pharm Blue Mint Antiseptic Mouth Rinse; Top Care Antiseptic Mouth Rinse; Ultra Fresh Antiseptic Mouth Rinse; Ultra Fresh Blue Mint Antiseptic Mouth Rinse; Valu-Rite Antiseptic Mouth Rinse; Venture Antiseptic Mouth Rinse; Venture Blue Mint Antiseptic Mouth Rinse; Vi-Jon Antiseptic Mouth Rinse; Vi-Jon Mint Antiseptic Mouth Rinse; Walgreens Antiseptic Mouth Rinse; Walgreens Fresh Mint Antiseptic Mouth Rinse; Wegmans Antiseptic Mouth Rinse; Wegmans Blue Mint Antiseptic Mouth Rinse; Weis Quality Antiseptic Mouth Rinse; Weis Quality Blue Mint Antiseptic Mouth Rinse; Western Family Antiseptic Mouth Rinse; Western Family Blue Mint Antiseptic Mouth Rinse

Table 11.2

Mouthrinses: Adverse Effects, Precautions and Contraindications

Generic name	Adverse effects	Precautions/contraindications
Chlorhexidine	Allergic reaction (skin rash, hives, swelling of face), alteration of taste, staining of teeth, staining of restorations, discoloration of tongue, increase in calculus formation, parotid duct obstruction, parotitis, desquamation of oral mucosa, irritation to lips or tongue, oral sensitivity	Permanent staining of margins of restorations or composite restorations Should not be used as sole treatment of gingivitis Contraindicated in patients with sensitivity to chlorhexidine
Cosmetic mouthrinses and mouthrinses for halitosis	Alcohol content in these mouthrinses can have a drying effect on the oral mucosa, particularly in people who have low salivary flow; however, the flowing agents in them may stimulate salivary flow	Should be used cautiously in young children and in people who have low salivary flow due to age or drugs Contraindicated in patients with allergic reactions Contraindicated in patients with oral ulcerations Contraindicated in patients with oral desquamative diseases
Essential oils	Burning sensation, bitter taste, drying out of mucous membranes	Should not be used as sole treatment of gingivitis Contraindicated in patients with oral ulcerations or desquamative diseases Contraindicated in children (because of high alcohol content)
Fluorides	Ulcerations of oral mucosa, fluorosis, osteosclerosis, diarrhea, bloody vomit, nausea, stomach cramps, black tarry stools, drowsiness, faintness, stomach cramps or pain, unusual excitement if swallowed	Chronic systemic overdose may induce fluorosis and changes in bone Contraindicated in patients with dental fluorosis Contraindicated in patients who exhibit fluoride toxicity from systemic ingestion Contraindicated in patients who have severe renal insufficiency
Oxygenating agents	Chemical burns of oral mucosa, decalcification of teeth, black hairy tongue	Should not be used for extended periods of time because of possible side effects mentioned at left Contraindicated for treatment of periodontitis or gingivitis
Prebrushing rinses	None reported	Negligible effects on plaque make these agents of little use in the treatment of carious lesions or periodontal diseases, including gingivitis
Sanguinarine	Allergic reaction (skin rash, hives, swelling of face), burning sensation, bitter taste	Should not be used as sole treatment of gingivitis Contraindicated in patients with sensitivity to sanguinaria extract

is absorbed is excreted primarily in the feces. Depending on the dose, chlorhexidine can be bacteriostatic or bactericidal. Bacteriostasis results from interference with bacterial cell wall transport systems. Bactericidal concentrations disrupt the cell wall, which leads to leakage of intracellular proteins.

Chlorhexidine can also be administered to subgingival sites in a controlled local delivery system called PerioChip. This delivery system consists of a small chip (4.0 mm × 5.0 mm × 0.35 mm) composed of a biodegradable hydrolyzed gelatin matrix that contains 2.5 mg of chlorhexidine gluconate. When inserted into a periodontal pocket that has a probing depth of 5 mm or greater, the chip releases chlorhexidine and maintains an antibacterial concentration in crevicular fluid for at least 7 days. As many as 8 chlorhexidine chips may be inserted at one visit. Because PerioChip degrades in 7 to 10 days, a second appointment to remove the chip is unnecessary. Additional placement may be necessary at 3-mo intervals for up to two successive cycles after the initial placement. Clinical studies have not demonstrated staining or adverse effects using this agent in a local delivery system, and the chlorhexidine chip may be a valuable adjunct to scaling and root planing.

Essential Oils

Antibacterial activity is created by a combination of essential oils (eucalyptol [0.092%], thymol [0.062%], methyl salicylate [0.06%] and menthol [0.042%]) in an alcohol-based (21.6-26.9%) vehicle. Essential oils have been implicated in inhibiting bacterial enzymes and reducing pathogenicity of plaque. The substantivity of these agents, also called phenolics, is poor.

Fluorides

Fluoride has been shown to reduce carious lesions dramatically in both children and adults. Fluoride ion is assimilated into the apatite crystal of enamel and stabilizes the crystal, making teeth more resistant to decay.

Fluoride also has been shown to help remineralize incipient carious lesions. The germicidal activity of these agents, which include various liquid formulations of stannous fluoride, is negligible.

Oxygenating Agents

Oxygenating agents release oxygen as an active intermediate, loosening debris in inaccessible areas. Oxygenating agents also have been reported to induce damage in bacterial cells by altering membrane permeability. The germicidal activity of these agents is negligible. The substantivity of oxygenating agents is poor.

Prebrushing Rinses

The exact mechanism that prebrushing rinses use to "loosen" plaque is not known and is questionable. However, it has been suggested that surface-active agents (sodium lauryl sulfate and sodium benzoate, for example) make plaque soluble and therefore easier to remove.

Sanguinarine and Other Herbal Agents

Sanguinarine is a benzophenanthridine alkaloid extract from the root of *Sanguinaria canadensis* that has broad-spectrum antibacterial activity. Sanguinarine has been reported to bind to reactive sulfhydryls, which causes the cell to be less enzymatically active.

Some mouthrinses contain a variety of mixtures of herbal agents (such as aloe vera, sodium carrageenan, ecchinacea, golden seal, bee propolis and many others). At this time, controlled long-term studies to ascertain the efficacy of these agents in patients are lacking.

Note: Although alcohol can denature bacterial cell walls, it serves as a vehicle in most mouthrinses.

Patient Advice

• The effectiveness of any mouthrinse is tied to the use of the agent as prescribed by the dentist. This means the proper dose, duration of time in the mouth and frequency of rinsing must be carefully followed. If a patient misses a dose, he or she should apply the mouthrinse as soon as possible; however, doubling the dose will offer no benefit.

- To receive the greatest antiplaque or anticaries benefit, the patient should rinse before retiring to bed.
- After using a mouthrinse, the patient should not rinse with water or drink anything for at least 30 min. Immediately drinking or rinsing with water will increase the drug's clearance from the mouth and reduce its effectiveness. Furthermore, changes in taste sensation may occur if the mouth is rinsed with water immediately after mouthrinse use.
- These mouthrinses should be kept out of the reach of young children, as their ingestion of 4 or more oz of rinses containing alcohol can cause alcohol intoxication.

Suggested Readings

Ciancio SG. Chemical agents: plaque control, calculus reduction and treatment of dentinal hypersensitivity. Periodontology 2000 1995;8:75-86.

Dawes C. Clearance of substances from the oral cavity—implications for oral health. In: Edgar WM, O'Mullane DM, eds. Saliva and oral health. 2nd ed. London: British Dental Association; 1996:67-80.

Fine DH. Chemical agents to prevent and regulate plaque development. Periodontology 2000 1995;8:87-107.

Kleinberg I, Westbay G. Oral malodor. Crit Rev Oral Biol Med 1990;1(4):247-59.

Mariotti A, Hefti A. Drugs for the control of supragingival plaque. In: Stitzel CR, Craig RE, eds. Modern pharmacology. 5th ed. Boston: Little, Brown; 1997:533-40.

Dentifrices

Oral hygiene is a critical aspect of all dental therapy. Proper oral hygiene reduces the buildup of dental plaque on tooth surfaces and reduces the incidence of dental caries as well as various types of periodontal diseases. Dentifrices—which help remove dental plaque by enhancing the mechanical scrubbing and cleaning power of a toothbrush—are pastes, gels or powders used with a toothbrush to aid in the cleaning of accessible tooth surfaces. Dentifrices typically contain abrasives (to remove debris and residual stain), foaming agents (a preference of consumers), humectants (to prevent loss of water from the preparation), thickening agents or binders (to stabilize dentifrice formulations and prevent separation of liquid and solid phases), flavoring (a preference of consumers) and therapeutic agents (see Table 11.3).

Depending on the dentifrice, the principal therapeutic outcomes can include reduction of caries incidence by assimilation of the fluoride ion into the apatite crystal of enamel (as a result of sodium fluoride, stannous fluoride or sodium monofluorophospate); reduction of tooth hypersensitivity by blocking the pain caused by fluid exchange between dentinal tubules and pulp (as a result of strontium chloride, sodium citrate or potassium nitrate); cosmetic whitening of teeth (as a result of hydrogen peroxide, papain/sodium citrate, or sodium tripolyphosphate and/or abrasives); reduction of calculus by chelation of divalent cations in saliva (as a result of pyrophosphates, zinc citrate or triclosan); and reduction of plaque formation by reducing enzymatic activity of microorganisms and by an antibacterial effect (as a result of triclosan, zinc citrate or stannous fluoride) (see Table 11.3).

A fluoride dentifrice containing calcium and phosphate has been introduced. Its manufacturer claims that supplemental calcium and phosphate incorporated into the dentifrice aid in the remineralization of incipient caries. The important role of calcium and phosphate in remineralization is well known, but abundant quantities of calcium and phosphate already exist in saliva. At press time, clinical studies were not available to determine if the calcium and phosphate in the dentifrice enhance its effectiveness beyond that of a conventional fluoride dentifrice.

Most dentifrices marketed to the public can be broadly classified as agents for

- antitartar activity (reduction of calculus formation),
- caries prevention,
- cosmetic effect (tooth whitening),
- gingivitis reduction,

Table 11.3

Components of Dentifrices

Ingredients	Function
Therapeutic ingredients	
Abrasives: Calcium carbonate, dehydrated silica gels, hydrated aluminum oxides, magnesium carbonate, phosphate salts, silicates	Remove debris and residual stain, whiten teeth
Fluoride	Reduces caries
Peroxides, sodium tripolyphosphate	Whiten teeth
Potassium nitrate, sodium citrate, strontium chloride	Reduce sensitivity
Pyrophosphates, triclosan, zinc citrate	Reduce calculus
Stannous fluoride, triclosan, zinc citrate	Reduce gingival inflammation
Additional ingredients	
Detergents: Sodium lauryl sulfate, sodium N-lauryl sarcosinate	Create foaming action and may help increase the solubility of plaque and accretions during brushing
Flavoring agents: Diverse and complex agents that may contain saccharin as a sweetener	Provide taste to dentifrice (consumer preference)
Humectants: Glycerol, propylene glycol, sorbitol	Prevent water loss
Thickening agents or binders: Mineral colloids, natural gums, seaweed colloids, synthetic celluloses	Stabilize formulations

- plaque formation reduction,
- reduction of tooth sensitivity.

Triclosan (2,4,4,'-Trichloro-2'-hydroxdi-phenyl ether) is an antiplaque/antigingivitis agent available in dentifrices. The addition of a copolymer called vinylmethyl-ether maleic acid (Gantrez) has been shown to improve the effectiveness of triclosan by enhancing its substantivity (that is, its retention by hard and soft surfaces). This formula (Colgate Total) has been approved by the Food and Drug Administration for sale in the United States and is ADA-accepted. Claims allowed are for the reduction of plaque, gingivitis, calculus and caries in all patients over the age of 6 y.

Accepted Indications

Dentifrices are used in dentistry for cosmetic purposes and to provide caries prevention, reduce tooth sensitivity, reduce calculus formation, reduce plaque formation, reduce gingivitis or provide a combination of all of these.

General Dosing Information

Depending on the patient's age and the dentifrice used (see Table 11.4), the usual adult dosage is approximately 1.5 mg of fluoride.

Dosage Adjustments

The actual maximum dose for each patient must be individualized depending on factors

Table 11.4
Antitartar, Cosmetic and Sensitivity-Reduction Dentifrices

Product	Therapeutic/active ingredient
Antitartar	
Aim Anti-Tartar Gel Formula with Fluoride	Zinc citrate, 0.76% sodium monofluorophosphate
Aquafresh Tartar Control Toothpaste ★	Tetrapotassium pyrophosphate, tetrasodium pyrophosphate, 0.221% sodium fluoride
Aquafresh Whitening Toothpaste ★	Sodium fluoride
Close-Up Tartar Control Gel	Zinc citrate, 0.76% sodium monofluorophosphate
Colgate Tartar Control Formula Gel Micro Cleaning Formula ★	Tetrasodium pyrophosphate, 0.15% sodium fluoride
Colgate Tartar Control Formula Toothpaste Micro Cleaning Formula ★	Tetrasodium pyrophosphate, 0.15% sodium fluoride
Colgate Tartar Control Plus Whitening Gel ★	0.243% sodium fluoride, 1% tetrasodium pyrophosphate
Colgate Total ★, Colgate Total Fresh Stripe ★	0.30% triclosan, 0.15% sodium fluoride
Crest Extra Whitening With Tartar Protection ★	0.243% sodium fluoride, 5.045% tetrasodium pyrophosphate
Crest MultiCare ★	Tetrasodium pyrophosphate, 0.15% sodium fluoride
Crest MultiCare Extra Whitening ★	0.243% sodium fluoride, 5.045% tetrasodium pyrophosphate
Crest Tartar Protection Fluoride Gel ★	Tetrapotassium pyrophosphate, disodium pyrophosphate, tetrasodium pyrophosphate, 0.15% sodium fluoride
Crest Tartar Protection Fluoride Toothpaste ★	Tetrapotassium pyrophosphate, disodium pyrophosphate, tetrasodium pyrophosphate, 0.15% sodium fluoride (1,100 ppm)
Prevent Tartar Prevention Toothpaste with Fluoride	Zinc chloride, 0.76% monofluorophosphate
Sensodyne Tartar Control Plus Whitening	0.145% sodium fluoride, 5.2% tetrasodium pyrophosphate, 0.1% calcium peroxide
Viadent Advanced Care Toothpaste	2% zinc citrate, 0.8% sodium monofluorophosphate

★ indicates a product bearing the ADA Seal of Acceptance.
* These dentifrices also possess caries-preventive properties.

Continued on next page

Table 11.4 (cont.)

Antitartar, Cosmetic and Sensitivity-Reduction Dentifrices

Product	Therapeutic/active ingredient
Cosmetic*	
Aquafresh Whitening Toothpaste ★	0.243% sodium fluoride, 10% sodium tripolyphosphate
Caffree Anti-Stain Fluoride Toothpaste	Fluoride
Colgate Platinum Tooth Whitener Toothpaste	2% tetrasodium phosphate, 10% aluminum oxide, 0.76% sodium monofluorophosphate
Colgate Tartar Control Plus Whitening Gel ★	0.243% sodium fluoride, 7% sodium tripolyphosphate, 24.5% silica
Crest Extra Whitening With Tartar Protection ★	0.243% sodium fluoride, 31.0% hydrated silica
Crest MultiCare Extra Whitening ★	0.243% sodium fluoride, 27.5% hydrated silica
Pearl Drops Baking Soda Whitening Toothpaste	Fluoride
Pearl Drops Extra Strength Whitening Toothpaste with Fluoride	Fluoride
Pearl Drops Whitening Gel	Fluoride
Pearl Drops Whitening Toothpolish with Fluoride	Fluoride
Rembrandt Age Defying Toothpaste	0.76% sodium monofluorophosphate, tribon, papain, dicalcium ortho phosphate, 6% carbamide peroxide
Rembrandt Dazzling White Toothpaste	0.76% sodium monofluorophosphate, 6% carbamide peroxide, citroxain
Rembrandt Whitening Toothpaste	44% dicalcium phosphate dihydrate, 0.76% sodium monofluorophosphate (1,000 ppm), citroxain
Sensodyne Extra Whitening	0.15% sodium monofluorophosphate, 0.1% calcium peroxide, 5.2% tetrapotassium pyrophosphate
Sensodyne Tartar Control Plus Whitening	0.145% sodium fluoride, 5.2% tetrasodium pyrophosphate, 0.1% calcium peroxide, silica

★ indicates a product bearing the ADA Seal of Acceptance.
* These dentifrices also possess caries-preventive properties.

Continued on next page

Table 11.4 (cont.)

Antitartar, Cosmetic and Sensitivity-Reduction Dentifrices

Product	Therapeutic/active ingredient
Gingivitis reduction*	
Colgate Total ★	0.30% triclosan, 0.15% sodium fluoride
Colgate Total Fresh Stripe ★	0.30% triclosan, 0.15% sodium fluoride
Crest Gum Care	0.45% stannous fluoride, 0.15% sodium fluoride
Viadent Advanced Care Toothpaste	2% zinc citrate, 0.8% sodium monofluorophosphate
Plaque reduction*	
Colgate Total ★	0.30% triclosan, 0.15% sodium fluoride
Colgate Total Fresh Stripe ★	0.30% triclosan, 0.15% sodium fluoride
Viadent Advanced Care Toothpaste	2% zinc citrate, 0.8% sodium monofluorophosphate
Viadent Fluoride Gel	Sanguinarine, 0.8% sodium monofluorophosphate
Viadent Fluoride Paste	Sanguinarine, 0.8% sodium monofluorophosphate
Sensitivity reduction*	
Aquafresh Sensitive Teeth Toothpaste	5% potassium nitrate, 0.15% sodium fluoride†
Colgate Sensitive Maximum Strength	5% potassium nitrate, 0.454% stannous fluoride
Crest Sensitivity Protection Fluoride Toothpaste ★	5% potassium nitrate, 0.15% sodium fluoride
Orajel Sensitive Pain-Relieving Toothpaste for Adults ★	5% potassium nitrate, 1.15% sodium monofluorophosphate
Oral-B Sensitive with Fluoride Paste	5% potassium nitrate, 0.14% sodium fluoride
Protect Sensitive Teeth Gel Toothpaste ★	5% potassium nitrate, 0.15% sodium fluoride
Rembrandt Whitening Toothpaste for Sensitive Teeth	5% potassium nitrate, 0.76% sodium monofluorophosphate, citroxain
Sensodyne Cool Gel Toothpaste	5% potassium nitrate, 0.13% sodium fluoride
Sensodyne Extra Whitening	0.15% sodium monofluorophosphate, 5% potassium nitrate

★ indicates a product bearing the ADA Seal of Acceptance.
* These dentifrices also possess caries-preventive properties.
† In sensitivity-reduction dentifrices, fluoride is the active agent only for caries prevention;
the exception is stannous fluoride, which has both caries-preventive and sensitivity-reducing properties.

Table 11.4 (cont.)

Antitartar, Cosmetic and Sensitivity-Reduction Dentifrices

Product	Therapeutic/active ingredient
Sensitivity reduction* (cont.)	
Sensodyne Fresh Mint Toothpaste	5% potassium nitrate, sodium fluoride
Sensodyne Original	5% potassium nitrate, 0.13% sodium fluoride
Sensodyne Tartar Control Plus Whitening	0.145% sodium fluoride, 5% potassium nitrate
Sensodyne Toothpaste for Sensitive Teeth and Cavity Protection with Baking Soda	5% potassium nitrate, 0.15% sodium fluoride

* These dentifrices also possess caries-preventive properties.

such as his or her size, age and physical status; ability to effectively rinse and expectorate; oral health; and sensitivity. Highly fluoridated dentifrices are not often prescribed for pediatric patients, and reduced maximum doses may be indicated for certain patients, such as those with physical or mental disabilities.

A list of caries prevention dentifrices with fluoride can be found on page 227.

Special Dental Considerations

Drug Interactions of Dental Interest
The following drug interactions and related problems involving dentifrices are potentially of clinical significance in dentistry.

Many of the ingredients of dentifrices, as well as products containing stannous fluoride, interact with chlorhexidine. Therefore, these agents should not be used concomitantly but, rather, used at least 30 min apart. Use of a chlorhexidine rinse followed immediately by a fluoride dentifrice may reduce the efficacy of each agent.

Cross-Sensitivity
Some patients can develop allergic reactions (skin rash, hives, desquamation) to dentifrices and should discontinue use of the product immediately.

Special Patients
Patients with physical or mental disabilities may have difficulty clearing dentifrices from the mouth. These patients should receive additional help from caretakers.

Patient Monitoring: Aspects to Watch
See Table 11.5.

Adverse Effects and Precautions
The incidence of adverse reactions to dentifrices is relatively low. Many reactions (burning or taste alterations) are temporary. Idiosyncratic and allergic reactions account for a small minority of adverse responses.

The adverse effects listed in Table 11.5 apply to all major types of dentifrices. Some patients cannot use tartar-control products because of the development of dentinal hypersensitivity or soft tissue irritation. For information on desensitizing agents, see Chapter 13. A small percentage of patients have an adverse reaction to sodium lauryl sulfates, a detergent that is added to some toothpastes. In such instances, switching to a dentifrice without sodium lauryl sulfate (such as Rembrandt or Sensodyne Gel) may be beneficial. Finally, preliminary information has suggested that toothpastes containing sanguinarine may be associated with oral

Caries Prevention Dentifrices (Active Ingredient: Fluoride*)

Aim Baking Soda Gel with Fluoride

Aim Extra Strength Toothpaste ★

Aim Regular Strength Gel with Fluoride

Aquafresh for Kids Toothpaste ★

Aquafresh Triple Protection Toothpaste ★

Arbor Fluoride Toothpaste ★

Arm and Hammer Dental Care Gel with Fluoride

Brooks Sodium Fluoride Toothpaste ★

Chateau Fluoride Toothpaste ★

Close-Up Fluoride Toothpaste

Close-Up Fluoride Gel

Colgate Cavity Protection Gel with Baking Soda ★

Colgate Cavity Protection Toothpaste with Baking Soda ★

Colgate Cavity Protection Toothpaste/Great Regular Flavor ★

Colgate Cavity Protection Toothpaste/Winterfresh Gel ★

Colgate Total ★

Colgate Total Fresh Stripe ★

Crest Cavity Protection Gel ★

Crest Cavity Protection Gel with Baking Soda ★

Crest Cavity Protection Toothpaste ★

Crest Cavity Protection Toothpaste with Baking Soda ★

Crest Gum Care

Crest Kids SparkleFun Cavity Protection Gel ★

Crest Multicare Toothpaste ★

Drug Emporium Fluoride Toothpaste ★

Enamelon

Equate Fluoride Toothpaste ★

Finast Fluoride Toothpaste ★

Food Lion Fluoride Toothpaste ★

Fred's Fluoride Toothpaste ★

Giant Eagle Fluoride Toothpaste ★

Gleem Toothpaste

Good Sense Fluoride Toothpaste ★

Grand Union Fluoride Toothpaste ★

Hannaford Fluoride Toothpaste ★

Homebest Fluoride Toothpaste ★

Hy-Vee Sodium Fluoride Toothpaste ★

Interplak Toothpaste with Fluoride

Kroger Fluoride Toothpaste ★

Leader Sodium Fluoride Toothpaste ★

Longs Fluoride Toothpaste ★

Meijer Fluoride Toothpaste ★

Mentadent Fluoride Toothpaste w/Baking Soda & Peroxide ★

Mouth Kote Toothpaste

My First Colgate Anti-Cavity Fluoride Toothpaste ★

Oral-B Sesame Street Fluoride Toothpaste ★

Oraline Fluoride Toothpaste ★

Oraline Kids Bubblegum

Osco Fluoride Toothpaste ★

Pepsodent Baking Soda Gel

Pepsodent Fluoride Toothpaste

Perrigo Fluoride Toothpaste ★

Price Chopper Fluoride Toothpaste ★

Quality Choice Mint Flavor Toothpaste ★

Raley's Fluoride Toothpaste ★

Sav-On Fluoride Toothpaste ★

Shane Fluoride Toothpaste ★

Shaw's Fluoride Toothpaste ★

Sheffield's Fluoride Toothpaste ★

Shoprite Fluoride Toothpaste ★

Swan Sodium Fluoride Toothpaste ★

Tom's Natural Baking Soda Toothpaste with Fluoride

Tom's Natural Toothpaste for Children with Fluoride

Tom's Natural Toothpaste with Calcium and Fluoride ★

Tom's Natural Toothpaste with Propolis and Myrrh

Top Care Sodium Fluoride Toothpaste

Topol Smoker's Fluoride Gel

Topol Smoker's Toothpaste with Fluoride

Ultra Brite Gel

Ultra Brite Toothpaste

Ultra Fresh Fluoride Toothpaste ★

Valu-Rite Fluoride Toothpaste ★

Walgreens Sodium Fluoride Toothpaste ★

Wegmans Fluoride Toothpaste ★

Weis Quality Fluoride Toothpaste ★

★ *indicates a product bearing the ADA Seal of Acceptance.*
* *Fluoride from either sodium fluoride, sodium monofluorophosphate or stannous fluoride.*

Table 11.5

Dentifrices: Adverse Effects, Precautions and Contraindications

Dentifrice type	Adverse effects	Precautions/contraindications
Antitartar formulas	Development of dentinal hypersensitivity and tissue irritation, but incidence is low	None of significance
Cosmetic formulas	Burning sensation, drying out of mucous membranes, taste alteration, gingival abrasion, enamel erosion	Not all discolorations of enamel (for example, enamel mottling, tetracycline staining, aging-extrinsic enamel) are responsive to extrinsic bleaching via dentifrices
Fluoride formulas	Fluorosis	Precautions include telling the caregivers of pediatric patients to make sure a pea-sized amount is used on toothbrush so that amount of fluoride ingested is minimized
Gingivitis-reducing formulas	None of significance	Products containing stannous fluoride may produce reversible staining of teeth
Plaque-reducing formulas	Allergic reaction, burning sensation, bitter taste	None of significance
Sensitivity-reduction formulas	Allergic reactions (most products contain parabens, to which some patients may be allergic)	Differential diagnosis is important to rule out other reasons for sensitivity—for example, cracked tooth or caries

leukoplakias; however, more data are required to establish a link between sanguinarine and oral lesions.

Pharmacology

Antitartar Formulas

The precise mechanism of supragingival calculus formation is not known. However, it is assumed that most calculus-reducing formulas reduce crystal growth on tooth surfaces. One way in which they accomplish this is the chelation of cations by dentifrices' active ingredient.

Cosmetic Formulas

Whitening of teeth can occur by two mechanisms. One method is mechanical, in which an abrasive is used to remove debris from the tooth. The other method involves the use of compounds that break down pigments that accumulate on or in tooth enamel. Several toothpastes have received the ADA Seal of Acceptance for whitening teeth. These products use either a special abrasive or a chemical to remove stain without damaging underlying tooth surfaces.

Fluoride Formulas

Fluoride has been shown to reduce carious lesions dramatically in both children and adults. Fluoride ion is assimilated into the apatite crystal of enamel and stabilizes the crystal, making it more resistant to decay. Fluoride also has been shown to remineralize carious lesions.

Gingivitis- and Plaque-Reduction Formulas

Triclosan is both a bisphenol and a nonionic germicide that is effective against gram-positive and gram-negative bacteria, and it has been shown to reduce plaque accumulation and decrease the severity of gingivitis. A dentifrice containing stabilized stannous fluoride has been shown to reduce gingivitis. The mechanism of action is thought to depend on the inhibition of bacterial metabolism and concomitant plaque acid reduction. Dentifrices containing zinc citrate have been reported to prevent the attachment of plaque to teeth and to be antibacterial. Dentifrices containing stannous fluoride also may be antibacterial.

Herbal Agents

Some toothpastes contain a variety of mixtures of herbal agents (such as aloe vera, sodium carrageenan, ecchinacea, golden seal and bee propolis). At press time, controlled, long-term studies to ascertain the efficacy of these agents in patients are lacking.

Sensitivity-Reduction Formulas

Two principal mechanisms of action have been proposed to reduce tooth sensitivity. It has been hypothesized that pain sensation in teeth can be reduced by blocking dentin tubule fluid exchange, by depolarizing pulpal nerves or by both means. Currently available sensitive-teeth formulas act via the topical application of agents to root surfaces, and dentifrices have been developed to precipitate drugs at the site of action.

Suggested Readings

Chikte UM, Rudolph MJ, Reinach SG. Anti-calculus effects of dentifrice containing pyrophosphate compared with control. Clin Prev Dent 1992;14(4):29-33.

Ismail AI. Fluoride supplements: current effectiveness, side effects, and recommendations. Community Dent Oral Epidemiol 1994;22(3):164-72.

Rolla G, Ellingsen JE. Clinical effects and possible mechanisms of action of stannous fluoride. Int Dent J 1994;44(1)(Supple):99-105.

Rolla G, Ogaard B, Cruz R de A. Clinical effect and mechanism of cariostatic action of fluoride-containing toothpastes: a review. Int Dent J 1991;41(3):171-4.

Stookey GK, DePaola PF, Featherstone JD, et al. A critical review of the relative anticaries efficacy of sodium fluoride and sodium monofluorophosphate dentifrices. Caries Res 1993;27(4):337-60.

Chapter 12

Systemic and Topical Fluorides

Kenneth H. Burrell, D.D.S., S.M.; Jarvis T. Chan, D.D.S., Ph.D.

With today's array of available systemic and topical fluoride products, it is not surprising that confusion abounds concerning their proper use. Factors that should be taken into account when considering a fluoride regimen are the age of the patient, the patient's caries rate and other caries-producing factors.

Age of the patient. Patients aged < 6 y are at risk of developing enamel fluorosis from excessive amounts of fluoride in the water supply, inappropriate and injudicious use of fluoride supplements and regular, inadvertent ingestion of fluoride-containing over-the-counter products. Ingestion of fluoride in food products also contributes to a child's total daily fluoride intake.

Improper use of fluoride supplements by itself can cause fluorosis. With the exception of incorrectly prescribed fluoride supplements, no other factors alone are thought to contribute to dental fluorosis. Patients should follow instructions on the labels of over-the-counter fluoride-containing products so that they can avoid unintended fluoride ingestion.

The patient's caries rate. Patients without caries or with no apparent risk of caries may require nothing more than the 0.7 to 1.2 parts per million fluoride in the municipal water supply or an appropriate fluoride-supplement dosage schedule, along with the daily use of a fluoride-containing dentifrice and semiannual postprophylaxis fluoride applications. Patients with low caries rates or a slight risk may require the additional use of a 0.05% sodium fluoride over-the-counter mouthrinse or a 0.4% stannous fluoride gel.

Patients with moderate-to-high caries rates and moderate-to-severe risk of caries may also require the daily use of neutral or acidulated 1.1% sodium fluoride gel.

Other caries-producing factors. A patient's existing fluoride regimen is an important part of his or her dental history, but, of course, it is not the only consideration when trying to determine treatment for caries. The patient's oral hygiene regimen, diet and medical history, and whether or not pit and fissure sealants have been placed on newly erupted teeth, must also be taken into account. Twice-daily brushing and once-daily interdental cleaning, usually with floss, should be adequate for most patients, provided these procedures are done properly and thoroughly. A well-balanced diet with a minimum amount of snacking also should reduce the risks of dental caries. Important events in a patient's medical history can change that regimen, however. Diminished salivary flow, or xerostomia, can be caused by medications, head and neck irradiation for cancer treatments and some diseases, such as Sjögren's syndrome. Xerostomia can increase the caries rate dramatically so that a patient's diet, oral hygiene and fluoride use may require modification after its onset.

Clinical judgment is important for successful treatment. Correct diagnosis as a result of careful history-taking, meticulous examination and competent interpretation of diagnostic tests can increase the likelihood of successful prevention or treatment outcome.

Systemic Fluorides

Accepted Indications

Fluoride in water supplies and fluoride supplements are considered to be long-term caries preventives by making fluoride available systemically while tooth enamel is forming. When fluoride levels in drinking water are below 0.6 ppm, a fluoride supplement should be considered (see Table 12.1). An analysis of the home drinking water may not be adequate, however. The patient's parents or guardians may need to be questioned about the child's usual source of drinking water. Many bottled waters do not contain optimal amounts of fluoride. Day care centers may have fluoridated drinking water that is at levels adequate to preclude prescribing a fluoride supplement.

General Dosing Information

The recommended concentration of fluoride in fluoridated water supply systems that offers the maximum reduction in dental caries with the minimal amount of enamel mottling or fluorosis varies with the annual average of maximum daily air temperature (people living in warmer climates tend to drink more water than those in cooler climates).

It may range from 0.7 ppm in Houston, Texas, to 1.2 ppm in Duluth, Minn.

The fluoride level in drinking water is a major factor in determining the dosage for fluoride supplements that are used for children between the ages of 6 mo and 16 y. Table 12.1 shows the recommended fluoride supplement dosage schedule.

Systemic dosing of fluoride supplements is typically prescribed in the form of either drops, tablets or dual-use topical/systemic swish-and-swallow solutions.

General dosage forms include tablets and lozenges available in 0.25 mg, 0.50 mg and 1 mg. Fluoride drops are available in various concentrations, which affects the number of drops per dose. Thus, it is important to specify the concentration of the drops prescribed. A combination fluoride supplement/mouthrinse is also available, with each 5 mL (one teaspoonful) containing 1 mg of fluoride from 2.20 mg of sodium fluoride and orthophosphoric acid.

Fluoridated salt. Salt fluoridation is not used in the United States but is used in some countries, such as Mexico and Switzerland, where water fluoridation is not possible. Fluoride has been shown to be effective at a concentration of 200-250 mg/kg of table salt.

Table 12.1

Systemic Fluoride Supplements: Recommended Dosage Schedule of the American Dental Association, the American Academy of Pediatric Dentistry and the American Academy of Pediatrics

Age	Fluoride ion level in drinking water (ppm)*		
	‹ 0.3 ppm	0.3-0.6 ppm	› 0.6 ppm
Birth-6 mo	None	None	None
6 mo-3 y	0.25 mg/day†	None	None
3-6 y	0.50 mg/day	0.25 mg/day	None
6-16 y	1.0 mg/day	0.50 mg/day	None

* 1.0 ppm = 1 mg/liter.
† 2.2 mg sodium fluoride contains 1 mg fluoride ion.

Fluoridated milk. A small number of studies have been conducted to determine the caries-inhibiting effects of fluoride in cow's milk. Although reductions in caries related to fluoridated milk have shown promise, more studies are required. There is concern that the effectiveness of fluorides in milk products may be reduced because fluoride combines with calcium to form calcium fluoride, which is poorly absorbed in the stomach. Fluoridated milk products are not available in the United States.

Fluoridated chewing gum. In several European countries, chewing gum is used as an adjunctive vehicle for delivering fluoride topically to teeth. The concentration of fluoride in these gums is approximately 0.25 mg of fluoride per stick of gum. Use of fluoridated chewing gums results in a salivary fluoride concentration similar to that achieved by using other fluoride sources such as dentifrices or mouthrinses. In addition, fluoride gums have the added advantage of simultaneously stimulating salivary flow and raising salivary and plaque pH. Such effects may be particularly advantageous to xerostomatic patients. However, there are, to date, no definitive clinical studies on the anticaries protective effect of these gums, and further studies are required before any conclusions regarding their efficacy can be reached.

Prenatal fluoride. The efficacy of prenatal dietary fluoride supplements in preventing dental caries has been well-established in animal studies. However, well-designed clinical studies to demonstrate the safety and efficacy of prenatal fluoride in preventing caries in human subjects still are lacking. Therefore, no definitive recommendations regarding the use of prenatal fluoride can be made. Furthermore, prenatal dietary fluoride supplements will not affect the permanent dentition because permanent teeth do not begin to develop in utero.

Maximum Recommended Doses

No more than 120 mg of fluoride should be dispensed per household at one time. One tablet of the prescribed dose should be taken per day with water or juice. Taking fluoride supplements with milk and other dairy products is not recommended because they can combine with the calcium to become poorly absorbed calcium fluoride. The tablet strength is determined by the concentration of fluoride in the patient's source of drinking water and the age of the child. Tables 12.1 and 12.2 show the maximum recommended dose: 1 mg per day.

Dosage Adjustments

The actual maximum dose for each patient must be individualized depending on the patient's weight, age, physical status and other dietary sources of fluoride intake. Reduced doses may be indicated for patients based on changes in their water supply's fluoride content, which may result from relocation or any adverse side effects experienced.

Special Dental Considerations

Drug Interactions of Dental Interest

Calcium-containing products and food interfere with the absorption of systemic fluoride.

Cross-Sensitivity

Allergic rash and other idiosyncratic reactions have rarely been reported. Gastric distress, headache and weakness have been reported in cases of excessive ingestion.

Special Patients

Fluoride supplements are not recommended for patients other than children living in areas with fluoride levels such as those described in Table 12.1.

Patient Monitoring: Aspects to Watch

Fluoride supplements can cause fluorosis if used in areas where drinking water contains fluoride levels greater than the levels outlined in Table 12.1.

Adverse Effects and Precautions

No adverse reactions or undesirable side effects have been reported when fluoride

Table 12.2

Systemic Fluorides: Dosage and Prescribing Information

Generic name	Brand name(s)	Child dosage*	Max child dosage
Sodium fluoride, drops—0.5 mg/mL fluoride	**Drops:** Luride ★, Pediaflor	½ dropperful = 0.25 mg 1 dropperful = 0.5 mg 2 droppersful = 1 mg	Prescribe no more than 200 mL per household
Sodium fluoride, drops—2 mg/mL fluoride	**Drops:** Karidium ★	2 drops = 0.25 mg 4 drops = 0.5 mg 8 drops = 1 mg	Prescribe no more than 30 mL per household
Sodium fluoride, drops—2.5 mg/mL fluoride	**Drops:** Fluor-A-Day ★	2 drops = 0.25 mg 4 drops = 0.5 mg 8 drops = 1 mg	Prescribe no more than 30 mL per household
Sodium fluoride, drops—5 mg/mL fluoride	**Drops:** Fluoritab ★	1 drop = 0.25 mg 2 drops = 0.5 mg 4 drops = 1 mg	Prescribe no more than 23 mL per household
Sodium fluoride, rinse—0.2 mg/mL fluoride	**Rinses:** Phos-Flur ★	1 mg fluoride/teaspoonful (0.2 mg fluoride/mL) swished for 1 min then swallowed	Prescribe no more than 500 mL per household
Sodium fluoride, tablets and lozenges—0.25 mg fluoride	**Tablets:** Fluor-A-Day ★, Fluoritab ★, Luride Lozi-Tabs ★ **Lozenges:** Fluor-A-Day ★	1 tablet or lozenge per day taken with water or juice and dissolved in mouth or chewed	Prescribe no more than 480 tablets or lozenges per household
Sodium fluoride, tablets and lozenges—0.5 mg fluoride	**Tablets:** Fluor-A-Day ★, Fluoritab ★, Luride Lozi-Tabs ★ **Lozenges:** Fluor-A-Day ★	1 tablet or lozenge per day taken with water or juice and dissolved in mouth or chewed	Prescribe no more than 240 tablets or lozenges per household
Sodium fluoride, tablets and lozenges—1 mg fluoride	**Tablets:** Fluor-A-Day ★, Fluoritab ★, Luride Lozi-Tabs ★ **Lozenges:** Fluor-A-Day ★	1 tablet or lozenge per day taken with water or juice and dissolved in mouth or chewed	Prescribe no more than 120 tablets or lozenges per household

★ indicates a product bearing the ADA Seal of Acceptance.
* These supplements are for children only. There is no dose for adult or geriatric patients.

supplements have been taken as directed. Excessive use may result in dental fluorosis, especially in areas where the fluoride level in drinking water is high. Therefore, fluoride supplements are not recommended where the water content of fluoride is at or above 0.6 ppm.

In children, acute ingestion of 10-20 mg of sodium fluoride can cause excessive salivation and gastrointestinal disturbances. Ingestion of 500 mg can be fatal. Oral or intravenous fluids containing calcium, or both, may be indicated.

Precautions. If the fluoride level is unknown, the drinking water must be tested for fluoride content before supplements are prescribed. For testing information, ask the local or state health department or dental school. Determining a proper dosage schedule can be a complex task if a patient has exposure to a number of different water supplies. Once a proper schedule is established, however, the effectiveness of the schedule requires the patient's long-term compliance.

Contraindications. The fluoride dosage schedule was designed to take into account the widespread use of fluorides that can contribute to the increased frequency and severity of fluorosis. Fluoride supplements are contraindicated for children drinking water with fluoride concentrations at or above 0.6 ppm.

Pharmacology

Systemic and Topical Fluorides

Mechanism of action/effect. After early studies showed that fluoride reduced the solubility of powdered enamel and dentin, investigators began trying to determine how fluoride works to reduce dental caries. However, the mechanism or mechanisms of action are still incompletely understood. Nevertheless, fluoride is thought to work in many ways. It has been speculated that a combination of actions work to reduce the severity and frequency of dental caries, which is the result of excessive demineraliza-tion in the demineralization-remineralization process. This excessive demineralization occurs after repeated acid attacks that result when bacterial plaque metabolizes sugars ingested during meals and snacks. Clinical manifestations of dental caries become evident when demineralization predomi-nates over time and upsets the demineraliza-tion-remineralization equilibrium. Fluoride reduces the demineralization of enamel and dentin by reducing the acid production of bacterial plaque and decreasing the solubility of apatite crystals. When fluoride is exposed to apatite crystals, it readily becomes incor-porated to reduce the dissolution of apatite during acid attacks. The presence of fluoride, therefore, inhibits demineralization and helps to maintain the equilibrium between demineralization and remineralization dur-ing acid attacks.

Absorption. Fluoride is absorbed in the gastrointestinal tract, 90% of it in the stom-ach. Calcium, iron or magnesium ions may delay absorption.

Distribution. After absorption, 50% of fluoride is deposited in bone and teeth.

Elimination. The major route of excretion is the kidneys. Fluoride is also excreted by the sweat glands, the tear glands, the gastroin-testinal tract and in breast milk.

Patient Advice

- Patients and their parents or guardians should be advised to take systemic fluorides as directed.
- Patients or their parents or guardians should notify the prescriber when their water supply has changed as the result of a move or a change in schools or by the addition of fluoride to the water supply.
- These products should be kept from children's reach; they are often formulated to have a pleasant taste and children there-fore are more likely to consume them if they are easily accessible.

Topical Fluorides

Accepted Indications

Topical preparations are used in the prevention and treatment of dental caries. Concentrations of 1,500 ppm or below are sold as over-the-counter preparations for the prevention of dental caries. Preparations that are prescribed for topical home use generally consist of higher concentrations of fluoride and are indicated for both treatment and prevention. Patients who are either at high risk of developing dental caries or who experience high caries rates are candidates for daily use of these products. However, high-concentration preparations that are usually applied annually or after dental prophylaxis in children are applied to prevent caries.

Some kinds of fluoride compounds at certain concentrations can be used to reduce dentinal hypersensitivity. Sodium fluoride (151,000 ppm fluoride ion), in equal amounts of kaolin and glycerin, has been shown to be effective for this purpose when professionally applied and burnished into affected areas using orangewood sticks. A water-free 0.4% (1,000 ppm fluoride ion) stannous fluoride gel has also been demonstrated to reduce dentinal hypersensitivity when patients use it daily at home. A dentifrice containing 0.454% stannous fluoride and 5% potassium nitrate also has been shown to reduce dentin hypersensitivity by tubular occlusion.

There is evidence that a stabilized 0.4% stannous fluoride toothpaste has been shown to reduce gingivitis with daily use.

General Dosing Information

Topical dosing is typically provided in the form of liquid solutions, gels, foams, varnishes, pastes, rinses and dentifrices. Concentrations can vary depending on oral health and sensitivity, the particular indication involved, region of treatment, response to previous or existing concentrations and doses of fluoride as well as individual patient characteristics such as age, weight, physical status, and ability to effectively rinse and expectorate. See Table 12.3.

Doses of topically applied solutions, gels, foams and varnishes are typically applied with a cotton swab, a toothbrush, a carrier or as a rinse. To control the dosing of high fluoride concentrations so that excessive amounts of fluoride are not in the mouth and to control salivary contamination, cotton rolls, a saliva ejector or high vacuum suction can be used. Because varnishes are applied to adhere to teeth for prolonged periods, all residual fluoride is swallowed. Between 0.3 and 0.5 mL of varnish is used per patient so that about 5-11 mg is ingested. This amount is consistent with ingestion calculations for other professionally applied fluoride preparations.

When it comes to fluoride dentifrices, more frequent brushing may be required, but this depends on the patient's caries risk. A 0.4% stannous fluoride gel might be considered as an alternative to brushing with a dentifrice, however. In this way, the patient can receive the benefit of the same fluoride exposure as with the dentifrice without a dentifrice's cleansing properties, which may not be necessary. Also, the cleansing properties of a dentifrice may not be desirable if topical application of fluoride is required more than twice a day.

Maximum Recommended Doses

The maximum recommended doses for topical fluoride formulations per procedure or appointment are listed in Table 12.4.

Dosage Adjustments

The actual maximum dose for each patient can be individualized depending on the patient's age and physical status, ability to effectively rinse and expectorate and oral health and sensitivity.

Special Dental Considerations

Cross-Sensitivity

Although allergies to fluoride probably do not exist, patients may be allergic to some of

Table 12.3

Topical Fluorides: Dosage and Prescribing Information

Generic name/ active ingredient	Brand name(s)	Adult dosage*	Max adult dosage
Professionally applied fluoride products			
Acidulated phosphate fluoride solutions, gels and foams (1.23% fluoride ion)	**Foams:** Butler Fluoride Foam, Laclede ★, Oral B Minute Foam **Gels:** Care-4 ★, Fluorident ★, FluoroCare Time Saver, Oral B Minute Gel, Perfect Choice ★, Pro-Dent$_X$ ★, Protect ★, Topex 00:60 Second Foam Fluoride, Topex 00:60 Second Fluoride Gel	5 mL of solution or gel with 12,300 ppm fluoride ion after dental prophylaxis per fluoride carrier	10 mL
2% neutral sodium fluoride solutions, gels or foams (0.90% fluoride ion)	Butler Fluoride Foam, FluoroCare Neutral, Neutra-Foam, Oral B Neutrafoam, Topex Neutral pH	5 mL of solution, gel or foam with 9,050 ppm fluoride ion after dental prophylaxis per fluoride carrier	10 mL
Fluoride-containing varnishes, 5% sodium fluoride (2.26% fluoride ion)	Duraflor, Duraphat, Fluor Protector	0.3-0.5 mL of varnish containing 22,600 ppm fluoride ion after dental prophylaxis	0.5 mL
Fluoride prophylaxis pastes (0.40% - 2% fluoride ion)	Butler Fluoride Prophylaxis Paste, Glitter, Masnasil, Prophy Gems, Radent, Teledyne Water Pik Prophylaxis Paste, Topex, Unipro Prophy Paste, Zircon F, Ziroxide	Use amount sufficient to polish the teeth (4,000-20,000 ppm fluoride ion)	Use no more than the amount required to polish the teeth
Prescription fluorides			
1.1% neutral or acidulated sodium fluoride gel or dentifrice (0.50% fluoride ion)	ControlRx, Karigel-N ★, Luride Lozi-Tabs, Oral B Neutracare, PreviDent Gel, PreviDent 5000 Plus, Pro-Dent$_X$ 1.1% Plus, Theraflur ★	4-8 drops on inner surface of each custom-made tray per day (5,000 ppm fluoride ion)	Maximum amount prescribed is one 24-mL plastic squeeze bottle; maximum adult dose is 16 drops/day
0.2% neutral sodium fluoride rinses (0.09% fluoride ion)	NaF rinse ★, Oral B Fluorinse, PreviDent ★	Recommended for use by children (905 ppm fluoride ion solution)	None
0.044% sodium fluoride and acidulated phosphate fluoride rinses (0.02% fluoride ion)	Phos-Flur ★	10 mL once daily after brushing (200 ppm fluoride ion solution)	Same as usual adult dosage

★ *indicates a product bearing the ADA Seal of Acceptance.*
* *Geriatric dosage is same as adult dosage.*

Continued on next page

Table 12.3 (cont.)
Topical Fluorides: Dosage and Prescribing Information

Generic name/ active ingredient	Brand name(s)	Adult dosage*	Max adult dosage
Over-the-counter fluorides			
Fluoride-containing dentifrices (0.10-0.15% fluoride ion)	See Chapter 11	Amount sufficient to cover toothbrush bristles: ≈ 1 g per day (1,000-1,500 ppm fluoride ion)	Twice a day or more as recommended
0.4% stannous fluoride gels (0.10% fluoride ion) and rinses	Alpha-Dent ★, Easy-Gel, Florentine II, Gel-Kam ★, Gel-Kam Oral Rinse, Gel-Tin ★, Oral B Stop, Perfect Choice ★, Plak Smacker ★, Periocheck Oral Med, Schein Home Care, Super-Dent ★	Amount sufficient to cover toothbrush bristles: ≈ 1 g per day (1,000 ppm fluoride ion)	Once a day or more as recommended
0.05% sodium fluoride rinses (0.02% fluoride ion)	Fluorigard, NaF rinse Acidulated ★, NaF rinse Neutral ★, Reach Act ★	10 mL of solution with 230 ppm fluoride ion	Rinse for 1 min, once daily

★ indicates a product bearing the ADA Seal of Acceptance.
* Geriatric dosage is same as adult dosage.

Table 12.4
Fluoride: Maximum Recommended Doses per Appointment

Form	Maximum Dose
1.23% acidulated phosphate fluoride solution, gel or foam	5 mL
Fluoride-containing varnish	0.3-0.5 mL
Fluoride toothpaste for children < age 6 y	Pea-sized amount (0.25 g)
1.1% neutral and acidulated sodium fluoride gel drops	0.2-0.4 mL
2% neutral sodium fluoride	5 mL
5% sodium fluoride	0.3-0.5 mL
0.05% sodium fluoride mouthrinse for children > age 6 y*	10 mL

* Mouthrinses are not recommended for children < age 6 y.

the ingredients in the various formulations. Some of the 1.23% acidulated phosphate fluoride solutions and gels and some dentifrices contain tartrazines used as color additives. They can cause allergic reactions, especially in patients with hypersensitivity to aspirin.

Adverse Effects and Precautions

Excessive ingestion of fluoride products can produce acute and chronic effects. Ingestion of quantities of fluoride as low as 1 mg per day have been shown to produce mild fluorosis in a small percentage of the population if the ingestion takes place during tooth crown development. The severity and frequency of fluorosis can increase in a population if the recommended dose is exceeded and if the quantity of daily fluoride ingestion increases. Chronic fluoride toxicity, or skeletal fluorosis, may occur after years of daily ingestion of 20-80 mg of fluoride; however, such heavy doses are far in excess of the average intake in the United States. There is no evidence that skeletal changes are produced by ingestion of therapeutic doses of fluoride, however.

Accidental ingestion of high concentrations of fluoride (> 1,500 ppm) can cause gastrointestinal disturbances such as excessive salivation, nausea, vomiting, abdominal pain and diarrhea. Central nervous system disturbances that have been observed include irritability, paresthesia, tetany and convulsions. Respiratory and cardiac failure have also been observed. See Table 12.5.

Dentifrices should not exceed 260 mg of fluoride ion. It is thought that the quantity of fluoride in dentifrice can exceed the 120-mg limit the American Dental Association has established for other fluoride-containing products because dentifrices contain humectants and detergents that act to induce vomiting.

Table 12.5

Topical Fluorides: Adverse Effects, Precautions and Contraindications

Type	Adverse effects	Precautions/contraindications
Professionally applied fluoride products		
Acidulated phosphate fluoride solutions, gels and foams (1.23% fluoride ion, 12,300 ppm fluoride ion)	**CNS:** Inadvertent ingestion can produce headaches and weakness; more severe instances of excessive ingestion can cause CNS problems such as irritability, paresthesia, tetany, convulsions, respiratory failure and cardiac failure; fluoride has direct toxic action on nerve tissue **GI:** Excessive salivation, nausea, vomiting **Hema:** Excessive amounts of fluoride can also cause electrolyte disturbances leading to hypocalcemia and hyperkalemia; hypoglycemia is a result of failure of enzyme systems **Musc:** Fluoride has a direct toxic action on muscle and nerve tissue	Some preparations may contain tartrazines (FDC Yellow No. 5), which are used as color additives; tartrazine-containing products are contraindicated in patients allergic to the compound; tartrazine can cause allergic reactions, including bronchial asthma; allergic response is rare, but is frequently observed in patients who also experience hypersensitivity to aspirin

Continued on next page

Table 12.5 (cont.)

Topical Fluorides: Adverse Effects, Precautions and Contraindications

Type	Adverse effects	Precautions/contraindications
Professionally applied fluoride products		
2% neutral sodium fluoride solutions or gels (9,050 ppm fluoride ion)	**CV:** Excessive amounts of fluoride can produce cardiac failure **CNS:** Excessive amounts of fluoride can produce irritability, paresthesia, tetany, convulsions; fluoride has direct toxic action on nerve tissue **GI:** Excessive amounts of fluoride can produce GI disturbances such as excess salivation, nausea, abdominal pain, vomiting and diarrhea **Hema:** Excessive amounts of fluoride can cause electrolyte disturbances leading to hypocalcemia and hyperkalemia. Hypoglycemia is a result of enzyme systems failure **Musc:** Fluoride has direct toxic action on muscle tissue **Resp:** Excessive amounts of fluoride can produce respiratory failure	Not to be used with other professionally applied topical fluoride preparations
Fluoride-containing varnishes, 5% sodium fluoride (2.26% fluoride ion, 22,600 ppm fluoride ion)	**CNS:** Inadvertent ingestion can produce headaches and weakness; more severe instances of excessive ingestion can cause CNS problems such as irritability, paresthesia, tetany, convulsions, respiratory failure and cardiac failure; fluoride has direct toxic action on nerve tissue **Hema:** Excessive amounts of fluoride can also cause electrolyte disturbances leading to hypocalcemia and hyperkalemia; hypoglycemia is a result of failure of enzyme systems **Musc:** Fluoride has a direct toxic action on muscle and nerve tissue	Not to be used in conjunction with other high-concentration topical fluoride solutions when varnish is applied to all tooth surfaces; use of some formulations can result in a temporary yellow discoloration of teeth, which patient can brush away 2-6 h after fluoride application
Fluoride prophylaxis pastes, 4,000-20,000 ppm fluoride	**Oral:** Excessive polishing may remove more fluoride from the enamel surface than fluoride prophylaxis paste can replace	Should be thoroughly rinsed from mouth on completion of prophylaxis

Continued on next page

Table 12.5 (cont.)

Topical Fluorides: Adverse Effects, Precautions and Contraindications

Type	Adverse effects	Precautions/contraindications
Prescription fluorides		
1.1% neutral or acidulated phosphate fluoride gel-drops (5,000 ppm fluoride ion)	**Oral:** Patients with mucositis may report irritation to the acidulated preparation	Repeated use of acidulated fluoride has been shown to etch glass filler particles in composite restorations and porcelain crowns, facings and laminates As with all fluoride products, children < age 6 y should be supervised to prevent their swallowing the product, which can lead to fluorosis, nausea and vomiting
0.2% neutral sodium fluoride rinse (905 ppm fluoride ion solution)	**General:** Allergic reaction could result from flavoring agent **GI:** Nausea and vomiting may result from inadvertent swallowing **Oral:** Irritation of oral tissues, especially in children with mucositis, may result from alcohol that might be part of the formulation	Should not be used in children < age 6 y because they cannot rinse without significant swallowing and this product is not for systemic use Should not be swallowed by children of any age and should be kept from their reach
Over-the-counter fluorides		
Dentifrice with 0.12-0.15% and 0.24% fluoride ion (1,000-1,500 ppm fluoride ion)	**General:** Allergic reactions thought to be caused by flavoring agents in some formulations (mint-flavored products have been reported to cause these reactions; however, as a variety of flavoring agents is available, patient should be advised to change to another flavor until a suitable product is found)	To prevent fluorosis, supervise children < age 6 y so that swallowing does not occur Accidental ingestion of a single dose, which contains 1-2 mg of fluoride ion, is not harmful Intentional ingestion of large amounts of fluoride toothpaste can cause gastric irritation, nausea and vomiting No single container should exceed 260 mg of fluoride ion (it is thought that quantity of fluoride in dentifrice can exceed the 120-mg limit ADA has established for other fluoride-containing products because dentifrices contain humectants and detergents that induce vomiting)
0.4% stannous fluoride gels (1,000 ppm fluoride ion)	**General:** Allergic reactions thought to be caused by flavoring agents in some formulations (mint-flavored products have been reported to cause these reactions; however, as a variety of flavoring agents is available, patient should be advised to change to another flavor until a suitable product is found) Reversible black stain may occur in pits and fissures and along cervical aspect of a tooth or teeth	Children < age 6 y should be supervised to prevent swallowing and fluorosis; accidental ingestion of a single dose (1- to 2-mg ribbon of gel) is not harmful Intentional ingestion of large amounts of gel can cause gastric irritation, nausea and vomiting No single container should exceed 120 mg of fluoride

Continued on next page

Table 12.5 (cont.)

Topical Fluorides: Adverse Effects, Precautions and Contraindications

Type	Adverse effects	Precautions/contraindications
Over-the-counter fluorides (cont.)		
0.05% sodium fluoride mouthrinses (230 ppm fluoride ion)	**General:** Allergic reactions thought to be caused by flavoring agents in some formulations (mint-flavored products have been reported to cause these reactions; however, as a variety of flavoring agents is available, patient should be advised to change to another flavor until a suitable product is found)	Children < age 6 y generally should not use this product because of their inability to rinse without swallowing; otherwise, accidental ingestion of a single dose is not harmful Intentional ingestion of several doses can cause gastric irritation, nausea and vomiting Some of these products contain alcohol to promote solubility of flavoring agents; these products should be kept out of children's reach and in childproof caps/packaging

Pharmacology

See the discussion earlier in this chapter.

Patient Advice

Although the gel form of 2% neutral sodium fluoride may be more easily applied, clinical evidence of its effectiveness has not been demonstrated. The original application schedule was 4 times per year and was for children at the specific ages of 3, 7, 10, and 13 y. Currently the caries-inhibiting properties of this solution are considered to be equivalent to the APF gels and solutions, which contain a higher concentration of fluoride (12,300 ppm).

Suggested Readings

Levy SM. Review of fluoride exposures and ingestion. Community Dent Oral Epidemiol 1994;22(3):173-80.

Newbrun E. Current regulations and recommendations concerning water fluoridation, fluoride supplements, and topical fluoride agents. J Dent Res 1992;71(5):1255-65.

Ripa LW. A critique of topical fluoride methods (dentifrices, mouthrinses, operator-, and self-applied gels) in an era of decreased caries and increased fluorosis prevalence. J Public Health Dent 1991;51(1):23-41.

Ripa LW. Review of the anticaries effectiveness of professionally applied and self-applied topical fluoride gels. J Public Health Dent 1989;49(5):297-309.

Warren DP, Chan JT. Topical fluorides: efficacy, administration, and safety. J Acad Gen Dent 1997;45(2):134-40, 142.

Whitford GM, Allmann DW, Shaked AR. Topical fluoride: effects on physiologic and biochemical process. J Dent Res 1987;66(5):1072-8.

Chapter 13

Desensitizing Agents

Martha Somerman, D.D.S., Ph.D.; Jarvis T. Chan, D.D.S., Ph.D.

Dentin hypersensitivity is characterized by a sharp pain produced in response to mild stimuli that usually disappears with removal of the stimulus. Root sensitivity is a significant problem for many patients and may be a result of, or associated with, scaling and root planing, periodontal surgery, gingival recession, toothbrush abrasion, attrition, erosion, trauma or chronic periodontal disease. It is important to rule out active pathology (for example, root fracture or root surface decay) before providing treatment for root sensitivity. In many situations, root sensitivity decreases with time, but when it does not, it results in extreme discomfort or an inability to eat or drink certain foods, inability to function outdoors in cold weather and, at times, poor oral hygiene that can result in periodontal-related problems. Unfortunately, ideal OTC and professional desensitizing agents with predictable outcomes have not been developed.

Desensitizing agents can be separated into two types: agents applied to the tooth by a practitioner and agents that are for home use. Table 13.1 provides information about currently available products for use in the clinical setting. A major concern with products for home use is the abrasiveness of the paste; however, all ADA-accepted toothpastes have safe levels of abrasive materials.

In-Office Products

Accepted Indications

In-office desensitizing agents are used to provide relief from thermal and tactile sensitivity on exposed root surfaces when pathological causes for pain have been ruled out. Agents containing fluoride also provide an anticaries function. Differential diagnoses for dentinal hypersensitivity are listed in Table 13.2.

Some of the desensitizing agents may be applied in conjunction with iontophoresis, which is the electrical transport of positively or negatively charged drugs across surface tissues. One of the uses of iontophoresis in dentistry is in the treatment of dentinal hypersensitivity with fluoride. Usually a 1% sodium fluoride solution is employed. Results are variable, and the time and cost of the treatment may limit patients' acceptance of it.

General Usage Information

Usage and Administration for Adults and Children

See Table 13.1 for information on usage and administration. As with any agents, if pain persists or worsens, the situation should be re-evaluated. Overuse can be detrimental to tooth structure. Therefore, continued sensitivity, after ruling out other symptoms, can be treated by changing the product versus increasing the dose. Use of increased amounts, beyond those

Table 13.1

Desensitizing Fluorides, Oxalates, Varnishes, Sealants and Bonding Agents: Usage Information

Generic name	Brand name(s)	Usage and administration for adults	Usage and administration for children	Content/form	Features/uses
Fluorides					
0.40% stannous fluoride, 1.09% sodium fluoride, 0.14% hydrogen fluoride (equivalent to 0.72% fluoride and 0.30% Sn)	Dentinbloc Dentin Desensitizer, Pro-Dent$_x$ Office Fluorides, Pro-Dent$_x$ Comfort Dentin Desensitizer, Gel-Kam ★	Dry dentin surface (isolation not necessary); dispense 10-12 drops into plastic dappen dish; apply saturated cotton pellets to sensitive area for 1 full min; use light pressure and do not burnish; have patient expectorate after application; to overcome pain threshold, sequential 1-min treatments may be required Do not apply with wooden stick	Caution must be taken in use of fluorides as desensitizing agents in children owing to possibility of fluorosis **Age < 12 y:** Not intended for this age group	Available in boxes of 50-unit dose treatments (0.75 g/unit)	Has been shown to form particles that block dentinal tubules, thereby providing temporary relief from pain associated with root-surface sensitivity
3.9% strontium chloride, 0.42% sodium fluoride	Health-Dent Desensitizer, Hema-Glu Desensitizer	See note above	See note above	**Gel:** 10 mL, 60 mL **Solution:** 10 mL	See note above
3.28% stannous fluoride	Stani-Max Pro	Dilute 1:1 with water, preferably distilled water, to provide a 1.64% SnF$_2$ rinse Use in office irrigation or rinse Recommended rinse after scaling and root planing	See note above	**Glycerin-based liquid:** 16-oz bottles	See note above
1.1% neutral sodium fluoride	NiteWhite NSF	Apply in a tray and wear as directed for 5 min/day	See note above	NA	See note above

★ indicates a product bearing the ADA Seal of Acceptance.
NA: Not available.

Continued on next page

Table 13.1 (cont.)

Desensitizing Fluorides, Oxalates, Varnishes, Sealants and Bonding Agents: Usage Information

Generic name	Brand name(s)	Usage and administration for adults	Usage and administration for children	Content/form	Features/uses
Oxalates					
2.7% potassium mono-oxalate	Protect	Dry dentin surface (isolation not necessary); dispense 10-12 drops into plastic dappen dish; apply saturated cotton pellets to sensitive area for 1 full min; use light pressure and do not burnish; have patient expectorate after application; to overcome pain threshold, sequential 1-min treatments may be required Do not apply with wooden stick	NR	½-oz bottle, 24 ampules/box	Chairside treatment of dentinal hypersensitivity; acidic reagents remove smear layer and demineralize root surface (and may also leave crystals of calcium oxalate on the root surface), which may decrease effectiveness of bond cements and adhesives' interaction with the root surface; therefore, surfaces treated with an oxalate should be pumiced before a bonding agent is used
Ferric oxalate (6% ferric oxalate)	Sensodyne Sealant [CAN]	See note above	NR	Available in ½-oz (15 mL) bottles with dispenser	See note above
Aluminum oxalate	Dentin Conditioners	See note above	NR	3 mL/5mL bottle with dispenser	See note above
Varnishes, sealants and bonding agents					
Varnishes: Sodium fluoride	Duraphat, Duraflor, Fluor Protector	Apply chairside according to manufacturer's recommendations	NR	50 mg/mL, 10-mL tube	**Varnishes:** Used for chairside treatment of dentinal hypersensitivity; varnishes occlude dentinal tubules

[CAN] indicates an agent available only in Canada.
NR: Not recommended.

Continued on next page

Table 13.1 (cont.)

Desensitizing Fluorides, Oxalates, Varnishes, Sealants and Bonding Agents: Usage Information

Generic name	Brand name(s)	Usage and administration for adults	Usage and administration for children	Content/form	Features/uses
Varnishes, sealants and bonding agents (cont.)					
Sealants: Active ingredient not listed	Barrier Dental Sealant, Pain-Free Desensitizer	Apply chairside according to manufacturer's recommendations	NR	2 component bottles of 5 mL each	Sealants appear to close dentinal tubules and protect pulp and reduce sensitivity to temperature extremes; compatible with all restorative materials, dental cements, and cavity liners
Bonding agents: Methacrylate polymer	All-Bond DS Desensitizer, Micro prime, Confi-Dental, Gluma Desensitizer	Apply chairside according to manufacturer's recommendations	NR	**All-Bond DS Desensitizer:** Kit contains two primers, cleanser, mixing well, brush handle and brush tips **Gluma Desensitizer, Confi-Dental:** available in small dispenser bottle **Micro prime:** 5-mL bottle	Bonding agents seal dentinal tubules and reduce fluid shifting

NR: Not recommended.

shown in Table 13.1, has not been reported to be effective in decreasing sensitivity.

Special Dental Considerations

- Fluorides interact with calcium-containing products—for example, to form calcium fluoride, which is poorly absorbed.
- Also, certain agents—for example, chlorhexidine—may decrease fluoride's ability to bind to root surfaces. Thus, after using fluoride agents, the patient should not rinse or eat for 1 h.
- Some agents are acidic and thus may cause sensitivity in patients with mucositis.

- Some acidic compounds—for example, oxalate—may cause dulling of porcelain ceramics and decreased effectiveness of bonding cements. Therefore, surfaces treated with oxalate should be pumiced before a bonding agent is used.

Special Patients

Pregnant and nursing women

There is no evidence that desensitizing agents are harmful to pregnant women or during breast feeding. While a minimal amount does cross the placental barrier if these agents are ingested and traces also are found in breast

Table 13.2

Differential Diagnoses for Dentinal Hypersensitivity

Pathology	Signs and symptoms	Clinical evaluation
Chipped tooth	Thermal sensitivity, pain from abrasion	Visual examination
Cracked tooth	Pain from pressure (biting)	Percussion, biting, application of dye to disclose fracture
Dental caries	Thermal sensitivity (cold), pain from pressure	Radiographic or clinical examination
Dentin hypersen-sitivity	Sharp, sudden, short pain; thermal sensitivity; pain from abrasion	Osmotic solution, thermal testing, mechanical abrasion, normal electrical pulp test
Fractured restoration	Thermal sensitivity, pain from pressure	Visual examination, biting on plastic or wood sticks
Postoperative sensitivity	Thermal sensitivity with moderate short pain	History of recent operative work
Trauma from occlusion	Thermal sensitivity, pain from pressure, mobility, wear facets, short pain	Occlusal equilibration

milk, no contraindications are reported when these agents are used as recommended.

Pediatric, geriatric and other special patients
In children, ingestion of high levels of fluoride will cause fluorosis of teeth and osseous changes. In older patients, there is no evidence suggesting a need to modify existing procedures.

Patient Monitoring: Aspects to Watch

- Persistent or increased pain: may require re-evaluation of differential diagnosis as well as consideration of alternative agents, therapies or both

Adverse Effects and Precautions

Fluorides

Fluoride preparations should be kept out of reach of children. On rare occasions, adverse reactions to fluorides, including skin rash, GI upset and headaches, may be noted. Such reactions are reversible upon discontinuing use. Fluoride should not be swallowed.

Patients with gingival sensitivity may be sensitive to the acidity of certain fluoride solutions.

Acidic fluoride solutions may cause dulling of porcelain and ceramic restorations.

Oxalates

Acids may decrease the effectiveness of bonding cements; thus, teeth treated with oxalates should be pumiced before application of bonding agents.

Varnishes, Sealants and Bonding Agents

No adverse effects or precautions have been reported.

Pharmacology

The general principle guiding the development of desensitizing agents is that the number of dental tubules exposed to the mouth correlates with sensitivity; thus, many of the agents are designed to occlude tubules. The most popular theory, the "hydrodynamic theory," is that sensitivity in this situation results from the movement of fluid through the exposed tubules, which results in activation of the nerves within the pulp, subsequently registered as pain. A strategy used to decrease sensitivity, based on the hydrodynamic theory, includes the development of agents that can depolarize nerves directly.

Another theory of dentin hypersensitivity is that of the "dentinal receptor mechanism," which proposes that odontoblasts play a more receptive role; however, agents that induce pain normally fail to evoke pain when applied to exposed dentin. Yet a third theory is that certain polypeptides present within the pulp can modulate nerve impulses within the pulp. Thus, therapies have been directed at agents or procedures or both that can depolarize nerves directly.

Patient Advice

- Patients should be aware that, in general, several factors must be carefully considered in treatment of tooth sensitivity: severity of the problem, physical findings and past treatment. Proper diagnosis is required before initiation of treatment, whether in office or at home.
- Patients must realize that use of a desensitizing agent may not prove effective over a short time (for example, less than 2 w).

Suggested Readings

Curro FA, ed. Tooth hypersensitivity. Dent Clin North Am 1990;July:34(3).

Pashley EL, Tao L, Pashley DH. Effects of oxalate on dentin bonding. Am J Dent 1993;3:116-8.

Richardson DW, Tao L, Pashley DH. Bond strengths of luting cements to potassium oxalate-treated dentin. J Prosthet Dent 1990;63:418-22.

Silverman G, German E, Hanna CB, et al. Assessing the efficacy of three dentifrices in the treatment of dentinal hypersensitivity. JADA 1997;127:191-201.

Home Use Products

Accepted Indications

Desensitizing toothpaste agents are used to provide relief from thermal and tactile sensitivity on exposed root surfaces when pathological causes for pain have been ruled out. In addition, these toothpastes contain fluoride to prevent caries.

General Usage Information

Usage and Administration

See Table 13.3 for general usage information on desensitizing toothpastes.

Special Dental Considerations

Following are special dental considerations for home use desensitizing agents, which are the same as or very similar to those for in-office products listed earlier in this chapter.

Drug Interactions of Dental Interest

- There is some suggestion of interaction of fluorides with calcium-containing products—for example, formation of calcium fluoride, which is poorly absorbed.
- Certain agents—for example, chlorhexidine—may decrease fluoride's ability to bind to the root surface. Thus, after using fluoride agents, the patient should not use any rinses or eat for 1 h.
- Some agents are acidic and thus may cause sensitivity in patients with mucositis.
- Some acidic compounds—for example, oxalate—may cause dulling of porcelain ceramics and decreased effectiveness of bonding cements. Therefore, pumicing the root surface before use of some desensitizing agents is recommended.

Special Patients

There is no evidence that desensitizing agents are harmful to pregnant women or during breast feeding. In children, high levels of fluoride will cause fluorosis of teeth and osseous changes. In older patients, no alteration of dose is required.

Patient Monitoring: Aspects to Watch

- Persistent or increased pain: may require re-evaluation of differential diagnosis and consideration of alternative agents, therapies or both

Adverse Effects and Precautions

No adverse effects are reported beyond those related to high-dose fluoride. Precautions include the underlying possibility of an undiagnosed serious dental problem that may need prompt dental care. Products should not be used more than 4 w unless recommended by the dentist. Keep out of reach of children. All patients, and especially those with severe dental erosion, should brush properly and lightly with any dentifrice to avoid further removal of tooth structure.

Pharmacology

The general principle guiding development of desensitizing agents, including toothpastes, is that the number of dental tubules exposed to the mouth correlates with sensitivity; thus, most agents are designed to occlude tubules. The most popular theory is that sensitivity in this situation is due to the movement of fluid through the exposed tubules, which results in activation of the nerves within the pulp and subsequently is registered as pain.

Patient Advice

- Patients should be aware that, in general, several factors must be carefully considered in treatment of tooth sensitivity: severity of the problem, physical findings and past treatment. Proper diagnosis is required before initiation of treatment, whether in office or at home.
- Patients must realize that use of a desensitizing agent will not prove effective over a short time unless the product is used for at least 2 w.

Suggested Readings

Curry FA, ed. Tooth hypersensitivity. Dent Clin North Am 1990;July:34(3).

Gilliam DG, Newman HN, Bulman JS, Davies EH. Dentifrice abrasivity and dental hypersensitivity. Results 12 weeks following cessation of 8 weeks' supervised use. J Periodontol 1992;63:7-12.

Kuroiwa M, Kodaka T, Kuroiwa M, Abe M. Dentin hypersensitivity. Occlusion of dentinal tubules by brushing with and without an abrasive dentifrice. J Periodontol 1994;65:291-6.

Ochardson R, Gangarosa LP Sr, Holland GR, Pashley DH. Towards a standard code of practice for evaluating the effectiveness of treatments for hypersensitive dentine. Arch Oral Biol 1994;39:1215-45.

Table 13.3

Desensitizing Toothpastes: Usage Information

Generic name	Brand name(s)	Usage and administration for adults	Usage and administration for children	Content/form	Features/uses
Sodium fluoride, 5% potassium nitrate	Aquafresh Sensitive Teeth, Arm & Hammer Dentacare, Crest Sensitivity Protection ★, Desensitize Plus, Oral-B Sensitive, Protect Sensitive Teeth ★, Sensodyne Cool Gel, Sensodyne Tartar Control	Apply toothpaste onto soft-bristle toothbrush; brush teeth thoroughly for at least 1 min tid (morning and evening) or as recommended by a dentist or physician; make sure to brush all sensitive areas of the teeth	**Age < 12 y:** Dentist or physician should be consulted before children use this product **Age < 6 y:** Children should be supervised when using this product; keep out of reach of children	**Tubes:** 1-, 6-oz	Fluoride products are used for prevention of cavities, and potassium nitrate is considered to decrease dentinal hypersensitivity through nerve inhibition; if pain persists more than 4 w, patient should be re-evaluated to determine cause of sensitivity
Sodium monofluorophosphate, 5% potassium nitrate	Den-Mat Sensitive, Orajel Sensitive Pain-Relieving Toothpaste ★, Rembrandt Whitening Sensitive, Sensodyne Fresh Mint, Sensodyne Original	See note above	See note above	**Tubes:** 1-, 6-oz	See note above
Stannous fluoride, 5% potassium nitrate	Colgate Sensitive Maximum Strength	See note above	See note above	**Tubes:** 4-oz	See note above
Strontium chloride 10%	Sensodyne-SC [CAN]	See note above	See note above	**Tubes:** 1-, 6-oz	Strontium chloride decreases dentinal hypersensitivity through tubule occlusion; if pain persists more than 4 w, patient should be re-evaluated to determine cause of sensitivity

★ indicates a product bearing the ADA Seal of Acceptance.
[CAN] indicates a product available only in Canada.

Chapter 14

Bleaching Agents

B. Ellen Byrne, R.Ph., D.D.S., Ph.D.

Tooth bleaching agents can be classified as to whether they are used for external or internal bleaching and whether the procedure is performed in the office by a dentist or at home by a patient. For tooth bleaching, hydrogen peroxide (H_2O_2) is used alone at levels of 35% or at 10% to 22% levels in a stable gel of carbamide peroxide (urea peroxide) that breaks down to form hydrogen peroxide (3.35% hydrogen peroxide from 10% carbamide peroxide), urea, ammonia and carbon dioxide. The Food and Drug Administration has not approved peroxide solutions for use as a home bleach, however.

The terms "whitening" and "bleaching," unfortunately, have been used interchangeably. While the mechanism is not completely understood, bleaching involves free radicals and breakdown of pigment, while whitening is accomplished by abrasive agents in the dentifrice (see Chapter 11).

Internal bleaching. Internal bleaching produces reliable results when used to eliminate intrinsic stains in dentin caused by blood breakdown products or endodontics or for stains in receded pulp chambers. However, bleaching should be confined to the dentin; bleaching the cementum, which provides an attachment for the periodontal ligament, has been associated with external root resorption. External root resorption below the gingival attachment is associated with internal bleaching on nonvital teeth that have sustained trauma, poorly sealed canal spaces or heating during the bleaching procedure. It is felt that the bleaching agent diffuses through the dentinal tubules and initiates an inflammatory resorptive response in the cervical area. Unfortunately, external cervical resorption is not seen for approximately 5 to 6 y after internal bleaching. The use of heat is not essential and should be avoided.

Internal bleaching is always performed in the dental office. There are two common approaches to internal bleaching: the "office bleach" (a one-time application) and the "walking bleach" (sealed inside the tooth for 2 to 3 days). The office bleaching agent is a mixture of Superoxol (30% hydrogen peroxide) and perborate, to which heat is applied by the use of a hot instrument, such as a ball burnisher or an electric heat-producing instrument, for 2 to 5 min to accelerate the bleaching process. Heat also has been associated with external root resorption. Walking bleach seals the Superoxol and perborate mixture inside the tooth for 2 to 3 days. The sodium perborate, a stable white powder that is soluble in water, decomposes into sodium metaborate and hydrogen peroxide, thus releasing nascent oxygen. The sodium perborate, which is mixed with the hydrogen peroxide, also releases oxygen. This combination is thought to be synergistic and very effective in bleaching. This technique is called "walking bleach" because the bleaching process actually occurs between dental appointments, during which time the bleaching agents are sealed in the pulp chamber.

External bleaching. External bleaching is indicated for teeth that are discolored from aging, fluorosis or staining due to the effects of tetracycline. External bleaching can be applied by the dentist or staff or can be applied by the patient in home-use bleaching. When dentist-administered and home-use bleaching are used together, it is called "dual bleaching."

Dentist-applied external bleaching can be accomplished with periodically repeated use of an office-bleaching agent. Dentist-applied bleaching procedures can be divided into two types:

- power bleaching with high concentrations of hydrogen peroxide (35% to 40%);
- assisted bleaching with high concentrations of carbamide peroxide (35% to 44%).

The power bleaching systems are gels that either are premixed or can be prepared chairside by the mixing of liquid bleach with powder. These products are caustic and, thus, can cause significant soft-tissue injury. The safest, most reliable gingival protection is a properly placed, sealed rubber dam. Assisted bleaches can be used to boost a home-bleaching program or as an easier, low-cost in-office bleaching method. Because carbamide peroxide is not as strong as hydrogen peroxide, it cannot yield the same results as hydrogen peroxide. Even though these assisted bleaches are not as caustic as high concentrations of hydrogen peroxide, they do have the capability to irritate the gingiva.

An etching gel containing phosphoric acid that is applied to selected dark areas increases the penetration of the bleach. Light is used to produce heat, which accelerates the bleaching process. The light/heat source can be a visible curing light, overhead operatory light or argon laser. Externally bleached teeth may need touch-up treatment every 1 or 2 y. Severely stained teeth may require more frequent retreatment.

Table 14.1

Types of Tooth Discoloration

Color of stain	Etiology	Ease or difficulty of bleaching
White	Fluorosis	Degree of difficulty depends on extent of fluorosis
Blue-gray	Dentinogenesis imperfecta, erythroblastosis fetalis, tetracycline	Deeply stained blue-gray discolorations, especially those associated with tetracycline, are more difficult to treat than yellow stains
Gray	Silver oxide from root canal sealers	Dark stains from root canal sealers seldom bleachable, should be treated restoratively
Yellow	Fluorosis, physiological changes due to aging, obliteration of the pulp chamber	Mild uniform yellow discoloration associated with aging or mild uniform fluorosis is easiest to treat
Brown	Fluorosis, caries, porphyria, tetracycline, dentinogenesis imperfecta	Stains that are deeper in color are more difficult to treat
Black	Mercury stain (amalgam), caries, fluorosis	Very dark or black stains from silver-containing root canal sealers or from mercury are seldom bleachable, should be treated restoratively
Pink	Internal resorption	Bleaching is not indicated; treatment consists of endodontics and calcium hydroxide treatment

Table 14.2

Professionally Applied Internal Bleaching Agents: Usage Information

Generic name	Brand name(s)	Indications	Usual adult dosage
30% hydrogen peroxide	Superoxol with sodium perborate ★	Yellow or black stains from endodontics or tetracycline; intrinsic stains when teeth have darkened from blood breakdown products, or in receded pulp chambers	Sealed into pulp chamber for up to 7 days

★ *indicates a product bearing the ADA Seal of Acceptance.*

Table 14.3

Professionally Applied External Bleaching Agents

Generic name	Brand name(s)
Power bleaches	
Hydrogen peroxide 35%	Hi Lite, 35% Hydrogen Peroxide Gel, Opalescence Xtra, Perfect White, Powergel, Quasarbrite, Starbrite Power Pack
Hydrogen peroxide 35-40%	Quick White
Assisted bleaches	
Carbamide peroxide 35%	Opalescence Quick, Quik Start
Carbamide peroxide 44%	44% Carbamide Peroxide
Hydrogen peroxide 15% and carbamide peroxide 28.5%	Whitespeed

Home bleaching, supervised by the dentist, is done by the patient at home using a custom-made plastic carrier that holds the bleach against the patient's teeth. After the desired result is achieved, overnight use on a periodic basis (1 to 4 times/mo) or daily use of a whitening dentifrice can maintain the lightening that has been achieved.

These products vary in their viscosity, flavor and packing. Most of the home-use bleaches are supplied with material for bleaching trays. In addition, these products contain various concentrations of carbamide peroxide, hydrogen peroxide or both; at least one contains no peroxide. The concentrations of carbamide peroxide range from 10% to 22%; the hydrogen peroxide concentrations range from 3% to 7.5%. The nonperoxide-containing product, Hi Lite 2, is an aqueous-based bleach for home use that contains a patented material called Hydroxylite as well as glycerin, water, cellulose gum and xanthan gum. This product is mainly indicated for patients who have experienced either tooth sensitivity or gingival irritation with use of other agents. It is also the choice for patients who are concerned about the free radicals that are created by any type of peroxide. Fluoride, potassium nitrate or both have been added to some products to reduce tooth sensitivity. The majority of side effects involving tooth sensitivity resolve within 24 to 48 h after use of the product is discontinued.

External bleaching is seldom permanent, lasting approximately 1 to 4 y, after which teeth gradually return to their original color. Usually, the younger the patient, the longer the bleaching will last. The more difficult it is to bleach a tooth, the more likely it is to discolor again. Bluish-gray stains seem to reappear more quickly than yellow stains. Because reoccurrence of staining is unpredictable, promises about longevity should not be made. Internal bleaching usually lasts longer than external bleaching.

The patient must understand that the bleaching agent will not lighten resin-based composite restorations as much as it will natural tooth structure. While there is evidence that resin-based composites will bleach, the results may not match those achieved in natural tooth structure. Patients should be informed that existing restorations will need to be replaced. There is in vitro evidence supporting the fact that bonding of resin-based composites to etched enamel after vital bleaching procedures results in a decreased bond strength. However, within hours to days, the bond strength returns to that achieved with nonbleached enamel. Restoration replace-

Table 14.4

Dentist-Dispensed Home Bleaching Agents

Generic name	Brand name(s)
Carbamide peroxide	
Carbamide peroxide 10%	Colgate Platinum Overnight Professional Whitening System ★, Colgate Platinum Professional Whitening System ★, Contrast P.M. 10% Whitening Gel ★, Nite White Classic ★, Opalescence ★, Patterson Brand Toothwhitening Gel ★, Rembrandt Lighten Bleaching Gel ★
Carbamide peroxide 10%, 15% and 20%	Contrast P.M.
Carbamide peroxide 10%, 15% and 22%	Rembrandt Bleaching Gel Plus
Carbamide peroxide 10% and 16%	Nite White Excel 2, Nite White Excel 2NSF, Nite White Excel 2Z, Zaris
Carbamide peroxide 11%, 13%, 16% and 21%	Trio
Carbamide peroxide 15% and 20%, both with 0.11% fluoride ion	Opalescence F, Opalescence PF
Hydrogen peroxide	
Hydrogen peroxide 4.5%	Perfecta 3/15 Extra Strength
Hydrogen peroxide 5.5% and 7.5%	Day White 2
Nonperoxide Hydroxylite	Hi Lite 2

★ indicates a product bearing the ADA Seal of Acceptance.

Table 14.5

Bleaching Agents: Possible Interactions With Other Substances

Substance used by patient	Interaction with bleaching agent	Dentist's actions
Alcohol	May possibly result in additive carcinogenicity because peroxides have mutagenic potential and may boost the effects of known carcinogens	Advise patients to avoid these products
Coffee	May compromise treatment results	See note above
Tea	May compromise treatment results	See note above
Heavy use of tobacco	May compromise treatment results; may possibly result in additive carcinogenicity because peroxides have mutagenic potential and may boost the effects of known carcinogens	See note above

Table 14.6

Bleaching Agents: Adverse Effects, Precautions and Contraindications

Body system	Adverse effects	Precautions/contraindications
General	Prolonged use of 30% or higher H_2O_2 can destroy cells, and for cells that are not destroyed, prolonged use may potentiate the carcinogenic effects of carcinogens	Patients should not smoke or use other potential carcinogens during treatment
Oral	Owing to acidic nature of some of these products, patients can experience transient dentin sensitivity High concentrations of H_2O_2, or Superoxol, used in office bleaching may produce what appear to be tissue burns—white areas on the gingiva that are caused by oxygen gas bubbles and are not true burns, although discomfort can feel like a burn	Patients with root sensitivity may not want to have treatment because treatment can aggravate sensitivity In cases of tissue burns (see description at left), rinse affected area for 1-5 min

ment should be delayed for about two w to allow for return of bond strength and color rebound after bleaching.

Accepted Indications

Types and causes of tooth discoloration and response to bleaching are provided in Table 14.1. Information on in-office bleaching techniques is provided in Tables 14.2 and 14.3; information on dentist-supervised home bleaching is provided in Table 14.4. Brown, blue-gray and gray stains are usually caused by caries, porphyria, fluorosis, dentinogenesis imperfecta and erythroblastosis fetalis.

They need microabrasion and restorative care and should not be bleached.

General Usage Information

Maximum Recommended Amounts
Average treatment time is generally 2-6 w. More difficult cases require extended treatment and may result in teeth that look chalky. In some patients, stains relapse when treatment is discontinued.

Usage Adjustments
Adult
When having bleaching done at the dental office, some patients, especially those with severe erosion, abrasion or recession, may find the combination of heat and peroxide uncomfortable. These patients are not good candidates for office bleaching. For at-home bleaching, the recommended wearing time varies greatly; the wearing times are determined by clinical study designs and vary considerably between products. The daily dosage is between ½ h and 10 h for one or two treatments per day.

Special Dental Considerations

Drug Interactions of Dental Interest
Possible interactions between substances such as therapeutics and bleaching agents are provided in Table 14.5.

Special Patients
Pregnant and nursing women
The long-term effects of using in-office or home bleaching agents on the teeth of pregnant women have not been studied; therefore, women who are pregnant or who have a reasonable expectation that they could become pregnant should not undergo treatment. Pregnancy risk category has not been determined.

Pediatric, geriatric and other special patients
Bleaching agents are not indicated for use in children. The gel should be kept away from children.

Patient Monitoring: Aspects to Watch
Long-term use can alter normal oral flora and can contribute to lingual papillary hypertrophy (hairy tongue) and *Candida albicans*.

Adverse Effects and Precautions
See Table 14.6 for adverse effects, precautions and contraindications for in-office and home use of bleaching agents.

Pharmacology
The mechanism of tooth bleaching is not fully understood; however, it is felt that the unstable peroxide breaks down to highly unstable free radicals. These free radicals chemically break larger pigmented organic molecules in the enamel matrix into smaller less pigmented constituents. Higher concentrations, such as 30% or higher, of hydrogen peroxide remove the enamel matrix, thereby creating microscopic voids that scatter light and increase the appearance of whiteness until remineralization occurs and the color partly relapses. When the morphology of unbleached teeth is compared to that of teeth that have been treated with lower concentrations of peroxide, such as carbamide peroxide 10%, the latter seem not to be affected; therefore, different bleaching materials and concentrations may have different modes of action.

The addition of carbopol, a carboxypoly-methylene polymer, prolongs the release of hydrogen peroxide from carbamide peroxide. Carbopol, a water-soluble resin used in many household products such as shampoo and toothpaste, is used as a thickening agent. It does not break down, nor does it increase the breakdown of the bleaching agent. The carbopol binds to the peroxide and triples or quadruples the active release time of peroxide. Products without carbopol are more fluid and bleach more slowly due to the reduced activity time and greater loss of bleach from the tray. See the box on page 256 for the ADA's statement on the safety of home-use tooth whitening products.

Patient Advice

The following advice pertains to patients who are using home bleaching agents:

- The more treatments per day, the faster the bleaching; however, this concentrated use of bleaching agents can also increase sensitivity.
- The bleaching agent should be tightly capped and refrigerated.
- The patient should not wear the appliance while eating.
- Users should discontinue treatment with the bleaching agent if the teeth, gums or bite become uncomfortable.
- The dentist should check the patient's mouth every 1-6 w to ensure that no damage has been done to the teeth, gums or dental restorations.

- Use of a whitening dentifrice after treatment may extend the whitening effect of the treatment.

Suggested Readings

Albers HF. Lightening natural teeth. ADEPT Report 1991;2(1):1-24.

Dishman MV, Covey DA, Baughan LW. The effect of peroxide bleaching on composite to enamel bond strength. Dent Materials 1994;9:33-6.

Harrington GW, Natkin F. External resorption associated with bleaching of pulpless teeth. J. Endod 1979;5:344-8.

Haywood VB, Leonard RH, Nelson CF, Brunson WD. Effectiveness, side effects and long-term status of night-guard vital bleaching. JADA 1994;125(9):1219-26.

Monaghan P, Trowbridge T, Lautenschlager E. Composite resin color change after vital tooth bleaching. J Prosth Dent 1992;67:778-81.

Reality: The information source for esthetic dentistry. Houston: Reality Publishing Co.; 1999.

Reality: The information source for esthetic dentistry. Houston: Reality Publishing Co.; 2000.

ADA Statement on the Safety of Home-Use Tooth Whitening Products

Over the last 10 years, the ADA Council on Scientific Affairs has monitored the development and proliferation of whitening or bleaching oral hygiene products intended for use by consumers at home.

Many of these products contain peroxide(s), while others contain agents that work by physical or chemical action to remove extrinsic or surface stains. They may be dispensed by dentists or purchased over the counter (OTC) and can be categorized into two major groups, as seen below.

Peroxide-containing whiteners or bleaching agents containing 3% hydrogen peroxide

Ten percent carbamide peroxide, which is equivalent to 3% hydrogen peroxide, is the most commonly used active ingredient in tooth-bleaching products. Carbamide peroxide breaks down into hydrogen peroxide and urea in aqueous solution, with hydrogen peroxide being the active bleaching agent. Other ingredients of peroxide-containing tooth whiteners may include glycerin, carbopol, sodium hydroxide and flavors.

Accumulated clinical data over the last 10 years on 10% carbamide peroxide with neutral acidity continue to support both the safety and the effectiveness of this tooth-whitening agent. The most commonly observed side effects of hydrogen or carbamide peroxide are tooth sensitivity to temperature changes and occasional irritation of oral mucosa. (This statement does not address side effects that may be associated with other ingredients in these formulations.) Tooth sensitivity often occurs during early stages of bleaching treatment. In most cases, an ill-fitting tray rather than the tooth-bleaching agent is the cause of mucosal irritation. Both of these conditions are generally transient and stop upon cessation of treatment.

The ADA advises patients to consult with their dentists to determine if bleaching is appropriate. This is especially important for patients with many fillings, crowns and extremely dark stains.

Dentifrices containing only polishing or other chemical agents

Dentifrices that contain only polishing or chemical agents improve tooth appearance by removing extrinsic or surface stains through a gentle polishing, chemical chelation or some other action.

A list of ADA-accepted whitening dentifrices and 10% carbamide peroxide, tray-applied tooth-whitening products is available on ADA.org (http://www.ada.org).

Chapter 15.

Drugs for Medical Emergencies in the Dental Office

Stanley F. Malamed, D.D.S.

Medical emergencies can and do occur in dental offices. Surveys have demonstrated that it is likely that at least one potentially life-threatening emergency situation will develop during a dentist's practice lifetime. (See Chapter 16 for a discussion of how to manage emergency situations.)

Each professional staff member in every dental office should be trained to recognize and manage any emergency situation that might arise.

Although certain categories of emergency drugs are suggested for the dental office emergency kit, it must be emphasized that administering emergency drugs will always be secondary to providing basic life support during an emergency. Indeed, during all emergency situations, health care professionals should strictly adhere to the P,A,B,C,D emergency management protocol:

P = position;
A = airway;
B = breathing;
C = circulation;
D = definitive treatment (which might include administration of drugs).

Because dentists' levels of training in emergency management can vary significantly, it is impossible to recommend any one list of emergency drugs or any one proprietary emergency drug kit that meets the needs and abilities of all dentists. For this reason, dentists should develop their own emergency drug and equipment kits, based on their level

of expertise in managing emergencies.

Although no state dental boards have established specific recommendations as to which emergency drugs and equipment a dentist must have available, state boards of dental examiners do mandate that certain drugs and items of emergency equipment be available in offices where dentists employ intramuscular or intravenous parenteral sedation or general anesthesia. Specialty groups, such as the American Dental Society of Anesthesiology, the American Association of Oral and Maxillofacial Surgeons and the Academy of Pediatric Dentistry, have instituted guidelines for the use of sedation and general anesthesia, which dictate the emergency drugs that must be readily available. The following drug categories are mandated by many state boards of dental examiners for doctors who have been permitted to use parenteral conscious sedation, deep sedation or general anesthesia:

- vasoconstrictor;
- corticosteroid;
- bronchodilator;
- muscle relaxant;
- opioid antagonist;
- benzodiazepine antagonist;
- antihistamine (histamine blocker);
- anticholinergic;
- cardiac medications: epinephrine, antidysrhythmic, vasodilator;
- antihypertensive.

Dentists should not include in the emergency kit any drug or item of emergency equipment they are not trained to use. For example, dentists who are not well-trained in tracheal intubation should not include a laryngoscope and endotracheal tubes in their emergency kits; likewise, dentists who are not proficient in venipuncture should not have an anticonvulsant drug, such as diazepam, in their kits because anticonvulsant drugs must be administered intravenously. Also, dentists should not use anticonvulsants if they are unable to ventilate a patient who is unconscious and apneic, as is likely to occur when anticonvulsant drugs are administered to terminate a seizure.

Table 15.1 lists four levels of drugs and medical equipment that can help the dentist design an emergency kit that will be suitable for the level of emergency preparedness of his or her dental office:

- Level 1 drugs are those deemed most important or critical;
- Level 2 drugs are less critical but can be included in the emergency drug kits of dentists trained to use them;
- Level 3 drugs are those employed for advanced cardiac life support;
- Level 4 includes antidotal drugs that are used to reverse the clinical actions of previously administered medications.

Accepted Indications

Table 15.2 describes the emergency clinical indications for injectable and noninjectable drugs.

General Dosing Information

Table 15.2 provides the dosing information for injectable and noninjectable drugs.

Special Dental Considerations

Drug Interactions of Dental Interest

Table 15.3 lists the possible interactions of injectable and noninjectable emergency drugs with other drugs.

Adverse Effects and Precautions

Table 15.4 lists the adverse effects and precautions related to injectable and noninjectable emergency drugs with other drugs.

Pharmacology

Injectable Drugs

Level 1 (Basic, critical drugs)

Epinephrine (1:1,000): Epinephrine, a sympathomimetic drug, acts on both α- and β-adrenergic receptors. It is the most potent α-adrenergic receptor agonist available. Clinical actions of benefit during anaphylaxis include increased systemic vascular resistance, increased arterial blood pressure, increased coronary and cerebral blood flow and bronchodilation.

Histamine blockers (diphenhydramine and chlorpheniramine): Histamine blockers appear to compete with histamine for cell-receptor sites on effector cells. These drugs also have anticholinergic and sedative properties.

Level 2 (Noncritical drugs)

Anticonvulsant (diazepam): Diazepam, a central nervous system (CNS) depressant that acts on parts of the limbic system, thalamus and hypothalamus, provides anticonvulsant effects.

Analgesic (morphine sulfate): Morphine exerts its primary effects on the CNS and organs containing smooth muscle. Pharmacological effects include analgesia, drowsiness, euphoria (mood alteration), reduction in body temperature (at low doses), dose-related respiratory depression, interference with adrenocortical response to stress (at high doses) and reduction of peripheral resistance with little or no effect on the cardiac index.

Vasoconstrictor (methoxamine): Methoxamine is an α-receptor agonist that produces a prompt and prolonged rise in blood pressure after parenteral administration. Methoxamine differs from most other sympathomimetic amines by having a predominantly peripheral action and lacking inotropic and chronotropic effects. Methoxamine also has less dysrhythmogenic potential than other sympathomimetic amines and rarely causes ventricular tachycardia, fibrillation or increased sinoatrial rate. A decrease in heart rate may occasionally be noted as the blood pressure increases. This is thought to be caused by a carotid sinus reflex. Methoxamine's constrictor action appears to be due to peripheral vasoconstriction rather than to a centrally mediated effect. Methoxamine also increases venous pressure.

Antihypoglycemic (glucagon, dextrose 50%): Glucagon, which causes an increase in blood glucose concentration, is used to treat hypoglycemia. It is effective in small doses, and no evidence of toxicity has been reported with its use. Glucagon acts only on liver glycogen by converting it to glucose. Intravenous administration of 50% dextrose also can be used to manage hypoglycemia.

Anti-inflammatory adrenal corticosteroid (hydrocortisone sodium succinate): Hydrocortisone sodium succinate has the same metabolic and anti-inflammatory actions as hydrocortisone. After intravenous administration of hydrocortisone sodium succinate, demonstrable effects are evident within 1 h and persist for a variable period. The preparation also may be administered IM.

Antihypertensive, antianginal, β-adrenergic blocking agents (esmolol, labetalol): Esmolol is a β_1 (cardioselective) adrenergic receptor blocking agent with rapid onset, a very short duration of action and no significant membrane-stabilizing or intrinsic sympathomimetic (partial agonist) activities at therapeutic doses. Esmolol inhibits β_1 receptors located chiefly in cardiac muscle. At higher doses, it can inhibit β_2 receptors located chiefly in the bronchial and vascular musculature. Clinical actions include a decrease in heart rate, an increase in sinus cycle length, prolongation of sinus node recovery time, prolongation of the A-H interval during normal sinus rhythm and during atrial pacing, and an increase in the antegrade Wenckebach cycle length.

Labetalol combines both selective competi-tive α_1-adrenergic blocking and nonselective competitive β-adrenergic blocking activity. Blood pressure is lowered more when the patient is in the standing rather than in the supine position, and symptoms of postural hypotension can occur. During IV dosing, the patient should not be permitted to move to an erect position unmonitored until ability to do so has been established. Labetalol is metabolized primarily through conjugation to glucuronide metabolites.

Anticholinergic, antidysrhythmic (atropine): Though commonly classified as an anticholinergic drug, atropine is more precisely an antimuscarinic agent. Atropine-induced parasympathetic inhibition can be preceded by a transient phase of stimulation. This is most notable in the heart, where small doses often first slow the rate before the more characteristic tachycardia develops owing to inhibition of vagal control. Compared with scopolamine, atropine's actions on the heart, intestine and bronchial smooth muscle are more potent and longer-lasting. Also unlike scopolamine, atropine, in clinical doses, does not depress the CNS, but may stimulate the medulla and higher cerebral centers.

Adequate doses of atropine abolish various types of reflex vagal cardiac slowing, or asystole. It also prevents or eliminates bradycardia, (asystole produced by injection of choline esters, anticholinesterase agents or other parasympathomimetic drugs) and cardiac arrest produced by vagal stimulation. Atropine can also lessen the degree of partial heart block when vagal activity is an etiologic factor.

Systemic doses can raise systolic and diastolic pressures slightly and can produce significant postural hypotension. Such doses also slightly increase cardiac output and decrease central venous pressure. Occasionally, therapeutic doses dilate cutaneous blood vessels, particularly in the blush area, producing atropine flush, and can cause atropine fever owing to suppression of sweat gland activity in infants and small children.

Atropine disappears from the blood rapidly

after administration and is metabolized primarily by enzymatic hydrolysis in the liver.

Level 3 (Advanced Cardiac Life-Support Drugs)

Endogenous catecholamine (epinephrine [1:10,000]): Epinephrine is an endogenous catecholamine with both α- and β-adrenergic activity. Clinical actions of benefit during cardiac arrest include increased systemic vascular resistance, increased arterial blood pressure, increased heart rate, increased coronary and cerebral blood flow, increased myocardial contraction and increased myocardial oxygen requirements and increased automaticity.

Anticholinergic, antidysrhythmic (atropine): See description under Level 2.

Antidysrhythmic (lidocaine): Lidocaine suppresses ventricular arrhythmias primarily by decreasing automaticity, by reducing the slope of Phase 4 diastolic depolarization. Its local anesthetic properties also may help to depress ventricular ectopy after acute myocardial infarction. During acute myocardial ischemia, the threshold for the induction of ventricular fibrillation is reduced. Some studies have shown that lidocaine elevates the fibrillation threshold; therefore, elevation of the fibrillation threshold correlates closely with blood levels of lidocaine.

Lidocaine usually does not affect myocardial contractility, arterial blood pressure, atrial arrhythmogenesis or intraventricular conduction. It can, on occasion, facilitate atrioventricular conduction.

Antidysrhythmic (procainamide): Procainamide effectively suppresses ventricular ectopy and may be effective when lidocaine has not achieved suppression of life-threatening ventricular dysrhythmias. Procainamide suppresses Phase 4 diastolic depolarization, reducing the automaticity of ectopic pacemakers. Procainamide also slows intraventricular conduction.

Antidysrhythmic (bretylium tosylate): Bretylium is a quaternary ammonium compound with both adrenergic and direct myocardial effects. Initially, bretylium releases norepinephrine from adrenergic nerve endings in direct relation to its concentration at the adrenergic terminal. These sympathomimetic effects, which persist for approximately 20 min, consist of transient hypertension, tachycardia and, in some patients, increases in cardiac output. Subsequently, inhibition of norepinephrine release from peripheral adrenergic terminals results in adrenergic blockade, which generally begins 15 to 20 min after injection and peaks 45 to 60 min later. During this time, clinically significant hypotension may develop, especially with changes in position. In addition, as bretylium blocks the uptake of norepinephrine into adrenergic nerve terminals, it potentiates the actions of exogenous catecholamines.

Bretylium elevates the ventricular fibrillation threshold; it also increases the action potential duration and effective refractory period without changes in the heart rate. Bretylium does not suppress Phase 4 depolarization or the spontaneous firing of Purkinje's fibers. The restoration of injured myocardial cell electrophysiology toward normal, as well as the increase of the action potential duration and effective refractory period without changing their ratio to each other, may be important factors in suppressing the reentry of aberrant impulses and decreasing induced dispersion of local excitable states.

Antidysrhythmic (verapamil): Verapamil is a calcium ion influx inhibitor (slow-channel blocker or calcium-ion inhibitor) that exerts its pharmacological effects by modulating the influx of ionic calcium across the cell membrane of the arterial smooth muscle as well as in conductile and contractile myocardial cells.

Alkalinyzing agent (sodium bicarbonate): Intravenous sodium bicarbonate therapy increases plasma bicarbonate, buffers excess hydrogen ion concentration, raises blood pH and reverses the clinical manifestations of acidosis. Administration of sodium bicarbonate does not facilitate ventricular defibrillation or survival in patients who have had a cardiac arrest.

Calcium salt (calcium chloride): Calcium ions increase the force of myocardial contraction. Calcium's positive inotropic effects are modulated by its action on systemic vascular resistance. Calcium can either increase or decrease systemic vascular resistance.

Level 4 (Antidotal Drugs)

Opioid antagonist (naloxone): Naloxone prevents or reverses the actions of opioids, including respiratory depression, sedation and hypotension. It also can reverse the psychotomimetic and dysphoric effects of agonist-antagonists such as pentazocine.

As a "pure" opioid antagonist, naloxone does not produce respiratory depression, psychotomimetic effects or pupillary constriction. In the absence of opioids or agonistic effects of other opioid antagonists, naloxone exhibits essentially no pharmacological activity.

Naloxone is a competitive antagonist for opioid receptor sites. The onset of action after IV administration is apparent within 2 min, with an only slightly slower onset after subcutaneous or IM administration. Duration depends on the route of administration; IM administration produces a more prolonged effect than IV administration. The need for repeated doses of naloxone depends on the dose, route of administration and the type of opioid being antagonized.

Naloxone is rapidly distributed in the body and is metabolized in the liver.

Benzodiazepine antagonist (flumazenil): Flumazenil, which antagonizes the actions of benzodiazepines on the CNS, competitively inhibits the activity at the benzodiazepine recognition site on the GABA/benzodiazepine receptor complex. Flumazenil has little or no agonist activity in humans. Flumazenil does not antagonize the CNS effects of drugs effecting GABA-ergic neurons by means other than the benzodiazepine receptor (that is, ethanol, barbiturates or general anesthetics) and does not reverse the effects of opioids.

Flumazenil antagonizes sedation, impairment of recall and psychomotor impairment produced by benzodiazepines in healthy human volunteers. The duration and degree of reversal of benzodiazepine effects are related to the dose and plasma concentration of flumazenil as well as that of the sedating benzodiazepine. Onset of reversal is usually evident within 1 to 2 min after IV injection. An 80% response is reached within 3 min, with peak effect noted at 6 to 10 min.

Noninjectable Drugs

Level 1 (Basic, critical drugs)

Vasodilators (nitroglycerin): The primary action of the vasodilator nitroglycerin is to relax vascular smooth muscle. Although venous effects predominate, nitroglycerin produces, in a dose-related manner, dilation of both venous and arterial beds. It decreases venous return to the heart and reduces systemic vascular resistance and arterial pressure. These effects lead to a decrease in myocardial oxygen consumption, resulting in a more favorable supply-demand ratio and the cessation of anginal discomfort.

Bronchodilator (albuterol): Compared with isoproterenol, albuterol has a preferential effect on β_2-adrenergic receptors. β_2-adrenergic receptors are the predominant receptors in bronchial smooth muscle. Recent data indicate that β-adrenergic receptors also exist in the human heart in a concentration from approximately 10 to 50%. The action of albuterol is attributable, at least in part, to stimulation through β-adrenergic receptors of ATP to cyclic-AMP. Increased cyclic-AMP levels are associated with bronchial smooth muscle relaxation and the inhibition of the release of mediators of immediate hypersensitivity from cells, especially mast cells.

Albuterol has a greater effect on the respiratory tract, in the form of bronchial smooth muscle relaxation, while producing fewer cardiovascular (CV) side effects than most bronchodilators at comparable doses. However, in some patients, albuterol, like other bronchodilators, can produce significant CV effects, such as increased pulse rate, blood pressure, symptoms such as palpitation and tremor, and/or electrocardiographic changes.

Antihypoglycemics (orange juice, regular [not diet] soft drinks): Antihypoglycemics are rapidly absorbed sources of glucose for the management of hypoglycemia.

Fibrinolytic (aspirin): Aspirin, in a dose of 81-325 mg, is recommended in the prehospital phase of out-of-hospital myocardial infarction. Its fibrinolytic properties may help in the reperfusion of ischemic myocardium.

Level 2 (Noncritical drugs)

Respiratory stimulant (aromatic ammonia, spirits of ammonia): Ammonia, which is a noxious-smelling vapor, acts by irritating the mucous membrane of the upper respiratory tract, thereby stimulating the respiratory and vasomotor centers of the medulla. This, in turn, increases respiration and blood pressure.

Suggested Readings

Fast TB, Martin MD, Ellis TM. Emergency preparedness: a survey of dental practitioners. JADA 1986;112:499-501.

Malamed SF. Managing medical emergencies. JADA 1993;124:40-53.

Office anesthesia evaluation manual. 4th ed. Rosemont, Ill.: American Association of Oral and Maxillofacial Surgeons; 1991.

Table 15.1

Levels and Types of Injectable and Noninjectable Drugs and Equipment for Emergencies in Dental Offices

Injectable drugs	Noninjectable drugs	Equipment
Level 1 (basic, critical drugs)		
Endogenous catecholamine: Epinephrine (1:1,000) **Histamine blocker:** Diphenhydramine, chlorpheniramine	**Oxygen** **Vasodilator:** Nitroglycerin **Bronchodilator:** Albuterol **Antihypoglycemic:** Orange juice, regular (not diet) soft drinks **Fibrinolytic:** Aspirin (chewable)	**Oxygen delivery system** including positive-pressure/demand valve, bag, valve, mask device, pocket mask; **high-volume suction and aspirator tips or tonsillar suction; syringes; tourniquets; Magill intubation; forceps**
Level 2 (noncritical drugs)		
Analgesic: Morphine sulfate **Anticonvulsant:** Diazepam **Antihypertensive:** Antianginal, ß-adrenergic blocking agents such as esmolol, labetalol **Antihypoglycemic:** Glucagon HCl, 50% dextrose **Glucocorticoid:** Hydrocortisone sodium succinate **Vasoconstrictor:** Methoxamine	**Anticholinergic:** Atropine **Respiratory stimulant:** Aromatic ammonia, spirits of ammonia	**Airway equipment:** Oropharyngeal or nasopharyngeal airways, or both; laryngoscope and endotracheal tubes **Equipment for intravenous infusion:** Infusion solution such as 5% dextrose and water (D5W); intravenous tubing; catheters, winged infusion sets, or both **Cricothyrotomy device**
Level 3 (advanced cardiac life-support drugs)		
Alkalinizing agent: Sodium bicarbonate **Analgesic:** Morphine sulfate **Antidysrhythmic:** Bretylium tosylate **Antidysrhythmic:** Lidocaine **Antidysrhythmic:** Procainamide **Antidysrhythmic:** Verapamil **Anticholinergic, antidysrhythmic:** Atropine **Calcium salt:** Calcium chloride **Endogenous catecholamine:** Epinephrine (1:10,000, for IV administration)		
Level 4 (antidotal drugs)		
Benzodiazepine antagonist: Flumazenil **Opioid antagonist:** Naloxone		

Table 15.2

Injectable and Noninjectable Emergency Drugs: Dosage and Prescribing Information

Generic name	Brand name(s)	Adult dosage (mg/kg)	Child dosage	PRC	Content/form	Indications
		Level 1 (basic, critical drugs)				
Anti-hypoglycemics (orange juice, nondiet soft drinks)	Many commercially available brands	Orange juice or regular (not diet) cola beverages are administered in 4-oz increments every 5-10 min until patient has returned to normal level of consciousness	Orange juice or regular (not diet) cola beverages are administered in 4-oz increments every 5-10 min until patient has returned to normal level of consciousness		**Liquids:** Available in 12-oz cans	For hypoglycemia in the conscious patient
Bronchodilator: Albuterol	Ventolin, Proventil	2 inhalations repeated every 4-6 h; for some patients, 1 inhalation q 4 h may be adequate; neither more frequent administrations nor a larger number of inhalations are recommended; if a previously effective dosage regimen fails to provide the usual relief, medical advice should be sought immediately, as this is a sign of seriously worsening asthma and requires reassessment of therapy	**Age < 14 y:** NE **Age ≥ 14 y:** 2 inhalations repeated every 4-6 h; for some patients, 1 inhalation q 4 h may be adequate; neither more frequent administrations nor a larger number of inhalations are recommended; if a previously effective dosage regimen fails to provide the usual relief, medical advice should be sought immediately, as this is a sign of seriously worsening asthma and requires reassessment of therapy	C	**Inhalation aerosol:** 0.09 mg/inhalation, 200 inhalations	For relief of bronchospasm in patients aged ≥ 4 y who have reversible obstructive airway disease; for prevention of exercise-induced bronchospasm in patients aged ≥ 4 y

Drug	Brand names	Usual dosage	PRC	Forms	Indications
Endogenous catecholamine (sterile solution): Epinephrine 1:1,000	Ana-Guard, Epi-Pen Auto-Injector	**To manage allergic reaction—IM or SC:** 0.2-1.0 mL (mg); small dose should be administered initially and increased, if necessary **Note:** When epinephrine is administered IM, buttocks should be avoided and mid-deltoid or vastus lateralis muscles should be used instead **To manage asthma and certain allergic reactions, such as angioedema, urticaria, serum sickness and anaphylaxis—SC:** 0.2-1.0 mL (mg); small dose should be administered initially and increased, if necessary; preferred route of administration is SC **For cardiac resuscitation—IV:** 0.5 mL (0.5 mg) diluted to 10 mL with sodium chloride injection **Note:** External cardiac compression should be continued after IV administration in patients who have had cardiac arrest to ensure distribution of the epinephrine to coronary circulation **Note:** Drug should be administered only when physical and electromechanical attempts at resuscitation have failed	C	**For asthmatic pediatric patients—SC:** 0.01 mg/kg or 0.3 mg/m² to a maximum of 0.5 mg; dose should be repeated every 4 h, if needed **To manage asthma and certain allergic reactions, such as angioedema, urticaria, serum sickness and anaphylaxis—SC:** 0.01 mg/kg or 0.3 mg/m² body surface to a maximum of 0.5 mg; dose should be repeated every 4 h, if needed; preferred route of administration is SC	**Note:** When diluted, can be administered IV; each mL contains 1 mg of epinephrine hydrochloride dissolved in water for injection, with sodium chloride added for isotonicity **Syringe:** IM 0.15 mg/0.3 mL Epi-Pen Jr. Autoinjector; IM 0.3 mg/0.3 mL Epi-Pen Autoinjector; IM, IV, SC 0.3mg/ 0.3 mL Ana-Guard **Vial—IM, IV, SC:** 0.1 mg/mL in 3- and 10-mL vials; 1.0 mg/mL in 3- and 10-mL vials	For relief of respiratory distress due to bronchospasm To provide rapid relief of hypersensitivity reactions from drugs and other allergens, anaphylaxis, anaphylactic shock
Fibrinolytic: Aspirin	Many commercially available brands	Chewable aspirin should be administered to presumed victim of myocardial infarction as soon as possible	C	Myocardial infarction is highly unlikely to develop in the pediatric age group	**Tablets:** 81-, 162-, 325-mg	For fibrinolysis in suspected myocardial infarction; administered in prehospital phase of management

PRC: Pregnancy risk category.
NE: Not established.

Continued on next page

Table 15.2 (cont.)

Injectable and Noninjectable Emergency Drugs: Dosage and Prescribing Information

Generic name	Brand name(s)	Adult dosage (mg/kg)	Child dosage	PRC	Content/form	Indications
			Level 1 (basic, critical drugs) (cont.)			
Histamine blocker: Chlorphen-iramine	Chlor-Trimeton, Chlor-Pro 10, generic	**IM or IV:** 4 mg tid-qid up to 40 mg/day **Overdosage:** Overdosage can be manifested by CNS symptoms ranging from depression to excitation; stimulation is particularly likely in children; atropine-like signs and symptoms—dry mouth; fixed, dilated pupils; flushing; gastrointestinal symptoms—also can develop	**IM or IV:** 2 mg tid-qid	C	**IV, IM:** 10 mg/mL	For allergic reactions, allergies, anaphylactic reactions, angioedema; mild, uncomplicated skin manifestation of urticaria and angioedema **Age ≥ 60 y:** More likely to cause dizziness, sedation and hypotension
Histamine blocker: Diphenhy-dramine	Benadryl	**IV or deep IM:** 10-50 mg; 100 mg, if required, to a maximum daily dose of 400 mg **Overdosage:** Overdosage can be manifested by CNS symptoms ranging from depression to excitation; stimulation is particularly likely in children; atropine-like signs and symptoms—dry mouth; fixed, dilated pupils; flushing; gastrointestinal symptoms—also can develop	**IV or deep IM:** 5 mg/kg/24 h or 150 mg/m²/24 h	B	**IV, IM:** 10 mg/mL, 50 mg/mL	For allergic reactions, allergies, anaphylactic reactions, angioedema; mild, uncomplicated skin manifestation of urticaria and angioedema **Age ≥ 60 y:** More likely to cause dizziness, sedation and hypotension

		Inhalation: Administered at a flow rate, calculated in L/min, that is adequate to alleviate the presenting signs and symptoms	NE	In compressed gas cylinders in a variety of sizes; portability of the oxygen cylinder is a desirable characteristic; a minimum supply for emergency use is one E-cylinder	Any emergency situation in which respiratory distress is evident
Oxygen					
Vasodilators, antianginals, antihypertensives, CV drugs: Nitroglycerin	Nitrostat, Nitrolingual Spray	**Oral—sublingual tablets:** One tablet (0.15–0.6 mg) should be dissolved under tongue or in buccal pouch at first sign of an acute anginal attack; dose may be repeated every 5 min until relief is obtained; if pain persists after administration of 3 tablets in a 15-min period, a physician should be notified **Oral—lingual aerosol spray:** At onset of an anginal attack, 1 (0.4–0.8 mg) or 2 metered doses should be sprayed onto or under the tongue; no more than 3 metered doses are recommended during a 15-min period; if chest pain persists, prompt medical attention is recommended **Overdosage:** Severe hypotension and reflex tachycardia, which can be managed by elevating the patient's legs and temporarily terminating administration of the drugs, can occur	C	**Sublingual tablets:** 0.15, 0.3, 0.4, 0.6 mg **Translingual spray:** Nitrolingual, 0.4, 0.8 mg/dose **Vaporoles:** amyl nitrite (yellow), 0.3 mL	For the prophylaxis, treatment and management of patients with angina pectoris

PRC: *Pregnancy risk category.*
NE: *Not established.*

Continued on next page

Table 15.2 (cont.)

Injectable and Noninjectable Emergency Drugs: Dosage and Prescribing Information

Generic name	Brand name(s)	Adult dosage (mg/kg)	Child dosage (mg/kg)	PRC	Content/form	Indications
			Level 2 (noncritical drugs)			
Analgesic: Morphine sulfate	Astramorph PF, Duramorph, generic; Epimorph [CAN], Morphine Forte [CAN], Morphine Extra-Forte [CAN], Morphine H.P. [CAN]	**IV:** small incremental doses of 2-5 mg every 5-30 min until desired effect is achieved **Overdosage:** Is characterized by respiratory depression with or without concomitant CNS depression; because respiratory arrest can result either through direct depression of respiratory center or as result of hypoxia, dentist's first action should be ensuring adequate respiratory exchange through provision of patent airway and institution of assisted or controlled ventilation **Note:** Naloxone, the opioid antagonist, is a specific antidote; usually given in 0.4-mg doses; should be administered IV simultaneously with respiratory resuscitation; naloxone injection and resuscitative equipment should be immediately available for administration in case of life-threatening or intolerable side effects **Note:** Low doses of IV-administered morphine have little effect on CV stability; high doses are excitatory, resulting from sympathetic hyperactivity and increase in circulating catecholamines **Note:** CNS excitation, resulting in convulsions, can accompany high doses of morphine administered IV **Note:** Dysphoric reactions and toxic psychoses have also been reported	In dentistry, not used with children	C	**Solution for injection—IM, IV, SC:** 2, 4, 5, 8, 10, 15 mg/mL	To manage pain that is not responsive to nonopioid analgesics; for treatment of pain and anxiety associated with acute myocardial infarction

			PRC	Solution	Use/Notes
Anticholinergic, antidysrhythmic: Atropine	Sal-Tropine ★, generic	**Injection—IM, IV, SC:** 0.5 mg (range, 0.4-0.6 mg) **As an antisialagogue before induction of anesthesia—IM:** 0.5 mg (range, 0.4-0.6 mg) **For bradyarrhythmias—IV:** 0.4-1 mg q 1-2 h, as needed; larger doses up to maximum of 2 mg may be required **Overdosage—IV, slow:** Physostigmine 1-4 mg rapidly abolishes delirium and coma caused by large doses of atropine (see Table 15.4 for adverse reactions) **Note:** Fatal dose level of atropine is not known; doses of 200 mg have been used, and doses as high as 1,000 mg have been given to adults	C	**Solution for injection—IM, IV, SC:** 0.1, 0.4, 0.5, 1 mg/mL and 0.4 mg/0.5 mL ampules	As an antisialagogue for preanesthetic medication; to restore cardiac rate and arterial pressure when vagal stimulation causes a sudden decrease in pulse rate and cardiac action; to lessen the degree of atrioventricular heart block when increased vagal tone is a major factor in conduction defect (as in some cases due to digitalis); to overcome severe bradycardia and syncope owing to hyperactive carotid sinus reflex
		Injection—IV: 0.01-0.33 mg/kg **Overdosage—IV, slow:** Physostigmine 0.5-1 mg rapidly abolishes delirium and coma caused by large doses of atropine (see Table 15.4 for adverse reactions) **Note:** In children, doses of 10 mg or less may be fatal; with a dose as low as 0.5 mg, undesirable minimal symptoms or responses of overdosage may occur, and these increase in severity and extent with larger doses of the drug (excitement, hallucinations, delirium and coma with dose of 10 mg or more)			
Anticonvulsant: Diazepam	D-Val, Valium	Should be individualized (titrated) for maximum beneficial effect **IV:** 1 mL (5 mg)/min until seizure ceases; maximum dose of 20 mg recommended by some authorities	D	**Solution for injection—IV:** 5 mg/mL	A useful adjunct in treating status epilepticus and severe recurrent convulsive seizures
		Older children—IV: 2-20 mg, depending on indication and its severity **Patients with status epilepticus and severe recurrent convulsive seizures—IV:** maximum of 30 mg			
Anticonvulsant: Midazolam	Versed	**IV:** 1 mL/min (1 mg) until seizure ceases **IM:** 10 mg	D	**Solution for injection—IV:** 1 mg/mL and 5 mg/mL (dilute to 1 mg/mL)	See note above
		IM: 0.2 mg/kg, may repeat q 10-15 min (maximum dose 10.0 mg)			

Continued on next page

★ indicates a product bearing the ADA Seal of Acceptance.
[CAN] indicates a drug available only in Canada.
PRC: Pregnancy risk category.

Table 15.2 (cont.)

Injectable and Noninjectable Emergency Drugs: Dosage and Prescribing Information

Generic name	Brand name(s)	Adult dosage (mg/kg)	Child dosage	PRC	Content/form	Indications
		Level 2 (noncritical drugs) (cont.)				
Anti-hypertensive, antianginal, β-adrenergic blocking agent: Esmolol	Brevibloc	**Injection:** Should be diluted to 10-mg/mL infusion by addition of two 2.5-g ampules to a 500-mL container of a compatible IV solution **For intra- or postoperative tachycardia or hypertension:** Not always advisable to slowly titrate dose of esmolol to a therapeutic effect; for immediate control of tachycardia, hypertension or both, give 80-mg (approximately 1 mg/kg) bolus dose over 30 s, then 150-μg/kg/min infusion, if necessary; adjust infusion rate, as necessary, up to 300 μg/kg/min to maintain desired heart rate/blood pressure **For intra- or postoperative tachycardia or hypertension, alternative method:** Loading dose infusion of 500 μg/kg/min for 1 min, then 4-min maintenance infusion of 50 μg/kg/min; if adequate therapeutic effect is not noted within 5 min, repeat same loading dose and follow with maintenance infusion increased to 100 μg/kg/min **Note:** Can be mixed with these IV solutions: 5% dextrose (D5) and water, D5 in lactated Ringer's, D5 in Ringer's, D5 and 0.45% sodium chloride, D5 and 0.9% sodium chloride, lactated Ringer's, 0.45% sodium chloride, 0.9% sodium chloride; is *not compatible with sodium bicarbonate injection* *(Continued on next page)*	NE	C	**Solution for injection—IV:** 2.5 g/10 mL, 100 mg/10 mL	For treatment of tachycardia and hypertension that occur intraoperatively and postoperatively during surgery or emergence from anesthesia

| Antihypertensive, antianginal, β-adrenergic blocking agent: Labetalol | Normodyne, Trandate (labetalol) | **Labetalol:** Intended for IV use in hospitalized patients

Overdosage: Acute toxicity, secondary to massive accidental overdosage of labetalol, has occurred, and result has been hypotension, bradycardia, drowsiness and loss of consciousness; patient should be placed in a supine position and legs should be raised to improve blood supply to brain; effects have resolved within 10 min, in some cases, with administration of a vasopressor agent

Note: Bradycardia can be treated with atropine; bronchospasm with a ß₂-agonist or a theophylline derivative or both; symptomatic hypotension can be managed with IV fluids, vasopressor agents or both | NE | | |
| | | **Overdosage:** Acute toxicity, secondary to massive accidental overdosage of esmolol, has occurred due to errors in dilution; result has been hypotension, bradycardia, drowsiness and loss of consciousness; patient should be placed in a supine position and legs should be raised to improve blood supply to brain; effects have resolved within 10 min, in some cases, with administration of a vasopressor agent

Note: Bradycardia can be treated with atropine; bronchospasm with a ß₂-agonist or a theophylline derivative or both; symptomatic hypotension can be managed with IV fluids, vasopressor agents or both | C | **Solution for injection—IV:** 5 mg/mL in 4-, 8-, 20-, 40-mL vials | For control of blood pressure in patients with severe hypertension |

Continued on next page

PRC: Pregnancy risk category.
NE: Not established.

Table 15.2 (cont.)

Injectable and Noninjectable Emergency Drugs: Dosage and Prescribing Information

Generic name	Brand name(s)	Adult dosage	Child dosage (mg/kg)	PRC	Content/form	Indications
Level 2 (noncritical drugs) (cont.)						
Anti-hypoglycemic: Dextrose 50%	generic	**IV:** 20-50 mL at a rate of 10 mL/min; most patients regain consciousness rapidly (5-10 min); additional 50 mL may be needed in some patients; supplementary carbohydrates should be given as soon as possible **Note:** Is generally well-tolerated	0.5-1 g/kg/dose; D50W is diluted 1:1, producing D25W to avoid hypertonicity **Note:** Supplementary carbohydrates should be given as soon as possible, especially to children or adolescent patients	C	50-mL glass ampules	For the management of severe hypoglycemic reactions (patients with Type I diabetes do not have as great a response to blood glucose levels as do stable Type II diabetes patients)
Anti-hypoglycemic: Glucagon hydrochloride	Glucagon; generic	1 mg by SC, IM or IV injection; patient usually awakens within 15 min; if response is delayed, there is no contraindication to administration of 1-2 additional doses of glucagon; however, in view of deleterious effects of cerebral hypoglycemia and depending on duration and depth of coma, use of parenteral glucose must be considered; IV glucose must be given if patient fails to respond to glucagon **Note:** Should not be administered at concentrations greater than 1 mg/mL **Note:** Is generally well-tolerated and no cases of overdosage of glucagon have been reported; if overdosage were to occur, it would not be expected to cause consequential toxicity, but would be expected to be associated with nausea, vomiting, gastric hypotonicity and diarrhea	**Weight > 20 kg—IM, IV, SC:** 1 mg **Weight < 20 kg—IM, IV, SC:** 0.5 mg or dose equivalent to 20-30 µg/kg; patient usually awakens within 15 min; if response is delayed, there is no contraindication to the administration of 1-2 additional doses of glucagon; however, in view of deleterious effects of cerebral hypoglycemia and depending on duration and depth of coma, use of parenteral glucose must be considered; IV glucose must be given if patient fails to respond to glucagon **Note:** Supplementary carbohydrates should be given as soon as consciousness returns, especially to children or adolescent patients	B	**Solution for injection—IM, IV, SC:** 1 mg/mL	For the management of severe hypoglycemic reactions **Note:** Patients with Type I diabetes do not have as great a response to blood glucose levels as do stable Type II diabetes patients

Drug category / Generic name	Brand / Other names	Dosage / Administration	Pediatric use	PRC	How supplied	Indications / Remarks
Anti-inflammatory adrenal corticosteroid: Hydrocortisone sodium succinate	A-hydroCort, Solu-Cortef, generic	Should be administered IV in emergency situations, but can also be administered IM; usual starting dose is 100 mg administered IV over 30 s	NE	C	**Solution for injection—IM, IV:** 100 mg in 1-mL vials, 250 mg in 2-mL vials, 500 mg in 4-mL vials, 1 g in 8-mL vials **Act-O-Vial System:** 100 mg, diluted to 50 mg/mL	For treating primary or secondary adrenocortical insufficiency as well as acute adrenocortical insufficiency; also for treatment of shock that proves unresponsive to conventional therapy if adrenocortical insufficiency exists or is suspected; to control severe or incapacitating allergic conditions intractable to adequate trials of conventional treatment in bronchial asthma and drug hypersensitivity reactions
Respiratory stimulants	Aromatic ammonia, spirits of ammonia	**Inhalation:** Vaporole containing ammonia is crushed between the user's fingers and held beneath patient's nose, thus permitting patient to inhale the ammonia	Though rarely indicated in children, dosage and method of administration same as for adults	NA	**Vaporoles:** 0.3 mL	Respiratory depression not induced by opioid analgesics; vasodepressor syncope
Vasoconstrictor, sympathomimetic agent: Methoxamine	Vasoxyl	**To correct hypotension—IM:** 10-15 mg; dose depends on degree of hypotension **To correct fall in systolic pressure to 60 mm/Hg or less—IV:** 3-5 mg; this dose can be accompanied by 10-15 mg IM for more prolonged effect **Whenever an emergency exists—IV:** 3-5 mg; this dose can be accompanied by 10-15 mg IM for more prolonged effect **Overdosage:** Can be manifested as undesirable elevation in blood pressure and/or bradycardia	NE	C	20 mg in 1-mL ampules	For the support or maintenance of blood pressure

Continued on next page

PRC: Pregnancy risk category.
NA: Not available.
NE: Not established.

Table 15.2 (cont.)

Injectable and Noninjectable Emergency Drugs: Dosage and Prescribing Information

Generic name	Brand name(s)	Adult dosage (mg/kg)	Child dosage	PRC	Content/form	Indications
Level 3 (advanced cardiac life-support drugs)						
Alkalinyzing agent: Sodium bicarbonate	generic	1 mEq/kg initially; maximum of 50% of this dose can be given for subsequent doses, which should not be given more frequently than every 10 min	1 mEq/kg/dose	C	**Injectable solution:** 4.2%, 5%, 7.5% and 8.4% in 5-, 10-, 50- and 500-mL vials	Because of absence of proven efficacy and numerous adverse effects, for use (if at all) only after application of more definitive and better substantiated interventions: prompt defibrillation, effective chest compression, endotracheal intubation and hyperventilation with 100% oxygen, and use of such drugs as epinephrine and lidocaine (these interventions take 10 min; thereafter, sodium bicarbonate therapy, although not recommended, can be considered in specific clinical circumstances, such as documented pre-existing metabolic acidosis with or without hyperkalemia)

| Analgesic: Morphine sulfate | Astramorph PF, Duramorph, generic; Epimorph [CAN], Morphine [CAN], Morphine Forte [CAN], Morphine Extra-Forte [CAN], Morphine H.P. [CAN] | Injection—IM, IV, SC: Small incremental doses of 2-5 mg q 5-30 min until desired effect is achieved

Overdosage: Is characterized by respiratory depression with or without concomitant CNS depression; because respiratory arrest can result either through direct depression of respiratory center or as result of hypoxia, dentist's first action should be ensuring adequate respiratory exchange through provision of patent airway and institution of assisted or controlled ventilation

Note: Naloxone, the opioid antagonist, is a specific antidote; usually given in 0.4-mg doses; should be administered IV simultaneously with respiratory resuscitation; naloxone injection and resuscitative equipment should be immediately available for administration in case of life-threatening or intolerable side effects

Note: Low doses of IV-administered morphine have little effect on CV stability; high doses are excitatory, resulting from sympathetic hyperactivity and increase in circulating catecholamines

Note: CNS excitation, resulting in convulsions, can accompany high doses of morphine administered IV

Note: Dysphoric reactions and toxic psychoses have also been reported | Analgesic—IV, very slow: 50-100 μg/kg | C | Solution for injection: 2, 4, 5, 8, 10, 15 mg/mL | To manage pain that is not responsive to nonopioid analgesics; for the treatment of pain and anxiety associated with acute myocardial infarction |

Continued on next page

[CAN] indicates a drug available only in Canada.
PRC: Pregnancy risk category.

Table 15.2 (cont.)

Injectable and Noninjectable Emergency Drugs: Dosage and Prescribing Information

Generic name	Brand name(s)	Adult dosage (mg/kg)	Child dosage (mg/kg)	PRC	Content/form	Indications
			Level 3 (advanced cardiac life-support drugs) (cont.)			
Anti-dysrhythmic agent: Bretylium tosylate	Bretylol, generic	**Injection—IM, IV:** Used clinically only for treatment of life-threatening ventricular dysrhythmias under constant electrocardiographic monitoring; meant for short-term use only; patients should be kept supine during course of bretylium therapy or be closely observed for postural hypotension **For immediate management of life-threatening ventricular dysrhythmias such as ventricular fibrillation or hemodynamically unstable ventricular tachycardia—IV, rapid:** 5 mg/kg; other usual cardiopulmonary resuscitative procedures, including electrical conversion, should be employed before and after injection in accordance with good medical practice; if ventricular fibrillation persists, the dosage can be increased to 10 mg/kg and repeated as necessary **Overdosage:** In the presence of life-threatening dysrhythmias, underdosing with bretylium probably presents a greater risk to patients than potential overdosage	5 mg/kg; may be increased to 10 mg/kg	C	**Solution for injection:** 50 mg/mL in 10-mL vials; 1 mg/mL generic	For prophylaxis and therapy of ventricular fibrillation; for treatment of life-threatening ventricular dysrhythmias (such as ventricular tachycardia) that have failed to respond to adequate doses of a first-line antidysrhythmic such as lidocaine

		PRC			
Antidysrhythmic Lidocaine	Xylocaine, generic	B	**Injection:** Bolus of 1 mg/kg, with additional bolus injections of 0.5 mg/kg repeated q 8-10 min, if needed, to total dose of 3 mg/kg; dosage should be reduced for debilitated and/or elderly patients, commensurate with their age and physical status **Overdosage:** Signs and symptoms of an overdose are described in Table 15.4; should convulsions or signs of respiratory depression and arrest develop, airway patency and adequacy of ventilation must be ensured immediately; when convulsions persist despite ventilation with oxygen, small increments of anticonvulsants, such as diazepam, may be administered IV	**Solution for injection:** 1%, 2%, 5% in vials and syringes	For the acute management of ventricular dysrhythmias such as those occurring in relation to acute myocardial infarction; drug of choice for suppression of ventricular tachycardia and ventricular fibrillation, as well as ventricular premature complexes in critically ill patients
Antidysrhythmic Procainamide	Pronestyl	C NE	**For ventricular tachycardia or premature ventricular complexes—IV:** 100 mg initially, then 50 mg q 5 min until one of the following has been observed: (1) the dysrhythmia has been suppressed, (2) hypotension has ensued, (3) the QRS complex has been widened by 50% of its original width or (4) total of 1 g has been administered **Overdosage:** After IV administration, transiently high plasma levels of procainamide can induce hypotension, affecting systolic pressure more than diastolic pressure, especially in hypertensive patients; such high plasma levels can also produce CNS depression, tremor and even respiratory depression; management of overdosage includes general positioning-, airway-, breathing- and circulation- supportive measures (P,A,B,C), close observation, monitoring of vital signs and, possibly, intravenous pressor agents and mechanical cardiorespiratory support	**Solution for injection:** 100 mg/mL in 10-mL syringes and vials; 500 mg/mL in 2-mL vials	Useful in suppressing premature ventricular complexes and recurrent ventricular tachycardia that cannot be controlled by lidocaine; rarely used to treat ventricular fibrillation because it takes so long to reach adequate blood levels even after intravenous administration; can also be used to convert supraventricular dysrhythmias

PRC: Pregnancy risk category.
NE: Not established.

Continued on next page

Table 15.2 (cont.)

Injectable and Noninjectable Emergency Drugs: Dosage and Prescribing Information

Generic name	Brand name(s)	Adult dosage (mg/kg)	Child dosage	PRC	Content/form	Indications
			Level 3 (advanced cardiac life-support drugs) (cont.)			
Anti-dysrhythmic: Verapamil	Calan, Iseptin, generic	**Injection—IV:** Bolus of 0.075-0.150 mg/kg (maximum 10 mg) over 1 min; peak therapeutic effects occur within 3-5 min of bolus injection **If initial response is inadequate:** Repeated doses of 0.15 mg/kg (maximum 10 mg) q 30 min after first dose **Overdosage:** Treat all verapamil overdoses as serious and maintain observation for at least 48 h under continuous hospital care	**Age 1-15 y:** Initially, 0.1-0.3 mg/kg (usual single dose 2-5 mg), not to exceed 5 mg; for repeat dose 30 min after initial dose, do not exceed 10 mg as a single dose	C	**Solution for injection:** 2.5 mg/mL in 2-mL ampules	For management of paroxysmal supraventricular tachycardia that does not require cardioversion
Calcium salt: Calcium chloride	generic	**Injection—IV, slow:** 2-4 mg/kg of a 10% solution and repeated at 10-min intervals if considered necessary **Overdosage:** Too rapid administration can lower blood pressure and produce cardiac syncope	**Injection:** 5-7 mg/kg; first dose should be infused slowly (no faster than 1 mL/min) and repeated once after 10 min, if required	C	**Solution in pre-filled syringes or ampules:** 10 mL of 10% solution of calcium chloride with 13.6 mEq of calcium (1 mL = 100 mg)	Only for treatment of acute hyperkalemia, hypocalcemia or calcium channel blocker toxicity
Endogenous catecholamine: Epinephrine (1:10,000)	Adrenalin	**IV or endotracheally:** 0.5-1.0 mg; higher range of doses should be used and repeated at least every 5 min	**IV or endotracheally:** 0.01 mg/kg (0.1 mL/kg of the 1:10,000 solution)	C	**Solution:** 1 mg epinephrine/10 mL of solution in syringes	For patients who have suffered cardiac arrest

Benzodiazepine antagonist: Flumazenil	Romazicon	**For reversal of conscious sedation or in general anesthesia—IV only:** Initially, 0.2 mg (2 mL) administered over 15 s; if desired level of consciousness has not been obtained after waiting an additional 45 s, further dose of 0.2 mg can be injected and repeated at 60-s intervals, where necessary, up to additional 4 doses to maximum total dose of 1 mg (10 mL); dose should be individualized according to patient's response; most patients respond to doses of 0.6-1 mg **Resedation:** Repeated doses can be administered at 20-min intervals, as needed **Repeat treatment:** No more than 1 mg (administered at 0.2 mg/min) should be administered at any one time; no more than 3 mg should be given in any 1-h period **Overdosage:** Large IV doses of flumazenil administered to healthy normal volunteers in absence of a benzodiazepine agonist produced no serious adverse reactions, severe signs or symptoms or clinically significant laboratory test abnormalities; reversal with an excessively high dose of flumazenil can produce anxiety, agitation, increased muscle tone, hyperesthesia and possible convulsions	Same as adult dosage	C	**Solution for injection:** 0.1 mg/mL in 5-, 10-mL multiple-use vials	For complete or partial reversal of sedative effects of benzodiazepines in cases in which general anesthesia has been induced and/or maintained with benzodiazepines or sedation has been produced with benzodiazepines for diagnostic and therapeutic procedures, and for management of an overdose of benzodiazepine

Continued on next page

PRC: Pregnancy risk category.

Table 15.2 (cont.)

Injectable and Noninjectable Emergency Drugs: Dosage and Prescribing Information

Generic name	Brand name(s)	Adult dosage (mg/kg)	Child dosage	PRC	Content/form	Indications
			Level 4 (antidotal drugs) (cont.)			
Opioid antagonist: Naloxone	Narcan ★, generic	**For reversal of respiratory depression—IV:** 0.1-0.2 mg IV q 2-3 min to desired degree of reversal (adequate ventilation and alertness without significant pain or discomfort); repeat doses may be required within 1-2 h, depending on amount, type (short- or long-acting) and time since last administration of opioid; supplemental IM doses of naloxone have been shown to produce a longer lasting effect **Note:** Can be injected IM, IV or SC, but most rapid onset of action follows IV use; IV route is recommended in emergency situations **Note:** Larger than necessary dosage of naloxone can result in significant reversal of analgesia and increase in blood pressure; in addition, too rapid a reversal can induce nausea, vomiting, sweating and circulatory stress **Note:** Because duration of action of some opioids can exceed that of naloxone, patient should be kept under continued observation and repeated doses of naloxone should be administered, if necessary **Note:** For partial reversal of opioid depression after use of opioids during surgery, smaller doses of naloxone are usually adequate; dose should be titrated according to patient's response **Overdosage:** In humans, no clinical experience with overdosage of naloxone	**For reversal of respiratory depression—IV:** Increments of 0.005 to 0.010 mg q 2- to 3-min to desired degree of reversal	B	**Solution for injection:** 0.02 mg/mL in 2-mL vials; 0.4 mg/mL in 1-, 2- and 10-mL vials; 1.0 mg/mL in 1-, 2-, 5- and 10-mL vials	For complete or partial reversal of opioid depression (including respiratory depression) induced by opioids, including natural and synthetic opioids, propoxyphene, methadone and the opioid antagonist analgesics nalbuphine, pentazocine and butorphanol; also indicated for suspected acute opioid overdosage

★ indicates a drug bearing the ADA Seal of Acceptance.
PRC: Pregnancy risk category.

Table 15.3

Injectable and Noninjectable Emergency Drugs: Possible Interactions With Other Drugs

Drug taken by patient	Interaction with emergency injectable and noninjectable drugs	Dentist's action
Level 1 (basic, critical drugs)		
Bronchodilator: Albuterol	Other sympathomimetic aerosol inhalers should not be used concomitantly with albuterol so as to minimize the risk of deleterious CV events Albuterol should be administered with extreme caution to patients receiving monoamine oxidase (MAO) inhibitors or tricyclic antidepressants because the action of albuterol on the CV system can be potentiated	In the case of an emergency, there is no situation in which a drug-to-drug interaction would be of concern
Histamine blockers: Diphenhydramine, chlorpheniramine	Histamine blockers have additive effects with alcohol and other central nervous system depressants such as sedatives, hypnotics and tranquilizers	See note above
Fibrinolytic: Aspirin	When used with NSAIDs, aspirin can increase the risk of GI bleeding and ulceration	See note above
Level 2 (noncritical drugs)		
Analgesic: Morphine	Depressant effects of morphine are potentiated by either concomitant administration or the presence of other central nervous system depressants such as alcohol, sedatives, histamine-blockers or psychotropic drugs such as monoamine oxidase inhibitors, phenothiazines, butyrophenones and tricyclic antidepressants	In the case of an emergency, there is no situation in which a drug-to-drug interaction would be of concern
Anticonvulsant: Diazepam, Midazolam	If combined with other psychotropic or anticonvulsant drugs—such as phenothiazines, opioids, barbiturates, monoamine oxidase inhibitors and other antidepressants—CNS and respiratory depressant actions of diazepam can be potentiated	See note above
Vasoconstrictor, sympathomimetic agent: Methoxamine	The constrictor effect of methoxamine can be markedly potentiated when administered in conjunction with monoamine oxidase inhibitors, tricyclic antidepressants, vasopressin or ergot alkaloids such as ergotamine, ergonovine or methylergonovine	See note above
Level 3 (advanced cardiac life-support drugs)		
Antidysrhythmic agent: Bretylium tosylate	The pressor effects of catecholamines, such as dopamine or norepinephrine, are enhanced by bretylium	In the case of an emergency, there is no situation in which a drug-to-drug interaction would be of concern
Injectable antidysrhythmic: Lidocaine	Lidocaine should be used with caution in patients with digitalis toxicity that is accompanied by atrioventricular block; concomitant use of β-blocking agents or cimetidine can reduce hepatic blood flow and thereby reduce lidocaine clearance	See note above

Continued on next page

Table 15.3 (cont.)

Injectable and Noninjectable Emergency Drugs: Possible Interactions With Other Drugs

Drug taken by patient	Interaction with emergency injectable and noninjectable drugs	Dentist's action
Level 3 (advanced cardiac life-support drugs) (cont.)		
Injectable antidysrhythmic: Procainamide	If other antidysrhythmic drugs are being administered, additive effects can occur with administration of procainamide, so a reduction in dosage may be necessary	In the case of an emergency, there is no situation in which a drug-to-drug interaction would be of concern
Antidysrhythmic agent: Verapamil	Concomitant therapy with β-adrenergic blockers and verapamil can result in additive negative effects on heart rate, atrioventricular conduction or cardiac contractility or both Concomitant administration of verapamil with oral antihypertensive agents will usually have an additive effect on lowering blood pressure; patients receiving this combination should be monitored appropriately	See note above
Calcium chloride: Calcium salt	Calcium increases ventricular irritability and can precipitate digitalis toxicity in those who are taking digitalis	See note above
Level 4 (antidotal drugs)		
Benzodiazepine antagonist: Flumazenil	Interaction with CNS depressants other than benzodiazepines has not been specifically studied; however, no deleterious interactions were seen when flumazenil was administered after opioids, inhalational anesthetics, muscle relaxants and muscle relaxant antagonists administered in conjunction with sedation or anesthesia	In the case of an emergency, there is no situation in which a drug-to-drug interaction would be of concern

Table 15.4

Injectable and Noninjectable Emergency Drugs: Adverse Reactions, Precautions and Contraindications

Type of drug	Adverse reactions	Precautions/contraindications
		Level 1 (basic, critical drugs)
Antihypoglycemics (orange juice, nondiet soft drinks)	None of significance to dentistry	These and other oral medications should not be administered to patients who are unconscious or unable to swallow; choking and aspiration can occur in such situations
Bronchodilator: Albuterol	**CNS:** Tremor (< 15%), dizziness (< 5%), nervousness (< 10%) **CV:** Adverse reactions to albuterol are similar to those of other sympathomimetic amines, although incidence of some CV events is less with albuterol than with isoproterenol; palpitations (10% albuterol; 15% isoproterenol), tachycardia (10% for both), increased blood pressure (< 5% for both) **GI:** Nausea (< 15%), heartburn (< 5%)	Albuterol should be used with caution in patients with CV disorders, especially coronary insufficiency, cardiac dysrhythmias and hypertension; in patients with convulsive disorders, hyperthyroidism, or diabetes mellitus and in patients who are unusually responsive to sympathomimetic amines Contraindicated in patients with a history of hypersensitivity to any of its components As with other inhaled β-adrenergic agonists, albuterol inhalation aerosol can produce paradoxical bronchospasm that can be life-threatening; fatalities have been reported in association with excessive administration of inhaled sympathomimetic drugs; though the precise cause of death is not known, cardiac arrest following the development of severe acute asthmatic crisis and subsequent hypoxia is suspected
Epinephrine 1:1,000	**General:** Transient and minor side effects of anxiety, headache, fear and palpitations may be noted with therapeutic doses, most often in patients with hyperthyroidism	Should be protected from exposure to light; solution should not be used if it is pinkish or darker than light yellow or if it contains a precipitate Is preferred treatment for life-threatening allergic reactions even though it contains sodium bisulfite, a product that in other drugs can cause allergic-type reactions, including anaphylaxis or life-threatening or less severe asthmatic episodes, in certain susceptible patients; because alternatives to using epinephrine in life-threatening situations may not be acceptable, presence of sulfite in this product should not deter dentist from administering it for treatment of serious allergic or other life-threatening situations
Fibrinolytic: Aspirin	Significant side effects, ulcers, hepatotoxicity warrant caution in patients with history of ulcers and liver disease	Known sensitivity to aspirin; may increase risk of bleeding in patients taking oral anticoagulants

Continued on next page

Table 15.4 (cont.)

Injectable and Noninjectable Emergency Drugs: Adverse Reactions, Precautions and Contraindications

Type of drug	Adverse reactions	Precautions/contraindications
Level 1 (basic, critical drugs) (cont.)		
Histamine blockers: Diphenhydramine, chlorpheniramine	**CNS:** Sedation, dizziness, sleepiness and disturbed coordination **GI:** Epigastric distress **Resp:** Thickening of bronchial secretions	Can diminish mental alertness in children; in young children, in particular, can produce excitation
Oxygen	None	Not indicated for patients experiencing hyperventilation
Vasodilators, antianginals, antihypertensives, CV drugs: Nitroglycerin	**General:** The most frequent (2%) adverse reaction associated with administration of nitroglycerin is headache; other adverse reactions that occur in less than 1% of patients receiving nitroglycerin include tachycardia, nausea, vomiting, apprehension, restlessness, muscle twitching, retrosternal discomfort, palpitations, dizziness and abdominal pain	Should be used with caution in patients with severe hepatic or renal disease Excessive hypotension, especially for prolonged periods, should be avoided because of potentially deleterious effects on brain, heart, liver, and kidneys from poor perfusion and attendant risk of ischemia, thrombosis and altered function of these organs; paradoxical bradycardia and increased angina pectoris can accompany nitroglycerin-induced hypotension Contraindicated in patients with hypersensitivity to nitroglycerin or other organic nitrates, hypotension or uncorrected hypovolemia, increased intracranial pressure and inadequate cerebral circulation
Level 2 (noncritical drugs)		
Analgesic: Morphine sulfate	**General:** Most frequently observed adverse reactions include constipation, lightheadedness, dizziness, sedation, nausea, vomiting, sweating, dysphoria and euphoria **Resp:** Most serious side effect is respiratory depression; because of delay in maximum CNS effect with IV-administered morphine (up to 30 min), rapid administration can result in overdosing	Should be administered with extreme caution in aged or debilitated patients, in patients with increased intracranial or intraocular pressure and in patients with head injury Care must be taken with patients who have decreased respiratory reserve (emphysema, severe obesity, kyphoscoliosis) Contraindicated for patients whose medical conditions would preclude IV administration of opioids: allergy to morphine or other opiates, acute bronchial asthma or upper airway obstruction Should be limited to use by those familiar with management of respiratory depression; facilities where morphine sulfate is administered must be equipped with resuscitative equipment, oxygen, injectable naxolone and other resuscitative drugs

Drug category	Adverse effects	Precautions
Anticholinergic, antidysrhythmic agent: Atropine	**General:** Adverse effects most often are a result of excessive dosage: palpitation, dilated pupils, difficulty in swallowing, hot, dry skin, thirst, dizziness, restlessness, tremor, fatigue and ataxia; toxic doses can lead to marked palpitation, restlessness and excitement, hallucinations, delirium and coma **CV:** Depression and circulatory collapse occur with severe intoxication; blood pressure declines and death due to respiratory failure can ensue as consequence of paralysis and coma	Should be administered with caution in all patients aged > 40 y; conventional systemic doses can precipitate acute glaucoma in susceptible patients, convert partial organic pyloric stenosis into complete urinary retention in patients with prostatic hypertrophy or cause inspiration of bronchial secretions and formation of dangerous viscid plugs in patients with chronic lung disease Except in doses ordinarily used for preanesthetic medication, is generally contraindicated for patients with glaucoma, pyloric stenosis or prostatic hypertrophy Is a highly potent drug, and due care is essential to avoid overdosage, especially with IV administration; children are more susceptible than adults to toxic effects of anticholinergic agents
Anticonvulsants: Diazepam, midazolam	**General:** Drowsiness, fatigue, ataxia **CV:** bradycardia, cardiovascular collapse, hypertension **CNS:** Confusion, depression, slurred speech, syncope **Hema:** Venous thrombosis, phlebitis at site of injection (diazepam) **Resp:** depressed respiration, apnea	Although seizures can be brought under control promptly, a significant proportion of patients experience a return of seizure activity, presumably due to short-lived effect of IV diazepam and midazolam; clinician should be prepared to re-administer drug When used IV, solution should be injected slowly (1 min for each mL given); small veins, such as those on dorsum of hand or wrist should be avoided (diazepam), and extreme care should be taken to avoid intra-arterial or extravascular administration
Antihypertensive, antianginal, β-adrenergic blocking agents: Esmolol, labetalol	**CV:** Most important adverse reaction is hypotension; symptomatic hypotension (dizziness, diaphoresis) occurs in 12% of patients receiving esmolol; asymptomatic hypotension occurs in 25% of patients; symptomatic postural hypotension occurs in 58% of patients receiving IV labetalol permitted to assume an erect posture within 3 h of administration, with increased sweating in 4%; peripheral ischemia occurs in 1% of patients, whereas less than 1% of patients experience pallor, flushing, bradycardia (heart rate < 50 beats per minute), chest pain, syncope, pulmonary edema or heart block *(Continued on next page)*	**Esmolol:** Infusion concentrations of 20 mg/mL of esmolol are associated with more serious venous irritation, including thrombophlebitis, than concentrations of 10 mg/mL; extravasation of 20 mg/mL can lead to a serious local reaction and possible skin necrosis; care should be taken when administering esmolol intravenously because sloughing of the skin and necrosis have been reported in association with infiltration and extravasation of intravenous infusions; 20-50% of patients treated with esmolol have experienced hypotension, generally defined as systolic pressure < 90 mmHg and/or diastolic pressure < 50 mmHg; about 12% of patients have been symptomatic (diaphoresis or dizziness) **Labetalol:** Symptomatic postural hypotension was observed in 58% of patients allowed to assume an upright position within 3 h of receiving IV injection *(Continued on next page)*

Continued on next page

Table 15.4 (cont.)

Injectable and Noninjectable Emergency Drugs: Adverse Reactions, Precautions and Contraindications

Type of drug	Adverse reactions	Precautions/contraindications
		Level 2 (noncritical drugs) (cont.)
Antihypertensive, antianginal, β-adrenergic blocking agents: Esmolol, labetalol (cont.)	**CNS:** Dizziness and somnolence occur in 3% of patients on esmolol and 9% with labetalol; confusion, headache and agitation in about 2% and fatigue in 1% of patients on esmolol **GI:** Nausea was reported in 7% of patients on esmolol, with vomiting in 1%; of patients on labetalol, 13% reported nausea and 4% reported vomiting; virtually all adverse reactions to esmolol and labetalol are dose-related **Resp:** Bronchospasm, wheezing, dyspnea, nasal congestion, rhonchi and rales have been reported in less than 1% of patients	**Labetalol and esmolol:** Increased risk of severe anaphylactic reaction in susceptible patients, who may prove unresponsive to doses of epinephrine usually used to treat allergic reactions; are both contraindicated in patients with sinus bradycardia, heart block greater than first degree, cardiogenic shock or overt heart failure; labetalol also contraindicated in patients with bronchial asthma Sympathetic stimulation is necessary for supporting circulatory function in congestive heart failure, and β blockade with either esmolol or labetalol carries potential hazard of further depressing myocardial contractility and precipitating more severe failure; continued depression of myocardium with β-blocking agents over period of time can, in some cases, lead to cardiac failure Patients with bronchospastic diseases should, in general, not receive β-blockers
Antihypoglycemic: Glucagon	**GI:** occasional nausea and vomiting, which can also occur with hypoglycemia	Helpful in treating hypoglycemia only if liver glycogen is available; is of little or no help for people who are in a state of starvation or for patients with adrenal insufficiency or chronic hypoglycemia; 50% dextrose should be considered for management of hypoglycemia in these situations Should be administered cautiously to patients with a history suggestive of insulinoma and/or pheochromocytoma; IV administration of glucagon will produce initial increase in blood glucose, but in patients with insulinoma, glucagon's ability to cause an insulin release can subsequently produce hypoglycemia; patient who is developing symptoms of hypoglycemia after a dose of glucagon should be given glucose orally, IV or by lavage, whichever is most appropriate Stimulates release of catecholamines, so should be used with caution in patients with pheochromocytoma because it could cause tumor to release catecholamines and thus produce sudden and marked increase in blood pressure Contraindicated in patients with known sensitivity to it or in patients with pheochromocytoma

Drug	Side Effects	Considerations
Anti-inflammatory adrenal corticosteroid: Hydrocortisone sodium succinate	Adverse reactions are extremely rare when adrenal corticosteroids are used in acute emergency situations; most significant adverse reactions to administration of adrenal corticosteroids are observed after use in long-term treatment	For patients receiving corticosteroid therapy who are subjected to unusual stress, increased dosage of rapidly acting corticosteroids before, during and after unusual stressful situation is indicated
Respiratory stimulant: Aromatic ammonia, spirits of ammonia	**Resp:** May induce brochospasm in asthmatics and others with chronic lung disease	Contraindicated in patients with chronic obstructive pulmonary disease or asthma because it can precipitate bronchospasm resulting from its irritating effects on the mucous membranes of the upper respiratory tract
Vasoconstrictor, sympathomimetic agent: Methoxamine	**General:** Contains potassium bisulfite, a bisulfite that can cause allergic-type reactions, including anaphylactic symptoms and life-threatening or less severe asthmatic episodes, in certain susceptible people; sulfite sensitivity is seen more frequently in asthmatic than in nonasthmatic patients **CV:** Excessive blood pressure elevations, particularly with high dosage, ventricular ectopic beats **CNS:** Headache (often severe), anxiety **GI:** Nausea, vomiting (often projectile) **Integ:** Sweating, pilomotor response	Like other vasoconstrictor agents, should be used with caution in patients with hyperthyroidism, bradycardia, partial heart block, myocardial disease or severe arteriosclerosis; caution should be exercised to avoid overdosage, which can cause undesirable high blood pressure and/or bradycardia; bradycardia can be abolished with atropine Contraindicated in patients who have severe hypertension or who are hypersensitive to methoxamine Administration of methoxamine to patients receiving monoamine oxidase inhibitors, tricyclic antidepressants or oxytocic agents (such as vasopressin or certain ergot alkaloids) can result in potentiation of constrictor effect

Level 3 (advanced cardiac life-support drugs)

Drug	Side Effects	Considerations
Alkalinyzing agent: Sodium bicarbonate	**General:** Overly aggressive use can result in metabolic alkalosis (associated with muscular twitching, irritability and tetany) and hypernatremia	None as used in cardiac arrest

Continued on next page

Table 15.4 (cont.)

Injectable and Noninjectable Emergency Drugs: Adverse Reactions, Precautions and Contraindications

Type of drug	Adverse reactions	Precautions/contraindications
		Level 3 (advanced cardiac life-support drugs) (cont.)
Antidysrhythmic agent: Bretylium tosylate	**CV:** Hypotension and postural hypotension **GI:** Nausea and vomiting (in about 3% of patients primarily after rapid IV administration)	Should be diluted for IV use; one vial or ampule of bretylium should be diluted with minimum of 50 mL of dextrose 5% injection or sodium chloride injection before IV use; rapid IV administration can cause severe nausea and vomiting; therefore, diluted solution should be administered over period > 8 min; however, when treating existing ventricular fibrillation, bretylium tosylate should be administered as rapidly as possible and can be given without being diluted No contraindications to the use of bretylium tosylate in patients with ventricular fibrillation or life-threatening refractory ventricular dysrhythmias Administration regularly results in postural hypotension, subjectively recognized by dizziness, lightheadedness, vertigo or faintness; some degree of hypotension is present in about 50% of patients when supine; due to initial release of norepinephrine from adrenergic postganglionic nerve terminals by bretylium, transient hypertension or increased frequency of ventricular premature complexes and other arrhythmias may occur in some patients
Antidysrhythmic agent: Verapamil	**CV:** Angina pectoris, atrioventricular dissociation, chest pain, claudication, myocardial infarction, palpitation, purpura and syncope **CNS:** Cerebrovascular accident, confusion, equilibrium disorders, insomnia, muscle cramps, paresthesia, psychotic symptoms, shakiness and somnolence **GI:** Diarrhea, dry mouth, GI distress, gingival hyperplasia	Because verapamil is highly metabolized by the liver, should be administered cautiously to patients with impaired hepatic function Contraindicated in patients with severe left ventricular dysfunction, hypotension (systolic pressure < 90 mmHg or cardiogenic shock, "sick sinus syndrome," second- or third-degree atrioventricular block, patients with atrial flutter or atrial fibrillation and an accessory bypass tract (for example, Wolff-Parkinson-White and Lown-Ganong-Levine syndromes) and patients with known hypersensitivity to verapamil Use should be avoided in patients with severe left ventricular dysfunction or moderate-to-severe symptoms of cardiac failure and in patients with any degree of ventricular dysfunction if they are receiving a β-adrenergic blocker; occasionally can produce decrease in blood pressure below normal levels, which can result in dizziness or symptomatic hypotension **Overdosage:** Treat all verapamil overdoses as serious and maintain observation for at least 48 h under continuous hospital care

Drug	Adverse effects	Precautions and contraindications
Anticholinergic, antidysrhythmic agent: Atropine	**General:** Adverse effects most often are a result of excessive dosage: palpitation, dilated pupils, difficulty in swallowing, hot, dry skin, thirst, dizziness, restlessness, tremor, fatigue and ataxia; toxic doses can lead to marked palpitation, restlessness and excitement, hallucinations, delirium and coma **CV:** Depression and circulatory collapse occur with severe intoxication; blood pressure declines and death due to respiratory failure can ensue as consequence of paralysis and coma	Should be administered with caution in all patients aged > 40 y; conventional systemic doses can precipitate acute glaucoma in susceptible patients, convert partial organic pyloric stenosis into complete urinary retention in patients with prostatic hypertrophy or cause inspiration of bronchial secretions and formation of dangerous viscid plugs in patients with chronic lung disease Except in doses ordinarily used for preanesthetic medication, is generally contraindicated for patients with glaucoma, pyloric stenosis or prostatic hypertrophy Is a highly potent drug, and due care is essential to avoid overdosage, especially with IV administration; children are more susceptible than adults to toxic effects of anticholinergic agents
Calcium salt: Calcium chloride	**General:** Rapid injection may cause complaints of tingling sensations, calcium taste, sense of oppression or "heat wave"	If heart is beating, rapid administration of calcium can slow cardiac rate; can produce vasospasm in coronary and cerebral arteries
Endogenous catecholamine: Epinephrine (1:10,000)	None that would indicate against use	Should not be mixed in same infusion bag with alkaline solutions such as sodium bicarbonate because solutions will increase rate of epinephrine's auto-oxidation; this is not of clinical significance when epinephrine is administered by IV bolus; epinephrine's positive inotropic and chronotropic effects can precipitate or exacerbate myocardial ischemia; doses in excess of 20 μg/min or 0.3 mg/kg/min frequently produce hypertension in patients who are not receiving CPR May induce or exacerbate ventricular ectopy, especially in patients who are receiving digitalis

Continued on next page

Chapter 15. Drugs for Medical Emergencies in the Dental Office **289**

Table 15.4 (cont.)

Injectable and Noninjectable Emergency Drugs: Adverse Reactions, Precautions and Contraindications

Type of drug	Adverse reactions	Precautions/contraindications
	Level 3 (advanced cardiac life-support drugs) (cont.)	
Injectable antidysrhythmic agent: Lidocaine	**General:** Adverse reactions similar to those of other amide local anesthetic agents; reactions usually dose-related, resulting from high plasma levels caused by excessive dosage, rapid absorption or inadvertent intravascular injection, or can result from patient's hypersensitivity; idiosyncrasy or diminished tolerance **CV:** Usually depressant; bradycardia, hypotension and CV collapse, which can lead to cardiac arrest; allergic reactions to amide anesthetics are extremely rare **CNS:** Reactions most common when lidocaine is used for ventricular dysrhythmias; reactions can be either excitatory or depressant or both: lightheadedness; nervousness; apprehension; euphoria; confusion; dizziness; drowsiness; tinnitus; blurred or double vision; vomiting; sensations of heat, cold, or numbness; twitching; tremors; convulsions; unconsciousness; respiratory depression and arrest	Caution should be employed when using lidocaine in patients with severe liver or kidney disease as accumulation of the drug or its metabolites can occur Should be used with caution in the treatment of patients with hypovolemia, severe congestive heart failure, shock and all forms of heart block Is contraindicated in patients with known history of hypersensitivity to amide-type local anesthetics To manage possible adverse reactions, resuscitative equipment, oxygen and other resuscitative drugs should be immediately available when lidocaine is used
Injectable antidysrhythmic agent: Procainamide	**CV:** Hypotension and serious cardiac rhythm disturbances such as ventricular asystole or fibrillation more common after IV administration **CNS:** Dizziness or giddiness, weakness, mental depression and psychosis with hallucinations	Patients should be closely observed for possible hypersensitivity reactions immediately after start of procainamide therapy, especially if sensitivity to procaine or local anesthetic is suspected Contraindicated in patients with complete heart block or to patients with allergy to procaine or other ester-type local anesthetics Contains sodium metabisulfite, a sulfite that can cause allergic-type reactions, including anaphylactic symptoms and life-threatening or less severe asthmatic episodes, in certain susceptible people; sulfite sensitivity is seen more frequently in asthmatic patients than in those without asthma

Benzodiazepine antagonist: Flumazenil	**CNS:** Serious adverse reactions have occurred in all clinical settings, with convulsions most commonly reported; has been associated with onset of convulsions in patients who are relying on benzodiazepine effects to control seizures, are physically dependent on benzodiazepines or who have ingested large doses of other drugs	**Use in resedation:** Improves alertness of patients recovering from procedure involving sedation or anesthesia with benzodiazepines, but should not be substituted for adequate period of postprocedure monitoring; availability of flumazenil does not reduce risks associated with use of large doses of benzodiazepines for sedation; patients should be monitored for resedation, respiratory depression or other persistent or recurrent agonist effects for adequate period after administration; resedation is least likely in cases in which flumazenil is administered to reverse low dose of short-acting benzodiazepine (< 10 mg midazolam) and is most likely in cases in which a large single or cumulative dose of a benzodiazepine has been given in the course of a long procedure along with neuromuscular-blocking agents and multiple anesthetic agents

Use in ambulatory patients: Effects can wear off before a long-acting benzodiazepine is completely cleared from body; in general, if a patient shows no signs of sedation within 2 h after 1-mg dose of flumazenil, serious resedation at a later time is unlikely; adequate period of observation must be provided for any patient in whom either a long-acting benzodiazepine (such as lorazepam) or large doses of a short-acting benzodiazepine (such as > 10 mg midazolam) have been used

Contraindicated in patients with known hypersensitivity to flumazenil or to benzodiazepines, patients who have been given benzodiazepines for control of a potentially life-threatening condition (such as control of intracranial pressure or status epilepticus) and patients who show signs of serious cyclic antidepressant overdose

Has been associated with seizures, most frequently in patients who have been receiving benzodiazepines for long-term sedation or in overdose cases in patients who are showing signs of a serious cyclic antidepressant overdose; practitioners should individualize dosage and be prepared to manage seizures; patients receiving flumazenil to reverse benzodiazepine effects should be monitored for resedation, respiratory depression or other residual effects for up to 120 min based on dose and duration of effect of benzodiazepine used |

Continued on next page

Table 15.4 (cont.)

Injectable and Noninjectable Emergency Drugs: Adverse Reactions, Precautions and Contraindications

Type of drug	Adverse reactions	Precautions/contraindications
		Level 4 (antidotal drugs)
Opioid antagonist: Naloxone	**General:** Abrupt reversal of opioid depression can result in nausea, vomiting, sweating, tachycardia, increased blood pressure and tremulousness; administration of larger-than-necessary doses of naloxone can result in significant reversal of analgesia and in excitement in postsurgical patients **CV:** Hypotension, hypertension, ventricular tachycardia and fibrillation and pulmonary edema	In addition to naloxone, other resuscitative measures (such as maintenance of a patent airway, artificial ventilation, cardiac massage and vasoconstrictor agents) should be available and employed, when needed, to counteract acute opioid poisoning Hypotension, hypertension, ventricular tachycardia and fibrillation, and pulmonary edema have been reported in postoperative patients, most of whom had pre-existing CV disorders or received drugs that may have similar adverse CV effects; therefore, naloxone should be used with caution in patients with pre-existing cardiac disease or patients who have received potentially cardiotoxic drugs Contraindicated in patients with known hypersensitivity Should be administered cautiously to patients who are known to be or suspected to be physically dependent on opioids; in such cases, abrupt and complete reversal of opioid effects can precipitate acute abstinence syndrome; after satisfactory response to naloxone, patient should be kept under continued observation and repeat doses should be administered, as needed, because duration of action of some opioids can exceed that of naloxone; naloxone is not effective against respiratory depression caused by use of nonopioid drugs

Chapter 16.

Managing Medical Emergencies in the Dental Office

Stanley F. Malamed, D.D.S.

Medical emergencies can and do occur in the dental office. In two independent surveys, 4,309 dentists reported 30,608 emergency situations that had arisen in their practices during a 10-year period. The reported emergencies—shown in the box, "Ten-Year Incidence of Emergency Situations Reported by Private Practice Dentists"—spanned a wide array, from usually benign but pressing problems such as syncope to catastrophic events such as cardiac arrest.

Given that medical emergencies do occur in the practice of dentistry, it is important for all members of the dental office staff to be able to rapidly recognize and to efficiently manage such potential problems. Taking the following measures should help dental staff members prepare for managing emergency situations:

- take American Heart Association or American Red Cross training in basic life support at the health care provider level;
- develop an in-office emergency response team that participates in regular simulated emergency drills;
- keep well informed about the availability of outside emergency assistance, such as that available by dialing 9-1-1;
- have emergency drugs and equipment available in the dental office.

Unfortunately, when emergencies occur, it is not always possible to immediately determine the precise nature of the problem. For example, a patient may report that he or she is having difficulty breathing, not suffering from an asthmatic attack or hyperventilation, or the initial complaint may be of a "tightness in my chest," not "I am suffering an anginal attack" or a myocardial infarction.

In the following discussion, the recognition and management of medical emergencies is based on clinical signs and symptoms that are commonly presented. Five categories are noted, including

- altered consciousness;
- convulsions;
- respiratory distress;
- drug-related emergencies (allergy and overdose);
- chest pain.

Remember P,A,B,C,D in Emergencies

To facilitate recall in times of duress, emergency management should be based on a concept of simplicity.

The following five steps are to be followed, in sequence, for all emergency situations:

- P (position),
- A (airway),
- B (breathing),
- C (circulation),
- D (definitive care).

P,A,B,C are the steps of basic life support and are used to ensure the adequate delivery of blood containing oxygen to the brain. Once this is ensured, then D—definitive care—can be implemented. This involves diagnosing

Syncope (15,407)	Cardiac arrest (331)
Mild allergic reaction (2,583)	Anaphylactic reaction (304)
Angina pectoris (2,552)	Myocardial infarction (289)
Postural hypotension (2,475)	Local anesthetic overdose (204)
Seizures (1,595)	Acute pulmonary edema (heart failure) (141)
Asthmatic attack (bronchospasm) (1,392)	Diabetic coma (109)
Hyperventilation (1,326)	Cerebrovascular accident (68)
"Epinephrine reaction" (913)	Adrenal insufficiency (25)
Insulin shock (hypoglycemia) (890)	Thyroid storm (4)

* *In actual numbers; information taken from Fast TB, Martin MD, Ellis TM. Emergency preparedness: a survey of dental practitioners. JADA 1986;112:499-501; and Malamed SF. Managing medical emergencies. JADA 1993;124:40-53. Situations reported are listed in order of frequency from most to least.*

the problem and, if possible, administering appropriate drug therapy (see Chapter 15) or seeking assistance in managing the problem.

Remembering P,A,B,C,D can save a life. The following explanations describe in more depth each step of the basic management protocol. This information provides direction for the dentist who encounters a medical emergency in the office, whether the victim (be it a patient or staff member) is conscious or unconscious.

P: Position the Patient

Unconscious Patient

Because the most common cause of unconsciousness is a drop in blood pressure (hypotension), the supine (horizontal) position with feet elevated 10 to 15 degrees is recommended (at least initially) for all unconscious patients. This position ensures an increased return of blood to the heart and improved delivery of blood to the brain.

Conscious Patient

In a conscious patient suffering a medical emergency, the heart is still functioning at least adequately; thus, positioning of the conscious person during a medical emergency is based solely on patient comfort. Asthmatics and patients complaining of chest pain will usually be more comfortable if permitted to sit upright.

A: Airway

Unconscious Patient

Performing a head tilt–chin lift maneuver (one hand on the patient's forehead, the other hand on the tip of the patient's chin, lifting the chin upwards while tilting the head upwards) is necessary because in 80% of unconscious patients, the airway will be totally obstructed by the tongue as its muscles relax and it falls into the pharynx.

Conscious Patient

In the conscious patient who can speak, airway management is unnecessary.

B: Breathing

Unconscious Patient

Assessment of ventilatory adequacy is necessary, using the "look, listen and feel" technique. If spontaneous ventilation is absent, rescue breathing must be started.

Conscious Patient

In the conscious patient who can speak, ventilatory management is unnecessary.

C: Circulation

Unconscious Patient

The carotid pulse is palpated for 5-10 s; if absent, chest compression is started.

Conscious Patient

In the conscious patient who can speak, chest compression is unnecessary.

D: Definitive Care

Definitive care consists of drug administration, seeking medical assistance in managing the problem, or both. If the doctor is certain of the diagnosis and has appropriate drugs available, then drug administration is warranted. If any doubt exists concerning the nature of the problem, do not administer any drug other than oxygen. **Note:** When in doubt, do not medicate.

Assistance should be obtained at any time the doctor feels it is needed, including if there is any doubt as to the nature of the emergency situation or if there is any doubt as to whether appropriate drugs or equipment are available, or if they are definitely not available.

Specific Emergencies

The remainder of this chapter covers specific emergency conditions:

- altered consciousness,
- seizures,
- respiratory distress,
- allergy,
- local anesthetic overdose,
- chest pain.

Altered Consciousness

Alterations in central nervous system (CNS) function lead to varying degrees of altered consciousness. Minimal CNS depression leads to a conscious patient's exhibiting altered (e.g., bizarre) behavior, whereas greater levels of CNS depression result in the loss of consciousness.

Managing the Unconscious Patient: What to Do

A definition of unconsciousness is lack of response to sensory stimulation. Syncope—also known as vasodepressor syncope, vasovagal syncope and fainting—remains the most common emergency seen in dental practice. It develops when the patient's body, responding to a real or perceived "fight-or-flight" type of stressful situation, directs blood into the skeletal muscles of the legs and arms of a patient seated upright or standing. In the absence of movement (for example, in the macho male who can "take it like a man" and sits still and does not inform the doctor of his anxiety, fear or pain), blood remains in the legs; as a result, circulating blood volume, cardiac output and cerebral blood flow all decrease. The brain is unable to function normally in the absence of an adequate blood flow (decreased glucose and oxygen supplies) and the signs and symptoms associated with syncope develop. These include pallor, nausea, sweating, feelings of dizziness or faintness and, finally, the loss of consciousness.

Position the Patient

Critical step: Position the patient supine (horizontal) with his or her feet elevated slightly (10 to 15 degrees) to increase blood flow to the brain.

Airway

Critical step: Maintain airway patency with head tilt–chin lift positioning.

Breathing

Assess breathing: Breathing is usually present in syncope. If not, ventilate with two full breaths.

Circulation

Assess circulation: Palpable pulse should be present. In syncope, bradycardia is normally present with a heart rate of 20 to 30 beats per min.

Recovery of consciousness in syncope is usually quite rapid (approximately 10-15 s) after proper positioning and airway management.

Definitive Care

- Loosen any tight clothing, such as collars and ties.
- Administer oxygen.
- Crush and hold aromatic ammonia vaporole beneath the patient's nose to help speed recovery.
- Monitor and record vital signs. For example, blood pressure typically will be lower

than baseline and bradycardia will be present. In this case, return of vital signs to baseline will be quite gradual.

- Postpone further dental care at this appointment. Dismiss patient in the care of a responsible adult, preferably a friend or relative. Do not permit a postsyncopal patient to drive a car or leave the office unescorted. Recovery from a period of syncope, however brief its duration, requires up to 24 h.

Important Points
- Because of the extremely brief duration of unconsciousness (approximately 10-15 s) seen with proper management of syncope, activation of emergency medical services is rarely necessary.
- When unconsciousness persists for more than 15 s after positioning and maintenance of the airway, calling emergency medical services (EMS) should be seriously considered, as syncope is unlikely to be the cause.
- Inadequate airway management during syncope or during any period of unconsciousness leads to tonic-clonic seizure activity, as the brain becomes progressively more hypoxic and finally anoxic. **Note:** Positioning (to increase cerebral blood flow) and airway management (to ensure that cerebral blood contains O_2) are the critical steps in management of any unconscious patient.
- Healthy children do not faint. Healthy children do not sit in a dental chair and "take it like a man," they behave like children. Movement of arms, legs and body maintain an adequate return of blood to the heart and brain, even when a patient may be seated upright. When a child appears to "faint," the steps P,A,B,C,D must be followed and EMS called immediately.

Managing Altered Consciousness: What to Do

Our definition of altered consciousness is a conscious patient's acting strangely. There are several causes of altered consciousness, including cerebrovascular accident (stroke), hyperthyroidism, hypothyroidism and drug ingestion, with hypoglycemia being the one most commonly encountered in the dental office.

With recent changes in the management of Type I diabetes requiring the more frequent injection of insulin, it is estimated that the incidence of hypoglycemic episodes will increase threefold. When the brain is deprived of adequate glucose, it is unable to function normally, producing clinical signs and symptoms of hypoglycemia: an appearance of mental confusion (which may be mistaken for inebriation, but can be differentiated in part because there is no alcohol odor on the breath), cool moist skin, a mild tremor, headache and a feeling of hunger. If severe, hypoglycemia can lead to the loss of consciousness. (**Note:** For treatment, see "Managing the Unconscious Patient: What to Do" earlier in this section; however, be advised that the patient will not regain consciousness in approximately 10 s as with vasodepressor syncope, so be sure to activate EMS.) Hypoglycemia can also lead to seizures. (**Note:** For treatment, see "Managing Seizures: What to Do" in the next section.)

Position the Patient
Position the patient comfortably; upright or semireclined is usually preferred.

Note: Conscious patients may be positioned in the most comfortable position during emergency situations. Unconscious patients are always (at least initially) placed supine with their feet elevated slightly.

Airway
The airway is adequately maintained by the conscious hypoglycemic patient.

Breathing
Breathing is adequately maintained by the conscious hypoglycemic patient.

Circulation
Circulation is adequately maintained by the conscious hypoglycemic patient.

Definitive Care

- If the patient is a known diabetic (look for Medic-Alert bracelet, check medical history, ask), ask if he or she has eaten or administered insulin recently.
- Administer sugar orally: suggestion— fruit juices or soft drinks, 4 oz every 5-10 min for 30 min. **Note:** For most Type I diabetics who are hypoglycemic, drinking orange juice is the most rapid means of alleviating the signs and symptoms of hypoglycemia, with sucking on candy the second fastest.
- Monitor and record vital signs: Blood pressure is typically at or near baseline and heart rate is rapid during hypoglycemia.
- If signs and symptoms resolve completely, dental treatment may continue if both the doctor and the patient are agreeable.
- The patient may be dismissed alone if, in the doctor's opinion, all signs and symptoms have resolved. If any doubt remains, discharge him or her into the custody of a responsible adult.
- Before dismissing the patient, determine a cause for the reaction (for example, "I didn't eat before the dental appointment") and modify future care to minimize this risk.
- If symptoms do not resolve following administration of oral sugar, activate EMS.
- If consciousness is lost, repeat P,A,B,C,D protocol and activate EMS procedures.

Important Points

- Never administer oral sugar to an unconscious patient.
- Whenever a diabetic patient exhibits the signs and symptoms listed above, assume hypoglycemia and administer sugar-rich liquids.

Seizures

The definition of seizures is generalized skeletal muscle contractions. **Note:** Seizure and convulsion are synonyms. Epilepsy implies recurrent, discrete seizures in which there is a disturbance of movement, sensation, behavior or consciousness.

The person most likely to have a seizure in the dental environment will be the patient or staff member with a history of epilepsy with poorly controlled seizures or a person with well-controlled epilepsy who is fearful of dentistry.

Local anesthetic overdose is another possible, though unlikely, cause of generalized tonic-clonic seizures, or GTCSs. GTCSs are present in about 90% of epileptics. Several distinct phases of the GTCS exist as follows.

1. Prodromal Phase

A prodromal phase, consisting of the aura, lasting from a few s to several h prior to the next phase. The aura serves as warning to the patient and doctor that the seizure has begun. Determine a patient's aura at a preliminary visit.

2. Tonic Phase

The patient loses consciousness and a brief (10-20 s) phase of generalized muscle rigidity (the tonic phase) is observed. The patient will arch the back and emit a strange crowing sound (the "epileptic cry") as air is expelled from the lungs.

3. Clonic Phase

The clonic phase, a phase of repetitive generalized skeletal muscle contraction and relaxation, usually lasts from 2 to 5 min. Muscle contraction may be violent or barely perceptible with intermediate gradations. The cardiovascular, respiratory and central nervous systems are all stimulated at this time.

4. Postictal Phase

Muscle contraction ends as the postictal phase—a stage of CNS, cardiovascular and respiratory system depression lasting from 10 to 30 min—begins. The patient is sleeping (physiological sleep) deeply and is difficult to arouse. Snoring may be heard, indicating partial airway obstruction. Gurgling, indicating fluid (vomitus, secretions, blood) in the airway may also be heard. Full recovery from GTCS requires up to 3 h.

Important Point

Status epilepticus is an acutely life-threatening situation in which a seizure is continuous for more than 5 min or when a seizure stops and returns before the patient regains consciousness.

Managing Seizures: What to Do

If a seizure occurs during dental treatment, leave the patient in the dental chair and remove all dental equipment from the mouth as expeditiously as possible. Then follow P,A,B,C,D as described below.

Position the Patient

Position the patient; all unconscious patients are to be placed in the supine position with their feet elevated slightly. **Note:** Elevation of the feet may be extremely difficult to accomplish during a seizure, but as the patient's blood pressure is quite elevated at this time, foot elevation is not critical.

Airway

The airway is usually adequately maintained by the patient during a GTCS. Little or no treatment is usually necessary by the rescuer.

Breathing

Breathing is usually adequate during a GTCS. Little or no airway management is necessary by the rescuer.

Circulation

Circulation is adequately maintained by the patient during a GTCS. Little or no treatment is usually necessary by the rescuer.

Definitive Care

- Activate EMS procedure as soon as the seizure begins.
- Protect victim from injury during clonic phase of seizure. **Note:** Gently hold arms and legs, permit limited movement, but do not restrain patient and prevent movement.

Important Point

Do not attempt to put anything into the mouth of a convulsing person. Most injury to victims of seizures occurs during the clonic phase as rescuers attempt to insert objects into the mouth (for example, tongue depressors wrapped in gauze) to "protect the victim" from injury. Fewer than 50% of persons suffering GTCS suffer any intraoral injury when left alone, with injury limited to soft-tissue bruising of the cheek, lateral border of the tongue or both.

Postseizure Phase

When the seizure ceases, repeat P,A,B,C.

Position the Patient

In the dental chair, maintain the patient in a supine position with his or her feet elevated. If lying on the floor, the patient should be turned onto his or her side after the seizure. This position aids in maintaining a patent airway.

Airway

Snoring is frequently present, requiring head tilt–chin lift. If necessary, the patient may be repositioned supine and then given the head tilt–chin lift positioning. If a gurgling sound is heard, suctioning of the pharynx is necessary.

Breathing

Spontaneous breathing is normally present.

Circulation

Adequate circulation is normally present in the postictal phase.

Definitive Care

Talk to the patient, explaining that "you are in the dental office, have had a seizure, and everything is OK." In the postictal phase, patients are disoriented and sleeping deeply. If a companion has accompanied the patient to the office, have the companion talk to the patient as the patient may respond more quickly to a familiar voice.

Recovery and Discharge

EMS is summoned at the start of the seizure for two reasons.

First, not all seizures stop within 5 min. Continuous seizures (status epilepticus) are life-threatening and mandate the administration of IV anticonvulsants (for example, diazepam or midazolam). Unless specifically trained in management of apneic patients, never consider the administration of anticonvulsant drugs. Emergency medical personnel are trained to administer anticonvulsants and to ventilate a nonbreathing patient.

Second, most patients (especially those with epilepsy) may be discharged in the care of a responsible adult after having seizures. However, where there is no history of seizures or where seizures last longer than 5 min, hospitalization may be required. Summoning medical assistance at the onset of seizures ensures their prompt arrival on the scene and an accurate evaluation of the postictal patient.

Respiratory Distress

Our definition of respiratory distress is a conscious patient's having difficulty breathing.

Possible causes of respiratory distress in a dental care situation include bronchospasm, hyperventilation and acute pulmonary edema. Whatever the actual cause of the respiratory problem (the actual cause may not be immediately obvious), it is important that the conscious patient who is having difficulty breathing (and likely to be quite apprehensive as a result) be managed expeditiously. Initial steps in management of respiratory distress are uniform (see "Managing Bronchospasm: What to Do" below).

Bronchospasm, the acute manifestation of asthma, is the most common cause of respiratory distress in dentistry. Acute episodes of bronchospasm are usually quite easily managed; however, bronchospasm is considered to be life-threatening when it persists despite the administration of two doses of the patient's bronchodilating aerosol drug. **Note:** This is termed "status asthmaticus." The incidence of asthma and the number of deaths from status asthmaticus have increased greatly in the past two decades. A bronchodilating aerosol inhaler should be included in the basic emergency drug kit. Asthmatic patients should be reminded to bring their own inhaler with them to every dental appointment. During an acute episode, the asthmatic patient will demonstrate difficulty in breathing. Wheezing is likely to be heard, along with breathing in short gasping inspirations and long noisy (wheezing) expirations. Sweating and flushing of the face and upper torso may be observed, along with use of accessory muscles of respiration.

When respiratory distress is related to pulmonary aspiration of a dental object or device, a chest radiograph should be ordered to determine if the foreign body is in the bronchi or lungs. When foreign body aspiration is considered a possibility, immediate referral to a physician is important. If the foreign body is not in the lung, a gastrointestinal series of radiographs might be of value. For most patients, fecal recovery can be considered.

Managing Bronchospasm: What to Do

Position the Patient
Position the patient comfortably: Patients in bronchospasm almost universally prefer the upright position.

Airway
The airway is adequately maintained during bronchospasm.

Breathing
Breathing is normally adequate during bronchospasm but is associated with the sound of wheezing (indicative of a partially obstructed airway produced by spasm of bronchial smooth muscle).

Circulation
Circulation is adequately maintained during bronchospasm. Blood pressure is usually slightly elevated while the heart rate is at baseline or slightly elevated.

Definitive Care
- Administer bronchodilator. The patient's bronchodilator aerosol inhaler should

be given to him or her. Permit asthmatic patients to administer the drug themselves, as they are accustomed to doing so. The acute episode will terminate within minutes, with the wheezing resolving and the work of breathing easing.

• Administer oxygen. Oxygen is of secondary importance to the bronchodilator and is usually not necessary; however, should the episode continue or if cyanosis appears, oxygen should be administered.

Recovery and Discharge

Once the typical acute episode of bronchospasm has passed, the patient essentially returns to a "normal state." If both the doctor and the patient agree, the planned dental treatment can proceed. Determine the cause of the episode (for example, sight of the dental syringe or a bloody gauze) and modify future treatment to minimize the likelihood of a recurrence.

The patient may be dismissed alone after the episode only if the doctor feels that recovery is complete.

Allergy

Allergy is a potentially life-threatening reaction. Fortunately, most allergy involves only the skin, producing itching, hives, rash and possibly edema. Signs and symptoms of allergy are produced by the chemical mediators of allergy, primarily histamine, released into tissue and circulating throughout the body. Other mediators include slow-reacting substance of anaphylaxis (SRS-A) and eosinophilic chemotactic factor of anaphylaxis. The rate of release of these chemicals, as well as the sites of their distribution, determine the severity of the allergic reaction. It is essential that allergy be treated aggressively. In general, the faster the onset of signs and symptoms, the more rapidly they progress and the more severe the reaction will become. The usual progression of a severe anaphylactic reaction is skin → eyes, nose, GI → respiratory system →

cardiovascular system (CVS). The following section describes proper management of a mild reaction.

Managing Mild Systemic Allergic Skin Reaction: What to Do

Airway, breathing and circulation must be evaluated to determine if the allergic skin reaction has progressed to involve either the respiratory system or the CVS. If the reaction involves either the cardiovascular or respiratory systems, management should proceed as described in the following section on anaphylaxis.

Position the Patient

Position the patient comfortably. The conscious patient suffering from a systemic skin reaction will usually be comfortable if seated upright or semireclined.

Airway

The patient experiencing a mild systemic allergic skin reaction can usually speak without difficulty. A high-pitched "crowing sound" is indicative of soft-tissue edema at the level of the larynx (laryngeal edema) and represents a life-threatening situation. If laryngeal edema is present, EMS must be activated immediately.

Breathing

In most patients with systemic skin reactions, breathing sounds will be normal. The presence of wheezing and of labored breathing indicates respiratory involvement—bronchospasm—necessitating activation of EMS and the administration of a bronchodilator (see "Respiratory Distress" section earlier in chapter).

Circulation

The CVS is rarely affected in an allergic skin reaction. However, if large amounts of chemical mediators are released into the CVS, vasodilation occurs, resulting in hypotension and tachycardia. The patient may feel faint or lose consciousness. Basic management of the unconscious patient is required (see "Altered Consciousness" section earlier in chapter).

In a systemic skin reaction with neither respiratory nor cardiovascular involvement, there is no immediate need to contact EMS, but definitive treatment must continue.

Definitive Care
- Administer oxygen.
- Administer histamine blocker. Parenteral administration of a histamine blocker is required to manage a systemic skin reaction and to minimize the risk of its progressing to involve either the respiratory or cardiovascular systems. Diphenhydramine (50 mg) or chlorpheniramine (10 mg) are administered either IV or IM (into either the mid-deltoid or vastus lateralis muscles).
- Permit the patient to recover. Following IM administration, histamine blockers require approximately 10-30 min to alleviate itching (the same response occurring within 2-4 min after IV administration). The skin reaction (hives) will remain.

Discharge of the Patient
The patient may be permitted to leave the dental office after being observed for at least 1 h if there is no evidence of a return or progression of the signs and symptoms.

Prescription
Prescribe oral histamine blockers for 3 days.

Note: Allergy must be treated aggressively. Whenever parenteral histamine blockers are administered, a 3-day regimen of an oral histamine blocker should be prescribed.

Managing Anaphylactic (Systemic Allergy) Reaction: What to Do

Our definition of anaphylaxis is a patient's experiencing a rapid-onset systemic allergic reaction involving either the respiratory system (dyspnea, wheezing), the CVS (tachycardia, hypotension) or both; this patient is in urgent need of emergency medical care.

Position the Patient
The patient, though conscious, typically exhibits signs of hypotension. Positioning is predicated on the maintenance of adequate blood flow to the brain; therefore, the supine position with feet elevated slightly is recommended, if possible. Modification might be necessary if respiratory distress is severe.

Airway
The airway need not be maintained as the patient is conscious and is communicating normally.

Breathing
Breathing is often adequate in this patient, although there is evidence of some respiratory compromise in wheezing and dyspnea.

Circulation
A palpable carotid pulse is usually present, although the rate may be rapid and the feel of the pulse "weak."

Definitive Care
- Activate EMS. When an allergic reaction involves either breathing, the CVS or both, emergency assistance should be sought immediately.
- Administer epinephrine. Epinephrine must be administered IM as soon as possible during acute allergic reactions. Using the preloaded syringe of 1:1,000 epinephrine, a dose of 0.3 mg (0.3 mL) is administered IM in the mid-deltoid, vastus lateralis or sublingual areas. The latter is preferred to the former as the sublingual region is more vascular, resulting in a more rapid absorption of the epinephrine.
- Administer oxygen.
- Monitor and record vital signs. Blood pressure, heart rate and rhythm, and respiratory rate and quality are monitored and recorded throughout the reaction.
- Readminister epinephrine, if needed. Epinephrine in a 0.3 mg dose is administered to the patient every 5 min until the clinical signs of bronchospasm and hypotension are relieved. Breathing should sound more normal (a soft whooshing

sound), and the patient should no longer exhibit labored breathing. The pulse rate will remain elevated (epinephrine produces tachycardia), but the strength of the pulse will improve (become stronger). Blood pressure will increase. Itching and hives will remain.

- Administer a histamine blocker. After relief of the respiratory and cardiovascular signs and symptoms, a parenteral histamine blocker is administered. Diphenhydramine or chlorpheniramine administered IM or IV will minimize the risk of a recurrence of cardiovascular and respiratory symptoms and will alleviate the itching.
- When emergency medical technicians (EMTs) arrive, the patient will be monitored aggressively (ECG, pulse oximetry), an IV infusion started and additional drugs administered. These might include additional histamine blockers and corticosteroids. The patient will usually require hospitalization for a period of time for observation and additional management.

Important Points
- The more rapid the onset of signs and symptoms, the more aggressively the allergic reaction must be treated.
- Allergic reactions involving the respiratory system, the CVS, or both, are life-threatening.
- Whenever allergic reactions involve the respiratory system or the CVS, aggressive management is essential to help ensure a positive outcome. The immediate administration of epinephrine is usually critical to success.

Local Anesthetic Overdose

Local anesthetic overdose is most likely to develop from the overadministration of the drug to a smaller, lighter-weight patient, such as a child or an elderly adult.

Peak blood levels of local anesthetic after intraoral administration develop in approximately 5-10 min with a "plain" local anesthetic, and 20-30 min with a local anesthetic containing a vasoconstrictor (e.g., epinephrine). As anesthetic blood levels increase, signs and symptoms of increasing CNS stimulation can be noted (paradoxically, these are caused by a progressive depression of the CNS), including increased talkativeness, increased apprehension, slurred speech and stuttering. With further increase in anesthetic blood levels, muscular twitching and, finally, generalized convulsions are observed.

Rapid IV administration of local anesthetics can also induce seizures. The onset of the seizure will be almost immediate, within seconds of the anesthetic's IV administration.

Local anesthetic–induced seizures will persist until the local anesthetic blood level falls below the "seizure threshold" for that particular anesthetic. Of significance is the fact that acidosis lowers the seizure threshold of local anesthetics. During seizures, lactic acid is produced as a result of muscular contraction, excessive carbon dioxide is retained and hypoxia occurs. The result is acidosis and a prolongation of the seizure. Airway management and adequate ventilation are absolutely critical in management of local anesthetic-induced seizures.

Managing Local Anesthetic Overdose: What to Do

Position the Patient
The unresponsive patient having a local anesthetic–induced seizure should be placed in the supine position.

Airway
The airway is usually adequately maintained during local anesthetic–induced seizures, but head tilt–chin lift positioning should be performed to ensure airway patency.

Breathing
Breathing is usually adequately maintained during local anesthetic–induced seizures. Oxygen should be administered to the patient during a local anesthetic–induced

seizure to minimize the risk of hypoxia, hypercapnia and acidosis.

Circulation
Circulation is usually adequately maintained during the seizure.

Important Point
Because acidosis lowers the seizure threshold during local anesthetic–induced seizures, the provision of adequate airway maintenance and ventilation is critical to a successful outcome. A number of devices are available for emergency use to aid in airway maintenance and should be included in an office emergency kit (if the doctor is trained in their use). Oxygen is the most important drug in managing local anesthetic overdose.

Definitive Care
- Activate EMS. Emergency assistance should be summoned whenever a serious adverse reaction occurs after drug administration.
- Manage seizures (see "Seizures" section earlier in chapter). Seizures will cease when local anesthetic blood level falls below its seizure threshold. The post-seizure stage is similar to that of generalized tonic-clonic seizure (CNS, CVS and respiratory depression), except that the patient will usually not be disoriented or mentally confused.
- Basic life support should be administered as indicated below.

Airway
Airway may require head tilt–chin lift positioning.

Breathing
Breathing may be depressed or absent, necessitating supplemental oxygen or controlled ventilation.

Circulation
Hypotension and tachycardia usually will be evident.

Recovery and Discharge
Patients who have had a serious local anesthetic overdose will usually be hospitalized

for definitive treatment and for a period of observation.

Chest Pain

The two most likely causes of chest pain in the dental office are angina pectoris and acute myocardial infarction (heart attack). It is often difficult to distinguish between the two conditions at the onset of "the pain," so initial management is directed at the more frequently occurring and easily treated cause: angina pectoris.

Managing Angina Pectoris: What to Do
Patients who have a history of stable angina pectoris are able to tell the doctor that "I am having an anginal attack," greatly simplifying diagnosis and management. Initially, the pain is described by the patient as a pressure, a heavy weight, a constricting feeling or a burning between the shoulder blades, substernally or radiating to the left neck, left mandible or epigastric region (stomach).

Anginal pain is alleviated by rest (3-8 min) or, more promptly, by administration of nitrates (nitroglycerin). Shortness of breath may also occur during the episode. In patients who have no history of chest pain, immediate activation of EMS is recommended.

Position the Patient
A conscious patient experiencing "chest pain" will almost always be more comfortable in an upright sitting position. As long as consciousness remains, this position is acceptable.

Airway
Airway is adequate.

Breathing
Breathing is adequate.

Circulation
Circulation should be monitored. Blood pressure may be near baseline, elevated slightly or somewhat lower. The heart rate will usu-

ally be increased with possible cardiac dysrhythmias noted.

Definitive Care

- Administer nitroglycerin. The patient's nitroglycerin should be used, with the patient self-administering his or her normal dose, usually 1 to 3 sublingual tablets or 1 to 3 translingual sprays. **Note:** Nitroglycerin alleviates anginal pain within 1-2 min, and the pain should not return.
- If chest pain subsides and does not return, dental treatment may continue after determining the cause of the acute episode (for example, inadequate pain control or severe dental anxiety). Modification of future dental care may be warranted.
- If the patient's nitroglycerin tablets are administered but the chest pain is not alleviated, administer a second dose using the nitroglycerin spray from the office emergency drug kit. If the chest pain subsides and does not return, urge the patient to get a "fresh supply" of nitroglycerin immediately.
- Where there is no history of chest pain or angina and the patient experiences the aforementioned episode, treatment will be similar (steps P,A,B,C,D above), with the exception that EMS should be summoned immediately. A patient suffering an initial episode of "chest pain" will usually be extremely frightened, feeling certain that "This is it, the big one!" EMT management usually will include transportation to the hospital for further diagnosis of the patient's cardiovascular condition.
- If chest pain subsides after nitroglycerin administration and subsequently returns, EMS should be summoned immediately. Treatment proceeds as described in the next section—"Managing Acute Myocardial Infarction: What to Do."

Important Point

Chest pain alleviated by nitroglycerin that returns is not anginal. Manage it as though it was an acute myocardial infarction.

Managing Acute Myocardial Infarction: What to Do

Anginal pain is almost always precipitated by an acute episode that increases the workload of the myocardium, such as fear, pain or exertion. Conversely, 55% of myocardial infarcts occur when the patient is at rest. Although the pain associated with acute myocardial infarction (MI) is often indistinguishable from anginal pain at the onset, MI is of longer duration, is more severe and does not respond well or at all to nitroglycerin.

The myocardium becomes ischemic during an MI, decreasing cardiac output and leading to signs and symptoms indicative of inadequate blood flow: pallor, sweating, nausea, lightheadedness, shortness of breath, generalized weakness, cool moist skin of an ashen-gray color and cyanosis of mucous membranes. Acute dysrhythmias (bradycardias, tachycardias, PVCs, ventricular tachycardia and ventricular fibrillation) and a very intense, crushing chest pain are all associated with MI.

Position the Patient

The upright position is normally favored by the patient experiencing crushing chest pain. If blood pressure decreases or if consciousness is lost, the supine position with feet elevated slightly must be assumed immediately.

Airway

The airway is usually maintained by the patient.

Breathing

Spontaneous ventilation is usually present.

Circulation

Monitor blood pressure and heart rate and rhythm. Blood pressure is usually decreased slightly or may be close to baseline during acute MI. The heart rate may vary from baseline to extremely slow to extremely rapid. Irregularities in the rhythm may be evident. The heart functions as a pump, circulating blood to the cells of the body. As long as there is a palpable (carotid) pulse and the patient remains conscious, the pump is still functional.

Definitive Care

- Administer oxygen via nasal cannula or nasal hood at a 4-6 L/min flow rate.
- Summon EMS, and perform the following procedures while awaiting EMS arrival:
  - Administer nitroglycerin. Administer a dose of two translingual sprays of nitroglycerin from the office emergency kit supply.
  - Continue to administer oxygen.
  - Administer a 325-mg dose of aspirin. Recent evidence indicates that chewing an aspirin, permitting it to be absorbed through the oral soft tissues, has a potentially beneficial effect in aiding in the recanalization of the coronary artery that has become occluded by a thrombus. The aspirin should not be swallowed whole, as this will delay onset of its thrombolytic actions.
  - Loosen constricting clothing (such as ties, collars).
  - Monitor and record vital signs.
  - Alleviate pain. Traditionally, pain of myocardial infarction has been managed with intravenous morphine (2 to 5 mg every 5 to 15 min). The combination of nitrous oxide (35%) and oxygen (65%) has been shown to be equianalgesic with morphine in managing the pain of MI. Additionally, nitrous oxide at a 35% concentration is a sedative, relaxing a scared patient, while the 65% oxygen is more than three times the ambient oxygen concentration.
  - Should the patient lose consciousness, reassess P,A,B,C and implement as necessary.
- On arrival, the EMTs will initiate monitoring (for example, electrocardiogram and pulse oximeter), an intravenous infusion, will administer appropriate advanced cardiac life support (ACLS) drugs and will transport the patient to the hospital emergency department for definitive management.

Suggested Readings

American Heart Association. Textbook of advanced cardiac life support. Dallas: American Heart Association; 1987.

Blakeslee S. Doctors announce new way to forestall effect of diabetes. New York Times; 1993;June 14:1,9.

Bosco DA, Haas DA, Young ER, Harrop KL. An anaphylactoid reaction following local anesthesia: a case report. Anesth Pain Control Dent 1993;2(2):87-93.

Fast TB, Martin MD, Ellis TM. Emergency preparedness: a survey of dental practitioners. JADA 1986;112:499-501.

Roberge RJ, Maciera-Rodriguez L. Seizure-related oral lacerations: incidence and distribution. JADA 1985; 111:279.

Thompson PL, Lown B. Nitrous oxide as an analgesic in acute myocardial infarction. JAMA 1976;235:924.

Section II.

Drugs Used in Medicine:
Treatment and Pharmacological
Considerations for Dental
Patients Receiving Medical Care

Chapter 17.

Cardiovascular Drugs

Steven Ganzberg, D.M.D., M.S.

Cardiovascular disease affects one in six men and one in seven women aged 45-64 y in the United States. The incidence increases to one in three people aged > 65 y. A wide array of medications, with considerably different mechanisms of action, are prescribed to treat these disorders. Primary mechanisms involve the renin-angiotensin system mediated via renal mechanisms and nervous system control via adrenergic supply. Not surprisingly, medications to treat hypertension modify these systems or associated receptor systems.

This chapter will discuss the medications used for the following cardiovascular disorders: dysrhythmias, congestive heart failure, angina, hypertension and hypercholesterolemia. The chapter is organized by drug class and provides a brief explanation of each. It should be noted that sildenafil (Viagra), which is used for erectile dysfunction, is included in the Antihypertensive Drugs section of this chapter because it is a vasodilator. (It originally was tested as an antihypertensive and did not succeed.)

Special Dental Considerations

Before performing any dental procedure with a patient who has cardiovascular disease, the dentist should evaluate the patient's blood pressure, heart rate and regularity of rhythm. Any change in medication regimen should be reviewed. It is important for patients to take their cardiovascular medications at their usual scheduled time, irrespective of a dental appointment, to minimize the possibility of rebound hypertension or tachycardia.

Noncompliance with medication regimens is not uncommon. The dentist should take special precautions to minimize the stress or pain of a dental procedure so that adverse cardiovascular responses are, in turn, minimized.

Many of these drugs can cause orthostatic hypotension. The dentist should have the patient sit up in the dental chair for 1-2 min after being in a supine position and monitor the patient when he or she is standing. Use of epinephrine or levonordefrin in local anesthetic solutions should be minimized, and extra care should be taken with aspiration to avoid intravascular injection. If local anesthetic solutions containing epinephrine are deemed necessary, it has been recommended that no more than 40 µg of epinephrine (0.04 mg or approximately two 1.8-cubic-centimeter cartridges of local anesthetic with 1:100,000 epinephrine) should be used for successive dental anesthetic injections in patients with cardiovascular disease. Vital sign monitoring may be of value between injections for selected patients with severe disease. Additional injections of local anesthetic with epinephrine can be given after approximately 5-10 min if vital signs are satisfactory. The use of gingival retraction cord with epinephrine is absolutely contraindicated in all patients with cardiovascular disease; this cord should be used with extreme caution, if at all, in other patients.

Patients taking some cardiovascular medications may also be taking anticoagulants. Therefore, before dental procedures involving bleeding are performed, consultation with the patient's physician may be indicated to adjust the anticoagulant dose as discussed in Chapter 22, Hematologic Drugs.

Antidysrhythmic Drugs

In cardiac dysrhythmia, some aspect of normal cardiac electrophysiology is disturbed. This may manifest in one or more of the following: the sinoatrial (SA) node, atrioventricular (AV) node, Bundle of His, Purkinje fibers or in cardiac muscle itself. Antidysrhythmic drugs modify aberrant electrophysiological processes to help restore or improve either an unacceptable rate, an unacceptable rhythm or both.

See Table 17.1 for basic information on antidysrhythmic drugs.

Table 17.1
Antidysrhythmic Drugs: Dosage and Prescribing Information

Generic name	Brand name(s)	Dosage range	Interactions with other drugs
Class IA			
Disopyramide	Norpace	150-200 mg q 6 h	Excessive quantities of either local anesthetic or epinephrine/levonordefrin can precipitate dysrhythmia
			These patients should avoid anticholinergics and sedating antihistamines
			Hepatic microsomal enzyme inducers, such as barbiturates, may increase metabolism of disopyramide
Procainamide	Procan, Promine, Pronestyl	500-1,000 mg q 4-6 h	Excessive quantities of either local anesthetic or epinephrine/levonordefrin can precipitate dysrhythmia
			Avoid use of anticholinergics and sedating antihistamines
Quinidine gluconate, quinidine sulfate	Cardoquin, Cinquin, Duraquin, Quinalan, Quinidex, Quiniglute, Quinora; Novoquinidin [CAN]	**Quinidine gluconate:** 324-660 mg q 6-12 h **Quinidine sulfate:** 200-600 mg q 6-8 h	Excessive quantities of either local anesthetic or epinephrine/levonordefrin can precipitate dysrhythmia
			Avoid use of anticholinergics and sedating antihistamines if possible
			Hepatic microsomal enzyme inducers, such as barbiturates, may increase metabolism of quinidine
			Medications containing potassium, such as IV penicillin G potassium, may potentiate quinidine effects
Class IB			
Lidocaine (cardiac)	Xylocaine, Xylocard	**IV only:** 0.75-3.0 mg/kg	Not applicable; used only in emergency situations
Mexiletine	Mexitil	200-400 mg q 8 h	Hepatic enzyme inducers, such as barbiturates, may decrease plasma levels

[CAN] indicates a drug available only in Canada.

Continued on next page

Table 17.1 (cont.)

Antidysrhythmic Drugs: Dosage and Prescribing Information

Generic name	Brand name(s)	Dosage range	Interactions with other drugs
Class IB (cont.)			
Phenytoin	Dilantin, Diphenylan, Phenytex	**IV only:** 50-100 mg q 10 min; maximum 50 mg/kg	**Acetaminophen (prolonged use):** Increased risk of hepatic toxicity **Aspirin:** Increased plasma concentration **CNS depressants:** Increased sedative effects **Corticosteroids, benzodiazepines, barbiturates:** Increased metabolism **Fluconazole, ketaconazole, metronidazole:** Decreased metabolism and increased plasma concentration **Lidocaine (high dose):** Increased risk of cardiac dysrhythmia
Tocainide	Tonocard	400-600 mg q 8 h	Hepatic enzyme inducers, such as barbiturates, may decrease plasma levels
Class IC			
Encainide	Encaid	25-50 mg q 8 h	Hepatic enzyme inducers, such as barbiturates, may decrease plasma levels
Flecainide	Tambocor	50-200 mg q 12 h	Hepatic enzyme inducers, such as barbiturates, may decrease plasma levels
Class II			
β-blockers	See Table 17.5, Adrenergic Blocking Agents	See Table 17.5, Adrenergic Blocking Agents	See Table 17.5, Adrenergic Blocking Agents
Class III			
Amiodarone	Cordarone	200-1,600 mg q day	Lidocaine or vasoconstrictors may produce hypotension and/or bradycardia
Bretylium	Bretylate, Bretylol	**For IV use:** 5-10 mg/kg	Increased toxicity with other antidysrhythmic agents
Sotalol	Betapace	80-160 mg q 12 h	See Table 17.5, Adrenergic Blocking Agents
Class IV			
Calcium channel blockers	See Table 17.8, Calcium Channel Blockers	See Table 17.8, Calcium Channel Blockers	See Table 17.8, Calcium Channel Blockers

Special Dental Considerations

If dental patients have been taking these drugs for long periods and their symptoms are under adequate control, the management of these patients in an outpatient dental setting without continuous cardiac monitoring is generally acceptable. Hypotension is commonly encountered. Quinidine is used for several dysrhythmias, but commonly for atrial fibrillation. Other Class I and Class III agents are frequently administered either intravenously or orally for severe cardiac dysrhythmias such as ventricular tachycardia. Class II and Class IV agents can be used for either hypertension or dysrhythmia control or angina. The dentist should consider ECG and continual vital-sign monitoring for patients with serious dysrhythmia. In addition, the dentist should follow the recommendations listed under Special Dental Considerations at the beginning of this chapter for all drugs in this category.

Use of large quantities of injected local anesthetics may have additive and possibly detrimental cardiac effects. Use of epinephrine or levonordefrin in local anesthetic solutions should be minimized, and extra care should be taken with aspiration to avoid intravascular injection. A stress-reduction protocol is appropriate.

Most Class I and Class III agents may, in rare cases, cause leukopenia, thrombocytopenia or agranulocytosis. Consider medication-induced adverse effects if gingival bleeding or infection occurs. Elective dental treatment should be deferred if hematologic parameters are compromised.

Quinidine and amiodarone can cause bitter or altered taste. Amiodarone can cause facial flushing.

In orofacial pain management, oral analogues of lidocaine, such as mexiletine, have been reported to be of some use in certain neuropathic pain states. The dentist using these drugs as therapeutic agents is presumed to be proficient in prescribing and managing these medications.

Drug Interactions of Dental Interest

The use of local anesthetics with or without vasoconstrictors is described earlier under Special Dental Considerations. There may be additive anticholinergic effects, such as dry mouth and constipation, with anticholinergic drugs and some sedating antihistamines. Additionally, the cardio-accelerating effect of these medications may be undesirable. Barbiturates, especially when chronically administered, may induce hepatic enzymes and decrease the plasma levels of many anti-dysrhythmics. Neuromuscular blockade during general anesthesia may be prolonged. Phenytoin interactions are covered in Chapter 20, Neurological Drugs, although this agent typically is used as an antidysrhythmic only in acute cases, for digitalis overdose.

Laboratory Value Alterations

- Most Class I and Class III agents may cause leukopenia, thrombocytopenia or agranulocytosis in rare cases. Bleeding times may be affected.
- Quinidine may cause anemia.
- Disopyramide may lower blood glucose levels.

Pharmacology

The antidysrhythmic drugs, classified in four groups from Class I to Class IV, modify the aberrant electrophysiological process to help restore more normal rate and rhythm. The classification of antidysrhythmic drugs is based on the predominant electrophysiological effect of each drug on the various components of the cardiac conduction system in regard to automaticity, refractoriness and responsiveness. Examples of conditions in which these drugs are useful include atrial fibrillation and other atrial dysrhythmias, emergency treatment of ventricular fibrillation, ventricular dysrhythmias (including premature ventricular contractions, or PVCs), ventricular tachycardia and drug-induced dysrhythmias.

Cardiac Glycosides

These drugs are used mainly to treat congestive heart failure and certain cardiac dysrhythmias such as atrial fibrillation. The two commonly used drugs in this category include digitoxin and digoxin.

See Table 17.2 for basic information on cardiac glycosides.

Special Dental Considerations

Increased gag reflex is possible. Bright dental lights may not be tolerated. The patient's anticoagulation status, as well as the patient's need for bacterial endocarditis prophylaxis, should be evaluated. In addition, the dentist should follow the recommendations listed under Special Dental Considerations at the beginning of this chapter for drugs in this category.

Drug Interactions of Dental Interest

Use of epinephrine or levonordefrin in local anesthetic solutions should be minimized, and extra care should be taken with aspiration to avoid intravascular injection.

Use of erythromycin may increase digitoxin absorption and toxicity.

Hepatic enzyme inducers (such as barbiturates), especially when used chronically, may increase digitalis metabolism.

Sudden increases in potassium, such as through rapid IV administration of penicillin G potassium or succinylcholine, may precipitate digitalis-induced dysrhythmia.

Pharmacology

These drugs increase the force of cardiac contraction and decrease heart rate. By these mechanisms, an enlarged heart is allowed to function more efficiently and its size may be reduced. Because of the rate-slowing effects of these drugs, they are also used to treat specific supraventricular tachycardias. The primary mechanisms of action include inhibition of the sodium-potassium adenosinetriphosphatase, or ATPase, pump and increases in the availability of myocardial Ca^{++} ions intracellularly. This drug has a narrow therapeutic index, which necessitates frequent plasma level determinations.

Table 17.2

Cardiac Glycosides: Dosage and Prescribing Information

Generic name	Brand name(s)	Dosage range	Interactions with other drugs
Digitoxin	Crystodigin, Digitaline	50-300 µg (0.05-0.3 mg) q day	Excessive epinephrine or levonordefrin in local anesthetic solutions may produce dysrhythmia
			Erythromycin may increase digitalis absorption
			Hepatic enzyme inducers, such as barbiturates, may increase digitalis metabolism, especially in chronic use
			Sudden increases in potassium, such as by rapid IV administration of penicillin G potassium or succinylcholine, may precipitate digitalis-induced dysrhythmia
Digoxin	Lanoxicaps, Lanoxin	50-350 µg (0.05-0.35 mg) q 12-24 h	See note above

Antianginal Agents

Angina pectoris, literally "pain in the chest," usually results from a lack of adequate oxygen for myocardial need (ischemia) secondary to coronary atherosclerosis. There are three types of angina—chronic stable exertional angina, Prinzmetal's angina and unstable angina. Chronic stable exertional angina usually occurs in patients when activity is such that myocardial oxygen requirement exceeds supply. These patients typically carry a sublingual tablet or spray nitroglycerin, which usually aborts attacks. Prinzmetal's angina is angina at rest. Unstable angina is, as the name implies, new-onset angina or worsening angina in a patient who was previously stable. No elective dental procedures should be performed for patients with unstable angina until medically stabilized.

Immediate-acting nitrates, long-acting nitrates, β-blockers and calcium channel blockers are used in the management of angina.

See Table 17.3 for basic information on antianginal drugs.

Special Dental Considerations

Patients with angina who are taking sublingual nitroglycerin on an as-needed basis should have this medication available at all dental appointments. In the event of chest pain during a dental visit, the prompt use of nitroglycerin is indicated. Supplemental oxygen and vital-sign monitoring are appropriate. Nitroglycerin in the dentist's emergency kit should be checked regularly, as its shelf life is generally short. This is especially true of sublingual nitroglycerin tablets after the container has been opened.

In addition, the dentist should follow the recommendations listed under Special Dental Considerations at the beginning of this chapter.

Nitroglycerin may cause flushing of the face, headache and xerostomia.

Drug Interactions of Dental Interest

Use of epinephrine or levonordefrin in local anesthetic solutions should be minimized, and extra care should be taken with aspiration to avoid intravascular injection. Opioids may have added hypotensive effects.

Laboratory value alterations

- Use of nitrate-based antianginal agents may increase the risk of methemoglobinemia. Pulse oximetry may overestimate oxygen saturation.

Pharmacology

Four types of drugs are used to treat angina. The nitrates, typified by nitroglycerin, are direct-acting vasodilators. A dual effect of increased coronary blood flow to ischemic areas coupled with reduction in venous tone leading to decreased myocardial workload account for nitroglycerin's antianginal activity. Long-acting nitrates, such as isosorbide dinitrate, are also somewhat effective; however, tolerance to these agents limits their long-term value. β-blockers, which block adrenergic responses, may be helpful in treating angina by decreasing myocardial rate and workload. Calcium channel blockers cause vasodilation and slow the heart rate, thus decreasing anginal attacks. Lastly, antiplatelet and anticoagulation agents, such as aspirin, may be of value in preventing myocardial infarction.

Antihypertensive Agents

Hypertension is common in the American population, affecting 15-20% of people. The risk of hypertension increases dramatically with age. Physiological blood pressure regulation is a complex interrelationship of multiple overlapping systems. Generally, ACE inhibitors or diuretics are considered first-line agents. Other medications—such as β-blockers, calcium channel blockers, α-blockers and direct-acting vasodilators—are then used, alone or in combination, to control blood pressure. The patient taking multiple antihypertensive agents should be consid-

Table 17.3

Antianginal Drugs: Dosage and Prescribing Information

Generic name	Brand name(s)	Dosage range	Interactions with other drugs
β-blockers	See Table 17.5, Adrenergic Blocking Agents	See Table 17.5, Adrenergic Blocking Agents	See Table 17.5, Adrenergic Blocking Agents
Calcium channel blockers	See Table 17.8, Calcium Channel Blockers	See Table 17.8, Calcium Channel Blockers	See Table 17.8, Calcium Channel Blockers
Erythrityl tetranitrate	Cardilate	5-10 mg q 6-8 h	Opioids may have added hypotensive effects Epinephrine and levonordefrin in local anesthetic solutions may contribute to onset of angina
Isosorbide dinitrate	Dilatrate SR, Iso-Bid, Isordil, Isotrate, Sorbitrate	**Oral, extended-release tablets:** 40-80 mg q 8-12 h **Oral, tablets:** 5-40 mg q 6 h **Sublingual or buccal:** 2.5-5 mg q 2-3 h	See note above
Nitroglycerin	Deponit, Klavikordal, Nitrocad, Nitrodisc, Nitro-Dur, Nitrogard, Nitroglyn, Nitroject, Nitrol, Nitrolin, Nitrolingual, Nitronet, Nitrong, Nitrospan, Nitrostat, Tridil	**Buccal:** 1 mg q 5 h **Extended oral:** 2.5-9 mg q 8-12 h **Sublingual:** 0.15-0.6 mg/dose **Topical, ointment:** 15-30 mg q 8-12 h **Transdermal, patch:** 0.1-0.6 mg/day	See note above
Pentaerythritol tetranitrate	Duotrate, Pentylan, Peritrate	**Oral, capsules and extended-release tablets:** 30-80 mg q 12 h **Oral, tablets:** 10-20 mg q 6 h	See note above

ered at increased risk of experiencing a hypertensive or hypotensive crisis.

Additionally, many of these drugs are used to treat orofacial pain conditions. β-blockers and calcium channel blockers are used to manage migraine and other conditions. Verapamil is used for prevention of cluster headache. β-blockers and α-blockers are used in the management of complex regional pain syndrome (sympathetically maintained pain). Intravenous phentolamine is currently being used as a diagnostic tool to help determine if pain is being influenced by the sympathetic nervous system. Clonidine is used for a variety of painful conditions. The dentist using these drugs as therapeutic agents is presumed to be proficient in prescribing and managing these medications.

Diuretics

Diuretic drugs generally exert an antihypertensive effect by increasing sodium and water excretion, thus decreasing blood volume. This decrease in blood volume decreases arterial tone and reduces myocardial workload. These drugs are commonly first-line agents and frequently are combined with other antihypertensives.

See Table 17.4 for basic information on diuretics.

Special Dental Considerations

Potassium-sparing diuretics may rarely cause agranulocytosis and thrombocytopenia. Consider medication-induced adverse effects if gingival bleeding or infection occurs. In addition, some patients taking diuretics may experience xerostomia, which may require special dental care.

In addition, the dentist should follow the recommendations listed under Special Dental Considerations at the beginning of this chapter.

Drug Interactions of Dental Interest

NSAIDs may antagonize natriuresis and the antihypertensive effects of some diuretics. Diflunisal, specifically, may increase the plasma concentration of hydrochlorothiazide. Excessive use of epinephrine or lev-onordefrin in local anesthetic solutions may antagonize the antihypertensive effects of these agents. All diuretics, except potassium-sparing agents, may enhance neuromuscular blockade during general anesthesia.

Laboratory Value Alterations

- Loop diuretics and thiazide diuretics can increase blood glucose levels.
- Potassium-sparing diuretics may rarely cause agranulocytosis and thrombocytopenia.

Pharmacology

The site of action of these drugs can be any portion of the kidney from the glomerulus to the distal tubule. Modulation of electrolyte and water reabsorption are common mechanisms of action. It should be noted that patients may be taking these drugs for conditions other than essential hypertension such as renal failure, glaucoma or congestive heart failure. A thorough health history review should provide the necessary information.

Table 17.4

Diuretics: Dosage and Prescribing Information

Generic name	Brand name(s)	Dosage range	Interactions with other drugs
Diuretics, loop			
Bumethanide	Bumex	0.5-2 mg q 8-12 h	**All diuretics:** NSAIDs may antagonize the diuretic effect, leading to fluid retention or loss of blood pressure control Excessive use of epinephrine or lev-onordefrin in local anesthetic solutions may antagonize antihypertensive effects **All diuretics except potassium-sparing:** Enhanced neuromuscular blockade possible
Ethacrynic acid	Edercin	50-400 mg/day	See note above
Furosemide	Furoside, Lasix, Myrosemide, Uritol; Novosemide [CAN]	20-120 mg/day	See note above

[CAN] indicates a drug available only in Canada.

Continued on next page

Table 17.4 (cont.)

Diuretics: Dosage and Prescribing Information

Generic name	Brand name(s)	Dosage range	Interactions with other drugs
Diuretics, potassium-sparing			
Amiloride	Midamor	5-20 mg/day	**All diuretics:** NSAIDs may antagonize the diuretic effect, leading to fluid retention or loss of blood pressure control Excessive use of epinephrine or levonordefrin in local anesthetic solutions may antagonize antihypertensive effects **All diuretics except potassium-sparing:** Enhanced neuromuscular blockade possible
Spironolactone	Aldactone; Novospiroton [CAN]	25-400 mg/day	See note above
Triamterene	Dyrenium	25-300 mg/day	See note above
Diuretics, thiazide			
Bendroflumethiazide	Naturetin	2.5-20 mg/day	**All diuretics:** NSAIDs may antagonize the diuretic effect, leading to fluid retention or loss of blood pressure control Excessive use of epinephrine or levonordefrin in local anesthetic solutions may antagonize antihypertensive effects **All diuretics except potassium-sparing:** Enhanced neuromuscular blockade possible
Benzthiazide	Exna, Hydrex	25-100 mg up to bid	See note above
Chlorothiazide	Diuril	250-1,000 mg/day	See note above
Chlorthalidone	Hygroton, Thalitone, Uridon; Apo-Chlorthalidone [CAN], Novo-Thalidone [CAN]	25-100 mg/day OR 100-200 mg every other day	See note above
Cyclothiazide	Anhydron	1-6 mg/day	See note above
Hydrochlorothiazide	Diuchlor H, Esidrix, Hydro-chlor, Hydro-D, HydroDIURIL, Oretic; Apo-Hydro [CAN], Neo-Codema [CAN], Novo-Hydrazide [CAN], Urozide [CAN]	25-100 mg up to bid	See note above
Hydroflumethiazide	Diucardin, Saluron	25-200 mg/day	See note above
Methyclothiazide	Aquatensen, Duretic, Enduron	2.5-10 mg/day	See note above

[CAN] *indicates a drug available only in Canada.*

Continued on next page

Table 17.4 (cont.)

Diuretics: Dosage and Prescribing Information

Generic name	Brand name(s)	Dosage range	Interactions with other drugs
Diuretics, thiazide (cont.)			
Metolazone	Diulo, Mykrox, Zaroxolyn	**Extended release:** 5-20 mg/day **Prompt release:** 0.5-1 mg/day	**All diuretics:** NSAIDs may antagonize the diuretic effect, leading to fluid retention or loss of blood pressure control Excessive use of epinephrine or levonordefrin in local anesthetic solutions may antagonize antihypertensive effects **All diuretics except potassium-sparing:** Enhanced neuromuscular blockade possible
Polythiazide	Renese	1-4 mg/day	See note above
Quinethazone	Hydromox	50-200 mg/day	See note above
Trichloromethiazide	Metahydrin, Naqua, Trichlorex	1-4 g/day	See note above
Diuretics, combination			
Amiloride + hydrochlorothiazide (HCTZ)	Moduretic	5 mg amiloride/50 mg HCTZ 1-2 times/day	**All diuretics:** NSAIDs may antagonize the diuretic effect, leading to fluid retention or loss of blood pressure control Excessive use of epinephrine or levonordefrin in local anesthetic solutions may antagonize antihypertensive effects **All diuretics except potassium-sparing:** Enhanced neuromuscular blockade possible
Spironolactone + HCTZ	Aldactazide, Spirozide	25-200 mg/day Available as 25 mg spironolactone/25 mg HCTZ and 50 mg spironolactone/50 mg HCTZ	See note above
Triamterene + HCTZ	Dyazide	37.5-300 mg/day triamterene/25-200 mg/day hydrochlorothiazide Available as 37.5 mg triamterene/25 mg HCTZ, 50 mg triamterene/25 mg HCTZ and 75 mg triamterene/50 mg HCTZ	See note above

Adrenergic Blocking Agents

Adrenergic blocking agents include β-blockers, α-blockers, and combined α- and β-blockers. These drugs are used to manage hypertension by decreasing sympathetic nervous system activity.

See Table 17.5 for basic information on adrenergic blocking agents.

Special Dental Considerations

Rarely, taste changes have been reported. In addition, the dentist should follow the recommendations listed under Special Dental Considerations at the beginning of this chapter.

Drug Interactions of Dental Interest

Vasoconstrictors in local anesthetics

β-blockers. Hypertension and bradycardia can occur when epinephrine or levonordefrin in local anesthetic solutions is administered to patients taking nonselective β-blockers. Vital sign monitoring before and after injection of local anesthetics containing vasoconstrictors is highly recommended. There is generally minimal interaction of local anesthetic solutions containing epinephrine or levonordefrin with the cardioselective β-blockers.

α-blockers. Hypotension and tachycardia can occur when epinephrine or levonordefrin in local anesthetic solutions is administered to patients taking α-blockers. Vital sign monitoring before and after injection of local anesthetics containing vasoconstrictors is highly recommended.

Combined α- and β-blocker. There is generally minimal interaction with local anesthetic solutions containing epinephrine or levonordefrin.

All adrenergic blocking agents

NSAIDs may partially antagonize the antihypertensive effects of these medications. Opioids may potentiate the hypotensive effect of these medications.

β-blockers only

These agents may decrease the clearance of injected local anesthetics from the peripheral circulation. Phenothiazines may increase the plasma concentration of both drugs.

Pharmacology

The peripheral adrenergic autonomic system principally consists of β_1, β_2, α_1 and α_2 receptors. Catecholamines, such as epinephrine and norepinephrine, act as agonists at these receptors, which have numerous physiological effects. In regard to blood pressure control,

- β_1 activity increases force and rate of cardiac contraction, thus causing tachycardia and increase in blood pressure;
- β_2 activity causes vasodilation in skeletal muscles, thus decreasing blood pressure;
- α_1 receptors cause peripheral vasoconstriction, thus causing an increase in blood pressure;
- α_2 activity causes a decrease in the release of norepinephrine, thus decreasing adrenergic tone.

Adrenergic blocking agents work on one or more of these receptors to alter the sympathetic nervous system response.

β-blockers

β-blockers provide blood pressure control by decreasing the force and rate of cardiac contraction. They are also useful in tachydysrhythmias and angina pectoris. β-blockers are either nonselective or cardioselective. The nonselective β-blockers are antagonists at both the β_1 and β_2 receptors. The cardioselective β-blockers are antagonists at predominantly the β_1 receptor. Because of this difference in receptor activity, patients taking β_1 cardioselective agents experience little interaction with epinephrine in local anesthetic solutions.

α-blockers

α-blockers block either the α_1 receptor (making them selective) or both the α_1 and α_2 receptors (making them nonselective). These drugs control blood pressure by decreasing peripheral vascular tone. Since activation of α_2 receptors decreases adrenergic tone, agents that block both α_1 and α_2 receptors may not be desirable in some patients.

Table 17.5

Adrenergic Blocking Agents: Dosage and Prescribing Information

Generic name	Brand name(s)	Dosage range	Interactions with other drugs
Nonselective β-blockers			
Carteolol	Cartol	2.5-10 mg/day	NSAIDs may partially antagonize antihypertensive effects of these medications
			Clearance of injected local anesthetics from peripheral circulation may decrease
			Opioids may potentiate hypotensive effect of these medications
			Hypertension and bradycardia can occur when epinephrine or levonordefrin in local anesthetic solutions is administered to patients taking nonselective β-blockers
Nadolol	Corgard; Syn-Nadolol [CAN]	40-240 mg/day	See note above
Oxprenolol	Trasicor	20-160 mg q 8 h	See note above
Penbutolol	Levatol	20 mg/day	See note above
Pindolol	Visken; Novo-Pindol [CAN], Syn-Pindol [CAN]	5-30 mg q 12 h	See note above
Propranolol	Detensol, Inderal; Apo-Propranolol [CAN], Novopronol [CAN]	80-640 mg/day	See note above
Sotalol	Betapace, Sotacor	80-160 mg q 12 h	See note above
Timolol	Blocadren; Apo-Timol [CAN]	10-30 mg q 12 h	See note above
Cardioselective β-blockers			
Acebutolol	Monitan, Sectrol	100-600 mg q 12 h	NSAIDs may partially antagonize antihypertensive effects of these medications
			Clearance of injected local anesthetics from peripheral circulation may decrease
			Opioids may potentiate hypotensive effect of these medications
Atenolol	Tenormin; Apo-Atenolol [CAN], Novo-Atenol [CAN]	25-200 mg/day	See note above
Betaxolol	Kerlone	10-20 mg/day	See note above

[CAN] indicates a drug available only in Canada.

Continued on next page

Table 17.5 (cont.)

Adrenergic Blocking Agents: Dosage and Prescribing Information

Generic name	Brand name(s)	Dosage range	Interactions with other drugs
Cardioselective β-blockers (cont.)			
Bisoprolol	Zebeta	2.5-10 mg/day	NSAIDs may partially antagonize antihypertensive effects of these medications Clearance of injected local anesthetics from peripheral circulation may decrease Opioids may potentiate hypotensive effect of these medications
Esmolol	Brevibloc	**IV infusion:** 10-50 mg bolus and/or maintenance—0.05-0.2 mg/kg/min	See note above
Metoprolol	Betalol, Durules, Lopressor, Toprol XL; Apo-Metoprolol [CAN], Novo-Metoprol [CAN]	50-400 mg/day	See note above
Combined α- and β-blocker			
Labetalol	Normodyne, Trandate	100-400 mg q 12 h	NSAIDs may partially antagonize antihypertensive effects of these medications Clearance of injected local anesthetics from peripheral circulation may decrease Opioids may potentiate hypotensive effect of these medications Hypotension and tachycardia can occur when epinephrine or levonordefrin in local anesthetic solutions is administered to patients taking α-blockers
α-blockers			
Phenoxybenzamine	Dibenzyline	10-40 mg q 8-12 h	**All α-blockers:** Hypotension and tachycardia can occur when epinephrine or levonordefrin in local anesthetic solutions is administered to patients taking α-blockers NSAIDs may partially antagonize antihypertensive effects of these medications Opioids may potentiate hypotensive effect of these medications
Phentolamine	Regitine	**IV only:** 5 mg 1-2 h before surgery	See note above
Prazosin	Minipress (α_1 selective)	1-15 mg/day in 2-3 divided doses	See note above
Terazosin	Hytrin (α_1 selective)	1-10 mg/day	See note above

[CAN] indicates a drug available only in Canada.

Combined α- and β-blocker

Labetalol blocks both α_1 and β_1/β_2 receptors with more activity at β-receptors than at α-receptors. Labetalol, the only combined α-blocker and β-blocker, thus possesses properties of a nonselective β-blocker and a vasodilator.

Direct-Acting Vasodilators

Direct-acting vasodilators include hydralazine, minoxidil, diazoxide, nitroglycerin and derivatives, as well as the calcium channel blockers, which are discussed in a separate section below. These drugs work directly on the peripheral vasculature to decrease arterial and/or venous tone. See Table 17.6 for basic information on direct-acting vasodilators.

Special Dental Considerations

Hydralazine may, rarely, cause agranulocytosis and thrombocytopenia. The dentist should consider medication effects if gingival bleed-ing or infection occurs. Facial flushing may occur. Excessive facial hair growth may be seen with minoxidil.

In addition, the dentist should follow the recommendations listed under Special Dental Considerations at the beginning of this chapter.

Drug Interactions of Dental Interest

Excessive use of epinephrine or levonordefrin in local anesthetic solutions may antagonize the antihypertensive effects of these agents. NSAIDs may partially antagonize the anti-hypertensive effects of these medications. Opioids may potentiate the hypotensive effect of these medications.

Laboratory Value Alterations

- Erythrocyte concentration, hemoglobin and hematocrit may be artificially decreased due to hemodilution.

Pharmacology

These agents provide hypertension control pre-dominantly by various direct actions on vascu-lar smooth muscle. The mechanism of action is

Table 17.6

Direct-Acting Vasodilators: Dosage and Prescribing Information

Generic name	Brand name(s)	Dosage range	Interactions with other drugs
Calcium channel blockers	See Table 17.8, Calcium Channel Blockers	See Table 17.8, Calcium Channel Blockers	See Table 17.8, Calcium Channel Blockers
Hydralazine	Apresoline; Novo-Hylazin [CAN]	50-75 mg q 6 h	NSAIDs may antagonize diuretic effect, leading to fluid retention or loss of blood pressure control Excessive use of epinephrine or levonordefrin in local anesthetic solutions may antagonize antihypertensive effects of these agents Opioids may potentiate hypotensive effect of these agents
Minoxidil	Loniten	10-100 mg/day	See note above
Nitrates	See Table 17.3, Antianginal Drugs	See Table 17.3, Antianginal Drugs	See Table 17.3, Antianginal Drugs

[CAN] indicates a drug available only in Canada.

believed to be mediated via nitric oxide, which alters Ca++ dependent muscular contractility and thus produces vascular muscle relaxation.

Vasodilator Used for Erectile Dysfunction

Erectile dysfunction is caused by organic, psychogenic or mixed etiologies. Diseases such as diabetes and peripheral vascular disease, as well as postsurgical sequelae such as those following prostatectomy, can cause erectile dysfunction. See Table 17.7 for basic information on a vasodilator used for erectile dysfunction.

Special Dental Considerations

Glossitis, stomatitis, gingivitis and xerostomia have been reported; however, a causal relationship to drug use is unclear.

Drug Interactions of Dental Interest

Erythromycin, ketaconazole and itraconazole may increase sildenafil plasma levels.

Pharmacology

The mechanism of erection of the penis involves release of nitric oxide (NO) in the corpus cavernosum during sexual stimulation. NO activates guanylate cyclase, which increases cGMP levels to produce smooth muscle relaxation and increase blood flow to the corpus cavernosum. Sildenafil inhibits the degradation of cGMP, thus increasing the effects of NO. At recommended doses, sildenafil has no effect in the absence of sexual stimulation.

Calcium Channel Blockers

Calcium channel blockers are commonly prescribed antihypertensive, antianginal and antidysrhythmic agents. See Table 17.8 for basic information on calcium channel blockers.

Special Dental Considerations

Gingival enlargement can occur with these agents. Meticulous oral hygiene can reduce these effects. If gingival enlargement occurs, the patient's physician should be consulted about changing the medication to a noncalcium channel blocker. Nimodipine may cause thrombocytopenia. Other agents rarely cause blood dyscrasias. Consider medication-induced adverse effects if gingival bleeding or infection occurs.

In addition, the dentist should follow the recommendations listed under Special Dental Considerations at the beginning of this chapter.

Drug Interactions of Dental Interest

Excessive use of epinephrine or levonordefrin in local anesthetic solutions may antagonize the antihypertensive effects of these agents. NSAIDs may partially antagonize the antihypertensive effects of these medications. Opioids may potentiate the hypotensive effect of these medications. There is a possible increased hypotensive effect with aspirin.

Pharmacology

These drugs decrease peripheral vascular tone by decreasing calcium influx in vascular smooth muscle. The antidysrhythmic effect is due primarily to decreasing the slow inward

---

Table 17.7

Vasodilator Used for Erectile Dysfunction: Dosage and Prescribing Information

Generic name	Brand name	Dosage range	Interactions with other drugs
Sildenafil	Viagra	25-100 mg/day	Erythromycin, ketaconazole and itraconazole may increase sildenafil plasma levels

Table 17.8

Calcium Channel Blockers: Dosage and Prescribing Information

Generic name	Brand name(s)	Dosage range	Interactions with other drugs
Bepridil	Bepadin	200-400 mg/day	Excessive use of epinephrine or levonordefrin in local anesthetic solutions may antagonize antihypertensive effects of these agents NSAIDs may partially antagonize antihypertensive effects of these medications Opioids may potentiate hypotensive effect of these agents Neuromuscular blockade may be intensified or prolonged
Diltiazem	Cardizem, Cardizem CD, Cardizem SR, Dilacor	**Oral, extended-release tablets:** 30-60 mg/day OR 20 mg bid **Oral, tablets:** 30-120 mg q 8 h	See note above
Felodipine	Renedil	5-20 mg/day	See note above
Flunarazine	Sibelium	10 mg/day	See note above
Isradipine	DynaCirc	2.5-10 mg q 12 h	See note above
Nicardipine	Cardene	20-40 mg q 8 h	See note above
Nifedipine	Adalat, Procardia; Apo-Nifed [CAN], Novo-Nifedin [CAN], Nu-Nifedin [CAN]	10-30 mg q 8 h	See note above
Nimodipine	Nimotop	60 mg q 4 h	See note above
Nisoldipine	Sular	10-60 mg/day	See note above
Verapamil	Calan, Calan SR, Isoptin, Verelan; Novo-Veramil [CAN], Nu-Verap [CAN]	120-480 mg/day	See note above

[CAN] indicates a drug available only in Canada.

Ca++ current in the cardiac conduction system. The agents also depress force and rate of cardiac contraction to various degrees. For instance, verapamil and diltiazem control heart rate more effectively than nifedipine, which acts more prominently by direct vasodilation.

Drugs Acting on the Renin-Angiotensin System

These drugs are considered first-line agents in the control of hypertension. By blocking the effects of angiotensin II, a potent vasoconstrictor, these agents decrease high blood pressure in many patients. See Table 17.9 for basic information on drugs acting on the renin-angiotensin system.

Special Dental Considerations

These agents may cause neutropenia or agranulocytosis. Consider medication-induced adverse effects if gingival bleeding or infection occurs. Angioneurotic edema may occur on the face, tongue or glottis. Coughing is a common side effect. Loss of taste has been reported, but rarely.

In addition, the dentist should follow the recommendations listed under Special Dental Considerations at the beginning of this chapter.

Drug Interactions of Dental Interest

Excessive use of epinephrine or levonordefrin in local anesthetic solutions may antagonize the antihypertensive effects of these agents. NSAIDs may partially antagonize the antihypertensive effects of these medications. Opioids may potentiate the hypotensive effect of these medications. Potassium-containing medications, such as penicillin G potassium administered IV, may exacerbate medication-induced hyperkalemia.

Laboratory Value Alterations

- Agranulocytosis and neutropenia may occur.

Pharmacology

Under normal conditions, the renin-angiotensin system provides for an increase in blood pressure when hypotension occurs. Renin released from the renal glomerulus leads to the formation of angiotensin I, which is converted to angiotensin II, primarily in the lung. Angiotensin II is a potent vasoconstrictor and also stimulates aldosterone release. The antihypertensive effect of these agents occurs when angiotensin II is blocked, either at the angiotensin II receptor or by decreased formation of angiotensin II itself. This latter effect occurs when angiotensin-converting enzyme (ACE) in the lung is inhibited, thus blocking the metabolism of angiotensin I to angiotensin

II. The term "ACE inhibitor" is therefore commonly used with these medications.

Centrally Acting Antihypertensive Agents

These drugs act in the central nervous system (CNS) to decrease peripheral sympathetic tone. See Table 17.10 for basic information on centrally acting antihypertensive agents.

Special Dental Considerations

A rebound hypertensive crisis may occur if patients abruptly stop taking drugs in this category prior to a dental appointment. Dental patients should be instructed to take their medications at the usual time irrespective of the time of their dental appointment.

These drugs may inhibit salivary flow. Parotid pain may occur.

In addition, the dentist should follow the recommendations listed under Special Dental Considerations at the beginning of this chapter.

Drug Interactions of Dental Interest

Excessive use of epinephrine or levonordefrin in local anesthetic solutions may antagonize the antihypertensive effects of these agents and produce a serious hypertensive crisis. NSAIDs may partially antagonize the antihypertensive effects of these medications. Opioids may potentiate the hypotensive and sedative effects of these medications. Other oral or IV sedative agents may be potentiated by these agents. There may be a decreased antihypertensive effect with tricyclic antidepressants. Methyldopa may increase the anticoagulant effect of coumarin anticoagulants.

Pharmacology

The mechanism of action of these agents is chiefly via a CNS α_2 agonist action. As the α_2 receptor decreases adrenergic tone, there is a decrease in sympathetic outflow. This causes a decrease in blood pressure and heart rate.

Table 17.9
Drugs Acting on the Renin-Angiotensin System: Dosage and Prescribing Information

Generic name	Brand name(s)	Dosage range	Interactions with other drugs
ACE inhibitors			
Benazepril	Lotensin	10-40 mg/day	Excessive use of epinephrine or levo-nordefrin in local anesthetic solutions may antagonize antihypertensive effects of these agents NSAIDs may partially antagonize antihypertensive effects of these agents Opioids may potentiate hypotensive effect of these agents Medications containing potassium, such as IV penicillin G potassium, may exacerbate medication-induced hyperkalemia
Captopril	Capoten	12.5-50 mg q 8 h	See note above
Enalapril	Vasotec	5-40 mg/day	See note above
Fosinopril	Monopril	10-80 mg/day	See note above
Lisinopril	Prinivil, Zestril	10-80 mg/day	See note above
Moexipril	Univasc	7.5-30 mg/day	See note above
Perindopril	Aceon	4-8 mg/day	See note above
Quinapril	Accupril	10-80 mg/day	See note above
Ramipril	Altace	2.5-20 mg/day	See note above
Trandolapril	Mavik	1-8 mg/day	See note above
Angiotensin II receptor antagonist			
Candesartan	Atacand	16-32 mg/day	See note above
Eprosartan	Teveten	400-800 mg/day	See note above
Irbesartan	Avapro	150-300 mg/day	See note above
Losartan	Cozaar	25-100 mg/day	See note above
Telmisartan	Micardis	40-80 mg/day	See note above
Valsartan	Diovan	80-320 mg/day	See note above

Table 17.10

Centrally Acting Antihypertensive Agents: Dosage and Prescribing Information

Generic name	Brand name(s)	Dosage range	Interactions with other drugs
Clonidine	Catapress, Catapres TTS, Dixarit	**Oral—maintenance:** 0.2-0.6 mg q 6 h **Transdermal:** 0.1-0.3 mg/day	Rebound hypertensive crisis may occur if patients abruptly stop taking these agents prior to a dental appointment Excessive use of epinephrine or levonordefrin in local anesthetic solutions may antagonize antihypertensive effects of these agents NSAIDs may partially antagonize antihypertensive effects of these agents Opioids may potentiate hypotensive and sedative effects of these agents Other oral or IV sedative agents may be potentiated by these agents
Guanabenz	Wytensin	4-16 mg q 12 h	See note above
Guanfacine	Tenex	1-3 mg/day	See note above
Methyldopa	Aldomet; Apo-Methyldopa [CAN], Dopamet [CAN]	250-1,000 mg q 8-12 h	See note above

[CAN] indicates a drug available only in Canada.

Neuronal Blocking or Depleting Agents

This diverse group of drugs is rarely prescribed today due to numerous undesirable side effects and the availability of other more efficacious agents. See Table 17.11 for basic information on neuronal blocking or depleting agents.

Special Dental Considerations

These drugs may inhibit salivary flow.

In addition, the dentist should follow the recommendations listed under Special Dental Considerations at the beginning of this chapter.

Drug Interactions of Dental Interest

Neuronal blocking or depleting agents can cause administered epinephrine or levonordefrin to have an exaggerated cardiovascular effect. Blood pressure and heart rate should be carefully monitored if local anesthetic solutions containing epinephrine are deemed essential. NSAIDs may partially antagonize the antihypertensive effects of these medications. Opioids may potentiate the hypotensive and sedative effects of these medications. Other oral or IV sedative agents may be potentiated by these agents. Phenothiazines may exhibit increased extrapyramidal reactions.

Pharmacology

These drugs act principally by depleting norepinephrine and other catecholamines from the adrenergic nerve endings. Therefore, decreases in heart rate, force of cardiac contraction and peripheral vascular resistance result. These drugs can have complex effects when initially administered.

Table 17.11

Neuronal Blocking or Depleting Agents: Dosage and Prescribing Information

Generic name	Brand name(s)	Dosage range	Interactions with other drugs
Deserpidine	Harmonyl	250-500 µg (0.25-0.5 mg)/day	Neuronal blocking or depleting agents can cause administered epinephrine to have an exaggerated cardiovascular effect
			Blood pressure and heart rate should be carefully monitored if local anesthetic solutions containing epinephrine are deemed essential
			NSAIDs may partially antagonize antihypertensive effects of these medications
			Opioids may potentiate hypotensive and sedative effects of these agents
			Effects of other oral or IV sedative agents may be potentiated by these agents
			Phenothiazines may produce increased extrapyramidal effects
Guanadrel	Hylorel	15-75 mg/day	See note above
Guanethidine	Ismelin	10-50 mg/day	See note above
Rauwolfia serpentina	Raudixin, Rauval, Rauverid, Wolfina	50-200 mg/day	See note above
Reserpine	Reserfia, Serpalan, Serpasil; Novoreserpine [CAN]	100-250 µg (0.1-0.25 mg)/day	See note above

[CAN] indicates a drug available only in Canada.

Anticholesterol Drugs

3-hydroxy-3-methylglutaryl coenzyme A (HMGCoA) reductase inhibitors are the primary drugs used to lower cholesterol, predominantly low-density lipoproteins (LDLs), also called "bad cholesterol." Drugs that lower LDLs can prevent the formation of, slow the progression of or decrease already-formed atherosclerotic plaques. This can lead to improved coronary blood flow and a decrease in morbidity and mortality associated with coronary artery disease.

Although not listed in detail in this text, resins (cholestyramine and colestipol), fibrates (clofibrate, gemfibrozil and fenofibrate) and niacin also may be of value, but they are more so in lowering triglyceride or increasing high-density lipoprotein (HDL) levels.

See Table 17.12 for dosage and prescribing information on anticholesterol drugs.

Special Dental Considerations

There are no specific dental considerations other than evaluating the overall cardiovascular risk in patients who are hypercholesteremic, as this indicates at least one risk factor for coronary artery disease.

Drug Interactions of Dental Interest

Use of erythromycin with lovastatin has been associated with increased risk of rhabdomyolysis and acute renal failure. Although this has not been reported for other HMGCoA reductase inhibitors, it is recommended that erythromycin not be given to patients taking any agent in this class.

Laboratory Value Alterations

- Levels of serum transaminase may increase.
- Creatinine kinase levels may increase, although this usually is not associated with myositis or rhabdomyolysis.

Pharmacology

The conversion of HMGCoA to mevalonate is the rate-limiting step in the synthesis of cholesterol, primarily in the liver. The inhibition of cholesterol synthesis by HMGCoA reductase inhibitors, which block this rate-limiting step, leads to upregulation of LDL receptors and a subsequent increase in degradation of LDLs. There also is a decrease in the synthesis of LDLs.

Adverse Effects

Table 17.13 lists adverse effects of cardiovascular medications.

Suggested Readings

Drugs for cardiac arrhythmias. Med Lett Drugs Ther 1991;33(846):55-60.

Follath F. Clinical pharmacology of antiarrhythmic drugs: variability of metabolism and dose requirements. J Cardiovasc Pharmacol 1991;17(Suppl 6):S74-6.

Friedman L, Schron E, Yusuf S. Risk-benefit assessment of antiarrhythmic drugs: an epidemiological perspective. Drug Saf 1991;6:323-31.

Kaplan NM, ed. Clinical hypertension. 6th ed. Baltimore: Williams & Wilkins; 1994.

Laragh JH, Brenner BM, eds. Hypertension: Pathology, diagnosis, and management. New York: Raven Press; 1990.

Muzyka BC, Glick M. The hypertensive dental patient. JADA 1997;128:1109-20.

Nichols C. Dentistry and hypertension. JADA 1997;128:1557-62.

Veterans Administration Cooperative Study Group on Antihypertensive Agents. Effects of treatment on morbidity in hypertension. JAMA 1967;202:1028-34.

Table 17.12

Anticholesterol Drugs: Dosage and Prescribing Information

Generic name	Brand name(s)	Dosage range	Interactions with other drugs
Atorvastatin	Lipitor	10-80 mg/day	Erythromycin may cause rhabdomyolysis and acute renal failure
Cerivastatin	Baycol	0.3 mg/day	See note above
Fluvastatin	Lescol	20-80 mg/day	See note above
Lovastatin	Mevacor	20-80 mg/day	See note above
Pravastatin	Pravachol	20-40 mg/day	See note above
Simvastatin	Zocor	20-80 mg/day	See note above

Table 17.13
Cardiovascular Drugs: Adverse Effects

Body system	Cardiac glycosides	Antianginal agents	Diuretics	Antihypertensive agents								
				Adrenergic blockers: β-blockers, labetalol	Adrenergic blockers: α-blockers	Direct-acting vasodilators	Vasodilator used for erectile dysfunction	Calcium channel blockers	ACE inhibitors	Centrally-acting antihypertensive agents	Neuronal blockers or depleters	Anticholesterol drugs
General	Allergic reaction	Allergic reaction	Allergic reaction	Allergic reaction	Allergic reaction	Allergic reaction lymphadenopathy, systemic lupus erythematosus	Allergic reaction to agent, flushing	Allergic reaction	Allergic reaction cough, Stevens-Johnson syndrome			Allergic reaction to agent
CV	Dysrhythmias, including ventricular fibrillation, bradycardia	Hypotension, tachycardia	Chest pain	Bradycardia, congestive heart failure, peripheral vascular insufficiency, dysrhythmias	Hypotension, tachycardia, palpitations, angina, edema	Angina, tachycardia, hypotension, sodium and water retention, edema	Hypotension, angina pectoris, dysrhythmia, syncope, myocardial ischemia, cardiac arrest	Angina, congestive heart failure, dysrhythmias, tachycardia, bradycardia, hypotension, edema	Angioedema, hypotension, tachycardia, chest pain	Palpitations, tachycardia, hypotension, congestive heart failure, water retention, Raynaud's phenomena	Angina, bradycardia, congestive heart failure, tachycardia, edema, hypotension	
CNS	Drowsiness, confusion, headache	Headache	Confusion, headache	Depression, confusion, dizziness, numbness, tingling of extremities and scalp, headache, nightmares, tiredness	Dizziness, headache, fatigue	Peripheral neuritis, headache, dizziness	Dizziness, neuropathy, parasthesias, tremor, vertigo, somnolence	Dizziness, drowsiness, anxiety, depression, insomnia, headache	Headache, nightmares	Depression, dizziness, nervousness, insomnia, headache, nightmares	Drowsiness, depression, weakness, fatigue, headache	Dizziness, headache, insomnia

System												
Endoc		Blurred vision, photophobia	Decreased libido	Decreased sexual ability	Priapism, impotence		Unstable diabetes, hyperglycemia, hyperuricemia		Impotence	Decreased libido	Difficulty in ejaculation, breast enlargement, impotence	
EENT		Blurred vision	Ototoxicity	Blurred vision		Nasal congestion, lacrimation	Abnormal vision, photosensitivity, blurred vision, nasal congestion, xerostomia			Dry eyes	Tinnitus, visual changes, diplopia, blurred vision, nasal stuffiness	Possible lens opacities
GI	Nausea, vomiting, loss of appetite, diarrhea, stomach pain	Nausea, vomiting	Stomach pain, nausea, vomiting, diarrhea, loss of appetite, cramps	Constipation, nausea, vomiting, stomach pain	Nausea, constipation	Anorexia, diarrhea, nausea, vomiting, constipation	Dyspepsia, esophagitis, diarrhea	Nausea, vomiting, diarrhea, stomach pain, constipation	Diarrhea, fatigue, nausea, bronchospasm	Nausea, vomiting, stomach cramps, constipation	Diarrhea, nausea, vomiting, constipation	Constipation, nausea, diarrhea, gas, heartburn, stomach pain
GU				Increased urination	Urinary frequency		UTI, priapism	Increased urination	Abnormal urination		Nocturia	Impotence

Continued on next page

Table 17.13 (cont.)

Cardiovascular Drugs: Adverse Effects

Body system	Cardiac glycosides	Antianginal agents	Diuretics	Antihypertensive agents								
				Adrenergic blockers: β-blockers, labetalol	Adrenergic blockers: α-blockers	Direct-acting vasodilators	Vasodilator used for erectile dysfunction	Calcium channel blockers	ACE inhibitors	Centrally acting antihypertensive agents	Neuronal blockers or depleters	Anticholesterol drugs
Hema			Rare leukopenia/agranulocytosis, thrombocytopenia (especially with loop diuretics), hyperuricemia, electrolyte imbalance	Leukopenia, thrombocytopenia	Lymphadenopathy	Blood dyscrasias	Anemia, leukopenia	Hyperkalemia	Neutropenia, agranulocytosis	Hyperglycemia	Thrombocytopenia and leukopenia with guanethidine, galactorrhea	
HB			Rare hepatic dysfunction	Hepatotoxicity		Abnormal liver function tests		Altered liver enzymes (dentist should/must request this information on lab values)	Pancreatitis			Acute pancreatitis, elevated transaminase levels

System											
Integ	Skin rash, flushing of face/neck, sweating, bluish extremities (may indicate overdose)	Increased sensitivity of skin to light			Allergic reaction, skin blisters	Sweating, urticaria		Skin rash	Itching, redness of skin, rash, sweating, alopecia	Skin rash, alopecia	Skin rash
Musc	Weakness		Back or joint pain			Myalgia, arthrosis	Arthritis	Joint pain		Muscle pain/tremor	Myalgia, arthrosis
Oral	Dry mouth, bluish lips (may indicate overdose)		Dry mouth, taste change	Dry mouth		Glossitis, stomatitis, gingivitis, xerostomia	Gingival enlargement, dry mouth	Loss of taste	Dry mouth, taste changes, parotid pain	Dry mouth	Glossitis, stomatitis, gingivitis, xerostomia
Renal		Nephrolith-iasis			Sodium and water retention, edema	Hyperurice-mia, periph-eral edema		Renal failure, nephrotic syndrome	Water retention		Hyperuricemia, peripheral edema
Resp			Broncho-spasm, shortness of breath, nasal congestion	Shortness of breath	Shortness of breath	Asthma, dyspnea, sinusitis, cough				Shortness of breath, bronchospasm	Asthma, dyspnea, sinusitis, cough

Chapter 18.

Respiratory Drugs

Martha Somerman, D.D.S., Ph.D.; Jarvis T. Chan, D.D.S., Ph.D.

A significant number of people in the general population have respiratory disorders that require the use of medications. Bronchial asthma is the most common respiratory disease the dentist encounters; therefore, he or she should be particularly familiar with drugs taken by patients with such conditions.

Asthma is characterized physiologically by reversible airway obstruction that results from constriction of the bronchial and bronchiolar muscles and hypersecretion of viscous mucus. Factors that can precipitate an asthmatic attack include respiratory infection, physical exertion, exposure to cold air or irritating gases, allergy and stress.

There are three major approaches to the treatment of asthma:

- use of anti-inflammatory drugs to reduce symptoms and bronchial hyperactivity;
- use of agents that reverse or inhibit bronchoconstriction;
- avoidance of causative factors.

Causative factors include indoor allergens and stress; thus, the dentist must be sensitive to the possibility of these factors provoking an asthmatic attack in a susceptible person while he or she is in the dental office. If a patient is using metered-dose inhalants, these inhalants should be readily accessible at his or her dental appointment.

The information in this chapter will provide summary data on special dental considerations for, use of, interactions of, adverse effects of and contraindications for drugs taken by and potentially given to people who have respiratory conditions.

When treating a patient with a respiratory condition, the dentist must determine the nature of the condition and which, if any, drugs the patient is taking for these conditions. The American Society of Anesthesiologists classification of asthma is provided in Table 18.1.

Glucocorticoids are covered in more detail in Chapter 6, while β-blockers are covered in Chapter 17.

Tables 18.2-18.5 provide general information on drugs used for respiratory diseases, including indications, typical dosage ranges and interactions with other drugs.

Special Dental Considerations

When it comes to treating patients with respiratory conditions, practitioners should keep the following important points in mind.

First, chronic obstructive pulmonary disease (COPD) is a respiratory disease of major medical concern; bronchial obstruction in this disease is irreversible, resulting in severe infections, heart disease and respiratory failure. Respiratory conditions and the use of inhalants can result in decreased salivary flow and associated problems, including caries and candidiasis. Therefore, patients should use fluoride rinses and should be observed for the need to use antifungal agents.

Reduction of stress may require the use of sedatives, especially when complex procedures are being performed. Stress reduction methods, including medications, may be required to prevent an asthmatic attack.

NSAIDs and aspirin are contraindicated in patients with respiratory conditions, as they

Table 18.1

American Society of Anesthesiologists Classification: Asthma

ASA class*	Description	Dental treatment modifications
II	Typical extrinsic or intrinsic asthma • Easily managed • Characterized by infrequent episodes • Does not require emergency care or hospitalization	Reduce stress as needed Determine triggering factors Avoid triggering factors Have bronchodilators available during dental treatment
III	Exercise-induced asthma • Often accompanied by fear • Patient with Class III asthma usually has history of emergency care or hospitalization	Follow ASA II modifications Administer sedation-inhalation with nitrous oxide, oxygen or oral benzodiazepines, if indicated
IV	Chronic asthma • Signs and symptoms of asthma present at rest	Obtain medical consultation before beginning treatment Provide only emergency care in office Defer elective care until respiratory status improves or until patient can be treated in controlled environment

Adapted with permission of the publisher from Malamed SF. Medical emergencies in the dental office. 4th ed. St. Louis: Mosby; 1993:198. Copyright © 1993 C.V. Mosby Co.
* Class I represents a healthy person with no asthma.

may prompt an asthmatic attack.

A semisupine chair position should be used for patients with respiratory diseases, especially for patients with COPD. To prevent orthostatic hypotension, patients should sit upright for a few minutes before being dismissed.

Inhalants that patients are using should be easily accessible during the dental appointment.

With patients receiving chronic steroid therapy, there is an enhanced concern about stress situations—such as the possibility of adrenal crisis—as well as increased susceptibility to infections.

With patients using β-adrenergic agonists, there is a concern about cardiovascular side effects. Most of the drugs in this category used to treat asthma are selective β_2 adrenergic agonists and thus act as bronchodilators. However, they do have some β_1 side effects, so there is a need to be aware of possible cardiovascular side effects (for example, tachycardia and hypertension).

Drug Interactions of Dental Interest
Avoid drugs that may precipitate an asthmatic attack: aspirin, NSAIDs and narcotics.

Special Patients
As a rule, inhalants are not recommended for use in children aged < 5 y. Also, these drugs may have hepatic and renal side effects that often are of more concern with children and older adults.

Adverse Effects, Precautions and Contraindications
Table 18.6 describes adverse effects associated with steroids and β_2 adrenergic blockers (whether taken orally or inhaled); Table 18.7 describes precautions and contraindications.

Pharmacology

Inhibitors of Chemical Mediators/ Anti-inflammatory Drugs
Cromolyn sulfate
Cromolyn sulfate has no direct bronchodilating activity, so it is active only when given by

Table 18.2

Inhibitors of Chemical Mediators/Anti-Inflammatory Drugs:
Dosage and Prescribing Information

Generic name	Brand name(s)	Indications/uses	Dosage range	Interactions with other drugs
Cromolyn				
Disodium cromoglycate/ cromolyn	Intal	Chronic asthma Not for acute attacks Prophylactic for exercise, cold air, environmental pollutants	Usually 2 puffs qid by metered-dose inhaler	None listed
Nedocromil sodium	Tilade; Rynacrom [CAN]	See note above	See note above	None listed
Glucocorticoids (inhalants)				
Beclomethasone dipropionate	Beclovent, Vanceril	Chronic asthma Severe asthma, rhinitis Chronic obstructive pulmonary disease, possibly in combination with β_2 adrenergic agents Not for acute treatment	**Inhalation:** Varies depending on extent of disease; usually 2 puffs tid-qid or 4 puffs bid Tablets/liquid also available	In general, more concerns of interactions with use of systemic glucocorticoids (see Chapter 6, Table 6.1 for details); for example, possible interactions with acetaminophen, amphotericin B or carbonic anhydrase inhibitors, anabolic steroids, antacids, antidiabetic agents, NSAIDs, digitalis glycosides, hepatic enzyme-inducing agents, some β_2-adrenergic agonists
Budesonide	Pulmicort [CAN]	See note above	0.5-1 mg via nebulizer bid	See note above
Flunisolide	AeroBid; Bronalide [CAN]	See note above	2 puffs bid	See note above
Triamcinolone acetonide	Azmacort	See note above	2 puffs tid-qid	See note above

[CAN] indicates a drug available only in Canada.

Table 18.3

Bronchodilators: Dosage and Prescribing Information

Generic name	Brand name(s)	Indications/uses	Dosage range	Interactions with other drugs
		β-adrenergic agonists		
Albuterol	Proventil, Ventolin; Novosalomol [CAN]	Usually, for acute situations with asthma and bronchospasm and to control acute symptoms, but long-acting β_2 selective agonists, such as salmeterol, are used for maintenance, often in combination with inhaled steroid Epinephrine compounds have both β_1 & β_2 agonist activity, thus use for bronchodilation is limited	**Inhalation, metered-dose inhaler:** 2-3 puffs q 3-4 h, not to exceed 12/day	Cardiovascular effects may be potentiated in patients receiving MAO inhibitors, tricyclic depressants, sympathomimetic agents, inhaled anesthetics
Bitolterol	Tornalate	See note above	See note above	See note above
Epinephrine/ epinephrine bitartrate/epinephrine HCI	Bronkaid Mist, Epi Pen, Epi Pen Jr., Medihaler-EpiAdrenalin, Primatene Mist Asthma Haler, Sus-Phrine, Sus-Phrine (parenteral); Vaponefrin[CAN]	See note above	See note above	See note above
Isoetharine HCl/isoetharine mesylate	Arm-a-Med, Bronkometer, Bronkosol, Day-lute, Dispos-a-Med, Dry-dose, Isoetharine	See note above	**Inhalation, metered-dose inhaler:** 1-2 puffs q 4 h **Solution:** 2.5-10 mg, usually not more than q 4 h **Syrup:** 2-4 mg tid or qid prn	See note above
Metaproterenol sulfate	Alupent, Metaprel	See note above	**Inhalation, metered-dose inhaler:** 2-3 puffs q 3-4 h, not to exceed 12/day	See note above
Pirbuterol acetate	Maxair	See note above	See note above	See note above
Salmeterol	Serevent	See note above	See note above	See note above
Terbutaline	Brethaire, Brethine, Bricanyl	See note above	See note above	See note above

[CAN] indicates a drug available only in Canada.

Continued on next page

Table 18.3 (cont.)

Bronchodilators: Dosage and Prescribing Information

Generic name	Brand name(s)	Indications/uses	Dosage range	Interactions with other drugs
Xanthines				
Aminophylline (theophylline ethylenediamine-xanthine), dyphylline, phyllocontin, somophyllin, somophyllin - DF; parolon [CAN]	Dilor, Dyflex, Lu Fyllin, Neothylline; Protophyline [CAN]	Usually chronic asthma and in combination with other asthmatic agents	**Inhalation, metered-dose inhaler:** 2-3 puffs q 3-4 h, not to exceed 12/day	Can alter metabolism of many other drugs and also other drugs may alter metabolism **Barbiturates, carba-mazepine, phenytoin, ketoconazole:** Decrease xanthine activity **Benzodiazepines:** Sedative effects may be decreased **Erythromycin, clin-damycin, ciprofloxacin, alcohol:** Decrease xanthine clearance **Halothane & CNS stimulants:** Increased risk of cardiac dysrhythmia
Theophylline	Choledyl, Oxitriphylline, Slo-Phyllin, Theo-24	See note above	See note above	See note above
Theophylline, theophylline sodium glycinate	Aquaphyllin, Bronkodyl, Quibron-T, Respbid, Slo-bid, Slo-Phyllin, Theoclear, Theodur Sprinkle, Theolair, Theospan-SR, Theostat, Theovent, Uniphyl	See note above	See note above	See note above

[CAN] indicates a drug available only in Canada.

Table 18.4

Anticholinergic Drugs: Dosage and Prescribing Information

Generic name	Brand name(s)	Indications/uses	Dosage range	Interactions with other drugs
Ipratropium bromide	Atrovent	Chronic obstructive pulmonary disease (not approved by FDA for asthma, but has proven useful in older, nonatopic patients who have chronic obstruction of airflow)	2-4 puffs tid/qid	Increased effects of systemic anti-cholinergic drugs

Table 18.5
Evolving Respiratory Therapies: Dosage and Prescribing Information

Generic name	Brand name(s)	Indications/uses	Dosage range	Interactions with other drugs
Allergen avoidance/ chemicals to denature allergens	generic	Prophylaxis	Not established	Not established
DNase inhibitors (Dornase Alfa)	Pulmozyme	For treatment of cystic fibrosis to reduce respiratory infection and improve pulmonary function	**Inhalation, nebulizer:** 2.5-5 mg/day Dose for children < age 5 y not established	Has not been studied
Immunosuppressive agents such as methotrexate	Methotrexate	Prophylaxis	Not labeled	Hepatotoxic drugs alter metabolism of methotrexate
Leukotriene antagonists and inhibitors	Zafirlukast (Accolate), Zileuton (Zyflo)	Prophylaxis and maintenance treatment of asthma	**Accolate:** 20 mg tid **Zyflo:** 600 mg qid	Zileuton metabolized by P450 system, thus will alter metabolism of other drugs including theophylline (decreased clearance, serum levels); warfarin (increased serum levels); propranolol (increased serum levels) Patients should be monitored for hepatic toxicity

inhalation. It is thought to act by stabilizing mast cells. In addition, cromolyn also may inhibit mast cell release of histamine, leukotrienes and other inflammatory mediators and inhibit calcium influx into mast cells. The result is decreased stimuli for bronchospasm. However, as it has no bronchodilating activity, cromolyn is useful only for prophylactic treatment and not for acute situations.

Glucocorticoids
See Chapter 6 for details.

Bronchodilators
β-adrenergic agonists
β-adrenergic agonists are used for treatment of acute bronchospasm. Ideal drugs act predominantly on β_2 adrenergic receptors and stimulate dilation of bronchial smooth muscles. This relaxes the airway's smooth muscle. β-adrenergic agents also inhibit release of substances from mast cells and thus prevent bronchoconstriction. Most adrenergic drugs have some β_1 activity; therefore, there is a need to monitor patients for cardio-

vascular effects, including increased force and rate of cardiac contraction. This is especially true of epinephrine. Note: Epinephrine usually is used for emergency situations such as rapid/acute asthmatic attack, in which case 0.2-0.5 mL of 1:1,000 solution is administered subcutaneously or intramuscularly.

Intramuscular injection of epinephrine into the buttocks should be avoided, because it could cause gas gangrene. The subcutaneous route is recommended for bronchodilatory purposes; for anaphylactic reactions, either the subcutaneous or the intramuscular route could be used.

Xanthines

Xanthines relax bronchial smooth muscle (in both acute and chronic situations, and often in combination with other drugs). Several mechanisms for this activity have been proposed, but none have been definitively proved.

These mechanisms include inhibition of phosphodiesterase, mobilization of calcium pools, inhibition of prostaglandin activity and decreased uptake of catecholamines.

Anticholinergic agents

Anticholinergic agents act on receptors to prevent smooth muscle contraction. They are marketed for inhalant treatment of chronic obstructive pulmonary disease, but this use is still under investigation.

Evolving Respiratory Therapies

New therapies continue to be targeted at decreasing inflammation. DNase inhibitors are thought to act by breaking up long extracellular DNA into smaller fragments. DNA is considered to contribute to thick sputum, especially in patients with cystic fibrosis. Leukotriene antagonists and inhibitors decrease leukotriene levels and thus decrease

Table 18.6

Respiratory Drugs: Adverse Effects

Body system	Cromolyn	Corticosteroids	Adrenergic agents	Xanthines	Anticholinergic agents
General	Minimal adverse effects	Owing to too-quick withdrawal: flare-up of underlying disease; acute adrenal insufficiency; also (rarely) pseudotumor cerebri	Many side effects related to ß₁ effect on cardiovascular system, especially with epinephrine	Flushing	In high environmental temperatures, risk of rare increase in body temperature; geriatric or debilitated patients may respond with excitement, agitation, drowsiness or confusion
CV		*Hypertension, cardiovascular collapse*	Palpitation, tachycardia, hypotension, angina, dysrhythmias (especially with epinephrine)	Palpitation, sinus tachycardia, hypotension, other dysrhythmias	Palpitation (rare)
CNS		Behavioral disturbances (rare)	Tremors, anxiety, insomnia, restlessness, hallucinations, flushing, irritability	Anxiety, restlessness, insomnia, dizziness, convulsions, headaches, light-headedness, muscle twitching	Anxiety, dizziness, headache

Italics indicate information of major clinical significance.

Continued on next page

Table 18.6 (cont.)

Respiratory Drugs: Adverse Effects

Body system	Cromolyn	Corticosteroids	Adrenergic agents	Xanthines	Anticholinergic agents
EENT		Cataracts, glaucoma, blurred vision	Dry nose, irritation of nose and throat		Blurred vision (rare)
Endoc		Growth arrest, hyperglycemia, suppression of HPA			
GI	Nausea, vomiting, anorexia	Increased GI upset, nausea, vomiting, peptic ulcers	Heartburn, nausea, vomiting, diarrhea	Nausea, vomiting, anorexia, diarrhea, dyspepsia, gastric distress	Nausea, vomiting, cramps
GU	Urinary frequency, dysuria		Difficulty in urination		
Hema		*Increased susceptibility to infection*			
HB				Hepatotoxicity	
Integ	Rash, urticaria, angioedema	Acne, poor or delayed wound healing, hirsutism, striae, ecchymoses		Urticaria	Rash (rare)
Metab		Catabolism, fat redistribution			
Musc	Joint pain/ swelling	Fractures, osteoporosis, muscular weakness	Muscle cramps		
Oral	Irritation, dryness of throat, burning mouth, bitter taste, possible candidiasis	Dry mouth, poor or delayed wound healing, petechiae, candidiasis	Taste changes, xerostomia, discoloration of teeth	Bitter taste, xerostomia	Xerostomia, stomatitis, metallic taste
Renal		Fluid, electrolyte abnormalities			
Resp			Bronchospasm	Increased rate of respiration	Cough, worsening of symptoms

Italics indicate information of major clinical significance.

Table 18.7

Respiratory Drugs: Precautions and Contraindications

Drug	Precautions and contraindications
Adrenergic agonists	Concern about possible β_1 side effects related to effects on heart in patients with tachydysrhythmias, hypertension, severe cardiac disease
	Some agents may appear in breast milk
	Should be used cautiously with patients who have hyperthyroidism, diabetes mellitus, prostatic hypertrophy, narrow-angle glaucoma, seizures
	Pregnancy risk category: C
	Epinephrine: *Contraindicated* in patients taking MAO inhibitors
Anticholinergic agents	Should be used cautiously with patients who have narrow-angle glaucoma, prostatic hypertrophy, bladder neck obstruction
	Pregnancy risk category: B
	Contraindicated for children < age 12 y
Corticosteroids	Possible bacterial/fungal infections
	Consider using semisupine position while carrying out dental treatment
	May require stress reduction
	Concern about possible adrenal crisis for patients taking high doses and/or receiving chronic therapy
	Pregnancy risk category: C
	Contraindicated for children < age 12 y
	Contraindicated in acute situations
Cromolyn	Should be used cautiously in lactating women and in patients with hepatic disease
	Pregnancy risk category: B
	Contraindicated for children < age 5 y
	Contraindicated in acute situations
Xanthines	Should be used cautiously in pediatric and elderly patients and patients who have congestive heart failure, cor pulmonale, hepatic disease, active peptic ulcer, diabetes, hyperthyroidism, hypertension, glaucoma, prostatic hypertrophy, tachydysrhythmias
	Pregnancy risk category: C

Italics indicate information of major clinical significance.

inflammatory activity of mast cells. In the area of allergen avoidance, there have been efforts to develop products that can control dust-mite allergens and that can denature allergens.

Suggested Readings

Abramowicz M, ed. Drugs for asthma. Med Lett Drugs Ther 1996;37(939):1-4.

Barnes PJ, Roger IW, Thomson NC, eds. Asthma: basic mechanisms and clinical management. 2nd ed. New York: Academic Press; 1992.

Call RS, Platt-Mills TAE. Drugs used in asthma and obstructive lung disease. In: Brody TM, Larner J, Minneman KP, Neu HC, eds. Human pharmacology: molecular to clinical. 2nd ed. St. Louis: Mosby; 1994:775-86.

Malamed SF. Medical emergencies in the dental office. 4th ed. St. Louis: Mosby; 1993:194-207.

Chapter 19

Gastrointestinal Drugs

B. Ellen Byrne, R.Ph., D.D.S., Ph.D.

"Heartburn" occurs daily in approximately 7% of the population. It is a symptom of reflux esophagitis, an irritation and inflammation of the esophageal mucosa caused by the reflux of acidic stomach or duodenal contents retrograde into the esophagus. Reflux esophagitis is commonly seen in gastroesophageal reflux disease (GERD) and peptic ulcer disease (PUD), which are considered together in this chapter because the same drugs are used to treat them. Other symptoms associated with GERD include regurgitation, dysphagia, bleeding and chest pain. Regurgitation is the most specific symptom of GERD and may result in morning hoarseness, laryngitis and pulmonary aspiration.

PUD is a heterogeneous group of disorders characterized by ulceration of the upper gastrointestinal tract. Peptic ulcer disease can occur at any place in the gastrointestinal (GI) tract that is exposed to the erosive action of pepsin and acid. It can be exacerbated by stress, alcohol, cigarette smoking, some foods and aspirin and aspirinlike drugs. Medical therapy for GERD and PUD consists mainly of neutralizing the stomach contents or reducing gastric acid secretions and using promotility agents to enhance peristalsis. Infections with a bacterium, *Helicobacter pylori*, also have been implicated in the pathogenesis of PUD, and eradication of this organism with antibiotics, bismuth compounds and an antisecretory agent has been shown to alter the natural course of peptic ulcer disease. Although the optimal regimen

to eradicate *H. pylori* and cure PUD has not been established, a number of combinations are effective. An antisecretory drug often is added to achieve more rapid relief from ulcer symptoms as well as ulcer healing. Antibiotics used in PUD therapy include amoxicillin, clarithromycin, metronidazole and tetracycline. The antisecretory drugs include H_2 receptor antagonists such as cimetidine and proton pump inhibitors such as omeprazole. Bismuth subsalicylate, the third drug in this triad, is found in Pepto-Bismol.

Diarrhea is usually caused by infection, toxins or drugs. Antidiarrheal agents can be sold over the counter or by prescription only. Virally or bacterially induced diarrhea is usually transient and requires only a clear liquid diet and increased fluid intake. Antimicrobial therapy may be indicated. Intravenous fluids may be required if dehydration occurs.

Drug- or toxin-induced diarrhea is best treated by discontinuing the causative agent when possible. Chronic diarrhea may be caused by laxative abuse, lactose intolerance, inflammatory bowel disease, malabsorption syndromes, endocrine disorders or irritable bowel syndrome. Treatment of chronic diarrhea should be aimed at correcting the cause of diarrhea rather than alleviating the symptoms.

"Gastroparesis" is the term for disorders causing gastric stasis. Nausea, vomiting, bloating, fullness and early satiety are signs of gastroparesis. Treatment is aimed at accelerating gastric emptying. This condition is often associated with diabetes.

Crohn's disease and ulcerative colitis are considered together because the same drugs are used to treat these disorders. Crohn's disease is a chronic inflammatory disease that can affect any part of the gastrointestinal system, from mouth to anus. The etiology is unknown. The most common symptoms are abdominal pain and diarrhea. Perirectal fissure with sinus formation and strictures is common.

Ulcerative colitis is an inflammatory disease of the gastrointestinal tract that is limited to the colon and rectum. Typically, patients with ulcerative colitis present with bloody diarrhea. The disease primarily affects young adults. The etiology is unknown. Management of both Crohn's disease and ulcerative colitis is aimed at decreasing the inflammation and providing symptomatic relief.

Nausea and vomiting usually are self-limiting events without serious sequelae. Protracted vomiting may result in dehydration, malnutrition, metabolic alkalosis, hyponatremia, hypokalemia and hypochloremia. Infants and children are at greatest risk.

Nausea and vomiting may occur in patients with inferior myocardial infarction or diabetic ketoacidosis, Addisonian crisis, acute pancreatitis or acute appendicitis.

Drug-induced nausea and vomiting are common in cancer chemotherapy. However, numerous other drugs—such as narcotics, antibiotics (erythromycin, quinolones, flucytosine, nitrofurantoin and tetracyclines), digoxin and theophylline—also may cause nausea and vomiting.

Viral gastroenteritis is the most common cause of nausea and vomiting. Bacterial infections, motion sickness and pregnancy are other frequently encountered etiologies of nausea and vomiting.

Treatment of nausea and vomiting can include removal or treatment of the underlying cause. Antiemetic therapy is indicated in patients with electrolyte disturbances secondary to vomiting, severe anorexia or weight loss. Antiemetic drugs are available over the counter and by prescription. If a patient is unable to retain oral medication, rectal and injectable routes of administration may be preferable. Many classes of drugs have been used to treat nausea and vomiting, including antihistamines, anticholinergics, seratonin antagonists, dopamine antagonists, phenothiazines, cannabinoids and butyrophenones.

Antidiarrheal Agents

Special Dental Considerations

There are no contraindications to the dental treatment of patients with diarrhea.

Most acute diarrhea is self-limiting. The opioids and anticholinergics used to treat diarrhea produce xerostomia; therefore, meticulous oral hygiene should be stressed. These drugs also produce drowsiness and this effect is additive with other CNS depressants, thereby producing greater drowsiness.

Drug Interactions of Dental Interest

Drugs used to treat diarrhea include opioids and absorbents. Drug interactions of concern with opioids (narcotics) would occur if the patient took another CNS depressant drug, such as alcohol, antidepressants, antianxiety agents, anticholinergics, antihistamines or barbiturates. This combination of drugs may seriously increase the side effect of either drug.

Adsorbent drugs such as bismuth salts and cholestyramine can bind with various drugs resulting in decreased adsorption of the drug and a decreased therapeutic response. If these drugs must be taken together it is best to space dosing by 6 h.

See Table 19.1 for general information on antidiarrheal agents.

Pharmacology

Antidiarrheal agents can be divided into antibiotic and nonantibiotic drugs. Antibiotics

Table 19.1

Antidiarrheal Agents: Dosage and Prescribing Information

Generic name	Brand name(s)	Dosage range (daily)	Interactions with other drugs
Adsorbents			
Bismuth subsalicylate*	Bismatrol Extra Strength, Pepto-Bismol, Pepto-Bismol Maximum Strength	524-4,200 mg	**Decreased effects:** Tetracyclines, uricosurics **Increased effects:** Aspirin, warfarin, anticoagulants, antidiabetic agents, oral or insulin
Cholestyramine	Questran, Questran Light	4-24 g	Concurrent use of cholestyramine may decrease absorption of fat-soluble vitamins, digoxin, diuretics, penicillin G, tetracyclines, coumadin, anticoagulants, vancomycin, thyroid hormones, phenylbutazine
Kaolin/pectin	Kaopectate, Kao-Span, Kapectolin, K-P	1.2-9 g; 60-120 mL after each loose bowel movement	Decreased absorption of orally administered clindamycin, tetracycline, penicillamine, digoxin, anticholinergics, antidyskinetics, lincomycins, loxapine, phenothiazines, thioxanthenes
Opioids			
Codeine	generic	60-120 mg	Increased effects with CNS depressants
Diphenoxylate HCl and atropine sulfate	Lomotil, Lofene, Logen, Locomot, Lonox, VI-Atro	15-20 mg; maintenance: 5 mg	Increases effects with CNS depressants, anticholinergics May cause drowsiness Avoid alcoholic beverages May suppress respiration in elderly, very ill, or patients with respiratory problems
Loperamide	Imodium A-D, Kaopectate II, Maalox Anti-Diarrheal, Pepto Diarrhea Control; Diarr-Eze [CAN]	4-16 mg	Concurrent use with opioid analgesic may increase risk of severe constipation
Paregoric	generic	5-40 mL (equivalent to 2-16 mg of anhydrous morphine)	At high doses, produces effects of opioids—dizziness, faintness, lightheadedness, antidiuretic effect, CNS effects, hypotension, ureteral spasm, xerostomia

[CAN] indicates a drug available only in Canada.
* Patients allergic to aspirin would be allergic to this drug as well.

are the mainstay of treatment of acute bacterial diarrhea. Whenever possible, antibiotics should be directed toward specific microorganisms either identified by culture or clinically suspected.

There are many commercial preparations sold for symptomatic relief of diarrhea. Controlled clinical trials have not proven the safety and effectiveness of most of them.

Adsorbents have been shown to increase stool consistency but do not decrease stool water content.

Anticholinergics relieve cramps by reducing contractile activity but have no effect on diarrhea.

Bismuth subsalicylate binds toxins and prevents bacteria from attaching to intestinal epithelium.

Cholestyramine has been shown to effectively bind *Clostridium difficile* toxins and perhaps other bacterial toxins.

The opioids have a profound effect on motility. These agents are generally contraindicated in dysentery.

In general, these nonspecific antidiarrheal agents should not be used as a substitute for oral rehydration and directed antibiotics.

Crohn's Disease and Ulcerative Colitis Drugs

Special Dental Considerations

There are no contraindications to the dental treatment of patients with Crohn's disease. The leukopenic and thrombocytopenic effects of sulfasalazine may increase the incidence of certain microbial infections, delay healing and increase gingival bleeding. If a patient has leukopenia or thrombocytopenia, dental treatment should be deferred until laboratory counts have returned to normal. Patients treated with glucocorticoids are likely to have a decreased resistance to infection and a poor wound healing response. Actual and potential sources of infection in the mouth

should be treated promptly. If surgical procedures are necessary, they should be as atraumatic, conservative and aseptic as possible. Prophylactic antibiotic coverage should be considered in most cases. Adrenal suppression owing to the administration of glucocorticoids is also a consideration. Depending on the dose and length of treatment, the patient may require an increased dose of glucocorticoids before undergoing stressful dental treatment.

For patients with ulcerative colitis, use of antibiotics may aggravate the problem. Antibiotics most often associated with ulcerative colitis are broad-spectrum penicillins.

Drug Interactions of Dental Interest

See Table 19.2 for general information on Crohn's disease and ulcerative colitis drugs.

Pharmacology

Crohn's disease is a chronic inflammatory condition of the gastrointestinal tract. Current therapy is directed at reducing inflammation and providing systematic relief. Initial treatment includes sulfasalazine antibiotics and nutritional support. Sulfasalazine (through its active component 5-aminosalicylic acid [5-ASA]) exerts an anti-inflammatory effect on the colon. Metronidazole is most commonly used and likely functions by reducing bacterial endotoxin and granuloma formation.

Second-line therapy includes the use of glucocorticoids for reduction of inflammation followed by the use of immunomodulating drugs, such as azothioprine, which also reduce inflammation.

Gastric Motility Disorder (Gastroparesis) Drugs

Special Dental Considerations

There are no contraindications to the dental treatment of patients with gastroparesis.

Table 19.2

Crohn's Disease and Ulcerative Colitis Drugs: Dosage and Prescribing Information

Generic name	Brand name(s)	Dosage range (daily)	Interactions with other drugs
Antibiotics			
Metronidazole	Flagyl, Metric 21, Protostat, generic; Novo-Nidazol [CAN], Trikacide [CAN]	1,500-2,000 mg	**Antabuse reaction:** Alcohol and alcohol-containing products Potentiates effects of anticoagulants Concurrent use of cimetadine may result in decreased serum metronidazole concentrations Should not be used concurrently with or 2 w after administration of disulfiram in alcoholic patients; may result in confusion and psychotic reactions
Bowel disease suppressant			
Sulfasalazine	Azulfidine; Salazopyrin [CAN]	1-4 g; maintenance 2 g	Increases half-life of oral hypoglycemics (chlorpropamide, acetohexamide), anticoagulants, anticonvulsants, hemolytics, hepatotoxic medications, methotrexate, phenylbutazone, sulfin pyrazone
Glucocorticoids			
Prednisone	**Syrup:** Liquid Pred **Tablets:** Meticorten, Orasone, Deltasone, Predicen-M, Sterapred, Sterapred DS	5-60 mg up to 250 mg	Decreases effect of salicylates Decreased effect with barbiturates, phenytoin, ritampin
Immunosuppressants			
Azathioprine	Imuran	1-5 mg/kg/day **Initial dose:** Up to 2.5 mg/kg/day **Maintenance dose:** Reduced from initial dose to minimum effective dose	Allopurinol increases azathioprine activity and toxicity Concurrent administration with immuno-suppressants may increase risk of infection and development of neoplasms Vaccines should not be administered for 3-12 mo after use

[CAN] indicates a drug available only in Canada.

Table 19.3

Gastric Motility Disorder (Gastroparesis) Drugs: Dosage and Prescribing Information

Generic name	Brand name(s)	Dosage range (daily)	Interactions with other drugs
Cisapride	Propulsid; Prepulsid [CAN]	60 mg q day (20 mg tid)	Because of increased gastrointestinal mobility and decreased gastric emptying time, absorption of oral medicaments from the stomach may be decreased, while absorption from the small intestine may be enhanced
			Decreased effect: anticholinergics
			Contraindicated for concomitant use with *clarithromycin, erythromycin,* troleandomycin, *fluconazole,* itraconazole, *ketoconazole, miconazole,* nefazodone, indinavir and ritonavir; potentially fatal owing to increased plasma concentrations of cisapride
Metoclopramide HCl	**Syrup:** Reglan, generic **Tablets:** Clopra, Octamide, Reclomide, Reglan, generic	40 mg q day (10 mg qid)	Because of increased gastrointestinal mobility and decreased gastric emptying time, absorption of oral medications from stomach may be decreased, while absorption from small intestine may be enhanced
			Enhanced CNS depression with opiate analgesics and alcohol

[CAN] indicates a drug available only in Canada.
Italics indicate information of major clinical significance.

Drug Interactions of Dental Interest

Drugs which treat gastroparesis increase gastrointestinal mobility and decrease gastric emptying time. Oral absorption from the stomach may be decreased while absorption from the small intestine may be enhanced.

Cisapride is a gastrointestinal promotility agent that enhances the release of acetylcholine in the myenteric plexus. This action increases gastrointestinal motility and accelerates gastric emptying of both liquids and solids. Serious cardiac dysrhythmias—including ventricular tachycardia, ventribular fibrillation, torsades de pointes and Q-T prolongation—have been reported in patients taking cisapride concomitantly with other drugs that inhibit CYP3A4, the enzyme that metabolizes cisapride. This interaction results in increased cisapride plasma concentrations with possible cardiotoxicity. In addi-

tion, concomitant use with grapefruit juice should be avoided, as the juice increases cisapride's bioavailability.

Cisapride is contraindicated for concomitant use with the macrolide antibiotics, antidysrhythmic agents, nonsedating antihistamines, azole antifungal agents, carbonic anhydrase inhibitors, histamine H_2 antagonists, loop diuretics, phenothiazines, protease inhibitors, tetracyclic antidepressants, thiazide diuretics, tricyclic antidepressants, bepridil, diltiazem, mibefradil and nefazodone.

See Table 19.3 for general information on gastric motility disorder drugs.

Pharmacology

Diabetic gastroparesis is a common GI complication of diabetes mellitus. Caused by delayed gastric emptying, the symptoms range from early satiety and bloating to severe gastric retention with nausea, vomiting and abdominal pain. Impaired gastric emptying is caused by abnormal motility of the stomach or a reduction in motor activity in the intestine. Metoclopramide affects gut motility through indirect cholinergic stimulation of the gut muscle, whereas cisapride stimulates GI motility by enhancing the physiological release of acetylcholine in GI smooth muscle.

Gastroesophageal Reflux Disease and Peptic Ulcer Disease Drugs

Special Dental Considerations

There are no contraindications to the dental treatment of patients with GERD or PUD; however, drugs that cause gastrointestinal injury should be avoided in patients with GERD or PUD. These drugs include erythromycin, aspirin, corticosteroids and nonsteroidal anti-inflammatory agents. Dental patients with GERD should be kept in a semisupine chair position for patient comfort because of the reflux effects of this disease. Xerostomia is a common side effect of the anticholinergic agents and meticulous oral hygiene must be emphasized. Many anticholinergic agents also induce orthostatic or postural hypotension. Therefore, dental patients treated with one of these agents should remain in the dental chair in an upright position for several minutes before being dismissed.

Drug Interactions of Dental Interest

Drugs used to treat GERD and PUD include antacids, H_2 histamine receptor antagonists, anticholinergics and promotility agents.

Antacids potentially interfere with the absorption of many drugs by forming a complex with these drugs or by altering gastric pH. Antacids containing metal cations (Mg^{2+}, Ca^{2+}, Al^{3+}) have a strong affinity for tetracy-

cline, and response to the antibiotic can vary according to the extent of the complex.

Antacids increase the intragastric pH, and this can decrease the absorption of drugs that require an acidic environment for dissolution and absorption. Conversely, enteric-coated drugs such as erythromycin may be released prematurely.

Most of these drug-antacid interactions can be minimized by administering each drug 2 h from the other.

The H_2 histamine receptor antagonist cimetadine can bind to the cytochrome P450 mixed-function oxidase system and can inhibit the biotransformation of drugs by the liver. This results in inhibition of metabolism and increased serum drug concentrations of the drug not metabolized. Serum levels of some benzodiazepines (diazepam, alprazolam, chlorodiazepoxide, midazolam, triazolam) have been shown to increase, resulting in enhanced sedation.

Anticholinergics can decrease gastric emptying time, which can increase the amount of drug absorbed or increase the degradation of a drug in the stomach, thus decreasing the amount of drug absorbed. Overall, this interaction appears to have minor significance.

See Table 19.4 for general information on GERD and PUD drugs.

Pharmacology

H_2 histamine receptor antagonists are effective for short-term treatment of GERD and PUD. These agents prevent histamine-induced acid release by competing with histamine for H_2 receptors.

Proton-pump inhibitors (such as omeprazole) act by irreversibly blocking the H^+/K^+-ATPase pump. It markedly inhibits both basal and stimulated gastric acid secretion.

Antacids act by neutralizing gastric acid and thus raising the gastric pH. This has the effect of inhibiting peptic activity, which practically ceases at pH 5. The antacids in common use are salts of magnesium and aluminum. Magnesium salts cause diarrhea

Table 19.4

Gastroesophageal Reflux Disease and Peptic Ulcer Disease Drugs:
Dosage and Prescribing Information

Generic name	Brand name(s)	Dosage range (daily)	Interactions with other drugs
Antacids			
Aluminum salts	Alternagel, Alu-Cap, Aluminum Hydroxide Gel, Alu-Tab, Amphojel, Phosphajel	10-60 mL; 300-10,080 mg	Decreased absorption of tetracyclines, digoxin, indomethacin, or iron salts, benzodiazepines
Calcium salts	Camalox, Marblen, Mylanta, Mylanta DS, Mylanta Soothing Lozenges, Robalate, Tums	2-16 tablets (500-10,000 mg)	Decreased absorption of tetracyclines
Magnesium salts and aluminum salts	Aludrox, Delcid, Gelusil, Gelusil II, Maalox, Maalox TC, Milk of Magnesia, Mylanta, Mylanta DS, Riopan	10-80 mL; 400-9,600 mg	Decreased absorption of tetraclines, digoxin
Anticholinergic acids			
Pirenzepine [CAN]	Gastrozepin [CAN]	100-150 mg	May cause blurred vision; with anticholinergics, possible decrease in gastric emptying time, which changes amount of drug absorbed (overall, this interaction is of minor significance)
Propantheline bromide	Pro-Banthine; Propanthel [CAN]	22.5-120 mg	May delay absorption of concurrently ingested drugs

Excessive cholinergic blockade may occur if given with belladonna alkaloids, synthetic or semisynthetic anticholinergics, antihistamines, phenothiazines, tricyclic antidepressants, or other psychoactive drugs

Increases intraocular pressure if given with glucocorticoids |
| Mepenzolate bromide | Cantil | 100-200 mg | May cause blurred vision; with anticholinergics, possible decrease in gastric emptying time, which changes amount of drug absorbed (overall, this interaction is of minor significance) |
| Methscopolamine bromide | Pamine | 10-20 mg | May cause blurred vision; with anticholinergics possible decrease in gastric emptying time, which changes amount of drug absorbed (overall this interaction is of minor significance) |

[CAN] indicates a drug available only in Canada.

Continued on next page

Table 19.4 (cont.)

**Gastroesophageal Reflux Disease and Peptic Ulcer Disease Drugs:
Dosage and Prescribing Information**

Generic name	Brand name(s)	Dosage range (daily)	Interactions with other drugs
H₂ histamine receptor antagonists			
Cimetidine	Tagamet; Novo-Cimetidine [CAN]	800-1,200 mg	Reduced absorption of ketoconazole, reduced hepatic clearance of lidocaine, benzodiazepines, metronidazole, warfarin-type anticoagulants, phenytoin, propanolol, nifedipine (chlordiazepoxide, diazepam), certain tricyclic antidepressants, theophylline
Famotidine	Pepcid, Pepcid AC; Ulcidine [CAN]	**Pepcid:** 40-640 mg **Pepcid AC:** 10-20 mg	None
Nizatidine	Axid; Apo-Nizatidine [CAN]	150-300 mg	Only in very high doses of aspirin (3,900 mg/day), elevated serum salicylate levels seen with 150 mg bid nizatidine
Ranitidine	Zantac; Nu-Ranit [CAN]	150-600 mg	None
Miscellaneous			
Metoclopramide HCl	Reglan	40-60 mg	Opioid analgesics increase CNS depression GI motility effects antagonized by anticholinergics and opioid analgesics Additive sedative effects with alcohol, sedatives, hypnotics, opioids or tranquilizers Use cautiously, if at all, with monoamine oxidase inhibitors May decrease absorption of digoxin May increase rate and/or extent of absorption of acetaminophen, tetracycline, levodopa, ethanol and cyclosporine
Misoprostol	Cytotec	400-800 μg	Increases diarrhea when given with magnesium-containing antacids
Omeprazole	Prilosec	20-40 mg; up to 360 mg in pathological hypersecretory conditions	Decreases effect of ketoconazole; increases effect of benzodiazepines, digoxin, phenytoin and warfarin
Sucralfate	Carafate; Sulcrate [CAN]	2-4 g	If taken concurrently, decreases absorption of tetracycline, cimetidine, digoxin, fluoroquinolone antibiotics, ketoconazoles, l-thyroxine, phenytoin, quinidine, ranitidine, theophylline

[CAN] indicates a drug available only in Canada.

and aluminum salts cause constipation, so mixtures of the two are used to maintain bowel function.

Drugs that protect the mucosa can do so by either forming a protective physical barrier over the surface of the ulcer (sucralfate) or enhancing or augmenting endogenous prostaglandins (misoprostol) to promote bicarbonate and mucin release and inhibit acid secretion.

Anticholinergic agents (such as propantheline bromide) have played a limited role in the treatment of PUD by inhibiting vagally stimulated gastric acid secretion. These agents are not considered first-line agents for treatment of PUD.

Antiemetic Drugs

Special Dental Considerations

The dentist should be aware of why the patient is taking a drug for nausea and vomiting. If the patient is receiving the drug for cancer chemotherapy, he or she may require palliative therapy for stomatitis. Patients with cancer may be taking chronic opioids for pain. The dentist should not prescribe additional drugs for pain without reviewing the patient's medication profile. Also, the dentist should avoid procedures or drugs that could promote nausea and vomiting. An increased gag reflex makes it difficult for the patient to undergo dental procedures such as obtaining

Table 19.5

Antiemetic Drugs: Dosage and Prescribing Information

Generic name	Brand name(s)	Type of emesis	Dosage range (daily)	Interactions with other drugs
Anticholinergic				
Scopolamine	Transderm-Scop, generic injection; Transderm-V [CAN]	Motion sickness, postoperative nausea	**Adult—transdermal:** 0.5 mg/72 h; 1 mg/72 h [CAN] **Child:** NR	Additive adverse effects with other anticholinergics
Antihistamines				
Buclizine	Bucladin-S	Motion sickness	**Adult—oral:** 50 mg 30 min before exposure and q 4-6 h **Child:** NR	Increased toxicity with CNS depressants, anticholinergics, neuroleptics and alcohol
Cyclizine	Marezine	Motion sickness	**Adult—IM or oral:** 50 mg 30 min before exposure (max 200 mg/day) **Child:** NR	See note above
Dimenhydrinate	Dramamine	Motion sickness	**Adult—IM, IV or oral:** 50-100 mg 30 min before exposure **Child:** NR	See note above
Meclizine	Antivert, Bonine	Motion sickness, vertigo (prophylaxis), radiotherapy-induced nausea and vomiting	**Adult—oral:** 25-50 mg 1 h before exposure; 25-100 mg/day; 50 mg 2-12 h before radiotherapy and before travel **Child < age 12 y:** NR	See note above

[CAN] indicates a drug available only in Canada.
NR: Not recommended.

Continued on next page

Table 19.5 (cont.)

Antiemetic Drugs: Dosage and Prescribing Information

Generic name	Brand name(s)	Type of emesis	Dosage range (daily)	Interactions with other drugs
Butyrophenones				
Droperidol	Inapsine	Chemotherapy, post-operative nausea and vomiting (prophylaxis)	**Adult—IV:** 7-20 µg/kg q 4 h **Child, for postoperative prophylaxis—IM or IV:** 20-75 µg/kg	CNS depressants may increase adverse effects
Haloperidol	Haldol	Chemotherapy, post-operative	**Adult—IM or oral:** 1-2 mg q 8 h	Carbamazepine and phenobarbital decrease effectiveness of haloperidol CNS depressants may increase adverse effects
Cannabinoids				
Dronabinol	Marinol	Chemotherapy	**Adult—oral:** 5 mg/m² 1-3 h before chemotherapy; max: 15 mg/m²/dose	Increased drowsiness with alcohol, benzodiazepines and barbiturates
Nabilone	Cesamet	Chemotherapy, post-operative, general	**Adult—oral:** 1-2 mg q 8-12 h; max: 6 mg/day	See note above
Dopamine antagonist				
Metoclo-pramide	Octamide, Reglan; Maxeran [CAN]	Chemotherapy, gastric stasis, postoperative	**Adult, for chemotherapy—IV or oral:** 1-2 mg/kg; max: 12 mg/kg/day **Adult, for postoperative nausea—IM:** 10-20 mg near the end of surgery **Adult, for stasis—oral:** 10 mg 30 min before meals and at bedtime	Anticholinergics decrease the action of metoclopramide Opioid analgesics increase CNS depression
Glucocorticoid				
Dexameth-asone	Decadron, Dexone, Hexadrol	Chemotherapy	**Adult—IV or oral:** 10-20 mg before chemotherapy	Barbiturates, phenytoin and rifampin decrease the effects of dexamethasone

[CAN] indicates a drug available only in Canada.

Continued on next page

Table 19.5 (cont.)

Antiemetic Drugs: Dosage and Prescribing Information

Generic name	Brand name(s)	Type of emesis	Dosage range (daily)	Interactions with other drugs
Phenothiazines				
Chlorpro-mazine	Thorazine	Postoperative	**Adult—IM or oral:** 12.5-25 mg q 4-6 h **Child—IM or oral:** 0.275-0.55 mg q 4-6 h	Additive with other CNS depressants
Prochlor-perazine	Compazine	Chemotherapy, post-operative, general	**Adult—IM or oral:** 5-10 mg q 3-4 h prn **Adult—rectal:** 25 mg bid	See note above
Promethazine	Anergan, Phenergan	Postoperative, motion sickness	**Adult—rectal:** 25 mg q 4-6 h prn	See note above
Thiethyl-perazine	Torecan	Chemotherapy, post-operative, general	**Adult—IM, oral or rectal:** 10 mg q 8 h	See note above
Serotonin antagonist				
Ondansetron	Zofran	Chemotherapy	**Adult and child > age 4 y— IV:** 0.15 mg/kg bolus over 15 min given 30 min before chemotherapy; repeat 4 and 8 h later	Decreased effect with barbiturates, carba-mazepine, rifampin, phenytoin and phenylbutazone
Miscellaneous				
Benzquin-amide	Emete-Con	Postoperative	**Adult—IM:** 0.5-1 mg/kg q 3-4 h	Increased toxicity with other CNS depressants
Dextrose, levulose, phosphoric acid	Emetrol	General	**Adult—oral:** 15-30 mL q 1-3 h prn	See note above
Diphenidol	Vontrol	Postoperative, chemotherapy, labyrinthine disturbances	**Adult—oral:** 25-50 mg q 4 h **Child > age 6 mo—oral:** 0.88 mg/kg q 4 h	See note above
Trimetho-benzamide	Tigan	General	**Adult—oral:** 250 mg q 6-8 h **Adult—IM or rectal:** 200 mg q 6-8 h	See note above

Table 19.6

Gastrointestinal Drugs: Adverse Effects

Body system	Antidiarrheal agents	Crohn's disease and ulcerative colitis drugs	Gastric motility disorder (gastroparesis) drugs	Gastroesophageal reflux disease and peptic ulcer disease drugs	Antiemetic drugs
General	**Bismuth subsalicylate:** Anxiety, confusion **Opioids:** Headache	**Azathioprine:** Pancreatitis **Glucocorticoids:** Insomnia, depression, flushing **Metronidazole:** Headache **Sulfasalazine:** Agranulocytosis, Stevens-Johnson syndrome	**Cisapride:** Headache **Metoclopramide:** Drowsiness, restlessness, agranulocytosis, extrapyramidal effects	**Anticholinergics:** Hyperpyrexia **H₂ histamine receptor antagonists:** Dizziness, headache, drowsiness **Metoclopramide:** Weakness, restlessness, drowsiness, insomnia, depression **Misoprostol:** Headache **Omeprazole:** Headache	**Antihistamines:** Drowsiness **Cannabinoids:** Altered mental perceptions ("high") **Glucocorticoids:** Euphoria, hyperglycemia, insomnia, psychosis **Ondansetron:** Headache **Phenothiazines:** Drowsiness **Scopolamine:** Confusion, drowsiness
CV	**Opioids:** Angioneurotic edema	**Glucocorticoids:** Hypertension	**Cisapride:** Tachycardia	**Anticholinergics:** Circulatory collapse, hypotension, tachycardia **Omeprazole:** Edema, tachycardia, bradycardia	**Butyrophenones, phenothiazines:** Hypotension **Cannabinoids:** Orthostatic hypotension **Glucocorticoids:** Mild fluid retention **Scopolamine:** Hypotension, tachycardia
CNS	**Opioids:** Sedation, drowsiness, depression	**Glucocorticoids:** Nervousness **Metronidazole:** Dizziness, convulsions		**Anticholinergics:** Delirium, hallucinations, psychosis **Metoclopramide:** Restlessness, drowsiness, insomnia, depression **Omeprazole:** Dizziness **Sucralfate:** Drowsiness, dizziness	**Antihistamines:** Confusion **Ondansetron:** Sedation
EENT	**Bismuth subsalicylate:** Buzzing in ears			**Anticholinergics:** Blurred vision	**Butyrophenones, phenothiazines:** Blurred vision

Continued on next page

Table 19.6 (cont.)

Gastrointestinal Drugs: Adverse Effects

Body system	Antidiarrheal agents	Crohn's disease and ulcerative colitis drugs	Gastric motility disorder (gastroparesis) drugs	Gastroesophageal reflux disease and peptic ulcer disease drugs	Antiemetic drugs
GI	**Bismuth subsalicylate:** Fecal impactions may occur in infants and debilitated patients **Cholestyramine:** Constipation, nausea and vomiting, irritation of perianal area **Kaolin/pectin:** Constipation, fecal impaction **Opioids:** Nausea and vomiting	**Azathioprine:** Nausea and vomiting **Metronidazole:** Nausea and vomiting, pseudomembranous colitis **Sulfasalazine:** Bleeding ulcers, nausea and vomiting	**Cisapride:** Diarrhea **Metoclopramide:** Diarrhea	**Antacids:** Constipation, stomach cramps; magnesium salts–diarrhea; calcium salts–constipation, flatulence **Anticholinergics:** Constipation **H$_2$ histamine receptor antagonists:** Diarrhea, nausea and vomiting **Metoclopramide:** Nausea, diarrhea **Misoprostol:** Diarrhea, constipation, nausea, vomiting, abdominal pain **Omeprazole:** Nausea, vomiting, diarrhea, constipation, irritable colon **Sucralfate:** Constipation, nausea, vomiting	**Butyrophenones, phenothiazines:** Constipation **Glucocorticoids:** GI bleeding **Metoclopramide:** Diarrhea **Ondansetron:** Diarrhea or constipation
GU	**Opioids:** Urinary retention			**Anticholinergics:** Urinary retention	
Hema		**Azathioprine:** Leukopenia, thrombocytopenia **Glucocorticoids:** Thrombocytopenia **Metronidazole:** Leukopenia **Sulfasalazine:** Leukopenia, neutropenia, thrombocytopenia			
HB		**Azathioprine:** Hepatotoxicity, jaundice **Sulfasalazine:** Renal failure			**Ondansetron:** Altered liver function

Continued on next page

Table 19.6 (cont.)

Gastrointestinal Drugs: Adverse Effects

Body system	Antidiarrheal agents	Crohn's disease and ulcerative colitis drugs	Gastric motility disorder (gastroparesis) drugs	Gastroesophageal reflux disease and peptic ulcer disease drugs	Antiemetic drugs
Integ	**Cholestyramine:** Rash, irritation of skin	**Glucocorticoids:** Poor wound healing, petechiae			
Musc				**Omeprazole:** Back pain; muscle, joint and leg pain	**Butyrophenones, phenothiazines:** Dystonias **Metoclopramide:** Dystonias
Oral	**Bismuth subsalicylate:** Discoloration of tongue (darkening due to bismuth) **Cholestyramine:** Irritation of tongue **Opioids:** Xerostomia	**Azathioprine:** Stomatitis, oral ulcerations **Glucocorticoids:** Xerostomia, oral candidiasis **Metronidazole:** Xerostomia, metallic taste, glossitis, stomatitis, change in taste **Sulfasalazine:** Stomatitis, glossitis	**Cisapride:** Xerostomia **Metoclopramide:** Xerostomia	**Antacids:** Aluminum hydroxide–chalky taste **Anticholinergics:** Xerostomia **Metoclopramide:** Xerostomia **Omeprazole:** Xerostomia, taste alterations **Sucralfate:** Metallic taste, xerostomia	**Antihistamines:** Xerostomia **Butyrophenones, phenothiazines:** Xerostomia **Scopalamine:** Xerostomia
Resp	**Kaolin/pectin:** Pneumoconiosis if large amounts inhaled			**Omeprazole:** Cough	

radiographs or impressions. Many antiemetic drugs cause xerostomia, so these patients should avoid mouthrinses containing alcohol because of its drying effects. They also should use sugarless gum or saliva substitutes or take sips of water.

Drug Interactions of Dental Interest

Antacids can decrease the absorption of many drugs, including tetracycline, digoxin, benzodiazepines, iron salts and indomethacin. Antihistamines, phenothiazines and buty-rophenones cause drowsiness. This drowsiness may be additive with that caused by other CNS depressants.

See Table 19.5 for general information on antiemetic drugs.

Pharmacology

Numerous pathways are capable of stimulating the vomiting center and chemoreceptor trigger zone in the brain, so it is not surprising that a wide variety of drugs can be used in treating nausea and vomiting. Phenothiazines

Table 19.7

Gastrointestinal Drugs: Precautions and Contraindications

Drug category	Precautions and contraindications
Antidiarrheals	**Adsorbents** *Bismuth subsalicylate:* Subsalicylates should be used with caution if patient is taking aspirin because of possible additive toxicity; use with caution in children < age 3 y; do not use subsalicylates in patients with influenza or chicken pox because of risk of Reye's syndrome; pregnancy risk category C (D in third trimester) *Cholestyramine:* Use with caution in patients with constipation; pregnancy risk category C *Kaolin/pectin:* May mask dehydration, may make recognition of parasitic causes of diarrhea more difficult; check with physician if diarrhea not controlled within 48 h and/or if fever develops; pregnancy risk category C **Opioids:** Use cautiously in patients who have hepatic disease, renal disease, severe liver disease, glaucoma, electrolyte imbalances or who are nursing mothers or children < age 2 y; pregnancy risk category C
Crohn's disease and ulcerative colitis drugs	**Azathioprine:** Use cautiously in patients who have severe hepatic and renal disease; pregnancy risk category D **Glucocorticoids:** Use cautiously in patients with diabetes mellitus, glaucoma, osteoporosis, renal disease, peptic ulcer, congestive heart failure; pregnancy risk category C **Metronidazole:** Use cautiously in patients who have *Candida* infections or are pregnant; pregnancy risk category B **Sulfasalazine:** Use cautiously in patients with hypersensitivity to sulfonamides or salicylates or impaired renal or hepatic function or who are nursing mothers; pregnancy risk category B
Gastric motility disorder drugs	**Cisapride:** Use cautiously in patients who have gastrointestinal hemorrhage, mechanical obstruction, perforation; potentially fatal with mycins (for example, erythromycin, clindamycin) and antifungal azoles (fluconazole, ketoconazole, miconazole, itraconazole); pregnancy risk category C **Metoclopramide:** Use cautiously in patients who have epilepsy, gastrointestinal hemorrhage, mechanical obstruction; pregnancy risk category B
Gastroesophageal reflux disease and peptic ulcer disease drugs	**Antacids:** Aluminum antacids—prolonged administration or large doses may cause hypophosphatemia; pregnancy risk category C Magnesium salts—use with caution in patients with renal impairment; pregnancy risk category B Calcium salts—use with caution in patients who are taking digitalis or have congestive heart failure or renal failure; pregnancy risk category C **Anticholinergic agents:** May cause agitation, mental confusion; may inhibit lactation; pregnancy risk category C **H₂ histamine receptor antagonists:** May cause agitation, reduce dosage in hepatic/renal disease; American Academy of Pediatrics has recommended that cimetidine not be taken by lactating mothers; pregnancy risk category B **Miscellaneous** *Sucralfate:* Use not established in children; pregnancy risk category B *Metoclopramide:* Should be used cautiously in patients with Parkinson's disease; dose should be modified for patients with renal failure; pregnancy risk category B *Omeprazole:* Pregnancy risk category C *Misoprostol:* Safety and efficacy not established in children < age 18 y; use with caution in elderly patients and patients with renal impairment; pregnancy risk category X

Continued on next page

Table 19.7 (cont.)
Gastrointestinal Drugs: Precautions and Contraindications

Drug category	Precautions and contraindications
Antiemetic drugs	**Antihistamines:** Use with caution in patients with narrow-angle glaucoma, prostatic hypertrophy; pregnancy risk category B
	Cannabinoids: Use with caution in patients with heart disease, hepatic disease or seizure disorders; pregnancy risk category B
	Glucocorticoids: Use with caution in patients with hypothyroidism, cirrhosis, hypertension, congestive heart failure, ulcerative colitis; pregnancy risk category C
	Metoclopramide: Use cautiously in patients with epilepsy, gastrointestinal hemorrhage, mechanical obstruction; pregnancy risk category B
	Ondansetron: Ondansetron should be used on a scheduled basis, not prn, as the data support use of this drug in prevention of nausea and vomiting and not as a rescue from nausea and vomiting once it starts; pregnancy risk category B
	Phenothiazines: May lower seizure threshold, so should be used cautiously in patients with seizure history; drug-induced Parkinson's syndrome can occur; the risk of tardive dyskinesia may be as high as 40% in elderly people; avoid use in patients with narrow-angle glaucoma, bone marrow depression, severe liver or cardiac disease; pregnancy risk category C
	Scopolamine: Contraindicated in patients with narrow-angle glaucoma, acute hemorrhage, gastrointestinal or genitourinary obstruction; anticholinergic agents are not well-tolerated by elderly people; should be used cautiously in patients with hepatic and renal impairment; pregnancy risk category C

and butyrophenones block dopamine receptors and are believed to act at the chemoreceptor trigger zone. Antihistamines and anticholinergics are effective in managing vomiting associated with vestibular disturbances by blocking acetylcholine receptors in the vestibular center. Metoclopramide is a dopamine antagonist that has both peripheral and central antiemetic actions. This drug accelerates gastric emptying, inhibits gastric relaxation and appears to block the chemoreceptor trigger zone. Ondansetron is a highly selective and potent antagonist of $5\text{-}HT_3$ (serotonin) receptors. Cannabinoids are believed to inhibit emesis by blocking descending impulses from the cerebral cortex. Glucocorticoids have demonstrated antiemetic activity in patients receiving cancer chemotherapy. Their mechanism of action is unknown.

Adverse Effects, Precautions and Contraindications

Adverse effects of gastrointestinal drugs are provided in Table 19.6. Gastrointestinal drug precautions and contraindications are provided in Table 19.7.

Suggested Readings

Anderson PO, Knoben JE, eds. Handbook of clinical drug data. 8th ed. Stamford, Conn.: Appleton & Lange; 1997.

Tatro DS, ed. Drug interactions facts: facts and comparisons. St. Louis: Facts and Comparisons; 1995.

Wells BG, DiPiro JT, Schwinghammer TL, Hamilton CW. Pharmacotherapy handbook. Stamford, Conn.: Appleton & Lange; 1998.

Young LY, Koda-Kimble MA, eds. Applied therapeutics: the clinical use of drugs. 6th ed. Vancouver, Wash.: Applied Therapeutics; 1995.

Chapter 20

Neurological Drugs

Steven Ganzberg, D.M.D., M.S.

Patients who are receiving ongoing treatment of neurological conditions may consult the dentist for oral health care. One of the more common neurological conditions dentists see among these patients is seizure disorders; they also may encounter other conditions such as Parkinson's disease, multiple sclerosis, Alzheimer's disease, myasthenia gravis and other myopathies, spasticity resulting from spinal cord injury, and poststroke syndrome. Long-term medication management is common. The dentist also may prescribe neurological drugs for treatment of pains of neuropathic origin as well as for primary headache syndromes, such as migraine, cluster and tension-type headaches. The dentist who undertakes treatment of these disorders is presumed to have advanced training or experience in diagnosis and management of these disorders. For general information on neurological drugs, see Tables 20.1-20.5.

Clinicians should review the condition and level of disease control (for example, quality of seizure control) of patients who have neurological conditions. If warranted, delay in elective dental treatment may be prudent pending medical consultation. Vital signs, including respiratory status, should be evaluated preoperatively. Adverse effects are provided in Table 20.6 and precautions/contraindications in Table 20.7.

Anticonvulsant Drugs

Anticonvulsant drugs typically are used to control epilepsy, a convulsive disorder characterized by intermittent excessive discharges of neurons. This dysregulation of neural function is frequently associated with altered or lost consciousness. Seizure disorders have been characterized as generalized, including tonic-clonic (grand mal) seizures, absence, partial, atonic and unclassified. Specific anticonvulsant agents have been shown to be superior for some types of seizures.

In orofacial pain management, anticonvulsants are useful in treating trigeminal neuralgia and other posttraumatic trigeminal neuropathies. Carbamazepine, phenytoin, valproic acid and its derivatives, and clonazepam (as well as baclofen, an antispastic) have been reported to be useful. A newer anticonvulsant, gabapentin, is also being investigated in this regard. Certain anticonvulsants have been reported to provide some benefit for migraine headache as well. These medications have numerous side effects, some life-threatening. The dentist prescribing an anticonvulsant drug is presumed to have established a proper diagnosis and to be fully aware of the drug's interactions, adverse effects and contraindications.

See Table 20.1 for basic information on anticonvulsant drugs, both commonly and rarely used (owing to pronounced side effects

Table 20.1

Anticonvulsant Drugs: Dosage and Prescribing Information

Generic name	Brand name(s)	Dosage range (daily)	Interactions with other drugs
Commonly used anticonvulsants			
Carbamazepine	Epitol, Tegretol; Apo-Carbamazepine [CAN], Novo-Carbamaz [CAN]	200-1,600 mg	**Acetaminophen (prolonged use):** Increased risk of hepatic toxicity **CNS depressants:** Increased sedative effects **Corticosteroids:** Increased metabolism **Propoxyphene, erythromycin/clarithromycin:** Decreased metabolism, increased risk of toxicity
Clonazepam	Klonopin	1.5-20 mg	**CNS depressants (for example, alcohol, opioids and sedative antihistamines):** May potentiate sedative side effects
Diazepam	D-Val, Valium, Valrelease, Vivol, Zetran; Apo-Diazepam [CAN], Novo-Dipam [CAN]	**Emergency treatment of seizures:** 0.1 mg/kg IV **Injection—preoperative:** 5-10 mg **Oral, extended-release capsules:** 15-30 mg/day **Oral, solution or tablets:** 2-10 mg bid-qid	See note above
Ethosuximide	Zarontin	500-1,500 mg	**Acetaminophen (prolonged use):** Increased risk of hepatic toxicity **CNS depressants:** Increased sedative effects **Corticosteroids:** Increased metabolism
Gabapentin	Neurontin	300-3,600 mg	**CNS depressants:** Increased sedative effects
Lamotrigine	Lamictal	50-500 mg/day **With valproic acid:** 25-200 mg/day	**Acetaminophen:** Decreased effect **CNS depressants:** Increased sedative effects
Phenobarbital	Ancalixir, Barbita, Luminal, Solfoton	60-250 mg	**CNS depressants:** Increased sedative effects **Corticosteroids:** Increased metabolism

[CAN] indicates a drug available only in Canada.

Continued on next page

Table 20.1 (cont.)

Anticonvulsant Drugs: Dosage and Prescribing Information

Generic name	Brand name(s)	Dosage range (daily)	Interactions with other drugs
Commonly used anticonvulsants (cont.)			
Phenytoin	Dilantin, Diphenylan, Phenytex	200-600 mg	**Acetaminophen (prolonged use):** Increased risk of hepatic toxicity **Aspirin:** Increased plasma concentration **CNS depressants:** Increased sedative effects **Corticosteroids, benzodiazepines, barbiturates:** Increased metabolism **Fluconazole, ketaconazole, metronidazole:** Decreased metabolism and increased plasma concentration **Lidocaine (high dose):** Increased risk of cardiac dysrhythmia
Primidone	Mysoline, Myidone, Sertan; Apo-Primidone [CAN]	100-2,000 mg	**Acetaminophen (prolonged use):** Increased risk of hepatic toxicity **CNS depressants:** Increased sedative effects **Corticosteroids:** Increased metabolism
Tiagabine	Gabitril	2-32 mg	**CNS depressants:** Increased sedative effects
Topiramate	Topamax	50-400 mg	See note above **Carbamazepine, phenytoin, valproic acid:** Decrease levels of topiramate
Valproic acid, divalproex sodium	Depakene, Depakote	5-60 mg/kg/day	**Aspirin/NSAIDs:** Increased risk of bleeding **CNS depressants:** Increased sedative effects
Rarely used anticonvulsants			
Acetazolamide	Acetazolam, Dazamide, Diamox, Storzolamide; Apo-Acetazolamide [CAN]	375-1,000 mg	**Aspirin:** Risk of salicylate toxicity
Ethotoin	Peganone	500-3,000 mg	**Acetaminophen (prolonged use):** Increased risk of hepatic toxicity **Aspirin:** Increased plasma concentration **CNS depressants:** Increased sedative effects **Corticosteroids, benzodiazepines, barbiturates:** Increased metabolism **Fluconazole, ketaconazole, metronidazole:** Decreased metabolism and increased plasma concentration **Lidocaine (high dose):** Increased risk of cardiac dysrhythmia

[CAN] indicates a drug available only in Canada.

Continued on next page

Table 20.1 (cont.)

Anticonvulsant Drugs: Dosage and Prescribing Information

Generic name	Brand name(s)	Dosage range (daily)	Interactions with other drugs
		Rarely used anticonvulsants (cont.)	
Mephenytoin	Mesantoin	50-1,200 mg	**Acetaminophen (prolonged use):** Increased risk of hepatic toxicity
			Aspirin: Increased plasma concentration
			CNS depressants: Increased sedative effects
			Corticosteroids, benzodiazepines, barbiturates: Increased metabolism
			Fluconazole, ketaconazole, metronidazole: Decreased metabolism and increased plasma concentration
			Lidocaine (high dose): Increased risk of cardiac arrhythmia
Mephobarbital	Mebaral	200-600 mg	**CNS depressants:** Increased sedative effects
			Corticosteroids: Increased metabolism
Metharbitol	Gemonil	100-800 mg	**CNS depressants:** Increased sedative effects
			Corticosteroids: Increased metabolism
Methsuximide	Celontin	300-1,200 mg	**Acetaminophen (prolonged use):** Increased risk of hepatic toxicity
			CNS depressants: Increased sedative effects
			Corticosteroids: Increased metabolism
Paramethadione	Paradione	900-2,400 mg	**CNS depressants:** Increased sedative effects
Phenacemide	Epiclase, Phenurone, Phetylureum	500-5,000 mg	**CNS depressants:** Increased sedative effects
Phensuximide	Milontin	500-3,000 mg	**Acetaminophen (prolonged use):** Increased risk of hepatic toxicity
			CNS depressants: Increased sedative effects
			Corticosteroids: Increased metabolism
Trimethadione	Tridione, Tridione Dulcets	900-2,400 mg	**CNS depressants:** Increased sedative effects

or inferior efficacy compared to that of newer agents).

Special Dental Considerations

Many commonly prescribed anticonvulsants can cause blood dyscrasias, especially carbamazepine, phenytoin and valproic acid. Stevens-Johnson syndrome can occur with many anticonvulsants, especially lamotrigine. Xerostomia and taste changes are common with many anticonvulsants. Topiramate can cause gingivitis. Consider these agents in the differential diagnosis of oral complaints if signs or symptoms warrant. Valproic acid/divalproex sodium may inhibit platelet aggregation.

Drug Interactions of Dental Interest

Anticonvulsants are frequently sedating. Sedative agents, including opioids, may potentiate this effect. Meperidine, especially when used in multiple doses, can promote seizures in patients with otherwise well-controlled seizure disorders.

Many anticonvulsants induce hepatic microsomal enzymes, causing decreased effectiveness or shorter duration of action of certain concomitantly prescribed drugs. Patients taking anticonvulsants may experience increased metabolism of concomitantly administered corticosteroids, benzodiazepines and barbiturates, a situation that leads to decreased effectiveness of these agents.

Prolonged use of acetaminophen may increase the risk of anticonvulsant-induced hepatic toxicity.

Propoxyphene, erythromycin and clarithromycin may result in decreased metabolism of carbamazepine and increased risk of toxicity.

Fluconazole, ketaconazole and metronidazole may result in decreased metabolism of phenytoin and related hydantoins and increased risk of toxicity. Aspirin may increase plasma concentrations of hydantoins, thereby leading to toxicity. For phenytoin, high doses of lidocaine may have additive cardiac depressant effects.

Laboratory Value Alterations

- With most anticonvulsants (except benzodiazepines, acetazolamide and gabapentin): leukopenia, thrombocytopenia, anemia or pancytopenia is possible.
- With hydantoin derivatives: increase in serum glucose possible.
- With acetazolamide: increase in serum glucose is possible.
- With valproic acid/divalproex sodium: bleeding time is increased.

Special Patients
Pediatric patients
Pediatric patients taking hydantoin derivatives are more prone than adults to gingival enlargement, coarsening of facial features (widening of nasal tip, thickening of lips) and facial hair growth.

Pharmacology

Anticonvulsants' primary action is to prevent the spread of abnormal neuronal depolarization from an epileptic focus without completely suppressing that focus. The pharmacological mechanisms of action are varied but generally involve, alone or in combination, stabilization of neuronal sodium channels, increasing γ–aminobutyric acid (GABA) tone, alteration of excitatory amino acid neurotransmission and alteration of calcium ion influx.

Antimyasthenic and Alzheimer's-Type Dementia Drugs

Myasthenia gravis is a progressive disease characterized by a decreased number of functional acetylcholine receptors at the neuromuscular junction, resulting in muscular weakness. Drugs to combat this disease impair acetylcholinesterase, the enzyme that degrades acetylcholine, thus increasing the relative concentration of available acetylcholine.

The Alzheimer's-type dementia drug, donepezil, is included in this discussion, as it is a reversible anticholinesterase drug. Current theories of Alzheimer's disease attribute some of the symptoms to a deficiency in central nervous system (CNS) cholinergic transmission. The use of donepezil for mild to moderate Alzheimer's disease shows variable, but clinically measurable, improvement in some patients.

See Table 20.2 for basic information on antimyasthenic and Alzheimer's-type dementia drugs.

Special Dental Considerations

The dentist should monitor vital signs, including respiratory status, before beginning dental treatment.

The dentist should evaluate the patient for possible postural hypotension by having him or her sit in the dental chair for a minute or two after being in a supine position and then evaluating him or her when standing.

These drugs may cause increased salivation. Anticholinergics are generally contraindicated.

Drug Interactions of Dental Interest

There may be a reduced rate of metabolism of ester local anesthetics.

High doses of local anesthetic may depress muscle function.

CNS depressants should be used with caution.

Pharmacology

Antimyasthenic drugs increase the amount of acetylcholine present at the neuromuscular junction by inhibition of acetylcholinesterase, the enzyme that degrades acetylcholine.

Table 20.2
Antimyasthenic and Alzheimer's-Type Dementia Drugs: Dosage and Prescribing Information

Generic name	Brand name(s)	Dosage range (daily)	Interactions with other drugs
Antimyasthenic drugs			
Ambenonium	Mytelase Caplets	15-200 mg	**Anticholinergics:** Should not be used without medical consultation **Lidocaine:** High doses may cause decreased muscle function
Neostigmine	Prostigmin	30-150 mg	**Anticholinergics:** Should not be used without medical consultation **Lidocaine:** High doses may cause decreased muscle function
Pyridostigmine	Mestinon, Regonol	60-1,500 mg	**Anticholinergics:** Should not be used without medical consultation **Lidocaine:** High doses may cause decreased muscle function
Alzheimer's-type dementia drugs			
Donepezil	Aricept	5-10 mg	**Anticholinergics:** Decreased activity **CNS depressants including opioids:** Use with caution, if at all, in patients with dementia

The increase in acetylcholine concentration improves muscular function.

The only currently available anti–Alzheimer's-type-dementia drug increases CNS cholinergic function by inhibiting the cholinesterase enzyme. In some patients, cognitive indices are improved.

Antiparkinsonism Drugs

Parkinson's disease is a CNS disorder characterized by resting tremor, frequently accompanied by involuntary mouth and tongue movements, rigidity of the limbs and trunk, postural instability and bradykinesia, including loss of facial expressions (masklike facies). Drooling is common owing to swallowing incoordination. A relative imbalance between dopamine, acetylcholine and GABA neurotransmission in the basal ganglia and related areas plays a significant role in the pathophysiology of this disorder. Antiparkinsonism drugs attempt to alter this neurotransmitter imbalance.

See Table 20.3 for basic information on antiparkinsonism drugs.

Special Dental Considerations

Many of these drugs can cause xerostomia. The dentist should consider them in the differential diagnosis of caries, periodontal disease or oral candidiasis.

If newly diagnosed mouthing movements (involuntary mouth and tongue movements and/or drooling) are seen, which may indicate a serious medication side effect, consul-

Table 20.3
Antiparkinsonism Drugs: Dosage and Prescribing Information

Generic name	Brand name(s)	Dosage range (daily)	Interactions with other drugs
Drugs acting on acetylcholine			
Benztropine	Cogentin; Apo-Benztropine [CAN], PMS-Benztropine [CAN]	1-6 mg	**Phenothiazines, butyrophenones, metoclopramide, and other dopamine antagonists:** Contraindicated in Parkinson's disease
Biperiden	Akineton	2-16 mg	**Anticholinergics:** Additive oral drying effect **CNS depressants:** Increased sedative effects with anticholinergics **Phenothiazines, butyrophenones, metoclopramide, and other dopamine antagonists:** Contraindicated in Parkinson's disease
Diphenhydramine	Benadryl, multiple OTC agents	100-300 mg	**CNS depressants:** CNS and respiratory depressive effects increase with administration of other CNS depressants **MAO inhibitors:** May increase anticholinergic effects
Ethopropazine	Parsidol, Parsitan	50-600 mg	**Phenothiazines, butyrophenones, metoclopramide, and other dopamine antagonists:** Contraindicated in Parkinson's disease

[CAN] indicates a drug available only in Canada.

Continued on next page

Table 20.3 (cont.)

Antiparkinsonism Drugs: Dosage and Prescribing Information

Generic name	Brand name(s)	Dosage range (daily)	Interactions with other drugs
Drugs acting on acetylcholine (cont.)			
Orphenadrine	Banflex, Disipal, Flexoject, Marflex, Myolin, Myotrol, Noradex, Norflex, Orflagen	150-250 mg	**Phenothiazines, butyrophenones, metoclopramide, and other dopamine antagonists:** Contraindicated in Parkinson's disease
Procyclinide	Kemadrin, Procyclid; PMS-Procyclinide [CAN]	7.5-20 mg	See note above
Trihexyphenidyl	Aparkane, Artane, Trihexane, Trihexy; Apo-Trihex [CAN]	10-15 mg	See note above
Drugs acting on dopamine			
Amantadine	Symmetrel	100-400 mg	**Phenothiazines, butyrophenones, metoclopramide, and other dopamine antagonists:** Contraindicated in Parkinson's disease
Bromocriptine	Parlodel	1.25-40 mg	See note above
Carbidopa-levodopa	Sinemet	30 mg/200 mg-300 mg/2,000 mg	**Phenothiazines, butyrophenones, metoclopramide, and other dopamine antagonists:** Contraindicated in Parkinson's disease **Vasoconstrictors:** Less likely than levodopa to stimulate interaction
Entacapone	Comton	200 mg with each dose of carbidopa-levodopa; max 600 mg/day	**Phenothiazines, butyrophenones, metoclopramide, and other dopamine antagonists:** Contraindicated in Parkinson's disease Use epinephrine/levonordefrin cautiously; when administered concomitantly, may produce exaggerated effects on blood pressure and heart rate
Levodopa	Dopar, Larodopa	500-8,000 mg	**Anticholinergics:** May have additive oral drying effects **Phenothiazines, butyrophenones, metoclopramide, and other dopamine antagonists:** Contraindicated in Parkinson's disease **Vasocontrictors in local anesthetic solution:** May have exaggerated effects

[CAN] indicates a drug available only in Canada.

Continued on next page

Table 20.3 (cont.)

Antiparkinsonism Drugs: Dosage and Prescribing Information

Generic name	Brand name(s)	Dosage range (daily)	Interactions with other drugs
Drugs acting on dopamine (cont.)			
Pergolide	Permax	0.05-5 mg	**Phenothiazines, butyrophenones, metoclopramide, and other dopamine antagonists:** Contraindicated in Parkinson's disease
Selegiline	Eldepryl, Deprenyl; Novo-Selegiline [CAN]	10 mg	**Meperidine (and possibly other opioids):** May cause hypertensive crisis
Tolcapone	Tasmar	100-600 mg/day	**Epinephrine/levonordefrin:** Use cautiously; when administered concomitantly, may produce exaggerated effects on blood pressure and heart rate
Miscellaneous			
Clonazepam	Klonopin	0.5-20 mg	**CNS depressants (for example, alcohol, opioids and sedating antihistamines):** May potentiate sedative side effects See Chapter 21, Psychoactive Drugs, for more information **Phenothiazines, butyrophenones, metoclopramide, and other dopamine antagonists:** Contraindicated in Parkinson's disease
Nadolol	Corgard	40-240 mg/day	**Injected local anesthetics:** Clearance from peripheral circulation may decrease; hypertension and bradycardia can occur when epinephrine or levonordefrin in local anesthetic solutions is administered to patients taking nonselective β-blockers **NSAIDs:** May partially antagonize antihypertensive effects of these medications **Opioids:** May potentiate hypotensive effect of these medications **Phenothiazines, butyrophenones, metoclopramide, and other dopamine antagonists:** Contraindicated in Parkinson's disease For more information, see Chapter 17
Propranolol	Detensol, Inderal; Apo-Propranolol [CAN], Novo-Pranol [CAN]	80-640 mg/day	See note above

[CAN] indicates a drug available only in Canada.

tation with the patient's physician may be appropriate.

Selegiline may cause circumoral burning.

The dentist should monitor the patient's vital signs during all dental visits. The dentist should ask the patient to sit upright in the dental chair for a minute or two after being in a supine position and then monitor the patient when standing.

Drug Interactions of Dental Interest

Patients taking levodopa, entacapone, tolcapone and high doses of selegiline may produce an exaggerated hemodynamic response to vasoconstrictors in local anesthetic solutions. The dentist should employ careful aspiration technique with limited vasoconstrictor (0.04 mg epinephrine). Additional vasoconstrictor may be used after monitoring of vital signs.

Dopamine antagonist medications, such as chlorpromazine, metoclopramide, and promethazine, which may be prescribed for nausea, are contraindicated in patients with Parkinson's disease.

Anticholinergics may have an additive oral drying effect and should be used with caution.

In patients taking high doses of selegiline, meperidine (and possibly other opioids) may cause a hyperthermic and possibly hypertensive crisis.

Pharmacology

Parkinson's disease is classically characterized by an imbalance in dopaminergic and cholinergic neurotransmission with contributions involving GABA neurotransmission in the nigrastriatum. Medications that act on dopamine increase its availability either by increasing the concentration of dopamine precursors (levodopa), decreasing the breakdown of precursors (carbidopa), acting as agonists at the dopamine receptor (bromocriptine, pergolide and amantadine) or decreasing the degradation of dopamine by MAO-B (selegiline). The catechol-O-methyl-transferase (COMT) inhibitor drugs enta-capone and tolcapone are used with carbidopa-levodopa (Sinemet) to decrease levodopa degradation, thus increasing levodopa plasma levels. Anticholinergic drugs, or antihistamines with some degree of anticholinergic activity, decrease cholinergic tone by blocking cholinergic receptors and improving the balance between dopaminergic and cholinergic transmission. GABA agonists such as clonazepam and other drugs, such as β-blockers, are also useful in some cases.

Antispastic Drugs

Patients taking antispastic drugs typically have spinal cord or other CNS lesions. Spasticity can occur in some neurological disorders, such as multiple sclerosis.

Baclofen also may be effective for the treatment of trigeminal neuralgia and other trigeminal neuropathies.

See Table 20.4 for basic information on antispastic drugs.

Special Dental Considerations

Baclofen may cause dry mouth. Dantrolene can infrequently cause blood dyscrasias. The dentist should consider these drugs in the differential diagnosis if oral signs and symptoms warrant it. Tizanidine may cause hypotension.

Drug Interactions of Dental Interest

These drugs may be sedating. Sedative agents, including opioids, may potentiate this effect.

Laboratory Value Alterations

- Dantrolene may infrequently cause blood dyscrasias.

Pharmacology

Antispastic drugs work directly on the muscle by decreasing calcium release from the sarcoplasmic reticulum (dantrolene), in the CNS by increasing GABA tone (baclofen) or by an α_2 agonist effect (tizanidine).

Table 20.4

Antispastic Drugs: Dosage and Prescribing Information

Generic name	Brand name(s)	Dosage range (daily)	Interactions with other drugs
Baclofen	Alpha-Baclofen, Lioresal	15-80 mg	**CNS depressants:** Increased sedative effects
Dantrolene	Dantrium (also used for malignant hyperthermia)	25-400 mg/day	**CNS depressants:** Increased sedative effects
Tizanidine	Zanaflex	8-24 mg/day	**CNS depressants:** Increased sedative effects

Vascular Headache Suppressants

There are numerous conditions that cause headache or facial pain. The majority of patients who list headache as a primary condition on the medical history will be diagnosed with migraine, tension-type or cluster headache. Numerous drugs are used to treat these conditions. They can be divided into symptomatic medications, abortive medications and preventive medications. Symptomatic medications include analgesics and antiemetics, both of which have been covered in other chapters and will not be listed here. These drugs generally are taken intermittently for severe head pain, as continued use can aggravate headache conditions.

Abortive medications include those drugs which, when taken at onset of or during a severe headache (such as migraine or cluster headache), will arrest the headache process and in some cases the associated symptoms (such as nausea and photophobia). These medications include ergotamines, "triptans," isomethep-tene mucate combinations and, in some cases, phenothiazines. These medications can have adverse cardiovascular consequences, but because they generally are taken on an intermittent basis not associated with a dental visit, they should not be of concern in dental care.

Preventive medications are varied and frequently draw from other drug categories. Various cardiovascular medications—including calcium channel blockers and β-blockers—are used for management of chronic headache. Likewise, most antidepressants and some anticonvulsants have been used for headache prevention.

Neuropathic facial pains, if they respond to medical treatment, are usually treated with anticonvulsant or antidepressant medications. Specific conditions may respond to baclofen, α-blockers or clonidine.

See Table 20.5 for basic information on vascular headache supressants. A thorough discussion of the pharmacological management of headache and facial pain is beyond the scope of this book. Headache suppressant medications, which have not been covered elsewhere in this text, will be presented.

Special Dental Considerations

Abortive headache medications are used only when needed for moderate-to-severe headache and generally not on the day of a dental appointment. If ergot preparations or a triptan are used within 12-24 h of a dental procedure, vasoconstrictor precautions similar to those for hypertensive patients should be followed. For preventive medications—for example, antidepressants, anticonvulsants or antihypertensives—the dentist should follow precautions listed for that specific category of drug.

Table 20.5

Vascular Headache Suppressants (Indicated for Headache Only): Dosage and Prescribing Information

Generic name	Brand name(s)	Dosage range (daily)	Interactions with other drugs
Dihydroergotamine	DHE-45	**IM or SC:** 1 mg; maximum 3 mg/day **IV:** 1 mg slow, maximum 2 mg/day	**Vasoconstrictors:** Increased hypertensive effect if used chronically
Ergotamine tartrate and caffeine	Cafergot, Ercaf, Ergocaff, Gotamine, Wigraine	1-2 mg at onset of headache; maximum 6 mg/day; not to be used more than 2 days/w	See note above
Ergotamine tartrate	Ergomar, Ergostat, Gynergen, Medihaler Ergotamine	1-2 mg at onset of headache; maximum 6 mg/day; not to be used more than 2 days/w, preferably at least 5 days apart	See note above
Isometheptene mucate, dichlorphenazone, acetaminophen	Midrin	4-8 capsules/day	See note above
Methysergide maleate	Sansert	4-6 mg	See note above
Naratriptan	Amerge	1-2.5 mg at onset of headache; can repeat 4 h later; maximum 5 mg/day	See note above
Rizatriptan	Maxalt	5-10 mg at onset of headache; can repeat 2 h later; maximum 30 mg/day	See note above
Sumatriptan succinate	Imitrex	6 mg SC at onset of headache; 25-100 mg orally at onset of headache; 5- or 20-mg nasal spray at onset of headache	See note above
Zolmitriptan	Zomig	2.5-5 mg at onset of headache; can repeat 2 h later; maximum 10 mg/day	See note above

The dentist who undertakes primary treatment of head and face pain is presumed to have established a proper diagnosis and to be fully aware of the interactions, adverse effects and contraindications of headache medications.

Drug Interactions of Dental Interest

Ergot derivatives may have hypertensive effects, in which case vasoconstrictors in local anesthetic solutions should be used cautiously.

For preventive medications, see the appropriate drug category.

Laboratory Value Alterations

- For preventive medications, see the appropriate drug category.
- Methysergide may cause blood dyscrasias.

Pharmacology

Numerous drugs are used for the management of headache and facial pain. The pharmacology reflects the condition that is to be treated. For example, migraine headache is thought to involve abnormal serotonergic transmission. Varied medications, such as antidepressants, ergots and specific antihistamines, alter serotonin neurotransmission and can be effective in the acute or preventive treatment of migraine. Trigeminal neuralgia responds to anticonvulsant medications by decreasing hyperactive neuronal function.

Treatment of headache and facial pain is beyond the scope of this text. For a more complete review of the pharmacological basis of headache and facial pain management, consult appropriate references.

Adverse Effects, Precautions and Contraindications

Table 20.6 presents adverse effects of neurological drugs; Table 20.7 presents precautions and contraindications.

Suggested Readings

Calne DB. Treatment of Parkinson's disease. New Engl J Med 1993;329:1021-7.

Fraser AD. New drugs for the treatment of epilepsy. Clinical Biochem 1996:29(2):97-110.

McQuay H, Carrol D, et al. Anticonvulsant drugs for the management of pain: a systematic review. Br Med J 1995;311(7012):1047-52.

Millard CB, Broomfield CA. Anticholinesterases: medical applications of neuro-chemical principles. J Neurochem 1995;64(5):1909-18.

Saper JR, Siberstein S, et al. Handbook of headache management. Baltimore: Williams & Wilkins; 1993.

The United States Pharmacopeial Convention, Inc. Drug information for the health care professional. 17th ed. Rockville, Md.: The United States Pharmacopeial Convention, Inc.; 1997.

Table 20.6

Neurological Drugs: Adverse Effects

Body system	Anticonvulsant drugs	Antimyasthenic and Alzheimer's-type dementia drugs	Antiparkinsonism drugs	Antispastic drugs	Vascular headache suppressants
General	Allergic reaction		If noticeable mouthing movements occur, consultation with patient's physician regarding this medication-related side effect may be appropriate	Allergic reaction	
CV	Hypotension, bradycardia, dysrhythmia	Hypotension, bradycardia, heart block, dysrhythmia, cardiac arrest	**Dopamine agonists:** Orthostatic hypotension, dysrhythmias, hypertension, Raynaud's phenomena **Anticholinergics:** Hypotension, tachycardia, ventricular fibrillation	Hypotension	Cardiac fibrosis, valvular thickening, hypertension, tachycardia, dysrhythmias
CNS	Dizziness, drowsiness, sedation, headache, insomnia, slurred speech, trembling, paresthesia	Increased muscarinic and nicotinic effects; dizziness, confusion, weakness, insomnia, fatigue, anorexia	**Dopamine agonists:** Involuntary movements, anxiety, dizziness, fainting spells or lightheadedness, confusion, headache, dyskinesia, insomnia, mood change, fever, hallucinations, excessive dreaming, drowsiness, fatigue **Anticholinergics:** Ataxia, drowsiness, nervousness, hallucinations, weakness, decreased sweating	Drowsiness, vertigo, dizziness, insomnia, euphoria, excitement, slurred speech, weakness, fatigue, headache	Headache, dizziness, confusion, drowsiness, tremor
EENT	Hiccups, diplopia, photophobia	Increased nasal discharge Increased lacrimation, miosis, blurred vision	**Dopamine agonists:** Stuffy nose, dry nose, blepherospasm, blurred vision, yellowing of the eyes **Anticholinergics:** Dry nose, blurred vision, mydriasis, eye pain	Tinnitus, nasal congestion, blurred vision, mydriasis	
Endoc	Hypoventilation, respiratory depression		**Anticholinergics:** Decreased breast milk production		
GI	Nausea, vomiting, dyspepsia, anorexia, weight loss, constipation	Nausea, vomiting, diarrhea	**Dopamine agonists:** Nausea, vomiting, dyspepsia, anorexia, weight loss, constipation, abdominal cramps, GI bleeding, severe diarrhea **Anticholinergics:** Nausea, vomiting	Nausea, vomiting, constipation	Nausea, vomiting

Continued on next page

Table 20.6 (cont.)

Neurological Drugs: Adverse Effects

Body system	Anticonvulsant drugs	Antimyasthenic and Alzheimer's-type dementia drugs	Antiparkinsonism drugs	Antispastic drugs	Vascular headache suppressants
GU		Urinary frequency/ urgency	**Dopamine agonists:** Urinary retention, difficulty in urinating, dark yellow or brown urine **Anticholinergics:** Urinary retention, difficulty in urinating	Urinary frequency	
Hema	Aplastic anemia, agranulocytosis, thrombocytopenia, exacerbation of porphyria, decreased platelet aggregation, blood dyscrasias (uncommon but possible with carbamazepine, phenytoin, valproic acid; can infrequently occur with phenobarbitol, primidone, ethosuximide, topirimate)		**Dopamine agonists:** Anemia, leukopenia, neutropenia for amantadine only	Blood dyscrasias (dantrolene only)	Blood dyscrasias
HB	Hepatitis			Elevated liver enzymes	Retroperitoneal fibrosis
Integ	Skin rash, Stevens-Johnson syndrome, urticaria	Rash, flushing	**Dopamine agonists:** Skin rash, increased sweating, yellowing of the skin **Anticholinergics:** Skin rash	Rash	Rash, flushing, hair loss
Musc	Weakness	Weakness, cramping	**Dopamine agonists:** Leg cramps, dyskinesia	Weakness	Muscle and joint pain
Oral	Dry mouth, glossitis **Topiramate:** Gingivitis	Increased salivation, circumoral burning	Many of these drugs can cause xerostomia **Dopamine agonists:** Xerostomia, involuntary mouth movements, drooling, altered taste **Anticholinergics:** Xerostomia	Xerostomia, taste changes	
Resp	Hypoventilation, respiratory depression	Respiratory depression, bronchospasm			

Table 20.7

Neurological Drugs: Precautions and Contraindications

Drug category	Precautions and contraindications
Anticonvulsants	Monitor vital signs, including respiratory status, prior to dental appointments
	Blood dyscrasias may occur (uncommon but possible with carbamazepine, phenytoin, valproic acid; can infrequently occur with phenobarbitol, primidone, ethosuximide)
	CNS depressants should be prescribed cautiously due to additive sedative effects; meperidine, especially when administered in multiple doses, may precipitate seizure activity
Antimyasthenic and Alzheimer's-type dementia drugs	Monitor vital signs, including respiratory status, prior to dental appointments
	Evaluate the patient for possible postural hypotension while he or she sits in the dental chair for a minute or two after having been in a supine position and likewise when standing
	Anticholinergic agents should be prescribed only upon consultation with physician
	CNS depressants should be prescribed cautiously owing to possible respiratory depression
Antiparkinsonism drugs	Evaluate the patient for possible postural hypotension while he or she sits in the dental chair for a minute or two after having been in a supine position and likewise when standing
	Dopamine antagonist medications that may be prescribed for nausea—such as chlorpromazine, metoclopramide and promethazine—are contraindicated in patients with Parkinson's disease
Antispastic drugs	CNS depressants should be prescribed cautiously owing to possible respiratory depression
Vascular headache suppressants	Vasoconstrictors should be used with caution within 24 h of administration of vascular headache suppressants owing to possible additive hypertensive effects; caution should be used at all times with methysergide

Chapter 21

Psychoactive Drugs

Steven Ganzberg, D.M.D., M.S.

Approximately one of every three people will suffer from a mental illness at some point in his or her life. Many of these people will be placed on a regimen of psychoactive drugs, which may influence dental management. Psychiatric medications include antidepressant, antianxiety, antipsychotic and antimanic drugs as well as sedatives and "sleeping pills" and drugs for attention deficit/hyperactivity disorders and other illnesses.

When members of the dental team are treating a patient taking psychoactive medications, common sense dictates that they should take care in their personal interactions with the patient. Efforts to minimize anxiety, although routine in dental practice, should be given high priority.

General psychiatric drug information is provided in Tables 21.1-21.6. Adverse effects of psychiatric drugs are provided in Table 21.7; precautions and contraindications are provided in Table 21.8.

Use of Psychoactive Drugs in Dental Practice

The prescription of psychoactive agents by dentists is indicated for a number of conditions, including acute anxiety associated with dental or oral surgery, management of bruxism and management of various orofacial pain conditions. These agents also have a place in dentistry for sedation and general anesthesia; this use is covered in Chapters 2 and 3.

Anxiety Associated With Dental or Oral Surgery

The benzodiazepines generally are regarded as the drugs of choice for oral preoperative anxiolysis in dental practice. These drugs have a high margin of safety, especially when used as a single dose 1 h before a dental visit. Diazepam historically has been used in this regard, but with the advent of newer agents with different phamacokinetic properties, other agents may be preferred. Diazepam is an inexpensive drug, with a rapid onset of action and a long half-life with active metabolites. At a dose of 5-10 mg, 1 h before a dental appointment, most adult patients will have some element of anxiolysis without significant sedation.

Another drug, triazolam, has a more rapid onset of action and the shortest half-life of any oral benzodiazepine, 1.5-5 h without active metabolites. This agent may provide less postoperative sedation, which may be desirable. The typical adult oral preoperative anxiolytic dosage for triazolam would be 0.25-0.5 mg 1 h before the dental appointment.

The intravenous drug midazolam has a similar pharmacokinetic profile to that of triazolam. This medication is now FDA-approved for oral use in children. Flurazepam, at 15-30 mg, also may be an acceptable agent based on its pharmacokinetic profile (half-life 2-3 h, peak plasma concentration 0.5-1 h), but this drug also has active metabolites.

With any of these agents, there should be minimal, if any, respiratory or cardiac depression when used alone. In elderly, medically compromised or smaller adult patients, the lower dose range should be prescribed initially. Some patients may experience significant sedation even at low doses. If oral premedication is prescribed, the patient must have a responsible adult escort present at all times until the effects of the sedative have worn off sufficiently. Patients who have taken an oral sedative before a dental appointment must not drive to or from the dental office. Patients should be cautioned about lingering sedative effects during the day and to avoid other central nervous system (CNS) depressants such as alcohol and opioids.

Management of Nocturnal Bruxism

If an acute anxiety-producing circumstance leads to severe bruxism, a short course of a benzodiazepine at bedtime can be efficacious. Typically, diazepam 5-10 mg at bedtime has been used owing to its muscle-relaxing properties and anxiolytic effect. Other benzodiazepines are also effective. In general, this type of benzodiazepine use should be limited to no more than 2 w to avoid issues of dependence, rebound insomnia and alteration of sleep architecture. Benzodiazepines are relatively contraindicated in a depressed patient unless approved by the patient's psychiatrist in advance. Patients should be cautioned about lingering sedative effects during the day and to avoid other CNS depressants such as alcohol and opioids.

The tricyclic antidepressants have come into increasing use for the long-term management of nocturnal bruxism unresponsive to intraoral orthotic therapy. Although not fully understood, bruxism appears to occur during transitional stages of sleep or during rapid-eye-movement (REM) sleep. The tricyclic antidepressants decrease the number of awakenings, shorten time spent in transitional stages of sleep, increase stage III and IV sleep, and markedly decrease time spent in REM sleep. These effects may be beneficial for some patients with bruxism. Common agents used include amitriptyline, nortriptyline or doxepin. These drugs are usually

started at 10 mg at bedtime and gradually titrated upward every few days. It is uncommon for most patients to require more than 50 mg at bedtime, which is substantially below the effective dose for use as an antidepressant.

These drugs are not benign. They have significant anticholinergic and antihistaminic side effects. They can cause cardiac dysrhythmias and may lower seizure threshold. In patients aged > 40 y, pretreatment electrocardiogram evaluation may be appropriate. The dentist prescribing antidepressants for this use is presumed to have established a proper diagnosis and to be fully aware of the drug's interactions, adverse effects and contraindications. When used as antidepressants, these drugs should be prescribed only by clinicians who have had special training in the diagnosis and management of depression.

Management of Orofacial Pain

Psychotropic drugs have a long history of use for chronic pain conditions. A full listing of indications and prescribing information is not appropriate for this text. For the properly trained dentist, the use of psychoactive drugs is appropriate for the management of orofacial conditions such as primary headaches, neuropathic and musculoskeletal pains.

Antidepressants are commonly used for a variety of chronic pain conditions (including myofascial pain syndrome and migraine headache). Phenothiazines can be a useful adjunct for some types of neuropathic pains, and lithium is indicated for cluster headaches. The dentist using these drugs as therapeutic agents is presumed to be proficient in prescribing and managing these medications.

Antianxiety Agents

Anxiety is a state of uneasiness of mind that resembles fear, but usually has no identifiable source. Anxiety has both physical and mental aspects. The anxious patient may be tachycardic, nauseated, diaphoretic or lightheaded. Although a patient may be diagnosed with a generalized anxiety disorder, at times clearly defined categories of anxiety apply. These categories include phobia, agoraphobia, panic attacks, obsessive-compulsive disorder, posttraumatic stress disorder and performance anxiety. Benzodiazepines, gamma-aminobutyric acid-A (GABA$_A$) agonists, are typically prescribed for these disorders. The development of dependence may limit the long-term use of these drugs in some patients. Oral overdose of benzodiazepines is rarely fatal unless combined with other central nervous system depressants such as opioids, barbiturates or alcohol. Another drug without dependence-producing characteristics, the selective serotonin agonist buspirone, may be effective for some generalized anxiety disorders.

β-blockers more recently have been prescribed as an adjunct to benzodiazepine treatment and for control of performance anxiety. Antidepressants are frequently prescribed for patients with coexisting anxiety and depression. The antihistamine hydroxyzine is sometimes used for selected cases of anxiety disorders and as an oral agent for pediatric sedation for dental treatment.

See Table 21.1 for general information on antianxiety agents. Other agents listed as sleep adjuncts, although not FDA-approved for treatment of anxiety, may be prescribed for these disorders. More information on sleep adjuncts appears later in this chapter.

Special Dental Considerations

These drugs may cause xerostomia and should be considered in the differential diagnosis of

Table 21.1

Antianxiety Agents: Dosage and Prescribing Information

Generic name	Brand name(s)	Dosage range (daily)	Interactions with other drugs
Benzodiazepines (See also Table 21.6, Sleep Adjuncts)			
Alprazolam	Alprazol, Alprazolam Intensol, Xanax, Xanax TS, generic; Apo-Alpraz [CAN], Nu-Alpraz [CAN]	0.75-4 mg	CNS depressants (for example, alcohol, opioids and sedating antihistamines) may potentiate sedative side effects
Bromazepam	Lectopam	6-30 mg	CNS depressants (for example, alcohol, opioids and sedating antihistamines) may potentiate sedative side effects
Chlordiazepoxide	Libritabs, Librium, Poxi, generic; Apo-Chlordiazepoxide [CAN], Novo-Poxide [CAN], Solium [CAN]	20-100 mg	Decreased metabolism with cimetidine and erythromycin CNS depressants (for example, alcohol, opioids and sedating antihistamines) may potentiate sedative side effects
Clonazepam	Klonopin, Rivotril; PMS-Clonazepam [CAN]	1.5-20 mg	CNS depressants (for example, alcohol, opioids and sedating antihistamines) may potentiate sedative side effects
Clorazepate	Gen-XENE, Tranxene, Tranxene-SD, Tranxene T-Tab, generic; Apo-Clorazepate [CAN], Novo-Clopate [CAN]	15-90 mg	CNS depressants (for example, alcohol, opioids and sedating antihistamines) may potentiate sedative side effects

[CAN] indicates a drug available only in Canada.

Continued on next page

Table 21.1 (cont.)
Antianxiety Agents: Dosage and Prescribing Information

Generic name	Brand name(s)	Dosage range (daily)	Interactions with other drugs
Benzodiazepines (cont.)			
Diazepam	Diazepam, D-Val, Valium, Valrelease, Zetran; Apo-Diazepam [CAN], Diazemuls [CAN], Novo-Dipam [CAN], PMS-Vivol [CAN]	2-40 mg	Decreased metabolism with cimetidine and erythromycin Decreased clearance with SSRI antidepressants
Halazepam	Paxipam	60-160 mg	CNS depressants (for example, alcohol, opioids and sedating antihistamines) may potentiate sedative side effects
Ketazolam	Loftran	15-30 mg	CNS depressants (for example, alcohol, opioids and sedating antihistamines) may potentiate sedative side effects
Lorazepam	Ativan, Lorazepam Intensol; Apo-Lorazepam [CAN], Novo-Lorazepam [CAN], Nu-Loraz [CAN]	2-9 mg	CNS depressants (for example, alcohol, opioids and sedating antihistamines) may potentiate sedative side effects Increased effect with morphine, MAO inhibitors, loxapine, tricyclic antidepressants
Oxazepam	Serax, generic; Apo-Oxazepam [CAN], Novoxapam [CAN]	30-120 mg	CNS depressants (for example, alcohol, opioids and sedating antihistamines) may potentiate sedative side effects Increased toxicity with anticoagulants, alcohol, tricyclic antidepressants, sedative hypnotics, MAO inhibitors
Prazepam	Centrax, generic	20-60 mg	CNS depressants (for example, alcohol, opioids and sedating antihistamines) may potentiate sedative side effects Increased toxicity with anticoagulants, alcohol, tricyclic antidepressants, sedative hypnotics, MAO inhibitors
Nonbenzodiazepines			
Buspirone	BuSpar	15-60 mg	CNS depressants (for example, alcohol, opioids and some antihistamines) may potentiate sedative side effects
Hydroxyzine	Anxanil, Atarax, E-Vista, Hydroxacen, Hydroxyzin, Hyzine-50, Quiess, Vistaril, Vistazine-50, Vistaject-25 or -50; Apo-Hydroxyzine [CAN], Novo-Multipax [CAN]	**Oral:** 50-100 mg dose **IM:** 50-100 mg, repeated as needed q 4-6 h	Increased toxicity with CNS depressants and anticholinergics

[CAN] indicates a drug available only in Canada.

caries, periodontal disease or candidiasis.

These drugs may cause orthostatic hypotension. After supine positioning, the dentist should ask the patient to sit upright in the dental chair for a minute or two and then monitor the patient when standing.

If these drugs are used for oral preoperative anxiolysis for dental procedures, a competent adult should drive the patient to and from the dental office. Assistance to and from the dental chair may be needed, especially for elderly patients.

Drug Interactions of Dental Interest

Antianxiety agents may have an additive sedative effect with concomitantly administered CNS depressants.

Absorption of diazepam and chlordiazepoxide is delayed with antacids.

The metabolism of chlordiazepoxide, diazepam and triazolam is decreased if they are administered with cimetidine and erythromycin.

The clearance of diazepam is decreased if it is administered with selective serotonin reuptake inhibitor (SSRI) antidepressants.

Special Patients

In elderly, medically compromised or smaller adult patients, the lower dose range should be prescribed initially. Some of these patients may experience significant sedation even at low doses.

Pharmacology

These agents are mainly benzodiazepines, which act at the $GABA_A$ receptor, a gated chloride-ion channel that has specific benzodiazepine and barbiturate receptor sites. Binding of benzodiazepines to the receptor complex opens the chloride channel to facilitate GABA receptor transmission. GABA is the main inhibitory neurotransmitter of the central nervous system. Activity of the GABA system provides antianxiety, sedative, anticonvulsant, amnestic and muscle-relaxing actions. Long-term use of benzodiazepines can lead to a withdrawal syndrome if

abruptly discontinued. The sedative and antianxiety effects of these drugs are used to advantage in promoting short-term sleep improvement. These drugs are hepatically metabolized to active or inactive metabolites for excretion in the bile or urine.

Buspirone, a serotonin ($5HT1_A$) receptor partial agonist with weak dopamine receptor activity, has shown some utility in the management of generalized anxiety. Its onset of action is delayed, thus making this drug a poor choice for management of acute anxiety.

The antihistamines hydroxyzine and diphenhydramine are seldom-used older agents that have sedative and anticholinergic effects independent of GABA action.

Antidepressants

Depression is a common mental illness that will affect at least 5 percent of the population at some time in life. A great number of these patients will be placed on antidepressants. Antidepressants are classified as heterocyclic (tricyclic, tetracyclic), monoamine oxidase inhibitors (MAOIs), selective serotonin reuptake inhibitors (SSRIs), and other miscellaneous agents. These drugs work by affecting neurotransmitter balance between serotonin, norepinephrine and, in some cases, dopamine in the CNS.

Implications in dental and oral surgery revolve around the use of vasoconstrictors in local anesthetics, medication side effects and issues of patient management.

See Table 21.2 for basic information on antidepressants and for epinephrine/levonordefrin interaction information.

Special Dental Considerations

Most of these drugs cause decreased salivary flow. Consider this in the differential diagnosis of caries, periodontal disease or oral candidiasis.

These drugs, in rare cases, cause blood dyscrasias and should be considered in the differential diagnosis of oral signs and symptoms.

Many of these drugs can cause orthostatic hypotension. The dentist should ask the patient to sit upright in the dental chair for a minute or two after being in a supine position and then monitor the patient when standing.

Amoxapine, and less commonly other antidepressants, can cause tardive dyskinesia or extrapyramidal symptoms, which are manifested as involuntary oral or facial movements. Management of bruxism, occlusal adjustments and bite registrations may be difficult to obtain. If newly diagnosed mouthing movements (involuntary mouth and tongue movements and/or drooling) are seen, which may indicate a serious medication side effect, consultation with the patient's physician may be appropriate.

Vanlafaxine can, rarely, cause trismus.

Drug Interactions of Dental Interest

There has been much misunderstanding about the use of local anesthetics with epinephrine for patients taking antidepressants. Local anesthetics with epinephrine are not absolutely contraindicated for any patient taking any antidepressant—including tricyclic or MAOI agents, both of which increase the concentration of norepinephrine in the synaptic cleft. The potential concern is that these drug combinations might lead to a hypertensive crisis. Because a major route of metabolism of exogenously administered catecholamine (such as epinephrine) involves catechol-O-methyl transferase (COMT), use of epinephrine or levonordefrin in patients taking MAOIs is not likely to be of concern. Antidepressants that block norepinephrine reuptake (tricyclics, tetracyclics, venlafaxine, nefazodone) could cause unwanted cardiovascular effects when epinephrine- or levonordefrin-containing local anesthetics are administered. It is prudent, therefore, to monitor vital signs for dental patients taking antidepressants that affect norepinephrine reuptake blockade or monoamine oxidase A (MAO-A) activity.

It is reasonable to administer no more than 40 µg of epinephrine in local anesthetic solutions (approximately one cartridge of local anesthetic with 1:50,000 epinephrine, two cartridges with 1:100,000 epinephrine, four cartridges with 1:200,000 epinephrine or two cartridges of local anesthetic with 1:20,000 levonordefrin) within a short period with careful aspiration technique. Additional anesthetic with vasoconstrictor may be administered if vital signs are acceptable. This may be particularly important in patients taking venlafaxine, which has been noted to produce a sustained increase in diastolic blood pressure and heart rate as a relatively common side effect. No vasoconstrictor contraindication exists for the SSRI antidepressants. Gingival retraction cord with epinephrine is contraindicated for all patients taking antidepressants other than SSRI and should be used with caution, if at all, in other patients.

Anticholinergics and antihistamines should be used cautiously due to additive xerostomia and CNS sedative effects.

CNS depressants (for example, alcohol, opioids and benzodiazepines) may potentiate sedative side effects.

Meperidine and dextromethorphan are specifically contraindicated in patients taking MAOIs. Hypermetabolic crisis may occur. Caution with other opioids is warranted.

Tricyclic antidepressants (which might be used for bruxism) are contraindicated with MAOIs and should be used cautiously with SSRIs unless their use is cleared by a psychiatrist.

The anticoagulant effect of coumarin agents is increased when most antidepressants, including tricyclic agents, are administered concomitantly.

Antidepressants may lower the seizure threshold.

The therapeutic effect of tricyclic antidepressants may be decreased by concurrent administration of barbiturates, anticonvulsants or other hepatic-enzyme–inducing drugs.

With cimetidine, fluoxetine, methylpheni-

Table 21.2

Antidepressants: Dosage and Prescribing Information

Generic name	Brand name(s)	Dosage range (daily)	Interactions with other drugs
Miscellaneous			
Bupropion	Wellbutrin	200-450 mg	**CNS depressants (alcohol, opioids, benzodiazepines):** Additive sedative side effects May induce hepatic microsomal enzymes; metabolism of many drugs may be increased
Mirtazapine	Remeron	7.5-45 mg	**CNS depressants (alcohol, opioids, benzodiazepines):** Additive sedative side effects Monitor vital signs for possible hypertensive crisis Administer no more than 40 µg epinephrine in local anesthetic solutions (two cartridges of 2% lidocaine with 1:100,000 epinephrine or its equivalent) within short period with careful aspiration technique; additional anesthetic with vasoconstrictor may be administered if vital signs are acceptable
Nefazodone	Serzone	200-600 mg	**CNS depressants (alcohol, opioids, benzodiazepines):** Additive sedative side effects Monitor vital signs for possible hypertensive crisis Administer no more than 40 µg epinephrine in local anesthetic solutions (two cartridges of 2% lidocaine with 1:100,000 epinephrine or its equivalent) within short period with careful aspiration technique; additional anesthetic with vasoconstrictor may be administered if vital signs are acceptable May inhibit metabolism of terfenadine/astemizole, which can lead to cardiac dysrhythmias Decreased metabolism of triazolam/alprazolam **Anticholinergics and antihistamines:** May produce additive xerostomia and CNS sedative effects
Trazodone	Desyrel, Trazon, Trialodone, generic	50-600 mg	**CNS depressants (alcohol, opioids, benzodiazepines):** Additive sedative side effects Anticholinergics and antihistamines may produce additive xerostomia and other CNS effects
Venlafaxine	Effexor	75-375 mg	**CNS depressants (alcohol, opioids, benzodiazepines):** Additive sedative side effects Monitor vital signs for possible hypertensive crisis Administer no more than 40 µg epinephrine in local anesthetic solutions (two cartridges of 2% lidocaine with 1:100,000 epinephrine or its equivalent) within short period with careful aspiration technique; additional anesthetic with vasoconstrictor may be administered if vital signs are acceptable

Continued on next page

Table 21.2 (cont.)

Antidepressants: Dosage and Prescribing Information

Generic name	Brand name(s)	Dosage range (daily)	Interactions with other drugs
Monoamine oxidase inhibitors			
Isocarboxazid	Marplan	10-60 mg	**CNS depressants (alcohol, opioids, benzodiazepines):** Additive sedative side effects Monitor vital signs for possible hypertensive crisis Administer no more than 40 µg epinephrine in local anesthetic solutions (two cartridges of 2% lidocaine with 1:100,000 epinephrine or its equivalent) within short period with careful aspiration technique; additional anesthetic with vasoconstrictor may be administered if vital signs are acceptable Meperidine is contraindicated, as it may cause hypermetabolic crisis; caution with other opioids is warranted **Anticholinergics and antihistamines:** Relatively contraindicated owing to additive xerostomia and other CNS effects
Phenelzine	Nardil	15-90 mg	See notes above
Tranylcypromine	Parnate	10-60 mg	See notes above
Selective serotonin reuptake inhibitors			
Citalopram	Celexa	20-60 mg	**CNS depressants (alcohol, opioids, benzodiazepines):** Additive sedative side effects No vasoconstrictor interaction Antifungal agents and erythromycin may increase the plasma levels of citalopram
Fluoxetine	Prozac	20-80 mg	**CNS depressants (alcohol, opioids, benzodiazepines):** Additive sedative side effects No vasoconstrictor interaction The elimination time of some benzodiazepines, especially diazepam, may be increased
Fluvoxamine	Luvox	50-300 mg	**CNS depressants (alcohol, opioids, benzodiazepines):** Additive sedative side effects No vasoconstrictor interaction Decreased clearance of triazolam, diazepam and midazolam

Continued on next page

Table 21.2 (cont.)

Antidepressants: Dosage and Prescribing Information

Generic name	Brand name(s)	Dosage range (daily)	Interactions with other drugs
Selective serotonin reuptake inhibitors (cont.)			
Paroxetine	Paxil	10-50 mg	**CNS depressants (alcohol, opioids, benzodiazepines):** Additive sedative side effects No vasoconstrictor interaction Anticholinergics and antihistamines may produce additive xerostomia and other CNS effects
Sertraline	Zoloft	50-200 mg	**CNS depressants (alcohol, opioids, benzodiazepines):** Additive sedative side effects No vasoconstrictor interaction
Tetracyclic agent			
Maprotiline	Ludiomil, generic	25-225 mg	**CNS depressants (alcohol, opioids, benzodiazepines):** Additive sedative side effects Monitor vital signs for possible hypertensive crisis Administer no more than 40 µg epinephrine in local anesthetic solutions (two cartridges of 2% lidocaine with 1:100,000 epinephrine or its equivalent) within short period with careful aspiration technique; additional anesthetic with vasoconstrictor may be administered if vital signs are acceptable Anticholinergics and antihistamines may provide additive xerostomia and CNS sedative effects
Tricyclic agents			
Amitriptyline	Elavil, Endep, Levate, generic; Apo-Amitriptyline [CAN], Novo-Triptyn [CAN]	10-300 mg	**CNS depressants (alcohol, opioids, benzodiazepines):** Additive sedative side effects Monitor vital signs for possible hypertensive crisis Administer no more than 40 µg epinephrine in local anesthetic solutions (two cartridges of 2% lidocaine with 1:100,000 epinephrine or its equivalent) within short period with careful aspiration technique; additional anesthetic with vasoconstrictor may be administered if vital signs are acceptable Anticholinergics and antihistamines may provide additive xerostomia and CNS sedative effects
Amoxapine	Asendin, generic	100-300 mg	See notes above
Clomipramine	Anafranil	75-250 mg	See notes above

[CAN] indicates a drug available only in Canada.

Continued on next page

Table 21.2 (cont.)

Antidepressants: Dosage and Prescribing Information

Generic name	Brand name(s)	Dosage range (daily)	Interactions with other drugs
Tricyclic agents (cont.)			
Desipramine	Norpramin, Pertofrane, generic	100-300 mg	**CNS depressants (alcohol, opioids, benzodiazepines):** Additive sedative side effects Monitor vital signs for possible hypertensive crisis Administer no more than 40 µg epinephrine in local anesthetic solutions (two cartridges of 2% lidocaine with 1:100,000 epinephrine or its equivalent) within short period with careful aspiration technique; additional anesthetic with vasoconstrictor may be administered if vital signs are acceptable Anticholinergics and antihistamines may provide additive xerostomia and CNS sedative effects
Doxepin	Sinequan, Triadapin, generic; Novo-Doxepin [CAN]	75-300 mg	See notes above
Imipramine	Impril, Norfranil, Tipramine, Tofranil, generic; Apo-Imipramine [CAN], Novo-Pramine [CAN]	75-300 mg	See notes above
Nortriptyline	Aventyl, Pamelor, generic	75-150 mg	See notes above
Protriptyline	Vivactil; Triptil [CAN]	5-60 mg	See notes above
Trimipramine	Rhotrimine, Surmontil, generic; Apo-Trimip [CAN], Novo-Tripramine [CAN]	50-200 mg	See notes above

[CAN] indicates a drug available only in Canada.

date and some estrogens (oral contraceptives), there is increased plasma concentration of trycyclic antidepressants.

Laboratory Value Alterations

- Blood glucose levels may increase or decrease.
- ECG changes are possible with tricyclic antidepressants, especially with pre-existing conduction abnormalities.

Special Patients

Side effects, such as xerostomia and orthostatic hypotension, are more pronounced in elderly patients.

Pharmacology

Antidepressants affect mood by altering the balance between serotonin, norepinephrine and dopamine in critical brain centers. Antidepressants, in general, increase the availability of neurotransmitters in the synaptic cleft, causing changes in the post-synaptic receptor. These changes take some time to develop, thus accounting for the delay in action of 2-4 w or longer for these drugs' mood-altering effects to become apparent. Due to the side-effect profile of many of the tricyclic and MAOI agents, the SSRIs are frequently chosen as first-line therapy for depression. In pain management, both norepinephrine and serotonin reuptake blockade appear to be important for an analgesic effect, so the tricyclics remain the preferred initial agents. Analgesia occurs well before the antidepressant effect and at low doses that are not effective for management of depression in many patients with chronic pain.

The heterocyclic (tricyclic and tetracyclic) and selective serotonin reuptake inhibitor (SSRI) antidepressants block the reuptake of the neurotransmitters into the presynaptic neuron, a partial mechanism by which neurotransmitter activity is modulated. The SSRIs, as their name implies, affect only serotonin reuptake. Because of the receptor selectivity of these agents, they generally possess the fewest side effects of any antidepressant type. The heterocyclic (tricyclic, tetracyclic) antidepressants affect norepinephrine and serotonin, as well as a number of other important neurotransmitters, but to varying degrees. Amoxapine possesses strong dopamine reuptake blocking effects. The MAOIs block the action of MAO-A, an enzyme found in the presynaptic neuron, which degrades serotonin and norepinephrine after reuptake. Buproprion is a weak reuptake blocker of dopamine and, to a lesser extent, norepinephrine and serotonin. Vanlafaxine and nefazadone both block reuptake of norepinephrine and serotonin but have slightly different side-effect profiles than the tricyclic agents. Mirtazapine is an α_2 antagonist affecting norepinephrine and, indirectly, serotonin.

Antimanic/Bipolar Disorder Drugs

Mania is a state of excessive excitement or enthusiasm and is frequently associated with hyperactivity or aggressive behavior. Approximately 90% of people who experience mania alternate these experiences with episodes of depression; this condition is termed "bipolar disorder" (manic-depression). Lithium carbonate is usually the drug of choice, although the anticonvulsants carbamazepine and divalproex sodium are also used.

See Table 21.3 for general information on antimanic/bipolar disorder drugs.

Special Dental Considerations: Lithium

Lithium can cause decreased salivary flow. Consider in the differential diagnosis of caries, periodontal disease or oral candidiasis.

Lithium can cause blood dycrasias and should be considered in the differential diagnosis of oral signs and symptoms.

Lithium can cause orthostatic hypotension. The dentist should monitor vital signs and, after supine positioning, ask the patient to sit upright in the dental chair for a minute or two and then monitor the patient when standing.

Drug Interactions of Dental Interest: Lithium

Vasoconstrictors in local anesthetics should be used with caution owing to lithium's hypotensive effects.

Opioids, alcohol and other hypotension-producing agents have additive hypotensive effects.

NSAIDs, except aspirin and sulindac, increase lithium's plasma concentration because of decreased renal clearance and should be prescribed, if at all, in consultations with the patient's psychiatrist.

Metronidazole increases plasma lithium concentration because of decreased renal clearance.

Table 21.3

Antimanic/Bipolar Disorder Drugs: Dosage and Prescribing Information

Generic name	Brand name(s)	Dosage range (daily)	Interactions with other drugs
Carbamazepine	Atretol, Epitol, Tegretol; Apo-Carbamazepine [CAN], Novo-Carbamaz [CAN], Nu-Carbamazepine [CAN], Tegretol Chewtabs [CAN]	200-1,200 mg or 60 mg/kg/day	**Acetaminophen (prolonged use):** Increased risk of hepatic toxicity **CNS depressants:** Increased sedative effects **Corticosteroids:** Increased metabolism **Propoxyphene, erythromycin/ clarithromycin:** Decreased metabolism, increased risk of toxicity
Divalproex	Depakote, Depakote Sprinkle; Epival [CAN]	500-4,000 mg	**Aspirin/NSAIDs:** Increased risk of bleeding **CNS depressants:** Increased sedative effects
Lithium	Carbolith, Cibalith-S, Duralith, Eskalith, Eskalith CR, Lithane, Lithizine, Lithobid, Lithonate, Lithotabs, generic	600-2,400 mg	**With NSAIDs, metronidazole, chlorpromazine:** Increased serum lithium concentration **With succinylcholine:** Prolonged paralysis may occur

[CAN] indicates a drug available only in Canada.

Tricyclic antidepressants (which may be used for bruxism) may lead to manic episodes.

Laboratory Value Alterations: Lithium
* Blood glucose may be increased.

Pharmacology

Lithium remains the primary treatment for prevention of mania and treatment of bipolar disorder. Although the mechanism of action is incompletely understood, the mood-stabilizing effects may be due to enhancement of the Na^+/K^+ ATPase pump, catecholamine neurotransmission, interference with inositol turnover in the brain or decreased activity of cyclic AMP. Lithium, a monovalent cation, is almost completely dependent on renal excretion for elimination. Coadministered drugs that affect renal function, such as NSAIDs, can increase the plasma concentration of this agent, which has a narrow therapeutic plasma concentration range.

Other agents useful for the treatment of mania, such as valproic acid and carba-mazepine, also have poorly understood mechanisms of action. The anticonvulsant mechanism of these agents is discussed in Chapter 20, Neurological Drugs.

Antipsychotic Agents

The term "psychotic" refers to behavior in which a person cannot distinguish between the real and the unreal. Although the term "psychotic state" denotes mental illness, it does not identify the etiology, such as schizophrenia, major depression, brain tumor or adverse drug reaction. Hallucinations, delusions and thought disorders are characteristic of a psychotic state. Antipsychotic drugs are prescribed to help patients organize chaotic and disorganized thinking. In the past, the terms "major tranquilizers" (denoting prominent sedative side effects) and "neuroleptics" (denoting parkinsonian-like side effects) were used, but the term "antipsychotic" is now preferred.

Table 21.4

Antipsychotic Agents: Dosage and Prescribing Information

Generic name	Brand name(s)	Dosage range (daily)	Interactions with other drugs
		Benzoxazole	
Risperidone	Risperdal	1-16 mg	**Epinephrine/levonordefrin:** Many antipsychotics can cause α-adrenergic receptor blockade; use of epinephrine-containing local anesthetic solutions may cause hypotension and tachycardia Monitor vital signs for possible hypertensive crisis Administer no more than 40 μg epinephrine in local anesthetic solutions (two cartridges of 2% lidocaine with 1:100,000 epinephrine or its equivalent) within short period with careful aspiration technique; additional anesthetic with vasoconstrictor may be administered if vital signs are acceptable **CNS depressants (alcohol, opioids, barbiturates):** Additive sedative effects **Anticholinergic drugs:** Additive anticholinergic effects
		Butyrophenone	
Haloperidol	Haldol, generic; Apo-Haloperidol [CAN], Novo-Peridol [CAN], Peridol [CAN]	1-100 mg	**Epinephrine/levonordefrin:** Many antipsychotics can cause α-adrenergic receptor blockade; use of epinephrine-containing local anesthetic solutions may cause hypotension and tachycardia Monitor vital signs for possible hypertensive crisis Administer no more than 40 μg epinephrine in local anesthetic solutions (two cartridges of 2% lidocaine with 1:100,000 epinephrine or its equivalent) within short period with careful aspiration technique; additional anesthetic with vasoconstrictor may be administered if vital signs are acceptable **CNS depressants (alcohol, opioids, barbiturates):** Additive sedative effects **Anticholinergic drugs:** Additive anticholinergic effects

[CAN] indicates a drug available only in Canada.

Continued on next page

Table 21.4 (cont.)
Antipsychotic Agents: Dosage and Prescribing Information

Generic name	Brand name(s)	Dosage range (daily)	Interactions with other drugs
Dibenzothiazepines			
Quetiapine	Seroquel	50-800 mg	**Epinephrine/levonordefrin:** Many antipsychotics can cause α-adrenergic receptor blockade; use of epinephrine-containing local anesthetic solutions may cause hypotension and tachycardia
			Monitor vital signs for possible hypertensive crisis
			Administer no more than 40 μg epinephrine in local anesthetic solutions (two cartridges of 2% lidocaine with 1:100,000 epinephrine or its equivalent) within short period with careful aspiration technique; additional anesthetic with vasoconstrictor may be administered if vital signs are acceptable
			CNS depressants (alcohol, opioids, barbiturates): Additive sedative effects
			Erythromycin and many antifungal agents may increase quetiapine plasma concentration
Dibenzoxapines			
Clozapine	Clozaril	25-900 mg	**Epinephrine/levonordefrin:** Many antipsychotics can cause α-adrenergic receptor blockade; use of epinephrine-containing local anesthetic solutions may cause hypotension and tachycardia
			Monitor vital signs for possible hypertensive crisis
			Administer no more than 40 μg epinephrine in local anesthetic solutions (two cartridges of 2% lidocaine with 1:100,000 epinephrine or its equivalent) within short period with careful aspiration technique; additional anesthetic with vasoconstrictor may be administered if vital signs are acceptable
			CNS depressants (alcohol, opioids, barbiturates): Additive sedative effects
			Anticholinergic drugs: Additive anticholinergic effects
Loxapine	Loxitane, Loxitane C, Loxitane IM; Loxapac [CAN]	30-250 mg	See notes above
Olanzapine	Zyprexa	10-100 mg	See notes above

[CAN] indicates a drug available only in Canada.

Continued on next page

Table 21.4 (cont.)

Antipsychotic Agents: Dosage and Prescribing Information

Generic name	Brand name(s)	Dosage range (daily)	Interactions with other drugs
Diphenylbutyl			
Pimozide	Orap	1-20 mg	**Epinephrine/levonordefrin:** Many antipsychotics can cause α-adrenergic receptor blockade; use of epinephrine-containing local anesthetic solutions may cause hypotension and tachycardia

Monitor vital signs for possible hypertensive crisis

Administer no more than 40 μg epinephrine in local anesthetic solutions (two cartridges of 2% lidocaine with 1:100,000 epinephrine or its equivalent) within short period with careful aspiration technique; additional anesthetic with vasoconstrictor may be administered if vital signs are acceptable

CNS depressants (alcohol, opioids, barbiturates): Additive sedative effects

Anticholinergic drugs: Additive anticholinergic effects |
| Indole derivatives | | | |
| Molindone | Moban Concentrate; Fluanoxol Depot [CAN] | 20-225 mg | **Epinephrine/levonordefrin:** Many antipsychotics can cause α-adrenergic receptor blockade; use of epinephrine-containing local anesthetic solutions may cause hypotension and tachycardia

Monitor vital signs for possible hypertensive crisis

Administer no more than 40 μg epinephrine in local anesthetic solutions (two cartridges of 2% lidocaine with 1:100,000 epinephrine or its equivalent) within short period with careful aspiration technique; additional anesthetic with vasoconstrictor may be administered if vital signs are acceptable

CNS depressants (alcohol, opioids, barbiturates): Additive sedative effects

Anticholinergic drugs: Additive anticholinergic effects |

[CAN] indicates a drug available only in Canada.

Continued on next page

Table 21.4 (cont.)
Antipsychotic Agents: Dosage and Prescribing Information

Generic name	Brand name(s)	Dosage range (daily)	Interactions with other drugs
Phenothiazines			
Acetophenazine	Tindal	40-120 mg	**Epinephrine/levonordefrin:** Many antipsychotics can cause α-adrenergic receptor blockade; use of epinephrine-containing local anesthetic solutions may cause hypotension and tachycardia
			Monitor vital signs for possible hypertensive crisis
			Administer no more than 40 μg epinephrine in local anesthetic solutions (two cartridges of 2% lidocaine with 1:100,000 epinephrine or its equivalent) within short period with careful aspiration technique; additional anesthetic with vasoconstrictor may be administered if vital signs are acceptable
			CNS depressants (alcohol, opioids, barbiturates): Additive sedative effects
			Anticholinergic drugs: Additive anticholinergic effects
Chlorpromazine	Largactil, Ormazine, Thorazine, Thorazine Concentrate, Thorazine Spansule, Thor-prom, generic; Chlorpromanyl-40 [CAN], Chlorpromanyl-5 [CAN], Largactil Liquid [CAN], Novo-Chlorpromazine [CAN]	30-1,000 mg	See notes above
Fluphenazine	Modecate, Moditen, Permitil, Prolixin	2.5-20 mg	See notes above
Mesoridazine	Serentil, Serentil Concentrate	25-150 mg	See notes above
Methotrimeprazine	Levoprome, Norinan	5-100 mg	See notes above
Pericyazine	Neuleptil	5-60 mg	See notes above
Perphenazine	Trilafon	4-64 mg	See notes above
Pipotiazine	Piportal L4	50-150 mg/q 4 w (parenteral only)	See notes above
Prochlorperazine	Stemetil, Vesprin	10-150 mg	See notes above
Promazine	Promazine, Sparine	40-1,000 mg	See notes above

[CAN] indicates a drug available only in Canada.

Continued on next page

Table 21.4 (cont.)

Antipsychotic Agents: Dosage and Prescribing Information

Generic name	Brand name(s)	Dosage range (daily)	Interactions with other drugs
Phenothiazines (cont.)			
Thiopropazate	Dartal [CAN]	20-100 mg	**Epinephrine/levonordefrin:** Many antipsychotics can cause α-adrenergic receptor blockade; use of epinephrine-containing local anesthetic solutions may cause hypotension and tachycardia Monitor vital signs for possible hypertensive crisis Administer no more than 40 µg epinephrine in local anesthetic solutions (two cartridges of 2% lidocaine with 1:100,000 epinephrine or its equivalent) within short period with careful aspiration technique; additional anesthetic with vasoconstrictor may be administered if vital signs are acceptable **CNS depressants (alcohol, opioids, barbiturates):** Additive sedative effects **Anticholinergic drugs:** Additive anticholinergic effects
Thioproperazine	Majeptil [CAN]	5-90 mg	See notes above
Thioridazine	Mellaril, Mellaril Concentrate, Mellaril-S, generic; Apo-Thioridazine [CAN], PMS-Thioridazine [CAN]	20-800 mg	See notes above
Trifluoperazine	Solazine, Stelazine, Terfluzine	1-40 mg	See notes above
Triflupromazine	Vesprin	80-150 mg (parenteral only)	See notes above

[CAN] indicates a drug available only in Canada.

Continued on next page

See Table 21.4 for general information on antipsychotic agents.

Special Dental Considerations

Many of these drugs can cause decreased salivary flow; the dentist should consider this in the differential diagnosis of caries, periodontal disease or oral candidiasis.

These drugs can cause blood dyscrasias (although this is less likely with risperidone and molindone). The dentist should consider this in the differential diagnosis of oral signs and symptoms.

Many of these drugs can cause orthostatic hypotension. After supine positioning, the dentist should ask the patient to sit upright in the dental chair for a minute or two and then monitor the patient when standing.

Extrapyramidal effects can cause involuntary oral or facial movements (although this is less likely with risperidone and clozapine). Management of bruxism, occlusal adjustments and bite registrations may be difficult. If newly diagnosed oral movements (involuntary mouth and tongue movements and/or drooling) are seen, this may indicate a seri-

Table 21.4 (cont.)
Antipsychotic Agents: Dosage and Prescribing Information

Generic name	Brand name(s)	Dosage range (daily)	Interactions with other drugs
		Thioxanthene	
Chlorprothixene	Taractan	75-600 mg	**Epinephrine/levonordefrin:** Many antipsychotics can cause α-adrenergic receptor blockade; use of epinephrine-containing local anesthetic solutions may cause hypotension and tachycardia
			Monitor vital signs for possible hypertensive crisis
			Administer no more than 40 µg epinephrine in local anesthetic solutions (two cartridges of 2% lidocaine with 1:100,000 epinephrine or its equivalent) within short period with careful aspiration technique; additional anesthetic with vasoconstrictor may be administered if vital signs are acceptable
			CNS depressants (alcohol, opioids, barbiturates): Additive sedative effects
			Anticholinergic drugs: Additive anticholinergic effects
Flupenthixol	Fluanxol [CAN]	3-12 mg	See notes above
Thiothixene	Intensol, Navane, Thiothixine HCl, generic	6-60 mg	See notes above
		Tricyclic agents	
Carbamazepine	Atretol, Epitol, Tegretol; Apo-Carbamazepine [CAN], Novo-Carbamaz [CAN], Nu-Carbamazepine [CAN], Tegretol Chewtabs [CAN]	200-1,200 mg	**Acetaminophen (prolonged use):** Increased risk of hepatic toxicity
			CNS depressants: Increased sedative effects
			Corticosteroids: Increased metabolism
			Propoxyphene, erythromycin/clarithromycin: Decreased metabolism, increased risk of toxicity

[CAN] indicates a drug available only in Canada.

ous medication side effect and the need for consultation with the patient's physician.

Drug Interactions of Dental Interest
With epinephrine/levonordefrin

Many anti-psychotics can cause α-adrenergic receptor blockade. Use of epinephrine-containing local anesthetic solutions may cause hypotension and tachycardia. It is prudent, therefore, to monitor vital signs for dental patients taking these medications. It is rea-sonable to administer no more than 40 µg of epinephrine in local anesthetic solutions (approximately one cartridge of local anesthetic with 1:50,000 epinephrine, two cartridges with 1:100,000 epinephrine, four cartridges with 1:200,000 epinephrine or two cartridges of local anesthetic with 1:20,000 levonordefrin) within a short period with careful aspiration technique. Additional anesthetic with vasoconstrictor may be administered if vital signs are acceptable.

CNS depressants such as alcohol, opioids and barbiturates have additive sedative effects.

Anticholinergic drugs have additive anticholinergic effects.

Tricyclic antidepressants (which may be used for bruxism) have additive anticholinergic effects; combined use of these drugs can lead to alteration of plasma concentration of either drug. Also, they are associated with a possible increased risk of neuroleptic malignant syndrome.

Laboratory Value Alterations
- ECG changes (Q, T wave changes, QT interval, ST depression, AV conduction changes) are possible.

Special Patients
If antipsychotic drugs are being used in elderly patients for an antiemetic effect, lower doses should be used.

Pharmacology
All antipsychotic drugs appear to produce reduction of dopamine synaptic activity in limbic forebrain centers as a common pathway of antipsychotic activity. It appears that action at the dopamine-2 receptor is particularly important. Some of the newer agents, such as clozapine, have significant influences at serotonergic receptors as well, which suggests that other neurotransmitters also play a role in affected midbrain dopamine neurotransmisson. Many of the side effects of these drugs relate to interaction at other receptor sites. α-adrenergic receptor blockade (causing orthostatic hypotension, reflex tachycardia and epinephrine interactions), antihistaminic effects (causing sedation and weight gain) and anticholinergic effects (causing dry mouth, constipation, tachycardia and difficulty in focusing the eyes) are common with many of these drugs.

Because these drugs produce effects on nigrostriatal pathways—an important area in Parkinson's disease—side effects such as tardive dyskinesia and neuroleptic malignant syndrome can occur with these agents. Other extrapyramidal reactions, such as akathisia (restlessness usually associated with some component of motor hyperactivity) or acute dystonic reactions such as oculogyric crisis (uncontrolled eye, face, or neck movements), can occur. Bruxism or other excessive oral movement disorders can be a drug-induced side effect.

These drugs typically undergo extensive hepatic metabolism by oxidation and glucuronidation to inactive metabolites, which are then excreted in the urine.

Drugs Used for Attention Deficit/Hyperactivity Disorder

Hyperactive children have difficulty keeping still for even a few minutes or may display impulsive behaviors. Children with attention deficit disorder (ADD) have difficulty concentrating on tasks and are easily distracted. These diagnoses should not be cavalierly applied to any child who is difficult to manage or is distracted easily; rather, a thorough medical and psychiatric evaluation, including an evaluation of the child's psychosocial functioning, is needed to render the diagnosis of ADD and/or hyperactivity. Interestingly, stimulant medications, with or without psychotherapy, are frequently used for treatment. There is increasing recognition of this disorder in adults.

See Table 21.5 for general information on drugs used for attention deficit/hyperactivity disorder.

Special Dental Considerations
Determine if the patient is taking any drug for attention deficit disorder or narcolepsy. Monitor vital signs because of possible sympathomimetic effects.

Many of these drugs can cause decreased salivary flow and should be considered in the differential diagnosis of caries, periodontal disease or oral candidiasis.

These drugs can, rarely, cause blood dyscrasias; the dentist should consider this in

Table 21.5

Drugs Used for Attention Deficit/Hyperactivity Disorder: Dosage and Prescribing Information

Generic name	Brand name(s)	Dosage range (daily)	Interactions with other drugs
Dextroamphetamine	Dexedrine, Dexedrine Spansule, Dextrostat, generic	5-60 mg	Can interact with vasoconstrictors in local anesthetic solutions; therefore, reasonable approach is to monitor vital signs for possible hypertensive crisis and administer no more than 40 µg epinephrine in local anesthetic solutions (two cartridges of 2% lidocaine with 1:100,000 epinephrine or its equivalent) within short period with careful aspiration technique; additional anesthetic with vasoconstrictor may be administered if vital signs are acceptable; if preoperative vital signs warrant, smaller quantities of vasoconstrictor or no vasoconstrictor may be indicated; additional anesthetic with vasoconstrictor may be administered if vital signs are acceptable **Meperidine:** Contraindicated in patients taking dextroamphetamine
Methylphenidate	Ritalin, Ritalin-SR, generic; PMS-Methylphenidate [CAN]	10-90 mg	Monitor vital signs for possible hypertensive crisis Administer no more than 40 µg epinephrine in local anesthetic solutions (two cartridges of 2% lidocaine with 1:100,000 epinephrine or its equivalent) within short period with careful aspiration technique; additional anesthetic with vasoconstrictor may be administered if vital signs are acceptable
Pemoline	Cylert	37.5-112.5 mg	Can interact with vasoconstrictors in local anesthetic solutions (to a lesser extent than methylphenidate and dextroamphetamine); therefore, reasonable approach is to administer no more than 40 µg epinephrine in local anesthetic solutions (two cartridges of 2% lidocaine with 1:100,000 epinephrine or its equivalent) within a short period with careful aspiration technique; if preoperative vital signs warrant, smaller quantities of vasoconstrictor or no vasoconstrictor may be indicated; additional anesthetic with vasoconstrictor may be administered if vital signs are acceptable

[CAN] indicates a drug available only in Canada.

Table 21.6

Sleep Adjuncts: Dosage and Prescribing Information

Generic name	Brand name(s)	Dosage range (daily)*	Interactions with other drugs
		Benzodiazepines	
Alprazolam	Alprazolam Intensol, Xanax, Xanax TS, generic; Apo-Alpraz [CAN], Novo-Alprazol [CAN], Nu-Alpraz [CAN]	0.75-4 mg	**CNS depressants (alcohol, opioids, sedating antihistamines):** May potentiate sedative side effects Delayed absorption with antacids for chlordiazepoxide and diazepam **Chlordiazepoxide, diazepam:** Decreased metabolism with cimetidine and erythromycin
Bromazepam	Lectopam	6-30 mg	**CNS depressants (alcohol, opioids, sedating antihistamines):** May potentiate sedative side effects
Diazepam	D-Val, Valrelease, Valium, Zetran; Apo-Diazepam [CAN], Diazemuls [CAN], Novo-Dipam [CAN], PMS-Diazepam [CAN], Vivol [CAN]	4-40 mg	Decreased metabolism with cimetidine and erythromycin Decreased clearance with SSRI antidepressants
Estazolam	ProSom	1-2 mg	**CNS depressants (alcohol, opioids, sedating antihistamines):** May potentiate sedative side effects
Flurazepam	Dalmane, generic; Apo-Flurazepam [CAN], Novo-Flupam [CAN], Somnol [CAN]	15-30 mg	See note above
Lorazepam	Ativan; Apo-Lorazepam [CAN], Novo-Lorazam [CAN], Nu-Loraz [CAN]	2-4 mg	See note above
Nitrazepam	Mogadon [CAN]	5-10 mg	See note above
Quazepam	Doral	7.5-15 mg	See note above
Temazepam	Restoril	7.5-15 mg	See note above
Triazolam	Halcion; Apo-Triazo [CAN], Gen-Triazolam [CAN], Novo-Triolam [CAN], Nu-Triazo [CAN]	0.125-0.5 mg	Decreased effect with phenytoin, phenobarbital; increased effect with CNS depressants, cimetidine, erythromycin

[CAN] indicates a drug available only in Canada.
* Dosage listed is single adult dose at bedtime.

Continued on next page

Table 21.6 (cont.)

Sleep Adjuncts: Dosage and Prescribing Information

Generic name	Brand name(s)	Dosage range (daily)*	Interactions with other drugs
		Nonbenzodiazepines	
Diphenhydramine	Benadryl, Compoz, Diphen, Nidryl, Nordryl, Nytol	25-100 mg	**CNS depressants (alcohol, opioids, sedating antihistamines):** May potentiate sedative side effects
Zopicione [CAN]	Imovane [CAN]	3.75-7.5 mg	See note above
Zolpidem	Ambien	10-20 mg	See note above

[CAN] indicates a drug available only in Canada.
* Dosage listed is single adult dose at bedtime.

the differential diagnosis of oral signs and symptoms.

Drug Interactions of Dental Interest

Vasoconstrictors in local anesthetics have possible additive sympathomimetic effects. Depending on vital signs, it is reasonable to administer no more than 40 µg of epinephrine in local anesthetic solutions (approximately one cartridge of local anesthetic with 1:50,000 epinephrine, two cartridges with 1:100,000 epinephrine, four cartridges with 1:200,000 epinephrine or two cartridges of local anesthetic with 1:20,000 levonordefrin) within a short period with careful aspiration technique. If vital signs warrant it, less vasoconstrictor should be used. Additional anesthetic with vasoconstrictor may be administered if vital signs are acceptable after a short period.

Tricyclic antidepressants (which may be used for bruxism) should be used with caution, because their metabolism is decreased by methylphenidate. Increased sympathomimetic effects are possible when tricyclic antidepressants are prescribed to patients taking dextroamphetamine because of norepinephrine reuptake blockade by tricyclics.

Anticholinergics have additive oral drying effects.

Meperidine is contraindicated due to the MAO-inhibitory effect of dextroamphetamine.

Pharmacology

Methylphenidate and pemoline appear to act by blocking dopamine reuptake. These drugs increase children's ability to pay attention and decrease their motor restlessness. Dextroamphetamine is a sympathomimetic amine that blocks the reuptake of dopamine and norepinephrine, inhibits MAO and releases catecholamines. Because of the stimulant effects, use of these drugs may result in weight loss, insomnia and tachycardia. These effects are particularly prominent with dextroamphetamine. These drugs are also used to treat narcolepsy.

Sleep Adjuncts

Sleep disorders include disorders in initiating or maintaining sleep, disorders of excessive somnolence, disorders of sleep-wake schedule and parasomnias (including nocturnal bruxism). Disorders of initiating and maintaining sleep are by far the most common complaints and will be addressed in this section.

The benzodiazepines, GABA$_A$ agonists, are the drugs most commonly prescribed for insomnia. Unfortunately, prolonged use can interfere with normal sleep architecture and be detrimental in the long term. The FDA indication for these drugs is for short-term use only, although they are frequently prescribed for many months or years. Dependence and rebound insomnia are frequently observed. Nevertheless, for short-term use, these agents are generally effective.

A recently introduced nonbenzodiazepine GABA$_A$ agonist, zolpidem, produces less disruption of sleep architecture and may have some effect in treating bruxism. The more sedating tricyclic antidepressants and trazadone also have been used for some patients who require long-term treatment, as have sedating antihistamines. The older barbiturate drugs, such as secobarbital and pentobarbital, are rarely used today for insomnia.

See Table 21.6 for general information on sleep adjuncts.

Special Dental Considerations

These drugs can cause xerostomia. The dentist should consider this in the differential diagnosis of caries, periodontal disease or candidiasis.

These drugs may cause orthostatic hypotension. The dentist should monitor vital signs, ask the patient to sit upright in the dental chair for 1-2 min after being in a supine position and then monitor the patient when standing.

If these drugs are used for preoperative anxiolysis for dental procedures, ensure that a competent adult drives the patient to and from the dental office. Assistance to and from the dental chair may be needed, especially for elderly patients.

Drug Interactions of Dental Interest

CNS depressants will have an additive effect with concomitantly administered CNS depressants.

Diazepam and chlordiazepoxide have delayed absorption with antacids.

The metabolism of chlordiazepoxide, diazepam and triazolam is decreased if they are administered with cimetidine and erythromycin.

The clearance of diazepam is decreased if it is administered with SSRI antidepressants.

Special Patients

In elderly, medically compromised or smaller adult patients, the lower dose range should be prescribed initially. Some of these patients may experience significant sedation even at low doses.

Pharmacology

See the description for antianxiety agents above.

Adverse Effects, Precautions and Contraindications

Table 21.7 provides adverse effects and Table 21.8 provides precautions and contraindications of psychoactive drugs.

Suggested Readings

American Psychiatric Association. Diagnostic and statistical manual of mental disorders (DSM-IV). 4th ed. Washington, D.C.: American Psychiatric Association; 1994.

Brown RS, Bottomley WK. The utilization and mechanism of action of tricyclic antidepressants in the treatment of chronic facial pain: a review of the literature. Anes Prog 1990;37:223-9.

Eschalier A, Mestre C, Dubray C, Ardid D. Why are antidepressants effective as pain relief? CNS Drugs 1994;2:261-7.

Mortimer AM. Newer and older antipsychotics: a comparative review of appropriate use. CNS Drugs 1994;2:381-6.

Okeson JP, ed. Orofacial pain: guidelines for assessment, diagnosis and management. Lombard, Ill.: Quintessence; 1996.

Tucker GJ. Psychiatric disorders in medical practice. In: Wyngaarden JB, Smith LH Jr., Bennett JC, eds. Cecil textbook of medicine. 19th ed. Philadelphia: Saunders; 1992.

The United States Pharmacopeial Convention. Drug information for the health care professional. 17th ed. Rockville, Md.: The United States Pharmacopeial Convention, Inc.; 1997.

Table 21.7

Psychoactive Drugs: Adverse Effects

Body system	Antianxiety agents and sleep adjuncts	Antidepressants—tricyclic, tetracyclic	Antimanic/bipolar disorder drugs	Antipsychotics	Drugs used for attention deficit/hyperactivity disorder	MAO inhibitors	Miscellaneous antidepressants (nefazodone, vanlafaxine, buproprion, mirtazapine)	SSRI antidepressants
General	Pain on injection of diazepam or lorazepam, physical and psychological dependence		**Lithium:** Bluish discoloration of fingers and toes			Peripheral edema, chest pain, headache, increased sweating, increased appetite, weight gain, fatigue	Headache, chest pain, peripheral edema, increased sweating	Chills, fever, joint/muscle pain, allergic reaction, swollen glands, headache, increased sweating, decreased appetite/weight, chest pain, weakness
CV	Hypotension, bradycardia, syncope	Dysrhythmias, tachycardia, bradycardia, hypotension	Tachycardia, bradycardia, irregular pulse	Hypotension, tachycardia	Tachycardia, hypertension, hypotension, dysrhythmias	Hypotension, tachycardia, hypertension, bradycardia, hypertension, dysrhythmias	Palpitations, hypertension, tachycardia, increased diastolic pressure and heart rate (vanlafaxine), hypotension	Tachycardia

Continued on next page

Table 21.7 (cont.)
Psychoactive Drugs: Adverse Effects

Body system	Antianxiety agents and sleep adjuncts	Antidepressants—tricyclic, tetracyclic	Antimanic/bipolar disorder drugs	Antipsychotics	Drugs used for attention deficit/hyperactivity disorder	MAO inhibitors	Miscellaneous antidepressants (nefazadone, vanlafaxine, buproprion, mirtazapine)	SSRI antidepressants
CNS	Drowsiness, amnesia, confusion, ataxia, dizziness, paradoxical excitement, depression, sweating, ataxia, headache, parasthesias	Anticholinergic effects; confusion, fatigue, seizures, delirium, hallucinations, nervousness, anxiety, restlessness, fine tremor, extrapyramidal symptoms, neuroleptic malignant syndrome	Lethargy, dizziness, trembling of hands, pseudotumor cerebri, fatigue, trembling, weakness	Akathisia, loss of balance, dizziness, fine tremor of hands/fingers, decreased seizure threshold, decreased sweating, psychotic behavior, memory loss, tardive dyskinesia, neuroleptic malignant syndrome	Agitation, nervousness, insomnia, drowsiness, headache, Tourette's syndrome, increased sweating	Orthostatic hypotension, sympathetic stimulation, parkinsonian syndrome, shakiness, trembling	Abnormal thinking, agitation, confusion, worsening depression, insomnia, orthostatic hypotension, mania, anxiety, trismus	Mania, hypomania, seizures, insomnia, sedation
Endoc	Irregular menses, decreased libido	Syndrome of inappropriate antidiuretic hormone	Diabetes insipidus, polydipsia, symptoms of hypothyroidism	Galactorrhea, impaired temperature regulation, priapism, menstrual changes, decreased libido, breast pain/swelling	Retarded growth, increase or decrease in libido	Decreased libido, decreased sexual ability, syndrome of inappropriate antidiuretic hormone	Sexual dysfunction, menstrual changes	Decreased libido, priapism (trazadone), hypoglycemia

	Col 1	Col 2	Col 3	Col 4	Col 5	Col 6	Col 7	Col 8
EENT	Blurred vision, diplopia, ear ringing, hyperacusis, nasal congestion	Blurred vision, eye pain, ear ringing	Visual problems	Blurred vision, cornea/lens changes, dry eyes, pigmentary retinopathy, nasal congestion	Blurred vision	Photophobia, blurred vision	Ear pain, ringing of ears, rhinitis, eye pain, blurred vision, pharyngitis	Vision changes
GI	Diarrhea, nausea, vomiting, appetite changes	Constipation, weight gain	Diarrhea, nausea, weight gain	Nausea, vomiting, stomach pain, constipation, weight gain	Nausea, vomiting, weight loss, anorexia, GI pain, diarrhea	Diarrhea, nausea, vomiting, constipation	Constipation, dyspepsia	Nausea, vomiting, constipation
GU		Difficulty in urinating, sexual dysfunction, gynecomastia, galactorrhea	Urinary urgency, renal disease	Difficulty in urinating			Urinary retention or frequency, vaginitis	Frequent urination, hyponatremia
Hema	Rare blood dyscrasias	Blood dyscrasias including aganulocytosis, leukopenia, thrombocytopenia	Leukocytosis	Blood dyscrasias	Blood dyscrasias including thrombocytopenia, leukopenia and anemia	Anemia, leukopenia	Thrombocytopenia, leukopenia	

Continued on next page

Table 21.7 (cont.)

Psychoactive Drugs: Adverse Effects

Body system	Antianxiety agents and sleep adjuncts	Antidepressants—tricyclic, tetracyclic	Antimanic/bipolar disorder drugs	Antipsychotics	Drugs used for attention deficit/hyperactivity disorder	MAO inhibitors	Miscellaneous antidepressants (nefazadone, vanlafaxine, buproprion, mirtazapine)	SSRI antidepressants
HB	Hepatic dysfunction	Cholestatic jaundice		Cholestatic jaundice, hepatotoxicity	Elevated liver enzymes	Hepatitis		
Integ	Rash, dermatitis	Alopecia, photosensitivity	Rash, eruptions	Photosensitivity, rash, itching	Rash		Itch/rash	Rash, hives, itching, flushing/redness of skin (including face/neck)
Musc	Rigidity, tremor	Fine tremor	Weakness, rigidity, tremor, twitching	Dystonic reactions			Neck rigidity	
Oral	Xerostomia	Xerostomia, tardive dyskinesia (especially amoza-pine), glossitis	Impaired taste, xerostomia	Dystonic oral/facial movements, xerostomia, tardive dyskinesia	Xerostomia		Taste changes, xerostomia, stomatitis, glossitis	Taste changes, xerostomia
Resp	Decrease in respiratory rate or apnea (with high dose or with other CNS depressants)	Asthma					Dyspnea, cough, bronchitis	Difficulty in breathing

Table 21.8

Psychoactive Drugs: Precautions and Contraindications

Drug category	Precautions/contraindications
Antidepressants	
General	Except for SSRIs, antidepressants can interact with vasoconstrictors in local anesthetic solutions, so it is prudent to monitor vital signs for dental patients taking these drugs; reasonable approach is to administer no more than 40 μg of epinephrine in local anesthetic solutions (approximately one cartridge of local anesthetic with 1:50,000 epinephrine, two cartridges with 1:100,000 epinephrine, four cartridges with 1:200,000 epinephrine or two cartridges of local anesthetic with 1:20,000 levonordefrin) within short period with careful aspiration technique; additional anesthetic with vasoconstrictor may be administered if vital signs are acceptable
	Can cause orthostatic hypotension; therefore, after supine positioning, dentist should ask patient to sit upright in the dental chair for 1-2 min and then monitor patient when standing
Tricyclic agents and tetracyclic agent*	Should not be prescribed to patients who have pre-existing cardiovascular disease without work-up
	Should be used cautiously, if at all, with fluoxetine
	If used in combination with other antidepressants, meperidine or dextromethorphan, may cause "serotonin syndrome," a condition of serotonin overload characterized by agitation, hyperthermia, sweating, shivering tremors and muscle rigidity
	May cause tardive dyskinesia or neuroleptic malignant syndrome
Selective serotonin reuptake inhibitors	If used in combination with other antidepressants, meperidine or dextromethorphan, may cause "serotonin syndrome," a condition of serotonin overload characterized by agitation, hyperthermia, sweating, shivering tremors and muscle rigidity
Monoamine oxidase inhibitors	Use of MAOIs in combination with other antidepressants, meperidine or dextromethorphan may cause "serotonin syndrome," a condition of serotonin overload characterized by agitation, hyperthermia, sweating, shivering tremors and muscle rigidity
	Meperidine: *Contraindicated for patients taking MAOIs*
Miscellaneous (nefazadone, vanlafaxine, buproprion, mirtazapine)	Use of these antidepressants (buproprion less than others) in combination with other antidepressants, or possibly meperidine or dextromethorphan, may cause "serotonin syndrome," a condition of serotonin overload characterized by agitation, hyperthermia, sweating, shivering tremors and muscle rigidity
	Vanlafaxine may produce sustained increased diastolic blood pressure and heart rate
	Nefazadone may increase plasma levels of terfenadine and astemizole, resulting in cardiac dysrhythmias

Italics indicate information of major clinical significance.
All heterocyclic agents are tricyclic except maprotiline, which is tetracyclic.

Continued on next page

Table 21.8 (cont.)

Psychoactive Drugs: Precautions and Contraindications

Drug category	Precautions/contraindications
Antianxiety agents	
General	Antianxiety agents, except buspirone and hydroyzine, can produce dependence and should not be prescribed for longer than 2 w unless for specific chronic pain complaints unresponsive to other treatments
	If used for an extended time, psychiatric consult may be advisable
	Should be used cautiously with other CNS depressant medications because of additive sedative effects
	Contraindicated in depressed patients without physician consultation and in patients with acute narrow-angle glaucoma
Antimanic/bipolar disorder drugs	
Lithium	Lithium toxicity can occur at or near therapeutic serum concentrations
	As lithium is eliminated almost exclusively via renal mechanisms, drugs that alter renal function—such as NSAIDs—should be used cautiously, if at all
	After supine positioning, dentist should ask patient to sit upright in dental chair 1-2 min and then monitor patient when standing
Antipsychotic drugs	
General	Many antipsychotics can cause α-adrenergic receptor blockade
	Use of epinephrine-containing local anesthetic solutions may cause hypotension and tachycardia, so it is prudent to monitor vital signs for dental patients taking these drugs; reasonable approach is to administer no more than 40 µg of epinephrine in local anesthetic solutions (approximately one cartridge of local anesthetic with 1:50,000 epinephrine, two cartridges with 1:100,000 epinephrine, four cartridges with 1:200,000 epinephrine or two cartridges of local anesthetic with 1:20,000 levonordefrin) within short period with careful aspiration technique; additional anesthetic with vasoconstrictor may be administered if vital signs are acceptable
	Can cause orthostatic hypotension; therefore, after supine positioning, dentist should ask patient to sit upright in dental chair for 1-2 min and then monitor patient when standing
	Many of these drugs can cause tardive dyskinesia (involuntary movements of facial, jaw and tongue muscles); consultation with patient's psychiatrist is appropriate, especially if mouthing movements are initially emergent or particularly severe
Drugs used for attention deficit/hyperactivity disorder	
General	Monitor vital signs before and after administration of epinephrine used in local anesthetic solutions as it may have an exaggerated effect
	Meperidine: *Contraindicated in patients taking amphetamines*

Italics indicate information of major clinical significance.

Continued on next page

Table 21.8 (cont.)

Psychoactive Drugs: Precautions and Contraindications

Drug category	Precautions/contraindications
	Sleep adjuncts
General	Sleep adjuncts, except buspirone and hydroxyzine, can produce dependence and should not be prescribed for longer than 2 w unless for specific chronic pain complaints unresponsive to other treatments
	If used for an extended time, psychiatric consultation may be advisable
	Should be used cautiously with other CNS depressant medications because of additive sedative effects
	Contraindicated in depressed patients without physician consultation and in patients with acute narrow-angle glaucoma

Italics indicate information of major clinical significance.

Chapter 22

Hematologic Drugs

Angelo J. Mariotti, D.D.S., Ph.D.

Hematologic disturbances involve a wide variety of diseases that affect erythrocyte production (anemia or erythrocytosis), leukocytes (leukopenia or leukocytosis), platelets (thrombocytopenia or thrombocytosis), homeostasis (hemorrhage) and normal growth of the lymphoreticular system. Because various drugs, including hormones, growth factors, vitamins and minerals, can directly or indirectly influence the blood as well as blood-forming organs, the treatment of hematologic disorders should always be directed to the specific cause of the disorder; accordingly, proper testing is an important factor in diagnosing the hematologic disturbance.

Antianemic Agents

Special Dental Considerations
Clinical signs of iron toxicity sometimes include bluish-colored lips, fingernails or palms of hands.

Drug Interactions of Dental Interest
Use of iron supplements reduces the absorption of tetracyclines.

Laboratory Value Alterations
The normal daily recommended intake of elemental iron for adolescent and adult males is 10 mg; for nonpregnant adolescent and adult females, the amount ranges from 10 to 15 mg. Common methods to ascertain iron levels in the human body usually measure iron indirectly via hemoglobin levels or hematocrits.

For adult males, the normal range of hemoglobin is 14 mg/dL-18 mg/dL and the normal hematocrit is 42%-52%. For adult females, the normal range of hemoglobin is 12 mg/dL-16 mg/dL and the normal hematocrit range is 37%-47%. Laboratory values falling below these ranges may indicate anemia.

See Table 22.1 for general information on antianemic agents.

Pharmacology
Iron supplements provide adequate amounts of iron necessary for erythropoeisis and increased oxygen transport capacity in the blood. Epoetin alfa induces erythropoeisis by stimulating erythroid progenitor cells to divide and differentiate into mature red blood cells.

Anticoagulant Agents

Special Dental Considerations
Early signs of overdose include bleeding from noninflamed gingivae on brushing or unexplained bruising on skin or in the mouth. In addition, the patient may exhibit purplish areas on the skin, unprovoked nosebleeds, prolonged and intense bleeding from minor cuts or wounds, or all of these. There is some controversy about whether patients receiving therapeutic levels of continuous anticoagulant therapy need to be removed from drug therapy before undergoing dental treatment (such as root planing or extractions). Although sound reasons exist to continue anticoagulation

Table 22.1

Antianemic Agents: Dosage and Prescribing Information

Generic name	Brand name(s)	Indications/uses	Dosage range*	Interactions with other drugs
Epoetin alfa	Epogen, Eprex, Procrit	A recombinant protein (identical to erythropoietin) that is used to treat anemias associated with renal failure and AIDS	**Adult, initial parenteral dose:** 50-100 units/kg 3 times/w **Adult, maintenance:** Should be lowest possible dose to maintain hematocrit at appropriate level **Child < age 12 y:** Not established	With an increase in red blood cells, iron supplements may need to be increased as well as antihypertensive agents, owing to a decrease in endogenous iron stores and increases in blood pressure, respectively
Ferrous fumarate	Femiron, Feostat, Fumerin, Hemocyte, Ircon, Palafer, Palmiron, Span-FF; Neo-Fer [CAN], Novo-Fumar [CAN]	Replacement therapy with iron supplements is used for the prevention and treatment of anemia induced by iron deficiency	**Adult, therapeutic—oral, tablets:** 200 mg tid-qid **Adult, prophylactic—oral, tablets:** 200 mg/day **Child, therapeutic—oral, tablets:** 3 mg/kg tid **Child, prophylactic—oral, tablets:** 3 mg/kg/day	Precautions should be taken not to use iron supplements concomitantly with acetohydroxamic acid, dimercaprol, etidronate, *tetracyclines*, alcohol, foods or medications containing bicarbonates, carbonates, oxalates or phosphates, milk or milk products, tea, whole-grain breads, coffee, calcium supplements, cimetidine, *ciprofloxacin*, deferoxamine, pancreatin, penicillamine, trientine
Ferrous gluconate	Fergon, Ferralet, Fertinic, Simron; Apo-Ferrous Gluconate [CAN], Novo-Ferrogluc [CAN]	See note above	**Adult, therapeutic—oral, capsules:** 325-650 mg qid **Adult, prophylactic—oral, capsules:** 325 mg/day **Child < age 2 y:** Dosage must be individualized by physician **Child > age 2 y, therapeutic—oral, capsules:** 16 mg/kg tid **Child > age 2 y, prophylactic—oral, capsules:** 8 mg/kg/day	See note above

[CAN] indicates a drug available only in Canada.
Italics indicate information of major clinical significance.
* Oral dosage forms for children and adults will differ depending on how drug is formulated.

Continued on next page

Table 22.1 (cont.)

Antianemic Agents: Dosage and Prescribing Information

Generic name	Brand name(s)	Indications/uses	Dosage range*	Interactions with other drugs
Ferrous sulfate	Feosol, Fer-In-Sol, Fero-Grad, Fero-Fradumet, Ferospae, Ferralyn Lanacaps, Ferra-TD, Mol-Iron, Slow Fe; Apo-Ferrous Sulfate [CAN], Novo-Ferrosulfate [CAN], PMS-Ferrous Sulfate [CAN]	Replacement therapy with iron supplements is used for the prevention and treatment of anemia induced by iron deficiency	**Adult, prophylactic—oral, capsules:** 300 mg/day **Adult, therapeutic—oral, capsules:** 300 mg bid-qid **Child, prophylactic—oral, capsules:** 5 mg/kg/day **Child, therapeutic—oral, capsules:** 10 mg/kg tid	Precautions should be taken not to use iron supplements concomitantly with acetohydroxamic acid, dimercaprol, etidronate, *tetracyclines*, alcohol, foods or medications containing bicarbonates, carbonates, oxalates or phosphates, milk or milk products, tea, whole-grain breads, coffee, calcium supplements, cimetidine, *ciprofloxacin*, deferoxamine, pancreatin, penicillamine, trientine

[CAN] *indicates a drug available only in Canada.*
Italics indicate information of major clinical significance.
* Oral dosage forms for children and adults will differ depending on how drug is formulated.

therapy during dental treatment, there also is a risk of hemorrhage in patients who are at therapeutic levels of anticoagulation. Generally, a patient who is taking anticoagulants and has an international normalized ratio (INR) of less than 3.0 is considered safe in undergoing scaling and root planing. Nonetheless, as the risk of localized bleeding after dental procedures (such as scaling, root planing and surgical procedures) can increase in a patient who is taking anticoagulants, the dentist must consult with the patient's physician to determine whether temporary reduction or withdrawal of the drug is advisable.

Drug Interactions of Dental Interest

All drug interactions affecting anticoagulants have not been identified; therefore, monitoring INR is recommended when any drug is added to or withdrawn from a patient's regimen.

Special Patients

Women of childbearing age should take additional nonhormonal precautions to prevent pregnancy when using anticoagulant agents. Anticoagulant use is not recommended during pregnancy or labor and delivery.

See Table 22.2 for general information on anticoagulant agents.

Pharmacology

These agents inhibit vitamin K γ-carboxylation of procoagulation factors II, VII, IX and X in the liver. Heparin potentiates the effects of antithrombin III and neutralizes thrombin.

Antidotes

Special Dental Considerations

In most cases, patients who receive folinic acid are suffering from toxicity (symptoms such as gastrointestinal bleeding and thrombocytopenia) owing to methotrexate, pyrimethamine or trimethoprim therapy for a neoplasm.

See Table 22.3 for general information on the antidote leucovorin.

Pharmacology

The principal use of leucovorin is to circumvent the actions of dihydrofolate reductase inhibitors.

Table 22.2

Anticoagulant Agents: Dosage and Prescribing Information

Generic name	Brand name(s)	Indications/uses	Dosage range	Interactions with other drugs
Acenocoumarol [CAN]	Sintrom [CAN]	Ensures flow of blood in vessels by preventing blood clotting and lysing of thrombi	Each dose of acenocoumarol must be individualized and adjusted according to appropriate coagulation test **Adult—oral, tablets:** 8-12 mg on first day, 4-8 mg on second day **Adult, maintenance—oral, tablets:** 1-10 mg, depending on prothrombin time tests **Child:** Not established	**Following drugs can increase anticoagulant activity:** *Acetaminophen*, allopurinol, aminosalicylates, amiodarone, anabolic steroids, *antibiotics, aspirin*, bromelains, cefamandole, cefoperazone, *chloral hydrate, chloramphenicol*, chymotrypsin, cimetidine, cinchophen, clofibrate, danzol, dextrothyroxine, diazoxide, diflunisal, disulfiram, *erythromycin*, ethacrynic acid, fenoprofen, gemfibrozil, glucagon, heparin, indomethacin, influenza vaccine, isoniazid, ketoconazole, meclofenamate, mefenamic acid, *meperidine*, methamazole, methotrexate, methyldopa, methylphenidate, *metronidazole*, miconazole, MAO inhibitors, nalidixic acid, nifedipine, phenylbutazone, plicamycin, propoxyphene, propylthiouracil, quinidine, quinine, *salicylates*, sulfinpyrazone, *sulfonamides*, sulindac, testolactone, thyroid hormones, tricyclic antidepressants, valproic acid, verapamil, vitamin A, vitamin E **Following drugs can decrease anticoagulant activity:** Antacids, ascorbic acid, *barbiturates, carbamazepine*, chlorobutanol, diuretics, estramustine, estrogens, ethchlorvynol, glutethimide, *griseofulvin*, laxatives, primidone, rifampin, vitamin K **Following drugs can increase or decrease anticoagulant activity:** Alcohol, cholestyramine, colestipol, contraceptives, corticotropin, cyclophosphamide, disopyramide, *glucocorticoids*, halperidol, mercaptopurine, phenytoin **Comments:** Oral surgical procedures can increase danger of hemorrhage from localized areas; before scaling and root planing or any surgical procedure, consultation with patient's physician is required
Anisindione	Miradon	Ensures flow of blood in vessels by preventing blood clotting and lysing of thrombi	Each dose of anisindione must be individualized and adjusted according to appropriate coagulation test **Adult and adolescent—oral, tablets:** 25-200 mg/day as indicated by prothrombin time levels **Child:** Not established	See note above

[CAN] indicates a drug available only in Canada.
Italics indicate information of major clinical significance.

Continued on next page

Table 22.2 (cont.)

Anticoagulant Agents: Dosage and Prescribing Information

Generic name	Brand name(s)	Indications/uses	Dosage range	Interactions with other drugs
Dicumerol	Dicumerol	Ensures flow of blood in vessels by preventing blood clotting and lysing of thrombi	Each dose of dicumerol must be individualized and adjusted according to appropriate coagulation test **Adult and adolescent—oral:** 25-200 mg/day **Child:** Not established	**Following drugs can increase anticoagulant activity:** *Acetaminophen,* allopurinol, aminosalicylates, amiodarone, anabolic steroids, *antibiotics, aspirin,* bromelains, cefamandole, cefoperazone, *chloral hydrate, chloramphenicol,* chymotrypsin, cimetidine, cinchophen, clofibrate, danzol, dextrothyroxine, diazoxide, diflunisal, disulfiram, *erythromycin,* ethacrynic acid, fenoprofen, gemfibrozil, glucagon, heparin, indomethacin, influenza vaccine, isoniazid, ketoconazole, meclofenamate, mefenamic acid, *meperidine,* methamazole, methotrexate, methyldopa, methylphenidate, *metronidazole,* miconazole, MAO inhibitors, nalidixic acid, nifedipine, phenylbutazone, plicamycin, propoxyphene, propylthiouracil, quinidine, quinine, *salicylates,* sulfinpyrazone, *sulfonamides,* sulindac, testolactone, thyroid hormones, tricyclic antidepressants, valproic acid, verapamil, vitamin A, vitamin E **Following drugs can decrease anticoagulant activity:** Antacids, ascorbic acid, *barbiturates,* carbamazepine, chlorobutanol, diuretics, estramustine, estrogens, ethchlorvynol, glutethimide, *griseofulvin,* laxatives, primidone, rifampin, vitamin K **Following drugs can increase or decrease anticoagulant activity:** Alcohol, cholestyramine, colestipol, contraceptives, corticotropin, cyclophosphamide, disopyramide, *glucocorticoids,* halperidol, mercaptopurine, phenytoin **Comments:** Oral surgical procedures can increase the danger of hemorrhage from localized areas; before scaling and root planing or any surgical procedure, a consultation with the patient's physician is required
Heparin	Calcilean, Calciparine, Hepalean, Heparin Leo, Liquaemin	Ensures flow of blood in vessels by preventing blood clotting and lysing of thrombi	Each dose of heparin must be individualized and adjusted according to appropriate coagulation test **Adult—IV:** 5,000 units, followed by 20,000-40,000 units over 24 h **Child—IV:** 50 units/kg followed by 20,000 units/m² /24 h	*Glucocorticoids,* ethacrynic acid, *salicylates,* anticoagulants (for example, coumarin), *antihistamines,* digitalis glycosides, nicotine, *tetracyclines,* streptokinase, urokinase, and so forth may interact with heparin, *aspirin,* sulfinpyrazone, cefamandole, cefoperazone, plicamycin, valproic acid, chloroquine, hydroxychloroquine, methimazole, propylthiouracil, nitroglycerine, probenecid and thrombolytic agents **Comments:** Oral surgical procedures can increase the danger of hemorrhage from localized areas; before scaling and root planing or any surgical procedure, consultation with patient's physician is required

| Warfarin | Coumadin, Panwarfin, Sofarin; Warfilone [CAN] | Ensures flow of blood in vessels by preventing blood clotting and lysing of thrombi | Each dose of warfarin must be individualized and adjusted according to appropriate coagulation test

Adult and adolescent—oral: 10-15 mg/day for 2-4 days, followed by 2-10 mg/day as indicated by prothrombin time levels

Child: Not established | **Following drugs can increase anticoagulant activity:** *Acetaminophen,* allopurinol, aminosalicylates, amiodarone, anabolic steroids, *antibiotics,* oral antidiabetic agents, *aspirin,* bromelains, cefamandole, cefoperazone, *chloral hydrate, chloramphenicol,* chymotrypsin, cimetidine, cinchophen, clofibrate, danzol, dextrothyroxine, diazoxide, diflunisal, disulfiram, *erythromycin,* ethacrynic acid, fenoprofen, gemfibrozil, glucagon, heparin, indomethacin, influenza vaccine, isoniazid, ketoconazole, meclofenamate, mefenamic acid, meperidine, methamazole, methotrexate, methyldopa, methylphenidate, *metronidazole,* miconazole, MAO inhibitors, nalidixic acid, nifedipine, phenylbutazone, plicamycin, propoxyphene, propylthiouracil, quinidine, quinine, *salicylates,* sulfinpyrazone, *sulfonamides,* sulindac, testolactone, thyroid hormones, tricyclic antidepressants, valproic acid, verapamil, vitamin A, vitamin E

Following drugs can decrease anticoagulant activity: Antacids, ascorbic acid, *barbiturates,* carbamazepine, chlorobutanol, diuretics, estramustine, estrogens, ethchlorvynol, glutethimide, *griseofulvin,* laxatives, primidone, rifampin, vitamin K

Following drugs can increase or decrease anticoagulant activity: Alcohol, cholestyramine, colestipol, contraceptives, corticotropin, cyclophosphamide, disopyramide, *glucocorticoids,* halperidol, mercaptopurine, phenytoin

Comments: Oral surgical procedures can increase the danger of hemorrhage from localized areas; before scaling and root planing or any surgical procedure, a consultation with the patient's physician is required |

[CAN] *indicates a drug available only in Canada.*
Italics indicate information of major clinical significance.

Table 22.3

Antidote: Dosage and Prescribing Information

Generic name	Brand name(s)	Indications/uses	Dosage range	Interactions with other drugs
Leucovorin	Wellcovorin, generic	Used in cancer chemotherapy when high doses of folic acid antagonists (that is, methotrexate, pyrimethamine or trimethoprim) are used	Various dosage regimens have been used; doctor who prescribes this medication should consult the literature, as most regimens are experimental **Adult—parenteral:** 10 mg/m^2 q 6 h until methotrexate blood levels fall below 5x10^{-8} m **Child:** Not established	Anticonvulsants (*barbiturate* or hydantoin), primidone and fluorouracil may interact with folinic acid

Italics indicate information of major clinical significance.

Antifibrinolytic Agent

Special Dental Considerations

Aminocaproic acid has been used for postsurgical hemorrhage after oral surgical procedures. See Chapter 5 for further discussion of this and other agents that modify blood coagulation.

Drug Interactions of Dental Interest

Aminocaproic acid and drugs containing estrogen may increase thrombus formation.

Special Patients

In women using oral contraceptives, concurrent use of aminocaproic acid increases the chance of thrombus formation.

See Table 22.4 for general information on the antifibrinolytic agent aminocaproic acid.

Pharmacology

This agent inhibits the activation of plasminogen.

Antithrombotic Agents

Special Dental Considerations

As increased risk of localized bleeding can occur after dental procedures (such as scaling, root planing and surgical procedures), the dentist should consider consulting the patient's physician to determine whether temporary reduction or withdrawal of the drug is advisable. It is recommended that these drugs be discontinued 10-14 days before any dental surgery. Ticlopidine also may induce neutropenia, leading to microbial infections, delayed healing and gingival bleeding. Dental work should be delayed if severe neutropenia occurs.

Drug Interactions of Dental Interest

There are additive effects of dipyridamole with aspirin on platelet aggregation. Therefore, there is a risk of increased bleeding when these agents are used with aspirin or (nonsteroidal anti-inflammatory drugs (NSAIDs).

Laboratory Value Alterations

Blood pressure and bleeding times should be monitored. Normal bleeding times range between 3 and 10 min, depending on the method used to determine bleeding times. Normal neutrophil levels are 3,000-7,000/cm^3.

See Table 22.5 for general information on antithrombotic agents.

Pharmacology

These agents either decrease or increase platelet aggregation.

Table 22.4
Antifibrinolytic Agent: Dosage and Prescribing Information

Generic name	Brand name(s)	Indications/uses	Dosage range	Interactions with other drugs
Aminocaproic acid	Amicar	Used to control hemorrhage induced following surgery or by hyperfibrinolysis-induced treatment	**Adult—oral:** 5 g in first h, followed by 1 g/h for 8 h or until appropriate response is achieved **Child—oral:** 0.1 g/kg for first h, followed by 0.0333 g/kg for 24 h or until appropriate response is achieved; total dose should not exceed 18 g	Estrogens, oral contraceptives containing estrogens and factor IX complex, in combination with aminocaproic acid, may increase the potential for thrombus formation

Table 22.5
Antithrombotic Agents: Dosage and Prescribing Information

Generic name	Brand name(s)	Indications/uses	Dosage range	Interactions with other drugs
Dipyridamole	Dipridacot, IV Persantine, Persantine; Apo-Dipyridamole [CAN], Novo-Dipiradol [CAN]	Used in conjunction with other anticoagulants to reduce chance of clotting problems associated with prosthetic heart valves	**Adult—oral:** 75-100 mg for 4 days with concomitant administration of an anticoagulant **Child:** NE	*Nonsteroidal anti-inflammatory drugs*, platelet aggregation inhibitors, *aspirin*, cefamandole, cefoperazone, cefotetan, pliamycin, valproic acid and thrombolytic agents may affect actions of this drug
Ticlopidine	Ticlid	Inhibits platelet aggregation and reduces chance of recurrent stroke in people who have had a thrombotic stroke	**Adult—oral:** 250 mg bid **Child:** NE	Anticoagulants (for example, coumarin derivatives), heparin, thrombolytic agents (for example, alteplase) and *aspirin* may increase the risk of bleeding when used with ticlopidine Antacids may decrease plasma concentrations of ticlopidine **Comments:** Prior to any dental surgery, patients should discontinue use of ticlopidine for 10-14 days in consultation with their physician In an emergency, the transfusion of fresh platelets may rectify hemostatic problems; in addition, ticlopidine may induce neutropenia and patient may elicit gingival bleeding, delayed healing and susceptiblity to infections; blood tests should be considered to determine neutrophil content and work delayed until blood counts return to normal

[CAN] indicates a drug available only in Canada.
Italics indicate information of major clinical significance.
NE: Not established.

Nutritional Supplements

Special Dental Considerations

Anemic patients may exhibit pallor in the mouth. Cyanocobalamin and folic acid are dietary supplements used to treat anemia.

Drug Interactions of Dental Interest

Antibiotics can interfere with the assay of serum vitamin B_{12} concentrations or serum folic acid concentrations. Sulfonamides will inhibit the absorption of folate.

See Table 22.6 for general information on nutritional supplements.

Pharmacology

These supplements provide adequate amounts of vitamin K or folic acid to prevent anemia.

Thrombolytic Agents

Special Dental Considerations

These agents are used intensively for short periods in a hospital setting; therefore, drug interactions are not normally observed in a dental office.

Drug Interactions of Dental Interest

Antibiotics (cefamandole, cefoperazone, cefotetan), aspirin and NSAIDs may increase the risk

Table 22.6
Nutritional Supplements: Dosage and Prescribing Information

Generic name	Brand name(s)	Indications/uses	Dosage range	Interactions with other drugs
Cyanocobalamin	Anacobin, Bedoz, Cobex, Crysta-mine, Crysti-12, Cyanoject, Cyomin, Rubion, Rubramin, Rubramin PC, generic	For prevention or treatment of pernicious anemia	**Adult—oral:** 0.001 mg/day, not to exceed 0.025 mg/day **Child ≤ age 1 y—oral:** 0.0007 mg/day **Child > age 1 y—oral:** 0.001 mg/day	Alcohol, aminosalicylates, colchicine, ascorbic acid and folic acid may reduce plasma concentration of cyanocobalamin *Antibiotics* can interfere with assay of serum vitamin B_{12} concentrations
Folic acid	Folvite; Apo-Folic [CAN], Novo-Folacid [CAN]	Replacement therapy with folic acid is used for prevention and treatment of anemia induced by folic acid deficiency	**Adult, as dietary supplement—oral:** 0.1 mg/day **Adult, for initial treatment of folic acid deficiency—oral:** 0.25-1 mg/day **Adult, for maintenance treatment of folic acid deficiency—oral:** 0.4 mg/day **Child, as dietary supplement—oral:** 0.1 mg/day **Child, for initial treatment of folic acid deficiency—oral:** 0.25-1 mg/day **Child, for maintenance treatment of folic acid deficiency—oral:** 0.1-0.4 mg/day, depending on child's age	*Analgesics,* anticonvulsants (hydantoin), carbamazepine, estrogens, aluminum- or magnesium-containing antacids, *antibiotics,* chlestyramine, methotrexate, pyrimethamine, triamterene, trimethoprim, *sulfonamides* and zinc supplements have been indicated to interact with folic acid

[CAN] indicates a drug available only in Canada.
Italics indicate information of major clinical significance.

of bleeding when used in conjunction with thrombolytic agents.

See Table 22.7 for general information on thrombolytic agents.

Pharmacology

These agents activate the endogenous fibrinolytic system by converting plasminogen to plasmin.

Adverse Effects, Precautions and Contraindications

Dental care professionals should be aware of the possible adverse effects of hematologic drugs (Table 22.8), as well as precautions and contraindications for their use (Table 22.9).

Suggested Readings

Becker RC, Gore JM. Cardiovascular therapies in the 1990s. An overview. Drugs 1991;41:345-57.

Corbett NE, Peterson GM. Review of the initiation of anticoagulant therapy. J Clin Pharm Ther 1995;20(4):221-4.

Freedman MD. Pharmacodynamics, clinical indications, and adverse effects of heparin. J Clin Pharmacol 1992;32:584-96.

Haines ST, Bussey HI. Thrombosis and the pharmacology of antithrombotic agents. Ann Pharm 1995;29:892-905.

Stern R, Karlis V, Kinney L, Glickman R. Using the international normalized ratio to standardize prothrombin time. JADA 1997;128:1121-2.

Stringer KA. Beyond thrombolysis: other effects of thrombolytic drugs. Ann Pharm 1994;28:752-6.

Workman ML. Anticoagulants and thrombolytics: what's the difference? AACN Clin Issues 1994;5:26-35.

Table 22.7
Thrombolytic Agents: Dosage and Prescribing Information

Generic name	Brand name(s)	Indications/ uses	Dosage range*	Interactions with other drugs
Alteplase, recombinant	Activase, Activase rt-PA, Lysatec rt-PA	Lysis of occluding thrombi in arterial or venous vessels	**Adult > 65 kg, for coronary arterial thrombosis—IV:** 100 mg over 3 h **Child:** Not established	Anticoagulants (for example, coumarin-derivative drugs), enoxaparin, heparin, antifibrinolytic agents (for example, aminocaproic acid), antihypertensive agents, cefamandole, cefoperazone, cefotetan, plicamycin, valproic acid, *corticosteroids*, ethacrynic acid, *salicylates, nonsteroidal anti-inflammatory drugs, aspirin*, indomethacin, phenylbutazone, platelet aggregation inhibitors, sulfinpyrazone, ticlopidine and thiotepa may interfere with this drug's actions
Anistreplase	Eminase	See note above	**Adult, for coronary arterial thrombosis—IV:** 30 units over 2-5 min **Child:** Not established	See note above
Streptokinase	Kabikinase, Streptase	See note above	**Adult, for coronary arterial thrombosis—IV:** 1,500,000 international units **Child:** Not established	See note above
Urokinase	Abbokinase, Abbokinase Open-Cath	See note above	**Adult, for coronary arterial thrombosis—IV:** 6,000 units/min **Child:** Not established	See note above

Italics indicate information of major clinical significance.
* Thrombolytic therapy should be accomplished in a hospital setting with appropriate personnel and equipment to monitor the patient. Each dose of drug must be individualized and adjusted according to the appropriate coagulation test.

Table 22.8
Hematologic Drugs: Adverse Effects

Body system	Antianemic agents	Anticoagulant agents	Antidote: Leucovorin	Antifibrinolytic agent: Aminocaproic acid	Antithrombotic agents	Nutritional supplements	Thrombolytic agents
General	**Epoetin alfa:** Chest pain **Ferrous drugs:** Soreness, contact irritation	**Heparin:** Pain, allergic reactions (anaphylaxis and anaphylactic shock), bleeding, chest pain **All other drugs in this category:** Bleeding	**Leucovorin:** Allergic reaction	Allergic reaction, unusual tiredness or weakness	**Dipyridamole:** Allergic reaction **Ticlopidine:** Bleeding complications	**Folic acid:** Allergic reaction	**All listed:** Allergic reaction, bleeding from wounds, fever, bleeding into subcutaneous spaces
CV	**Epoetin alfa:** Hypertension, tachycardia			Hypotension, thromboembolism	**Dipyridamole:** Angina pectoris		Hypotension, stroke, cholesterol or fat embolism
CNS	**Epoetin alfa:** Seizures **Ferrous drugs:** Drowsiness			Dizziness, lightheadedness	**Dipyridamole:** Dizziness, lightheadedness		
EENT				Tinnitus	**Ticlopidine:** Tinnitus		
GI	**Ferrous drugs:** Stomach pain, cramping, diarrhea, vomiting, constipation, nausea	**All but heparin:** Diarrhea, nausea		Gastrointestinal irritation (nausea, diarrhea)	**Dipyridamole:** Gastrointestinal irritation (diarrhea, nausea) **Ticlopidine:** Diarrhea, indigestion, nausea, abdominal pain		

Body System					
GU		**All but heparin:** Renal damage	Bladder obstruction		
Hema		**All but heparin:** Agranulocytosis		**Ticlopidine:** Agranulocytosis, thrombocytopenia	
HB		**All but heparin:** Hepatotoxicity		**Ticlopidine:** Hepatitis	
Integ	**Epoetin alfa:** Allergic reactions (rash, hives) **Ferrous drugs:** Bluish-colored lips and palms of hand; rash, hives	**Heparin:** Coldness or bluish tinge of extremities, necrosis of skin		**Ticlopidine:** Rash	**Cyanocobalamin:** Allergic reactions (rash, hives) **Folic acid:** Rash
Musc	**Ferrous drugs:** Muscle pain	**Heparin:** Peripheral neuropathy	Myopathy		
Oral	**Ferrous drugs:** Metallic taste				
Renal			Renal failure		
Resp	**Epoetin alfa:** Shortness of breath			**Dipyridamole:** Dyspnea	**Folic acid:** Bronchospasm

Table 22.9
Hematologic Drugs: Precautions and Contraindications

Antianemic agents	Anticoagulant agents	Antidote: Leucovorin	Antifibrinolytic agent: Aminocaproic acid	Antithrombotic agents	Nutritional supplements	Thrombolytic agents
Epoetin alfa: May cause increase in blood pressure; therefore, blood pressure should be monitored at frequent intervals; hypertensive patients must comply with their antihypertensive regimen Rapid rise of the hematocrit has been associated with medical problems and must be monitored twice/w Low iron levels will decrease efficacy of epoetin Renal function should be monitored in patients with impaired renal function Pregnancy risk category: C	**Acenocoumarol, anisindione, dicumeral, warfarin:** Congenital defects have been reported in pregnant women taking coumarin-like anticoagulants Owing to the deficiency of vitamin K, infants are more susceptible to anticoagulants *Contraindicated* in patients with history of miscarriage, aneurysm, any type of hemorrhage (for example, cerebrovascular), hypertension, hemophilia, thrombocytopenia, severe diabetes, recent childbirth, endocarditis, recent surgery (for example, ophthalmic, neurosurgery), pericarditis, impaired renal function, trauma, impaired hepatic function Pregnancy risk category: X	**Leucovorin:** May increase seizures in children *Contraindicated* in patients with pernicious anemia, vitamin B_{12} deficiency, impaired renal function, sensitivity to folinic acid Pregnancy risk category: C	May cause hypotension and bradycardia and should be carefully considered when prescribed to patients with cardiovascular problems In a few cases, this medication has caused acute renal failure *Contraindicated* in patients with hypersensitivity to this medication Pregnancy risk category: C	**Dipyridamole:** Contraindicated in patients with unstable angina pectoris, collateral blood vessels and hypotension Pregnancy risk category: B	**Cyanocobalamin:** Contraindicated in patients with Leber's disease and sensitivity to this drug Pregnancy risk category: C	**All thrombolytic agents:** Contraindicated in patients with aneurysm, arteriovenous malformations, active bleeding, brain tumors, cerebrovascular accident, recent surgery, recent trauma, hypertension, anaphylaxis to streptokinase or anistreplase, recent childbirth, coagulation defects, endocarditis, mitral stenosis **Alteplase, recombinant; anistreplase; streptokinase:** Pregnancy risk category—C **Urokinase:** Pregnancy risk category—B

Ferrous fumarate, ferrous gluconate, ferrous sulfate: Tumors have been reported at injection site for iron dextran	Heparin: Geriatric women (aged > 60 y) may be more susceptible to bleeding during therapy	Ticlopidine: Use should be discontinued 10-14 days before any surgical procedure	Folic acid: Contraindicated in treatment of pernicious anemia, as irreversible neurologic problems may occur; also contraindicated in patients with hypersensitivity to this drug
Use of iron supplements is contraindicated in patients with hemochromatosis, hemosiderosis, hemolytic anemia, thalassemia, alcoholism, asthma, hepatitis, kidney disease, enteritis, colitis, peptic ulcer, rheumatoid arthritis, allergy to iron	May cause osteoporosis in lactating women	Contraindicated in patients with active bleeding, hemophilia, hemapoietic disorders (for example, neutropenia), impaired hepatic function, gastrointestinal ulceration, recent surgery, recent trauma, impaired renal function and sensitivity to this drug	Pregnancy risk category: A
Pregnancy risk category: C	Contraindicated in patients with history of miscarriage, aneurysm, any type of hemorrhage (for example, cerebrovascular), hypertension, hemophilia, thrombocytopenia, severe diabetes, recent childbirth, endocarditis, recent surgery (for example, ophthalmic, neurosurgery), pericarditis, impaired renal function, trauma, impaired hepatic function	Pregnancy risk category: B	
	Pregnancy risk category: C		

Italics indicate information of major clinical significance.

Chapter 23

Endocrine/Hormonal Drugs

Angelo J. Mariotti, D.D.S., Ph.D.

Hormones are chemical substances that are secreted from various organs into the blood stream and have specific regulatory effects on target tissues. The general functions of hormones can be divided into reproduction; growth and development; homeostasis of the internal environment; and energy production, use and storage.

Although the effects of hormones are diverse and complex, hormones can be divided into two broad categories according to their chemical structure: polypeptides and steroids. The polypeptides or amino acid derivates represent a majority of hormones. This category comprises hormones that are secreted from a variety of organs (such as brain, pancreas, thyroid and adrenal glands) and include large polypeptides (such as luteinizing hormone), medium-sized peptides (such as insulin), small peptides (such as thyrotropin-releasing hormone), dipeptides (such as thyroxine) and single amino acid byproducts (such as histamine).

The remaining hormones are derivatives of cholesterol and are called steroid hormones. Similarly to the polypeptide hormones, steroid hormones are secreted from a variety of organs (such as adrenal glands, testis and ovary). But unlike the polypeptide hormones, they are more uniform in their chemical structure, because each steroid hormone must contain a cyclopentanoperhydrophenanthrene ring system (for example, estradiol).

Hormones, regardless of their chemical structure, have common characteristics. First, hormones are found in low concentrations in the blood circulation. Most polypeptide hormone concentrations in the blood range from 1 to 100 femtomolar, while thyroid and steroid hormone concentrations range between picomolar and micromolar concentrations. Second, hormones must be directed to their sites of action, and this is most commonly accomplished by special protein molecules (receptors) that recognize specific hormones. Polypeptide hormone receptors are proteins that are fixed on the cell membrane; thyroid and steroid hormone receptors are proteins located inside the cell.

Although most drugs are considered to be substances foreign to the body, naturally occurring substances such as hormones can be used as drugs and can exert important effects on the body. Furthermore, analogs of hormones also have been synthesized to produce important therapeutic effects. In addition, various drugs affect the synthesis, secretion or degradation of hormones as well as antagonize their cellular effects (hormone antagonists).

Androgens

Special Dental Considerations

Androgens can exacerbate patients' inflammatory status, causing erythema and an increased tendency toward gingival bleeding. A controlled oral hygiene program that combines professional cleanings and plaque control will minimize androgen-induced sequelae.

Drug Interactions of Dental Interest

Androgens are responsible for the growth and development of male sex organs and for the maintenance of secondary sexual characteristics in males. Androgens can be used for replacement therapy in androgen-deficient men or for treatment of certain neoplasms. Androgens may enhance the actions of oral anticoagulants, oral hypoglycemic agents and glucocorticoids.

See Table 23.1 for general information on androgens.

Pharmacology

Androgens bind to intracellular androgen receptors that regulate RNA and DNA in target tissues.

Estrogens

Special Dental Considerations

Estrogens can exacerbate patients' inflammatory status, causing erythema and an increased tendency toward gingival bleeding. In some instances, estrogens have been reported to induce gingival overgrowths. A controlled oral hygiene program that combines professional cleanings and plaque control will minimize estrogen-induced sequelae.

Drug Interactions of Dental Interest

Estrogens are responsible for the growth and development of female sex organs and for the maintenance of secondary sexual characteristics in women. Estrogens can be used to treat a variety of estrogen-deficiency states, as well as for certain neoplasms. Estrogen may change the requirements for oral anticoagulants, oral hypoglycemics, insulin or barbiturates.

See Table 23.2 for general information on estrogens.

Pharmacology

Estrogens bind to intracellular estrogen receptors that regulate RNA and DNA in target tissues.

Insulin

Special Dental Considerations

Patients with diabetes mellitus are at risk of developing periodontal disease. A thorough evaluation of the mouth followed by a controlled oral hygiene program—including regular oral examinations, professional cleanings and plaque control—are recommended. Because diabetics have an increased risk of developing leukopenia and thrombocytopenia, an increased frequency of infection, altered wound healing and gingival bleeding are possible. Dental treatment should be delayed if leukopenia or cytopenia occurs.

People who have either type 1 or type 2 diabetes mellitus can experience untoward effects in the dental office. These can occur when a patient's insulin dose is not correctly titrated and blood glucose levels are either too low or too high. In patients whose diabetes is well-controlled by insulin (or other hypoglycemic agents), these concerns are minimized by proper medication in conjunction with proper diet. Signs of hyperglycemia are listed in the box on the page 424.

Drug Interactions of Dental Interest

Insulin can be used for the treatment of patients with either insulin-dependent or noninsulin-dependent diabetes mellitus. Corticosteroids may enhance blood glucose levels, and large doses of salicylates and nonsteroidal anti-inflammatory drugs may increase the hypoglycemic effect of insulin.

Laboratory Value Alterations

- Values for leukocytes in leukopenia: less than 4,000 cells per cubic millimeter as opposed to the normal values, 5,000-10,000 cells/mm^3.
- Values for platelets in thrombocytopenia: less than 20,000 platelets/mm^3 as opposed to the normal values of 150,000-350,000 platelets/mm^3.

See Table 23.3 for general information on insulin.

Table 23.1

Androgens: Dosage and Prescribing Information

Generic name	Brand name(s)	Indications/uses	Dosage range	Interactions with other drugs
Fluoxymes-terone	Android-F, Halotestin	Androgens are anabolic steroid hormones used for treatment of androgen deficiency, delayed male puberty, catabolic processes, anemia as well as for treatment of some types of breast neoplasms	Drug therapy with androgens should be at lowest effective dose, with amount of drug individualized and adjusted to obtain desired effect. Regular monitoring by a physician is necessary	Anticoagulants (coumarin- or indandione-derivative), oral hypoglycemics, insulin and cyclosporine may affect actions of androgens
Methyltestos-terone	Android-10, Metandren, Oreton, Testred	See note above	See note above	See note above
Nandrolone	Deca-Durabolin, Durabolin, Hybolin Decanoate, Hybolin-Improved, Kabolin, Neo-Durabolic	See note above	See note above	See note above
Oxandrolone	Oxandrin	See note above	See note above	See note above
Oxymetholone	Anadrol-50, Anapolon 50	See note above	See note above	See note above
Stanozolol	Winstrol	See note above	See note above	See note above
Testosterone	Andro 100, Andro-Cyp 100, Andro-Cyp 200, Andro L.A. 100, Andro L.A. 200, Andryl 200, Delatest, Delatestryl, depAndro 100, depAndro 200, Depotest, Depo-Testosterone, Depo-Testosterone Cypionate, Duratest-100, Duratest-200, Durathate-200, Everone, Histerone-50, Histerone-100, Malogen, Malogex, T-Cypionate, Testa-C, Testamone 100, Testaqua, Testex, Testoderm, Testoject-50, Testoject-LA, Testone L.A. 200, Testred Cypionate 200, Testrin-P.A., Virilon IM	See note above	See note above	See note above

Table 23.2

Estrogens: Dosage and Prescribing Information

Generic name	Brand name(s)	Indications/uses	Dosage range	Interactions with other drugs
Chlortrianisene	TACE	Estrogens are steroid hormones used for treatment of estrogen deficiency, atropic vaginitis, vulvar squamous hyperplasia, menopause, uterine bleeding, osteoporosis, and some types of breast and prostatic neoplasms	Drug therapy with estrogens should be at the lowest effective dose, with amount of drug individualized and adjusted to obtain desired effect Estrogens may be administered in a cyclic or continuous regimen depending on the indication for use Regular monitoring by a physician is necessary	Bromocriptine, *corticosteroids*, cyclosporine, and some *antibiotics* may affect actions of estrogens
Conjugated estrogen	Congest, Premarin, Premarin Intravenous	See note above	See note above	See note above
Diethylstilbestrol	Honvol, Stilphostrol	See note above	See note above	See note above
Esterified estrogens	Estratab, Menest; Neo-Estrone [CAN]	See note above	See note above	See note above
Estradiol	Clinagen LA 40, Deladiol-40, Delestrogen, depGynogen, Depo-Estradiol, Depogen, Dioval 40, Dioval XX, Dura-Estrin, Duragen-20, Duragen-40, E-Cypionate, Estrace, Estraderm, Estragyn LA 5, Estra-L 40, Estro-Cyp, Estrofem, Estroject-LA, Estro-L.A., Estro-Span, Femogex, Gynogen L.A. 20, Gynogen L.A. 40, Menaval-20, Valeregen-10, Valeregen-20, Valeregen-40	See note above	See note above	See note above
Estrone	Aquest, Estragyn 5, Estro-A, Kestrone-5, Wehgen	See note above	See note above	See note above
Estropipate	Ogen, Ogen .625, Ogen 1.25, Ogen 2.5, Ortho-Est	See note above	See note above	See note above
Ethinyl estradiol	Estinyl	See note above	See note above	See note above
Quinestrol	Estrovis	See note above	See note above	See note above

[CAN] indicates a drug available only in Canada.
Italics indicate information of major clinical significance.

Signs of hypoglycemia	Signs of hyperglycemia
Anxiety	Xerostomia
Blood pressure normal or increased	Blood pressure normal or decreased
Breath normal in odor	Smell of acetone on breath
Breathing may be stertorous but at normal depth and rate	Breathing is deep and fast
Confusion, inability to concentrate	Warm and dry skin
Cool and moist skin	Loss of appetite
Hunger	Normal or depressed reflexes
Hyperactive reflexes	Lethargy
Lethargy	Gradual onset of symptoms
Rapid onset of symptoms	Rapid, normal or thready pulse
Rapid pulse	
Tired, weak	
Unsteadiness	
Vision problems	

Pharmacology

Insulin binds to fixed receptors on the cell membrane to control the storage and metabolism of carbohydrates, proteins and lipids.

Oral Contraceptives

Special Dental Considerations

Oral contraceptives can exacerbate patients' inflammatory status, causing erythema and an increased tendency toward gingival bleeding. In some instances, oral contraceptives have been reported to induce gingival enlargement.

All studies recording changes in gingival tissues associated with oral contraceptives were completed when contraceptive concentrations were at much higher levels than are available today. A recent clinical study evaluating the effects of oral contraceptives on gingival inflammation in young women found these hormonal agents to have no effect on gingival tissues. From these data, it appears that current compositions of oral contraceptives probably are not as harmful to the periodontium as were the early formulations. Nonetheless, a controlled oral hygiene program that includes regular oral examinations, professional cleanings and plaque control will minimize the effects of oral contraceptives.

These drugs also may increase the incidence of local alveolar osteitis after extraction of teeth.

Drug Interactions of Dental Interest

Oral contraceptives are used primarily to prevent ovulation. The effectiveness of oral contraceptives may be decreased by penicillin, chloramphenicol, oral neomycin, sulfonamides, barbiturates, glucocorticoids, griseofulvin and tetracyclines.

See Table 23.4 for general information on oral contraceptives.

Pharmacology

Oral contraceptives prevent conception by suppressing ovulation, preventing nidation or slowing migration of sperm to the ovum.

Oral Hypoglycemic Agents

Special Dental Considerations

Patients with diabetes mellitus are at risk of developing periodontal disease. In patients whose diabetes is well-controlled by hypoglycemic agents, concerns are minimized with proper medication, proper diet and proper oral hygiene. It is recommended that these patients receive a thorough evaluation of the mouth followed by a controlled oral hygiene program that includes regular oral examinations, professional cleanings and plaque control. Owing to an increased risk of leukopenia and thrombocytopenia in diabetic patients, an increased frequency of infection, altered wound healing and gingival bleeding is possible. Dental treatment should be delayed if leukopenia or cytopenia occurs.

Drug Interactions of Dental Interest

Oral hypoglycemic agents can be used only for the treatment of type 2 diabetes mellitus. Glucocorticoids may decrease the effectiveness of oral hypoglycemic agents. Nonsteroidal anti-inflammatory drugs and salicylates may increase the risk of hypoglycemia. See the box on the previous page for a listing of signs of hypoglycemia.

Laboratory Value Alterations

- Values for leukocytes in leukopenia: less than 4,000 cells per cubic millimeter as opposed to the normal values of 5,000-10,000 cells/mm^3.
- Values for platelets in thrombocytopenia: less than 20,000 platelets/mm^3 as opposed to the normal values of 150,000-350,000 platelets/mm^3.

See Table 23.5 for general information on oral hypoglycemic agents.

Pharmacology

Oral hypoglycemics lower blood glucose levels by stimulating the functioning of β cells of the pancreatic islets to secrete insulin.

Progestins

Special Dental Considerations

Progestins can exacerbate patients' inflammatory status, causing erythema and an increased tendency toward gingival bleeding. In some instances, progestins have been reported to induce gingival enlargement. A controlled oral hygiene program that includes regular oral examinations, professional clean-ings and plaque control will minimize the effects of progestins.

Drug Interactions of Dental Interest

Progestins are responsible for maintenance of the female reproductive system in pregnant and nonpregnant women. Progestins are used for the treatment of certain female hormone imbalances as well as for the treatment of some neoplasms. Drug interactions with progestins are limited and involve drugs not normally prescribed by dentists.

See Table 23.6 for general information on progestins.

Pharmacology

Progestins bind to intracellular progesterone receptors that regulate RNA and DNA in target tissues.

Thyroid Hormones

Special Dental Considerations

Patients with well-controlled hypothyroidism can receive any dental treatment. Dental treatment should be delayed in patients whose thyroid symptoms are not appropriately controlled pharmacologically.

Drug Interactions of Dental Interest

Thyroid hormones, a mixture of liothyroxin and levothyroxine, are necessary for the homeostasis of the human body. Liothyroxin and/or levothyroxine are used for replacement therapy in patients with diminished thyroid function. Glucocorticoids and sympathomimetic agents may interfere with the actions of the drugs.

See Table 23.7 for general information on thyroid hormones.

Pharmacology

Thyroid hormones bind to nuclear thyroid hormone receptors that regulate catabolic and anabolic effects necessary for homeostasis.

Table 23.3

Insulin: Dosage and Prescribing Information

Generic name	Brand name(s)	Indications/uses	Dosage range	Interactions with other drugs
Extended insulin zinc	Humulin-U, Humulin U Ultralente, Lente Iletin, Lente Iletin I, Lente Iletin II, Lente Insulin, Lente L, Ultralente Insulin, Ultralente U; Novolin ge Ultralente [CAN]	Insulin is used in treatment of type 1 dependent and type 2 diabetes mellitus	Amount of insulin and timing of insulin administration can vary dramatically among different patients; consequently, dosage and administration of insulin must be individualized and adjusted by physician to obtain desired blood glucose level in the patient **Adult—maintenance, SC:** 0.5-1.0 unit/kg/day	Amphetamines, baclofen, oral contraceptives, *corticosteroids*, danazol, dextrothyroxine, thiazide diuretics, *epinephrine*, estrogens, ethacrynic acid, furosemide, molindone, phenytoin, thyroid hormones and triamterene may enhance blood glucose concentrations, and dosage of either insulin or these drugs must be adjusted Alcohol, anabolic steroids, disopyramid, guanethidine, MAO inhibitors, *large doses of salicylates and nonsteroidal anti-inflammatory analgesics* may increase hypoglycemic effect of insulin β-adrenergic blocking agents may increase risk of either hypoglycemia or hyperglycemia
Insulin	Humulin R, Insulin-Toronto, Novolin R, Regular Iletin, Regular Iletin I, Regular Iletin II, Regular Insulin, Velosulin Human; Novolin ge Toronto [CAN]	See note above	Amount of insulin and timing of insulin administration can vary dramatically among different patients; consequently, dosage and administration of insulin must be individualized and adjusted by physician to obtain desired blood glucose level in the patient	See note above

Insulin zinc	Humulin L, Humulin-L, Novolin L; Novolin ge Lente [CAN]	See note above	See note above	See note above
Isophane insulin	Humulin 10/90, Humulin 20/80, Humulin 30/70, Humulin 40/60, Humulin 50/50, Humulin 70/30, Humulin N, Humulin-N, Novolin 70/30, Novolin ge 10/90, Novolin ge 20/80, Novolin ge 30/70, Novolin ge 40/60, Novolin ge 50/50, Novolin ge NPH, Novolin N, NPH Iletin, NPH Iletin I, NPH Iletin II, NPH Insulin	See note above	See note above	See note above
Prompt insulin zinc	Semilente Insulin	See note above	See note above	See note above

[CAN] indicates a drug available only in Canada.
Italics indicate information of major clinical significance.

Table 23.4

Oral Contraceptives: Dosage and Prescribing Information

Generic name	Brand name(s)	Indications/uses	Dosage range	Interactions with other drugs
Desogestrel (progestin), ethinyl estradiol (estrogen)	Desogen, Marvelon, Ortho-Cept	Oral contraceptives are a combination of estrogens and/or progestins used for prevention of pregnancy	Use of oral contraceptives depends on the preparation; monophasic, biphasic and triphasic combination oral contraceptives are taken for 21 days followed by a 7-day period during which no pills are taken; progesterone-only contraceptives (see Table 23.6, Progestins) are taken daily without interruption or can be injected IMI (for example, medroxyprogesterone)	Bromocriptine, anticoagulants (coumarin- or indandione-derivative) *corticosteroids*, cyclosporine, tricyclic antidepressants and some *antibiotics* (for example, *ampicillin, chloramphenicol, neomycin, penicillin V, sulfonamides, tetracyclines*) may affect actions of estrogens
Ethynodiol diacetate (progestin), ethinyl estradiol (estrogen)	Demulen 1/35, Demulen 1/50, Demulen 30, Demulen 50, Nelulen 1/35E, Nelulen 1/50E	See note above	See note above	See note above
Levonorgestrel (progestin), ethinyl estradiol (estrogen)	Levlen, Mini-Ovral, Nordette, Tri-Levlen, Triphasil, Triquilar	See note above	See note above	See note above
Norethindrone (progestin), ethinyl estradiol (estrogen)	Brevicon, Brevicon 0.5/35, Brevicon 1/35, GenCept 0.5/35, GenCept 1/35, GenCept 10/11, Genora 0.5/35, Genora 1/35, Jenest, ModiCon, N.E.E. 1/35, N.E.E. 1/50, Nelova 0.5/35E, Nelova 1/35E, Nelova 10/11, Norethin 1/35E, Norinyl 1+35, Ortho 0.5/35, Ortho 1/35, Ortho 7/7/7, Ortho 10/11, Ortho-Novum 1/35, Ortho-Novum 7/7/7, Ortho-Novum 10/11, Ovcon-35, Ovcon-50, Synphasic, Tri-Norinyl	See note above	See note above	See note above

Italics indicate information of major clinical significance..

Continued on next page

Table 23.4 (cont.)

Oral Contraceptives: Dosage and Prescribing Information

Generic name	Brand name(s)	Indications/uses	Dosage range	Interactions with other drugs
Norethindrone (progestin), mestranol (estrogen)	Genora 1/50, Nelova 1/50M, Norethin 1/50M, Norinyl 1/50, Norinyl 1+50, Ortho-Novum 0.5, Ortho-Novum 1/50, Ortho-Novum 1/80, Ortho-Novum 2	Oral contraceptives are a combination of estrogens and/or progestins used for prevention of pregnancy	Use of oral contraceptives depends on the preparation; monophasic, biphasic and triphasic combination oral contraceptives are taken for 21 days followed by a 7-day period during which no pills are taken; progesterone-only contraceptives (see Table 23.6, Progestins) are taken daily without interruption or can be injected IMI (for example, medroxyprogesterone)	Bromocriptine, anticoagulants (coumarin- or indandione-derivative) *corticosteroids*, cyclosporine, tricyclic antidepressants and some *antibiotics* (for example, *ampicillin, chloramphenicol, neomycin, penicillin V, sulfonamides, tetracyclines*) may affect actions of estrogens
Norethindrone acetate (progestin), ethinyl estradiol (estrogen)	Loestrin 1/20, Loestrin 1.5/30, Minestrin 1/20	See note above	See note above	See note above
Norgestimate (progestin), ethinyl estradiol (estrogen)	Cyclen, Ortho-Cyclen, Ortho Tri-Cyclen, Tri-Cyclen	See note above	See note above	See note above
Norgestrel (progestin), ethinyl estradiol (estrogen)	Lo/Ovral, Ovral	See note above	See note above	See note above

Italics indicate information of major clinical significance..

Table 23.5

Oral Hypoglycemic Agents: Dosage and Prescribing Information

Generic name	Brand name(s)	Indications/uses	Dosage range	Interactions with other drugs
Acetohexamide	Dimelor, Dymelor	Oral hypoglycemics are used in treatment of type 2 diabetes mellitus	Amount of oral hypoglycemic agents and timing of administration of oral hypoglycemic agents can vary dramatically among different patients; consequently, dosage, administration and type of oral hypoglycemic agents must be individualized and adjusted by physician to obtain desired blood glucose level in patient	Blood glucose concentrations may be increased with concomitant use of oral hypoglycemic agents and adrenocorticoids, amphetamines, anticonvulsants (for example, hydantoin), baclofen, bumetanide, calcium channel blocking agents, chlorthalidone, oral contraceptives, danazol, dextrothyroxine, *epinephrine*, ethacrynic acid, furosemide, glucagon, molindine, *large doses of salicylates*, thiazide diuretics, thyroid hormones and triamterene Blood glucose concentrations may be decreased with concomitant use of oral hypoglycemic agents and androgens, allopurinol, *nonsteroidal anti-inflammatory drugs*, insulin, *chloramphenicol*, clofibrate, MAO inhibitors, *salicylates* and *sulfonamides* β-adrenergic blocking agents may increase risk of either hypoglycemia or hyperglycemia
Chlorpropamide	Chlorpropamide	See note above	See note above	See note above
Glipizide	Glucotrol	See note above	See note above	See note above
Glyburide	Albert Glyburide, DiaBeta, Euglucon, Gen-Glybe, Glynase PresTab, Micronase; Apo-Glyburide [CAN], Novo-Glyburide [CAN]	See note above	See note above	See note above
Tolazamide	Tolamide, Tolinase, Tol-Tab	See note above	See note above	See note above
Tolbutamide	Mebenol, Orinase; Apo-Tolbutamide [CAN], Novo-Butamide [CAN]	See note above	See note above	See note above

[CAN] indicates a drug available only in Canada.
Italics indicate information of major clinical significance.

Table 23.6

Progestins: Dosage and Prescribing Information

Generic name	Brand name(s)	Indications/uses	Dosage range	Interactions with other drugs
Hydroxypro-gesterone	Hy/Gestrone, Hylutin, Pro-Depo, Prodrox, Pro-Span	Progestins are steroid hormones used for treatment of female hormonal imbalances, endome-triosis, contracep-tion, maintenance of pregnancy as well as for treatment of uter-ine corpus, metastatic endometrial and metastatic renal carcinomas	Drug therapy with progestins should be at lowest effective dose, with amount of drug individual-ized and adjusted to obtain desired effect; regular monitoring by a physician is necessary	Bromocriptine in combi-nation with progestins may cause amenorrhea or galactorrhea
Medroxypro-gesterone	Amen, Curretab, Cycrin, Depo-Provera, Provera	See note above	See note above	See note above
Megestrol	Megace	See note above	See note above	See note above
Norethindrone	Aygestin, Micronor, Morlutate, Norlutin, Nor-QD	See note above	See note above	See note above
Norgestrel	Ovrette	See note above	See note above	See note above
Progesterone	Gesterol 50	See note above	See note above	See note above

Antithyroid Agents

Special Dental Considerations

Dental treatment should be delayed in patients with hyperthyroidism whose symp-toms are not appropriately controlled phar-macologically or surgically. Antithyroid hormones are a group of drugs used to decrease the production of thyroid hormones. Because these agents have the potential to depress cells in the bone marrow, the incidence of microbial infections can increase, resulting in delayed healing and gingival bleeding. A patient who is using antithyroid drugs may exhibit leukopenia, thrombocytopenia or both, and any dental work should be deferred until blood counts return to normal.

Drug Interactions of Dental Interest

Methimazole and propylthiouracil are used in the treatment of patients with hyperthy-roidism before surgery or radiotherapy. These drugs can cause mouth sores, sialadenopathy, loss of taste, gingival bleeding and delayed wound healing.

See Table 23.8 for general information on antithyroid hormones.

Pharmacology

Antithyroid hormones inhibit the synthesis of thyroid hormones by interfering with the oxidation of iodide to iodine, thereby block-ing the synthesis of thyroxine.

Table 23.7

Thyroid Hormones: Dosage and Prescribing Information

Generic name	Brand name(s)	Indications/uses	Dosage range	Interactions with other drugs
Levothyroxine	Eltroxin, Leo-T, Levoxine, Synthroid	Thyroid hormones include natural and synthetic products used for treatment of hypothyroidism (replacement therapy), suppression of goiter growth and some thyroid neoplasms	Thyroid hormone therapy is generally begun with low doses and gradually increased, with amount of drug individualized and adjusted to obtain euthyroid state **Adult, maintenance:** 60-120 mg/day	*Glucocorticoids,* anticoagulants, cholestyramine, colestipol, estrogens, ketamine, maprotiline and *sympathomimetics* may interfere with actions of these drugs
Liothyronine	Cytomel	See note above	Thyroid hormone therapy is generally begun with low doses and gradually increased, with the amount of drug individualized and adjusted to obtain euthyroid state	See note above
Liotrix	Thyrolar	See note above	See note above	See note above
Thyroglobulin	Proloid	See note above	See note above	See note above
Thyroid	Armour Thyroid, Thyrar, Thyroid Strong, Westhroid	See note above	See note above	See note above

Italics indicate information of major clinical significance.

Adverse Effects, Precautions and Contraindications

Table 23.9 presents adverse effects of endocrine/hormonal drugs; Table 23.10 presents precautions and contraindications.

Suggested Readings

Galloway JA, Hooper SA, Spradlin CT, et al. Biosynthetic human proinsulin. Review of chemistry, in vitro and in vivo receptor binding, animal and human pharmacology studies, and clinical trial experience. Diabetes Care 1992;15:666-92.

Gray H, O'Rahilly S. Toward improved glycemic control in diabetes. What's on the horizon? Arch Intern Med 1995;155:1137-42.

Ilarde A, Tuck M. Treatment of non-insulin-dependent diabetes mellitus and its complications. A state of the art review. Drugs Aging 1994;4:470-91.

Johnson JL, Felicetta JV. Hypothyroidism: a comprehensive review. J Am Acad Nurse Pract 1992;4:131-8.

Mariotti A. Sex steroid hormones and cell dynamics in the periodontium. Crit Rev Oral Biol Med 1994;5:27-53.

Shepard AR, Eberhardt NL. Molecular mechanisms of thyroid hormone action. Clin Lab Med 1993;13:531-41.

Table 23.8

Antithyroid Hormones: Dosage and Prescribing Information

Generic name	Brand name(s)	Indications	Dosage range	Interactions with other drugs
Methimazole	Tapazole	Hyperthyroidism, thyrotoxic crisis	The dosage should be titrated to the individual needs of each patient Generally, the oral dose ranges from 15-60 mg/day depending on severity of disease The duration of the dosage is usually 6-8 w or until the patient becomes euthyroid For thyrotoxic crisis, the oral dose is 15-20 mg every 4 h during the first day **Maintenance:** 5-30 mg/day	Amiodarone, iodinated glycerol or potassium iodide may decrease the effects of antithyroid agents Response to oral anticoagulants and digitalis glycosides may increase, and the patient's metabolic status may decrease
Propylthiouracil	Propyl-Thyracil [CAN]	Hyperthyroidism, thyrotoxic crisis	The dosage should be titrated to the individual needs of each patient **Oral:** 300-900 mg/day until the patient becomes euthyroid **Maintenance:** 50-600 mg/day; dose can be given all at once or split into 4 applications	See notes above

[CAN] indicates a drug available only in Canada.

Table 23.9

Endocrine/Hormonal Drugs: Adverse Effects

Body system	Androgens	Estrogens	Insulin	Oral contraceptives	Oral hypoglycemics	Progestins	Thyroid hormones	Antithyroid hormones
General	Edema	Edema, anorexia, headache	Untoward effects of insulin occur when patient's insulin dose is not correctly titrated and blood glucose levels are either too low or too high, allergy	Edema, anorexia, headache, fever	Untoward effects of oral hypoglycemics occur when the individual's dose is not correctly titrated and blood glucose levels are either too low or too high, allergy	Edema, fever	Allergy	Mild and transient fever, arthralgia, arthritis, throat infection, dizziness, listlessness, muscle aches
CV					Increased risk of cardiovascular mortality, congestive heart failure (chlorpropamide only)			Vasculitis
CNS				Mental depression		Mental depression	Pseudotumor cerebri	Headache
Endoc	**Only in males:** Breast soreness, gynecomastia, priapism, nonspecific acute epididymitis, prostatic carcinoma, benign prostatic hypertrophy. **Only in females:** amenorrhea, oligomenorrhea	Breast pain or tenderness, gynecomastia, amenorrhea, breakthrough bleeding, menorrhagia	Insulin resistance	Breast pain or tenderness, gynecomastia, amenorrhea, breakthrough bleeding, menorrhagia, changes in vaginal bleeding pattern, galactorrhea		Changes in vaginal bleeding pattern, galactorrhea	Hyperthyroidism	Changes in menstrual cycle, goiter

	1	2	3	4	5	6	7
GI	Gastrointestinal irritation, diarrhea	Diarrhea, abdominal cramping, nausea		Diarrhea, abdominal cramping, nausea	Constipation, diarrhea, nausea		Constipation
GU	Bladder irritability (only in males)	Thromboembolism		Thromboembolism	Antidiuretic effect (chlorpropamide only), impaired renal function	Thrombo-embolic disorders	Nephritis, renal vasculitis (propylthiouracil)
Hema	Erythrocytosis				Eosinophilia, agranulocytosis, aplastic anemia, bone marrow depression		Agranulocytosis, aplastic anemia, hypoprothrombinemia (propylthiouracil), thrombocytopenia
HB	Hepatic dysfunction; hepatic necrosis			Hepatitis, gallbladder obstruction		Hepatitis, gallbladder obstruction	Cholestatic jaundice, hepatic necrosis
Integ	Acne; increased hair growth in pubic region		Fat atrophy at injection site and fat hypertrophy	Acne, increased body and facial hair		Acne, increased body and facial hair	Skin rash or itching, dry and/or puffy skin
Oral	Gingival inflammation and bleeding	Gingival inflammation and bleeding		Gingival inflammation and bleeding		Gingival inflammation and bleeding	Mouth sores, sialodenopathy, loss of taste
Peripheral nervous system							Peripheral neuropathy
Pulmonary							Interstitial pneumonitis

Table 23.10

Endocrine/Hormonal Drugs: Precautions and Contraindications

Drug category	Precautions/contraindications
Androgens	Increased risk of hepatic neoplasms with long-term, high-dose therapy
	In children, androgens can cause precocious puberty in boys, virilization in girls and premature closure of epiphyseal plates
	Precautions should be taken when administering androgens to patients with cardiac failure, cardi-renal disease, nephritis, nephrosis, myocardial infarction, diabetes mellitus, impaired hepatic function, hyperglycemia and benign prostatic hypertrophy
	Pregnancy risk category: X
	Contraindicated in patients taking other potentially hepatotoxic drugs
	Contraindicated in male patients with breast cancer or prostatic cancer
Estrogens	Increased risk of endometrial cancer in postmenopausal women
	In children, estrogens can cause precocious puberty in girls and prematurely close the epiphyseal plates
	Precautions should be taken when administering estrogens to patients with endometriosis, gallstones, hepatic dysfunction, hypercalcemia, thromboembolic disorders and uterine fibroids
	Pregnancy risk category: X
	Contraindicated in patients with breast cancer, neoplasms of reproductive organs or undiagnosed vaginal bleeding
Insulin	Should be used cautiously with patients who have high fever, hyperthyroidism, severe infections, diabetic ketoacidosis, trauma or surgery, hypothyroidism, diarrhea, nausea and impaired renal function
	Pregnancy risk category: A
Oral contraceptives	Increased risk of hepatic cancer in women using these drugs for > 8 y
	In children, oral contraceptives can cause precocious puberty in girls and prematurely close epiphyseal plates
	Should be used cautiously with patients who have endometriosis, gallstones, hepatic dysfunction, hypercalcemia, mental depression, hypertension, hepatic dysfunction, renal dysfunction and uterine fibroids
	Pregnancy risk category: X
	Contraindicated in patients with breast cancer, neoplasms of the reproductive organs, hepatic tumors, cerebrovascular disease, cholestatic jaundice, thromboembolic disorders or undiagnosed vaginal bleeding
Oral hypoglycemics	Should be used cautiously with patients who have adrenal insufficiency, pituitary insufficiency, high fever, impaired thyroid function, impaired hepatic function, impaired renal function and malnourishment
	Pregnancy risk category: C
	Contraindicated in patients with acidosis, severe burns, diabetic coma, severe infections, and major surgery or trauma

Italics indicate information of major clinical significance.

Continued on next page

Table 23.10 (cont.)

Endocrine/Hormonal Drugs: Precautions and Contraindications

Drug category	Precautions/contraindications
Progestins	Should be used cautiously with patients who have asthma, cardiac insufficiency, epilepsy, diabetes mellitus, hyperlipemia, mental depression and thromboembolic disorders
	Pregnancy risk category: X
	Contraindicated in patients with breast cancer or cancer of reproductive organs, hepatic disease, incomplete abortion, suspected pregnancy and undiagnosed vaginal bleeding
Thyroid hormones	Should be used cautiously with patients who have adrenocortical insufficiency, cardiovascular disease, hyperthyroidism, pituitary insufficiency or thyrotoxicosis
	Pregnancy risk category: A
Antithyroid hormones	Thyroid carcinomas have occurred with people using propylthiouracil
	The incidence of agranulocytosis is more likely in people > age 40 y
	Patients should be instructed in proper oral hygiene; however, owing to the possibility of poor wound healing and sores in the oral cavity, proper instruction in the use of oral hygiene aids (such as toothpicks, floss, toothbrush) is necessary to prevent unnecessary trauma
	Pregnancy risk category: D (small amounts of these drugs can be transferred to breast milk)

Italics indicate information of major clinical significance.

Chapter 24

Drugs Used for Connective-Tissue Disorders and Oral Mucosal Diseases

Martin S. Greenberg, D.D.S.

This chapter describes the drugs used to treat diseases of the oral mucosa as well as the major drugs used to manage connective-tissue diseases. Because dentists have a sizeable responsibility for the diagnosis and management of diseases affecting the oral mucosa, the chapter emphasizes the clinical application of these drugs. The section devoted to connective-tissue disease highlights the effect of this group of drugs on oral health and the precautions necessary when providing dental treatment for patients receiving drug therapy for this group of diseases.

Connective-Tissue Disorder Drugs

The connective-tissue diseases are a group of disorders with a prominent feature of tissue damage caused by the patient's own immune system. These diseases are often classified as autoimmune, but the cause of tissue damage is complex and often caused by immune complexes as well as autoantibodies. The major connective-tissue diseases include lupus erythematosus, rheumatoid arthritis, scleroderma (systemic sclerosis), dermatomyositis, mixed connective-tissue disease and Sjögren's syndrome.

See Table 24.1 for general information on connective-tissue disorder drugs.

Lupus Erythematosus Drugs

Lupus erythematosus is caused by the formation of autoantibodies to nuclear components, particularly DNA. Tissue damage may result directly from autoantibodies or more commonly from immune complexes composed of antigen, antibody and complement, which cause an inflammatory reaction involving skin, mucosa, internal organs (particularly the kidneys and brain) or joints.

Discoid lupus is confined to the skin and mucosa and causes skin lesions with scales that project into hair follicles (follicular plugging). Typical oral lesions of discoid lupus appear as a mixture of inflammation, atrophy, ulceration and keratosis. The lesions easily may be confused with lichen planus or, occasionally, leukoplakia. Systemic lupus is a multisystem disease with a strong genetic component that most commonly affects women in their childbearing years. Patients with systemic lupus have skin and mucosal lesions as well as renal, central nervous, cardiovascular and hematologic systemic manifestations. Patients with systemic lupus may have discoid lupus-type oral lesions or nonspecific ulcers caused by vasculitis. Dentists should be suspicious of the possibility of systemic lupus when a woman between the ages of 20 and 40 y develops oral lesions with symptoms of other involvement such as joint pains or skin lesions.

The lesions of discoid lupus often respond

Table 24.1

Connective-Tissue Disorder Drugs and Oral Mucosal Disease Drugs: Dosage and Prescribing Information

Generic name	Brand name(s)	Indications	Dosage range	Interactions with other drugs
Analgesics				
Nonsteroidal anti-inflammatory agents	See Chapter 4	See Chapter 4	See Chapter 4	See Chapter 4
Anticholinergic agent				
Pilocarpine	See Chapter 10	See Chapter 10	See Chapter 10	See Chapter 10
Antihistamine				
Diphen-hydramine	Benadryl	Topical anesthesia and relief of itching	5 cc as oral rinse and expectorate bid-qid	**CNS depressants and MAO inhibitors:** Should be used cautiously when administered concomitantly
Anti-inflammatory agent				
Amlexanox	Aphthasol	Recurrent aphthous ulcers	Apply ¼-in. ribbon of paste to ulcers qid	None
Antimalarial agent				
Hydroxy-chloroquine	Plaquenil	Discoid lupus erythematosus, systemic lupus erythematosus, rheumatoid arthritis, malaria	40-800 mg daily	**Penicillamine:** Concurrent use likely to increase the risk of serious hematologic and/or renal adverse effects
Gold compound				
Gold sodium thiomalate	Myochrysine	Active rheumatoid arthritis	10-50 mg	**Penicillamine:** Concurrent use likely to increase the risk of serious hematologic and/or renal adverse effects
Immunosuppressive drugs				
Azathioprine	Imuran	Prevention of organ transplant rejection, rheumatoid arthritis, lupus erythematosus, other connective-tissue diseases	50-200 mg daily	**Allopurinol:** Requires dose reduction **ACE inhibitors:** Increased anemia and leukopenia Increased leukopenia with drugs that affect leukocyte production

Continued on next page

Table 24.1 (cont.)

Connective-Tissue Disorder Drugs and Oral Mucosal Disease Drugs: Dosage
and Prescribing Information

Generic name	Brand name(s)	Indications	Dosage range	Interactions with other drugs
Immunosuppressive drugs (cont.)				
Cyclophos-phamide	Cytoxan; Procytox [CAN]	Anticancer drug, steroid-sparing agent in connective-tissue diseases	Changes with specific disease	Potentiates succinylcholine during general anesthesia High dosage of phenobarbital increases leukopenia
Cyclosporine	Sandimmune	Topically, for erosive lichen planus; prevention of organ transplant rejection	5-cc rinse/day	**Clarithromycin, erythromycin, fluconazole, itraconazole, ketaconazole:** Increase toxicity of cyclosporine
Penicillamine D	Cuprimine, Depen	Rheumatoid arthritis, scleroderma, Wilson's disease	Changes with specific disease	Should not be used with other drugs that depress bone marrow, such as gold sodium thiomalate, cytotoxic drugs or phenylbutazone
Local anesthetic				
2% Lidocaine viscous	Xylocaine Viscous	Topical relief of mucous membrane irritation	As needed	None when used topically
Recurrent aphthous stomatitis drugs				
Colchicine	generic	Antigout drug; can be useful for severe recurrent aphthous ulcers	0.6 mg tid	**CNS depressants, sympathomimetic drugs:** Colchicine may enhance response to these drugs **Vitamin B$_{12}$:** Decreased absorption
Pentoxifylline	Trental	Peripheral vascular disease; also used for diabetic ulcers and neuropathy; some uncontrolled studies indicate possible use with major aphthous ulcers	400 mg bid-tid	**Antihypertensive agents:** Effect increased by pentoxifylline **Cimetidine:** Increases levels of pentoxifylline
Retinoid				
Isotretinoin	Accutane	Inhibition of keratinization and sebaceous gland function	10-50 mg/day	**Carbamazepine:** Isotretinoin increases clearance of this drug **Vitamin A products:** May increase toxicity

[CAN] indicates a drug available only in Canada.

Continued on next page

Table 24.1 (cont.)

Generic name	Brand name(s)	Indications	Dosage range	Interactions with other drugs
Sedative-hypnotic agent				
Thalidomide	Thalomid	Erythema nodosum leprosum, severe resistant major aphthous stomatitis, Behçet's syndrome	50-300 mg daily	Decreases sedative effects of barbiturates, alcohol, chlorpromazine, reserpine
Sulfone				
Dapsone	Avlosulfon	Pemphigoid, leprosy, malaria, dermatitis, herpetiformis	50-300 mg daily	**Cimetidine:** Decreases methemoglobinemia **Rifampin:** Lowers dapsone levels **Trimethoprim:** Raises dapsone levels Use caution with any drug that induces hemolysis

to use of topical and intralesional glucocorticoids (see Chapter 6 for a discussion of those drugs). Patients with discoid lupus that does not respond to this therapy may be placed on systemic therapy with antimalarial agents such as hydroxychloroquine (Plaquenil). Patients with mild to moderate manifestations of lupus are treated symptomatically for joint pains and skin or mucosal lesions. Patients with serious organ involvement such as kidney or central nervous system manifestations are treated with systemic glucocorticoids alone or glucocorticoids in combination with immunosuppressive drugs such as azathioprine or cyclophosphamide.

Rheumatoid Arthritis Drugs

Rheumatoid arthritis (RA) is a systemic inflammatory disease whose chief manifestation is destruction of the synovial membrane that spreads to the joint cartilage. Susceptibility to the disease has a strong hereditary basis, and an infectious etiology is suspected but not proven. RA chiefly manifests itself as symmetrical swelling and pain of the joints in people between the ages of 30 and 50 y. Because RA is a systemic disease, generalized manifestations such as weakness, fatigue and subcutaneous nodules are also common.

A form of RA, Felty's syndrome, affects the blood, causing anemia and a decrease in white blood cells and platelets. Dentists treating patients who have this syndrome must be aware of the potential for infection and bleeding. Involvement of the temporomandibular joints is common, but it is a major problem for only a small percentage of patients.

Dentists treating patients with RA must be aware of the drugs prescribed and their possible effect on dental treatment. The major classes of drugs used to treat RA include the following:

- nonsteroidal anti-inflammatory drugs (NSAIDs), which can increase bleeding after surgery;
- gold sodium thiomalate, which can cause oral ulcers, decreased white blood cells and decreased platelets; patients receiving systemic gold should receive periodic hematologic evaluations, and dentists per-

forming surgical procedures on such patients should obtain the results of recent laboratory tests;

- penicillamine D, which may cause decreased white blood cells and platelets, drug-induced pemphigus with oral lesions or nephrotic syndrome; patients must have periodic hematologic evaluation; loss of taste has also been reported;
- systemic glucocorticoids (see Chapter 6);
- immunosuppressive drugs (see Chapter 27).

Scleroderma Drugs

Patients with scleroderma (systemic sclerosis) develop fibrosis of the skin and internal organs owing to the overproduction of collagen. Tightening of the skin, especially around the face and hands, is a characteristic of the disease. Raynaud's phenomenon, ischemia and blanching of the fingers caused by vasoconstriction are common. Patients with this form of scleroderma may develop fibrosis of the heart, kidney or lung, and dentists treating these patients should consult with the managing physician regarding the extent of organ involvement before performing dental treatment.

Drugs frequently used to treat scleroderma include the following:

- penicillamine D (see RA above);
- systemic glucocorticoids (see Chapter 6);
- immunosuppressive drugs (see Chapter 27).

Calcium channel blockers such as nifedipine are used to manage Raynaud's phenomenon. These drugs may cause gingival enlargement that can be minimized by good oral hygiene.

Dermatomyositis Drugs

Patients with dermatomyositis have skin lesions and muscle weakness. The term "polymyositis" is used when patients have only muscle involvement. The disease may occur alone or in association with an underlying malignancy or another connective-tissue disease. Oral involvement may include weakness of the palatal muscles and oral mucosal lesions.

Treatment of dermatomyositis includes use of high doses of systemic glucocorticoids (Chapter 6) and cytotoxic immunosuppressive drugs (Chapter 27).

Mixed Connective-Tissue Disease Drugs

Patients with mixed connective-tissue disease (MCTD) have signs and symptoms that overlap more than one connective-tissue disease. MCTD is considered a separate disorder as patients have a distinct laboratory finding of high levels of autoantibodies to nuclear ribonucleoprotein. The drugs taken by patients with MCTD are determined by the particular overlap syndrome. They take the same drugs described above for use with lupus, RA, scleroderma and dermatomyositis.

Sjögren's Syndrome Agents

Sjögren's syndrome (SS) is an autoimmune disease that primarily affects the lacrimal and salivary glands but also may be associated with other connective-tissue diseases or lymphoma. Primary SS, which occurs primarily in women (at a 9:1 ratio), causes destruction of salivary and lacrimal gland tissue and leads to severe xerostomia and dry eyes. Oral manifestations include an increased incidence of dental caries and candidiasis owing to a decrease in both the detergent and the antibacterial properties of saliva. Patients with SS also have difficulty wearing dentures. People with secondary SS have dry eyes and mouth in association with any one of the connective-tissue diseases described above, most frequently RA. A major concern of clinicians managing patients who have SS is the high incidence of lymphoma in people with this condition. The diagnosis of SS is made by testing for salivary and lacrimal gland function and abnormal serologic findings and detection of inflammatory foci in biopsy specimens of minor salivary glands.

The medical management of xerostomia in patients with SS includes use of topical rinses, such as artificial saliva substitutes, and use of pilocarpine to increase salivary flow. Pilocarpine 5 mg taken three times daily 30 min before meals increases salivary flow for patients who still have functional salivary gland tissue. The most common side effects of pilocarpine include sweating and gastrointestinal symptoms. Pilocarpine should not be used for patients with asthma, chronic bronchitis, narrow-angle glaucoma or chronic obstructive pulmonary disease. It should also be used with caution in patients with severe cardiovascular disease. See Chapter 10 for further information on xerostomia and agents used to treat it.

Special Dental Considerations

Drug Interactions of Dental Interest

Many of the drugs taken by patients receiving treatment for a connective-tissue disease may have a profound effect on both oral disease and the safety of dental treatment. Dentists treating a patient with a connective-tissue disease must take a careful drug history and understand the potential side effects of the drugs the patient is taking and how they may affect the safety of dental treatment. Many of the drugs described in this chapter affect the hematologic and immune systems and, therefore, increase the risk of both infection and bleeding. Long-term glucocorticoid or immunosuppressive drug therapy, for example, may require significant modification of the dental treatment plan. Dentists may be consulted to treat oral and dental complications of connective-tissue diseases, such as oral mucosal lesions in patients who have lupus or xerostomia in patients who have SS. Knowledge of the use of topical and intralesional glucocorticoids for patients with lupus and pilocarpine for patients with SS can be an important component of good medical therapy.

Lupus. Dentists should be aware of a disorder called "drug-induced lupus," which occurs when patients develop symptoms and signs of lupus triggered by drug therapy. Drugs most frequently associated with drug-induced lupus include hydralazine, procainamide, penicillamine D and oral contraceptives. Dentists should also be aware that drug therapy may exacerbate systemic lupus. Antibiotics such as penicillin and sulfonamides as well as NSAIDs have been reported to cause lupus flare-ups. Dentists should check with the treating medical specialist before prescribing these drugs for patients with lupus.

Scleroderma. Scleroderma of the face results in a progressive decrease in oral opening that leads to difficulty with both oral home care and dental treatment. Difficulty with proper oral hygiene increases the risk of dental caries, especially when scleroderma is complicated by xerostomia as a result of secondary SS.

Sjögren's syndrome. Patients with SS systemic manifestations may be receiving therapy from their internist with antimalarial drugs such as hydroxychloroquine, particularly when there is joint involvement. Systemic glucocorticoids and/or immunosuppressive drugs also are used to manage severe systemic manifestations of SS. Patients receiving antimalarial therapy should be closely monitored for the development of blood dyscrasias, including neutropenia and agranulocytosis. Patients receiving antimalarials may develop dark pigmentation of the skin and mucosa and may ask their dentist about the cause of a pigmented area discovered on the oral mucosa.

Laboratory Value Alterations

Many drugs used to treat connective-tissue diseases—such as immunosuppressive drugs, gold sodium thiomalate and penicillamine—may cause bone marrow depression. Patients taking these drugs should have a hematologic evaluation, including a white blood cell and platelet count, before undergoing dental and oral surgical procedures.

Adverse Effects, Precautions and Contraindications

Table 24.2 lists adverse effects related to connective-tissue disorder drugs.

Table 24.2

Connective-Tissue Disorder Drugs and Oral Mucosal Disease Drugs: Adverse Effects

Body system	Analgesics	Anticholinergic agent	Antimalarial agent	Gold compounds	Immunosuppressive drugs	
	NSAIDs	Pilocarpine	Hydroxy-chloroquine	Gold sodium thiomalate	Azathioprine	Cyclophos-phamide
General	See Chapter 4	See Chapter 10			Increased risk of neoplasm, increased risk of infections, birth defects, fever, malaise	Risk of malignancy, sterility, risk of infections, birth defects
CV						Cardiotoxicity at high doses
CNS			Emotional changes, psychosis, vertigo, deafness, convulsions, muscle weakness	Hallucinations, confusion, seizures		
Endoc						Amenorrhea, sterility
EENT			Retinopathy, corneal deposits			
GI				Nausea, vomiting, diarrhea, ulcerative colitis	Nausea, vomiting, diarrhea	
GU				Renal adenomas	Depressed spermatogenesis	Hemorrhagic cystitis, fibrosis of bladder
Hema			Leukopenia, thrombocytopenia, anemia	Anemia, thrombocytopenia, leukemia	Leukopenia, thrombocytopenia, immune deficiency, anemia	Immune deficiency, leukopenia, thrombocytopenia, anemia

Italics indicate information of major clinical significance.
* S.T.E.P.S.: System for Thalidomide Education and Prescribing Safety prescriber registry.
† G6PD: Glucose-6-phosphate dehydrogenase.

Immuno-suppressive drugs (cont.)	Recurrent aphthous stomatitis drugs		Retinoid	Sedative-hypnotic agent	Sulfone
Penicillamine D	Colchicine	Pentoxifylline	Isotretinoin	Thalidomide	Dapsone
Risk of birth defects, drug-induced lupus, fever, arthralgia, lymphadenopathy			Pregnancy risk factor X; must not be used by women who are pregnant or may become pregnant	*Severe, life-threatening birth defects; prescribers must register with S.T.E.P.S.**	Test for G6PD† deficiency before use, dapsone hypersensitivity syndrome (fever, lymphadenopathy, rash, hepatoxicity)
		Mild hypotension			
Myasthenia gravis, sensory neuropathy, motor neuropathy	Peripheral neuritis	Dizziness, agitation, headache	Fatigue, headache, depression	Peripheral neuropathy, drowsiness, dizziness, sedation, bradycardia	Peripheral neuropathy, headache
Thyroiditis, mammary hyperplasia	Azoospermia (rare)		Elevated levels of triglycerides		
		Earache	Itching in eyes, nasal dryness		Photophobia
Anorexia, vomiting	Nausea, vomiting, diarrhea, anorexia	Dyspepsia, nausea		Constipation, diarrhea	Nausea, vomiting, pancreatitis
Hematuria				*Cannot be used during pregnancy— patient must have pregnancy test before and during use, birth control counseling required*	
Aplastic anemia, thrombocytopenia, leukopenia	Bone marrow depression (rare), aplastic anemia			Neutropenia	Hemolytic anemia, methemoglobinemia

Continued on next page

Table 24.2 (cont.)

Connective-Tissue Disorder Drugs and Oral Mucosal Disease Drugs: Adverse Effects

	Analgesics	Anticholin-ergic agent	Antimalarial agent	Gold compounds	Immunosuppressive drugs	
Body system	NSAIDs	Pilocarpine	Hydroxy-chloroquine	Gold sodium thiomalate	Azathioprine	Cyclophos-phamide
HB	See Chapter 4	See Chapter 10		Hepatitis, jaundice	Hepatotoxicity, elevated liver enzymes	
Integ			Dermatitis, alopecia	Rashes (common), pruritis, exfoliative dermatitis	Rashes	Alopecia, rash, pigmentation
Oral				Ulcers (common), stomatitis (common), dysgeusia (metallic taste), glossitis	Candidiasis, deep fungal infections, recurrent herpes simplex infections	Candidiasis, deep fungal infections, recurrent herpes simplex infections, oral ulcers
Renal				Nephrotic syndrome, glomeru-lonephritis		
Resp				Interstitial pneumonitis		Interstitial pul-monary fibrosis with long-term use of high doses

Italics indicate information of major clinical significance.

Immuno-suppressive drugs (cont.)	Recurrent aphthous stomatitis drugs		Retinoid	Sedative-hypnotic agent	Sulfone
Penicillamine D	Colchicine	Pentoxifylline	Isotretinoin	Thalidomide	Dapsone
Hepatitis	Hepatotoxicity				
Pemphigus, pruritis, rash, alopecia, lichen planus	Alopecia, rash		Burning sensation, redness	Rash	
Pemphigus, lichen planus					
Nephrotic syndrome, glomerulopathy, hematuria, proteinuria				Nephrotic syndrome	Nephrotic syndrome
Goodpasture's syndrome, bronchitis					

Pharmacology

Gold sodium thiomalate. The mechanism that makes this drug an effective anti-inflammatory agent for patients with rheumatoid arthritis is unknown. It is effective in reducing synovitis in patients with active joint inflammation.

Hydroxychloroquine. This is an antimalarial drug that also is effective in the treatment of discoid and systemic lupus erythematosis. The mechanism of action in patients with lupus is not understood.

Immunosuppressive drugs. Azathioprine is an immunosuppressive drug used to prevent graft rejection in organ transplant patients. It also is effective for the management of some autoimmune and connective-tissue diseases owing to its effect on lymphocyte response and delayed hypersensitivity.

Cyclophosphamide is used in cancer chemotherapy, which also suppresses the immune response and therefore is useful in the management of autoimmune and connective-tissue diseases such as pemphigus and lupus erythematosus.

Nonsteroidal anti-inflammatory drugs. Pharmacological information on these drugs is provided in Chapter 4.

Penicillamine D. This drug decreases the level of rheumatoid factor related to immunoglobulin M. It also depresses the activity of T-lymphocytes.

Oral Mucosal Disease Drugs

This portion of the chapter will discuss the therapy for the major oral mucosal diseases not covered in other chapters.

Erythema Multiforme Drugs

Erythema multiforme (EM) is an acute inflammatory disease that may affect the mucosa, the skin or both. EM that involves multiple sites—including the mouth, conjunctiva, skin and genitals—is called Stevens-Johnson syndrome. Toxic epidermal necrolysis is a severe, life-threatening form of EM in which large areas of skin peel away, leaving the patient susceptible to fluid and electrolyte imbalance as well as secondary infection. EM may be caused by drug reactions or reactions to microorganisms. Drugs that most commonly cause EM include sulfonamides, oxicam NSAIDs (such as piroxicam), allopurinol and anticonvulsant drugs such as phenytoin and carbamazepine. Herpes simplex virus is the microorganism most commonly responsible for episodes of EM, and recurrent herpes infections are believed to be the most common cause of recurrent episodes of EM. Mycoplasma infections also trigger cases of EM.

The oral lesions associated with EM can be extensive and cause severe ulceration of the lips and intraoral mucosa. Patients may have oral lesions as the sole or chief manifestation of EM. Extensive oral lesions are frequently present as part of generalized EM.

The management of mild cases of oral EM includes supportive care with topical anesthetic agents, such as viscous lidocaine. Severe cases of EM in adults frequently are treated with a short course of systemic glucocorticoids. The use of glucocorticoids to treat EM has been controversial, but recently published findings have demonstrated both relief of symptoms and shortened healing times with few significant side effects when the drug is administered to adults. Children treated with glucocorticoids for EM have a higher incidence of side effects, particularly gastrointestinal bleeding or secondary infection. Patients with recurrent episodes of EM caused by herpes simplex virus benefit from prophylaxis with antiherpes drugs such as acyclovir or valacyclovir. Patients with severe stomatitis resulting from EM or other causes may obtain temporary relief with the use of topical anesthetic agents such as viscous lidocaine.

Lichen Planus Drugs

Lichen planus (LP) is a chronic mucocutaneous disease that affects the skin, mucosal surfaces or both. The oral mucosa is a common site of involvement, and LP oral lesions can present as reticular white lines, white plaques, areas of desquamation or ulcers. LP also is the most common cause of desquamative gingivitis. When LP is characterized by ulceration, desquamation or blisters, it is called "erosive LP." The etiology of the disease is unknown, but LP is divided into idiopathic and lichenoid reactions. Patients with idiopathic LP have no identifiable underlying trigger for the disease, whereas patients with lichenoid reactions have an underlying cause such as drug therapy, contact allergy or a systemic disease such as hepatitis C. The lesions of idiopathic LP and lichenoid reactions cannot be reliably distinguished either clinically or histologically; therefore, dentists or dental specialists who manage patients with oral LP should obtain a thorough history to rule out a possible underlying cause, particularly in severe cases of erosive LP. The drugs most commonly associated with LP include angiotensin-converting enzyme (ACE) inhibitors such as captopril, β-blockers and NSAIDs. Allergic reactions to dental materials (such as amalgam or gold) that are directly in contact with the lesions also have been reported as a cause of LP.

Proper management of oral LP includes an attempt to identify an underlying cause, such as a lichenoid drug reaction, and then to control symptomatic lesions with topical or, occasionally, systemic agents. Topical glucocorticoids are the most effective agents for a majority of patients with lesions symptomatic of erosive LP. The effectiveness of topical glucocorticoids when managing desquamative gingival lesions can be improved by fabrication of a soft splint or mouthguard that covers the gingiva and holds the glucocorticoid in place more effectively. In severe cases, the topical glucocorticoid may be supplemented with intralesional glucocorticoid injections. Plaquelike lesions of LP, which require therapy, have been successfully managed with the use of topical retinoids such as tretinoin. Cyclosporine, an immunosuppressive drug used to prevent graft rejection in organ trans-

plant patients, has been used topically to treat oral LP. The usefulness of this therapy is limited because it is significantly more expensive than the use of topical glucocorticoids.

Patients should be informed that LP is a chronic disease that may last for many years and that treatment is designed to control the lesions, not cure the disease. Because data strongly suggest that patients with oral LP have an increased risk of developing oral cancer, patients with LP should be evaluated periodically for the presence of suspicious lesions.

Mucous Membrane Pemphigoid Drugs

Mucous membrane pemphigoid (MMP), also called "cicatricial pemphigoid," is a chronic, blistering autoimmune disease caused by antibodies that destroy proteins in the basement membrane of the epithelium, thus causing separation of the epidermis from the dermis. The oral mucosa is the most common site of involvement in MMP, and desquamation of the gingiva is the most common oral manifestation. Involvement of the conjunctiva may lead to blindness, and in some cases the genital, tracheal and esophageal mucosa also may be affected. Diagnosis is made by biopsy of lesions that should be studied by means of both routine histology and direct immunofluorescence.

Oral lesions of MMP initially are treated with potent topical glucocorticoids, which can be more effective when held in place with occlusive dental splints if gingival or palatal lesions are involved. Intralesional glucocorticoids can be used when extensive localized lesions do not respond to topical glucocorticoids alone. Systemic therapy may be necessary to control severe cases of MMP. Systemic therapy found effective in some cases includes dapsone, tetracycline, immunosuppressive drugs (such as azathioprine) and systemic glucocorticoids. These drugs can have serious side effects and should be prescribed only by a dental or medical specialist trained in managing patients who are taking these drugs.

Pemphigus Vulgaris Drugs

Pemphigus vulgaris (PV) is an autoimmune disease caused by antibodies that destroy the attachment between epithelial cells and cause separation of the cells (called "acantholysis") and blister formation. PV may occur alone or in association with other autoimmune diseases, such as myasthenia gravis. The blistering and peeling of the skin and mucosa are potentially fatal if not treated. The oral mucosa is often the initial site of involvement, and PV is frequently diagnosed by biopsy of oral lesions using both routine histology and direct immunofluorescence. Most cases of PV are of unknown origin, but a minority of cases are caused by a reaction to drugs, particularly penicillamine or captopril. Paraneoplastic pemphigus is a form of PV triggered by neoplasms, such as lymphomas.

Systemic glucocorticoid therapy is the mainstay of treatment of PV. Adjuvant therapy with immunosuppressive drugs such as azathioprine allows the clinician to use lower doses of systemic glucocorticoids, which reduces the risk of serious side effects.

Recurrent Aphthous Stomatitis Drugs

Recurrent aphthous stomatitis (RAS) is a disease of unknown etiology, but it is clear that the tendency to develop RAS is inherited. RAS affects approximately 15% of the population and is commonly seen in dental patients. The disease is characterized by recurring oral ulcers with no other signs or symptoms of disease on other mucosal or skin surfaces and no evidence of involvement of other organ systems. Dentists managing patients with recurring oral ulcers should eliminate the possibility of other serious disorders that can cause recurring oral ulcers, such as connective-tissue disease, blood dyscrasias or human immunodeficiency virus (HIV) infection, by obtaining a thorough history and performing a careful examination. In severe or unusual cases, laboratory tests may be necessary to eliminate the possibility of underlying systemic disease. RAS is divided into minor and major forms. Patients with the minor form experience ulcers that are less than 1 cm in diameter and heal in 10 to 14 days. The major form of RAS is less common and causes ulcers that are greater than 1 cm in diameter, take weeks to months to heal and cause scarring.

The mainstay of treatment for RAS is the use of topical glucocorticoids. High-potency glucocorticoids such as fluocinonide placed directly on the lesion shorten the healing time of the lesion and increase patient comfort in a majority of cases, but do not prevent the formation of new lesions. Less potent glucocorticoids appear to have little effect. Other topical preparations that can decrease the healing time of RAS include amlexanox paste (Aphthasol) and topical tetracycline mouthrinses. The latter therapy may cause candidiasis or allergic reactions.

Patients with severe major aphthea may not experience adequate relief from topical preparations. Drugs that have been reported effective in reducing the number of ulcers in some cases of major RAS include colchicine, pentoxifylline and dapsone. Pentoxifylline is a methylxanthine related to caffeine, which is used chiefly to treat peripheral vascular disease because of its effect on the flexibility of red blood cells. Because it also has an effect on leukocytes, it appears useful for a number of inflammatory diseases. There have been several reports and uncontrolled trials of the successful use of pentoxifylline for the treatment of severe aphthous stomatitis.

Thalidomide has been shown to reduce the incidence and severity of RAS in both HIV and non-HIV patients, but it must be used with extreme caution in women of childbearing years owing to its potential for causing severe life-threatening and deforming birth defects. Clinicians prescribing thalidomide must be registered with the System for Thalidomide Education and Prescribing Safety Prescriber Registry, and patients receiving the drug must be carefully counseled regarding proper use of birth control methods during treatment with this drug. Other side effects of thalidomide include peripheral neuropathy, drowsiness and gastrointestinal disturbances.

See Table 24.1 for general information on oral mucosal disease drugs.

Special Dental Considerations

Topical glucocorticoids. Treatment with topical glucocorticoids is common for patients with inflammatory diseases involving the oral mucosa. Topical glucocorticoids are largely synthetic derivatives of hydrocortisone with an 11 B hydroxyl group required for anti-inflammatory action. The topical glucocorticoids are effective anti-inflammatory agents; these agents' effectiveness results from a combination of activities, including increased vasoconstriction, decreased migration of leukocytes, decreased complement activity and decreased fibroblast proliferation.

Long-term repeated use of topical glucocorticoids may cause resistance to the anti-inflammatory effects owing to tachyphylaxis, which primarily results from a decreased ability to cause vasoconstriction. Discontinuing the use of the drug for 3-4 days restores the normal response. Vasoconstriction is an important part of the action of topical glucocorticoids, and the potency of these drugs is established by an assay that measures vasoconstriction.

Topical glucocorticoids are grouped according to their potency. Examples of drugs in each group are as follows:

- Group 1: ultra high potency—betamethasone dipropionate 0.05%, clobetasol 0.05%;
- Group 2: high potency—fluocinonide 0.05%, desoximetasone 0.25%, 0.05%;
- Group 3: medium potency—betamethasone dipropionate 0.05%, triamcinolone acetonide 0.5%;
- Group 4: lower potency—triamcinolone acetonide, fluocinolone acetonide.

The effect of topical glucocorticoids on the desquamative lesions of LP may be enhanced by the use of soft occlusive dental splints that fit over the teeth and hold the glucocorticoid onto the attached gingiva, increasing contact of the glucocorticoid and preventing the medication from being washed away by saliva. The most frequent complication of the long-term use of topical glucocorticoids when treating chronic oral mucosal lesions such as LP or MMP is oral candidiasis. The incidence of candidiasis can be decreased by the concomitant use of topical antifungal agents such as nystatin suspension or clotrimazole troches. Dentists prescribing prolonged use of topical glucocorticoids must carefully instruct patients regarding safe use in the mouth, warn about overuse, and periodically monitor patients who are using these medications for extensive oral lesions.

Intralesional glucocorticoids. Patients with chronic, severe lesions of LP, MMP or major RAS that do not respond to topical glucocorticoids may be helped by the use of intralesional glucocorticoids. Depot glucocorticoids developed for intralesional use such as triamcinolone hexacetonide 5 mg/cc are useful in managing resistant lesions in patients with major aphthae, LP or MMP.

Systemic glucocorticoids. Many clinicians recommend a short course of systemic glucocorticoids for the management of EM. Use of systemic glucocorticoids in the management of chronic oral mucosal disease should be rare and for short periods to manage acute, severe exacerbations of diseases such as LP that are not life-threatening.

Retinoids. Retinoids include vitamin A and its synthetic analogues. Systemic retinoids such as isotretinoin (13-cis-retinoic acid) and etretinate have been shown to promote healing of premalignant oral leukoplakias in a significant number of cases and to reduce the incidence of second cancers in patients with a history of head and neck malignancies. Systemic retinoids have the potential for inducing serious side effects, such as severe birth defects; benign intracranial hypertension (pseudotumor cerebri); an increase in plasma triglycerides, high-density lipoproteins and cholesterol; and liver toxicity. Patients taking systemic retinoids may also develop mucocutaneous signs such as cheilitis and conjunctivitis. Topical retinoids have been used to treat oral mucosal leukoplakia and LP. The white plaques or reticulated lesions of LP have been reversed with the use of topical tretinoin. Mucosal irritation may result from use of topical retinoids.

Dapsone. Dapsone, a synthetic sulfone, was used initially to treat leprosy and malaria. In the 1950s, the drug's anti-inflammatory properties became known, and it was used to successfully treat a number of inflammatory disorders, particularly those with neutrophil-rich infiltrates such as dermatitis herpetiformis. In oral medicine, dapsone is used most frequently to treat mucous membrane pemphigoid, although, according to some controlled studies, it also has been used in severe refractory cases of major aphthous ulcers, pemphigus and LP. Side effects of dapsone are common, and the drug should be prescribed by a clinician experienced in its use. The most common side effects are hemolytic anemia and methemoglobinemia, and most patients receiving the drug will demonstrate a decrease in hemoglobin. Anemia can be minimized by concurrent use of cimetidine and vitamin C. The use of dapsone is contraindicated in patients with glucose-6-phosphate dehydrogenase (G6PD) deficiency. Before prescribing dapsone, the clinician must screen the patient for this deficiency.

Thalidomide. This drug, which originally was prescribed for the treatment of nausea in pregnant women, was banned in the United States because it causes severe birth defects and fetal death. The drug was approved for limited use in 1998 for the treatment of erythema nodosum leprosum, but it also has been shown to be beneficial in the management of severe minor and major recurrent aphthous ulcers in some patients, including some patients with HIV infection. The drug

may be prescribed to pregnant women only by specially registered physicians or dentists who have received formal education on the risk of fetal abnormalities. Use of thalidomide for recurrent aphthous stomatitis should be reserved for patients with severe intractable forms of the disease who have not responded to other less toxic forms of therapy. In addition to birth defects, the side effects of thalidomide include peripheral neuropathy, constipation, drowsiness and neutropenia.

Adverse Effects, Precautions and Contraindications

Table 24.2 lists adverse effects related to oral mucosal disease drugs.

Pharmacology

Colchicine. Colchicine suppresses white blood cell function by interfering on the cellular level with microtubule formation, inhibiting lysosomal degranulation and increasing the level of cyclic AMP. This decreases both the chemotactic and the phagocytic activity of neutrophils.

Cyclosporine. Cyclosporine is an immunosuppressive drug used to prevent graft rejection in organ transplant patients. It has a potent effect on the reponse of T-lymphocytes and cell-mediated immunity. It also has been used to treat connective-tissue and autoimmune diseases.

Dapsone. Dapsone is a sulfone that has been used for its antibacterial properties for more than 50 years. It continues to be used to treat leprosy, malaria and *Pneumocystis carinii* infections in people with HIV. The anti-inflammatory properties of dapsone are unrelated to its antibacterial actions, but diseases that respond favorably to the drug are associated with significant neutrophil infiltration. There is evidence that dapsone suppresses neutrophil function by interfering with the myeloperoxidase-H_2O_2-halide cytotoxic function of neutrophils, as well as inhibiting the synthesis of prostaglandins by neutrophils.

Retinoids. This class of drugs has a major effect on cellular growth and cell differentiation. The use of these drugs can reverse keratinization and premalignant changes. There also is evidence that retinoids have anti-inflammatory properties.

Thalidomide. This drug was marketed as a nonaddictive sedative until its severe teratogenic properties became known and its use was discontinued. More recently, it has been used for its immune-modulating effects and its angiogenesis-inhibiting properties, which are believed to result from suppression of tumor necrosis factor α and inhibition of leukocyte migration.

Viscous lidocaine. Pharmacological information on this drug is provided in Chapter 1.

Suggested Readings

Birnkrant D. Thalidomide for aphthous ulcers in HIV infection. N Engl J Med 1997;337:1086-87.

Greenberg MS. Immunologic diseases. In: Lynch MA, Brightman VJ, Greenberg MS, eds. Burket's oral medicine. 9th ed. Philadelphia: JB Lippincott; 1994:575-84.

Greenberg MS. Ulcerative, vesicular and bullous lesions. In: Lynch MA, Brightman VJ, Greenberg MS, eds. Burket's oral medicine. 9th ed. Philadelphia: JB Lippincott; 1994:11-50.

Lozada-Nur F, Silverman S Jr. Erythema multiforme. Oral Surg Oral Med Oral Pathol 1978;46:628-36.

Ship JA. Recurrent aphthous ulcers: a review of diagnosis and treatment. Oral Surg Oral Med Oral Pathol Oral Radiol Endod 1996;81:141-7.

Chapter 25

Skeletal Muscle Relaxants

Margaret M. Grisius, D.D.S.

Skeletal muscle relaxants have a myriad of indications in dentistry. They may be used to reduce facial pain from muscle spasms associated with temporomandibular disorders and trismus after dental or oral surgical procedures. Drugs that work at the neuromuscular junction are used for muscle relaxation in general anesthesia. In addition, centrally acting muscle relaxants such as benzodiazepines are commonly used as antianxiety agents for patients undergoing dental procedures.

Muscle relaxants are divided into two major therapeutic groups: neuromuscular blockers and spasmolytics. Neuromuscular blockers are peripherally acting agents used primarily in combination with general anesthetics to induce muscle relaxation and, thus, provide an optimal surgical working condition. Spasmolytics are centrally acting agents used to reduce spasticity in a variety of neurologic conditions such as cerebral palsy, inflammation and multiple sclerosis. Drugs within this class of muscle relaxants also are commonly used for antianxiety effects and to induce amnesia. Amnesia is an important quality in a sedation regimen. If a patient reacts poorly to a procedure but has no recollection of his or her reaction, he or she will most likely not develop apprehension regarding further procedures.

The skeletal muscles are innervated by large myelinated nerve fibers that originate in the large motor neurons of the spinal cord. The nerve ending joins the muscle at the neuromuscular junction. When the action potential in the nerve reaches the nerve terminal, a neurotransmitter is released. In the case of skeletal muscle, the neurotransmitter is acetylcholine. Acetylcholine is released into the synaptic cleft, which allows it to bind to its receptor on the muscle membrane. This binding results in a conformational change that increases the permeability of the muscle terminal to potassium and sodium ions, leading to skeletal muscle contraction. The released acetylcholine is removed from the end plate by diffusion and rapid enzymatic destruction by acetylcholinesterase.

Neuromuscular Blockers

Neuromuscular blocking agents are used to produce paralysis and are structurally similar to acetylcholine. These drugs can be divided into depolarizing and nondepolarizing agents. Neuromuscular blocking agents are potentially hazardous medications and should be administered only by highly trained clinicians in a setting where respiratory and cardiovascular resuscitation are immediately available; therefore, they are not used routinely in the dental office.

This chapter provides a summary of neuromuscular blocking agents; however, these drugs are to be used only by clinicians trained in sedation and general anesthesia. Those administering any kind of general anesthetic or sedative should be well-versed in the drug's applications and contraindications. This text is not intended to be comprehensive in terms of information on sedative/general anesthetic agents. Specific details on these drugs can be found in Chapter 3 and in anesthesia texts.

Depolarizing Neuromuscular Blockers

Succinylcholine provides rapid induction of paralysis to facilitate intubation of the trachea during induction of anesthesia. The most common use of succinylcholine in dental practice is to break a laryngospasm that occurs in a patient undergoing conscious sedation. The intravenous dose of succinylcholine to treat laryngospasm is 0.2-0.5mg/kg. If intravenous access is unavailable, 2-5mg/kg can be given sublingually or intramuscularly. Neuromuscular blocking agents are administered parenterally.

See Table 25.1 for general information on succinylcholine.

Special Dental Considerations

The sustained depolarization produced by initial administration of succinylcholine is manifested initially by transient generalized skeletal muscle contractions known as fasciculations. Various degrees of increased muscle tension in the masseter muscles may develop with succinylcholine, especially in pediatric patients. In extreme cases, trismus can occur and make it difficult to open the mouth for intubation of the trachea. Patients who develop trismus with succinylcholine administration are prone to developing malignant hyperthermia.

Head, neck, abdomen and back myalgia can occur postoperatively owing to muscle fasciculation associated with depolarization.

Succinylcholine is a general anesthetic agent and should be used only by clinicians trained in sedation and general anesthesia. Those administering any kind of general anesthetic or sedative should be well-versed in the drug's applications and contraindications.

Drug interactions of dental interest

Succinylcholine causes paralysis and does not have anesthetic or analgesic effects. Therefore, the dentist must ensure that not only paralysis but also adequate anesthesia has been achieved before performing procedures.

No interactions/contraindications are reported regarding the use of succinylcholine with general anesthetic for dental procedures performed in a surgical setting.

Laboratory value alterations

- Hyperkalemia sufficient to cause cardiac arrest may follow administration of succinylcholine; patients at risk include those with denervation of skeletal muscle, major burns, multiple trauma or upper motor neuron injury.

Pharmacology

Succinylcholine is an example of a depolarizing neuromuscular blocker and is the only one used clinically. It binds to the acetylcholine receptor and causes a prolonged depolarization of the postsynaptic membrane. This initial depolarization causes muscle contraction, which is seen clinically as muscle fasciculations throughout the patient's body. The duration of these initial contractions is short. The sustained depolarization of the postsynaptic membrane does not allow the function of acetylcholine to take place, because a depolarized membrane cannot respond to the release of acetylcholine.

These agents are metabolized by plasma cholinesterase, an enzyme found in the bloodstream but not in the synaptic cleft. Therefore, the duration of a depolarizing muscle relaxant is related to the rate of diffusion from the neuromuscular junction. In rare cases, a patient may have an atypical plasma cholinesterase that is not as effective in metabolizing the drug. In such patients, the action of depolarizing agents may be significantly prolonged. The function of a patient's plasma cholinesterase activity can be evaluated according to his or her dibucaine number. Dibucaine is an amide local anesthetic that reduces the function of normal cholinesterase to a greater degree than it diminishes atypical

Table 25.1

Succinylcholine: Dosage and Prescribing Information

Generic name	Brand name(s)	Indications	Dosage range	Interactions with other drugs
Succinylcholine	Anectine Chloride, Quelicin, Sucostrin	Laryngospasm, adjunct to general anesthesia	**Laryngospasm—IM, sublingual:** 2-5 mg/kg **Laryngospasm—IV:** 0.2-0.5 mg/kg	**Cyclophosphamide, aminoglycosides, clindamycin:** May increase bradycardia **Diazepam:** Decreases neuromuscular blockade **Digoxin:** Increases dysrhythmias (because of potassium changes) **Opioid analgesics and inhalation anesthetics:** May increase risk of sinus arrest **Promazine, oxytocin, phenothiazines, quinidine, β-blocking agents, procainamide, lidocaine, lithium, trimethaphan, furosemide, magnesium, chloroquine, acetylcholine, anticholinesterases, amphotericin B, thiazide diuretics (because of electrolyte imbalances):** Increase neuromuscular blockade

cholinesterase. This number reflects the quality, but not the quantity, of plasma cholinesterase. Any dentist administering a drug metabolized by plasma cholinesterase to a patient with a suspected history of plasma cholinesterase deficiency should obtain a dibucaine number to assess the quality of the patient's plasma cholinesterase enzyme system.

Adverse Effects, Precautions and Contraindications

Succinylcholine is used for paralysis as an adjunct to general anesthetic. This drug should be administered only by a clinician with advanced training in the practice of general anesthesia. This drug should not be administered unless facilities for intubation, artificial respiration and oxygen therapy and reversal agents are immediately available.

Many medications used for general anesthesia are potential triggers for malignant hyperthermia, and clinicians should be aware

of this potentially fatal hypermetabolism of skeletal muscle.

Cardiac dysrhythmias—including sinus bradycardia, junctional rhythm and sinus arrest—have occurred after administration of succinylcholine. The succinylcholine mimics acetylcholine at the cardiac postganglionic muscarinic receptors and induces cardiac dysrhythmias.

Transient increases in ocular pressure are seen 2-4 min after injection of succinylcholine. Theoretically, succinylcholine may contribute to extrusion of intraocular contents in patients with open eye injuries.

Fasciculations induced by succinylcholine lead to unpredictable increases in gastric pressure and may cause gastric fluid to pass into the esophagus and pharynx, thus resulting in pulmonary aspiration.

Table 25.2 presents adverse effects of succinylcholine; Table 25.3 lists precautions and contraindications associated with this agent.

Nondepolarizing Neuromuscular Blockers

Nondepolarizing neuromuscular blockers have a duration of action longer than that of depolarizing agents, which makes them useful for prolonged muscle relaxation in the operating room and the intensive care unit. The duration of action of nondepolarizing muscle relaxants depends on their redistribution to inactive tissue sites as well as on their metabolism and clearance from the body. Nondepolarizing muscle relaxants—such as vecuronium—are categorized as long-acting, intermediate-acting and short-acting.

Special Dental Considerations
Drug interactions of dental interest
No interactions/contraindications are reported regarding the use of nondepolarizing neuromuscular blockers with general anesthetic for dental procedures.

Special patients
Nondepolarizing neuromuscular blockers have limited ability to cross lipid membrane barriers. Therefore, this class of drugs does not affect the fetus.

Pharmacology
Nondepolarizing neuromuscular blockers act through competitive inhibition of acetylcholine. Portions of the structure of these drugs are similar to that of acetylcholine, which enables them to bind at the same receptor as that neurotransmitter. When the majority of acetylcholine receptors are bound by neuromuscular blockers, acetylcholine can no longer bind to the receptor. This mechanism produces the profound muscle relaxation characteristic of this class of skeletal muscle relaxants. The use of these drugs is primarily limited to muscle relaxation for general anesthesia.

The majority of nondepolarizing drugs are eliminated through renal excretion; however,

Table 25.2

Succinylcholine: Adverse Effects

Body system	Adverse effects
CV	Bradycardia, hypotension, hypertension, cardiac dysrhythmias, tachycardia
Endoc	Hyperkalemia, malignant hyperthermia
EENT	Increased intraocular pressure
GI	Increased intragastric pressure, salivation
Hema	Myoglobinuria
Integ	Rash, itching, erythema
Musc	Postoperative stiffness, myalgia
Resp	Apnea, bronchospasm, circulatory collapse

Table 25.3

Succinylcholine: Precautions and Contraindications

Generic name	Precautions/contraindications
Succinylcholine	Contraindicated in patients susceptible to malignant hyperthermia or who have a hypersensitivity to the drug
	Contraindicated in patients with skeletal muscle myopathies
	Contraindicated after acute phase of injury in patients with major burns, multiple trauma, extensive denervation of skeletal muscle or upper motor neuron injury
	Should be used cautiously in children and adolescents and in patients with pre-existing hyperkalemia with myotonia or with fractures or muscle spasms
	Should be used cautiously in patients with low plasma cholinesterase (e.g., those who are pregnant or have severe liver disease, cirrhosis, cancer)

some also undergo metabolism in the liver, ester hydrolysis or Hoffman elimination. Regardless of how these agents are metabolized, their duration of action is determined primarily by how rapidly they are redistributed to the peripheral tissues.

Adverse Effects, Precautions and Contraindications

Nondepolarizing neuromuscular blockers should be administered only by clinicians with advanced training in anesthesia. These drugs should not be administered unless facilities for intubation, artificial respiration and oxygen therapy and reversal agents are immediately available.

Nondepolarizing neuromuscular blockers cause cardiovascular effects, and the dentist should take into consideration these agents' specific cardiovascular manifestations when selecting the appropriate agents for a patient. These cardiac effects usually are transient and vary because of these agents' interactions with other medications. Many drugs used in anesthetic practice can trigger malignant hyperthermia; clinicians should consider this when obtaining the patient's medical history before beginning treatment.

Skeletal muscle fasciculations do not occur with onset of action of nondepolarizing neuromuscular blocking agents.

This category of medications is highly ionized at physiologic pH and has limited lipid solubility, resulting in a small volume of distribution primarily in the extracellular fluid. They have limited ability to cross lipid membrane barriers. Therefore, this class of drugs has few central nervous system effects and minimal oral and renal absorption; it also does not affect the fetus.

Spasmolytics

Spasmolytics are used in the dental office primarily to relieve anxiety, treat postprocedural trismus and treat muscle spasms of the head and neck (temporomandibular disorders). These agents often are used in conjunction with heat, physical therapy, rest and analgesics. Some of these agents have anxiolytic properties that may help reduce muscle tension. The etiology of temporomandibular disorders is complex and involves a variety of potential factors such as patient anxiety, joint pathology and muscle spasms. It should be noted that, in general, muscle relaxants are not the primary treatment for every type of facial pain.

Spasmolytics may be used to manage spasticity owing to systemic disease. Spasticity refers to abnormalities of regulation of skeletal muscle tone that result from lesions in the central nervous system (CNS). The pathophysiology of spasticity is poorly understood. A predominant component of such conditions is hyperexcitability of tonic stretch reflexes. Tendon jerks are exaggerated, painful flexor spasms occur and muscle weakness, with a loss of dexterity, almost always occurs. The most effective agents for control of spasticity include two that act directly on the CNS (baclofen and diazepam) and one that acts directly on skeletal muscle (dantrolene).

Table 25.4 presents general information on spasmolytics.

Benzodiazepines

More than 2,000 benzodiazepines have been synthesized. Among these, several are recommended as spasmolytics: chlordiazepoxide, clonazepam, diazepam, lorazepam and midazolam. Clonazepam is used mostly for its anticonvulsant properties but is used sometimes in the treatment of panic disorders. Although benzodiazepines exert similar clinical effects, differences in their pharmacokinetic properties have led to varying therapeutic applications. Chlordiazepoxide and diazepam are considered the prototypic drugs of their class.

The action of benzodiazepines is the result of potentiating the neural inhibition that is mediated by γ-aminobutyric acid (GABA). Diazepam acts on all GABA synapses by binding to the GABA-benzodiazepine receptor complex.

Benzodiazepines have sedative-hypnotic, muscle relaxant, anxiolytic and anticonvulsant effects. The antianxiety effects of this class of drugs make them an excellent choice for preoperative oral sedation in the fearful dental patient.

Most benzodiazepines reduce sleep latency and reduce the number of awakenings. They can be used for insomnia, but prescribing for this purpose should be done only by a clinician who is an expert in sleep disorders. Prolonged use of benzodiazepines for insomnia can have serious detrimental effects on the sleep cycle. When administered intravenously, diazepam can be used to break status epilepticus in patients who suffer from grand mal seizures.

Chlordiazepoxide. Chlordiazepoxide is the original prototype for the benzodiazepines. It has been demonstrated to have sedative, anxiolytic and weak analgesic properties. Chlordiazepoxide is used for treatment of anxiety disorders, short-term anxiety and preoperative anxiety. It is not recommended for the management of stress associated with everyday life. Paradoxical reactions, including excitement and rage, have been reported, especially in psychiatric patients and hyperactive pediatric patients.

Clonazepam. General medical use of clonazepam includes use for treatment of seizures and panic disorders. In dentistry, it has been used for treatment of acute myofascial pain and burning mouth syndrome. No formal recommendations of dosage have been made for its use in this area, and it is usually given in doses similar to those used for panic disorders.

Diazepam. Diazepam is useful as an anxiolytic and as a spasmolytic. When administered intravenously, diazepam can be used to break status epilepticus in patients who suffer from grand mal seizures.

Lorazepam. Lorazepam produces excellent amnesia. Unfortunately, its peak onset can occur as long as 2-4 h after oral administration. Its long duration and slow onset make it impractical as an oral sedative for outpatient procedures.

Midazolam. Midazolam is a rapid-onset, short-acting benzodiazepine that is commonly used intravenously for conscious sedation in an outpatient environment. It has good anxiolytic and amnesic effects, making it an excellent choice for IV sedation.

Special Dental Considerations

Benzodiazepines in general do not have any adverse interactions with dental materials. No special precautions are required for local

Table 25.4

Spasmolytics: Dosage and Prescribing Information

Generic name	Brand name(s)	Indications	Dosage range	Interactions with other drugs
Benzodiazepines				
Chlordiaze-poxide	Librium, Libritabs, Mitran, Resposans-10	Acute myofascial pain and burning-mouth syndrome Anxiety, preprocedural phobia, panic attacks Depression Muscle spasms, conscious sedation, status epilepticus Desired amnesia, antiemetic adjunct Alcohol withdrawal, seizures Transient insomnia	**Oral:** 5-10 mg (agent-specific dosages)	**Anticonvulsants:** Should be used cautiously in patients taking benzodiazepines **CNS depressants (such as alcohol):** These potentiate benzodiazepines' side effects (respiratory distress); patients should be warned of potentially serious interactions with ethanol **Cimetidine and erythromycin:** Decrease benzodiazepine metabolism **General anesthetics or opioids:** Used concomitantly with benzodiazepines, can produce apnea **SSRI antidepressants:** Decrease benzodiazepine clearance
Clonazepam	Klonopin	See note above	See note above	See note above
Diazepam	Valium, Valrelease	See note above	See note above	See note above
Lorazepam	Ativan	See note above	See note above	See note above
Midazolam	Versed	See note above	See note above	See note above
Benzodiazepine antagonist				
Flumazenil	Romazicon	Overdose of benzodiazepine, reversal of benzodiazepine effects	**Benzodiazepine overdose—IV:** 0.4-1 mg; onset will occur in 1-2 min, with peak effect occurring 6-10 min after administration; if a long-acting benzodiazepine has been given, the patient should be re-evaluated about every 20-30 min to see if repeat doses of flumazenil are necessary	Interactions with CNS depressants other than benzodiazepines have not been studied

Continued on next page

Table 25.4 (cont.)

Spasmolytics: Dosage and Prescribing Information

Generic name	Brand name(s)	Indications	Dosage range	Interactions with other drugs
Other spasmolytics				
Baclofen	Atrofen, Lioresal; Alpha-Baclofen [CAN], PMS-Baclofen [CAN]	Spasticity associated with multiple sclerosis, cerebral spasticity Unlabeled uses include intractable pain relief, bladder spasticity	15 mg bid; max: 100 mg/day	**Benzodiazepines, antihypertensive agents, opioid analgesics:** Increase effect of baclofen **Lithium:** Decreases effect of baclofen
Dantrolene	Dantrium	Chronic muscle spasticity associated with stroke, multiple sclerosis, cerebral palsy Malignant hyperthermia	**Chronic spasticity:** 25 mg q day; max: 100 mg tid **Malignant hyperthermia—oral:** 4-8 mg/kg/day for 1-3 days	**Estrogens (hepatotoxicity), CNS depressants (sedation), MAO inhibitors, phenothiazines, clindamycin (increased neuromuscular blockade), verapamil (hyperkalemia and cardiac depression), warfarin, clofibrate, tolbutamide:** Increase toxicity of dantrolene Should be used cautiously in combination with other hepatotoxic medications and CNS depressants
Spasmolytics for acute local spasm				
Carisoprodol (also available in combinations containing aspirin or codeine)	Rela, Sodol, Soma; Dolaren [CAN]	As adjunct to rest and physical therapy in treatment of acute myofascial pain and muscle spasm	350 mg qid, with last dose at bedtime	**Other CNS depressants (including alcohol):** Concomitant use should be avoided, as it may potentiate side effects
Chlorzoxazone	Blanex, Chlorofon-F, Flexaphen, Lobac, Miflex, Mus-Lac, Paraflex, Parafon Forte DSC, Pargen Fortified, Polyflex, Skelex	See note above	500 mg tid-qid; max: 750 mg tid-qid	See note above

[CAN] indicates a drug available only in Canada.

Continued on next page

Table 25.4 (cont.)

Spasmolytics: Dosage and Prescribing Information

Generic name	Brand name(s)	Indications	Dosage range	Interactions with other drugs
Spasmolytics for acute local spasm (cont.)				
Cycloben-zaprine	Cycoflex, Flexeril; Novo-Cycloprine [CAN]	As adjunct to rest and physical therapy in treatment of acute myofascial pain and muscle spasm	20-40 mg/day in divided doses (usually 10 mg tid); max: 60 mg/day; recommended that use be limited to 2-3 w	**Anticholinergic agents:** Should be coadministered with caution **Other CNS depressants (including alcohol):** Concomitant use should be avoided, as it may potentiate side effects **Tricyclic antidepressants:** Are structurally related to cyclobenzaprine, so should be coadministered with caution
Methocarbamol	Delaxin, Marbaxin, Robamol, Robaxin	See note above	1-4.5 g/day in 3-6 divided doses	**Other CNS depressants (including alcohol):** Concomitant use should be avoided, as it may potentiate side effects
Orphenadrine	Banflex, Flexon, Marflex, Noradex, Norflex	**Dental:** Treatment of acute myofascial pain **Medical:** Adjunctive treatment for acute muscle spasm	**IM or IV:** 60 mg q 12 h **Oral:** 100 mg bid	See note above

[CAN] indicates a drug available only in Canada.

anesthetic administration in conjunction with their use. Xerostomia is a common side effect that reverses itself when use of the medication is discontinued.

Drug interactions of dental interest

CNS depressants (alcohol, barbiturates, opioids) may enhance sedation and respiratory depression.

Patients with convulsant disorders may experience an increase in grand mal seizure activity with benzodiazepines; therefore, an increase in their standard anticonvulsant medication may be indicated.

Theophylline may antagonize the sedative effects of midazolam. Cimetidine may increase midazolam's serum concentrations.

Laboratory value alterations

- Isolated reports of benzodiazepine-associated neutropenia and jaundice exist, so periodic blood counts and liver function tests are recommended during long-term benzodiazepine therapy.

Special patients

Patients with narrow-angle glaucoma should not receive benzodiazepines.

Benzodiazepines should not be administered to pregnant or nursing women. An increased risk of congenital malformations is associated with the use of tranquilizers during the first trimester of pregnancy.

Long-acting benzodiazepines have been associated with falls in elderly people and should be avoided in this patient population.

Pharmacology

Benzodiazepines are metabolized by the cytochrome p-450 system in the liver and then are excreted by the kidney. The rate of elimination depends on the drug's half-life. The duration of action of specific benzodiazepines ranges from short to very long.

Benzodiazepines with long half-lives accumulate during repeated dosages and even with a single dose. This is of particular concern in elderly people, in whom half-life may be increased two- to fourfold. Several benzodiazepines, such as diazepam (see below), produce active metabolites when they are metabolized. Metabolites of lorazepam and oxazepam are inactive and, therefore, make these drugs safer than diazepam for patients with liver disease.

Chlordiazepoxide. Chlordiazepoxide's mechanism of action is not known. Animal studies suggest that it acts on the limbic system of the brain (which is involved with emotional response).

Clonazepam. The mechanism of action of clonazepam is not fully understood. Its proposed pharmacologic effects are related to its ability to increase GABA activity. Peak concentrations of clonazepam are reached 1-4 h after oral administration. The elimination half-life is about 30-40 h.

Diazepam. The metabolism of diazepam warrants special attention. Diazepam is metabolized into desmethyldiazepam, an active metabolite. Desmethyldiazepam can reenter the bloodstream through the enterohepatic circulation and produce delayed-onset sedation. Therefore, even after the initial effects of diazepam have disappeared, the patient must not engage in any potentially dangerous activity for 24 h. Diazepam is known to act on the limbic system and induce a calming effect. The peak onset of diazepam occurs 30-60 min after oral administration.

Lorazepam. Lorazepam acts on the CNS, resulting in a tranquilizing effect. IM onset of hypnosis is 20-30 min. Duration of action is 6-8 h.

Midazolam. Midazolam is a short-acting, water-soluble benzodiazepine that depresses the CNS.

Adverse Effects, Precautions and Contraindications

Benzodiazepines can be expected to cause varying degrees of lightheadedness, motor incoordination, ataxia, impaired psychomotor and mental function, confusion, amnesia, dry mouth and bitter taste. Other side effects include headache, blurred vision, vertigo, nausea, vomiting, epigastric distress, joint pain, chest pain and incontinence. Anticonvulsant benzodiazepines can increase the frequency of seizures in patients with epilepsy. Benzodiazepines can have paradoxical effects such as nightmares, restlessness, hallucinations, paranoia, depression, unusual uninhibited behavior and occasional suicidal ideation. When the drug is administered in oral doses at the intended time of sleep, weakness and other previously mentioned side effects may not be noticed. It is considered undesirable if the drug was administered at bedtime and side effects persist during waking hours.

Benzodiazepines have a low incidence of abuse and dependence; however, the possibility must not be overlooked. Mild dependence may occur in patients who have taken benzodiazepines for a prolonged period. Tolerance to benzodiazepines can develop.

Benzodiazepines slightly reduce alveolar ventilation in preanesthetic doses. This group of drugs may cause CO_2 narcosis in patients with chronic obstructive pulmonary disease. Apnea can occur when benzodiazepines are given during general anesthesia or in combination with opioids. Cases have been reported in which respiratory distress has occurred when patients have combined benzodiazepines with other CNS depressants such as alcohol. Patients should be warned of potentially serious interactions with ethanol.

Because their cognitive and motor function may be impaired, patients should be advised not to drive or participate in other potentially dangerous activities.

A specific benzodiazepine should be avoided if a patient has a known hypersensitivity to it. It should be noted that a cross-sensitivity between various benzodiazepines may exist. Benzodiazepines should not be used in patients who have CNS or respiratory depression or who are comatose. Benzodiazepines should not be administered to pregnant or nursing women. An increased risk of congenital malformations is associated with the use of tranquilizers during the first trimester of pregnancy. Patients with narrow-angle glaucoma should not receive benzodiazapines.

Clonazepam. Clonazepam should not be used in patients with a history of adverse reactions to benzodiazepines. It should be administered with caution to patients with liver disease or impaired renal function. Clonazepam may increase the incidence or precipitate the onset of grand mal seizures. It has not been shown to interfere with the pharmacokinetics of phenytoin, carbamazepine or phenobarbital. Valproic acid administered concomitantly with clonazepam may produce absence status.

Hypersalivation has been reported with the use of clonazepam; the dentist should consider this when selecting a medication for a patient who has difficulty controlling salivary flow. However, xerostomia is a more common complaint.

Diazepam. Diazepam should not be given to any patient with acute narrow-angle glaucoma. Precautions should be taken when it is administered to patients with a history of seizure disorders, chronic obstructive pulmonary disease or liver failure.

Midazolam. Theophylline may antagonize the sedative effects of midazolam. Cimetidine may increase serum concentrations. CNS depressants increase sedation and respiratory depression.

Benzodiazepine Antagonist: Flumazenil

Flumazenil is a benzodiazepine antagonist that binds to the GABA/benzodiazepine receptor in the CNS. This antagonist has been shown to reverse the effects of sedation, amnesia and respiratory depression in humans. If a benzodiazepine overdose is observed, flumazenil can be administered IV to reverse the effects of the benzodiazepine. Onset of reversal will occur in 1-2 min, with peak reversal occurring 6-10 min after administration. If a long-acting benzodiazepine has been given, the patient should be re-evaluated about every 20-30 min to see if repeat doses of flumazenil are necessary.

Special Dental Considerations
Drug interactions of dental interest
CNS depressants (alcohol, barbiturates, opioids), if used concurrently, may enhance sedation and respiratory depression.

Adverse Effects, Precautions and Contraindications
Side effects of the benzodiazepine antagonists include dizziness, drowsiness, somnolence, confusion and respiratory depression. Cardiovascular effects include palpitations, chest pain and syncope.

Patients may experience anorexia, xerostomia, vomiting and diarrhea.

Other Spasmolytics
Baclofen. Baclofen, a derivative of the inhibitory neurotransmitter GABA, functions as a GABA agonist in the brain as well as in the spinal cord. Baclofen may reduce substance P and, therefore, pain; it also may function as a spasmolytic. It is most effective for spasticity associated with multiple sclerosis and traumatic spinal cord lesions. In dentistry, it can be used for temporomandibular dystonia and is helpful in some cases of trigeminal neuralgia.

Baclofen is especially helpful in alleviating

the spasticity of multiple sclerosis and spinal cord injury when administered intrathecally. Baclofen is as effective as, but much less sedating than, diazepam in reducing spasticity. It also does not reduce general muscle strength, as happens with other spasmolytics such as dantrolene.

Dantrolene. Dantrolene is indicated for spasticity secondary to upper motor neuron disease (multiple sclerosis, stroke, cerebral palsy) and is not indicated for spasms caused by rheumatic disorders. Treatment for chronic spasticity requires gradual titration until the patient experiences maximum effect. Dantrolene also is used for the management of malignant hyperthermia. This is a rare, dominantly inherited syndrome that is precipitated by the use of inhalation anesthetics or neuromuscular blocking agents. Vigorous muscle contraction occurs, leading to a rapid and dangerous rise in body temperature, renal failure and rhabdomyolysis. Dantrolene is administered IV immediately during an attack, or it may be administered prophylactically to patients who are susceptible to this syndrome.

Special Dental Considerations

Baclofen. No information has been reported indicating the need for special precaution when baclofen is used with local anesthetics and vasoconstrictors.

Dantrolene. The safety of long-term use of dantrolene in humans has not been established.

Drug interactions of dental interest

Baclofen. Lithium decreases the effect of baclofen. Benzodiazepines, antihypertensive agents and opioid analgesics increase baclofen's effect. Increased toxicity is noted when baclofen is administered concomitantly with CNS depressants, alcohol and monoamine oxidase inhibitors. Increased short-term memory loss is noted when baclofen is taken with tricyclic antidepressants.

Dantrolene. Hepatotoxicity has occurred more frequently in women older than 35 y of age who are receiving estrogen therapy while taking dantrolene. The exact interaction is unclear, and caution must be exercised when estrogen and dantrolene are given together.

Cardiovascular collapse has been reported on rare occasion in patients taking both dantrolene and verapamil; therefore, this combination is not recommended. Dantrolene potentiates vecuronium-induced neuromuscular blocking.

Increased toxicity also occurs with concomitant administration of CNS depressants (sedation), MAO inhibitors, phenothiazines, clindamycin (which increase neuromuscular blockade), verapamil (associated with hyperkalemia and cardiac depression), warfarin, clofibrate and tolbutamide.

Laboratory value alterations

- Liver function tests should be obtained on a regular basis to monitor for hepatotoxicity with dantrolene.
- Leukopenia, throbocytopenia and aplastic anemia also have been reported with dantrolene, and patients should be monitored for hematologic abnormalities.

Special patients

Dantrolene. Dantrolene's safety in women who are pregnant or may become pregnant has not been established. Its long-term side effects in the pediatric population younger than 5 y of age has not been established.

Pharmacology

Baclofen. Baclofen is rapidly absorbed and has a half-life of 3-4 h.

Dantrolene. Dantrolene acts directly on the skeletal muscle by reducing the amount of calcium released from the sarcoplasmic reticulum.

Adverse Effects, Precautions and Contraindications

Baclofen. Side effects include dizziness, drowsiness, somnolence, confusion and respiratory depression. Cardiovascular effects include palpitations, chest pain and syncope.

Patients taking baclofen may experience

anorexia, xerostomia, vomiting and diarrhea.

Dantrolene. Dantrolene has a serious side effect of hepatotoxicity; therefore, hepatic function should be monitored after this drug is administered. Active hepatic disease, such as hepatitis and cirrhosis, is a contraindication for use of dantrolene. Long-term use should be discontinued if clear benefits are not evident. This agent should be used with caution in patients with impaired pulmonary and cardiac function resulting from myocardial disease. Cardiovascular side effects may include pleural effusion with pericarditis.

Other side effects include weakness, confusion, lightheadedness, drowsiness, severe diarrhea, abdominal cramps, urinary retention, erectile dysfunction, blurred vision and fatigue. These side effects usually are temporary and can be reduced by using a small initial dose and slowly increasing the dose until the optimal amount is reached. Diarrhea can be severe and require discontinuation of use of dantrolene.

Patients should be cautioned against driving or participating in potentially hazardous activities while taking dantrolene.

Photosensitivity has been associated with dantrolene, and patients taking it should be cautioned to avoid sun exposure.

Taste changes have been noted with dantrolene.

No information has been reported indicating the need for special precautions when dantrolene is used concomitantly with local anesthetics and vasoconstrictors.

Spasmolytics for Acute Local Spasm

Many spasmolytic drugs are indicated for the treatment of temporary relief of muscle spasm caused by trauma. Cyclobenzaprine is considered the prototype of this group of drugs. It is structurally related to the tricyclic antidepressants and has similar properties. It is believed to act at the brainstem. Other drugs in this category include carisoprodol, chlorzoxazone, methocarbamol and orphenadrine. These medications are not helpful in the treatment of muscle spasm that is caused by spinal cord injury, CNS disease or systemic disease.

Carisoprodol. Carisoprodol is used for acute skeletal muscle pain in conjunction with rest, physical therapy and other measures used to manage acute skeletal muscle spasm.

Chlorzoxazone. Chlorzoxazone is indicated as an adjunct to rest, physical therapy and other measures for the relief of acute, painful musculoskeletal conditions.

Cyclobenzaprine. Cyclobenzaprine relieves muscle spasm of local origin without interfering with muscle function. It is used as an adjunct to rest and physical therapy for relief of acute painful muscle spasms.

Methocarbamol. Methocarbamol is recommended as an adjunct to rest, physical therapy and other measures to manage acute skeletal muscle spasm.

Orphenadrine. Orphenadrine is used with rest and physical therapy for the treatment of acute skeletal muscle spasms. It is intended for short-term use only, and no studies of its long-term efficacy and safety have been published.

Special Dental Considerations

No complications have been reported with dental treatment of patients taking spasmolytics used for acute local spasm.

Cyclobenzaprine. It is recommended that cyclobenzaprine be used only for short periods (2 w), as research demonstrating its effectiveness and safety for prolonged use has not been conducted. This is not likely to be an issue, as the drug is indicated for the treatment of acute painful muscle spasm of short duration.

Drug interactions of dental interest

Cyclobenzaprine. Cyclobenzaprine is closely related to tricyclic antidepressants; it also may interact with monoamine oxidase inhibitors and potentially can lead to hyperpyretic crisis, convulsions and death. It should not be used concomitantly with, or within 14 days of use of, MAO inhibitors. It should be used with caution in patients taking anticholinergic medications.

Laboratory value alterations

- Chlorzoxazone: Liver enzyme changes may occur with use, suggesting hepatic toxicity. Therefore, the dentist should consider monitoring the patient's liver function.
- Cyclobenzaprine: This drug is indicated for short-term use and significant laboratory value changes are not expected. Thrombocytopenia and leukopenia have been reported only rarely, and no causal relationship has been established.
- Methocarbamol may cause inaccurate results in screening tests for 5-hydroxyindoleacetic acid and vanillylmandelic. The dentist should inform the patient's physician when prescribing methocarbamol.

Special patients

Carisoprodol. No reports have been published of studies testing this drug's effect on pregnant or nursing women; therefore, it is suggested that use of carisoprodol be avoided in such patients. The drug is not recommended for use in children.

Chlorzoxazone. No reports have been published of studies testing this drug's effect on pregnant or nursing women; therefore, it is suggested that use of chlorzoxazone be avoided in such patients. There are no established guidelines for its use in children, so it should not be administered to pediatric patients.

Cyclobenzaprine. Animal studies have not demonstrated that cyclobenzaprine poses a risk to the fetus or affects fertility. It has not been determined if this drug is excreted in breast milk; therefore, it should be used cautiously in nursing women.

Methocarbamol. Methocarbamol's safety in pregnant and lactating women has not been established, and it is not known if methocarbamol is excreted in breast milk. Safety in children younger than age 12 y has not been established.

Orphenadrine. No studies have been conducted testing orphenadrine's safety in pregnant and nursing women. Neither have

pediatric safety and efficacy studies been performed. This agent should be used with caution in patients with coronary insufficiency, cardiac decompensation, tachycardia, palpitations and dysrhythmia.

Pharmacology

Carisoprodol. Carisoprodol is centrally acting and blocks interneuronal activity in the spinal cord. Its onset is rapid and lasts 6 h. Its exact mechanism of action is not clear, but it is known that carisoprodol does not directly act on skeletal muscle.

Chlorzoxazone. Chlorzoxazone acts primarily at the spinal cord and the subcortical areas of the brain, where it inhibits multisynaptic reflex arcs involved in producing skeletal muscle spasm of varying etiology. Its exact mode of action has not been identified. This drug does not directly relax tense skeletal muscles. Peak blood levels of chlorzoxazone are detected 1-2 h after oral administration.

Cyclobenzaprine. Cyclobenzaprine primarily acts within the CNS at the brainstem, as opposed to the spinal cord levels. It does not act at the neuromuscular junction or directly on skeletal muscle.

Methocarbamol. The drug's mechanism of action has not been determined, but it may be linked to the drug's CNS depressive abilities.

Orphenadrine. The mode of action of orphenadrine is not clear, but it may be related to its analgesic action. Orphenadrine has mild anticholinergic activity and analgesic properties. It does not directly relax skeletal muscles.

Adverse Effects, Precautions and Contraindications

Table 25.5 presents adverse effects of spasmolytics; Table 25.6 lists precautions and contraindications associated with these agents.

Carisoprodol. Carisoprodol is metabolized by the liver and secreted by the kidneys and should be used with caution in patients with impaired liver or kidney function. Other adverse reactions may include drowsiness, malaise, dizziness, lightheadedness, epigastric distress, tachycardia, postural hypotension, facial flushing and, occasionally, idiosyncratic reaction. Seizure threshold may be lowered in patients with convulsive disorders. Patients should be advised of CNS effects and avoid driving and drinking alcohol.

Chlorzoxazone. Cardiovascular side effects include tachycardia and chest pain. Syncope, depression, dizziness, lightheadedness, headaches, trembling, hiccups and shortness of breath have been reported. Angioedema is a noted side effect. Serious and potentially fatal hepatotoxity has been reported with the use of this drug. The mechanism of this is not known, and factors predisposing patients to hepatotoxity have not been identified. Patients should be instructed to report early signs of toxicity such as dark urine, anorexia or upper-right-quadrant pain. Liver enzymes should be monitored if this drug is administered on a long-term basis. Other adverse reactions may include drowsiness, malaise, lightheadedness and, occasionally, overstimulation. Idiosyncratic reactions have been manifested as severe muscle weakness, confusion and ataxia. Patients may note a discoloration of the urine as a result of a phenolic metabolite of chlorzoxazone. This discoloration has no clinical significance.

Cyclobenzaprine. Cyclobenzaprine's potential side effects include drowsiness, malaise, tachycardia and dysrhythmia. Cyclobenzaprine may enhance the effects of alcohol, barbiturates and other CNS depressants. Cyclobenzaprine should be used with caution in patients who have a history of urinary retention, closed-angle glaucoma and increased intraocular pressure. It is contraindicated in patients who are taking MAO inhibitors or who have hyperthyroidism, congestive heart failure or dysrhythmias. This drug has no reported interactions with dental materials. No information has been reported indicating the need for special precautions with concomitant use of local anesthetics/vasocon-strictors. Patients may experience xerostomia while taking cyclobenzaprine.

Methocarbamol. Methocarbamol has CNS depressant effects. Patients taking CNS depressants should be cautioned not to combine methocarbamol with alcohol or other CNS depressants. Renal impairment has occurred on rare occasions as a side effect of methocarbamol use. Lightheadedness, dizziness, drowsiness, nausea, blurred vision, headache and fever are common side effects. The drug should be used with caution in patients with renal disease, hepatic disease, seizure disorders, myasthenia gravis and addictive personality.

Orphenadrine. As with all spasmolytic agents, orphenadrine may cause lightheadedness, drowsiness and syncope. This medication contains sodium bisulfate and may cause severe allergic reactions in patients with sulfite sensitivity. Sulfite sensitivity is seen more frequently in asthmatic patients. On rare occasions, aplastic anemia has been reported with orphenadrine use. It has mild anticholinergic effects, which may result in dry mouth and constipation. Other side effects include urinary retention, tachycardia, palpitations, blurred vision, dilation of pupils or gastric irritation. This drug can cause increased ocular tension and is contraindicated in patients with glaucoma. Orphenadrine also is contraindicated in people with pyloric or duodenal obstruction, prostate hypertrophy or obstruction of the bladder, cardiospasm and myasthenia gravis.

Suggested Readings

1999 physicians' desk reference. 53rd ed. Montvale, N.J.: Medical Economics Company; 1998.

Goodman LS, Gilman A, Gilman AG. Goodman and Gilman's the pharmacological basis of therapeutics. 8th ed. New York: Pergamon Press; 1990.

McCaughey W, Clarke RSJ, Fee JPH, Wallace WFM. Anaesthetic physiology and pharmacology. New York: Churchill Livingstone; 1997.

Neidle EA, Yagiela JA. Pharmacology and therapeutics for dentistry. 4th ed. Philadelphia: C.V. Mosby Co.; 1998.

Table 25.5

Spasmolytics: Adverse Effects*

Body system	Benzodi-azepines	Baclofen	Dantrolene	Spasmolytics for acute local spasm				
				Cariso-prodol	Chlorzox-azone	Cycloben-zaprine	Metho-carbamol	Orphena-drine
CV	Hypotension	Hypo-tension, palpitations (in < 1% of population), syncope	Tachycardia, erratic blood pressure, phlebitis	Postural hypo-tension, tachycardia		Tachycardia, dysrhyth-mia, palpi-tations, postural hypotension	Postural hypoten-sion, brady-cardia	Drowsiness, dizziness, tachycardia, palpitations
CNS	Drowsiness, confusion, depression, fatigue, tremors, ataxia, slurred speech	Drowsiness, vertigo, dizziness, slurred speech, euphoria, depression (with sudden withdrawal), halluci-nations	Fatigue, drowsiness, slurred speech	Dizziness, weakness, headache, tremors, depression, insomnia, ataxia, irritability		Syncope, ataxia, dizziness, tremors, hypertonia, insomnia, anxiety, paresthesia, depressed mood	Dizziness, weakness, drowsiness, seizures	Halluci-nations, agitation, tremors
EENT	Blurred vision	Taste disorder	Excess tearing	Diplopia, temporary vision changes	Burning eyes	Diplopia, tinnitus	Diplopia, blurred vision, nystagmus, temporary vision loss	Nystagmus, increased ocular pres-sure, dilated pupils
GI	Nausea	Nausea, anorexia, diarrhea	Diarrhea, constipation, nausea, vomiting	Nausea, vomiting, hiccups, epigastric distress	Nausea, vomiting	Vomiting, anorexia, diarrhea, gastritis, gastroin-testinal pain, flatu-lence, abnormal liver func-tion, hepa-titis (rare)	Nausea, vomiting, hiccups	Nausea, vomiting, constipation
GU	Urinary retention, incontinence	Enuresis, urinary retention, impotence, urinary fre-quency, hematuria				Urinary frequency or retention	Black, brown, or green urine	Decreased urination, urinary hesitancy or retention

* Spasmolytics are centrally acting; therefore, side effects noted for one drug can be anticipated for all. Reactions for one drug vs. another may be more or less remarkable.

Continued on next page

Table 25.5 (cont.)

Spasmolytics: Adverse Effects*

Body system	Benzodi-azepines	Baclofen	Dantrolene	Spasmolytics for acute local spasm				
				Cariso-prodol	Chlorzox-azone	Cycloben-zaprine	Metho-carbamol	Orphena-drine
Hema	Neutropenia		Thrombo-cytopenia	Leukopenia			Hemolysis	Aplastic anemia
HB			Hepatitis, abnormal liver function tests			Abnormal liver function		
Integ		Rash	Hair growth, rash, sweating	Facial flush-ing, idio-syncratic reactions (skin rash, pruritis, erythemia multiforme, angioneu-rotic edema)	Angio-neurotic edema		Rash	Rash, pruritis
Musc	Weakness, tremors	Weakness, paresthesia	Weakness	Weakness, tremors	Trembling	Local weakness		Weakness, tremors
Oral	Xerostomia	Xerostomia				Ageusia, xerostomia	Metallic taste	Xerostomia
Renal		Need for monitoring of renal function						
Resp		Dyspnea	Respiratory depression	Idiosyncra-tic reaction (asthmatic attack)	Shortness of breath			Nasal congestion (infrequent)

* Spasmolytics are centrally acting; therefore, side effects noted for one drug can be anticipated for all. Reactions for one drug vs. another may be more or less remarkable.

Table 25.6

Spasmolytics: Precautions and Contraindications

Generic name	Precautions/contraindications
Benzodiazepines	
Benzodiazepines	Contraindicated in patients with acute narrow-angle glaucoma or untreated glaucoma
	Contraindicated in patients with existing CNS depression or respiratory depression and in comatose patients
	Contraindicated in pregnant or nursing women
	Should be used cautiously in patients with chronic obstructive pulmonary disease and liver disease
Benzodiazepine antagonist	
Flumazenil	Contraindicated in patients with known hypersensitivity to flumazenil or benzodiazepines; with patients who have signs of serious cyclic antidepressant overdose; with patients given benzodiazepines for life-threatening illness such as intracranial pressure
	Should be used cautiously in patients with head injury
	Should be used cautiously in cases of mixed-drug overdose, as toxic effects of other drugs may emerge
	Use of flumazenil has been associated with seizures; clinicians should individualize doses and be prepared to manage seizures
Other spasmolytics	
Baclofen	Should be used cautiously in patients with impaired renal function
	Abrupt withdrawal should be avoided
Dantrolene	Extremely hepatotoxic and is contraindicated in patients with liver disease
Spasmolytics for acute local spasm	
Carisprodol	Contraindicated in patients with porphyria
	Should be used cautiously in patients with renal or hepatic dysfunction
Chlorzoxazone	Serious fatal hepatocellular toxicity has been reported (rarely); should be used cautiously in patients with hepatic disease
Cyclobenzaprine	Contraindicated for concomitant use with, or use within 14 days of use of, MAO inhibitors
	Contraindicated for patients with hyperthyroidism, recent myocardial infarction, dysrhythmias, cardiac conduction disturbances, congestive heart failure
	Should be used cautiously in patients with urinary hesitancy or glaucoma
Methocarbamol	Should be used cautiously in patients with renal disease, hepatic disease, seizure disorders, myasthenia gravis, addictive personality disorder
Orphenadrine	Contraindicated for patients with tachycardia, coronary insufficiency
	Should be used cautiously in patients with cardiac dysrhythmias

Chapter 26

Therapeutics in Renal and Hepatic Disease

B. Ellen Byrne, R.Ph., D.D.S., Ph.D.

The dosage of many drugs that are normally cleared by the kidney must be adjusted in patients with renal disease, as well as those with hepatic disease. If such adjustments are not made, drug accumulation and toxicity are likely to occur during renal dysfunction. The goal of therapy in a patient with renal impairment is to achieve unbound drug serum concentrations similiar to those that have been associated with optimal response in patients with normal renal function. Drug dosage in those with renal failure can be accomplished by one of two methods:

- keeping the dose the same and lengthening the dosing interval (interval prolongation method); or
- reducing the dose and keeping the dose interval constant (dose reduction method).

The interval prolongation method is convenient because the same doses used in patients with normal renal function are given less frequently. This method is most practical for drugs with long half-lives; however, this approach may result in marked fluctuations in high and low serum concentration and should be avoided where the drug has a narrow therapeutic index. The dose reduction method allows the drug to be given at the usual intervals but in less convenient doses. More constant serum concentrations are achieved with this method. This may be more beneficial in instances in which it is desirable to maintain concentrations above a given threshold.

No controlled studies have been performed to establish the relative efficacy of these two methods for drug-dose alterations in patients with renal insufficiency. And as neither of these two dosage adjustment methods is optimal for all agents, clinicians often will combine these two approaches by giving lower doses at a less prolonged dosing interval.

Drug dosage adjustments for hepatically eliminated drugs in patients with liver disease or dysfunction are difficult to predict. This is due to the complexity of hepatic metabolism, which involves numerous metabolic pathways that are variably affected in hepatic dysfunction. In renal disease, creatinine serves as an endogenous marker to predict the clearance of renally eliminated drugs. Unfortunately, in hepatic dysfunction, there are no reliable endogenous markers to accurately predict a drug's hepatic clearance. Because of this difficulty in predicting hepatic drug clearance, unnecessary and potentially hepatotoxic medications are best avoided. When drug therapy is indicated with agents that undergo hepatic elimination, it is prudent to use the lowest doses possible to achieve the desired therapeutic effect. The use of serum drug concentrations is necessary when treating patients with liver failure.

Special Dental Considerations

Drug Interactions of Dental Interest

Patients with renal disease usually receive a large variety of drugs. This creates great potential for numerous drug interactions. For example, one drug may displace another drug from protein binding sites. This increases the free unbound fraction of the drug and also increases its pharmacological activity. This also will change the amount of drug to be dialyzed. Before adding any drug to a patient's drug regimen, the dentist should review the drug combinations and screen for adverse interactions.

Laboratory Value Alterations

Aberrant renal function test results can be caused by medications. The consequences of this can be costly, time-consuming and misleading to the dentist, resulting in deleterious clinical results.

- Serum creatinine: aspirin competes with receptors for creatinine secretion, causing increased creatinine.
- Urate: increases with administration of salicylates and acetaminophen (nonenzymatic analytical method).
- Urine color: changes with administration of metronidazole (darkens on standing).
- Urine protein: false positive reaction occurs with administration of salicylates, cephalosporin or penicillin.

Drug Dosing in Renal Impairment

The drugs listed in Table 26.1 include drugs that could be given by the dentist. The drugs have been listed in alphabetical order independent of their classification of use. The brand names given are only representative, not all-inclusive. A brief summary of the route of elimination—that is, renal excretion, hepatic metabolism, presence of active metabolites—for each drug is also provided. The half-life (t ½) of drug elimination from the body is given for people with normal renal function and for anephric patients, those with end-stage renal disease (creatinine clearance [CrCl] < 10 mL/min). Dosing guidelines for three categories of renal disease are included. Dosing recommendations for the category "CrCl > 50 mL/min" usually represent normal dosage regimens. The effect of dialysis on drug removal is also described.

Suggested Readings

Aweeka FT. Appendix: drug reference table. In: Schrier RW, Gambertoglio JG, eds. Handbook of drug therapy in liver and kidney disease. Boston: Little, Brown; 1991: 285-371.

Aweeka FT. Drug dosing in renal failure. In: Young L, Koda-Kimble MA, eds. Applied therapeutics: the clinical use of drugs. 6th ed. Vancouver, Wash.: Applied Therapeutics Inc.; 1995:32.1-32.21.

Benet LZ, Williams RL. Appendix II: design and optimization of dosage regimens. In: Bennett WM. Guide to drug dosage in renal failure. Clin Pharmacokinet 1988; 15:326-51.

Goodman Gilman A, et al., eds. Goodman and Gilman's the pharmacological basis of therapeutics. New York: Pergamon Press; 1990:1650-1737.

Table 26.1

Drug Dosing in Renal Impairment: General Information

Generic name	Brand name(s)	Metabolism and elimination	Normal (t ½[h])*	Anephric (t ½[h])	Dose change with renal failure (CrCl† >50 mL/min)††	Dose change with renal failure (CrCl 10-50 mL/min)	Dose change with renal failure (CrCl <10 mL/min)	Effect of dialysis	Dose change in liver failure
Acetaminophen	Tylenol; Panadol [CAN]	Hepatic conjugation, oxidated metabolites are hepatotoxic; 3% excreted unchanged	1-4	1.9-2.5	q 4-6 h	q 4-6 h	q 4-6 h	Slightly/moderately dialyzed	Avoid
Acyclovir	Zovirax; Avirax [CAN]	76-82% excreted unchanged renally; 14% hepatic metabolism	1.5-3.3	20	No change	q 12-24 h	50% every 24 h	Dialyzed	No change
Amoxicillin	Amoxil, Trimox, Wymox; Apo-Amoxi [CAN], Novamoxin [CAN], Nu-Amoxi [CAN]	Hepatic metabolism 12-28%; 50-88% excreted unchanged	0.5-2.3	7-20	No change	q 6-12 h	q 12-14 h	Moderately dialyzed	No change
Ampicillin	OmniPen, PrinciPen, Totcillin, Apo-Ampi [CAN], Novo-Ampicillin [CAN]	76-88% excreted unchanged; 12-24% metabolism	0.5-1.5	20	No change	q 6-12 h	q 12-18 h	Moderately dialyzed	No change
Carbamazepine	Tegretol	Extensive metabolism; renal excretion; 1-2% unchanged and active metabolites	10-20	Half-life unknown in patient without kidney function	No change	No change	No change	Slightly dialyzed	Decrease

Cefaclor	Ceclor	70% excreted unchanged; <10% hepatic metabolism	0.6-1.0	1.5-4.7	No change	50-100% every 8 h	25-50% every 8-12 h	Moderately dialyzed	No change
Cephalexin	Keflex, C-Lexin, generic	85-95% excreted unchanged	1.0-1.9	20-40	No change	q 12 h	q 24 h	Moderately dialyzed	No change
Chloral hydrate	Noctec, generic	Rapidly metabolized to active trichloroethanol	7-14	Half-life unknown in patient without kidney function	q 24 h	Avoid	Avoid	Dialyzed	Decrease
Chlordiazepoxide	Librium, Libritabs, generic	Hepatic metabolism to active metabolites < 1% excreted unchanged	5-30	No change	q 6-8 h	q 6-8 h	q 12 h	Not/slightly dialyzed	Decrease
Clavulanic acid with amoxicillin	Augmentin	34-52% excreted unchanged; 26% unchanged in feces	0.8-1.2	2.6-4.0	No change	q 8 h	q 12-24 h	Dialyzed	No change
Clindamycin	Cleocin, generic	85% hepatic metabolism to active and inactive metabolites; 10% excreted unchanged in urine and 5% in feces	2-4	1.6-3.4	No change	No change	No change	Not dialyzed	Decrease

Continued on next page

[CAN] indicates a drug available only in Canada.
* Half-life in hours.
† CrCl: creatinine clearance.
†† mL/min: milliliters per minute.

Table 26.1 (cont.)
Drug Dosing in Renal Impairment: General Information

Generic name	Brand name(s)	Metabolism and elimination	Normal (t ½[h])*	Anephric (t ½[h])	Dose change with renal failure (CrCl† >50 mL/min)††	Dose change with renal failure (CrCl 10-50 mL/min)	Dose change with renal failure (CrCl <10 mL/min)	Effect of dialysis	Dose change in liver failure
Codeine phosphate, codeine sulfate	Generic	Hepatic metabolism; 5-17% excreted unchanged	2.5-3.5	No change	No change	Decrease dose 25%	Decrease dose 50%	Unknown	Decrease
Diazepam	D-Val, Diazepam Intensol, Valium, Valrelease, Zetran, generic	Hepatic metabolism to active metabolites via N-demethylation and hydroxylation; renal excretion	20-70	37	q 8 h	q 8 h	q 8 h	Not dialyzed	Decrease
Doxycycline	Doxy Film, Monodox, Doxy-Caps, Doryx, Vibramycin, Vibratabs, generic	10-20% hepatic metabolism; 30% intraluminal gut wall; 40% excreted unchanged renally; 20-40% excreted in feces	14-24	14-36	No change	No change	No change	Not dialyzed	Decrease
Erythromycin	E-Mycin, Ery-Tab, Erythro, Erythrocin, generic	Hepatic metabolism 85-95% to inactive metabolites; 5-15% excreted unchanged	1.5-30	4-6	No change	No change	No change	Slightly dialyzed	Decrease
Ibuprofen	Advil*, Excedrin IB, Ibuprin, Ibuprofen, Motrin, Rufen	Hepatic metabolism 40-60% excreted in urine as unchanged drug and metabolites	2	2	No change	No change	No change	Not dialyzed	Unknown

Ketoconazole	Nizoral	51% hepatic metabolism; 45% excreted unchanged in feces and 3% unchanged renally	3-8	3-8	No change	No change	No change	Not dialyzed	Decrease
Lorazepam	Ativan, generic	Extensive glucuronide conjugation in the liver; excreted renally	8-24	28	q 8 h	q 8 h	q 8 h	Not/slightly dialyzed	Decrease
Meperidine	Demerol	Hepatic hydrolysis and conjugation, active normeperidine metabolite, 10% excreted unchanged	3.2	Half-life unknown in patient without kidney function	q 3-4 h	q 6 h (decrease dose 25%)	q 8 h (decrease dose 50%)	Unknown	Decrease
Metronidazole	Flagyl, Metric 21, Protostat, generic	Hepatic oxidation and glucuronide conjugation; 60-80% renal excretion, 20% excreted unchanged	8	q 8 h	q 8 h	q 8-12 h	q 12-24 h	Rapidly dialyzed	Decrease
Minocycline	Minocin, generic	60-75% hepatic metabolism; < 10% excreted unchanged renally; 20-34% excreted in feces	11-26	14-30	No change	No change	No change	Not dialyzed	Decrease

★ indicates a drug bearing the ADA Seal of Acceptance.
* Half-life in hours.
† CrCl: creatinine clearance.
†† mL/min: milliliters per minute.

Continued on next page

Table 26.1 (cont.)

Drug Dosing in Renal Impairment: General Information

Generic name	Brand name(s)	Metabolism and elimination	Normal (t ½[h])*	Anephric (t ½[h])	Dose change with renal failure (CrCl >50 mL/min)††	Dose change with renal failure (CrCl 10-50 mL/min)	Dose change with renal failure (CrCl <10 mL/min)	Effect of dialysis	Dose change in liver failure
Morphine	Astramorph PF Injection, Duramorph Injection, Infumorph Injection, MS Contin, Oramorph, Rescudose, Roxanol	Hepatic metabolism; 85% renal excretion, 10% excreted unchanged	2-3	2-3	No change	Decrease dose 25%	Decrease dose 50%	Unknown	Decrease
Naloxone	Narcan Injection *	Rapidly metabolized via N-dealkylation and glucuronidation, 70% renal excretion within 72 h	1.0-1.5	Half-life unknown in patient without kidney function	No change	No change	No change	Unknown	No change
Naproxen	Aleve, Anaprox, Anaprox DS EC-Naprosyn, Naprosyn	Hepatic metabolism in inactive metabolites; <1% excreted unchanged in urine	10-18	10-18	No change	No change	No change	Not dialyzed	Decrease
Oxazepam	Serax, generic	Extensive glucuronide conjugation in the liver; renal and fecal excretion	4-25	24-91	q 8 h	q 8 h	q 8 h	Not dialyzed	No change

Continued on next page

Penicillin G	Pentids, Bicillin L-A, Permapen, Wycillin, generic	Hepatic metabolism 19%; 50% excreted unchanged	0.4-0.9	6-19	No change	50-100% every 8-12 h	25-50% every 12 h	Moderately dialyzed, 30-50 mL/min	No change
Penicillin V potassium	Beepen-VK, Betapen-VK, Ledercillin VK, Pen.Vee K	Hepatic metabolism <30%; mostly renal	0.5-1	Unknown	q 6 h	q 6 h	q 6-8 h	Unknown	No change
Pentazocine	Talwin, Talwin-Nx	Hepatic metabolism; hydroxylation 2-15% excreted changed	2	2-3	No change	Decrease dose by 25%	Decrease dose by 50%	Unknown	Decrease
Pentobarbital	Nembutal, generic	Hepatic hydroxylation; <1% excreted unchanged	18-48	27	q 8-24 h	q 8-24 h	q 8-24 h	Slightly dialyzed	Decrease
Phenobarbital	Solfoton, Barbita, generic	Hepatic metabolism; renal excretion; 10-40% unchanged and active metabolites	100	Half-life unknown in patient without kidney function	No change	No change	Slight decrease	Moderately dialyzed	Decrease
Propoxyphene	Darvon	30-70% first-pass metabolism; 7% excreted unchanged	9-15	12-20	q 4 h	q 4 h	Avoid	Not dialyzed	Decrease
Salicylates (aspirin)	Anacin, Aspiritab, Bayer, Empirin, Norwich, St. Joseph	Converted to salicylic acid by peripheral enzymes; hepatic metabolism of salicylic acid	2-20 (dose-dependent)	2-20 (dose-dependent)	q 4 h	q 4-6 h	Avoid	Dialyzed	Avoid

★ *indicates a drug bearing the ADA Seal of Acceptance.*

* *Half-life in hours.*

† *CrCl: creatinine clearance.*

†† *mL/min: milliliters per minute.*

Table 26.1 (cont.)

Drug Dosing in Renal Impairment: General Information

Generic name	Brand name(s)	Metabolism and elimination	Normal (t ½[h])*	Anephric (t ½[h])	Dose change with renal failure (CrCl [mL/min])†† >50 mL/min	Dose change with renal failure (CrCl 10-50 mL/min)	Dose change with renal failure (CrCl <10 mL/min)	Effect of dialysis	Dose change in liver failure
Temazepam	Restoril	Extensive conjugation to inactive metabolites	10-15	10-15	q 12 h	q 12 h	q 12 h	Not dialyzed	No change
Tetracycline	Achromycin V, Sumycin, Tetracyn	48-70% excreted unchanged renally; <30% excreted through hepatic/biliary/fecal route	6-15	33-80	q 6 h	Avoid	Avoid	Slightly dialyzed	Use with caution
Thiopental (IV)	Pentothal, Thiopentone, generic	Hepatic metabolism; renal elimination is minimal	10	6-18	No change	No change	Decrease dose by 25%	Unknown	Decrease
Triazolam	Halcion	Extensive glucuronide conjugation to slightly active metabolites; little renal excretion, fecal excretion	2.3-2.8	Half-life unknown in patient without kidney function	q 12 h	q 12 h	q 12 h	Not dialyzed	No change

* Half-life in hours.
† CrCl: creatinine clearance.
†† mL/min: milliliters per minute.

Chapter 27

Drugs for Neoplastic Disorders

Sol Silverman Jr., M.A., D.D.S.; Alan M. Kramer, M.D.

More than 1.1 million new cases of cancer are diagnosed in the United States each year. In spite of improvements in surgical techniques and radiation therapy, only about half of these people will survive their disease. To diminish this high rate of mortality, chemotherapeutic drugs have become an increasingly important part of treatment regimens. These agents are used as single agents or in combination with other treatments. The intent of using these agents with many neoplasms is cure; however, they are more often used for palliation, to gain partial control over the growths and thus prolong life, or as adjuvants to improve response rates in radiation and surgical approaches. Additionally, these drugs are important in bone-marrow and stem-cell transplantations, which are used increasingly to improve tumor control.

The drugs used for neoplastic disorders can create cytotoxicity-induced immunosuppression, which can lead to significant symptoms and affect survival. Because the oral mucosae and microbial flora are extremely sensitive to immunosuppression, maintaining optimal oral and dental health becomes a key factor in patient management and outcomes.

Many agents are used to attack neoplastic cells through a variety of biochemical processes. They have efficacies for both solid and hematopoietic cancers. Response rates depend on the type of neoplasm, the combination of antineoplastic drugs and the patient's physical status and tolerance. Because these agents

are detoxified either in the liver or kidneys, these organs must be functional.

For oral and pharyngeal malignancies, these agents are used primarily as adjuvants to radiation, with the aim of improving responses to radiation. By far the best results for control of nasopharyngeal carcinomas have been achieved by the combination of radiation therapy and chemotherapy. However, in such cases, chemotherapy also accentuates the adverse effects of radiation.

The choice of drug(s) and dosage regimen(s) depends on response rates derived from multi-institutional and group cooperative studies. The toxic side effects of these agents, as well as response rates, are the factors that limit their application. These effects often limit dental procedures required for optimal oral health and create oral problems that lead to dysfunction and pain and require professional help (see box, "Guidelines for Dental Care of Patients Undergoing Chronic or Periodic Drug Treatment for Neoplastic Disorders"). Adverse side effects vary from patient to patient. Management by altering treatment, prescribing medications or instituting empirical procedures depends on the severity and the effects of patient outcomes.

Classification of Antineoplastic Drugs

Alkylating Agents

Alkylating agents are the oldest and most widely used class of anticancer drugs, being the major components of the combination

Dental clinical and radiographic evaluation
- Dental caries, periapical lesions, periodontal disease, bone abnormalities
- Oral mucosal lesions

Consultation with primary care physician/ oncologist
- Tumor site, type, stage
- Prognosis
- Medication(s)
- Other systemic diseases
- Suggested premedications
- Past treatment, next treatment

Dental treatment plan
- Immediate: Remove all sources of infection to prevent pain and bacteremia
- Long-term: Promote optimal function and esthetics and prevent infections

Optimal oral hygiene
- Pretreatment prophylaxis
- Initiation of fluoride applications
- Mouthrinses as tolerated (such as chlorhexidine)
- Home care instructions
- Orient patient to the side effects of treatment (such as mucositis) and hygiene modifications (such as soft brushes)

Limitations of treatment
- Infection risk: Leukopenia when white blood cell counts are < 1,500 mm³ (if procedure necessary, use antibiotics)
- Bleeding risk: Thrombocytopenia when platelet count is < 100,000 mm³ (extractions, cutting, invasive procedures)
- Candidiasis (yeast overgrowth): Use of topical/systemic antifungal drugs
- Mucositis: Use of topical/systemic analgesic, anti-inflammatory and antimicrobial agents

---

chemotherapy regimens for disseminated solid tumors and for high-dose/stem-cell-support treatment regimens. Aklyating agents interfere with DNA synthesis by causing cross-linking, which can lead to cell death via several pathways. Examples of alkylating agents are cyclophosphamide, cisplatin and nitrogen mustard.

Antibiotics

Antibiotics are a class of cytotoxic agents naturally derived from microbial fermentation broths that include bacteria, fungi and related organisms. Their mechanisms involve intercalation with DNA base pairs, thereby interfering with DNA synthesis. Examples of antibiotics are bleomycin and doxorubicin.

Antimetabolites

Antimetabolites are one of the more diversified and best characterized types of the chemotherapeutic agents in use. Both RNA and DNA syntheses are interrupted by competitive inhibition of purine and pyrimidine nucleosides and of folic acid. Examples are methotrexate, hydroxyurea, 5-fluorouracil, cytarabine and gemcitabine.

Biologic Agents

Biologic agents produce antitumor effects primarily by stimulating natural host defense mechanisms. Examples of these agents are interferons, interleukin-2, monoclonal antibodies, tumor vaccines and retinoids (isotretinoin).

Hormonal Agents

Hormonal agents are used in the hormonally responsive cancers, such as breast, prostate and endometrial carcinomas. As a group they have both cytostatic and cytocidal activity, which is largely mediated by secondary messengers via cytoplasmic and nuclear receptors. Examples of hormonal agents are tamoxifen, prednisone, androgens and estrogens, letrozole and flutamide.

Miscellaneous Antineoplastic Agents

There are miscellaneous other antineoplastic agents. Taxanes are novel agents that promote the formation of microtubules and stabilize them by preventing depolymerization. Examples are paclitaxel and docetaxel, which are used in breast, lung and ovarian cancers. Topoisomerase I inhibitors are a group of agents derived from cantothecin. They kill cancer cells by inhibiting the production of the enzyme topoisomerase I, which is essential to DNA replication. Examples are topotecan and irinotecan, used in refractory colon and ovarian cancers. Vinca alkaloids are part of a group of agents that interfere with microtubule assembly, thereby inhibiting the mitosis phase of the cell cycle. Examples are vinblastine, vincristine and a new agent, vinorelbine. These agents are used in patients with lymphomas, Kaposi's sarcoma, lung cancer and breast cancer.

Agents Under Investigation

Researchers are studying the use of vitamin A analogues (e.g., 13-cis retinoic acid [Accutane]), as well as the use of antioxidants beta carotene or vitamin A ester, combined with vitamins C (ascorbic acid) and E (alpha-tocopherol). Daily ingestion may help control precancerous oral lesions (leukoplakia), and/or help prevent additional primary head and neck cancers in patients already being treated for head and neck cancer. While antioxidant vitamins have no evident clinical adverse side effects, 13-cis retinoic acid may cause skin dryness, pruritus, rash, angular cheilitis, photosensitivity and an increase in blood triglycerides. Optimal dosages and combinations have not yet been established and are currently under study.

Table 27.1 provides general information on selected antineoplastic drugs in several commonly used categories: alkylating agents, antibiotics, antimetabolites, biologic agents and hormonal agents, as well as miscellaneous agents also used in cancer therapy.

Special Dental Considerations

The patient's response to chemotherapeutic agents, many of which suppress white blood cells and platelets, influences the timing and types of dental procedures. The dentist's main concern before providing care to a patient receiving chemotherapy relates to adequate numbers of white blood cells (because of concerns about infection) and blood platelets (because of concerns about excessive bleeding). The marrow suppression usually is cyclical, and there are periods during which the risks of infection and bleeding are minimal.

Before the dentist undertakes any dental procedure involving a patient with cancer, he or she should contact the patient's primary care physician regarding the need for any premedication. This includes the use of antibiotics to protect against bacteremias.

Because many medications used by dental clinicians to control oral complaints (signs and symptoms) may put an extra burden on a patient's ability to detoxify drugs, the dentist should notify the physician before using such medications. It is important to coordinate medical and dental treatment to minimize complications for the patient.

Careful clinical and radiographic examination followed by any indicated corrective procedure are essential to minimize subsequent complications of dental pain, abscesses, poor hygiene and periodontal disease that may occur during cancer therapy. This is an important step in prevention, because dental infections that occur when the patient is temporarily compromised while undergoing chemotherapy can create critical problems in patient care and recovery.

Nausea and vomiting often complicate patient progress because of poor hygiene, inadequate food and liquid intake, pain and discomfort, malaise and depression. However, it is essential that patients maintain optimal oral hygiene by using appropriate brushing and flossing techniques as well as mouthrinses. If mouthrinses that contain alcohol (e.g., chlorhexidine, antimicrobial mouthwash) cause discomfort, then blander mouthrinses (such as baking soda rinses) should be used. Some reports have stated that a daily rinse with chlorhexidine may reduce the risk of developing candidiasis (candidal overgrowth)

Table 27.1

Antineoplastic Agents and Related Drugs: Prescribing Information*

Generic name	Brand name(s)	Indications	Interactions with other drugs
Alkylating agents			
Carboplatin	Paraplatin	Brain, endometrial, head and neck, non–small-cell lung, ovarian cancers; seminoma	**Anticonvulsant drugs:** When administered with carboplatin, these may become subtherapeutic **Autotoxic drugs:** Carboplatin may potentiate these, leading to hearing loss **Nephrotoxic drugs (such as cyclosporine):** Carboplatin potentiates nephrotoxicity of these drugs
Cisplantin	Platinol	See note above; also cervical cancer, osteosarcoma, soft-tissue sarcoma	**NSAIDs, aminoglycosides:** Cisplantin increases these drugs' potential for nephrotoxicity and ototoxicity
Cyclophosphamide	Cytoxan	Breast and lung cancers; lymphoma, myeloma, sarcomas	**Barbiturates and any drugs that stimulate liver metabolic enzymes:** May increase the rate of hepatic conversion of cyclophosphamide to its toxic metabolites
Ifosamide	Ifex	Lung and testicular cancer; non-Hodgkin's lymphoma, sarcomas	**Allopurinol, chloral hydrate, chloroquine, cimetidine, glucocorticoids, imipramine, phenobarbital, phenytoin, phenothiazides:** When administered concomitantly with ifosamide, may accentuate hemotologic, digestive system and central nervous system abnormalities **Nephrotoxic medications (nonsteroidal anti-inflammatory drugs, or NSAIDs):** May increase ifosamide's nephrotoxic effects
Antibiotics			
Bleomycin	Blenoxane	Head and neck, testicular cancers; lymphomas; malignant pleural effusions	**Nephrotoxic agents:** May alter elimination and increase toxicity of bleomycin
Doxorubicin	Adriamycin	Bladder, breast cancers; myeloma, neuroblastoma, sarcomas; acute lymphocytic leukemia; Wilms' tumor	**Cyclophosphamide:** May induce hemorrhagic cystitis at an increased rate if administered concomitantly with doxorubicin **6-mercaptopurine:** Associated hepatotoxicity may increase with concomitant administration of doxorubicin

* *Doses are not provided, as they vary widely depending on which drug combinations are used.*

Continued on next page

Table 27.1 (cont.)

Antineoplastic Agents and Related Drugs: Prescribing Information*

Generic name	Brand name(s)	Indications	Interactions with other drugs
Antimetabolites			
Azathioprine	Imuran	As adjunct for prevention of rejection in renal transplantation; also used in severe rheumatoid arthritis	**Allopurinol, angiotensin-converting enzyme (ACE) inhibitors, cotrimoxazole, warfarin:** When administered concomitantly with azathioprine, these agents interfere with liver detoxification, depress red and white blood cell counts and inhibit anticoagulant effects
5-fluorouracil	Adrucil, Flurorouracil	Breast, colon, esophageal, head and neck, pancreatic, rectal, stomach cancers	**Diazepam and droperidol:** Incompatible
Hydroxyurea	Hydrea	Chronic myelogenous leukemia; head and neck, ovarian cancer; melanoma	NE
Methotrexate	Mexate	Bladder, breast, gestational trophoblastic, head and neck cancers; osteosarcoma; acute lymphocytic leukemia	**NSAIDs (diclofenac, indomethacin, naproxen, phenylbutazone):** Severe methotrexate toxicity with low to moderate doses **Salicylates and other weak organic acids:** Concomitant administration can result in toxic plasma concentrations of methotrexate
Biologic agents			
Interferons	Intron-A, Referon-A	Chronic myelogenous leukemia, hairy cell leukemia, HIV-associated Kaposi's sarcoma, melanoma	**Theophylline:** Reduced clearance when administered concomitantly with interferons
Monoclonal antibodies: Rituximab, trastuzumab	Herceptin, Rituxan	Relapsed low-grade follicular non-Hodgkin's lymphoma (CD-20-positive); patients with breast cancer who are positive for human epidermal growth factor receptor-2	NE
Retinoid: Isotretinoin	Accutane	Control of leukoplakia, prevention of sequential head and neck sarcomas	**Vitamin A:** Toxicity may be potentiated by isotretinoin

Doses are not provided, as they vary widely depending on which drug combinations are used.
NE: Not established.

Continued on next page

Table 27.1 (cont.)

Antineoplastic Agents and Related Drugs: Prescribing Information*

Generic name	Brand name(s)	Indications	Interactions with other drugs
Hormonal agents			
Glucocorticoids: Dexamethasone, prednisone	Decadron, Sterapred	Lymphoma, myeloma	**Antacids:** Concurrent use may decrease absorption **Hepatotoxic medications (ketoconazole, sulfamethoxazole, trimethoprim):** Hepatotoxic effects may be increased by concomitant administration with glucocorticoids
Tamoxifen	Nolvadex, Tamone; Novo-Tamoxifen [CAN]	Estrogen receptor–positive primary breast tumor; prevention of breast cancer in women at high risk of developing it	**Hepatotoxic drugs:** May increase hepatoxicity of tamoxifen
Miscellaneous antineoplastic agents			
Docetaxel	Taxotere	Breast, head and neck, lung, prostate cancers	**Erythromycin, ketoconazole, midazolam:** May inhibit metabolism of docetaxel
Etoposide	VePesid	Ewing's sarcoma; relapsed lymphoma; small-cell lung, testicular cancers	**Renally excreted drugs (cisplatin, cyclosporine A, ifosamide):** Prior or concomitant treatment with these agents may decrease clearance of etoposide
Gemcitabine	Gemzar	Colon, lung, pancreatic cancers	No confirmed interactions
Paclitaxel	Taxol	Breast, gastric, head and neck, lung, ovarian cancers	**Cisplatin:** If administered concomitantly with paclitaxel, may cause synergistic neurotoxicity; if administered before paclitaxel, may increase myelosuppression **Ketoconazole:** May inhibit metabolism of paclitaxel
Vinorelbine	Navelbine	Breast, lung, ovarian cancers; Hodgkin's lymphoma	**Cisplatin:** If administered concomitantly with vinorelbine, may increase myelosuppression **Mitomycin-C:** If administered concomitantly with vinorelbine, can cause acute pulmonary reactions

[CAN] indicates a drug available only in Canada.
* Doses are not provided, as they vary widely depending on which drug combinations are used.

and mucositis. Because of frequent instances of gingival sensitivity, soft toothbrushes or even gelfoam-type applicators are needed to apply a flavor-free toothpaste or baking soda.

Oral Conditions Associated With Cancer Therapy

Mucositis

Mucositis, or stomatitis, is a pathologic process of inflammation and ulceration probably caused by a combination of suppression of epithelial growth, mucosal ulceration and bacterial overgrowth. It is a common manifestation of induced leukopenia. The oral mucosal reaction usually is associated with pain, which interferes with nutrition and hydration. This can significantly alter a patient's course of recovery and become a major complaint and therapeutic problem.

Mucositis is best managed by maintaining optimal oral hygiene and waiting for the critical white blood cell recovery. During this period, controlling pain with medication is important for maintaining the patient's comfort and nutritional intake. Antibiotics, antifungal drugs and antiviral agents are often necessary. These medications are administered by the medical team. Short-course glucocorticoid therapy (using agents such as prednisone) is often helpful in reducing inflammation and discomfort. Sometimes a mild mouthwash made up of anti-inflammatory, antifungal and antihistamine solutions is helpful.

Xerostomia

Because many antineoplastic drugs affect the salivary glands and suppress saliva production, subsequent oral dryness can be bothersome and interfere with eating, speech and hygiene. If hyposalivation is prolonged, it can also cause dental caries and promote candidiasis.

Fortunately, this hyposalivation is almost always transient. Therefore, conservative approaches are usually sufficient. These approaches include sucking on ice chips, taking frequent sips of water, sucking on sugarless candy, chewing sugarless gum and using saliva substitutes that provide temporary lubrication. More severe or longer-lasting xerostomia can be palliated by the use of systemic sialogogues (such as pilocarpine 5 mg tid or qid or bethanechol 25-50 mg tid or qid) (see Chapter 10).

Taste

Some agents used to control neoplastic growth affect the sensitive taste buds. Use of these agents often forms the basis for patients' complaints of altered food tastes (dysgeusia), or a "bad taste in the mouth." In some patients, this may even cause food aversion and further complicate their maintenance of adequate caloric intake. This complaint usually is a transient, direct response to a drug or combination of drugs.

Infections

Bone-marrow suppression is a common response to many antineoplastic drugs. This response often will reduce a normal white blood cell count of more than 4,000 cells/mm^3 to less than 2,000, and sometimes even to zero. The ensuing leukopenia lowers a patient's ability to control the proliferation of microorganisms.

Overgrowth of bacteria, viruses and fungi that stems from drug-induced leukopenia can complicate patient care and the course of the disease. The main concern with bacterial overgrowth is the possibility of bacteremia, fevers of undetermined origin and patient morbidity and mortality.

Reactivation of the herpes simplex virus commonly occurs in the patient who is immunocompromised. The diagnosis is based on clinical suspicion combined with smears or cultures. Because of the acute nature of the viral infection, diagnosis and treatment are combined by instituting an antiviral drug along with the selected diagnostic technique.

Fungal overgrowth is usually caused by

leukopenia, xerostomia and poor hygiene. The organism is candidal, most often *Candida albicans*. Different species of the organism may have implications regarding responses to antifungal drugs. As with bacteria and foci of infection, the possibility of candidemia exists.

Identifying a causative agent of the infection is important. The medical team will prescribe the appropriate medications. It is important to rule out dental sources by examining the teeth, gingiva and mucosal surfaces.

Bleeding

Bleeding may be the result of a reduction of blood platelets, which occurs along with the marrow suppression and leukopenia. As platelet levels decrease to below 100,000/mm^3, the patient's risk of experiencing hemorrhage, either spontaneous or in response to trauma, increases. Therefore, it is important that the clinician have knowledge of a patient's blood status before beginning dental procedures.

Dental anomalies

In children, antineoplastic drug therapy may result in various dental anomalies. When a drug is given during tooth development, it may result in delayed eruption, noneruption, malformations of crowns and/or roots, and discolorations of the crown. While the clinical features and the patient's history can be fairly conclusive as to the cause of such conditions, the differential diagnosis still must include genetic dental dysplasia, hypoparathyroidism, and adverse influences of excess fluoride and broad-spectrum antibiotics.

Drug Interactions of Dental Interest

Because combinations of drugs, dosage ranges and patient profiles and responses differ so greatly, it is necessary to maintain contact with the patient's physician to determine palliation and therapeutic dosages, expected side effects and potential drug interactions. Interactions, if they do occur, are most commonly related to detoxification and elimination of drug products, resulting in high and potentially toxic drug levels in the blood. In turn, toxic manifestations are related to the efficiency of the drug, and the blood levels required for beneficial pharmacologic response are balanced against potential adverse side effects.

Laboratory Value Alterations

- Values for leukocytes in leukopenia: less than 3,000 cells per cubic millimeter as opposed to the normal values, 5,000-10,000 cells/mm^3.
- Values for platelets in thrombocytopenia: less than 50,000 platelets/mm^3 as opposed to the normal values, 150,000-350,000 platelets.

Special Patients

Pregnant and nursing women

Chemotherapy is contraindicated in pregnant and nursing women.

Pediatric, geriatric and other special patients

In children, depending on the type of tumor and the patient's age and size, neoplastic drugs might affect tooth development.

In some geriatric patients and patients with disabilities, the dental treatment plan depends on the patient's overall prognosis, the type of tumor, the patient's medical status (in terms of general well-being) and the patient's ability to comply with protocols and self-care regimens.

Adverse Effects, Precautions and Contraindications

Table 27.2 lists adverse effects related to antineoplastic drugs.

The following precautions and contraindications apply to all antineoplastic agents: concerns of myelosuppression, hepatotoxicity, nephrotoxicity, ototoxicity and gastrointestinal upset. All antineoplastic drugs are classified in pregnancy risk category D.

Pharmacology

In general, aklylating agents, intercalators and antibiotics damage or disrupt DNA, block activity of topoisomerases or alter RNBS structure. Antimetabolites block or decrease synthesis of both RNA and DNA. Steroids interfere with transcription, while plant alkaloids disrupt mitosis. Biologic agents stimulate natural host defense mechanisms. Taxanes are considered spindle poisons—but, unlike the vinca alkaloids, the taxanes allow microtubular assembly to occur and block disassociations.

Suggested Readings

2000 physicians' desk reference. 54th ed. Montvale, N.J.: Medical Economics Company; 2000.

Appelbaum FR. The use of bone marrow and peripheral blood stem cell transplantation in the treatment of cancer. CA Cancer J Clin 1996;46:142-64.

Krakoff IH. Systemic treatment of cancer. CA Cancer J Clin 1996;46:134-41.

Schubert MM, Peterson DE, Lloyd M. Oral complications. In: Thomas E, Blume KG, Foreman SJ, eds. Hemapoietic cell transplantation. 2nd ed. Oxford, England: Blackwell Science; 1999:751-63.

Silverman S Jr. Oral cancer: complications of therapy. Oral Surg Oral Med Oral Pathol Oral Radiol Endod 1999;88:122-6.

Table 27.2
Antineoplastic Agents and Related Drugs: Adverse Effects

Body system	Alkylating agents			Antibiotics		Antimetabolites		
	Cisplatin	Cyclophos-phamide	Melphalan (nitrogen mustard)	Bleomycin	Doxoru-bicin	5-fluoro-uracil	Methotrexate	
CV	Bradycardia, dysrhythmias				Dysrhyth-mias, ECG changes			
CNS	Peripheral neuropathy						Dizziness, convulsions, headache, confusion, hemiparesis, malaise, fatigue, chills, fever	
Endoc			Amenorrhea				Menstrual irregularities, defective spermato-genesis	
EENT	*Ototoxicity, optic neuritis, blurred vision*							
GI	*Very emetogenic*	Nausea, vomiting, diarrhea	Nausea, vomiting, diarrhea	Nausea, vomiting, diarrhea	Nausea, vomiting, diarrhea	Nausea, vomiting, diarrhea	Nausea, vomiting, anorexia, diarrhea, hepatotoxicity, cramps, ulcer, gastritis, GI hemorrhage, abdominal pain, hematemesis	

Italics indicate information of major clinical significance.
CPT: Carnitine palmityltransferase.

Biologic agents	Hormonal agents		Miscellaneous antineoplastic agents					
Retinoids	Prednisone	Tamoxifen	CPT-II	Gem-citabine	Paclitaxel	Taxanes	Vinorelbine
	Hypertension	Chest pain			Bradycardia, severe CV events		
		Weakness, light-headedness, depression, dizziness, headache, mental confusion, hot flashes			*Cumulative neurotoxicity:* Sensory neuropathy, motor neuropathy, autonomic neuropathy, myopathy		
Triglyceridemia	Hyperglycemia	Hypercalcemia					
		At high doses: Ocular lesions, retinopathy, corneal opacity, blurred vision					
		Nausea, vomiting, weight gain	Nausea, vomiting, diarrhea	Nausea, vomiting, diarrhea	*Nausea, vomiting*	Nausea, vomiting, diarrhea	Nausea, vomiting, diarrhea

Continued on next page

Table 27.2 (cont.)
Antineoplastic Agents and Related Drugs: Adverse Effects

Body system	Alkylating agents			Antibiotics		Antimetabolites	
	Cisplatin	Cyclophos-phamide	Melphalan (nitrogen mustard)	Bleomycin	Doxoru-bicin	5-fluoro-uracil	Methotrexate
GU	Hypocalcemia, hypokalemia Hypomagnesemia Hypophosphatemia	Hyperurecemia	Bladder irritation				Urinary retention, renal failure, hematuria, azotemia, uric acid nephropathy
Hema	*Myelosuppression*	Bone marrow suppression	*Myelosuppression*		Bone marrow suppression	Bone marrow suppression	*Myelosuppression*
HB	Increased liver enzymes						
Integ	Papilledema		Alopecia, vasculitis, rash, urticaria		Alopecia	Dermatitis, photosensitivity, dry skin	Rash, alopecia, dry skin, urticaria, photosensitivity, vasculitis, petechiae, ecchymosis, acne, alopecia
Oral	Stomatitis	Stomatitis	Stomatitis, oral ulceration	Stomatitis	Stomatitis	Stomatitis	Ulcerative stomatitis, gingivitis, bleeding
Renal	*Nephrotoxicity*		*Nephrotoxicity*				*Nephrotoxicity*
Resp			Fibrosis, dysplasia	Interstitial pneumonitis, pulmonary fibrosis			

Italics indicate information of major clinical significance.
CPT: Carnitine palmityltransferase.

| Biologic agents | Hormonal agents | | Miscellaneous antineoplastic agents | | | | |
Retinoids	Prednisone	Tamoxifen	CPT-II	Gem-citabine	Paclitaxel	Taxanes	Vinorelbine
		Vaginal bleeding and/or discharge, endometriosis, priapism, possible endometrial cancer, pruritus vulvae					
		Myelo-suppression	Bone marrow suppression	Bone marrow suppression	*Myelo-suppression*	Bone marrow suppression	Bone marrow suppression
Increased liver enzymes					*Abnormal liver function*		
Dry skin		*Rash, alopecia*			*Dermatitis, alopecia, erythema, swelling*		
	Fluid retention	*Nephro-toxicity*			*Nephro-toxicity*		
		Pulmonary embolism					

Section III.

Drug Issues in Dental Practice

Chapter 28

Oral Manifestations of Systemic Agents

B. Ellen Byrne, R.Ph., D.D.S., Ph.D.

Many commonly prescribed medications are capable of causing adverse oral drug reactions. The oral manifestations of drug therapy are often nonspecific and vary in significance. These undesirable effects can mimic many disease processes, such as erythema multiforme. They may also be very characteristic of a particular drug reaction (as in the case of phenytoin and gingival enlargement).

Oral Manifestations

Oral manifestations can be divided into 15 broad categories: abnormal hemostasis, altered host resistance, angioedema, coated tongue (black hairy tongue), dry socket, dysgeusia (altered taste), erythema multiforme, gingival enlargement, leukopenia and neutropenia, lichenoid lesions, movement disorders, salivary gland enlargement, sialorrhea (increased salivation), soft-tissue reactions and xerostomia.

In Tables 28.1-28.15, each of the 15 oral manifestations of systemic drugs is related to specific types of drugs that may cause it. In Table 28.16, systemic drugs that may have oral manifestations are listed by their generic names and are linked to the associated manifestation(s).

Abnormal Hemostasis

Abnormal hemostasis is seen with drugs that interfere with platelet function or that decrease coagulation by depressing prothrombin synthesis in the liver. Patients using such medications require a bleeding profile before extensive dental procedures.

Altered Host Resistance

Altered host resistance occurs when the microflora of the mouth is altered, resulting in an overgrowth of organisms that are part of the normal oral flora. Bacterial, fungal and viral superinfections all occur as a result of drug therapy. Broad-spectrum antibiotics and corticosteroids, as well as xerostomia, radiation and side effects of cancer chemotherapy (and AIDS), can elicit episodes of oral candidiasis. Oropharyngeal candidiasis or thrush has been associated with the use of orally inhaled and oral systemic corticosteroids, while pharyngeal candidiasis has been associated with the use of nasally inhaled and oral systemic corticosteroids. Treatment includes elimination of the causative factor, if possible, combined with use of an antifungal agent, such as nystatin suspension, clotrimazole troche or ketoconazole tablets. Various conditions such as diabetes, leukemia, lymphomas and AIDS can also render a patient more susceptible to oral candidal infections.

Angioedema

Angioedema is the result of drug-induced hypersensitivity reactions and can be life-threatening when it involves the mucosal and submucosal layers of the upper aerodigestive tract. Mild angioedema is treated with antihistamines. In more severe cases where the airway is threatened, the emergency treatment is managed the same way as in the case of an anaphylactic reaction. It may occur at any time during treatment with a drug; however, many times it will follow the first dose of a drug.

Coated Tongue (Black Hairy Tongue)

The most common discoloration of the tongue is a condition known as black hairy tongue. This results from hypertrophy of the filiform papillae. This condition is asymptomatic. The color is usually black, but may be various shades of brown. The exact mechanism by which this condition is produced is unknown and there is no effective treatment for this condition.

Dry Socket

Dry socket, or alveolar osteitis, is the result of lysis of a fully formed blood clot before the clot is replaced with granulation tissue. The incidence of dry socket seems to be higher in patients who smoke and in female patients who take oral contraceptives. Dry socket can be minimized in patients taking oral contraceptives if extractions are performed during days 23-28 of the tablet cycle.

Dysgeusia

Dysgeusia is manifested in taste alterations; medication taste; unusual taste; bitter, peculiar and metallic taste; taste perversion; and changes in taste and distaste for food. Xerostomia, malnutrition, neurological deficiencies and olfactory deficiencies also can be responsible for taste changes. Although the operative mechanism is unclear, there is some evidence that medications alter taste by affecting trace metal ions, which interact with the cell membrane proteins of the taste pores. There is no treatment other than withdrawal of the drug.

Erythema Multiforme

Erythema multiforme is a syndrome consisting of symmetrical mucocutaneous lesions that have a predilection for the oral mucosa, hands and feet. It presents initially as erythema, and vesicles and erosions develop within hours. Erythema multiforme usually has its onset from 1-3 w after the person begins taking the offending drug. Skin lesions can have concentric rings of erythema, producing the "target" or "bull's-eye"

appearance that is associated with this condition. The lesions are normally self-limiting but will persist if the patient continues to take the offending drug. Oral lesions heal without scarring.

Gingival Enlargement

Gingival enlargement has been associated with numerous types of systemic drug therapy, and usually becomes apparent in the first 3 mo after drug therapy begins. Clinically, the overgrowth starts as a diffuse swelling of the interdental papillae, which then coalesces for a nodular appearance. Many theories have been suggested to explain the overgrowth. The most attractive theory is that it is a direct effect of the drug or its metabolites on certain subpopulations of fibroblasts, which are capable of greater synthesis of protein and collagen. Many studies have shown a clear relationship between a patient's oral hygiene status and the extent of overgrowth. Also, mouth breathing and other local factors such as crowding of teeth, significantly relate to the occurrence of gingival enlargement.

Leukopenia and Neutropenia

Many drugs can alter a patient's hematopoietic status. These effects can take the form of leukopenia, agranulocytosis and neutropenia. These conditions can have a variety of effects in the mouth: increased infections, ulcerations, nonspecific inflammation, bleeding gingiva and significant bleeding after a dental procedure. Treatment includes discontinuing use of the suspected offending drug and replacing it with a structurally dissimilar agent if continued therapy is indicated.

Lichenoid Lesions

Lichenoid lesions seen with systemic use of drugs differ from actual lichen planus in that the condition resolves when the patient discontinues taking the offending drug. Patients have pain after ulcerations have developed. Buccal mucosa and lateral borders of the tongue are most often involved, and characteristic white striations (Wickham's striae) usually occur.

Movement Disorders

Movement disorders in the muscles of facial expression and mastication can be brought on by systemic drug therapy. These side effects include pseudoparkinsonism (rigidity, bradykinesia, tremor), akathisia (restlessness) and involuntary dystonic movements such as tardive dyskinesia. Tardive dyskinesia is characterized by repetitive, involuntary movements, usually of the mouth and tongue, secondary to long-term neuroleptic drug treatment. This type of movement, once developed, cannot be controlled and is usually irreversible. Tardive dyskinesia occurs in approximately 20% of all patients who take neuroleptic medications regularly. These patients may find it difficult to communicate, eat and use removable oral prostheses.

Salivary Gland Involvement

Salivary gland problems can appear as salivary gland swelling or pain and can resemble mumps. Differential diagnosis must include salivary gland infections, obstructions and neoplasms. The mechanism of salivary gland enlargement is unknown, and the treatment is discontinuing the use of the offending drug.

Sialorrhea

Any drug that works by increasing cholinergic stimulation by directly stimulating parasympathetic receptors (such as pilocarpine) or by inhibiting the action of cholinesterase (such as neostigmine) may cause sialorrhea or increased salivation.

Soft-Tissue Reactions

Soft-tissue problems include discoloration, ulcerations, stomatitis and glossitis. Gingivitis is inflammation of the gingiva, while gingival enlargement is an overgrowth of fibrous gingival tissue. Gingival overgrowth usually becomes apparent in the first 3 mo after the patient starts taking the drug and is most rapid in the first year. There are many theories on the cause of the gingival overgrowth. The most likely theory is that the drug or one of its metabolites directly stimulates a population of fibroblasts to synthesize more protein and collagen. This condition is aggravated by poor oral hygiene, mouth breathing and crowded teeth.

Xerostomia

Xerostomia, defined as dry mouth or a decrease in salivation, is a frequently reported side effect. This effect may be exaggerated during prolonged drug use by elderly people and may be even more pronounced when several drugs causing dry mouth are taken simultaneously. Possible nondrug causes of xerostomia include dehydration, salivary gland infection, neoplasm, obstruction, radiation to the mouth, diabetes mellitus, nutritional deficiencies, Sjögren's syndrome and drugs that either stimulate sympathetic activity or depress parasympathetic activity.

Suggested Readings

Felder RS, Millar SB, Henry RH. Oral manifestations of drug therapy. Spec Care Dentist 1988;8(3):119-24.

Lewis IK, Hanlon JT, Hobbins MJ, Beck JD. Use of medications with potential oral adverse drug reactions in community-dwelling elderly. Spec Care Dentist 1993; 13(4):171-6.

Mott AE, Grushka M, Sessle BJ. Diagnosis and management of taste disorders and burning mouth syndrome. Dent Clin North Am 1993;37(1):33-71.

Walton JG. Dental disorders. In: Davies DM, ed. Textbook of adverse drug reactions. 4th ed. Oxford, England: Oxford University Press; 1991:205-29.

Zelickson BD, Rogers RS. Oral drug reactions. Dermatol Clin North Am 1987;5(4):695-708.

Table 28.1

Abnormal Hemostasis: Associated Drugs

Generic name	Brand name(s)
Anticoagulant agents	
Anisindione	Miradon
Dalteparin	Fragmin
Danaparoid	Orgaran
Enoxaparin	Lovenox
Heparin	Hepalean
Warfarin	Coumadin
Antithrombotic agents	
Abciximab	ReoPro
Anagrelide	Agrylin
Clopidogrel	Plavix
Dipyridamole	Persantine
Sulfinpyrazone	Anturane
Ticlopidine	Ticlid
Nonsteroidal anti-inflammatory drugs (NSAIDs)	
Aspirin	Various brand names
Diclofenac	Cataflam, Voltaren; Apo-Diclo [CAN]
Diflunisal	Dolobid; Apo-Diflunisal [CAN]
Etodolac	Lodine ★
Ibuprofen	Advil ★, Motrin, Nuprin, Rufen; Actiprofen [CAN]
Indomethacin	Indocin; Indocid [CAN]
Ketoprofen	Orudis; Rhodis [CAN]

★ indicates a product bearing the ADA Seal of Acceptance.
[CAN] indicates a drug available only in Canada.

Continued on next page

Table 28.1 (cont.)

Abnormal Hemostasis: Associated Drugs

Generic name	Brand name(s)
Nonsteroidal anti-inflammatory drugs (NSAIDs) (cont.)	
Ketorolac	Toradol
Meclofenamate	Meclomen
Mefenamic acid	Ponstel; Ponstan [CAN]
Naproxen	Aleve, Anaprox, Naprosyn; Naxen [CAN]
Oxaprozin	Daypro
Piroxicam	Feldene
Tolmetin	Tolectin

[CAN] indicates a drug available only in Canada.

Table 28.2

Altered Host Resistance (Microflora Imbalance): Associated Drugs

Generic name	Brand name(s)
Antibiotics	
Aminoglycoside: Gentamicin	Garamycin; Cidomycin [CAN]
Cephalosporin: Cefaclor	Ceclor; Apo-Cefaclor [CAN]
Fluoroquinolone: Ciprofloxacin	Cipro
Macrolide: Erythromycin	E.E.S., E. Mycin, Eryc, PCE; Erybid [CAN]
Penicillin: Amoxicillin	Amoxil; Novamoxin [CAN]
Sulfonamide: Sulfisoxazole	Gantrisin
Tetracycline: Doxycycline	Vibramycin
Antidiabetic agent	
Insulin	Humulin

[CAN] indicates a drug available only in Canada.

Continued on next page

Table 28.2 (cont.)

Altered Host Resistance (Microflora Imbalance): Associated Drugs

Generic name	Brand name(s)
Antidiabetic (oral hypoglycemic) agents	
Acetohexamide	Dymelor; Dimelor [CAN]
Chlorpropamide	Diabinese
Diazoxide	Proglycem
Glipizide	Glucotrol
Glyburide	DiaBeta
Metformin	Glucophage
Tolazamide	Tolinase
Tolbutamide	Orinase; Mobenol [CAN]
Antineoplastic agent	
Tamoxifen	Nolvadex
Glucocorticoids (nasal)	
Beclomethasone dipropionate (solution)	Beconase
Dexamethasone (aerosol)	Decadron Turbinaire
Flunisolide (solution)	Nasalide
Triamcinolone (aerosol)	Nasocort
Glucocorticoids (oral inhalation)	
Beclomethasone dipropionate (aerosol)	Beclovent, Vanceril
Dexamethasone (aerosol)	Decadron, Respihaler
Flunisolide (aerosol)	AeroBid, AeroBid-M
Triamcinolone (aerosol)	Azmacort

[CAN] indicates a drug available only in Canada.

Continued on next page

Table 28.2 (cont.)
Altered Host Resistance (Microflora Imbalance): Associated Drugs

Generic name	Brand name(s)
Glucocorticoids (oral)	
Betamethasone	Celestone; Betnelan [CAN]
Cortisone acetate	Cortone
Dexamethasone	Decadron, Deronil, Dexone, Hexadrol; Dexasone [CAN]
Methylprednisolone	Medrol
Immunosuppressant agent	
Cyclosporin A	Sandimmune

[CAN] indicates a drug available only in Canada.

Table 28.3
Angioedema: Associated Drugs

Generic name	Brand name(s)
Angiotensin-converting enzyme (ACE) inhibitors (antihypertensive agents)	
Benazepril	Lotensin
Captopril	Capoten
Enalapril	Vasotec
Fosinopril	Monopril
Lisinopril	Prinivil, Zestril
Moexipril	Univasc
Quinapril	Accupril
Ramipril	Altace
Angiotensin II receptor antagonist	
Losartan	Cozaar

Continued on next page

Table 28.3 (cont.)

Angioedema: Associated Drugs

Generic name	Brand name(s)
Antianxiety agent	
Midazolam	Versed
Antifungal agent	
Ketoconazole	Nizoral
Antirheumatic agent (disease-modifying gold compound)	
Auranofin	Ridaura
Cholinesterase inhibitors	
Donepezil	Aricept
Tacrine	Cognex

Table 28.4

Coated Tongue (Black Hairy Tongue): Associated Drugs

Generic name	Brand name(s)
Antianxiety agents	
Diazepam	Valium; Novo-Dipam [CAN]
Lorazepam	Ativan; Nu-Loraz [CAN]
Antibiotics	
Amoxicillin	Amoxil
Amoxicillin/clavulanic acid	Augmentin; Clavulin [CAN]
Penicillin V potassium	PenVeeK, V-Cillin K; Nadopen-V [CAN]
Tetracycline	Robitet

[CAN] indicates a drug available only in Canada.

Continued on next page

Table 28.4 (cont.)

Coated Tongue (Black Hairy Tongue): Associated Drugs

Generic name	Brand name(s)
Anticonvulsant agent	
Clonazepam	Klonopin
Antidepressant agents	
Amitriptyline	Elavil; Novo-Triptyn [CAN]
Nortriptyline	Aventyl, Pamelor
Muscle relaxant	
Cyclobenzaprine	Flexeril
Nonsteroidal anti-inflammatory drug (NSAID)	
Ketoprofen	Orudis
Urinary tract anti-infective agent	
Nitrofurantoin	Macrodantin

[CAN] indicates a drug available only in Canada.

Table 28.5

Dry Socket (Increased Incidence): Associated Drugs

Generic name	Brand name(s)
Oral contraceptives	
Ethinyl estradiol	Estinyl
Ethinyl estradiol and ethynodiol	Demulen
Ethinyl estradiol and levonorgestrel	Levlen, Levora, Nordette, Tri-Levlen, Triphasil
Ethinyl estradiol and norethindrone	Brevicon, Genora, Loestrin, Ortho-Novum
Ethinyl estradiol and norgestrel	Lo/Ovral, Ovral

Table 28.6

Dysgeusia (Taste Disturbances): Associated Drugs

Generic name	Brand name(s)
Anorexiant agents	
Benzphetamine	Didrex
Diethylopropion	Tenuate
Mazindol	Sanorex, Mazanor
Phendimetrazine	Anorex SR, Bontril PM
Phentermine	Ionamin
Antianemic agent	
Iron	Numerous iron-containing vitamins and iron supplements
Antianxiety agent	
Midazolam	Versed
Antidysrhythmic agents	
Amiodarone	Cordarone
Encainide	Enkaid
Flecainide	Tambocor
Mexiletine	Mexitil
Moricizine	Ethmozine
Procainamide	Pronestyl
Propafenone	Rythmol
Antiarthritic (disease-modifying) agents	
Allopurinol	Zyloprim
Auranofin	Ridaura

Continued on next page

Table 28.6 (cont.)

Dysgeusia (Taste Disturbances): Associated Drugs

Generic name	Brand name(s)
Antiarthritic (disease-modifying) agents (cont.)	
Aurothioglucose	Solganal
Penicillamine	Cuprimine
Antibiotics	
Cefamandol	Mandol
Clarithromycin	Biaxin
Lincomycin	Lincocin
Metronidazole	Flagyl
Procaine penicillin	Wycillin
Tetracycline	Achromycin
Anticonvulsant agent	
Carbamazepine	Tegretol
Antidiabetic agents	
Metformin	Glucophage
Tolbutamide	Orinase
Antiemetic agents	
Dolasetron	Anzemet
Granisetron	Kytril
Ondansetron	Zofran

Continued on next page

Table 28.6 (cont.)

Dysgeusia (Taste Disturbances): Associated Drugs

Generic name	Brand name(s)
Antifungal agents	
Amphotericin B	Fungizone
Griseofulvin	Fulvicin; Grisovin [CAN]
Antihistamine	
Azelastine	Astelin
Antilipidemic agents	
Cholestyramine	Questran
Clofibrate	Atromid-S
Antineoplastic agents	
Azathioprine	Imuran
Bleomycin	Blenoxane
5-fluorouracil	Adrucil
Methotrexate	Folex
Vincristine	Oncovin
Antiparkinsonism agent	
Levodopa	Dopar
Antipsychotic agent	
Lithium	Eskalith, Lithane; Carbolith [CAN]
Antithyroid agent	
Methimazole	Tapazole

[CAN] indicates a drug available only in Canada.

Continued on next page

Table 28.6 (cont.)

Dysgeusia (Taste Disturbances): Associated Drugs

Generic name	Brand name(s)
β-adrenergic blocking agents	
Acebutolol	Sectral
Atenolol	Tenormin
Betaxolol	Kerlone
Bisoprolol	Zebeta
Carteolol	Cartrol
Metoprolol	Lopressor
Nadolol	Corgard
Pindolol	Visken
Penbutolol	Levatol
Propranolol	Inderal
Timolol	Blocadren
Carbonic anhydrase inhibitor	
Acetazolamide	Diamox
Cardiovascular agents	
Amrinone	Inocor
Bretylium	Bretylol
Captopril	Capoten
Diltiazem	Cardizem

Continued on next page

Table 28.6 (cont.)

Dysgeusia (Taste Disturbances): Associated Drugs

Generic name	Brand name(s)
Cardiovascular agents (cont.)	
Dipyridamole	Persantine
Enalapril	Vasotec
Nifedipine	Procardia
Spironolactone	Aldactone
CNS stimulant agent	
Dextroamphetamine	Dexedrine
Dental agent	
Chlorhexidine	Peridex ★
Glucose-elevating agent	
Diazoxide (oral)	Proglycem
Muscle relaxant agent	
Baclofen	Lioresal
Nonsteroidal anti-inflammatory drug (NSAID)	
Phenylbutazone	Butazolidin
Respiratory inhalant product	
Cromolyn sodium	Intal, Nasalcrom (OTC)
Smoking cessation agents	
Nicotine polacrilex (chewing gum)	Nicorette
Nicotine topical patches	Habitrol, NicoDerm

★ indicates a product bearing the ADA Seal of Acceptance.
OTC: Over the counter.

Table 28.7

Erythema Multiforme: Associated Drugs

Generic name	Brand name(s)
Antibiotics	
Clindamycin	Cleocin
Penicillin V potassium	PenVeeK, V-Cillin K, Veetids
Tetracycline	Achromycin
Anticonvulsant agents	
Carbamazepine	Tegretol
Phenytoin	Dilantin
Antidiabetic (oral hypoglycemic) agent	
Chlorpropamide	Diabinese
Barbiturates	
Pentobarbital	Nembutal
Phenobarbital	Luminal
Secobarbital	Seconal
Nonsteroidal anti-inflammatory drug (NSAID)	
Phenylbutazone	Butazolidin
Sulfonamides	
Sulfacytine	Renoquid
Sulfamethizole	Thiosulfil Forte
Sulfamethoxazole	Gantanol
Sulfisoxazole	Gantrisin

Table 28.8

Gingival Enlargement: Associated Drugs

Generic name	Brand name(s)
Anticonvulsant agent	
Phenytoin	Dilantin
Cardiovascular agents (calcium channel blockers)	
Diltiazem	Cardizem
Felodipine	Plendil
Nifedipine	Procardia
Verapamil	Calan
Immunosuppressant agent	
Cyclosporin A	Sandimmune

Table 28.9

Leukopenia and Neutropenia: Associated Drugs

Generic name	Brand name
Angiotensin-converting enzyme inhibitor	
Captopril	Capoten
Antibiotic	
Chloramphenicol	Chlormycetin
Antidiabetic (oral hypoglycemic) agent	
Tolbutamide	Orinase
Antidysrhythmic agent	
Tocainide	Tonocard
Antiprotozoal agent	
Quinine	Quinamm

Continued on next page

Table 28.9 (cont.)

Leukopenia and Neutropenia: Associated Drugs

Generic name	Brand name
Antipsychotic agents (phenothiazines)	
Chlorpromazine	Thorazine
Chlorprothixene	Taractan
Fluphenazine	Prolixin
Haloperidol	Haldol
Mesoridazine	Serentil
Perphenazine	Trilafon
Prochlorperazine	Compazine
Promazine	Sparine
Thioridazine	Mellaril
Trifluoperazine	Stelazine
Barbiturates	
Amobarbital	Amytal
Mephobarbital	Mebaral
Pentobarbital	Nembutal
Phenobarbital	Luminal
Primidone	Mysoline
Secobarbital	Seconal
Nonsteroidal anti-inflammatory drug (NSAID)	
Phenylbutazone	Butazolidin

Table 28.9 (cont.)
Leukopenia and Neutropenia: Associated Drugs

Generic name	Brand name
Sulfonamides	
Sulfacytine	Renoquid
Sulfamethizole	Thiosulfil Forte
Sulfamethoxazole	Gantanol
Sulfisoxazole	Gantrisin

Table 28.10
Lichenoid Reactions: Associated Drugs

Generic name	Brand name(s)
Angiotensin-converting enzyme (ACE) inhibitor (antihypertensive agent)	
Captopril	Capoten
Antidiabetic (oral hypoglycemic) agent	
Chlorpropamide	Diabinese
Antihypertensive agent	
Methyldopa	Aldomet
Diuretic agent	
Furosemide	Lasix
Nonsteroidal anti-inflammatory drugs (NSAIDs)	
Diflunisal	Dolobid
Flurbiprofem	Ansaid
Ibuprofen	Advil ★, Motrin, Nuprin, Rufen

★ indicates a product bearing the ADA Seal of Acceptance.

Table 28.11

Movement Disorders: Associated Drugs

Generic name	Brand name(s)
Antidepressant agent	
Amoxapine	Asendin
Antiparkinsonian agent	
Levodopa	Dopar, Larodopa
Antipsychotic agents (phenothiazines)	
Acetophenazine	Tindal
Chlorpromazine	Thorazine
Chlorprothixene	Taractan
Clozapine	Clozaril
Fluphenazine	Prolixin
Haloperidol	Haldol
Loxapine	Loxitane
Mesoridazine	Serentil
Perphenazine	Trilafon
Prochlorperazine	Compazine
Promazine	Sparine
Risperidone	Risperdal
Thioridazine	Mellaril
Thiothixene	Navane
Trifluoperazine	Stelazine
Gastrointestinal stimulants	
Cisapride	Propulsid
Metoclopramide	Reglan

Table 28.12
Salivary Gland Involvement: Associated Drugs

Generic name	Brand name(s)
Antihypertensive agents	
Bendroflumethiazide	Naturetin
Chlorothiazide	Diuril
Clonidine	Catapres; Dixarit [CAN]
Guanethidine	Ismelin
Hydrochlorothiazide	HydroDIURIL; Urozide [CAN]
Hydroflumethiazide	Diucardin
Methyclothiazide	Enduron; Duretic [CAN]
Methyldopa	Aldomet
Antipsychotic agent	
Lithium	Eskalith
Nonsteroidal anti-inflammatory drug (NSAID)	
Phenylbutazone	Butazolidin

[CAN] indicates a drug available only in Canada.

Table 28.13
Sialorrhea: Associated Drugs

Generic name	Brand name(s)
Cholinergic agents	
Bethanechol	Urecholine
Tacrine	Cognex
Respiratory inhalant product	
Cromolyn sodium	Intal, Nasalcrom (OTC)

OTC: Over the counter.

Table 28.14

Soft-Tissue Reactions*: Associated Drugs

Generic name (reaction)	Brand name(s)
Antiacne agent	
Isotretinoin (G)	Accutane
Antianxiety agent	
Meprobamate (S)	Equanil
Antiarthritic (disease-modifying) agents	
Auranofin (G, S)	Ridaura
Aurothioglucose (G, S)	Solganal
Gold sodium thiomalate (S)	Myochrysine
Antibiotics	
Minocycline (D)	Minocin
Ampicillin (U)	Omnipen
Anticoagulant agent	
Warfarin (U)	Coumadin
Antilipidemic agent	
Clofibrate (S)	Atromid-S
Antihypertensive agents	
Captopril (G, S)	Capoten
Guanadrel (G)	Hylorel
Methyldopa (D)	Aldomet
Chelating agent	
Penicillamine (D)	Cuprimine

* (D): discoloration; (G): glossitis; (P): pigmentation; (S): stomatitis; (U): ulceration.

Continued on next page

Table 28.14 (cont.)

Soft-Tissue Reactions*: Associated Drugs

Generic name (reaction)	Brand name(s)
Cytotoxic (antineoplastic) agents	
Busulphan (D)	Myleran
Carboplatin (S)	Paraplatin
Carmustin (D)	BiCNU
Hydroxyurea (G, S)	Hydrea
Lomustine (S)	CeeNU
Mercaptopurine (G)	Purinethol
Methotrexate (G, S)	Folex
P-cyclophosphamide (P)	Cytoxan
Vincristine (S)	Oncovin
Heavy metals	
Lead (P)	No brand names
Mercury (P)	No brand names
Immunosuppressant agent	
Azathioprine (G, S)	Imuran
Nonsteroidal anti-inflammatory drugs (NSAIDs)	
Aspirin (U)	Various brand names
Ibuprofen (U)	Advil ★, Motrin
Indomethacin (U)	Indocin
Ketoprofen (U)	Orudis
Ketorolac (U)	Toradol

*(D): discoloration; (G): glossitis; (P): pigmentation; (S): stomatitis; (U): ulceration.
★ indicates a product bearing the ADA Seal of Acceptance.

Continued on next page

Table 28.14 (cont.)

Soft-Tissue Reactions*: Associated Drugs

Generic name (reaction)	Brand name(s)
Oral contraceptives	
Ethinyl estradiol (D)	Estinyl
Ethinyl estradiol/ethynodiol (D)	Demulen
Ethinyl estradiol/levonorgestrel (D)	Levlen, Levora, Nordette, Tri-Levlen, Triphasil
Ethinyl estradiol/norethindrone (D)	Brevicon, Ortho-Novum
Ethinyl estradiol/norgestrel (D)	Lo/Ovral, Ovral

* (D): discoloration; (G): glossitis; (P): pigmentation; (S): stomatitis; (U): ulceration.

Table 28.15

Xerostomia: Associated Drugs

Generic name	Brand name(s)
Anorexiant agents	
Diethylpropion	Tenuate, Tepanil
Phendimetrazine	Anorex
Phentermine	Adipex-P, Fastin, Ionamin
Sibutramine	Meridia
Antiacne agent	
Isotretinoin	Accutane
Antianxiety agents	
Alprazolam	Xanax
Chlordiazepoxide	Librium
Diazepam	Valium
Lorazepam	Ativan

Continued on next page

Table 28.15 (cont.)
Xerostomia: Associated Drugs

Generic name	Brand name(s)
Antianxiety agents (cont.)	
Meprobamate	Equanil, Miltown
Oxazepam	Serax
Prazepam	Centrax
Anticholinergic/antispasmodic agents	
Atropine	Atropisol
Belladonna alkaloids	Bellergal-S
Chlordiazepoxide/clidinium	Librax
Dicyclomine	Bentyl
Hyoscyamine	Anaspaz
Hyoscyamine/atropine/phenobarbital/scopolamine	Donnatal, Kinesed
Isopropamide	Darbid
Methantheline	Banthine
Methscopolamine	Pamine
Oxybutynin	Ditropan
Oxyphencyclimine	Daricon
Propantheline	Pro-Banthine
Scopolamine	Transderm-Scop
Anticonvulsant agent	
Carbamazepine	Tegretol
Antidepressant agents	
Amitriptyline	Elavil, Endep
Amitriptyline/perphenazine	Etrafon

Continued on next page

Table 28.15 (cont.)
Xerostomia: Associated Drugs

Generic name	Brand name(s)
Antidepressant agents (cont.)	
Amoxapine	Asendin
Desipramine	Norpramin, Pertofrane
Doxepin	Sinequan
Fluoxetine	Prozac
Imipramine	Tofranil
Isocarboxazid	Marplan
Maprotiline	Ludiomil
Nortriptyline	Aventyl, Pamelor
Paroxetine	Paxil
Phenelzine	Nardil
Sertraline	Zoloft
Tranylcypromine	Parnate
Trazodone	Desyrel
Antidiarrheal agents	
Diphenoxylate/atropine	Lomotil
Loperamide	Imodium AD
Antidysrhythmic agents	
Diopyramide	Norpace
Mexiletine	Mexitil
Tocainide	Tonocard

Continued on next page

Table 28.15 (cont.)

Xerostomia: Associated Drugs

Generic name	Brand name(s)
Antihistamines	
Astemizole	Hismanal
Brompheniramine	Dimetane
Brompheniramine/phenylpropanolamine	Dimetapp
Chlorpheniramine	Chlor-Trimeton
Clemastine	Tavist
Cyproheptadine	Peractin
Diphenhydramine	Benadryl
Hydroxyzine	Vistaril
Loratadine	Claritin
Promethazine	Phenergan
Tripelennamine	Pyribenzamine (PBZ)
Triprolidine/pseudoephedrine	Actifed
Antihypertensive agents	
Captopril	Capoten
Clonidine	Catapres
Doxazocin	Cardura
Enalapril	Vasotec
Guanethidine	Ismelin
Lisinopril	Zestril
Losartan	Cozaar
Methyldopa	Aldomet

Continued on next page

Table 28.15 (cont.)
Xerostomia: Associated Drugs

Generic name	Brand name(s)
Antihypertensive agents (cont.)	
Metoprolol	Lopressor
Nadolol	Corgard
Nifedipine	Procardia
Prazosin	Minipress
Reserpine	Serpasil
Terazosin	Hytrin
Antinausea agents	
Dimenhydrinate	Dramamine
Hydroxyzine	Atarax, Vistaril
Meclizine	Antivert
Antiparkinsonism agents	
Benztropine mesylate	Cogentin
Biperiden	Akineton
Carbidopa/levodopa	Sinemet
Ethopropazine	Parsidol
Levodopa	Larodopa, Dopar
Orphenadrine HCl	Marflex
Pramipexole	Mirapex
Ropinirole	Requip
Tolcapone	Tasmar
Trihexyphenidyl	Artane

Continued on next page

Table 28.15 (cont.)
Xerostomia: Associated Drugs

Generic name	Brand name(s)
Antipsychotic agents	
Amitriptyline/perphenazine	Triavil
Chlorpromazine	Thorazine
Clozapine	Clozaril
Haloperidol	Haldol
Lithium	Eskalith
Loxapine	Loxitane
Molindone	Moban
Pimozide	Orap
Prochlorperazine	Compazine
Promazine	Sparine
Quetiapine	Seroquel
Risperidone	Risperdal
Thioridazine	Mellaril
Thiothixene	Navane
Trifluoperazine	Stelazine
Bronchodilators	
Albuterol	Proventil, Ventolin
Isoproterenol	Arm-a-Med, Isopro, Isuprel, Vapo-Iso
Cholinesterase inhibitor	
Donepezil	Aricept

Continued on next page

Table 28.15 (cont.)

Xerostomia: Associated Drugs

Generic name	Brand name(s)
Decongestant agent	
Phenylpropanolamine/chlorpheniramine	Ornade
Diuretics	
Amiloride	Midamor
Chlorothiazide	Diuril
Furosemide	Lasix
Hydrochlorothiazide	HydroDiuril, Esidrix
Triamterene	Dyrenium
Triamterene/hydrochlorothiazide	Dyazide, Maxzide
Muscarinic receptor antagonist	
Tolterodine	Detrol
Muscle relaxant agents	
Cyclobenzaprine	Flexeril
Orphenadrine	Norflex
Narcotic analgesics	
Codeine	Generic
Hydromorphone	Dilaudid
Levorphanol	Levo-Dromoran
Meperidine	Demerol
Methadone	Dolophine
Morphine	MS Contin
Oxymorphone	Numorphan ★

★ *indicates a product bearing the ADA Seal of Acceptance.*

Continued on next page

Table 28.15 (cont.)

Xerostomia: Associated Drugs

Generic name	Brand name(s)
Narcotic analgesics (cont.)	
Pentazocine	Talwin
Propoxyphene	Darvon
Tramadol	Ultram
Nonsteroidal anti-inflammatory drugs (NSAIDs)	
Diflunisal	Dolobid
Fenoprofen	Nalfon
Ibuprofen	Advil ★, Motrin, Rufen
Naproxen	Aleve, Anaprox, Naprosyn
Phenylbutazone	Butazolidin
Piroxicam	Feldene
Sedatives	
Flurazepam	Dalmane
Temazepam	Restoril
Triazolam	Halcion
Serotonin agonist	
Rizatriptan	Maxalt
Smoking cessation agents	
Nicotine polacrilex (chewing gum)	Nicorette
Nicotine topical patches	Habitrol, NicoDerm

★ *indicates a product bearing the ADA Seal of Acceptance.*

Table 28.16
Drugs and Associated Oral Manifestations

Generic name	Brand name(s)	Drug category	Associated manifestation(s)
Abciximab	ReoPro	Antithrombotic	Abnormal hemostasis
Acebutolol	Sectral	β-adrenergic blocker	Dysgeusia
Acetazolamide	Diamox	Carbonic anhydrase inhibitor	Dysgeusia
Acetohexamide	Dymelor	Antidiabetic (oral hypoglycemic)	Altered host resistance
Acetophenazine	Tindal	Antipsychotic	Movement disorders
Albuterol	Proventil, Ventolin	Bronchodilator	Xerostomia
Allopurinol	Zyloprim	Antiarthritic (disease-modifying)	Dysgeusia
Alprazolam	Xanax	Antianxiety	Xerostomia
Amiodarone	Cordarone	Antidysrhythmic	Dysgeusia
Amitriptyline	Elavil, Endep	Antidepressant	Xerostomia, coated tongue
Amitriptyline/ perphenazine	Etrafon, Triavil	Antidepressant, antipsychotic	Xerostomia
Amobarbital	Amytal	Barbiturate	Leukopenia and neutropenia
Amoxapine	Asendin	Antidepressant	Xerostomia, movement disorders
Amoxicillin	Amoxil	Antibiotic (penicillin)	Coated tongue, altered host resistance
Amoxicillin/clavulanic acid	Augmentin	Antibiotic	Coated tongue
Amphotericin B	Fungizone	Antifungal	Dysgeusia
Ampicillin	Omnipen	Antibiotic	Soft-tissue reaction (U)*
Amrinone	Inocor	Cardiovascular	Dysgeusia
Anagrelide	Agrylin	Antithrombotic	Abnormal hemostasis

*indicates a soft-tissue reaction. (D): discoloration; (G): glossitis; (P): pigmentation; (S): stomatitis; (U): ulceration.

Continued on next page

Table 28.16 (cont.)

Drugs and Associated Oral Manifestations

Generic name	Brand name(s)	Drug category	Associated manifestation(s)
Anisindione	Miradon	Anticoagulant	Abnormal hemostasis
Aspirin	Anacin, A.S.A., Ascriptin, Aspergum, Bayer Aspirin, Bufferin, Ecotrin, Empirin, Zorprin	NSAID	Soft-tissue reaction (U)*, abnormal hemostasis
Astemizole	Hismanal	Antihistamine	Xerostomia
Atenolol	Tenormin	β-adrenergic blocker	Dysgeusia
Atropine	Atropisol	Anticholinergic/antispasmodic	Xerostomia
Auranofin	Ridaura	Antiarthritic (disease-modifying)	Soft-tissue reaction (G, S), dysgeusia, angioedema
Aurothioglucose	Solganal	Antiarthritic (disease-modifying)	Soft-tissue reaction (G, S), dysgeusia
Azathioprine	Imuran	Immunosuppressant, antineoplastic	Soft-tissue reaction (G, S), dysgeusia
Azelastine	Astelin	Antihistamine	Dysgeusia
Baclofen	Lioresal	Muscle relaxant	Dysgeusia
Beclomethasone dipropionate (nasal, aerosol)	Beconase, Becotide	Corticosteroid (inhaled)	Altered host resistance
Belladonna alkaloids	Bellergal-S	Anticholinergic/antispasmodic	Xerostomia
Benazepril	Lotensin	ACE inhibitor	Angioedema
Bendroflumethiazide	Naturetin	Antihypertensive	Salivary gland involvement
Benzphetamine	Didrex	Anorexiant	Dysgeusia
Benztropine mesylate	Cogentin	Antiparkinsonism	Xerostomia
Betamethasone	Celestone	Corticosteroid (oral)	Altered host resistance
Betaxolol	Kerlone	β-adrenergic blocker	Dysgeusia
Bethanechol	Urecholine	Cholinergic	Sialorrhea

indicates a soft-tissue reaction. (D): discoloration; (G): glossitis; (P): pigmentation; (S): stomatitis; (U): ulceration.

Continued on next page

Table 28.16 (cont.)

Drugs and Associated Oral Manifestations

Generic name	Brand name(s)	Drug category	Associated manifestation(s)
Biperiden	Akineton	Antiparkinsonism	Xerostomia
Bisoprolol	Cartrol	β-adrenergic blocker	Dysgeusia
Bleomycin	Blenoxane	Antineoplastic	Dysgeusia
Bretylium	Bretylol	Cardiovascular	Dysgeusia
Brompheniramine	Dimetane	Antihistamine	Xerostomia
Brompheniramine/ phenylpropanolamine	Dimetapp	Antihistamine	Xerostomia
Busulphan	Myleran	Cytotoxic agent	Soft-tissue reaction (D)*
Captopril	Capoten	Cardiovascular, ACE inhibitor	Xerostomia, soft-tissue reaction (G, S), dysgeusia, angioedema, lichenoid reaction
Carbamazepine	Tegretol	Anticonvulsant	Xerostomia, dysgeusia, erythema multiforme
Carbidopa/levodopa	Sinemet	Antiparkinsonism	Xerostomia
Carboplatin	Paraplatin	Cytotoxic agent	Soft-tissue reaction (S)
Carmustine	BiCNU	Cytotoxic agent	Soft-tissue reaction (D)
Cefaclor	Ceclor	Antibiotic (cephalosporin)	Altered host resistance
Cefamandol	Mandol	Antibiotic	Dysgeusia
Chloramphenicol	Chlormycetin	Antibiotic	Leukopenia and neutropenia
Chlordiazepoxide	Librium	Antianxiety	Xerostomia
Chlordiazepoxide/ clidinium	Librax	Anticholinergic/ antispasmodic	Xerostomia
Chlorhexidine	Peridex ★	Dental agent	Dysgeusia

★ indicates a product bearing the ADA Seal of Acceptance.
* indicates a soft-tissue reaction. (D): discoloration; (G): glossitis; (P): pigmentation; (S): stomatitis; (U): ulceration.

Continued on next page

Table 28.16 (cont.)

Drugs and Associated Oral Manifestations

Generic name	Brand name(s)	Drug category	Associated manifestation(s)
Chlorothiazide	Diuril	Diuretic	Xerostomia, salivary gland involvement
Chlorpheniramine	Chlor-Trimeton	Antihistamine	Xerostomia
Chlorpromazine	Thorazine	Antipsychotic	Xerostomia, leukopenia and neutropenia, movement disorders
Chlorpropamide	Diabinese	Antidiabetic (oral hypoglycemic)	Erythema multiforme, altered host resistance, lichenoid reaction
Chlorprothixene	Taractan	Antipsychotic	Leukopenia and neutropenia, movement disorders
Cholestyramine	Questran	Antilipidemic	Dysgeusia
Ciprofloxacin	Cipro	Antibiotic (fluoroquinolone)	Altered host resistance
Cisapride	Propulsid	GI stimulant	Movement disorder
Clarithromycin	Biaxin	Antibiotic	Dysgeusia
Clemastine	Tavist	Antihistamine	Xerostomia
Clindamycin	Cleocin	Antibiotic	Erythema multiforme
Clofibrate	Atromid-S	Antilipidemic	Soft-tissue reaction (S)*, dysgeusia
Clonazepam	Klonopin	Anticonvulsant	Coated tongue
Clonidine	Catapres	Antihypertensive	Xerostomia, salivary gland involvement
Clopidogrel	Plavix	Antithrombotic	Abnormal hemostasis
Clozapine	Clozaril	Antipsychotic	Xerostomia, movement disorders
Codeine	None	Narcotic analgesic	Xerostomia
Cortisone acetate	Cortone	Corticosteroid (oral)	Altered host resistance

* indicates a soft-tissue reaction. (D): discoloration; (G): glossitis; (P): pigmentation; (S): stomatitis; (U): ulceration.

Continued on next page

Table 28.16 (cont.)

Drugs and Associated Oral Manifestations

Generic name	Brand name(s)	Drug category	Associated manifestation(s)
Cromolyn sodium	Intal, Nasalcrom	Respiratory inhalant	Dysgeusia, sialorrhea
Cyclobenzaprine	Flexeril	Muscle relaxant	Xerostomia, coated tongue
Cyclosporin A	Sandimmune	Immunosuppressant	Gingival enlargement, altered host resistance
Cyproheptadine	Peractin	Antihistamine	Xerostomia
Dalteparin	Fragmin	Anticoagulant	Abnormal hemostasis
Danaparoid	Orgaran	Anticoagulant	Abnormal hemostasis
Desipramine	Pertofrane	Antidepressant	Xerostomia
Desopyramide	Norpace	Antidysrhythmic	Xerostomia
Dexamethasone (nasal, aerosol)	Decadron, Decadron Turbinaire	Corticosteroid (oral), corticosteroid (inhaled)	Altered host resistance
Dextroamphetamine	Dexedrine	CNS stimulant	Dysgeusia
Diazepam	Valium	Antianxiety	Xerostomia, coated tongue
Diazoxide	Proglycem	Antidiabetic (oral hypoglycemic)	Altered host resistance, dysgeusia
Diclofenac	Cataflam, Voltaren	NSAID	Abnormal hemostasis
Dicyclomine	Bentyl	Anticholinergic/ antispasmodic	Xerostomia
Diethylpropion	Tenuate, Tepanil	Anorexiant	Xerostomia, dysgeusia
Diflunisal	Dolobid	NSAID	Xerostomia, abnormal hemostasis, lichenoid reaction
Diltiazem	Cardizem	Cardiovascular (calcium channel blocker)	Dysgeusia, gingival enlargement
Dimenhydrinate	Dramamine	Antinauseant	Xerostomia

Continued on next page

Table 28.16 (cont.)

Drugs and Associated Oral Manifestations

Generic name	Brand name(s)	Drug category	Associated manifestation(s)
Diphenhydramine	Benadryl	Antihistamine	Xerostomia
Diphenoxylate/atropine	Lomotil	Antidiarrheal	Xerostomia
Dipyridamole	Persantine	Cardiovascular	Dysgeusia, abnormal hemostasis
Dolasetron	Anzemet	Antiemetic	Dysgeusia
Donepezil	Aricept	Cholinesterase inhibitor	Angioedema, xerostomia
Doxazocin	Cardura	Antihypertensive	Xerostomia
Doxepin	Adapin, Sinequan	Antidepressant	Xerostomia
Enalapril	Vasotec	Cardiovascular	Xerostomia, dysgeusia, angioedema
Encainide	Enkaid	Antidysrhythmic	Dysgeusia
Enoxaparin	Lovenox	Antithrombotic	Abnormal hemostasis
Erythromycin	E.E.S., E. Mycin, ERYC	Antibiotic (macrolide)	Altered host resistance
Ethinyl estradiol	Estinyl	Estrogen	Soft-tissue reaction (D)*, dry socket
Ethinyl estradiol/ethynodiol	Demulen	Oral contraceptive	Soft-tissue reaction (D), dry socket
Ethinyl estradiol/levonorgestrel	Levlen, Levora, Nordette, Tri-Levlen, Triphasil	Oral contraceptive	Soft-tissue reaction (D), dry socket
Ethinyl estradiol/norethindrone	Brevicon, Genora, Loestrin, Ortho-Novum	Oral contraceptive	Soft-tissue reaction (D), dry socket
Ethinyl estradiol/norgestrel	Lo/Ovral, Ovral	Oral contraceptive	Soft-tissue reaction (D), dry socket
Ethopropazine	Parsidol	Antiparkinsonism	Xerostomia
Etodolac	Lodine ★	NSAID	Abnormal hemostasis

★ indicates a product bearing the ADA Seal of Acceptance.
* indicates a soft-tissue reaction. (D): discoloration; (G): glossitis; (P): pigmentation; (S): stomatitis; (U): ulceration.

Continued on next page

Table 28.16 (cont.)

Drugs and Associated Oral Manifestations

Generic name	Brand name(s)	Drug category	Associated manifestation(s)
Felodipine	Plendil	Cardiovascular	Gingival enlargement
Fenoprofen	Nalfon	NSAID	Xerostomia
5-fluorouracil	Adrucil	Antineoplastic	Dysgeusia
Flecainide	Tambocor	Antidysrhythmic	Dysgeusia
Flunisolide (nasal, inhalation)	AeroBid, Nasalide	Corticosteroid (inhaled)	Altered host resistance
Fluoxetine	Prozac	Antidepressant	Xerostomia
Fluphenazine	Prolixin	Antipsychotic	Leukopenia and neutropenia, movement disorders
Flurazepam	Dalmane	Sedative	Xerostomia
Flurbiprofen	Ansaid	NSAID	Lichenoid reaction
Fosinopril	Monopril	ACE inhibitor	Angioedema
Furosemide	Lasix	Diuretic	Xerostomia, lichenoid reaction
Gentamicin sulfate	Garamycin	Antibiotic (aminoglycoside)	Altered host resistance
Glipizide	Glucotrol	Antidiabetic (oral hypoglycemic)	Altered host resistance
Glyburide	DiaBeta	Antidiabetic (oral hypoglycemic)	Altered host resistance
Gold sodium thiomalate	Myochrysine	Antirheumatic (disease-modifying)	Soft-tissue reaction (S)*
Granisetron	Kytril	Antiemetic	Dysgeusia
Griseofulvin	Fulvicin	Antifungal	Dysgeusia

*indicates a soft-tissue reaction. (D): discoloration; (G): glossitis; (P): pigmentation; (S): stomatitis; (U): ulceration.

Continued on next page

Table 28.16 (cont.)

Drugs and Associated Oral Manifestations

Generic name	Brand name(s)	Drug category	Associated manifestation(s)
Guanadrel	Hylorel	Antihypertensive	Soft-tissue reaction (G)*
Guanethidine	Ismelin	Antihypertensive	Xerostomia
Haloperidol	Haldol	Antipsychotic	Xerostomia, leukopenia and neutropenia, movement disorders
Heparin	Hepalean	Anticoagulant	Abnormal hemostasis
Hydrochlorothiazide	Esidrix, HydroDIURIL	Diuretic	Xerostomia, salivary gland involvement
Hydromorphone	Dilaudid	Narcotic analgesic	Xerostomia
Hydroxyurea	Hydrea	Cytotoxic agent	Soft-tissue reaction (G, S)
Hydroxyzine	Atarax, Vistaril	Antihistamine, antinauseant	Xerostomia
Hyoscyamine	Anaspaz	Anticholinergic/ antispasmodic	Xerostomia
Hyoscyamine/ atropine/phenobarbital/ scopolamine	Donnatal, Kinesed	Anticholinergic/ antispasmodic	Xerostomia
Ibuprofen	Advil ★, Motrin, Nuprin, Rufen	NSAID	Xerostomia, soft-tissue reaction (U), abnormal hemostasis, lichenoid reaction
Imipramine	Tofranil	Antidepressant	Xerostomia
Indomethacin	Indocin	NSAID	Soft-tissue reaction (U), abnormal hemostasis
Insulin	Humulin	Antidiabetic	Altered host resistance
Iron	Feosol	Antianemic	Dysgeusia
Isocarboxazid	Marplan	Antidepressant	Xerostomia

★ *indicates a product bearing the ADA Seal of Acceptance.*
* *indicates a soft-tissue reaction. (D): discoloration; (G): glossitis; (P): pigmentation; (S): stomatitis; (U): ulceration.*

Continued on next page

Table 28.16 (cont.)

Drugs and Associated Oral Manifestations

Generic name	Brand name(s)	Drug category	Associated manifestation(s)
Isopropamide	Darbid	Anticholinergic/ antispasmodic	Xerostomia
Isoproterenol	Isoprel	Bronchodilator	Xerostomia
Isotretinoin	Accutane	Antiacne	Xerostomia, soft-tissue reaction (G)*
Ketoconazole	Nizoral	Antifungal	Angioedema
Ketoprofen	Orudis	NSAID	Soft-tissue reaction (U), abnormal hemostasis, coated tongue
Ketorolac	Toradol	NSAID	Soft-tissue reaction (U), abnormal hemostasis
Lead	generic	Heavy metal	Soft-tissue reaction (P)
Levodopa	Dopar, Larodopa	Antiparkinsonism	Xerostomia, dysgeusia, movement disorders
Levorphanol	Levo-Dromoran	Narcotic analgesic	Xerostomia
Lincomycin	Lincocin	Antibiotic	Dysgeusia
Lisinopril	Zestril	Antihypertensive	Xerostomia, angioedema
Lithium	Eskalith	Antipsychotic	Xerostomia, dysgeusia, salivary gland involvement
Lomustine	CeeNU	Cytotoxic agent	Soft-tissue reaction (S)
Loperamide	Imodium AD	Antidiarrheal	Xerostomia
Loratadine	Claritin	Antihistamine	Xerostomia
Lorazepam	Ativan	Antianxiety	Xerostomia, coated tongue

*indicates a soft-tissue reaction. (D): discoloration; (G): glossitis; (P): pigmentation; (S): stomatitis; (U): ulceration.

Continued on next page

Table 28.16 (cont.)

Drugs and Associated Oral Manifestations

Generic name	Brand name(s)	Drug category	Associated manifestation(s)
Losartan	Cozaar	ACE inhibitor (antihypertensive)	Angioedema, xerostomia
Loxapine	Loxitane	Antipsychotic	Xerostomia, movement disorders
Maprotiline	Ludiomil	Antidepressant	Xerostomia
Mazindol	Sanorex	Anorexiant	Dysgeusia
Meclizine	Antivert	Antinauseant	Xerostomia
Meclofenamate	Meclomen	NSAID	Abnormal hemostasis
Mefenamic acid	Ponstel	NSAID	Abnormal hemostasis
Meperidine	Demerol	Narcotic analgesic	Xerostomia
Mephobarbital	Mebaral	Barbiturate	Leukopenia and neutropenia
Meprobamate	Equanil, Miltown	Antianxiety	Xerostomia, soft-tissue reaction (S)*
Mercaptopurine	Purinethol	Cytotoxic agent	Soft-tissue reaction (G)
Mercury	generic	Heavy metal	Soft-tissue reaction (P)
Mesoridazine	Serentil	Antipsychotic	Leukopenia and neutropenia, movement disorders
Metformin	Glucophage	Antidiabetic (oral hypoglycemic)	Altered host resistance, dysgeusia
Methadone	Dolophine	Narcotic analgesic	Xerostomia
Methantheline	Banthine	Anticholinergic/ antispasmodic	Xerostomia
Methimazole	Tapazole	Antithyroid	Dysgeusia
Methotrexate	Folex	Antineoplastic	Soft-tissue reaction (G, S), dysgeusia

* indicates a soft-tissue reaction. (D): discoloration; (G): glossitis; (P): pigmentation; (S): stomatitis; (U): ulceration.

Continued on next page

Table 28.16 (cont.)

Drugs and Associated Oral Manifestations

Generic name	Brand name(s)	Drug category	Associated manifestation(s)
Methscopolamine	Pamine	Anticholinergic/ antispasmodic	Xerostomia
Methyclothiazide	Enduron; Duretic [CAN]	Antihypertensive	Salivary gland involvement
Methyldopa	Aldomet	Antihypertensive	Xerostomia, soft-tissue reaction (D)*, salivary gland involvement, lichenoid reaction
Methylprednisolone	Medrol	Corticosteroid (oral)	Altered host resistance
Metoclopramide	Reglan	GI stimulant	Movement disorders
Metoprolol	Lopressor	Antihypertensive, β-adrenergic blocker	Xerostomia, dysgeusia
Metronidazole	Flagyl	Antibiotic	Dysgeusia
Mexiletine	Mexitil	Antidysrhythmic	Dysgeusia, xerostomia
Midazolam	Versed	Antianxiety	Angioedema, dysgeusia
Minocycline	Minocin	Antibiotic	Soft-tissue reaction (D)
Moexipril	Univasc	ACE inhibitor	Angioedema
Molindone	Moban	Antipsychotic	Xerostomia
Morieizine	Ethmozine	Antidysrhythmic	Dysgeusia
Morphine	MS Contin	Narcotic analgesic	Xerostomia
Nadolol	Corgard	Antihypertensive	Xerostomia, dysgeusia
Naproxen	Aleve, Anaprox, Naprosyn	NSAID	Xerostomia, abnormal hemostasis
Nicotine polacrilex (chewing gum)	Nicorette	Smoking cessation agent	Xerostomia, dysgeusia
Nicotine topical patches	Habitrol, NicoDerm	Smoking cessation agent	Xerostomia, dysgeusia

[CAN] indicates a drug available only in Canada.
* indicates a soft-tissue reaction. (D): discoloration; (G): glossitis; (P): pigmentation; (S): stomatitis; (U): ulceration.

Continued on next page

Table 28.16 (cont.)

Drugs and Associated Oral Manifestations

Generic name	Brand name(s)	Drug category	Associated manifestation(s)
Nifedipine	Procardia	Cardiovascular (calcium channel blocker)	Xerostomia, dysgeusia, gingival enlargement
Nitrofurantoin	Macrodantin	Urinary tract anti-infective	Coated tongue
Nortriptyline	Aventyl, Pamelor	Antidepressant	Xerostomia, coated tongue
Ondansetron	Zofran	Antiemetic	Dysgeusia
Orphenadrine	Norflex	Muscle relaxant	Xerostomia
Orphenadrine HCl	Marflex	Antiparkinsonism	Xerostomia
Oxaprozin	Daypro	NSAID	Abnormal hemostasis
Oxazepam	Serax	Antianxiety	Xerostomia
Oxybutynin	Ditropan	Anticholinergic/ antispasmodic	Xerostomia
Oxymorphone	Numorphan ⋆	Narcotic analgesic	Xerostomia
Oxyphencyclimine	Daricon	Anticholinergic/ antispasmodic	Xerostomia
P-cyclophosphamide	Cytoxan	Cytotoxic agent	Soft-tissue reaction (P)*
Paroxetine	Paxil	Antidepressant	Xerostomia
Penbutolol	Levatol	β-adrenergic blocker	Dysgeusia
Penicillamine	Cuprimine	Chelating agent, antiarthritic (disease modifying)	Soft-tissue reaction (D), dysgeusia
Penicillin G	Pfizerpen	Antibiotic	Erythema multiforme, altered host resistance
Penicillin V potassium	Pen-Vee K, V-Cillin K	Antibiotic	Coated tongue
Pentazocine	Talwin	Narcotic analgesic	Xerostomia

⋆ *indicates a product bearing the ADA Seal of Acceptance.*
indicates a soft-tissue reaction. (D): discoloration; (G): glossitis; (P): pigmentation; (S): stomatitis; (U): ulceration.

Continued on next page

Table 28.16 (cont.)

Drugs and Associated Oral Manifestations

Generic name	Brand name(s)	Drug category	Associated manifestation(s)
Pentobarbital	Nembutal	Barbiturate	Leukopenia and neutropenia, erythema multiforme
Perphenazine	Trilafon	Antipsychotic	Leukopenia and neutropenia, movement disorders
Phendimetrazine	Anorex	Anorexiant	Xerostomia, dysgeusia
Phenelzine	Nardil	Antidepressant	Xerostomia
Phenobarbital	Luminal	Barbiturate	Leukopenia and neutropenia, erythema multiforme
Phentermine	Adipex-P, Fastin, Ionamin	Anorexiant	Xerostomia, dysgeusia
Phenylbutazone	Butazolidin	NSAID	Xerostomia, dysgeusia, leukopenia and neutropenia, salivary gland involvement, erythema multiforme
Phenylpropanolamine/ chlorpheniramine	Ornade	Decongestant	Xerostomia
Phenytoin	Dilantin	Anticonvulsant	Gingival enlargement, erythema multiforme
Pimozide	Orap	Antipsychotic	Xerostomia
Pindolol	Visken	β-adrenergic blocker	Dysgeusia
Piroxicam	Feldene	NSAID	Xerostomia, abnormal hemostasis
Pramipexole	Mirapex	Antiparkinsonism	Xerostomia
Prazepam	Centrax	Antianxiety	Xerostomia
Prazosin	Minipress	Antihypertensive	Xerostomia
Primidone	Mysoline	Barbiturate	Leukopenia and neutropenia
Procainamide	Pronestyl	Antidysrhythmic	Dysgeusia

Continued on next page

Table 28.16 (cont.)

Drugs and Associated Oral Manifestations

Generic name	Brand name(s)	Drug category	Associated manifestation(s)
Procaine penicillin	Wycillin	Antibiotic	Dysgeusia
Prochlorperazine	Compazine	Antipsychotic	Xerostomia, leukopenia and neutropenia, movement disorders
Promazine	Sparine	Antipsychotic	Xerostomia, leukopenia and neutropenia, movement disorders
Promethazine	Phenergan	Antihistamine	Xerostomia
Propafenone	Rythmol	Antidysrhythmic	Dysgeusia
Propanolol	Inderal	β-adrenergic blocker	Dysgeusia
Propantheline	Pro-Banthine	Anticholinergic/antispasmodic	Xerostomia
Propoxyphene	Darvon	Narcotic analgesic	Xerostomia
Quetiapine	Seroquel	Antipsychotic	Xerostomia
Quinapril	Accupril	ACE inhibitor	Angioedema
Quinine	Quinamm	Antiprotozoal	Leukopenia and neutropenia
Quinolone antibiotic: ciprofloxacin	Cipro	Antibiotic	Altered host resistance
Ramipril	Altace	ACE inhibitor	Angioedema
Reserpine	Serpasil	Antihypertensive	Xerostomia
Risperidone	Risperdal	Antipsychotic	Xerostomia, movement disorders
Rizatriptan	Maxalt	Sedative	Xerostomia
Ropinirole	Requip	Antiparkinsonism	Xerostomia

Continued on next page

Table 28.16 (cont.)

Drugs and Associated Oral Manifestations

Generic name	Brand name(s)	Drug category	Associated manifestation(s)
Scopolamine	Transderm-Scop	Anticholinergic/ antispasmodic	Xerostomia
Secobarbital	Seconal	Barbiturate	Leukopenia and neutropenia, erythema multiforme
Sertraline	Zoloft	Antidepressant	Xerostomia
Sibutramine	Meridia	Anorexiant	Xerostomia
Spironolactone	Aldactone	Cardiovascular	Dysgeusia
Sulfacytine	Renoquid	Sulfonamide	Leukopenia and neutropenia, erythema multiforme
Sulfamethizole	Thiosulfil Forte	Sulfonamide	Leukopenia and neutropenia, erythema multiforme
Sulfamethoxazole	Gantanol	Sulfonamide	Leukopenia and neutropenia, erythema multiforme
Sulfinpyrazone	Anturane	Antithrombotic	Abnormal hemostasis
Sulfisoxazole	Gantrisin	Sulfonamide	Leukopenia and neutropenia, erythema multiforme, altered host resistance
Tacrine	Cognex	Cholinergic	Sialorrhea, angioedema
Tamoxifen	Novadex	Antineoplastic	Altered host resistance
Temazepam	Restoril	Sedative	Xerostomia
Terazosin	Hytrin	Antihypertensive	Xerostomia
Tetracycline	Achromycin, Robitet, Vibramycin	Antibiotic	Dysgeusia, coated tongue, altered host resistance
Thioridazine	Mellaril	Antipsychotic	Xerostomia, leukopenia and neutropenia, movement disorders

Continued on next page

Table 28.16 (cont.)

Drugs and Associated Oral Manifestations

Generic name	Brand name(s)	Drug category	Associated manifestation(s)
Thiothixene	Navane	Antipsychotic	Xerostomia, movement disorders
Ticlopidine	Ticlid	Antithrombotic	Abnormal hemostasis
Timolol	Blocadren	β-adrenergic blocker	Dysgeusia
Tocainide	Tonocard	Antidysrhythmic	Leukopenia and neutropenia, xerostomia
Tolazamide	Tolinase	Antidiabetic (oral hypoglycemic)	Altered host resistance
Tolbutamide	Orinase	Antidiabetic (oral hypoglycemic)	Leukopenia and neutropenia, altered host resistance, dysgeusia
Tolcapone	Tasmar	Antiparkinsonism	Xerostomia
Tolmetin	Tolectin	NSAID	Abnormal hemostasis
Tolterodine	Detrol	Muscarinic receptor antagonist	Xerostomia
Tramadol	Ultram	Narcotic analgesic	Xerostomia
Tranylcypromine	Parnate	Antidepressant	Xerostomia
Trazodone	Desyrel	Antidepressant	Xerostomia
Triamcinolone	Azmacort	Corticosteroid (inhaled)	Altered host resistance
Triamterene	Dyrenium	Diuretic	Xerostomia
Triamterene/ hydrochlorothiazide	Dyazide, Maxzide	Diuretic	Xerostomia
Triazolam	Halcion	Sedative	Xerostomia
Trifluoperazine	Stelazine	Antipsychotic	Xerostomia, leukopenia and neutropenia, movement disorders

Continued on next page

Table 28.16 (cont.)

Drugs and Associated Oral Manifestations

Generic name	Brand name(s)	Drug category	Associated manifestation(s)
Trihexyphenidyl	Artane	Antiparkinsonism	Xerostomia
Tripelennamine	Pyribenzamine (PBZ)	Antihistamine	Xerostomia
Triprolidine/pseudo-ephedrine	Actifed	Antihistamine	Xerostomia
Verapamil	Calan	Cardiovascular	Gingival enlargement
Vincristine	Oncovin	Antineoplastic (cytotoxic)	Soft-tissue reaction (S)*, dysgeusia
Warfarin	Coumadin	Anticoagulant	Soft-tissue reaction (U), abnormal hemostasis

* indicates a soft-tissue reaction. (D): discoloration; (G): glossitis; (P): pigmentation; (S): stomatitis; (U): ulceration.

Chapter 29.

Infection Control Strategies for the Dental Office

Chris H. Miller, Ph.D.

Infection control consists primarily of a series of standard procedures designed to reduce the number of microbes shared among people. In the office, this involves protection of patients, protection of the dental team and protection of the people in the community from microbes in the office. Infection control is accomplished by using universal precautions and by using products, equipment and procedures that will prevent or reduce exposure of people to microbes by

- preventing contamination of objects or surfaces and
- killing microbes and/or removing them from objects or surfaces.

Infection control guidelines for dentistry have been presented by the American Dental Association and the Centers for Disease Control and Prevention. The U.S. Department of Labor has established the Bloodborne Pathogens Standard for protection of employees from exposure to pathogens present in human body fluids. This standard covers employees who could come into contact with blood and other potentially infectious body fluids (for example, saliva in dentistry) as a result of performing their jobs. It indicates that it is the employer's responsibility to protect employees from this type of occupational exposure. Compliance with this standard in dentistry involves activity in seven areas:

- preparing a written exposure control plan for the workplace;

- training employees at their initial appointment with annual updates about this standard, the spread and prevention of bloodborne diseases, hepatitis B vaccination, engineering and work practice controls, personal protective equipment, and all other exposure control policies and procedures;

- practicing universal precautions with emphasis on engineering and work practice controls; providing, using, maintaining and disposing of personal protective equipment; washing hands; minimizing spattering and spraying of blood and other body fluids; minimizing injuries caused by sharps; ensuring proper packaging of specimens, contaminated equipment and regulated waste; decontaminating surfaces soiled with blood or other body fluids; handling waste and contaminated laundry properly;

- making the hepatitis B vaccination series available to covered employees at no cost to the employees;

- making a confidential medical evaluation and follow-up available to employees who are exposed to blood or other body fluid at work;

- using warning labels, signs and/or color-coding to identify biohazards such as regulated waste and contaminated laundry;

- maintaining records of employee training and confidential employee medical records (documentation of hepatitis B vaccination or vaccination refusal, and of postexposure medical evaluations).

Detailed descriptions of infection control procedures in dentistry can be obtained from a number of publications. Table 29.1 summarizes infection control procedures used in dentistry.

Although a considerable amount of published information about infection control in dentistry exists, this chapter provides a listing of representative infection control products and equipment. This listing is organized into five major categories based on groups of infection control procedures. These categories are presented in Table 29.2.

Understanding the philosophy of the categories listed in Table 29.2 may help clarify the reasons for the specific procedures listed.

Aseptic techniques. Aseptic techniques, in general, are aimed at reducing the spread of microbes from a potential source of contamination. The main source of microbes in the dental office is the patient's mouth. Thus, various aseptic techniques are used to limit the escape of microbes from a patient's mouth. These include the rubber dam that physically prevents most of the salivary microbes from escaping the mouth, high-volume evacuation that takes away microbes as they escape the mouth, preprocedure mouthrinsing that reduces the number of live microbes that can escape the mouth during the appointment, and disposable instruments that allow microbes on an item to be discarded so they cannot be spread to someone else. Other aseptic techniques reduce the

Table 29.1

Summary of Infection Control Procedures Used in Dentistry

Path of microbe spread	Infection control procedure to prevent spread
Patient to dental team	Wash hands
	Use gloves, mask, protective eyewear
	Use protective clothing
	Handle sharps carefully • recap needles safely • discard sharps in proper containers • use instrument cassettes to reduce instrument handling • use mechanical cleaning to reduce instrument handling • return sharps to resting position carefully • use tongs to pick up needles, scalpel blades, glass • use heavy gloves for instrument handling
	Use a rubber dam
	Have patients use an antimicrobial mouthrinse before receiving care
	Use high-volume evacuation
	Obtain immunizations
Dental team to patient	Use gloves, mask, protective clothing
	Wash hands
	Handle sharps carefully inside and outside of the mouth
	Sterilize instruments and handpieces
	Clean and disinfect contaminated surfaces
	Obtain immunizations

Continued on next page

Table 29.1 (cont.)

Summary of Infection Control Procedures Used in Dentistry

Path of microbe spread	Infection control procedure to prevent spread
Patient to patient	Sterilize instruments and handpieces before reuse
	Package instruments before sterilization to maintain sterility
	Use surface covers
	Clean and disinfect contaminated surfaces
	Wash and properly glove hands
	Use disposable items (such as syringe tips, prophy angles)
	Use clean/sterile supplies
	Change mask and protective clothing
	Control retraction of water into dental unit
	Maintain quality of treatment water
Office to community	Dispose of waste properly
	Disinfect impressions and appliances before shipping
	Decontaminate items sent out for repair
	Place specimens in proper containers before shipping
	Remove protective clothing before leaving office
	Place contaminated laundry in proper container before shipping
	Wash hands
Community to patient	Maintain quality of treatment water

number of microbes in treatment water, which can serve as a source of microbes. Another aseptic technique is handwashing, which is described in Chapter 9. Some procedures—such as the use of "hands-free" sink faucets—are included under aseptic techniques because they do not fit well in other categories but do interfere with the spread of microbes.

Barrier protection. Barrier protection techniques are used to prevent microbes from directly contacting our bodies. The barriers of gloves, eyewear, masks and protective clothing interfere with the transfer of the microbes from patients' mouths to one's eyes, skin, mouth, nose and clothing.

These barriers also help prevent the dental team's contact with microbes on opera-

tory surfaces, contaminated instruments, in the air and in cleaning solutions. Gloves prevent transfer of microbes on the hands of dental team members to patients, and wearing masks keeps respiratory microbes of the dental team from reaching open tissue in patients' mouths.

Instrument processing. Instrument processing converts contaminated instruments and handpieces into sterile instruments and handpieces ready to use on another patient. It not only allows for the cleaning and sterilizing of instruments but also for the maintenance of sterility (through packaging) until the instruments are presented at chairside for the next patient. Cleaning instruments facilitates subsequent sterilization, and using an ultrasonic cleaner or a washer/disinfector

Table 29.2

Major Categories of Infection Control Products

Infection control category	Infection control procedures	Table of related products
Aseptic techniques	Controlling spattering of oral fluids Controlling contamination Using disposables	Tables 29.3 and 29.4
Barrier protection	Using gloves, masks and eyewear Using protective clothing	Tables 29.5 and 29.6
Instrument processing	Cleaning, packaging, sterilizing instruments Monitoring the sterilization process	Table 29.7
Surface asepsis	Cleaning and disinfecting Covering surfaces	Table 29.8
Waste management	Identifying biohazards and containing regulated waste	Table 29.9

(rather than hand-scrubbing) reduces the direct handling of these contaminated sharps. Packaging the rinsed and dried instruments before placing them in a sterilizer protects the instruments after they are removed from the sterilizer and during transport to chairside or storage. The packaging maintains instrument sterility until they are used on a patient.

The cleaned and packaged instruments are heat-processed in a steam sterilizer (auto-clave), a dry heat sterilizer or the unsaturated chemical vapor sterilizer. The sterilization process is monitored routinely by using spore-tests called biological indicators (BI). The BI consist of highly resistant bacterial spores of *Bacillus stearothermophilus* (used to monitor steam and unsaturated chemical vapor sterilizers) or *Bacillus subtilis* (used for monitoring the dry heat sterilizer). Chemical indicators in the form of tape, strips, tabs and special markings on packaging material indicate exposure to heat or to sterilizing conditions. These indicators identify packages that indeed have been processed through a steril-

izer and are ready to use. Plastic items that are destroyed in a heat sterilizer are cleaned, rinsed, dried and sterilized by submersion in a liquid sterilant at room temperature for 6-12 h.

Surface asepsis. There are two approaches to surface asepsis: using surface covers to prevent a surface from becoming contaminated, and cleaning and disinfecting the surface after it becomes contaminated. Surfaces with deep grooves or protected sites that cannot be effectively cleaned should be covered with a protective barrier rather than disinfected (for example, chair, view-box, some handpiece control units, and electrical/light switches or buttons; grooved knobs; three-way syringe buttons; light handles; some sink faucets; cameras; and lenses). Surfaces that are flat and smooth or easily cleanable can be cleaned and disinfected (for example, countertops, chair arms, bracket tables, trays). Usually, a combination of these two approaches is used in an office.

Waste management. The key aspect of proper waste management in the dental office is to first identify what is regulated waste (defined below); then avoid direct contact with that waste; and finally contain the waste so that when it is treated, transported or finally discarded it will not contaminate people or surfaces.

Regulated waste in dentistry is defined by OSHA as

- liquid or semiliquid blood or saliva in dentistry;
- items contaminated with blood or saliva that would release these substances in a liquid or semiliquid state if compressed;
- items caked with dried blood or saliva that are capable of releasing these materials during handling;
- contaminated sharps; and
- pathological wastes (for example, tissue and teeth) containing blood or saliva.

The listings in Tables 29.3-29.9 provide a categorized guide to some representative infection control products and equipment. These lists do not include all infection control products or equipment. Also, the actual listing of an item does not denote its superiority to any other product listed or not listed, nor does it guarantee the availability, quality or proper functioning of the items. In some instances, identical products may be listed under different brand names.

The American Dental Association has an acceptance program for five categories of infection control products: antimicrobial mouthrinses, disposable prophy angles, handwashing agents, sterilization packaging materials and gloves. Latex gloves should not be used on patients who are allergic to latex. Handwashing agents are described in Chapter 9. Gloves, disposable prophy angles and sterilization packaging materials bearing the ADA Seal of Acceptance (as of the date of this writing) are identified in these tables with a green star ★.

Suggested Readings

ADA Council on Scientific Affairs and ADA Council on Dental Practice. Infection control recommendations for the dental office and the dental laboratory. JADA 1996;127(5):672-80.

Centers for Disease Control and Prevention. Recommended infection control practices for dentistry, 1993. MMWR 1993;41(RR-8):1-12.

Cottone JA, Terezhalmy GT, Molinari JA. Practical infection control in dentistry. Baltimore: Williams & Wilkins; 1996.

Miller CH. Infection Control. Dent Clin North Am 1996;40(2):437-56.

Miller CH, Palenik CJ. Infection control and management of hazardous materials for the dental team. 2nd ed. St. Louis: Mosby; 1998.

U.S. Department of Labor, Occupational Safety and Health Administration. Controlling occupational exposure to bloodborne pathogens in dentistry. Washington, D.C.: U.S. Department of Labor, Occupational Safety and Health Administration; 1992: OSHA publication no. 3129.

Table 29.3

Asepsis: Techniques and Associated Products

Generic name	Brand name(s)	Techniques and uses
Controlling contamination		
Antiretraction valve	Check valve	Needed in some dental units to reduce the retraction of water (and oral fluids) up through handpiece and three-way syringe into waterlines
Dental unit clean-water delivery system	Self-Contained Clean Water System, Self-Contained Water System	Provides for the use of water other than municipal water to improve the quality of treatment water for patient care

Also provides a means of disinfecting unit waterlines |

Continued on next page

Table 29.3 (cont.)

Asepsis: Techniques and Associated Products

Generic name	Brand name(s)	Techniques and uses
Controlling contamination (cont.)		
Dental unit water treatment system	Ariel IGN500, Bio2000, DCI UV Light System, Odyssey I	Provides antimicrobial treatment of dental unit water
Dental unit waterline treatment system	Ultra Kleen	Provides periodic antimicrobial treatment of waterlines
Sterile water delivery system	AquaSept, AseptiWater system, MicroSWP, Sterile water system, SteriWater system	Provides sterile water during patient care and eliminates use of dental unit waterlines
Waterline filter	Clearline, Clearline Plus, DentaPure, PALL Dental Unit Filtration System	Filters out microbes from dental unit water
Water analysis	MicroTest Labs, Micrylium Labs	Analyzes dental unit water for number of bacteria
Evacuation system cleaner	Pour-ta-Clear, ProE-Vac, Purevac, Ramclean, Sani-Treet Plus, Shock-ta-Clear, Surge, Turbo-Vac, Vac-K ta-Clear, Vacusol	Helps clean debris from evacuation lines
Hands-free faucet	Aquaflow, Automatic Faucet (infrared), WaterSense controller	Reduces the chances of cross-contamination during handwashing by preventing contact with potentially contaminated faucets
Transport container	Safe-T-Bag ICD	Allows specimens to be shipped in a safe manner
Controlling spatter		
Aerosol reduction during air-polishing	JetShield	Evacuates microbes escaping from the patient's mouth in aerosols generated by ultrasonic scaler
Aerosol reduction system	Safety suction	Evacuates microbes escaping from the patient's mouth in aerosols
Preprocedure antimicrobial mouthrinse	Listerine ★, Peridex ★, PerioGard	Temporarily reduces the number of microbes in the patient's mouth so that fewer will escape during care
Rubber dam	Dental Dam, Dental Dam: Non-latex, Rubber Dam	Reduces escape of microbes from patient's mouth during care

★ *indicates a product bearing the ADA Seal of Acceptance.*

Table 29.4

Asepsis: Techniques and Associated Disposable Products

Generic name	Brand name(s)	Techniques and uses
Air/water syringe tip	Safe-Tips EZ, Sani-Tip	Eliminates the need to clean and sterilize reusable tips, which may be difficult to clean
Bite block	Dispos-a-Bite	Replaces permanent bite blocks on panoramic radiograph machine
Chain-free bib	Sani-tab Chain-free Towel	Eliminates need for holders
Curing light probe	SaniCure	Eliminates the need to cover curing light tips
Eyewear	Eye Clasps	Eliminates need to decontaminate reusable eyewear; also can be used to protect patient's eyes during care
High-volume evacuation tip and saliva ejector tip	Evacuator/Ejector Tips, Oratip Evacuation Tips	Eliminate the need to clean and sterilize reusable tips
Napkin/bib holder	Disposa Chain, Bib-Its	Allows holders to be discarded along with napkin and eliminates need to clean and sterilize reusable napkin chains
Nitrous oxide mask liner	Porter/Brown Scavenging Systems	Permits use of a single-use personal mask liner for conscious sedation system
Prophy angle	Butler, Densco ★, Denticator ★, Nupro, Pivot, Schein, Teledyne, Young	Eliminates need to clean and sterilize reusable angles
Saliva ejector tip	Saliva ejector baskets, Saliva ejector screens	Eliminates need to clean and decontaminate reusable tips
Vacuum trap	Disposa-Trap, eezClean Screen, Evacuation Screens, Evac-u-Trap, Solids Collector Screens	Eliminates need to clean and decontaminate reusable traps, thus reducing chances of exposure to microbes

★ indicates a product bearing the ADA Seal of Acceptance.

Table 29.5

Barrier Protection: Gloves

Generic name	Brand name(s)	Techniques and uses
Glove liners	Stretch Knit All-day	Cotton gloves worn under patient care or utility gloves by those who may have skin reactions to the outer gloves
Heavy utility gloves	Asep-Gluv, Heavy Duty Nitrile, Latex Utility, Nitrile Decontamination	Used to prevent direct contact with contaminated items and surfaces during operatory clean-up and instrument processing **Note:** Heavy gloves may give the hands more protection from sharp objects, but such gloves are not puncture-proof
Nonlatex patient-care gloves	Accu-Gard Vinyl Examination, N-Dex Nitrile, ProTouch Vinyl Examination, TactyLite Non-latex, Triflex, Tru-Touch Stretch Vinyl, Vinylite	Used by those who may have a hyper-sensitivity to latex allergens
Nonsterile latex examination gloves	Accutouch Latex Examination ★, Accutouch Powder-Free Latex Examination ★, ADENNA Latex Examination LPX Powder ★, Allegiance Latex Dental ★, Allerjoy Latex Examination ★, Amerglo Deluxe Latex ★, Aster Powdered Latex Examination ★, Audra Latex Examination ★, Baldur Powdered Latex Examination ★, Baldur Powder-Free Latex Examination ★, Bio-Flex Dental Latex Examination ★, Blossom Powdered Latex Examination ★, Blossom Powder-Free Textured Latex Examination ★, Cranberry Latex Examination ★, Defend Latex Examination ★, DermaClean X-AM Powder-Free Latex Examination ★, Exam-Perfect Latex Examination ★, Exam-Perfect Powder-Free Latex Examination ★, Guardian Latex Examination ★, Guardian Powder-Free Latex Examination ★, Health+Aid Premium Latex Examination ★, Health-Tec Derma Grip Smooth Powder-Free Latex Examination ★, Insurex Latex Examination ★, KLH Silky Touch Latex Examination ★, Malaytex Latex Examination ★, Marsin Latex Examination ★, Medical Dental Latex ★, Millennium Fusion S2 Powder-Free Latex Examination ★, Neutraderm Latex Examination ★, Perfect Saver Powdered Latex Examination ★, Perfect Saver Powder-Free Latex Examination ★, Perfect Touch Latex Examination ★, Posi-Shield Powdered Latex Examination ★, Posi-Shield Powder-Free Siliconized Latex Examination ★, Posi-Shield Powder-Free Textured Latex Examination ★, *(continued on next page)*	For intraoral use during nonsurgical procedures to prevent direct contact with patient's oral fluids and to protect patient from contact with microbes on hands Also may be worn to prevent contact with contamination when handling inanimate objects

★ *indicates a product bearing the ADA Seal of Acceptance.*

Continued on next page

Table 29.5 (cont.)

Barrier Protection: Gloves

Generic name	Brand name(s)	Techniques and uses
Nonsterile latex examination gloves (cont.)	Powder Free Plus Latex ★, QualiTouch Ambidextrous Latex ★, QualiTouch L/R Fitted Latex ★, Quantum Latex Examination ★, Redwood Latex Examination ★, Rite-Dent Latex Examination ★, Savacare Latex Examination ★, Sensi Grip Latex Examination ★, Spectrum ★, Supergloves Latex Examination ★, Supergloves Textured Powder Free Latex Examination ★, Tri-Clean 110 Latex Examination ★, Tronex Latex Examination ★, Tronex Powder-Free Latex Examination ★, Ultra Plus Latex Examination ★, Ultra Plus Powderless Latex Examination ★, Ultra+Seal Latex Examination ★, Uniflex Powdered Latex Examination ★, Uniseal Latex Examination ★, Vital Shield Gold Non-Sterile Medical Examination ★, Waterforde Latex Examination ★	
Overgloves	Operatory Overgloves, Overgloves, ProBarrier Glove Sox	May be used to cover up contaminated patient-care gloves when it is necessary to leave chairside and possibly touch other surfaces Are removed to expose the original patient-care gloves when returning to care for the patient, protecting surfaces and patients from unnecessary contamination
Sterile latex gloves	Surgeons', Classic Sterile Latex, Micro-Touch Latex Surgical, Natraflex Surgeons'	For intraoral use during surgical procedures to prevent direct contact with patient's oral fluids and to protect patient from contact with microbes on hands

★ indicates a product bearing the ADA Seal of Acceptance.

Table 29.6

Barrier Protection: Masks, Eyewear, Clothing

Generic name	Brand name(s)	Techniques and uses
Masks		
Mask, earloop	Com-Fit , Cone Classic, Ear Loop Face, Ear Loop Procedure, InstaGard, Isofluid, Isolite, Shield High Efficiency Face, Sofloop Earloop, Vital Defense Pleated Surgical	Used to prevent sprays and spatter of blood, saliva, or other contaminated fluids from contacting mucous membranes of nose and lips Will reduce inhalation of some airborne particles Can reduce contamination of patient with respiratory particles from dental team member Are retained by two elastic bands that are placed over ears
Mask, single retention band	Defend Conpleat, Com-Fit, Aseptex Fluid Resistant, Molded face, Shield High Efficiency Face, Surgine	Retained by a single elastic band that is placed around back of head
Mask, tie-on	Barrier Extra Protection Face, Fog-Free Surgical, Tie-On Surgical	Retained by two pairs of nonelastic straps that tie in back of head
Protective clothing		
Disposable clothing	Barrier Scrub Apparel, Cover Gown, Criterion Shield Gown, Dental Cover Gown, Disposable Gowns, Sof-Therm Jackets	Used to prevent contaminated material from reaching work clothes, street clothes, undergarments, or skin Is changed when visibly soiled and before leaving work area and is not worn out of office
Reusable protective clothing	Various brands	Examples include uniforms, clinic coats, lab coats and gowns used to prevent contaminated material from reaching work clothes, street clothes, undergarments, skin Is changed when visibly soiled and before leaving the work area and is not worn out of the office Is handled in same manner as contaminated laundry, using personal protective equipment and leakproof biohazard bags or containers May be laundered in office or by outside laundry service
Protective eyewear		
Eyeglasses	Barrier Protective Glasses, Eyesaver glasses, Fog Free Enfog Safety Eyeglasses, ProSpec, ProVision Safety Glasses, SmartPractice Mono Lens	Used to protect eyes from sprays and spatter of blood, saliva, other contaminated fluids and from solid projectiles
Clip-on side shields	Side Shields, Disposable Side Shields	Attach to eyeglasses to prevent contamination or injury to eyes by particles entering from side
Goggles	Barrier Protective Goggles, Cover Goggles	Are more heavy-duty; fit close to skin around eyes and are frequently used over corrective glasses
Faceshields	Disposable Face Shield, ProSpec Shield, Sofloop Faceshield Plus Mask	Used to provide more protection to eyes and face usually worn instead of eyeglasses; some are attached to a mask

Table 29.7

Instrument Processing: Techniques and Associated Products

Generic name	Brand name(s)	Techniques and uses
Precleaning and cleaning solutions		
Enzymatic solution	BioSonic Enzymatic Ultrasonic Cleaner, Biozyme, Bosworth Vigilance, Clean & Simple, Coezyme, Crosszyme, Denta-zyme, Enzol, IMS Enzymax, Maxizyme, MetriZyme, ProEZ, Security Holding Solution	May facilitate removal of blood or other proteinaceous material from instruments before packaging and sterilization
Mechanical cleaners	BioSonic Ultrasonic Cleaner, Dental Thermal Disinfector, Health Sonics Ultrasonic Cleaner, Henry Schein Ultrasonic Cleaner, Pro-Sonic Cleaning System, Quantrex Ultrasonic Cleaner, Tuttnauer Ultrasonic Cleaner, Ultrasonic Cleaning System	Washer/disinfectors or ultrasonic cleaners that remove blood, saliva, dental materials, other debris and some associated microbes from instruments Used in place of the dangerous method of hand-scrubbing instruments
Nonenzymatic solution	BioSonic General Purpose Ultrasonic Cleaning Solution, BioSonic Germicidal Cleaning Solution, Dri-Clave, General Purpose Cleaner, GP Plus Ultrasonic Solution, IMS Instrument Daily Clean, Nonionic Multipurpose Ultrasonic, ProClense, Pro-Sonic, Restore Ultrasonic Cleaner, UltraClean	Used to facilitate removal of blood, saliva, dental materials, other debris, and some associated microbes from instruments prior to packaging and sterilization
Rust inhibitors		
Rust inhibitor	Anti-Rust Powder, Credo Clave, Surgical Milk, Vapor Phase	Retards corrosion of carbon steel items and surfaces to be processed through a steam sterilizer
Sterilization packaging material		
Cassette	IMS Cassettes, Instrument Cassettes, Instrument Delivery Cassettes	Perforated metal or plastic/resin container used to house instruments at chairside and during all of instrument processing (mechanical cleaning, rinsing, drying, packaging, sterilization, storage and distribution) Reduces dangerous direct handling of contaminated sharp instruments during processing
Paper/"plastic" pouch	Assure Plus Self-sealing ★, Assure Self-sealing ★, ATI Self-sealing, Carerite Nylon ★, Crosstex ★, Defend Self-sealing ★, Handpiece Headquarters ★, Harken Assure Self-seal ★, Henry Schein Self Seal ★, Kenpak Self-sealing ★, Medi-Plus Self-sealing ★, Medi-Plus Sterilization ★, Patterson Self-sealing ★, Peel Vue + Autoclave/Chemiclave ★, ProView Plus Sterilization ★, Sterility Assurance Pouches	Used with steam or unsaturated chemical vapor sterilizers Keeps instruments separated and protects them from recontamination after removal from sterilizer and during storage and distribution for use on next patient "Plastic" portion allows easy identification of package contents May be self-sealing or is sealed with sterilization tape Chemical indicators are present on paper portions

★ *indicates a product bearing the ADA Seal of Acceptance.*

Continued on next page

Table 29.7 (cont.)

Instrument Processing: Techniques and Associated Products

Generic name	Brand name(s)	Techniques and uses
Sterilization packaging material (cont.)		
Nylon tubing	Nyclave (steam), DH/Nyclave (dry heat), ProPak Nylon Sterilization, ProView Plus, Sani-Tube, Septodont Tubing	Used with steam or dry heat sterilizers Keeps instruments separated and protects them from recontamination after removal from sterilizer and during storage and distribution for use on next patient Is see-through, supplied on a roll in different widths, and sealed with a heat-sealer or sterilization tape
Wrap	CRS Wrap, Sterilization Wrap	Designed specifically for wrapping instrument cassettes or other items before they are processed through a sterilizer; some wraps are for steam and others may be used in dry heat sterilizers
Other	Re-Bag	Has necessary approval to be reused if handled properly
Sterilization packaging equipment		
Heat sealer	Crosstex Heat Sealer, Heat Sealer and Cutter, Nyclave Impulse Heat Sealer, Schein Heat Sealer, Septodont Heat Sealer, SPS Medical Heat Sealer	Used to seal nylon tubing packaging material
Sterilizers		
Steam autoclave	Barnstead/Thermolyne, Eagle Sterilizer, Midmark, Porter Sterilizer, Statim Cassette Sterilizer, Tuttnauer, Validator Plus	Uses steam under pressure to kill microbes remaining on previously cleaned and packaged instruments or other items Operates at 121°C to 134°C at exposure times ranging from 30 to 2.5 min Yields good penetration of heat into packages Causes corrosion of carbon steel items, and produces wet packs that should be dried before handling
Oven-type dry heat sterilizer	Schein dry heat sterilizer, Steri-Dent dry heat sterilizer	Uses dry heat to kill microbes remaining on cleaned and packaged instruments or other items Operates at 320°F for 1-2 h; no corrosion occurs
Rapid heat-transfer–type dry heat sterilizer	Cox Rapid Heat Transfer Sterilizer, Guardian	Uses circulated dry heat to kill microbes remaining on previously cleaned and packaged instruments or other items Operates at 375°F for 6-20 min; no corrosion occurs

Continued on next page

Table 29.7 (cont.)

Instrument Processing: Techniques and Associated Products

Generic name	Brand name(s)	Techniques and uses
Sterilizers (cont.)		
Unsaturated chemical vapor sterilizer	Harvey Chemiclave Required Chemical Solution (VapoSteril, VapoCide)	Uses unsaturated chemical vapors from formaldehyde and alcohol to kill microbes remaining on cleaned and packaged instruments or other items Operates at 134°C for 20 minutes; no corrosion occurs
Liquid sterilants for heat-labile plastic and rubber items		
Glutaraldehyde	Banicide (2.5% acidic), Banicide Plus (3.4% alkaline), Cida-Steryl 28 (2.0% alkaline), Cida-Steryl Plus (3.4% alkaline), Coecide XL (2.0% alkaline), Coecide XL Plus (3.4% alkaline), Cidex (2.4% alkaline), Cidex Plus (3.4% alkaline), MaxiCide (2.4% alkaline), MaxiCide Plus (3.4% alkaline), MetriCide (2.6% alkaline), MetriCide 28 (2.5% alkaline), MetriCide Plus 30 (3.4% alkaline), ProCide (2.4% alkaline), ProCide NS (2.4% alkaline, no surfactant), ProCide Plus (3.4% alkaline), SmartPractice (2.5% alkaline), SmartPractice (3.4% alkaline)	Used to sterilize previously cleaned items (usually made of plastic or rubber) that will be destroyed if processed through a heat sterilizer Not recommended for use on instruments that can be heat-sterilized or as a surface disinfectant Alkaline glutaraldehyde brands must be prepared properly and used container dated to monitor the 14- to 30-day use life Items being processed must be previously cleaned, rinsed and dried, then completely submerged for 10 h of contact time and thoroughly rinsed Avoid contact with skin, eyes and other mucous membranes
Hydrogen peroxide phosphoric acid	Sporox	See notes above; completely submerge for 6 h of contact time and thoroughly rinse
Chemical indicators		
Integrators for steam	ProChek S, SteriGauge, Vapor Line	Chemical indicators that change color or form after certain steam sterilizer conditions (temperature, time, presence of steam) have been achieved
Process indicator	ATI (dry heat-labels/strips), ATI (steam-strip), ATI (steam-tape), IMS Autoclave tape, ProChek ID (dry heat-strip), ProChek ID (steam-tape), SPS Medical (steam, dry heat, chemical vapor), Sure-Check strips (steam, chemical vapor)	Chemical indicator that changes color very soon after exposure to a certain temperature achieved in a sterilizer

Continued on next page

Table 29.7 (cont.)

Instrument Processing: Techniques and Associated Products

Generic name	Brand name(s)	Techniques and uses
Biological monitoring		
Mail-in spore testing service (for steam, dry heat, chemical vapor sterilizers)	ConFirm mail-in, Maxitest, Monitoring Services, PassPort mail-in	Use and functioning of heat sterilizers are routinely monitored by using biological indicators (highly resistant bacterial spores); some states require this spore testing weekly and others require it monthly; with a mail-in spore testing service, tests are sent to dental office, where they are routinely processed through sterilizer and mailed back to the service for analysis; service telephones office if a sterilization failure is detected and sends a written report to office on all test results
In-office spore testing systems (for steam, dry heat, chemical vapor sterilizers)	ConFirmST Culture Kit/Incubator, SporView Culture Set/Incubator	Dental office purchases proper spore strips, culture tubes and proper incubator system for in-office analysis of tests
In-office spore testing (for steam)	Assert Spore vials/Incubator, Attest Spore vials/Incubator, Biosign Spore vials/Incubator, ConFirm Ampules/Incubator, Proof Plus Spore vials/Incubator, SporAmpule Ampules/Incubator, Spor-Test Spore strips/Incubator	Dental office purchases proper spore test vials and incubator for in-office analysis of tests; vials contain both the spores and the culture medium
Spore strips (*Bacillus stearothermophilus* and/or *Bacillus subtilis*)	Spore strips	Are strips of filter paper impregnated with appropriate bacterial spores and are used in spore testing sterilizers; their use requires culture tubes containing proper growth medium and an incubator
Liquid sterilants		
Glutaraldehyde concentration monitor	Cidex Plus test strips, Cidex Test Strips, Cold Sterilog, Maxi-Strip, MetriTest, ProChek G	Chemically estimates concentration of alkaline glutaraldehyde sterilant being used for sterilization; with time, glutaraldehyde becomes inactivated, and this test estimates when concentration is below that which achieves sterilization

Table 29.8

Surface Asepsis: Techniques and Associated Products

Generic name	Brand name(s)	Techniques and uses
Surface covers		
Surface covers	Clear ProTection, Disposable Protectors, Disposa-Shield, Disposable Sleeves, ProBarrier, Sani-Shield, Simplastic, Surface Barriers	Used as barriers to prevent contamination of surfaces with microbes and/or patient materials such as blood or saliva; barriers are to be impervious to moisture (for example, made of plastic) and are usually used on surfaces or items that cannot easily be cleaned and disinfected (for example, knurled knobs; three-way syringe handle; electrical switches on the unit, light, chair, or radiographic unit and view-box; sink faucets; hoses; cameras); covers are carefully replaced with fresh covers between patients, surfaces that are covered need not be cleaned and disinfected between patients unless underlying surface accidentally becomes contaminated
Surface disinfectants		
Alcohol-based phenolics	Asepti-Steryl, Citrace, Coe-Spray, DisCide, Lysol I.C.	Used to disinfect surfaces that may be contaminated with microbial pathogens and/or patient materials such as blood or saliva; such surfaces may include countertops, handles, trays, supply containers and small nonsterilizable items Surfaces to be disinfected are to be cleaned first; disinfectants used in dentistry should at least be registered with the Environmental Protection Agency (as indicated on the product label under "Reg. No.") and be tuberculocidal As kill time for different microbes may vary, contact time for disinfection step should be longest microbial kill time indicated on product label for disinfection
Alcohol-based quaternary ammonium compound	Asepticare TB, CaviCide, DisCide-TB, DisCide Ultra, GC Spray-Cide, MetriGuard, Precise QTB, SaniTex Plus	See note above
Chlorine-based	Dispatch	See note above
Iodophor	Asepti-IDC, Biocide, IodoFive, Iodophor	See note above
Sodium bromide and chlorine	MicroStat 2	See note above
Water-based dual phenolics	BiArrest-2, Birex$_{se}$, Lysol I.C., Omni II, ProPhene Plus, ProSpray	See note above
Water-based tri-phenolics	Asepti-phene 128, Dencide, Tri-Cide	See note above

Table 29.9

Waste Management: Techniques and Associated Products

Generic name	Brand name(s)	Techniques and uses
Biohazard communication		
Signs and labels	ProTector Labels and Signage, Signs and Labels	Are used as warnings (for example, "biohazard") or for safety information (for example, "eyewash station")
Sharps management		
Recapping device	Aim Safe, Monotray, ProTector Needle Sheath Prop, Protector Recapper, Recap-it	Helps prevent needlesticks by holding (stabilizing) needle cap to allow insertion of used needle back into cap for later reuse on same patient or for removal and disposal
Safety syringe	Safe-Mate, Safety Plus, UltraSafe Aspirating Syringe	Helps prevent needlesticks by providing protective shield around needle
Waste disposal		
Biohazard bag	Dis-pose, Labcraft Biohazard Autoclave Bag, ProTector Infectious Waste Bags	Used to contain non-sharp solid regulated waste during storage, treatment and/or transport for disposal; examples of such waste are cotton rolls or gauze pads that are saturated or caked with blood or saliva so that liquid or semiliquid material is released when compressed; items that are merely spotted or damp with blood or saliva are not considered as regulated waste Should be leak-proof, closable and color-coded red or marked with a biohazard symbol; should be opened during heat-sterilization treatment, closed during transport, placed in a second appropriate biohazard bag if outside is contaminated and properly labeled with office name and address for transport in some states where indicated
Sharps container	DisposiNeedle System Sharps-a-Gator, Sharps Collector, Sharps Infectious Waste, Sharps Tainer	Used to contain contaminated sharps during storage, treatment and/or transport for disposal; contaminated sharps are regulated waste and are anything that can puncture skin or that can become a sharp if broken (such as needles, scalpel blades, wire, anesthetic carpule, broken instruments, wedges) Sharps containers are to be puncture-resistant, leak-proof on sides and bottom, closable and color-coded red or marked with a biohazard symbol Should be located near where sharps are used or found; maintained in an upright position; not allowed to overflow; opened during heat-sterilization treatment; closed during transport; properly labeled with office name and address for transport in some states where indicated

Chapter 30.

Substance Abuse

Linda Kittelson, M.S., R.N., C.S.A.D.C.

This chapter offers information to help practitioners safely manage patients who have or are suspected of having substance abuse problems, including alcohol abuse.

Consider the following points:
- Without some intelligent skepticism, a dentist can become an easy target for someone seeking to exploit a health care provider who has a license to prescribe controlled substances.
- Without appropriate protections, dental offices can be vulnerable to theft of medications, nitrous oxide, needles and syringes and prescription pads.
- Without some understanding of drug dependence, dentists may prescribe inappropriately for an active user or mismanage analgesia for a recovering addict or alcoholic.

Defining Addiction

In 1986, the ADA House of Delegates adopted the ADA Policy Statement on Chemical Dependency (Resolution 64H-1986), the opening statement of which is "The ADA recognizes that chemical dependency is a disease that affects all of society."

"Addiction" is defined by the American Society of Addiction Medicine as "a disease process characterized by the continued use of a specific psychoactive substance despite physical, psychological or social harm." Addiction is not a result of moral failing, poor upbringing or indulgent or unfortunate circumstances. Ongoing research gives growing support to defining addiction as a genetically based "brain disease." Characteristics of addiction are as follows:
- The use of the substance may be continuous or periodic.
- The addict experiences impaired control over the substance use, meaning there is an inability to limit use of the substance or the quantity and/or frequency of use. The behavioral consequences of use become increasingly unpredictable.
- Preoccupation is manifested in excessive, focused attention on the substance—its acquisition, its effects and its use—often to the exclusion of other issues that are more important.
- The addict experiences physical, psychological or social consequences that are substance-related problems. These may include withdrawal syndromes; liver disease; neurological impairment; gastritis; impaired cognition; mood lability or alteration; problems with anger control or anxiety management; occupational impairment; marital/relationship dysfunction; and/or legal, financial and spiritual problems.
- The addict expresses denial, a hallmark of addiction, representing a range of psychological maneuvers designed to eliminate or reduce awareness of problems with the substance.

The incidence of addiction in the general population is commonly thought to be about 10%. Here are some guiding principles to keep in mind:
- People who have one or more close family members with an addiction are at signifi-

cantly greater risk of developing the disease themselves.

- Substance abuse is underdiagnosed in women.
- Addicts come from all racial and ethnic groups, from all socioeconomic groups and from all educational levels. While some will look unkempt, most will come to a dental office looking like the professionals, laborers, teachers, students, PTA members or card-carrying senior citizens that they are.

The Dentist's Role With Addicted Patients

In 1989, the ADA House of Delegates augmented its 1986 statement with a policy on provision of dental care for patients who are or have been chemically dependent. The statement reads, in part, "The use of certain therapeutic agents in dental treatment may have effects on the health and relapse potential of the recovering chemically dependent patient." Furthermore, the statement reads, "It is the professional responsibility of the practicing dentists in the United States to be aware of chemical dependency as an illness and to address the issues of appropriate dental care in the chemically dependent population."

It is important that the dentist be aware of a patient's substance use history. Questions included in the ADA health history form will help the dentist do this. It should be noted that the use of this information will be subject to state confidentiality law, and also may be subject to federal, state and local antidiscrimination laws.

Recognizing Addicted Patients

Some addicted patients may not reveal their history of substance abuse. To arm themselves for dealing with patients such as these, dentists should become aware of the symptoms of substance abuse.

The symptoms of substance dependence will vary with the substance used. Substances of abuse can be grouped into 11 categories: alcohol, amphetamines, caffeine, cannabis (marijuana), cocaine, hallucinogens, inhalants, nicotine, opioids, phencyclidine hydrochloride (PCP) and sedatives/hypnotics/anxiolytics.

Symptoms of dependence

Alcohol dependence is one of the more prominent forms of dependence. Its symptoms include the following:

- **Physical:** Tremors, facial "spider veins," blackouts (temporary amnesia induced by consumption of a large quantity of alcohol), gastritis, esophagitis, liver disease, elevated blood pressure, weight gain or loss, neglect of physical appearance, bruises or other injuries, odor of alcohol on breath at inappropriate times.
- **Emotional/psychological:** Mood swings, irritability, depression, remorse, resentfulness, defensiveness about or denial of a problem, difficulty in concentration, chronic anger.
- **Social/behavioral:** Unpredictability, unreliability, arrests for driving under the influence (DUI) and other legal problems, conflict with significant others, family members adapting behaviors to accommodate drinking, financial problems and occupational impairment.

Many of the aforementioned symptoms will also be apparent in the abuse of other substances. Table 30.1 is included as a reference for the uses and effects of controlled substances which, by definition, have abuse potential.

Drug-seeking behaviors

Drug-seeking patients use various techniques and manipulations to acquire substances or prescriptions:

- contacting the dentist at inopportune times—such as at the end of the day or on a weekend—when it is impossible or inconvenient for the dentist to conduct a complete examination;
- claiming to be from out of town, "just passing through," or that they are in the middle of a procedure with a dentist in another town and forgot to bring their prescription medications;

- appearing very knowledgeable about their dental conditions and about which pain medications are and are not effective for them;
- requesting an antibiotic first, then following up with a request for pain medication;
- engaging the dentist in what may seem to be an innocent conversation about drug supplies or prescribing practices, the effects of nitrous oxide, security procedures or similar topics;
- looking through the Yellow Pages to find dentists new to an area;
- claiming allergy to non-narcotic analgesics;
- asking for pharmaceutical samples in addition to prescriptions;
- claiming to have lost their prescriptions.

Key Points Dentists Should Remember

- Patients who are IV drug users are at increased risk of acquiring hepatitis B and C, bacterial endocarditis, human immunodeficiency virus and opportunistic infections.
- Alcoholic patients are at increased risk of developing oral cancer, post-trauma osteomyelitis, poor healing, impaired clotting function and drug interactions.
- Cocaine users are at increased risk of experiencing cerebrovascular accident, myocardial infarction, cardiac dysrhythmias and reduced gas exchange capabilities of the lungs.
- Patients with a history of addiction are likely to need more analgesia than those without such a history. Even a simple operative procedure will require increased amounts of anesthesia and time.
- If at all possible, the dentist should use only non-narcotic analgesics with patients who have addictions. Ibuprofen 600-800 mg is recommended; the dentist may wish to consider tid dosing the day before and the day of oral surgery.
- Potential problems with liver function may interfere with the metabolism of amide-type local anesthetics, cause increased bleeding time or interfere with

the metabolism of antibiotics. The dentist should use caution in prescribing acetaminophen or aspirin to a patient with active alcoholism because of the risks of liver toxicity or gastritis and increased bleeding time.
- Patients with active alcoholism will require a wound healing time 20%-50% longer than the norm, owing to decreased collagen formation and decreased protein and albumin levels.
- Patients with addictive disorders are more likely to be smokers as well; their increased risk of oral cancer requires a thorough head and neck examination.
- Advise the patient to refrain from drinking alcohol 2 h before and 2 h after taking antibiotics.
- Avoid administering pretreatment tranquilizers and advise the patient not to premedicate himself or herself.
- The optimum treatment time for addicted patients is in the morning, for a maximum of 1-1½ h.
- Patients who use nonprescribed substances (over-the-counter or illicit) may experience adverse reactions from concomitant use of prescribed substances.
- The use of some substances is contraindicated in patients recovering from substance dependence. Tramadol and butorphanol, for example, while not scheduled drugs, have abuse potential in patients who have a history of substance dependence. Avoid the use of medications containing alcohol. Patients expect their health providers to know their history and to prescribe safely for them.
- Patients taking disulfiram will experience an adverse reaction, potentially life-threatening, upon exposure to alcohol in any form.
- Patients receiving opioid antagonist therapy (naltrexone) will have an altered response to analgesia.

Table 30.2 provides a summary of some prescribing considerations for dentists who have patients with a history of substance abuse or dependence.

Table 30.1

Controlled Substances: Uses and Effects

Drugs	CSA schedules	Trade or other names	Medical uses	Physical dependence
Anabolic Steroids				
Nandrolone (decanoate, phenpropionate)	III	Nortestosterone, Durabolin, Deca-Durabolin, Deca	Anemia, breast cancer	Unknown
Oxymetholone	III	Anadrol-50	Anemia	Unknown
Testosterone (cypionate, enanthate)	III	Depo-Testosterone, Delatestryl	Hypogonadism	Unknown
Cannabis				
Hashish and hashish oil	I	Hash, Hash Oil	None	Unknown
Marijuana	I	Pot, Acapulco Gold, Grass, Reefer, Sinsemilla, Thai Sticks	None	Unknown
Tetrahydrocannabinol	I,II	THC, Marinol	Antinauseant	Unknown
Depressants				
Barbiturates	II,III,IV	Amytal, Florinal, Nembutal, Seconal, Tuinal, Phenobarbital, Pentobarbital	Anesthetic, anticonvulsant, sedative hypnotic, veterinary euthanasia agent	High-Moderate
Benzodiazepines	IV	Ativan, Dalmane, Diazepam, Librium, Xanax, Serax, Valium, Tranxene, Verstran, Versed, Halcion, Paxipam, Restoril	Antianxiety, sedative, anticonvulsant, hypnotic	Low
Chloral hydrate	IV	Noctec, Somnos, Felsules	Hypnotic	Moderate
Glutethimide	II	Doriden	Sedative, hypnotic	High
Other depressants	I,II,III,IV	Equanil, Miltown, Noludar, Placidyl, Valmid, Methaqualone	Antianxiety, sedative, hypnotic	Moderate
Hallucinogens				
Amphetamine variants	I	2, 5-DMA, STP, MDA, MDMA, Esctasy, DOM, DOB	None	Unknown
LSD	I	Acid, Microdot	None	None
Mescaline and peyote	I	Mescal, Buttons, Cactus	None	None
Phencyclidine and analogs	I,II	PCE, PCPy, TCP, PCP, Hog, Loveboat, Angel Dust	None	Unknown
Other hallucinogens	I	Bufotenine, Ibogaine, DMT, DET, Psilocybin, Psilocyn	None	None

Psychological dependence	Tolerance	Duration (hours)	Usual method	Possible effects	Effects of overdose	Withdrawal syndrome
Anabolic Steroids						
Unknown	Unknown	14-21 days	Injected	Virilization, acne, testicular atrophy, gynecomastia, aggressive behavior, edema	Unknown	Possible depression
Unknown	Unknown	24	Oral			
Unknown	Unknown	14-28 days	Injected			
Cannabis						
Moderate	Yes	2-4	Smoked, oral	Euphoria, relaxed inhibitions, increased appetite, disorientation	Fatigue, paranoia, possible psychosis	Occasional reports of insomnia, hyperactivity, decreased appetite
Moderate	Yes	2-4	Smoked, oral			
Moderate	Yes	2-4	Smoked, oral			
Depressants						
High-Moderate	Yes	1-16	Oral, injected	Slurred speech, disorientation, drunken behavior without odor of alcohol	Shallow respiration, clammy skin, dilated pupils, weak and rapid pulse, coma, possible death	Anxiety, insomnia, tremors, delirium, convulsions, possible death
Low	Yes	4-8	Oral, injected			
Moderate	Yes	5-8	Oral			
Moderate	Yes	4-8	Oral			
Moderate	Yes	4-8	Oral			
Hallucinogens						
Unknown	Yes	Variable	Oral, injected	Illusions and hallucinations, altered perception of time and distance	Longer, more intense "trip" episodes, psychosis, possible death	Unknown
Unknown	Yes	8-12	Oral			
Unknown	Yes	8-12	Oral			
High	Yes	Days	Oral, smoked			
Unknown	Possible	Variable	Smoked, oral, injected, sniffed			

Continued on next page

Table 30.1 (cont.)

Controlled Substances: Uses and Effects

Drugs	CSA schedules	Trade or other names	Medical uses	Physical dependence
Narcotics				
Codeine	II,III,V	Tylenol w/Codeine, Empirin w/Codeine, Robitussin A-C, Fiorinal w/Codeine, APAP w/Codeine	Analgesic, antitussive	Moderate
Fentanyl and analogs	I,II	Innovar, Sublimaze, Alfenta, Sufenta, Duragesic	Analgesic, adjunct to anesthesia, anesthetic	High
Heroin	I	Diacetylmorphine, Horse, Smack	None in U.S., analgesic, antitussive	High
Hydrocodone	II,III	Tussionex, Vicodin, Hycodan, Lorcet	Analgesic, antitussive	High
Hydromorphone	II	Dilaudid	Analgesic	High
Methadone and LAAM	I,II	Dolophine, Methadose, Levo-alpha-acetylmethadol, Levomethadyl acetate	Analgesic, treatment of dependence	High
Morphine	II	Duramorph, MS-Contin, Roxanol, Oramorph SR	Analgesic	High
Oxycodone	II	Percodan, Percocet, Tylox, Roxicet, Roxicodone	Analgesic	High
Other narcotics	II,III,IV,V	Percodan, Percocet, Tylox, Opium, Darvon, Talwin*, Buprenorphine, Meperidine (Pethidine), Demerol	Analgesic, antidiarrheal	High-Low
Stimulants				
Amphetamine/methamphetamine	II	Biphetamine, Desoxyn, Dexedrine, Obetrol, Ice	Attention deficit disorder, narcolepsy, weight control	Possible
Cocaine**	II	Coke, Flake, Snow, Crack	Local anesthetic	Possible
Methylphenidate	II	Ritalin	Attention deficit disorder, narcolepsy	Possible
Other stimulants	I,II,III,IV	Adipex, Didrex, Ionamin, Melfiat, Plegine, Captagon, Sanorex, Tenuate, Tepanil, Prelu-2, Preludin	Weight control	Possible

*Designated a narcotic under the Controlled Substances Act (CSA).
**Not designated a narcotic under the CSA.
Source: Drugs of Abuse, 1996 edition. Washington, D.C.: U.S. Department of Justice, Drug Enforcement Administration; 1996.

Guarding Against Drug Theft

A number of safeguards can be implemented in the office to help protect the dentist from being targeted as a source of controlled substances. These measures should be implemented subject to applicable laws, including those regarding confidentiality. Suggestions include the following:

- Store narcotics in locked cabinets away from patient areas and well out of view of patients.
- Never leave medications unattended in a

Psychological dependence	Tolerance	Duration (hours)	Usual method	Possible effects	Effects of overdose	Withdrawal syndrome
Narcotics						
Moderate	Yes	3-6	Oral, injected	Euphoria, drowsiness, respiratory depression, constricted pupils, nausea	Slow and shallow breathing, clammy skin, convulsions, coma, possible death	Watery eyes, runny nose, yawning, loss of appetite, irritability, tremors, panic, cramps, nausea, chills and sweating
High	Yes	10-72	Injected, transdermal patch			
High	Yes	3-6	Injected, sniffed, smoked			
High	Yes	3-6	Oral			
High	Yes	3-6	Oral, injected			
High	Yes	12-72	Oral, injected			
High	Yes	3-6	Oral, smoked, injected			
High	Yes	4-5	Oral			
High-Low	Yes	Variable	Oral, injected			
Stimulants						
High	Yes	2-4	Oral, injected, smoked	Increased alertness, excitation, euphoria, increased pulse rate & blood pressure, insomnia, loss of appetite	Agitation, increased body temperature, hallucination, convulsions, possible death	Apathy, long periods of sleep, irritability, depression, disorientation
High	Yes	1-2	Sniffed, smoked, injected			
High	Yes	2-4	Oral, injected			
High	Yes	2-4	Oral, injected			

room, regardless of whether or not a patient is present.

- Keep prescription pads out of sight and, preferably, in a locked cabinet.
- When writing prescriptions, give quantities in words as well as numbers (for example, if writing for 12 Tylenol no. 3, specify "twelve Tylenol no. 3" as well).

- Do not use prescription blanks preprinted with your U.S. Drug Enforcement Agency (DEA) number.
- Be suspicious of patients who request specific medications and/or dosages.
- Use the lowest effective doses and non-controlled substances as much as possible (it is important, however, to manage acute

pain aggressively enough that patients experience relief).

- Prescribe in small quantities—a 2- to 3-day supply should be adequate for most dental procedures.
- Keep a tally in the patient record of quantities of controlled substances prescribed so as not to exceed a reasonable cutoff point.
- Maintain strict inventory control of any controlled substances stored in the office, and do not keep substances in stock that are not used in the office.
- If you or your office staff phone in prescriptions to the pharmacy, do so out of hearing range of patients in the office or waiting room. Information that can be gleaned, and possibly exploited, by eavesdropping includes the staff member's name, brand name, dosage, and quantity of drug in a usual prescription, the dentist's DEA number, whether refills are authorized, and anything else typically included in phone orders from a particular office.
- Follow appropriate procedures for securing nitrous oxide tanks.
- Do not prescribe medications over the phone for unknown patients.
- Investigate suspicious stories, such as treatment begun by another dentist in another community, by calling the other dentist.
- When treating patients who are recovering from substance abuse, coordinate their pain management with their primary physicians.

Actions Dentists Should Take on Recognizing Addicted Patients

When a dentist suspects a substance abuse problem in a patient, the appropriate response will vary, depending on the patient and the situation. It is important to keep in mind the obligation to practice within ethical guidelines and legal mandates, and also to protect one's practice and professional license from exploitation or abuse. Some of the possible actions to take, subject to applicable confidentiality and other laws, are as follows:

- Express concern to a patient and provide him or her with phone numbers for a local treatment facility, community mental health center or substance abuse counselor. Such brief intervention may be an effective catalyst to action.
- Express concern to a family member and offer to be of support in urging the patient to seek help.
- Notify local pharmacies of any suspicions of prescription abuse.
- Contact local police about suspicious behavior, such as requests made of you to prescribe illegally.
- If appropriate, share concerns with your patient's physician.

Suggested Readings

American Dental Association Transactions 1986:519, Resolution 64H-1986.

American Dental Association. ADA policy statement on provision of dental care for patients who are or have been chemically dependent. Chicago: American Dental Association; 1989.

American Psychiatric Association. Diagnostic and statistical manual of mental disorders: DSM–IV. 4th ed. Washington, D.C.: American Psychiatric Association; 1994.

American Society of Addiction Medicine. Principles of addiction medicine. 2nd ed. Chevy Chase, Md.: American Society of Addiction Medicine; 1998.

Drugs of abuse. Washington, D.C.: U.S. Department of Justice, Drug Enforcement Administration; 1996.

Glick M. Medical considerations for dental care of patients with alcohol-related liver disease. JADA 1997;128(1):61-70.

Table 30.2

Substances of Abuse: Dental Implications

Abused substance	Facts to aid in diagnosis	Drugs that may interact	Dental implications
Alcohol	Patient may appear drunk or drowsy and have slurred speech. Odor of alcohol may be present. Patient may have difficulty maintaining position of head	Other central nervous system (CNS) depressants (such as opioid analgesics) enhance alcohol-induced respiratory depression. Metronidazole interacts with alcohol to produce flushing, hypotension, nausea and vomiting	Alcohol-containing mouthrinses and liquid medications that contain high concentrations of alcohol should be avoided in dental treatment of recovering alcoholics. Recovering alcoholics with liver disease may require a lower dose of medications containing acetaminophen
Amphetamines	Patient may act jittery, irritable, unable to sit still. Patient may exhibit tremors, dilated pupils, increased blood pressure and heart rate	Intravascular injection of local anesthetics containing vasoconstrictors may enhance amphetamine-induced increase in blood pressure	Measure blood pressure preoperatively; if high (diastolic > 110 mm), reschedule procedure. Methamphetamine users have been reported to have high caries index; avoid local anesthetics containing vasoconstrictors within 24 h of use
Barbiturates	Patient may appear drunk or drowsy and have slurred speech. Patient may have difficulty maintaining position of head	Other CNS depressants (such as opioid analgesics) may enhance barbiturate-induced respiratory depression	Dose of opioids should be reduced to avoid enhanced respiratory depression
Benzodiazepines	These CNS depressants are favorites among drug abusers	Other CNS depressants (such as opioid analgesics) may enhance benzodiazepine-induced respiratory depression	Dose of opioids should be reduced to avoid enhanced respiratory depression. Xerostomia is a frequent side effect and may lead to increased caries
Cocaine	Patient may act jittery, irritable, unable to sit still. Patient may exhibit tremors, dilated pupils, increased blood pressure and heart rate	Intravascular injection of local anesthetics containing vasoconstrictors may enhance cocaine-induced increase in blood pressure and heart rate; cardiac arrest	Avoid local anesthetics containing vasoconstrictors; within 6 h of use, local anesthetics without vasoconstrictors may be used

Continued on next page

Note: As a general rule, patients in recovery from chemical dependency, including alcohol, should not be given any psychoactive drug, such as nitrous oxide or benzodiazepines.
Source: Hal Crossley, D.D.S., Ph.D.

Table 30.2 (cont.)

Substances of Abuse: Dental Implications

Abused substance	Facts to aid in diagnosis	Drugs that may interact	Dental implications
Inhalants	Most, if not all, inhalants are excreted via the lungs within a few hours will have an odor on breath	Most inhalants are CNS depressants	Chronic inhalant abuse may cause liver damage, decreasing rate of inactivation of prescribed or over-the-counter drugs such as acetaminophen and thus increasing their toxicity
	Patient who has abused an inhalant within a few hours will have an odor on breath	Other CNS depressants (such as opioid analgesics) may enhance inhalant-induced respiratory depression	
Lysergic acid diethylamide (LSD)	Patient may appear disoriented and confused	No confirmed interactions with dental drugs	None of significance to dentistry
	Patient may exhibit dilated pupils, increased blood pressure and heart rate		
Marijuana	Patient may appear sedated and lethargic and have bloodshot eyes	No confirmed interactions with dental drugs	None of significance to dentistry
	Heart rate may be increased but blood pressure will be decreased		
Nicotine	Patient may have history of use	No confirmed interactions with dental drugs	See Chapter 31, Cessation of Tobacco Use
	Patient may exhibit staining of teeth and oral tissues, malodor characteristic of smokers		
Opioids	Patient may appear drowsy, lethargic, disoriented and confused	Other CNS depressants (such as sedatives or hypnotics) may enhance opioid-induced respiratory depression	Opioid users in recovery or actively using drugs may require increased dose of opioid analgesics to achieve analgesia
	Pupils may be constricted	Patients taking naltrexone, an opioid antagonist, during recovery may exhibit decreased effect of opioid analgesics	Avoid prescribing opioid-type analgesics postoperatively in patients recovering from opioid addiction
	Arms may exhibit scars from previous injuries or needle marks		Opioid users exhibit profound xerostomia with increased craving for sweets, resulting in rampant caries
Phencyclidine hydrochloride (PCP)	This anesthetic agent may program CNS depression with paradoxical CNS excitation accompanied by hallucinations	Other CNS depressants may enhance PCP-induced respiratory depression	None of significance to dentistry

Note: *As a general rule, patients in recovery from chemical dependency, including alcohol, should not be given any psychoactive drug, such as nitrous oxide or benzodiazepines.*
Source: *Hal Crossley, D.D.S., Ph.D.*

Chapter 31.

Cessation
of Tobacco Use

Robert E. Mecklenburg, D.D.S., M.P.H.; Martha Somerman, D.D.S., Ph.D.

It is well-established that smoking is a leading cause of death in the world; it leads to nearly one of every five deaths in the United States. Tobacco use causes or contributes to various oral diseases and adverse conditions, with periodontal diseases being the most common among them. The risk is directly proportional to intensity and duration of exposure. Tobacco use adversely affects certain dental care and treatment prognoses—for example, wound healing, periodontal therapy, dental implants, cosmetic dentistry and cancer therapy. Smoking during pregnancy increases risks for fetal oral clefts and tooth anomalies. Long-term smokers often have serious health conditions that must be managed during dental treatment and may disrupt or compromise care.

Dentists may be the first health care providers exposed to the signs and symptoms of oral cancer and other diseases that result from smoking or chewing tobacco. Signs and symptoms related to cancer may include oral sores that do not heal; lumps in the head and neck region; thickened white, red or mixed patches on the oral mucosa (oral leukoplakia); or difficulty in chewing, swallowing or moving the tongue or jaw. The importance of a thorough dental examination for patients who use tobacco products cannot be overemphasized. Careful extra- and intraoral examination may lead to early detection and may decrease the chance for metastases to occur. Some forms of oral malignancies are aggressive, so prompt diagnosis is critical. Beyond this, the correlation of smoking with certain dental diseases warrants careful evaluation of patients who use tobacco products.

All forms of tobacco contain toxins, carcinogens and nicotine, which is the most commonly used addictive drug.

Nicotine, the chief alkaloid in tobacco and the active agent in all nicotine replacement pharmaceutical agents, binds stereoselectively to nicotinic-cholinergic receptors at the autonomic ganglia, in the adrenal medulla, at neuromuscular junctions and in the brain. Two types of central nervous system (CNS) effects are believed to be the basis of nicotine's positive reinforcing properties. A stimulating effect is exerted mainly in the cortex via the locus caeruleus, and a reward effect is exerted in the limbic system. At low doses, the stimulant effects predominate; at high doses, the reward effects predominate. Nicotine activates neurohormonal pathways, releasing acetylcholine, norepinephrine, dopamine, serotonin, vasopressin, β-endorphin and, at higher levels, growth hormone and adrenocorticotropic hormone.

Once dependence is established, use continues, even when the user understands the risks involved and makes attempts to quit. Nicotine dependence is defined as a chronic, progressive, relapsing disease. Patients with this disease must be treated and retreated with these characteristics in mind.

Nicotine dependence also has been defined as a brain disease embedded in a social context. People, generally young people, begin using tobacco for sociocultural reasons. These social stimuli are soon reinforced by internal drug-desiring cues and drug-seeking and drug-using behavior. Thus, it is insufficient to treat nicotine-dependent patients solely with FDA-approved pharmacological agents; treatment needs to include behavioral interventions as well. Indeed, reinforcing patients' motivation to quit and helping them develop coping skills are primary services. Behavioral counseling services sometimes are provided without pharmacological assistance, as is the case with most youths and pregnant women. However, FDA-approved pharmacological agents, when used in conjunction with recommended behavioral interventions, significantly increase long-term quit rates (6 mo or longer).

Helping patients quit is practical in every clinical setting and can be done by any clinician. A few moments of assistance from a clinician can be significantly more effective than self-help methods. Minimum assistance includes identifying whether patients use tobacco, advising users to stop, strengthening their interest in quitting and, for those who make a commitment to quit, equipping them with coping skills needed during the quitting process and providing follow-up support. Nicotine patches, polacrilex gum, nasal sprays, oral inhalers used alone or together with an antidepressant are to be used in combination with, not as substitutes for, support and follow-up programs. Some of the literature available to dentists as guides to helping patients stop using tobacco includes the following:

- *How to Help Your Patients Stop Using Tobacco: A National Cancer Institute Manual for the Oral Health Team,* National Cancer Institute, National Institutes of Health, Bethesda, Md.;
- *Tobacco Cessation Resource Packet and Smokeless Tobacco Resource Packet,* American Dental Association, Council on Access,

Prevention and Interprofessional Relations, Chicago;
- *Treating Tobacco Use and Dependence,* Agency for Health Care Research and Quality (AHRQ), Rockville, Md.;
- *Tobacco Effects in the Mouth: An NCI and NIDR Guide for Health Professionals,* National Cancer Institute, National Institutes of Health, Bethesda, Md.

The publications and World Wide Web sites referenced at the end of this chapter provide further information.

This chapter provides an overview of the rationale for clinical participation in tobacco-use cessation programs and an outline for using intervention procedures.

Clinical Practice Guidelines for Tobacco-Use Cessation

It has been established that dentists are as effective as physicians and other clinicians in helping patients stop using tobacco. It is important to do so for several reasons:

- It is ethical. Many oral diseases and adverse health conditions are caused or exacerbated by tobacco use. It is a major risk factor in the development of periodontal diseases. Risk prevention and reduction meet professional criteria for beneficence and nonmalfeasance.

- It is moral. Half of the people who smoke will die of a smoking-related illness. One of every four smokers will die prematurely, losing on average two decades of life. Tobacco-use cessation intervention services are more effective in terms of life-years saved than is any other dental service, including providing CPR and infection control. Common human decency does not permit standing passively aside when patients are at such high risk of experiencing preventable disease, disability and death.

- It is evidence-based. A large and growing body of scientific evidence shows that even minimum clinical interventions are effective; that moderate, longer-duration treatments are more effective than brief treatments; and that specific pharmaceutical agents are effective components of treatment.

- It is practical. Recommended methods are brief and simple and have been shown to significantly increase patient quit rates in virtually any type of practice setting.
- It is cost-effective. Long-term tobacco users develop chronic conditions; these become patient management problems that consume time and may lead to interrupted services and eventually loss of patients from practice because of tobacco-related disability and death. Among tobacco-using patients, many dental treatments are not an option, have a poor prognosis and/or are at special risk of failure.

Minimum Clinical Intervention

Minimum clinical intervention consists of the following steps, as described by AHRQ:

1. Ask patients about their tobacco use. Implement an officewide system that ensures that tobacco-use status is obtained and recorded for each patient at each office visit.

2. In a clear, strong and personalized manner, urge every tobacco-using patient to quit. If possible, associate the patient's tobacco use with an existing health condition. Ask for the patient's reasons to quit and reinforce those reasons.

3. Assist the patient in establishing a quit plan. Advise the user to

- set a quit date, ideally within 2 w;
- inform friends, family and coworkers of plans to quit and ask for support;
- remove tobacco from home, car and workplace and avoid using it in these places;
- review previous quit attempts—what helped and what led to relapse;
- anticipate challenges—including nicotine withdrawal—particularly during the critical first few weeks.

Give advice on successful quitting:

- total abstinence is essential—not even a single puff, dip or chew;

- drinking alcohol is strongly associated with relapse, so avoid any use of alcohol;
- having other users in the household hinders successful quitting, so seek their cooperation in not using tobacco in the patient's presence.

Encourage use of an FDA-approved pharmaceutical cessation agent.

- Nicotine replacement agents used during the first 2-3 mo of the quitting process produce significant reductions in craving for tobacco, but with wide variation in effect among individual patients. People who use nicotine delivered by patches, nasal sprays and oral inhalers have approximately double the long-term quit rates of those who use behavioral interventions alone. Nicotine gum also is effective for many patients.
- A non-nicotine tablet, bupropion sustained release (SR), is effective in countering nicotine reward and withdrawal effects. It approximately doubles long-term quit rates.
- Every patient should be offered an FDA-approved pharmaceutical cessation agent, except when such agents are medically contraindicated.

Provide culturally and educationally appropriate materials on cessation techniques.

4. Arrange follow-up care and counseling. Schedule follow-up contacts, either in person or by telephone. A first follow-up contact should be within 2 w of the quit date, preferably during the first week; a second contact should occur within the first month; and further follow-up contacts should occur as needed throughout the recovery period.

- Recognize and congratulate the patient on success.
- If a lapse occurs, ask for recommitment to total abstinence. This is a common experience, as nicotine dependence is a chronic, relapsing disease.
- Remind the patient that a lapse can be used as a learning experience and review the circumstances that cause it. Assist the patient in identifying alternative behaviors.

Table 31.1

General Information: Tobacco-Use Cessation Drugs

Generic name	Brand name(s)	Indications/uses	Dosage range	Interactions with other agents
Centrally acting non-nicotine agent				
Bupropion SR	Zyban	As part of a comprehensive behavioral tobacco-use cessation program to relieve nicotine withdrawal symptoms	150 mg/day for 3 days, then 150 mg bid for 7-12 w **Note:** Patient should choose a "stop tobacco use" date 1-2 w after use of bupropion begins, because drug takes 1 w to reach required levels for effectiveness See manufacturer's instructions	Contraindicated for simultaneous use with monoamine oxidase (MAO) inhibitors, other medications containing bupropion, alcohol, antipsychotic agents, hepatic enzyme inducers and inhibitors, levodopa; such agents may inhibit bupropion metabolism so that plasma levels increase, thereby increasing risk of seizures
Nicotine inhalation system				
Nicotine inhalation system	Nicotrol Inhaler	As part of a comprehensive behavioral tobacco-use cessation program to relieve nicotine withdrawal symptoms	Up to 80 puffs in 20 min through mouthpiece Begin with 6-16 cartridges/ 24 h; after 12 (or fewer) w, reduce dose gradually See manufacturer's instructions	Should not be used with other tobacco products owing to risk of nicotine toxicity Tobacco-use cessation, with or without nicotine replacement, may require adjustment of doses of other medications
Nicotine nasal spray				
Nicotine nasal spray	Nicotrol NS	As part of a comprehensive behavioral tobacco-use cessation program to relieve nicotine withdrawal symptoms	One spray in each nostril 8-16 times/day; patient should not sniff or inhale and should wait 2-3 min before blowing nose Pump should be primed before first use only or when not used in preceding 24 h See manufacturer's instructions	Should not be used with other tobacco products owing to risk of nicotine toxicity Tobacco-use cessation, with or without nicotine replacement, may require adjustment of doses of other medications

Continued on next page

Table 31.1 (cont.)

General Information: Tobacco-Use Cessation Drugs

Generic name	Brand name(s)	Indications/uses	Dosage range	Interactions with other agents
Nicotine polacrilex gum				
Nicotine polacrilex	Nicorette, Nicorette DS, Nicorette Mint, Nicorette Mint DS; Nicorette Mint Plus [CAN], Nicorette Plus [CAN]	As part of a comprehensive behavioral tobacco-use cessation program to relieve nicotine withdrawal symptoms	Depending on stage of treatment and patient's health, weight and level of nicotine dependence, dosage can be 2 or 4 mg/dose, taken in 1 piece every 1-2 h for 6 w, then 1 piece every 2-4 h for 2 w, then 1 piece every 4-8 h for 2 w Typically, 9-12 pieces/day, not to exceed 24 pieces/day Should be chewed until tingling is felt (which means nicotine is being released); when tingling stops, chewing can be resumed See manufacturer's instructions	Should not be used with tobacco products owing to risk of nicotine toxicity Tobacco-use cessation, with or without nicotine replacement, may require adjustment of doses of other medications Coffee, wine, colas and fruit juices taken within 15 min before or during use of polacrilex may decrease salivary pH and thereby decrease absorption of nicotine; therefore, patient should rinse mouth with water before using nicotine gum and refrain from ingesting acidic foods or beverages while using the gum
Transdermal nicotine system				
Nicotine transdermal patches*	Habitrol, NicoDerm CQ, Nicotrol, Prostep; Habitrol [CAN], Nicoderm [CAN], Nicotrol [CAN]	As part of a comprehensive behavioral tobacco-use cessation program to relieve nicotine withdrawal symptoms	Depending on stage of treatment and patient's health, weight and level of nicotine dependence, dosage can range from 7 to 22 mg/day Entire course of nicotine substitution and gradual withdrawal takes between 6 and 8 w, depending on brand and size of initial dose See manufacturer's instructions	Should not be used with other tobacco products owing to risk of nicotine toxicity Tobacco-use cessation, with or without nicotine replacement, may require adjustment of doses of other medications Following agents may require decreased dose of nicotine on cessation of tobacco use: acetaminophen, adrenergic antagonists (for example, prazosin and labetalol), caffeine, imipramine, insulin, oxazepam, pentazocine, propranolol, theophylline Adrenergic agonists (for example, isoproterenol and phenylephrine) may require increased dose on cessation of tobacco use

[CAN] indicates a drug available only in Canada.
* See Table 31.2 for further information on transdermal patches.

- Identify problems encountered and anticipate challenges in the immediate future.

Providing social support, skills training and problem-solving techniques and prescribing an FDA-approved pharmacological agent are the three most effective treatment strategies. Social support outside the treatment context also is effective.

A more intensive tobacco-use cessation program may be offered if it is determined that such a program is appropriate. Ideally, programs should offer at least four sessions, each at least 10 min in length, over a period of at least 2 w and preferably 12 w. Individual and group counseling are both effective.

The dentist should refer the patient to an intensive tobacco-use cessation program if brief intervention attempts are not successful, if the patient prefers intensive treatment or if the dentist believes such a program is appropriate. The dentist always should follow up with patients who have been referred to such programs. Former users need a lifetime of periodic reinforcement.

Special Considerations

1. If a tobacco user does not want to quit, the clinician should ask questions at each visit that help the patient identify reasons to quit and barriers to quitting. The clinician should pledge to assist the patient when he or she is ready to quit.

2. All treatment strategies apply as well to adolescents who use tobacco. Clinicians should be emphatic and nonjudgmental, and should personalize the encounter to the adolescent's individual situation. FDA-approved pharmacological agents may be considered for adolescents who are motivated to quit and who exhibit symptoms of nicotine dependence.

3. Fear of weight gain is an impediment to tobacco-use cessation for many. The clinician should inform users that some weight gain may be expected, but that it is a minor risk compared to that associated with continued tobacco use. Patients should tackle one problem at a time—first striving to feel confident that they have quit using tobacco for good, then working to reduce weight gain, if any. Use of nicotine gum or bupropion SR may delay weight gain.

4. Pregnant women should be strongly encouraged to quit for the duration of their pregnancies. Because of the serious risks of smoking to the pregnant smoker and the fetus, whenever possible, pregnant smokers should be offered extended or augmented psychosocial interventions beyond advice to quit. Minimum interventions should be offered if more intensive interventions are not feasible. The clinician should deliver a motivational message regarding the impact of tobacco use on both the pregnant smoker and the fetus. Pharmacotherapy should be used during pregnancy only when a pregnant woman is otherwise unable to quit and when the likelihood of quitting, with its potential benefits, outweighs the risks of the pharmacotherapy and potential continued smoking. Risks associated with the use of the nonnicotine agent bupropion SR have not been studied in humans; the teratology risk is negligible in animals.

5. Brief interventions should be offered to patients who have a psychiatric comorbidity and/or multiple drug dependencies. Although it is not necessary to assess psychiatric comorbidity before initiating tobacco-use cessation treatment, such assessment may be helpful in that it allows the clinician to prepare for an increased likelihood of relapse or for exacerbation of the comorbid condition in response to nicotine withdrawal. Referral to a specialist may be indicated in some instances.

In general, the more intense the treatment, the more effective it is in producing long-term abstinence from tobacco. If repeated quit attempts using minimum clinical interventions do not result in long-term abstinence, a patient may be considered for referral to a clinician who is competent in providing more intensive individual care. More intensive group counseling has not been shown to be more effective than individual counseling,

Table 31.2

Transdermal Nicotine Patches: Dosage Information

Brand name	Usual initial dose	Adjusted initial dose*	First weaning dose	Second weaning dose	Sample instructions	Plasma nicotine concentration from maximum dose
Habitrol	21 mg/day for 4-8 w (recommended duration: 6 w)	14 mg/day for 4-8 w (recommended duration: 6 w)	14 mg/day for 2-4 w (recommended duration: 2 w)	7 mg/day for 2-4 w (recommended duration: 2 w)	**Prescription:** Habitrol 21 mg/day, box of 30, apply one patch daily upon awakening	**Minimum:** 9 ng/mL **Average:** 13 ng/mL **Maximum:** 17 ng/mL
NicoDerm CQ	21 mg/day for 4-8 w (recommended duration: 6 w)	14 mg/day for 4-8 w (recommended duration: 6 w)	14 mg/day for 2-4 w (recommended duration: 2 w)	7 mg/day for 2-4 w (recommended duration: 2 w)	**Over the counter:** NicoDerm CQ 21 mg/day, 1-2 box(es) of 14, apply one patch daily upon awakening	**Minimum:** 11 ng/mL **Average:** 17 ng/mL **Maximum:** 23 ng/mL
Nicotrol	15 mg/day for 4-12 w (recommended duration: 6 w)	None recommended	None recommended	None recommended	**Over the counter:** Nicotrol 15 mg/day, 1-2 box(es) of 14, apply one patch daily upon awakening and remove patch at bedtime	**Minimum:** 3 ng/mL **Average:** 9 ng/mL **Maximum:** 13 ng/mL
Prostep	22 mg/day for 4-8 w	11 mg/day for 4-8 w	11 mg/day for 2-4 w	None recommended	**Prescription:** Prostep 22 mg/day, 1-4 box(es) of 7, apply one patch daily upon awakening	**Minimum:** 5 ng/mL **Average:** 11 ng/mL **Maximum:** 16 ng/mL

* Adjusted for patients weighing < 100 lb, patients who have cardiovascular disease or patients who smoke < half pack of cigarettes/day.

but it is a useful method for some patients. Referrals to more intensive individual or group programs are different than referrals made for patients whose relapses stem from psychiatric comorbidity and/or multiple drug dependencies.

Guides to help dentists strengthen their clinical tobacco-use cessation skills and related tobacco-use intervention materials are available from the National Cancer Institute's Cancer Information Service (1-800-4-CANCER), the National Institute of Dental and Craniofacial Research's Oral Health Information Clearing House (301-496-4261), or the American Dental Association's Council on Access, Prevention and Professional Relations (1-312-440-2860). In addition, practitioners may obtain copies of the clinical practice guideline on smoking cessation from the Agency for Health Care Research and Quality (AHRQ) Publication Clearinghouse (1-800-358-9295).

General information on tobacco-use cessation drugs is provided in Table 31.1; more specific dosage information for transdermal nicotine systems appears in Table 31.2. Some products are available over the counter.

Special Dental Considerations

Drug Interactions of Dental Interest

Centrally acting non-nicotine agent: bupropion SR

Bupropion SR (Zyban) is used in tobacco-use cessation programs as a centrally acting non-nicotine agent. Its interactions with many drugs—including alcohol, antipsychotic agents, hepatic enzyme inducers and inhibitors, levodopa and MAO inhibitors—are of concern, as many of these potentiate the risk of seizures. The use of bupropion SR is contraindicated for patients who are being treated with Wellbutrin (which is also bupropion), antipsychotics, antidepressants, theophylline or systemic steroids, as well as for patients who abruptly discontinue use of a benzodiazepine or another agent that lowers the seizure threshold.

Nicotine replacement systems

Tobacco-use cessation, with or without nicotine replacement, may alter the pharmacokinetics of certain concomitantly administered medications. Use of tobacco-use cessation products may require a simultaneous decrease in dose of certain medications, such as acetaminophen, caffeine, imipramine, oxazepam, pentazocine, propranolol, theophylline, insulin and adrenergic antagonists (for example, prazosin and labetalol). However, it may require an increase in dose of others, such as adrenergic agonists (for example, isoproterenol and phenylephrine).

Transdermal systems relieve withdrawal symptoms by release of nicotine into the bloodstream via the skin, while nicotine polacrilex products release nicotine into the bloodstream via the oral mucosa. Possible advantages of transdermal nicotine patches vs. gums for use in cessation programs include control of dose and lack of issues related to unpleasant taste, gastrointestinal distress or mandibular stress. Importantly, both treatments result in about one-quarter the peak nicotine plasma concentration found in smokers; furthermore, nicotine replacement drugs do not produce carbon monoxide, hydrogen cyanide and other toxic substances in tobacco smoke and tobacco that are linked with cardiovascular disease and cancer risks. The substances in smokeless tobacco also increase risks for cardiovascular and cancer morbidity and mortality as well as for oral diseases and adverse conditions.

Special Patients
Pregnant women

Bupropion SR is in pregnancy risk category B. It crosses the placenta barrier; thus, precautions should be used in administering this drug to women who are pregnant or planning to have children. In addition, bupropion SR and its metabolites pass into breast milk; thus, the agent is contraindicated for patients who are breast-feeding children. (There is

Table 31.3

Tobacco-Use Cessation Drugs: Adverse Effects

Body system	Centrally acting non-nicotine agent	Nicotine inhalation system	Nicotine nasal spray	Nicotine polacrilex gum	Transdermal nicotine systems
CV	*Hypertension*	Edema, cardiac irritability, *hypertension*	Edema, cardiac irritability, *hypertension*	Edema, cardiac irritability, *hypertension*	*Hypertension*
CNS	*Insomnia, seizures* (related to dose)	Anorexia, dizziness, *headache*, insomnia	Anorexia, dizziness, *headache*, insomnia	Anorexia, dizziness, *headache*, insomnia	Dizziness, *headache*, insomnia, abnormal dreams
EENT	None of significance to dentistry	*Pharyngitis* During first w, local irritant effects, including cough, mouth and throat irritation	*Pharyngitis* During first w, local irritant effects, including nasal irritation, runny nose, throat irritation, watering eyes, sneezing, coughing	*Pharyngitis*, hoarseness	None of significance to dentistry
Endoc	None of significance to dentistry	Dysmenorrhea	Dysmenorrhea	Dysmenorrhea	Dysmenorrhea
GI	Altered appetite	*GI upset, nausea, vomiting, eructation, increased appetite*	*GI upset, nausea, vomiting, eructation, increased appetite*	*GI upset, nausea, vomiting, eructation, increased appetite*	Diarrhea, dyspepsia, nausea, GI upset, *increased appetite*
Integ	None of significance to dentistry	Erythema, flushing, itching, rash, hypersensitivity	Erythema, flushing, itching, rash, hypersensitivity	Erythema, flushing, itching, rash, hypersensitivity	Cutaneous hypersensitivity, rash, increased sweating, erythema
Musc	None of significance to dentistry	None of significance to dentistry	None of significance to dentistry	Muscle pain	Arthralgia, back pain
Oral	Xerostomia	Xerostomia, increased susceptibility to oral fungal infections	Xerostomia, increased susceptibility to oral fungal infections	Aphthous ulcers, altered taste, excess salivation, glossitis, *jaw ache*, hiccups	Altered taste, xerostomia
Resp	None of significance to dentistry	None of significance to dentistry	None of significance to dentistry	None of significance to dentistry	Chest pain, increased cough

Italics indicate information of major clinical significance.

Table 31.4

Tobacco-Use Cessation Drugs: Precautions and Contraindications

Drug	Precautions	Contraindications
Centrally acting non-nicotine agent: bupropion SR	Associated with dose-dependent risk of seizures; risk related to patient factors, clinical situation and concurrent medication, all of which should be considered before prescription is given Dose should not be > 300 mg/day for tobacco-use cessation	Contraindicated for patients with anorexia or bulimia nervosa, bipolar disorders, CNS tumor, head trauma, history of drug abuse, hepatic or renal function impairment, recent history of myocardial infarct, unstable heart disease, psychosis, seizure disorders Contraindicated for simultaneous use with monoamine oxidase inhibitors Contraindicated for patients with sensitivity to bupropion (Wellbutrin)
Nicotine inhalation system	Can be toxic and addictive Should be kept out of reach of children and pets Patient should stop smoking completely on initiating therapy Should be used with caution and only when the benefits of use (including nicotine replacement in a smoking cessation program) outweigh risks for patients with following conditions: coronary heart disease, serious cardiac dysrhythmias, vasospastic disease, renal or hepatic impairment, hyperthyroidism, pheochromocytoma, insulin-dependent diabetes and active peptic ulcers Not recommended for use with children or for patients with history of drug abuse and dependence, because of nicotine's addictive nature	Contraindicated for continuous use of > 6 mo Contraindicated for patients who have asthma or chronic nasal disorders Contraindicated for patients during immediate postmyocardial infarction period, patients with serious arrhythmias or severe or worsening angina pectoris, pregnant women Contraindicated for patients who have hypersensitivity or allergy to nicotine or to any component of therapeutic system
Nicotine nasal spray	See note above	Contraindicated for continuous use of > 3 mo Contraindicated for patients who have asthma or chronic nasal disorders Contraindicated for patients during immediate postmyocardial infarction period, patients with serious arrhythmias or severe or worsening angina pectoris, pregnant women Contraindicated for patients who have hypersensitivity or allergy to nicotine or to any component of therapeutic system

Continued on next page

Table 31.4 (cont.)

Tobacco-Use Cessation Drugs: Precautions and Contraindications

Drug	Precautions	Contraindications
Nicotine polacrilex gum	Can be toxic and addictive Should be kept out of reach of children and pets Patient should stop smoking completely on initiating therapy Should be used with caution and only when the benefits of use (including nicotine replacement in a smoking cessation program) outweigh risks for patients with following conditions: coronary heart disease, serious cardiac dysrhythmias, vasospastic disease, renal or hepatic impairment, hyperthyroidism, pheochromocytoma, insulin-dependent diabetes and active peptic ulcers Not recommended for use with children or for patients with history of drug abuse and dependence, because of nicotine's addictive nature May have oral side effects, including interactions with restorative materials, xerostomia and pharyngeal and oral inflammation Treatment should be discontinued if patient experiences severe or persistent local skin reactions at the site of application	Contraindicated for patients who are nonsmokers, are in immediate postmyocardial infarction period, have severe or worsening angina pectoris, have active temporomandibular joint disease or are pregnant Contraindicated for patients with active temporomandibular joint disorders, history of GI disorders Contraindicated for patients who wear dental prostheses if gum's sticking to dental work becomes a problem Contraindicated for patients who have hypersensitivity or allergy to nicotine or to any component of therapeutic system
Transdermal nicotine system	See note above, with exception of paragraph on oral side effects	Contraindicated for continuous use of > 3 mo Contraindicated for patients during immediate postmyocardial infarction period, patients with serious arrhythmias or severe or worsening angina pectoris, pregnant women Contraindicated for patients who have hypersensitivity or allergy to nicotine or to any component of therapeutic system

potential for adverse reactions—such as seizures—in infants.)

There is some concern that smoking during pregnancy builds nicotine tolerance in the fetus. Although bupropion has a low abuse potential and there is no evidence that it harms the fetus, every effort should be made to help pregnant women quit without the assistance of this or any other FDA-approved pharmaceutical agent for smoking cessation.

Geriatric and pediatric patients

Older people are more sensitive to the anticholinergic, sedative and cardiovascular side effects of antidepressants. In addition, they often have age-related renal and hepatic problems that may require dose adjustment.

All nicotine replacement products deliver nicotine at levels that are lower than that self-administered via use of tobacco products. There is no evidence that age is itself a consideration in establishing dosing strengths and schedules.

Use of tobacco-use cessation medications with children has not been evaluated.

Adverse Effects, Precautions and Contraindications

It is imperative for a dentist who is involved directly in providing tobacco-use cessation programs for patients to understand the positive and negative features of such a program. Table 31.3 lists adverse effects associated with tobacco-use cessation drugs; Table 31.4 lists precautions and contraindications for their use. Please note, as stated in Table 31.4, that nicotine drugs are contraindicated for patients who have malignant hypertension and for patients in the immediate postmyocardial infarct period.

Pharmacology

Centrally Acting Non-nicotine Agent: Bupropion SR

An understanding of the brain's molecular and cellular function related to exposure to various addictive substances is developing rapidly. All drugs of dependence seem to work in the same area of the mesolimbic system, although each uses slightly different mechanisms at the neuronal synaptic junction. This is important, as bupropion SR appears to act on the two critical centers involved: the nucleus accumbens for dopamine release/ reward signals and the locus caeruleus for penalty/withdrawal signals.

Bupropion is primarily metabolized to hydroxybupropion by the CYP2B6 isoenzyme. Therefore, the potential exists for a drug interaction between bupropion SR and drugs that affect the CYP2B6 isoenzyme metabolism, such as orphenadrine and cyclophosphamide. No systemic data have been collected on the metabolism of bupropion SR after concomitant administration with other drugs or, alternatively, the effect of concomitant administration of bupropion SR on the metabolism of other drugs. The metabolism of bupropion SR may be induced by some drugs—such as carbamazepine, phenobarbital and phenytoin—and inhibited by others, such as cimetidine.

Nicotine Replacement Systems

Nicotine, through interactions that occur via nicotine-specific receptors, is a potent ganglionic and CNS stimulant. Therefore, the rationale for using all nicotine replacement agents is to slowly decrease the serum levels of nicotine and thereby reduce the severity of withdrawal symptoms and, ultimately, stop the smoking behavior. Also, the change to replacement agents from inhaled nicotine results in lower and slower activity doses of nicotine. Moreover, this method eliminates exposure to associated particulates, carcinogens and gases in smoke.

Nicotine inhalation systems

These systems deliver nicotine at low concentrations, in vapor form (via a cartridge attached to a mouthpiece); absorption occurs mainly through oral and pharyngeal mucosa.

Nicotine nasal spray

Nasal spray delivers nicotine more rapidly than gum or transdermal systems. The rationale behind the nasal spray system is that the more rapid rise in nicotine concentration that it provides, analogous to that derived from smoking, may help patients who have not been successful with other programs. However, the nasal spray may have a higher dependency potential than other pharmacotherapeutic nicotine delivery systems.

Nicotine polacrilex gum

Nicotine gum releases nicotine into the bloodstream via the oral mucosa.

Nicotine transdermal systems

Nicotine patches release nicotine into the bloodstream via the skin.

Other Pharmacotherapeutic Agents

Clonidine, an antihypertensive agent, and nortriptyline, a tricyclic antidepressant, have been found to be effective smoking cessation drugs. However, neither has been approved by the FDA for smoking cessation; therefore, although they might be prescribed for that purpose by physicians, they should not be considered for use in dental practice. In addition, Wellbutrin (a proprietary name for bupropion) is used as an antidepressant and is not approved under that name by the FDA for use in smoking cessation treatment.

Suggested Readings

Agency for Healthcare Research and Quality Web site. Available at: "http://www.ahrq.gov".

Fiester S, Goldstein M, Resnick M, et al. Practice guideline for the treatment of patients with nicotine dependence. Am J Psychiatry 1996; 153(10) (Supplement 31).

Fiore MC, Bailey WE, Cohen SJ, et al. Smoking cessation. Clinical practice guideline no. 18. Rockville, Md.: U.S. Department of Health and Human Services, 1996. AHCPR publication no. 96-0692.

Hughes JR, Goldstein MG, Hurt RD, Shiffman S. Recent advances in the pharmacotherapy of smoking. JAMA 1999;281:72-6.

Hurt RD, Sachs DPL, Glover ED, et al. A comparison of sustained-release bupropion and placebo for smoking cessation. N Engl J Med 1997;337:1195-1202.

Ostrowski DJ, DeNelsky GY. Pharmacologic management of patients using smoking cessation aids. Dent Clin North Am 1996;40:779-801.

Research, Science and Therapy Committee. Position paper: tobacco use and the periodontal patient. J Periodontol 1996;67:51-6.

Smoking cessation. Agency for Healthcare Research and Quality clinical practice guideline no. 18. Available at: "http://text.nlm.nih.gov/ftrs/pick?collect=ahcpr&dbName=smkc&cd=1&t=951421995".

Tobacco control. American Cancer Society Web site. Available at: "http://www.cancer.org/tobacco/index.html".

Chapter 32

Legal Implications of Using Drugs in Dental Practice

Kathleen M. Todd, J.D.; Jill Wolowitz, J.D., LL.M.

Editor's note: This chapter is based on a 1992 article by Linda M. Wakeen, J.D., that originally appeared in the *Journal of Public Health Dentistry.*[1]

Dentists often fear that they need a law license to practice their profession successfully in today's climate of excessive federal regulation and burgeoning litigation. This fear is sometimes manifested when doctors face difficult choices about the types of drugs they prescribe in their practices.

Two types of approval processes can assist dentists in making difficult choices: the federal Food, Drug, and Cosmetic Act approval process, and the American Dental Association's Seal of Acceptance Program. Overall, a dentist who prescribes a drug approved by the U.S. Food and Drug Administration in a manner that is consistent with the label approved by the FDA—according to the approved directions for dosage, indications for usage and so forth—can feel relatively confident that the drug is safe and effective for its approved uses. Similarly, products that bear the ADA's Seal have been found by the ADA Council on Scientific Affairs to meet ADA guidelines for safety and effectiveness. An FDA-approved, ADA-accepted drug is a wise choice.

However, the wise choice may not always be the reasonable choice. In court, a doctor will be judged according to the applicable standard of care. Generally, doctors are judged according to a reasonableness standard; in a malpractice action, courts look to see how a reasonably prudent doctor would have acted in the same or similar circumstances. This means the doctor must be able to show at all times that his or her decision about which drug to prescribe was reasonable.

For example, it would be unreasonable to prescribe a drug approved for pain relief to a patient who has no pain. Although the safety and efficacy of the drug may be well established by the FDA, prescribing the drug for a pain-free patient would be inappropriate and might well constitute a breach of the standard of care.

Conversely, there may be instances in which it is reasonable for a doctor to prescribe an approved drug for a nonapproved use or even to prescribe a non–FDA-approved drug. In this situation, in the absence of state regulations that might prohibit the use of a non–FDA-approved drug, the doctor's actions will be judged primarily by the same standard of reasonableness that would be used in a typical dental or medical malpractice action. However, the analysis is trickier, because some jurisdictions have found that use of nonapproved drugs or use of approved drugs in nonapproved ways is prima facie negligence—in other words, negligence on the face of it. Such a finding places the burden on the doctor to justify the scientific basis for his or her decision, to show that a reasonably prudent doctor acting in the same or similar circumstances would have made the same decision. In some situations, it may be appropriate to obtain specific informed consent for the use prescribed.

Overall, the law defers to the doctor's need and ability to exercise independent professional judgment in the prescription of all drugs but holds doctors accountable for the results of negligent decisions. This chapter will discuss the legal ramifications of various decisions that are made in the context of making difficult prescription choices.

Use of FDA-Approved Drugs for Unapproved Uses

Generally, the FDA does not regulate dentists and physicians.[2,3] Thus, if an approved drug is shipped in interstate commerce with an approved package insert, and neither the shipper nor the recipient intends that it be used for an unapproved purpose, all requirements of the Food, Drug, and Cosmetic Act (the Act) are satisfied. Once the drug is in a local pharmacy, a dentist or physician may lawfully prescribe a different dosage for his or her patient, or may otherwise vary the conditions of use from those approved in the package insert, without informing or obtaining the approval of the FDA.[2-4]

The FDA has itself explained that Congress did not intend the FDA to interfere with medical practice or to regulate the practice of medicine between the doctor and the patient. Congress recognized that patients have the right to seek civil damages in the courts if there should be evidence of malpractice and declined to place any legislative restrictions on the medical profession.[2,5,6] (The FDA stated in an issue of FDA Drug Bulletin, "Accepted medical practice often includes drug use that is not reflected in approved drug labeling."[5] And in Chaney vs. Heckler, the court stated, "Congress would have created havoc in the medical profession had it required physicians to follow the expensive and time-consuming

procedure of obtaining FDA approval before putting drugs to new uses."[6]) These pronouncements also should apply to the practice of dentistry, although the FDA has not made any specific statements to that effect.

In 1997, Congress adopted sweeping reforms of the Food Drug and Cosmetic Act via the Food and Drug Administration Modernization Act (FDAMA).[7] The FDAMA was approved in part because Congress recognized that the "prompt approval of safe and effective new drugs and other therapies is critical to the improvement of the public health so that patients may enjoy the benefits provided by these therapies to treat and prevent illness and disease."[8]

Nothing in the FDAMA changes the FDA's fundamental position on noninterference in the doctor-patient relationship. However, the Act does make it easier for drug manufacturers to promote off-label or unapproved uses for their drug products by abolishing the previous prohibition on dissemination of information about unapproved uses of drugs and medical devices. It allows, among other things, a manufacturer to disseminate certain written information (primarily a reprint or copy of a peer-reviewed article) concerning the safety, effectiveness or benefit of a use not described in the approved labeling of a drug or device if the manufacturer meets the specific requirements set forth in the Act.[9] The manufacturer must include with the information to be disseminated a prominently displayed statement disclosing that the information concerns a use of a drug or device that has not been approved or cleared by the Food and Drug Administration.

The FDA's policy on dissemination of information on off-label uses was the subject of long-standing litigation initiated by the Washington Legal Foundation. In July 1999, the U.S. District Court of the District of Columbia ruled that the FDAMA was unconstitutional to the extent that it impermissibly restrained a manufacturer's First Amendment right to disseminate truthful and non-misleading information about its product.[10] The FDA appealed to the U.S. Court of Appeals for the District of Columbia. In February 2000, the appeals court dismissed the FDA's appeal after FDA attorneys assured the court during oral argument that the agency did not interpret the FDAMA to give the agency new powers to prohibit or sanction constitutionally protected speech. In dismissing the appeal, the court vacated a district court injunction against FDA enforcement of the act. However, the appellate court did not disturb the district court's opinion about the limits the First Amendment places on the FDA's ability to regulate manufacturers' communications about off-label uses of drugs and devices.[11]

Determining Liability in Malpractice Cases

Although FDA does not regulate the prescription by doctors of FDA-approved drugs, doctors are subject to civil liability for their actions. Thus, while it is not uncommon for doctors to prescribe approved drugs for unapproved purposes, in doing so they take upon themselves the burden of justifying their actions and assume potential liability if a mistake is made. In a typical dental or medical malpractice case, the plaintiff must prove these elements[12]:

- the existence of a duty, created by a doctor-patient relationship between the plaintiff and defendant;
- evidence of the standard of care owed by the defendant doctor to the plaintiff;
- evidence that the standard of care was violated or breached;
- proof that the breach of the standard of care was the proximate cause of the plaintiff's injury.

Generally, the standard of care in a malpractice case must be established through the use of expert testimony. The rationale for this rule is that laypeople (in other words, jurors) cannot comprehend technical information without expert assistance.[13-15]

Courts have relied heavily on FDA-approved uses for approved drugs as evidence of the standard of care. In a malpractice action involving administration of a drug, some courts have gone so far as to hold that a drug manufacturer's clear and explicit instructions regarding the proper manner of administering a drug, accompanied by specific warnings of the hazards encountered in its improper administrations, are prima facie evidence of the standard of care. Under these decisions, no expert testimony is needed for the plaintiff to show the standard of care.

For example, in Haught vs. Maceluch,[16] the Physicians Desk Reference (PDR), which publishes drug manufacturers' instructions and package inserts, was cited as independent evidence of the medical standard for the administration of the drug oxytocin (Pitocin). This drug induces or augments labor. In the Haught case, the plaintiff claimed the defendant physician was negligent for failing to recognize well-established signs of fetal distress and to take appropriate action, and that the defendant negligently administered Pitocin. At trial, the court accepted evidence directly from the PDR that specifically contraindicated the use of Pitocin when fetal distress is suspected. The court held that the PDR established the standard because the physician ignored two important indicators of fetal distress.

In another case, a physician was found to have ignored the manufacturer's instructions for the intravenous injection of promazine hydrochloride (Sparine), as well as the warnings about complications that would arise from its improper administration.[17] The court relied directly on the FDA-approved manufacturer's instructions as evidence of the standard of care. The court held that where a drug manufacturer recommends to the medical profession the conditions under which its drug should be prescribed, the disorders it is designed to relieve, and the precautionary measures that should be observed and warns of the dangers inherent in its use, a doctor's deviation from such recommendations is prima facie evidence of negligence.[17,18] This evidence creates a reputable presumption that the doctor acted negligently and requires the doctor to come forward at trial with evidence as to why he or she was not negligent in deviating from the instructions.

Is it sufficient to follow manufacturer's instructions?

These cases represent an extreme view. Other cases, even from the same jurisdictions as the cases discussed above, have been careful to require that the manufacturer's instructions be absolutely clear and explicit before the courts will presume negligence. In Young vs. Cerniak,[19] for example, the defendant physicians were accused of deviating from the standard of care in failing to administer a proper dosage of the anticoagulant heparin. The plaintiff had an expert witness who relied at trial not on the manufacturer's instructions about the appropriate dosage, but on texts and treatises of experts in the field. The manufacturer's instructions were not, in the appellate court's opinion, explicit about the proper dosage and method of administration of the drug, and did not contain warnings about undesirable results if the physician deviated from the precise instructions. Moreover, the defendant physicians' experts testified that the manufacturer's recommendations contained one acceptable procedure for determining dosage, but the defendants followed an equally acceptable alternative method. The appellate court held that the manufacturer's instructions were not evidence of the standard of care, and the trial court had erred by telling the jury that the drug company's recommendations were a standard against which defendant's conduct was to be measured.

Similarly, in Nicolla vs. Fasulo,[20] an oral surgeon was sued for injuries allegedly resulting from his prescribing the drug oxycodone and acetaminophen (Percodan). The plaintiff asked the court to instruct the jury that the defendant would be prima facie negligent if the defendant deviated from the manufacturer's recommendations contained in the PDR. The appellate court held that the trial judge acted appropriately by refusing the request, because there was no clear and explicit contraindication or warning about Percodan in the PDR from which the defendant deviated.

Product inserts and expert testimony

An even more common approach is to allow product inserts and their parallel PDR references into evidence to show the standard of care, but only if expert testimony is also presented to explain the standard to the jury. This rule was followed in the case of Morlino vs. Medical Center of Ocean County.[21,22] In Morlino, a physician prescribed the antibiotic ciprofloxacin hydrochloride to the plaintiff, who was 8 mo pregnant and suffering from acute pharyngitis. Earlier treatment with another antibiotic had been ineffective. The plaintiff's fetus died 1 day after she ingested the drug. Experts for the plaintiff testified that a reasonable and prudent physician would not have used ciprofloxacin in a pregnant patient and pointed to the explicit warning in the PDR against such use. The defendant physician acknowledged that he was familiar with the PDR warning but produced an expert who testified that the suspected infectious agent (Haemophilus influenzae) was much more risky to the mother and the developing fetus than ciprofloxacin. The defendant argued that it was reasonable for him to prescribe ciprofloxacin in these circumstances.

The jury rendered a verdict for the defendant, and the plaintiff appealed. On appeal, the plaintiff argued that the jury should have been allowed to find that the physician was prima facie negligent for deviating from the PDR warning, without reference to conflicting expert testimony. The appellate court disagreed. It reasoned that to have allowed the jury to find that failure to follow the PDR warning alone was negligence would force a physician to follow the PDR directives or automatically suffer the consequences of a malpractice action. The court pointed out the differences between a package insert and accepted medical practice. The former is based on the rigorous proof a regulatory agency demands, the latter on the clinical judgment of a doctor based on the doctor's training, experience and skill and the specific needs of the individual patient. The court (quoting Peter H. Rheinstein, Drug Labeling as Standard for Medical Care, 4 J. Legal Med. 22, 24 [1976]) held that one cannot be taken as a standard for the other.[21]

The cases discussed above deal with the use of FDA-approved drugs for unapproved purposes, or the simple use of drugs in a manner inconsistent with the manufacturer's instructions. There are no reported cases discussing a dentist's use of an ADA-accepted drug. It is logical to assume, however, that if the dentist used the drug in the manner recommended by the manufacturer, the dentist would certainly try to introduce testimony about the product's acceptance by the ADA as evidence of the reasonableness of the dentist's action. When the ADA accepts a dental product, all of the claims made by the manufacturer about the product are also reviewed and approved. In fact, attorneys representing dentists frequently contact the ADA to find out whether a product used by a dentist bears the ADA Seal.

In summary, dentists and physicians may prescribe and use FDA-approved drugs in ways that differ from the uses approved by the FDA. Doctors should always base these decisions on sound professional judgment and should recognize that the decisions may need to be justified if the doctor is accused of malpractice.

Failure to Obtain Adequate Informed Consent

A related issue that needs to be considered is whether a doctor must obtain a special informed consent from a patient if the doctor prescribes an FDA-approved drug for a nonapproved purpose. A doctor's failure to obtain adequate informed consent can form a basis of liability to a patient that is separate and distinct from a negligence claim.

Traditionally, the standard of disclosure has been based on the customary practice of the community. Thus, courts look at what risks of treatment a reasonably prudent doctor would disclose in similar circumstances.[23,24] A more contemporary approach focuses on a lay standard of disclosure. While this approach varies by jurisdiction, courts generally look at what information a reasonable patient would consider material to the decision about whether or not to undergo treatment or diagnosis.[25-29]

The case of Reinhardt vs. Colton[30] is informative on the issue of informed consent in the context of using FDA-approved drugs for unapproved uses. In this case, the plaintiff's physician prescribed the drug penicillamine for the treatment of rheumatoid arthritis. At the time the drug was prescribed for her, it was used by other doctors to treat rheumatoid arthritis, but it was not approved by the FDA for this purpose. Penicillamine has the potential to cause many side effects, including destruction of the capacity to make red blood cells, which causes aplastic anemia. The plaintiff developed aplastic anemia after using penicillamine and brought suit against her physician.

One of the theories on which she based her lawsuit was a theory of "negligent nondisclosure of risk." Under this theory (a contemporary version of lack of informed consent), the plaintiff was required to prove that the physician had a duty to know of a risk or alternative treatment plan, that the physician had a duty to disclose the risk or alternative, that the duty was breached and that the plaintiff was harmed because of the nondisclosure of the risk. The standard used to judge the duty to disclose was based on the significance that a reasonable person in the plaintiff's position would have attached to the risk or the alternative in deciding whether to consent to treatment.

At trial, there was conflicting testimony about whether the plaintiff was informed that the use of penicillamine for rheumatoid arthritis was not approved by the FDA. However, the important testimony was the doctor's own statement about the risks of aplastic anemia associated with using the drug, the wide recognition of this risk in the medical community and other testimony about whether the patient had been sufficiently warned about this risk. The court held that this testimony was sufficient to create an issue that had to be decided by the jury.

The case shows that standard principles of informed consent, just like standard principles of negligence, govern the doctor's treatment decisions. It may not be necessary always to disclose whether a particular drug or device has been approved by the FDA. The overall analysis will focus on the total circumstances, as well as on whether the doctor acted within the applicable standard of care and informed the patient of risks and alternatives in a manner consistent with the standard applicable in the doctor's jurisdiction.

Use of Drugs Not Approved by the FDA

As discussed in the previous section, the FDA does not generally have jurisdiction over the practice of dentistry or medicine. Therefore, the FDA cannot, as a general rule, take action against a dentist or physician who prescribes drugs that do not have FDA approval.

Pharmacy as Manufacturer

An exception to this general principle arises if a dentist or physician places bulk orders from a pharmacy for unapproved prescription drugs. In this situation, the doctor may not be exempt from regulation by the FDA. For example, the FDA has stated that the dental drug called Sargenti Paste, Sargenti Compound, or N2 is an unapproved new drug (letter from Carl C. Peck, M.D., director, Center for Drug Evaluation and Research, Food and Drug Administration, to Newell Yaple, D.D.S., secretary, Ohio State Dental Board, Aug. 12, 1991).[31] Single prescriptions for individual patients may be lawfully prepared by pharmacies according to the Food, Drug, and Cosmetic Act, but bulk shipments by pharmacists to dentists are not permitted. The maximum amount of the formulation that the FDA permits to be dispensed is five grams (letter from Carl C. Peck, M.D., to Newell Yaple, D.D.S., Aug. 12, 1991). Conceivably, the FDA could take enforcement action against a dentist who ordered Sargenti Paste in bulk from a pharmacy.

A note about the above situation: Under the "pharmacy" exception to the Act, pharmacies are exempt from regulation under the act if they are regularly engaged in dispensing prescription drugs or devices, on prescriptions of practitioners licensed to administer such drugs or devices to patients under the care of such practitioners in the course of their professional practice, and if they do not manufacture, prepare, propagate, compound, or process drugs or devices for sale other than in the regular course of their business of dispensing or selling drugs or devices at retail. On the other hand, where a pharmacy compounds drugs in bulk, and sells them at wholesale prices with nationwide distribution, the pharmacy becomes a "manufacturer" under the act and is subject to FDA regulation. Relevant factors used to determine whether a pharmacy qualifies for the "pharmacy" exception to the Act are

- whether particular drugs are being compounded on a regular basis, as opposed to periodic compounding of different drugs,
- whether drugs are being compounded primarily for individual patient prescriptions as opposed to orders contemplating larger amounts for office use,
- the geographic area of distribution,
- whether any form of advertising or promotion is being used,
- the percentage of gross income received from sales of particular compounded drugs, and

- whether particular compounded drugs are being offered at wholesale prices.[32]

A dentist's use of non–FDA-approved drugs could conceivably also be limited by state law or by rules issued by a state licensing board. Some years ago, the Ohio State Dental Board considered a rule that would have prohibited dentists in that state from using any drug or medication not approved by the FDA in the treatment of patients. The rule was not adopted.

Use of Drugs Not Accepted by the ADA

The American Dental Association does not require its members to use only products that bear the ADA Seal of Acceptance. This policy reflects the voluntary nature of the ADA's Seal Program.

While the Seal is an important indicator that a product meets ADA guidelines for safety and efficacy, the fact that a product has not been evaluated by the ADA Council on Scientific Affairs does not necessarily mean the product is unsafe or ineffective. Therefore, while a dentist may rely on the existence of the Seal as an indicator of safety and efficacy, lack of the Seal should not be used to create any presumptions about the safety or efficacy of the unaccepted product.

Unproven Reliability and Effectiveness

Potential civil liability in a malpractice suit remains the most significant legal consequence of using a non–FDA-approved drug. In this area of inquiry, the existence of informed consent can be crucial, but will not always be enough to protect a doctor from later claims of negligence. Another crucial fact is whether alternative drugs of known effectiveness and proven reliability were available. In some cases, the outcome seems to depend upon the apparent egregiousness of the doctor's conduct.

The case of Sullivan vs. Henry illustrates the problems that can arise when a doctor prescribes a non–FDA-approved drug.[33]

Sullivan involved a general physician who diagnosed his patient with cancer, determined it could not be treated with conventional cancer therapies and suggested that the patient try amygdalin (Laetrile). Use of Laetrile was not approved by the FDA except for investigational use by experts qualified by scientific training and experience to investigate the safety and efficacy of the drug. The doctor in this case was not participating in such an investigation.

The patient was informed about the experimental nature of her treatment with Laetrile and knew that the drug was not approved by the FDA. The key issue was whether the physician acted negligently in choosing this course of treatment. The defendant asserted that he should win as a matter of law because he acted reasonably and within the standard of care. In opposition to that claim, the plaintiffs (the patient's family) produced affidavits from expert witnesses stating that Laetrile was not listed in the PDR, was a known poison with no known benefits and was unsafe at any dosage. Another expert for the plaintiffs expressed the opinion that the defendant doctor did not fully explore the nature of the patient's malignancy. This raised questions about the doctor's conclusion that conventional cancer therapies, such as chemotherapy and radiotherapy, were not suitable for this patient's cancer. These facts created a jury question as to whether the defendant was negligent.

It is interesting to note that the plaintiffs' expert in Sullivan focused on the potential that experimental treatment was unnecessary. Failure to prescribe a drug of known effectiveness and proven reliability, which could have been used instead of a non–FDA-approved drug, may constitute a breach of the standard of care. This occurred in Blanton vs. U.S.,[34] in which the plaintiff was asked to participate in an experiment to test whether the drug $Rh_0(D)$ immune globulin (HypRho-D) had effectiveness beyond its FDA-approved shelf life. The plaintiff, a hospital patient, refused to participate in the experiment, but she received the drug anyway by mistake.

The court noted that this was not a simple case of the plaintiff receiving one drug that was inaccurately represented as another. Rather, the drug was in effect a "new drug" that was not FDA-approved, and "it was administered despite the availability of a drug of known effectiveness and proven reliability." The court held that the hospital, by administering the drug to plaintiff without her consent, violated "accepted medical standards."[34 (at 362)] While this case involved a hospital's conduct, not that of a physician or dentist, the rationale could be extended to a health professional as well.

Duty of Disclosure

In truly egregious cases, courts may look beyond a negligence theory to impose liability on doctors who act improperly in prescribing non–FDA-approved therapies. For example, in Nelson vs. Gaunt, the plaintiff received from the defendant a series of silicone injections for breast augmentation.[35] The uncontested evidence showed that at the time the plaintiff received the injections, the FDA considered silicone injections dangerous for use in human body tissues, and only persons who obtained a special permit to administer the injections under scientific circumstances could use silicone for this purpose. The defendant physician not only had no such permit, but he told the plaintiff that the substance was safe, inert and had absolutely no side effects. He did not tell her the name of the substance, the fact that it could be used only for the purposes of scientific research, that even under those conditions its use required state or federal approval, and that he did not have a permit to perform the injections.

These facts, the court found, went beyond an ordinary negligence theory and even beyond a claim of battery, which would exist if, for example, a doctor performed an operation without the patient's consent. The theory applicable on these facts was fraud, based on the physician's fiduciary duty to disclose information to the patient that may be relevant to a meaningful decision-making process and necessary to form the basis of an intelligent consent by the patient to the proposed treatment. In this case, the court found, the doctor provided the patient with false and misleading information and knowingly concealed information that was material to the cause of the plaintiff's injuries.[35 (at Cal Rptr 174)]

The fact that a doctor is participating in an FDA-approved clinical investigation is not in itself sufficient to protect the doctor from claims of negligence. In a case involving use of a medical device, Daum vs. Spinecare Medical Group, Inc.,[36] a physician was required to defend himself against the charge that he failed to obtain the patient's informed consent to use the investigational device—a metal screw—in spinal fusion surgery. Applicable federal and state laws incorporated in the manufacturer's protocol for clinical trials required that patients be informed of the device's investigational status, give written consent to participate in the trial and be provided with a copy of their consent form.

The patient claimed that he was not told that the device was investigational or provided with the consent form until he was sedated and on a gurney being wheeled to the operating room; this raised an issue of whether the patient's consent was truly informed. However, the immediate question for the appellate court was whether the jury could find that simple failure to comply with the rules for conduct of the clinical trial, including the rule on informed consent, was negligence per se. The court held that it could, reasoning that the physician was not required to participate in the clinical trials but that once he did, he was required to abide by its rules. The jury was entitled to consider the physician's failure to comply with the rules on informed consent as evidence of negligence per se, shifting to the physician the burden of proving that he did what might reasonably be expected of a person of ordinary prudence, acting under similar circumstances who desired to comply with the law. There is no reason to believe that the court would not apply the same rule to a new drug.

Conclusion

Dentists, in using drugs in their practices, need to be cognizant of the status of those agents within the FDA and the ADA. However, the more important concern is to exercise sound professional judgment in making choices and to be sure that patients are fully cognizant of material information concerning their treatments and the alternatives available to them.

1. Wakeen LM. Legal implications of using drugs and devices in the dental office. J Public Health Dent 1992;52(6):403-8.
2. See 21 U.S.C.A. §360(g) (West 1972 and Supp. 1997).
3. See also 21 CFR Part 130, Legal Status of Approved Labeling for Prescription Drugs; Prescribing for Uses Unapproved by the Food and Drug Administration, Aug. 15, 1972.
4. Beck JM, Azari ED. FDA, off-label use, and informed consent: debunking myths and misconceptions. Food and Drug Law J 1998;53:71-104.
5. See also "Use of Approved Drugs for Unlabeled Indications," 12 FDA Drug Bulletin 4 (April 1982).
6. See also Chaney vs. Heckler, 718 F.2d 1174, 1180 (D.C. App. 1983), rev'd on other grounds, 470 U.S. 821 (1985).
7. Pub L No. 105-115, 111 Stat. 2296 (1997).
8. 21 U.S.C.A. 279g.
9. 21 U.S.C.A. 360aaa, et seq., Requirements for dissemination of treatment information on drugs or devices.
10. Washington Legal Foundation vs. Henney, 56 F.Supp.2d 81 (D.D.C. 1999).
11. Washington Legal Foundation v. Henney, 202 F.3d 331 (D.C. Cir., 2000).
12. See, e.g., Winkjer vs. Herr, 277 N.W.2d 579, 583 (N.D. 1979).
13. See, e.g., Blackwell vs. Hurst, 46 Cal.App.4th 939, 942 (Cal. App. 1996).
14. See, e.g., Rallings vs. Evans, 930 S.W.2d 259, 262 (Texas Ct. App. 1996).
15. See, e.g., Ellis vs. Oliver, 323 S.C. 121, 125 (1996).
16. Haught vs. Maceluch, 681 F.2d 291 (5th Cir. 1982).
17. Ohligschlager vs. Proctor Community Hospital, 303 N.E.2d 392 (Ill. 1973).
18. See also Mulder vs. Parke Davis & Company, 181 N.W.2d 882 (Minn. 1970).
19. See Young vs. Cerniak, 467 N.E.2d 1045 (Ill. App. 1984).
20. See Nicolla vs. Fasulo, 557 N.Y.S.2d 539 (App. Div. 1990).
21. Morlino vs. Medical Center of Ocean County, 295 N.J.Super. 113, 122 (1996).
22. See also Ramon vs. Farr, 770 P.2d 131 (Utah 1989).
23. See, e.g., Ross vs. Hodges, 234 So.2d 905 (Miss. 1970).
24. See, e.g., Aiken vs. Clary, 396 S.W.2d 668 (Mo. 1965).
25. See, e.g., Cobbs vs. Grant, 502 P.2d 1 (Cal. 1972).
26. See, e.g., Wilkinson vs. Vesey, 295 A.2d 676 (R.I. 1972).
27. See also Pa. Stat. Ann. Tit. 40, §1301.103 (Purdon Supp. 1997).
28. See also R.I. Gen. Laws §9-19-32 (1996).
29. See also Wash. Rev. Code Ann.§7.70.050(1)(c) (West Supp. 1997).
30. Reinhardt vs. Colton, 337 N.W.2d 88 (Minn. 1983).
31. See 21 U.S.C. §360(g)(1).
32. See Cedars North Towers Pharmacy, Inc. vs. United States of America, 824 CCH Food-Drug-Cosmetics Law Reporter par 38,200 (S.D.Fla. 1978).
33. Sullivan vs. Henry, 287 S.E.2d 652 (Ga.App. 1982).
34. Blanton vs. United States, 428 F.Supp. 360 (D.D.C. 1977).
35. Nelson vs. Gaunt, 125 Cal.App.3d 623 (1981).
36. Daum vs. Spinecare Medical Group, Inc., 52 Cal. App.4th 1285 (Cal.App.1997).

Appendixes and Index

U.S. and Canadian Schedules for Controlled Substances

U.S. Classifications

Schedule	Definition
I	No recognized legal medical use; used in research with appropriate registration
II	Most stringent classification for drugs; these drugs have legitimate medical use and very high abuse potential; inventory and distribution are tightly controlled; prescriptions not refillable
III	Significant abuse potential, but less than Schedule II; up to 5 authorized refills within 6 months
IV	Abuse potential lower than Schedule III; up to 5 authorized refills within 6 months
V	Lowest abuse potential; prescriber may authorize as many refills as desired; some drugs in this class may be available without a prescription

Canadian Classifications

Schedule	Definition
N (Narcotics)	Products containing narcotics; depending on the preparation, may be subject to strict or lesser regulatory controls
C (Controlled Drugs, Controlled Drugs Preparations)	Non-narcotic preparations with abuse potential (includes schedules E, F, G, H); depending on content, various regulatory controls apply

Schedules for Controlled Substances

Drug	United States	Canada
Heroin, LSD, peyote, marijuana, mescaline, phencyclidine	Schedule I (CI)	Schedule H
Opium, fentanyl, morphine, meperidine, methadone, oxycodone (and combinations), hydromorphone, codeine (single-drug entity), cocaine	Schedule II (CII)	Schedule N
Short-acting barbiturates	Schedule II	Schedule C
Amphetamine, methylphenidate	Schedule II	Schedule G
Codeine combinations, hydrocodone combinations, glutethimide, paregoric, phendimetrazine, thiopental, testosterone, other androgens	Schedule III (CIII)	Schedule F
Benzodiazepines (e.g., diazepam, midazolam), chloral hydrate, meprobamate, phenobarbital, propoxyphene (and combinations), pentazocine (and combinations), methohexital	Schedule IV (CIV)	Schedule F
Antidiarrrheals and antitussives with opioid derivatives	Schedule V (CV)	

Appendix B.

U.S. Food and Drug Administration Pregnancy Classifications

Classification	Definition
A	No risk demonstrated to the fetus in any trimester
B	No adverse effects in animals; no human studies available
C	Only given after risks to the fetus are considered; animal studies have shown adverse reactions; no human studies available
D	Definite fetal risks; may be given in spite of risks if needed in life-threatening situations
X	Absolute fetal abnormalities; not to be used at any time during pregnancy

Appendix C.

Agents That Affect the Fetus and Nursing Infant

Angelo J. Mariotti, D.D.S., Ph.D.

A teratogen is a drug or chemical that induces alterations in the formation of cells, tissues and organs and thus creates physical defects in a developing embryo or fetus. Teratogens act via a number of diverse mechanisms to ultimately damage the developing fetus. Drug-induced teratogenic changes can occur only during organogenesis; however, drug-induced toxicological changes affect the fetus after completion of tissue or organ formation because these drugs induce degenerative changes in formed tissue or organs. Unfortunately, the teratogenic or toxicological potential of many drugs has not been evaluated in utero.

To be safe, drugs that are known to be innocuous to the embryo or fetus should be the drugs of choice in the dental management of pregnant women. Drugs with unknown teratogenic or toxicological potential should be prescribed in consultation with the patient's obstetrician and used sparingly. Drugs with known teratogenic or toxicological effects should not be considered for use during dental procedures.

To aid health care providers, the U.S. Food and Drug Administration has developed a rating system for drugs that affect the fetus. The five categories the FDA uses to evaluate drug effects during pregnancy are shown in Appendix B.

The first list below comprises drugs that require special precautions when used during pregnancy. Many of these drugs are not teratogenic, but the potential side effect of each agent may affect the embryo or fetus; therefore, each drug should be carefully investigated. If you have questions about any drug that might cause problems during pregnancy, contact an obstetrician or the Organization of Teratology Information Services (1-888-285-3410 or "http://orpheus.ucsd.edu/otis/home.html") for agencies in your region that deal with potential harmful drugs to pregnant women.

The second list is of drugs that are excreted in breast milk.

Pregnancy Caution Information List

Alprazolam (systemic)

Amitriptyline (systemic)

Amobarbital (systemic)

Aprobarbital (systemic)

Ascorbic acid (systemic)

Aspirin, alone and in combination (systemic)

Atropine (systemic)

Bupivacaine (parenteral-local)

Butabarbital, alone and in combinations (systemic)

Butorphanol (systemic)

Caffeine (systemic)

Calcium carbonate (oral-local)

Carbamazepine (systemic)

Cefoxitin (systemic)

Chloral hydrate (systemic)

Chloramphenicol (systemic)

Chlordiazepoxide, alone and in combination (systemic)

Ciprofloxacin (ophthalmic)

Clarithromycin (systemic)

Clonazepam (systemic)

Clonidine (systemic)

Continued on next page

Clorazepate (systemic)
Clotrimazole
Codeine
Cortisone (systemic)
Cyanocobalamin Co 57 (systemic)
Demeclocycline (systemic)
Desoximetasone
Dexamethasone
Diclofenac (systemic)
Diflunisal
Epinephrine
Erythromycin estolate
Ethchlorvynol (systemic)
Etidocaine (parenteral-local)
Etodolac (systemic)
Fenoprofen (systemic)
Fentanyl (systemic)
Fluconazole (systemic)
Flurazepam (systemic)
Flurbiprofen (systemic)
Griseofulvin (systemic)
Halazepam (systemic)
Haloperidol (systemic)
Halothane (systemic)
Hydralazine (systemic)
Hydrocodone (systemic)
Hydrocortisone (systemic)

Hydromorphone (systemic)
Hyoscyamine (systemic)
Ibuprofen (systemic)
Indomethacin (systemic)
Iodine (topical)
Ketazolam (systemic)
Ketoprofen (systemic)
Ketorolac (systemic)
Labetalol (systemic)
Lidocaine (parenteral-local)
Lorazepam (systemic)
Meclizine (systemic)
Meclofenamate (systemic)
Mefenamic acid (systemic)
Meperidine (systemic)
Methadone (systemic)
Metronidazole (systemic)
Miconazole (vaginal)
Minocycline (systemic)
Morphine (systemic)
Naproxen (systemic)
Neomycin (oral-local)
Nicotine (systemic)
Nitrous oxide (systemic)
Norfloxacin (systemic)
Ofloxacin (ophthalmic)
Orphenadrine, aspirin and caffeine (systemic)

Oxazepam (systemic)
Oxycodone (systemic)
Oxytetracycline (systemic)
Paregoric (systemic)
Penbutolol (systemic)
Pentazocine (systemic)
Phenobarbital (systemic)
Phenylbutazone (systemic)
Prednisone (systemic)
Procaine (parenteral-local)
Promazine (systemic)
Promethazine (systemic)
Propoxyphene (systemic)
Pseudoephedrine (systemic)
Rifampin (systemic)
Salicylic acid (topical)
Salsalate (systemic)
Secobarbital (systemic)
Sufentanil (systemic)
Sulindac (systemic)
Tetracaine (parenteral-local)
Tetracycline (systemic)
Triamcinolone (systemic)
Triazolam (systemic)
Vitamin A (systemic)

Drugs Excreted in Breast Milk

Ampicillin
Antihistamines*
Aspirin
Atropine
Barbiturates
Cephalexin*
Cephalothin*
Chloral hydrate
Chloramphenicol
Codeine
Corticosteroids
Demeclocycline*

Diazepam
Diphenhydramine*
Erythromycin*
Fluorides*
Lincomycin*
Meperidine
Meprobamate
Methacycline
Methadone
Morphine
Narcotics
Oxacillin*

Penicillins*
Pentazocine*
Phenobarbital
Propantheline bromide*
Propoxyphene
Salicylates
Scopolamine*
Streptomycin
Tetracyclines*
Thiopental sodium*

* No adverse effects reported.
Source: United States Pharmacopeial Convention, Inc. Drug information for the health care professional.
Vol. I. 1995: Rockville, Md.: United States Pharmacopeial Convention, Inc.; 1995:3027-32.

Prevention of Bacterial Endocarditis

Prevention of Bacterial Endocarditis: A Statement for the Dental Profession

ADA Council on Scientific Affairs

The new American Heart Association (AHA) recommendations for the prevention of bacterial endocarditis represent a substantial departure from past guidelines. The new recommendations reflect a better understanding of the disease and its potential prevention. Major changes involve the indications for prophylaxis, antibiotic choice and dosing, ancillary procedures that may reduce bacteremic risk, a detailed discussion of mitral valve prolapse and greater attention to the medicolegal aspects of endocarditis.

Previously, antibiotic prophylaxis was suggested for dental procedures associated with any amount of bleeding. Now, only those that are associated with significant bleeding are recommended for prophylaxis as dictated by clinical judgment. This allows for a substantial number of dental procedures to be eliminated from the prophylaxis recommendation. A table is provided that delineates dental treatment procedures into those that may be associated with significant bleeding and those that pose negligible or no bacteremic risk. Recommended antibiotic prophylaxis regimens now consist of a single preprocedural dose; no second dose is recommended. If the clinical decision is made not to premedicate and significant unanticipated bleeding occurs, the dental professional may then begin the antibiotic and continue the procedure. A gentle prerinse with chlorhexidine can be employed, but gingival (subgingival) irrigation is not recommended due to conflicting data on efficacy in bacteremia reduction, the lack of data establishing that gingival irrigation will reduce endocarditis, its own potential for causing bacteremias and the lack of any standardized regimen.

It is recommended that all identified at-risk patients be strongly encouraged to maintain good oral health via professional and home care and plaque control procedures. This is particularly true for patients prior to cardiovascular surgical procedures. It is acknowledged that plaque control may induce bacteremias, but with much less or negligible risk as compared to a mouth with ongoing inflammation. The recommendations identify at-risk patients both medically and dentally.

Importantly, the medicolegal aspects of bacterial endocarditis are thoroughly addressed in the new recommendations, particularly regarding causation. The incubation period for most cases of endocarditis is defined, as are several factors that must be considered before attempting to attribute cause and effect to a given invasive procedure. It is acknowledged that most endocarditis is not associated with invasive procedures and that professional dental care is responsible for only a small percentage of endocarditis cases. However, antibiotic prophylaxis is still recommended prior to dental procedures associated with significant bleeding in high- and moderate-risk patients who are at a much greater risk of endocarditis than the general population. These recommendations are not intended as the standard of care, and practitioners should use their own clinical judgment in individual cases or special circumstances.

The new AHA recommendations for the prevention of bacterial endocarditis better define at-risk patients and the dental procedures to be covered by antibiotic prophylaxis. As a result, these new recommendations should aid in both patient and practitioner compliance, and diminish the adverse effects of prophylaxis including its role in promoting the development of microbial antibiotic resistance.

Prevention of Bacterial Endocarditis: Recommendations by the American Heart Association

The following tables are reprinted with permission of the publisher from Dajani AS, Taubert KA, Wilson W, et al. Prevention of Bacterial Endocarditis: Recommendations by the American Heart Association. JAMA 1997; 277:1794-801.

Cardiac Conditions Associated With Endocarditis.[1-21]

Endocarditis Prophylaxis Recommended

High-risk category

Prosthetic cardiac valves, including bioprosthetic and homograft valves

Previous bacterial endocarditis

Complex cyanotic congenital heart disease (e.g., single ventricle states, transposition of the great arteries, tetralogy of Fallot)

Surgically constructed systemic pulmonary shunts or conduits

Moderate-risk category

Most other congenital cardiac malformations (other than above and below)

Acquired valvar dysfunction (e.g., rheumatic heart disease)

Hypertrophic cardiomyopathy

Mitral valve prolapse with valvar regurgitation and/or thickened leaflets

Endocarditis Prophylaxis Not Recommended

Negligible-risk category (no greater than the general population)

Isolated secundum atrial septal defect

Surgical repair of atrial septal defect, ventricular septal defect, or patent ductus arteriosus (without residua beyond 6 mo)

Previous coronary artery bypass graft surgery

Mitral valve prolapse without valvar regurgitation

Physiologic, functional or innocent heart murmurs

Previous Kawasaki disease without valvar dysfunction

Previous rheumatic fever without valvar dysfunction

Cardiac pacemakers (intravascular and epicardial) and implanted defibrillators

Continued on next page

Dental Procedures and Endocarditis Prophylaxis.[22-25]

Dental extractions

Periodontal procedures including surgery, scaling and root planing, probing and recall maintenance

Dental implant placement and reimplantation of avulsed teeth

Endodontic (root canal) instrumentation or surgery only beyond the apex

Subgingival placement of antibiotic fibers or strips

Initial placement of orthodontic bands but not brackets

Intraligamentary local anesthetic injections

Prophylactic cleaning of teeth or implants where bleeding is anticipated

Restorative dentistry† (operative and prosthodontic) with or without retraction cord‡

Local anesthetic injections (nonintraligamentary)

Intracanal endodontic treatment; post placement and buildup

Placement of rubber dams

Postoperative suture removal

Placement of removable prosthodontic or orthodontic appliances

Taking of oral impressions

Fluoride treatments

Taking of oral radiographs

Orthodontic appliance adjustment

Shedding of primary teeth

* Prophylaxis is recommended for patients with high- and moderate-risk cardiac conditions.
† This includes restoration of decayed teeth (filling cavities) and replacement of missing teeth.
‡ Clinical judgment may indicate antibiotic use in selected circumstances that may create significant bleeding.

Reprinted with permission of the publisher from Dajani AS, Taubert KA, Wilson W, et al. Prevention of Bacterial Endocarditis: Recommendations by the American Heart Association. JAMA 1997;277:1794-801.

Prophylactic Regimens for Dental, Oral, Respiratory Tract, or Esophageal Procedures.[26-29]

Situation	Agent	Regimen*
Standard general prophylaxis	Amoxicillin	**Adults:** 2.0 g orally 1 h before procedure **Children:** 50 mg/kg orally 1 h before procedure
Unable to take oral medications	Ampicillin	**Adults:** 2.0 g intramuscularly (IM) or intravenously (IV) within 30 min before procedure **Children:** 50 mg/kg IM or IV within 30 min before procedure

* Total children's dose should not exceed adult dose.   Continued on next page

Reprinted with permission of the publisher from Dajani AS, Taubert KA, Wilson W, et al. Prevention of Bacterial Endocarditis: Recommendations by the American Heart Association. JAMA 1997;277:1794-801.

Prophylactic Regimens for Dental, Oral, Respiratory Tract, or Esophageal Procedures.[26-29] (cont.)

Situation	Agent	Regimen*
Allergic to penicillin	Clindamycin	**Adults:** 600 mg orally 1 h before procedure
		Children: 20 mg/kg orally 1 h before procedure
	OR	
	Cephalexin† or cefadroxil†	**Adults:** 2.0 g orally 1 h before procedure
		Children: 50 mg/kg orally 1 h before procedure
	OR	
	Azithromycin or clarithromycin	**Adults:** 500 mg orally 1 h before procedure
		Children: 15 mg/kg orally 1 h before procedure
Allergic to penicillin and unable to take oral medications	Clindamycin	**Adults:** 600 mg IV within 30 min before procedure
		Children: 20 mg/kg IV within 30 min before procedure
	OR	
	Cefazolin†	**Adults:** 1.0 g IM or IV within 30 min before procedure
		Children: 25 mg/kg IM or IV within 30 min before procedure

* Total children's dose should not exceed adult dose.
† Cephalosporins should not be used in individuals with immediate-type hypersensitivity reaction (urticaria, angioedema, or anaphylaxis) to penicillins.

Reprinted with permission of the publisher from Dajani AS, Taubert KA, Wilson W, et al. Prevention of Bacterial Endocarditis: Recommendations by the American Heart Association. JAMA 1997;277:1794-801.

1. Steckelberg JM, Wilson WR. Risk factors for infective endocarditis. Infect Dis Clin North Am. 1993;7:9-19.
2. Saiman L, Prince A, Gersony WM. Pediatric infective endocarditis in the modern era. J Pediatr. 1993;122:847-853.
3. Gersony WM, Hayes CJ, Driscoll DJ, et al. Bacterial endocarditis in patients with aortic stenosis, pulmonary stenosis, or ventricular septal defect. Circulation. 1993;87(suppl I):121-126.
4. Prabhu SD, O'Rourke RA. Mitral valve prolapse. In: Braunwald E, series ed, Rahimtoola SH, volume ed. Atlas of Heart Diseases: Valvular Heart Disease Vol XI. St. Louis, Mo: Mosby-Year Book Inc;1997:10.1-10.18.
5. Boudoulas H, Wooley CF. Mitral valve prolapse. In: Emmanouilides GC, Riemenschneider TA, Allen HD, Gutgesell HP, eds. Moss and Adams Heart Disease in Infants, Children, and Adolescents Including the Fetus and Young Adult. 5th ed. Baltimore, Md: Williams & Wilkins; 1995; 1063-1086.
6. Carabello BA. Mitral valve disease. Curr Probl Cardiol. 1993;7:423-478.
7. Devereux RB, Hawkins I, Kramer-Fox R, et al. Complications of mitral valve prolapse: disproportionate occurrence in men and older patients. Am J Med. 1986; 81:751-758.
8. Danchin N, Briancon S, Mathieu P, et al. Mitral valve prolapse as a risk factor for infective endocarditis. Lancet. 1989;1:743-745.
9. MacMahon SW, Roberts JK, Kramer-Fox R, et al. Mitral valve prolapse and infective endocarditis. Am Heart J. 1987;113:1291-1298.
10. Marks AR, Choong CY, Sanfilippo AJ, Ferre M, Weyman AE. Identification of high-risk and low-risk subgroups of patients with mitral-valve prolapse. N Engl J Med. 1989;320:1031-1036.
11. Devereux RB, Frary CJ, Kramer-Fox R, Roberts RB, Ruchlin HS. Cost-effectiveness of infective endocarditis prophylaxis for mitral valve prolapse with or without a mitral regurgitant murmur. Am J Cardiol. 1994;74:1024-1029.
12. Zuppiroli A, Rinaldi M, Kramer-Fox R, Favili S, Roman MJ, Devereux RB. Natural history of mitral valve prolapse. Am J Cardiol. 1995;75:1028-1032.
13. Wooley CF, Baker PB, Kolibash AJ, et al. The floppy, myxomatous mitral valve, mitral valve prolapse, and mitral regurgitation. Prog Cardiovasc Dis. 1991;33:397-433.
14. Morales AR, Romanelli R, Boucek RJ, Tate LG, Alvarez RT, Davis JT. Myxoid heart disease: an assessment of extravalvular cardiac pathology in severe mitral valve prolapse. Human Pathol. 1992;23:129-137.
15. Weissman NJ, Pini R, Roman MJ, Kramer-Fox R, Andersen HS, Devereux RB. In vivo mitral valve morphology and motion in mitral valve prolapse. Am J Cardiol. 1994;73:1080-1088.
16. Nishimura RA, McGoon MD, Shub C, et al. Echocardiographically documented mitral-valve prolapse. N Engl J Med. 1985;313:1305-1309.
17. McKinsey DS, Ratts TE, Bisno AL. Underlying cardiac lesions in adults with infective endocarditis. Am J Med. 1987;82:681-688.
18. Devereux RB, Kramer-Fox R, Kligfield P. Mitral valve prolapse: causes, clinical manifestations, and management. Ann Intern Med. 1989;111:305-317.
19. Stoddard MF, Prince CR, Dillon S, Longaker RA, Morris GT, Liddell NE. Exercise-induced mitral regurgitation is a predictor of morbid events in subjects with mitral valve prolapse. J Am Coll Cardiol. 1995;25:693-699.
20. Awadallah SM, Kavey REW, Byrum CJ, Smith FC, Kveselis DA, Blackman MS. The changing pattern of infective endocarditis in childhood. Am J Cardiol. 1991;68:90-94.
21. Durack DT. Prevention of infective endocarditis. N Engl J Med 1995;332:38-44.
22. Cheitlin MD, Alpert JS, Armstrong WF, et al. ACC/AHA guidelines for the clinical application of echocardiography: a report of the American College of Cardiology/American Heart Association Task Force on Practice Guidelines (Committee on Clinical Application of Echocardiography). Circulation. 1997;95:1686-1744.
23. Pallasch TJ, Slots J. Antibiotic prophylaxis and the medically compromised patient. Periodontol 2000. 1996;10:107-138.
24. Bender IB, Naidorf IJ, Garvey GJ. Bacterial endocarditis: a consideration for physicians and dentists. J Am Dent Assoc. 1984;109:415-420.
25. Guntheroth WG. How important are dental procedures as a cause of infective endocarditis? Am J Cardiol. 1984;54:797-801.
26. Dajani AS, Bisno AL, Chung KJ, et al. Prevention of bacterial endocarditis. JAMA. 1990;264:2919-2922.
27. Durack DT. Prevention of infective endocarditis. N Engl J Med 1995;332:38-44.
28. Dajani AS, Bawdon RE, Berry MC. Oral amoxicillin as prophylaxis for endocarditis: what is the optimal dose? Clin Infect Dis. 1994;18:157-160.
29. Rouse MS, Steckelberg JM, Brandt CM, Patel R, Miro JM, Wilson WR. Efficacy of azithromycin or clarithromycin for the prophylaxis of viridans group streptococcus experimental endocarditis. Antimicrob Agents Chemother. 1997; 41:1673-6.

Antibiotic Prophylaxis for Dental Patients With Total Joint Replacements

Advisory Statement: Antibiotic Prophylaxis for Dental Patients With Total Joint Replacements

American Dental Association; American Academy of Orthopaedic Surgeons

Approximately 450,000 total joint arthroplasties are performed annually in the United States. Deep infections of these total joint replacements usually result in failure of the initial operation and the need for extensive revision. Due to the use of perioperative antibiotic prophylaxis and other technical advances, deep infection occurring in the immediate postoperative period resulting from intraoperative contamination has been markedly reduced in the past 20 years.

Patients who are about to have a total joint arthroplasty should be in good dental health prior to surgery and should be encouraged to seek professional dental care if necessary. Patients who already have had a total joint arthroplasty should perform effective daily oral hygiene procedures to remove plaque (for example, by using manual or powered toothbrushes, interdental cleaners or oral irrigators) to establish and maintain good oral health. The risk of bacteremia is far more substantial in a mouth with ongoing inflammation than in one that is healthy and

employing these home oral hygiene devices.[1]

Bacteremias can cause hematogenous seeding of total joint implants, both in the early postoperative period and for many years following implantation.[2] It appears that the most critical period is up to 2 years after joint placement.[3] In addition, bacteremias may occur in the course of normal daily life and concurrently with dental and medical procedures.[4-6] It is likely that many more oral bacteremias are spontaneously induced by daily events than are dental treatment-induced.[6] Presently, no scientific evidence supports the position that antibiotic prophylaxis to prevent hematogenous infections is required prior to dental treatment in patients with total joint prostheses.[1] The risk/benefit[7,8] and cost/effectiveness[7,9] ratios fail to justify the administration of routine antibiotic prophylaxis. The analogy of late prosthetic joint infections with infective endocarditis is invalid, as the anatomy, blood supply, micro-organisms and mechanisms of infection are all different.[10]

It is likely that bacteremias associated with acute infection in the oral cavity,[11,12] skin, respiratory, gastrointestinal and urogenital systems and/or other sites can and do cause late implant infection.[12] Any patient with a total joint prosthesis with acute orofacial infection should be vigorously treated as any other patient with elimination of the source of the infection (incision and drainage, endodontics, extraction) and appropriate therapeutic antibiotics when indicated.[1,12] Practitioners should maintain a high index of suspicion for any unusual signs and symptoms (such as fever, swelling, pain, joint that is warm to touch) in patients with total joint prostheses.

Antibiotic prophylaxis is not indicated for dental patients with pins, plates and screws, nor is it routinely indicated for most dental patients with total joint replacements. This position agrees with that taken by the ADA Council on Dental Therapeutics[13] and the American Academy of Oral Medicine,[14] and is similar to that taken by of the British Society for Antimicrobial Chemotherapy.[15] There is limited evidence that some immunocompromised patients with total joint replacements (Box, "Patients at Potential Increased Risk of Hematogenous Total Joint Infection") may be at higher risk for hematogenous infections.[12,16-21] Antibiotic prophylaxis for such patients undergoing dental procedures with a higher bacteremic risk (as defined in the box "Incidence Stratification of Bacteremic Dental Procedures") should be considered

using an empirical regimen (Box, "Suggested Antibiotic Prophylaxis Regimens"). In addition, antibiotic prophylaxis may be considered when the higher-risk dental procedures (again, as defined in the box "Incidence Stratification...") are performed on dental patients within 2 years post-implant surgery,[3] on those who have had previous prosthetic joint infections and on those with some other conditions (Box, "Patients at Potential Increased Risk...").

Occasionally, a patient with a total joint prosthesis may present to the dentist with a recommendation from his or her physician that is not consistent with these guidelines. This could be due to lack of familiarity with the guidelines or to special considerations about the patient's medical condition that are not known to the dentist. In this situation, the dentist is encouraged to consult with the physician to determine if there are any special considerations that might affect the dentist's decision on whether or not to premedicate, and may wish to share a copy of these guidelines with the physician if appropriate. After this consultation, the dentist may decide to follow the physician's recom-

---

Patients at Potential Increased Risk of Hematogenous Total Joint Infection.*

Immunocompromised/immunosuppressed patients

Inflammatory arthropathies: rheumatoid arthritis, systemic lupus erythematosus

Disease-, drug- or radiation-induced immunosuppression

Other patients

Insulin-dependent (Type 1) diabetes

First 2 years following joint placement

Previous prosthetic joint infections

Malnourishment

Hemophilia

* Based on Ching and colleagues,[12] Brause,[16] Murray and colleagues,[17] Poss and colleagues,[18] Jacobson and colleagues,[19] Johnson and Bannister,[20] and Jacobson and colleagues.[21]

Incidence Stratification of Bacteremic Dental Procedures.*

Dental extractions

Periodontal procedures including surgery, subgingival placement of antibiotic fibers/strips, scaling and root planing, probing, recall maintenance

Dental implant placement and reimplantation of avulsed teeth

Endodontic (root canal) instrumentation or surgery only beyond the apex

Initial placement of orthodontic bands but not brackets

Intraligamentary local anesthetic injections

Prophylactic cleaning of teeth or implants where bleeding is anticipated

Restorative dentistry§ (operative and prosthodontic) with/without retraction cord**

Local anesthetic injections (nonintraligamentary)

Intracanal endodontic treatment; post placement and buildup

Placement of rubber dam

Postoperative suture removal

Placement of removable prosthodontic/orthodontic appliances

Taking of oral impressions

Fluoride treatments

Taking of oral radiographs

Orthodontic appliance adjustment

* Adapted with permission of the publisher from Dajani AS, Taubert KA, Wilson W, et al.[22]
† Prophylaxis should be considered for patients with total joint replacement that meet the criteria in the box "Patients at Potential Increased Risk of Hematogenous Total Joint Infection." No other patients with orthopedic implants should be considered for antibiotic prophylaxis prior to dental treatment/procedures.
‡ Prophylaxis not indicated.
§ This includes restoration of carious (decayed) or missing teeth.
** Clinical judgment may indicate antibiotic use in selected circumstances that may create significant bleeding.

Suggested Antibiotic Prophylaxis Regimens.*

Patient type	Regimen
Patients not allergic to penicillin: cephalexin, cephradine or amoxicillin	2 grams orally 1 h prior to dental procedure
Patients not allergic to penicillin and unable to take oral medications: cefazolin or ampicillin	Cefazolin 1 g or ampicillin 2 g intramuscularly or intravenously 1 h prior to the procedure
Patients allergic to penicillin: clindamycin	600 mg orally 1 h prior to the dental procedure
Patients allergic to penicillin and unable to take oral medications: clindamycin	600 mg IM/IV 1 h prior to the procedure

* No second doses are recommended for any of these dosing regimens.

mendation or, if in the dentist's professional judgment antibiotic prophylaxis is not indicated, may decide to proceed without antibiotic prophylaxis. The dentist is ultimately responsible for making treatment recommendations for his or her patients based on the dentist's professional judgment. Any perceived potential benefit of antibiotic prophylaxis must be weighed against the known risks of antibiotic toxicity; allergy; and development, selection and transmission of microbial resistance.

This statement provides guidelines to supplement practitioners in their clinical judgment regarding antibiotic prophylaxis for dental patients with a total joint prosthesis. It is not intended as the standard of care nor as a substitute for clinical judgment as it is impossible to make recommendations for all conceivable clinical situations in which bacteremias originating from the oral cavity may occur. Practitioners must exercise their own clinical judgment in determining whether or not antibiotic prophylaxis is appropriate.

The ADA/AAOS Expert Panel consisted of Robert H. Fitzgerald Jr., M.D.; Jed J. Jacobson, D.D.S., M.S., M.P.H.; James V. Luck Jr., M.D.; Carl L. Nelson, M.D.; J. Phillip Nelson, M.D.; Douglas R. Osmon, M.D.; and Thomas J. Pallasch, D.D.S. The staff liaisons were Clifford W. Whall Jr., Ph.D., for the ADA, and William W. Tipton Jr., M.D., for the AAOS.

1. Pallasch TJ, Slots J. Antibiotic prophylaxis and the medically compromised patient. Periodontology 2000 1996;10:107-38.
2. Rubin R, Salvati EA, Lewis R. Infected total hip replacement after dental procedures. Oral Surg Oral Med Oral Pathol 1976;41(1):13-23.
3. Hansen AD, Osmon DR, Nelson CL. Prevention of deep prosthetic joint infection. Am J Bone Joint Surg 1996;78-A (3):458-71.
4. Bender IB, Naidorf IJ, Garvey GJ. Bacterial endocarditis: a consideration for physicians and dentists. JADA 1984;109:415-20.
5. Everett ED, Hirschmann JV. Transient bacteremia and endocarditis prophylaxis: a review. Medicine 1977;56:61-77.
6. Guntheroth WG. How important are dental procedures as a cause of infective endocarditis? Am J Cardiol 1984;54:797-801.
7. Jacobsen JJ, Schweitzer SO, DePorter DJ, Lee JJ. Antibiotic prophylaxis for dental patients with joint prostheses? A decision analysis. Int J Technol Assess Health Care 1990;6:569-87.
8. Tsevat J, Durand-Zaleski I, Pauker SG. Cost-effectiveness of antibiotic prophylaxis for dental procedures in patients with artificial joints. Am J Public Health 1989;79:739-43.
9. Norden CW. Prevention of bone and joint infections. Am J Med 1985;78(6B):229-32.
10. McGowan DA. Dentistry and endocarditis. Br Dent J 1990;169:69.
11. Bartzokas CA, Johnson R, Jane M, Martin MV, Pearce PK, Saw Y. Relation between mouth and haematogenous infections in total joint replacement. Br Med J 1994;309:506-8.
12. Ching DWI, Gould IM, Rennie JAN, Gibson PII. Prevention of late haematogenous infection in major prosthetic joints. J Antimicrob Chemother 1989;23: 676-80.
13. Council on Dental Therapeutics. Management of dental patients with prosthetic joints. JADA 1990; 121:537-8.
14. Eskinazi D, Rathbun W. Is systematic antimicrobial prophylaxis justified in dental patients with prosthetic joints? Oral Surg Oral Med Oral Pathol 1988;66:430-1.
15. Cawson RA. Antibiotic prophylaxis for dental treatment: for hearts but not for prosthetic joints. Br Dent J 1992;304:933-4.
16. Brause BD. Infections associated with prosthetic joints. Clin Rheum Dis 1986;12:523-35.
17. Murray RP, Bourne MH, Fitzgerald RH Jr. Metachronous infection in patients who have had more than one total joint arthroplasty. J Bone Joint Surg [Am] 1991;73(10):1469-74.
18. Poss R, Thornhill TS, Ewald FC, Thomas WH, Batte NJ, Sledge CB. Factors influencing the incidence and outcome of infection following total joint arthroplasty. Clin Orthop 1984;182:117-26.
19. Jacobson JJ, Millard HD, Plezia R, Blankenship JR. Dental treatment and late prosthetic joint infections. Oral Surg Oral Med Oral Pathol 1986;61:413-17.
20. Johnson DP, Bannister GG. The outcome of infected arthroplasty of the knee. J Bone Joint Surg [Br] 1986;68(2):289-91.
21. Jacobson JJ, Patel B, Asher G, Wooliscroft JO, Schaberg D. Oral Staphylcoccus in elderly subjects with rheumatoid arthritis. J Am Geriatr Soc 1997;45:1-5.
22. Dajani AS, Taubert KA, Wilson W, et al. Prevention of bacterial endocarditis: Recommendations by the American Heart Association. From the Committee on Rheumatic Fever, Endocarditis and Kawasaki Disease, Council on Cardiovascular Disease in the Young. JAMA 1997;277:1794-1801.

A Legal Perspective on Antibiotic Prophylaxis

Kathleen M. Todd, J.D.

The Advisory Statement on Antibiotic Prophylaxis for Dental Patients with Total Joint Replacements reflects growing concern about the development of microbial resistance owing to the inappropriate use of antibiotics and recognizes that there are risks as well as benefits involved in the use of antibiotics. It delineates the limited circumstances in which antibiotic prophylaxis should be considered for dental patients who have had total joint replacements and cautions physicians and dentists to weigh the perceived potential benefits of antibiotic prophylaxis against the known risks of antibiotic toxicity, allergies and the development of microbial resistance.

But what should the dentist do if the patient brings to the appointment a recommendation for premedication from his or her physician with which the dentist disagrees? Should the dentist ignore the physician's recommendation or simply defer to the physician's judgment?

Neither approach is prudent from a risk management perspective. On the one hand, the physician's recommendation may be based on facts about the patient's medical condition that are not known to the dentist. On the other, the physician may not be familiar with this advisory statement or that premedication may be indicated for some dental procedures but not for others. The careful dentist will attempt to ascertain the basis for the physician's recommendation and to acquaint the physician with the reasons why the dentist disagrees. Ideally, consensus can be reached. Most dentists would be uncomfortable with the thought of the physician's testifying in a malpractice suit that the dentist failed to follow the physician's treatment recommendation. However, the dentist who blindly follows the physician's recommendation, even though it conflicts with the dentist's professional judgment, will not be able to defend himself or herself by claiming "the devil made me do it" if the patient sues. The courts recognize that each independent professional is ultimately responsible for his or her own treatment decisions.

The answer to this dilemma may lie in the concept of informed consent, which acknowledges the patient's right to autonomous decision making. Informed consent usually can be relied on to protect from legal liability the practitioner who respects the patient's wishes, as long as the practitioner is acting within the standard of care. However, for informed consent to be legally binding, it is incumbent on the practitioner to inform the patient of all reasonable treatment options and the risks and benefits of each. In the situation in question, the dentist would be prudent to inform the patient when the dentist's treatment recommendations differ from those of the patient's physician and even encourage the patient to discuss the treatment options with his or her physician before making a decision. All discussions with the patient and the patient's physician should be well-documented. Of course, allowing the patient to choose assumes that both the dentist's and the physician's treatment recommendations are acceptable.

Dentists are not obligated to render treatment that they deem not to be in the patient's best interest, simply because the patient requests it. In such circumstances, referral to another practitioner may be the only solution. ■

The above information should not be construed as legal advice or a standard of care. A dentist should always consult his or her own attorney for answers to the dentist's specific legal questions.

The material in this appendix first appeared in the following two sources:

American Dental Association and American Academy of Orthopaedic Surgeons. Advisory statement: antibiotic prophylaxis for dental patients with total joint replacements. JADA 1997;128:1004-7.

Todd K. A legal perspective on antibiotic prophylaxis. JADA 1997;128:1007-8.

Appendix F.

Antibiotic Use in Dentistry

ADA Council on Scientific Affairs

Microbial resistance to antibiotics is increasing at an alarming rate. In the last few years, penicillin resistance in *Streptococcus pneumoniae* has risen from virtually zero to 25-60% of all isolates. Such penicillin resistance is increasing in viridans streptococci, and a significant number of *Prevotella* and *Porphyromonas* isolates exhibit β-lactamase production. Hospital epidemics of vancomycin-aminoglycoside-methicillin–resistant staphylococci and vancomycin-resistant, β-lactamase–producing enterococci contribute significantly to the 150,000 annual deaths in United States hospitals that result from nosocomial septicemias.

The major cause of this public health problem is the use of antibiotics in an inappropriate manner, leading to the selection and dominance of resistant microorganisms and/or the increased transfer of resistance genes from antibiotic-resistant to antibiotic-susceptible microorganisms. Inappropriate antibiotic use includes faulty dosing (too low a dose, too long a duration), wrong choice of antibiotic (microorganisms not likely to be sensitive), improper combination of antibiotics and therapeutic or prophylactic use in unwarranted and unproven clinical situations.

Antibiotics are properly employed only for the management of active infectious disease or the prevention of metastatic infection (such as infective endocarditis) in medically high-risk patients. Antibiotic prophylaxis to prevent medical perioperative surgical infections is documented effective in high-risk surgical procedures (cardiovascular, neurological, orthopedic) when the antibiotics are employed intraoperatively (begun shortly before and terminated shortly after the surgery). The use of antibiotics after routine dental treatment to prevent infection has generally not been proven effective. However, the use of antimicrobial therapy may be of benefit in selective surgical procedures and their postoperative management on an empirical basis, and further research in this area is encouraged.

Dentistry has been relatively conservative with antibiotic use and has likely not contributed greatly to the worldwide problems of antibiotic microbial resistance. Adherence to the above principles of antibiotic use will continue and even improve our record of judicious use of antibiotics. Antibiotics are one of the few kinds of drugs that affect not only a single patient but entire populations of individuals through their collective effects on microbial ecology. Our responsibility lies not only with our own patients but with a world of such patients.

This statement was adopted by the Council on Scientific Affairs in September 1996. It first appeared in ADA Council on Scientific Affairs. Antibiotic use in dentistry. JADA 1997;128:648.

Nitrous Oxide in the Dental Office

ADA Council on Scientific Affairs; ADA Council on Dental Practice

The safe use of nitrous oxide in the dental office has been an issue the ADA has monitored for many years. In 1977, an ad hoc committee convened by the Association published a report on the potential health hazards of trace anesthetics in dentistry.[1] Also in 1977, the National Institute of Occupational Safety and Health (NIOSH) reported that, by using several control measures, nitrous oxide levels of approximately 50 parts per million were achievable in dental operatories during routine dental anesthesia/analgesia.[2] A few years later, in 1980, the ADA Council on Dental Materials, Instruments and Equipment recommended that effective scavenging devices be installed and monitoring programs be instituted in dental offices in which nitrous oxide is used, and the council indicated that using these methods or devices would assist in keeping the levels of nitrous oxide at the lowest possible level.[3]

NIOSH continued its activities relating to nitrous oxide concentrations in the dental office and, in 1994, published an alert called "Request for Assistance in Controlling Exposures to Nitrous Oxide During Anesthetic Administration."[4] In the same year, NIOSH also reported on field evaluations and laboratory studies evaluating nitrous oxide scavenging systems and modifications in attempts to achieve the current NIOSH recommended exposure limit of 25 ppm during administration. NIOSH concluded that nitrous oxide levels may be controlled to about 25 ppm by maintaining leak-free delivery systems and using proper exhaust rates, better-fitting masks and auxiliary exhaust ventilation.[5]

In 1995 the ADA Council on Scientific Affairs convened an expert panel to review scientific literature on nitrous oxide and to revise recommendations on controlling nitrous oxide concentrations in the dental office. What follows is an overview of the conclusions reached by that panel.

Conclusions and Recommendations of the Expert Panel

Nitrous oxide continues to be a valuable agent for the control of pain and anxiety. However, chronic occupational exposure to nitrous oxide in offices not using scavenging systems may be associated with possible deleterious neurological and reproductive effects on dental personnel. Limited studies show that as little as three to five hours per week of unscavenged nitrous oxide exposure could result in adverse reproductive effects. In contrast, in dental offices using nitrous oxide scavenging systems, there has been no evidence of adverse health effects.[6] It is strongly recommended, therefore, that while there is no consensus on a recommended exposure limit to nitrous oxide, appropriate scavenging systems and methods of administration should be adopted. A protocol for controlling nitrous oxide is outlined below.

Recommendations for Controlling Nitrous Oxide Exposure

The expert panel identified a number of recommendations that are important to consider in the safe and effective use of nitrous oxide:

- The dental office should have a properly installed nitrous oxide delivery system. This includes appropriate scavenging equipment with a readily visible and accurate flow meter (or equivalent measuring device), a vacuum pump with the capacity for up to 45 L of air per min per workstation, and a variety of sizes of masks to ensure proper fit for individual patients.
- The vacuum exhaust and ventilation exhaust should be vented to the outside (for example, through the vacuum system) and not in close proximity to fresh-air intake vents.
- The general ventilation should provide good room air mixing.
- Each time the nitrous oxide machine is first turned on and every time a gas cylinder is changed, the pressure connections should be tested for leaks. High-pressure–line connections should be tested for leaks on a quarterly basis. A soap solution may be used to test for leaks. Alternatively, a portable infrared spectrophotometer can be used to diagnose an insidious leak.
- Prior to first daily use, all nitrous oxide equipment (reservoir bag, tubings, mask, connectors) should be inspected for worn parts, cracks, holes or tears. Replace as necessary.
- The mask may then be connected to the tubing and the vacuum pump turned on. All appropriate flow rates (that is, up to 45 L/min or per manufacturer's recommendations) should be verified.
- A properly sized mask should be selected and placed on the patient. A good, comfortable fit should be ensured. The reservoir (breathing) bag should not be over- or underinflated while the patient is breathing oxygen (before administering nitrous oxide).
- The patient should be encouraged to minimize talking and mouth breathing while the mask is in place.
- During administration, the reservoir bag should be periodically inspected for changes in tidal volume and the vacuum flow rate should be verified.
- On completing administration, 100% oxygen should be delivered to the patient for 5 min before removing the mask. In this way, both the patient and the system will be purged of residual nitrous oxide. Do not use an oxygen flush.
- Periodic (semiannual interval is suggested) personal sampling of dental personnel, with emphasis to chairside personnel exposed to nitrous oxide, should be conducted (for example, use of diffusive sampler [dosimeters] or infrared spectrophotometer).

Research Priorities

The expert panel identified a number of areas that require high-priority research:

- the elucidation of biological mechanisms that result in the adverse health effects associated with exposure to nitrous oxide;
- studies to gain a full understanding of the potential health effects of chronic low-level exposure to nitrous oxide, with emphasis on prospective studies that use direct nitrous oxide exposure measurement;
- the investigation of possible cognitive effects related to exposure to low levels of nitrous oxide;
- the development of equipment to evaluate and control exposure to nitrous oxide;
- the study of ventilation systems and air-exchange mechanisms for dental office designs;
- the evaluation of advantages associated with the use of nitrous oxide in combination with other sedative drugs.

The councils will continue to work with industry and the research community to address research and development needs that will further reduce occupational exposure to nitrous oxide.

1. ADA Ad Hoc Committee on Trace Anesthetics as Potential Health Hazard in Dentistry. Reports of sub-committees of the ADA Ad Hoc Committee on Trace Anesthetics as Potential Health Hazard in Dentistry: review and current status of survey. JADA 1977;95(10):787-90.
2. Whitcher CE, Zimmerman DC, Piziali RL. Control of occupational exposure to N2O in the dental operatory. Cincinnati: National Institute of Occupational Safety and Health, 1977; DHEW publication no. (NIOSH) 77-171.
3. Council on Dental Materials, Instruments and Equipment. Council position on nitrous oxide scavenging and monitoring devices. JADA 1980;101(1):62.
4. Alert: request for assistance in controlling exposures to nitrous oxide during anesthetic administration. Cincinnati: U.S. Department of Health and Human Services, Public Health Service, Centers for Disease Control, National Institute of Occupational Safety and Health, 1994; DHHS publication no. (NIOSH) 94100.
5. Technical report: control of nitrous oxide in dental operatories. Cincinnati: U.S. Department of Health and Human Services, Public Health Service, Centers for Disease Control and Prevention, National Institute of Occupational Safety and Health, Division of Physical Sciences and Engineering, Engineering Control Technology Branch, 1994; DHHS publication no. (NIOSH) 94-129.
6. Rowland AS, Baird DD, Weinberg CR, Shore DL, Shy CM, Wilcox AJ. Reduced fertility among women employed as dental assistants exposed to high levels of nitrous oxide. N Engl J Med 1992;327:993-7.

This material first appeared in ADA Council on Scientific Affairs and ADA Council on Dental Practice. Nitrous oxide in the dental office. JADA 1997; 128:864-5.

Appendix H.

Normal Laboratory Values for Adults

Hematologic Examinations

Examination	Range
Blood cells	
Erythrocytes (RBC) (per mm³)	
Men	4,100,000-5,900,000
Women	3,800,000-5,500,000
Leukocytes (WBC) (per mm³)	4,100-12,300
Differential leukocytes (per mm³)	
Segmented neutrophils	2,500-6,000 (40-60%)
Band neutrophils	0-500 (0-5%)
Juvenile neutrophils	0-100 (0-1%)
Myelocytes	0 (0%)
Lymphocytes	1,000-4,000 (15.5-46.6%)
Monocytes	200-800 (2.8-12.9%)
Eosinophils	50-300 (0-6%)
Basophils	0-100 (0-2.3%)
Platelets (Plt) (per mm³)	140,000-450,000

Continued on next page

Hematologic Examinations (cont.)

Examination	Range
Blood cells (cont.)	
Hemoglobin (Hgb) (g/100 mL)	
Men	13-17.5
Women	11.6-16.2
Hemoglobin, total glycolated (percentage)	4-8
Hematocrit (HcT) (percentage)	
Men	40-52
Women	35-47
Erythrocyte sedimentation rate (ESR) (mm/h)	
Men	1-13
Women	1-20
Mean corpuscular volume (MCV) (mm³)	86-98
Mean corpuscular hemoglobin (MCH) (pg/cell)	28-33
Mean corpuscular hemoglobin concentration (MCHC) (g/dL)	32-36
Coagulation screening tests	
Bleeding time	3-9 min
Coagulation time (Lee-White) (glass)	5-15 min
International normalized ratio (INR)	1
Prothrombin time	less than 2 s deviation from control
Activated partial thromboplastin time (aPTT)	25-37 s
Thrombin time (TT)	± 5 s of control

Chemical Constituents of Blood

Constituent	Range
Proteins (g/100 mL)	
Total serum protein	6.0-8.4
Albumin, serum	3.5-5.0
Globulin, serum	2.3-3.5
A/G ratio	1.5:1-3.1
Lipids (mg/dL)	
Cholesterol, total	
Men	140-284
Women	140-252
HDL cholesterol	40-60
LDL cholesterol	65-170
Triglycerides	30-170

Continued on next page

Chemical Constituents of Blood (cont.)

Constituent	Range
Enzymes	
Amylase	4-25 U/mL
Creatine phosphokinase—CPK (mU/mL)	
Men	5-55
Women	5-35
Lactate dehydrogenase—LDH (IU/L)	
Men	86-272
Women	82-249
Phosphatase (alkaline)	31-121 IU/L
Transaminases	
Aspartate transaminase (AST) (SGOT) (IU/L)	
Men	6-37
Women	5-37
Alanine transaminase (ALT) (SGPT) (IU/L)	
Men	6-46
Women	6-37
Urea nitrogen—BUN	
Urea nitrogen—BUN	4-24 mg/100 mL
Uric acid	
Men	2.4-8.7
Women	2.1-6.9
Creatinine (mg/100 mL)	
Men	0.5-1.3
Women	0.4-1.2
BUN/creatinine	
BUN/creatinine	7-20
Oxygen saturation (arterial)	
Oxygen saturation (arterial)	96-100%
PO_2	
PO_2	75-100 mm Hg
PCO_2	
PCO_2	35-45 mm Hg
CO_2 combining power	
CO_2 combining power	24-34 mEq/L
pH	
pH	7.35-7.45

Continued on next page

Chemical Constituents of Blood (cont.)

Constituent	Range
Electrolytes and inorganic constituents	
Chloride (Cl-serum)	94-111 mEq/L
Sodium (serum)	135-145 mEq/L
Potassium (serum)	3.5-5.0 mEq/L
Calcium (serum)	9-11 mg/100 mL
Phosphorus (serum) (mg/100 mL)	
Adults	2.3-5.1
Children	4-6.5
Iron, total	50-150 µg/100 mL
Total base	143-155 mEq/L
Glucose, fasting	
Glucose, fasting	70-110 mg/100 mL
Bilirubin (mg/100 mL)	
Total	0.3-1.2
Direct	0.0-0.2
Bromsulfalein (BSP)	Less than 5% retention (45 min)

Urine Analysis

Component	Range
Macroscopic (fresh specimen)	
Color	clear yellow
Specific gravity	1.010-1.025
pH	4.8-7.5
Microscopic	
Bacteria	0 (single specimen)
Leukocytes	0-few (single specimen) up to 1,800,000/24 h
Erythrocytes	0-few (single specimen) up to 500,000/24 h
Casts (hyaline)	0 (single specimen) up to 5,000/24 h
Chemical components	
Glucose	0 (single specimen) less than 100 mg/100 mL (24-h specimen)
Albumin	0 (single specimen) 10-150 mg/24 h
Ketones	0 (single specimen) less than 50 mg/24 h
Creatinine clearance	150-180 L/day/1.73 m^2 surface area

Appendix I.

Weights and Measures

Common Metric Measurements and Their Abbreviations

Metric measurement	Abbreviation
Weight	
gram	g
kilogram	kg
milligram	mg
microgram	μg
Volume	
liter	L
milliliter	mL
microliter	μL

Common Metric Equivalents

Metric measurement	Abbreviation
Weight	
0.000001 gram (g)	1 microgram (μg)
0.001 g	1 milligram (mg)
1 g	1,000 milligrams (mg)
	1,000,000 μg
1 kg	1,000 g
Volume	
0.001 milliliter (mL)	1 microliter (μL)
1 mL	0.001 liter (L)
1,000 mL	1 L

Measures of Volume

Metric	Apothecary
5 milliliters (mL)	1 dram
	1 teaspoonful
30 mL	1 fluid ounce
480 mL	1 pint
960 mL	1 quart

Measures of Weight

Metric	Apothecary
1 gram (g)	15 grains (gr)
4 g	60 gr
	1 dram
30 g	1 ounce (oz)
1 kilogram (kg)	2.2 pounds (lb)
60 milligram (mg)	1 gr

Appendix J.

Calculation of Local Anesthetic and Vasoconstrictor Dosages

Stanley F. Malamed, D.D.S.

Local Anesthetic Dosages

Percentage concentration	= mg/mL	x 1.8 = mg/cartridge
0.5	5	9
1	10	18
1.5	15	27
2	20	36
3	30	54
4	40	72

Vasoconstrictor Concentrations (Equivalency Formula and Use)

Dilution OR	mg/mL x 1.8	= mg/cartridge	Recommended use
1:1,000	1.0		Anaphylaxis (IM, SC)
1:10,000	0.1		Cardiac arrest (IV)
1:20,000	0.05	0.09	Local anesthesia; levonordefrin
1:50,000	0.02	0.036	Local anesthesia; epinephrine
1:80,000	0.0125	0.0225	Local anesthesia; epinephrine (UK)
1:100,000	0.01	0.018	Local anesthesia; epinephrine
1:200,000	0.005	0.009	Local anesthesia; epinephrine

HIV and Common Antiretroviral Medications

Michael Glick, D.M.D.

Treatment regimens for human immunodeficiency (HIV) disease are accompanied by a long list of prophylactic and maintenance medications. Prophylactic medications usually are indicated when the patient's immune system has deteriorated to a point at which opportunistic infections can be expected. The more common medications include anti–*Pneumocystis-carinii*-pneumonia (PCP) agents such as trimethoprim sulfamethoxazole; anticytomegalovirus agents such as oral ganciclovir; antifungal medications such as itraconazole and fluconazole; and antimycobacteria agents such as rifampin and isoniazid. Many of these medications interact with other medications commonly used in dentistry.

However, the fastest progress in treatment for HIV disease is in the field of antiretroviral medications. These medications directly or indirectly inhibit HIV replication through dif-

ferent mechanisms. Nucleoside reverse transcriptase inhibitors (NRTIs) and non-nucleoside reverse transcriptase inhibitors (NNRTIs) act as competitive inhibitors to an enzyme, reverse transcriptase, that the virus carries for the purpose of transcribing the viral RNA into viral DNA. The newest group is protease inhibitors. These medications prevent breakdown of proteins, produced by the HIV-infected cell, into appropriate sizes for viral production. Continuous development of antiretroviral medications will challenge all health care workers treating HIV-infected patients to keep apprised of new agents that usually are associated with a high degree of toxicity.

The table below presents antiretroviral medications used for HIV disease, which may interact with a number of drugs prescribed by dentists.

Common Antiretroviral Medications: Dental Considerations

Generic name	Brand name(s)	Interactions with drugs used in dentistry	Adverse effects relevant in dentistry
Nucleoside reverse transcriptase inhibitors (NRTIs)			
Abacavir	Ziagen	U	Xerostomia
Didanosine (ddI)	Videx	Reduces efficacy of itraconazole and ketoconazole, so these drugs should be administered more than 2 h apart from ddI administration	Peripheral neuropathy, xerostomia
		Reduces efficacy of quinolone and tetracyclines, so these drugs should be administered 2 h before or 6 h after ddI administration	

U: *Unavailable.*

Continued on next page

Common Antiretroviral Medications: Dental Considerations (cont.)

Generic name	Brand name(s)	Interactions with drugs used in dentistry	Adverse effects relevant in dentistry
Nucleoside reverse transcriptase inhibitors (NRTIs) (cont.)			
Lamivudine (3TC)	Epivir	U	None noted
Stavudine (ddC)	Zerit	U	Peripheral neuropathy
Zalcitabine (ddC)	HIVID	U	Peripheral neuropathy, oral ulcerations
Zidovudine (AZT, ZDV)	Retrovir	U	Anemia, neutropenia
Zidovudine + lamivudine	Combivir	U	None noted
Non-nucleoside reverse transcriptase inhibitors (NNRTIs)			
Delavirdine	Rescriptor	Inhibits cytochrome p-450 enzymes Levels decreased by phenobarbitol Increases levels of clarithromycin, dapsone Administration of buffered medications should be avoided within 2 h of delavirdine administration Contraindicated for concomitant administration with midazolam	None noted
Efavirenz	Sustiva	Induces cytochrome p-450 enzymes Increases levels of clarithromycin Concurrent use with midazolam, triazolam and clarithromycin should be avoided	Hallucinations, xerostomia
Nevirapine	Viramune	Induces cytochrome p-450 enzymes	None noted
Protease inhibitors*			
Amprenavir	Agenerase	U	Oral paresthesia
Indinavir	Crixivan	Inhibits cytochrome p-450 enzymes Avoid concurrent use with midazolam and triazolam Levels increased by ketaconazole	Thrombocytopenia
Nelfinavir	Viracept	Inhibits cytochrome p-450 enzymes Avoid concurrent use with midazolam and triazolam	None noted

U: Unavailable.

* Protease inhibitors have been associated with reactivation of hepatitis, diabetes mellitus, diminished response to narcotics, and an increased incidence of intraoral human papillomavirus infection.

Continued on next page

Common Antiretroviral Medications: Dental Considerations (cont.)

Generic name	Brand name(s)	Interactions with drugs used in dentistry	Adverse effects relevant in dentistry
Protease inhibitors* (cont.)			
Ritonavir	Norvir	Inhibits cytochrome p-450 enzymes (potent) Increases levels of clarithromycin Decreases levels of trimethoprim-sulfamethoxazole Contraindicated for concomitant administration with diazepam, meperidine, midazolam, piroxicam, propoxyphene	Dysgeusia
Saquinavir	Fortovase, Invirase	Inhibits cytochrome p-450 enzymes Levels decreased by dexamethasone	None noted
Ribonucleotide reductase inhibitors			
Hydroxyurea	Hydra	U	Bone marrow suppression, oral ulcerations
Nucleotide reverse transcriptase inhibitors			
Adefovir	Preveon	U	Anemia

U: Unavailable.

* Protease inhibitors have been associated with reactivation of hepatitis, diabetes mellitus, diminished response to narcotics, and an increased incidence of intraoral human papillomavirus infection.

Appendix L.

Sample Prescriptions and Prescription Abbreviations

Sample Prescriptions

The following prescriptions are not all-inclusive; they are provided only as examples of prescriptions commonly written by dentists. Drugs are listed by generic name in these examples. Those listed as drug combinations are available under a variety of brand names. Selection of any particular drug for inclusion in these examples in no way indicates recommendation of that agent over another. Abbreviations are presented for prescription directions. However, if in doubt, write the directions out.

Antibiotic for Patients Requiring Antibiotic Premedication

Drug	#	Directions	Abbreviated directions
Penicillin			
Amoxicillin capsules 500 mg	4	Sig: 4 capsules 1 hour before procedure	Sig: 4 caps 1 h ā procedure
For patients allergic to penicillins			
Clindamycin 150 mg	4	Sig: 4 capsules 1 hour before procedure	Sig: 4 caps 1 h ā procedure
Cephalexin capsules 500 mg*	4	Sig: 4 capsules 1 hour before procedure	Sig: 4 caps 1 h ā procedure
Azithromycin 250 mg	2	Sig: 2 capsules 1 hour before procedure	Sig: 2 caps 1 h ā procedure
Clarithromycin 500 mg	1	Sig: 1 tablet 1 hour before procedure	Sig: 1 tab 1 h ā procedure

Cephalosporins should not be used in patients with immediate-type hypersensitivity reaction (urticaria, angioedema or anaphylaxis) to penicillins.

To Reduce Excess Salivation

Drug	#	Directions	Abbreviated directions
Propantheline bromide 7.5 mg	6	Sig: 1-2 tablets ½ hour before procedure	Sig: 1-2 tab ½ h ā procedure
Atropine sulfate 0.3 mg	9	Sig: 2-3 tablets ½ hour before procedure	Sig: 2-3 tab ½ h ā procedure

To Increase Salivation

Drug	#	Directions	Abbreviated directions
Pilocarpine 5 mg	30	Sig: 1-2 tablets three times daily	Sig: 1-2 tab tid

To Reduce Patient Anxiety Before a Dental Procedure

Drug	#	Directions	Abbreviated directions
Diazepam 5 mg	V	Sig: 1-2 tablets 1 hour before sleep; 1-2 tablets 1 hour before procedure	Sig: 1 tab 1-2 hs; 1 tab 1-2 h ā procedure
Hydroxyzine pamoate 50 mg	V	Sig: 2 tablets 1 hour before sleep; 1-2 tablets 1 hour before procedure	Sig: 2 tab 1 hs; 1-2 tab 1 h ā procedure
Triazolam 0.25 mg	V	Sig: 1 tablet ½ hour before sleep; 1 tablet ½-1 hour before procedure	Sig: 1 tab ½ hs, 1 tab ½-1 h ā procedure
Alprazolam 0.5 mg	V	Sig: 1-2 tablets at bedtime; 1-2 tablets 1 hour before procedure	Sig: 1-2 tabs hs; 1-2 tabs 1 h ā procedure
Lorazepam 0.5 mg	V	Sig: 1-2 tablets at bedtime; 1-2 tablets 1 hour before procedure	Sig 1-2 tabs hs; 1-2 tabs 1 h ā procedure

V: Varies with number of appointments.

For Analgesia

Drug	#	Directions	Abbreviated directions
For mild-to-moderate pain			
Ibuprofen 400 mg	18	Sig: 1 tablet every 4-6 hours as needed; maximum daily dose 8 tablets	Sig: 1 tab q 4-6 h for pain MDD 8 tab
Acetaminophen with codeine #3 (30 mg)	24	Sig: 1-2 tablets every 4 hours as needed for pain; maximum daily dose 12 tablets	Sig: 1-2 tab q 4 h for pain MDD 12 tab
Ketoprofen 25 mg or 50 mg	12	Sig: 1 tablet every 6-8 hours as needed; maximum daily dose 300 mg	Sig: 1 tab q 6-8 h for pain MDD 300 mg
For moderate to moderate-to-severe pain (unresponsive to NSAIDs)			
Hydrocodone bitartrate 5 mg and acetaminophen 500 mg, 650 mg or 750 mg	18	Sig: 1 tablet every 4 hours; maximum daily dose 6 tablets, acetaminophen 4,000 mg	Sig: 1 tab q 4 h MDD 6 tab, acetaminophen 4,000 mg
Oxycodone HCl 5 mg and acetaminophen 325 mg or 500 mg	18	Sig: 1 tablet every 6 hours; maximum daily dose 4 tablets, acetaminophen 4,000 mg	Sig: 1 tab q 6 h MDD 4 tab, acetaminophen 4,000 mg

Continued on next page

For Analgesia (cont.)

Drug	#	Directions	Abbreviated directions
For severe pain			
Hydromorphone HCl 2 mg	30	Sig: 1-2 tablets every 4-6 hours as needed for pain; maximum daily dose 8 tablets	Sig: 1-2 tab q 4-6 h for pain MDD 8 tab
Oxycodone Hcl 5 mg	30	Sig: 1-2 tablets every 4-6 h for pain; maximum daily dose 8 tablets	Sig: 1-2 tab q 4-6 h for pain MDD 8 tab

For Infections in the Mouth and Adjacent Tissues

Drug	#	Directions	Abbreviated directions
Penicillin V potassium 500 mg	30	Sig: 2 tablets at once, then 1 tablet every 6 hours until gone	Sig: 2 tabs stat, then 1 tab q 6 h until gone
Amoxicillin 500 mg	28	Sig: 1 capsule every 8 hours until gone	Sig: 1 cap q 8 h until gone
Metronidazole 250 mg	28	Sig: Take 1 tablet every 6 hours until gone	Sig: 1 tab q 6 h until gone
Clindamycin 150 mg	28	Sig: Take 1 capsule every 6 hours until gone	Sig: 1 cap q 6 h until gone
Erythromycin 250 mg	30	Sig: 2 tablets initially, 1 tablet every 6 hours until gone	Sig: 2 tab stat, 1 tab q 6 h until gone
Minocycline HCl 100 mg	15	Sig: 2 capsules initially, 1 capsule twice daily until gone	Sig: 2 cap stat, 1 cap bid until gone
Tetracycline HCl 250 mg	30	Sig: 2 capsules initially, 1 capsule every 6 hours until gone	Sig: 2 cap stat, 1 cap q 6 h until gone
Cephalexin 250 mg	30	Sig: 2 capsules initially, 1 capsule every 6 hours until gone	Sig: 2 cap stat, 1 cap q 6 h until gone

For Oral Candidiasis

Drug	#	Directions	Abbreviated directions
Nystatin oral suspension 100,000 units/mL	480 mL	Sig: Rinse for 2 minutes and swallow one teaspoonful four times daily until symptoms disappear	Sig: one teaspoonful qid, rinse 2 min and swallow
Chlorhexidine 0.12 %	16 oz	Sig: 0.5 oz twice a day as a rinse until symptoms disappear	Sig: 0.5 oz bid as rinse
Clotrimazole troche 10 mg	70	Sig: 1 troche by mouth five times daily	Sig: 1 troche po 5 times d

For Angular Cheilitis (Fungal Etiology)

Drug	#	Directions	Abbreviated directions
Nystatin 100,000 units/g ointment	15-g tube	Sig: Apply to lesion 4 times a day until healing occurs	Sig: Apply to lesion qid until healing occurs
Nystatin 100,000 units/g and triamcinolone 0.1% ointment	15-g tube	Sig: Apply to lesion 2-3 times a day until healing occurs	Sig: Apply to lesion bid-tid until healing occurs

For Mild-to-Moderate Lichen Planus or Mucous Membrane Pemphigoid

Drug	#	Directions	Abbreviated directions
Fluocinonide gel .05%	15 g	Sig: Apply with cotton swab to affected areas twice daily	Sig: Apply c̄ cotton swab bid

For Mild Allergic Reactions

Drug	#	Directions	Abbreviated directions
Diphenhydramine HCl 50 mg	30	Sig: 1 capsule every 4 hours as needed	Sig: 1 cap qid prn

For Herpetic Infections

Drug	#	Directions	Abbreviated directions
Penciclovir 1% cream	2-g tube	Sig: Apply to affected area every 2 hours while awake	Sig: Apply q 2 h while awake

Prescription Abbreviations

Abbreviation	Term	Abbreviation	Term	Abbreviation	Term
ā	before	h	hour	s̄, sine	without
ac	before meals	hs, HS, hor som	at bedtime	sig	write on the label
aq, H2O	water	non rep, nr, NR	do not repeat	s̄s̄, ss	one-half
bid	2 times a day	pc	after eating	stat	immediately
c̄, c	with	po	by mouth	tab	tablet
cap	capsule	prn	as needed	tid	3 times a day
d	day	qh	each hour		
gtt	drops	qid	4 times a day		

Appendix M.

Drugs That Cause Photosensitivity

B. Ellen Byrne, R.Ph., D.D.S., Ph.D.

Photosensitivity reactions may be caused by systemic or topical drugs, perfumes, cosmetics or sunscreens. Even brief exposures to sunlight in warm or cold weather can cause intense cutaneous reactions in patients with drug-induced photosensitivity. Individual sensitivity varies widely.

Suggested Readings

Allen JE. Drug-induced photosensitivity. Clin Pharm 1993;12:580-7.

Anderson PO, Knoben JE, Troutman WG. Handbook of clinical drug data 1997-1998. 8th ed. New York: McGraw-Hill Professional Publishing; 1999.

Drugs that may cause photosensitivity. Pharmacist's Letter PHARM-FaxBACK document no. 120617. Available from: Pharmacist's Letter, 2453 Grand Canal Blvd., Suite A, P.O. Box 8190, Stockton, Calif. 95203, by subscription.

Drugs that cause photosensitivity. Medical Letter 1995;37(946):35-6.

Drugs That Cause Photosensitivity

Generic name	Brand name
Antidepressants	
Amitriptyline	Elavil, Endep; Levate [CAN], Novo-Triptyn [CAN]
Amoxapine	Asendin
Clomipramine	Anafranil; Apo-Clomipramine [CAN]
Desipramine	Norpramin; Pertofrane [CAN], PMS-Desipramine [CAN]
Doxepin	Sinequan; Apo-Doxepin [CAN], Triadapin [CAN]
Imipramine	Norfranil, Tipramine, Tofranil; Apo-Imipramine [CAN], Impril [CAN], Novo-Pramine [CAN]
Isocarboxazid	Marplan
Maprotiline	Ludiomil
Mirtazapine	Remeron
Nortriptyline	Aventyl, Pamelor
Phenelzine	Nardil
Protriptyline	Vivactil; Triptil [CAN]
Sertraline	Zoloft
Trazodone	Desyrel
Trimipramine	Surmontil; Apo-Trimip [CAN], Rhotrimine [CAN]
Venlafaxine	Effexor

[CAN] indicates a drug available only in Canada.

Continued on next page

Drugs That Cause Photosensitivity (cont.)

Generic name	Brand name
Antihistamines	
Cetirizine	Zyrtec; Reactine [CAN]
Cyproheptadine	Periactin; PMS-Cyproheptadine [CAN]
Dimenhydrinate	Dramamine; Gravol [CAN], Traveltabs [CAN]
Diphenhydramine	Benadryl; AllerDryl [CAN]
Hydroxyzine	Anxanil, Atarax, Vistaril; Apo-Hydroxyzine [CAN], Multipax [CAN], PMS-Hydroxyzine [CAN]
Loratadine	Claritin
Antihypertensive agents	
Captopril	Capoten; Apo-Capto [CAN], Novo-Captopril [CAN], Nu-Capto [CAN]
Diltiazem	Cardizem, Dilacor-XR, Tiamate, Tiazac; Apo-Diltiaz [CAN], Novo-Diltiazem [CAN], Nu-Diltiaz [CAN]
Methyldopa	Aldomet; Dopamet [CAN], Mediment [CAN], Novomedopa [CAN]
Minoxidil	Loniten; Apo-Gain [CAN], Gen-Minoxidil [CAN]
Nifedipine	Adalat, Procardia; Adalat PA [CAN], Apo-Nifed [CAN]
Antimicrobial agents	
Azithromycin	Zithromax
Ciprofloxacin	Cipro
Clofazimine	Lamprene
Dapsone	Avlosulfon
Demeclocycline*	Declomycin
Doxycycline*	Doryx, Doxy, Vibramycin; Apo-Doxy [CAN], Doxycin [CAN]
Enoxacin	Penetrex
Flucytosine	Ancobon; Ancotil [CAN]
Griseofulvin	Fulvicin-U/F, Grisactin, Gris-PEG; Grisovin FP [CAN]
Lomefloxacin	Maxaquin
Minocycline	Dynacin, Minocin; Apo-Minocycline [CAN]
Nalidixic acid	NegGram
Norfloxacin	Noroxin
Ofloxacin	Floxin
Oxytetracycline	Terramycin
Pyrazinamide	generic; PMS-Pyrazinamide [CAN], Tebrazid [CAN]
Sulfadiazine	generic
Sulfamethizole	Thiosulfil Forte
Sulfamethoxazole	Gantanal, Urobak; Apo-Sulfamethoxazole [CAN]
Sulfamethoxazole and trimethoprim	Bactrim, Cotrim, Septra, Sulfatrim; Apo-Sulfatrim [CAN], Novo-Trimel [CAN], Nu-Cotrimox DS [CAN], Roubac [CAN]
Sulfisoxazole	Gantrisin
Tetracycline	Achromycin, Sumycin, Tetracyn; Apo-Tetra [CAN], Novo-Tetra [CAN]
Trimethoprim	Proloprim, Trimpex

[CAN] indicates a drug available only in Canada.
* indicates an agent with which reactions occur more frequently.

Continued on next page

Drugs That Cause Photosensitivity (cont.)

Generic name	Brand name
Antiparasitic agents	
Chloroquine	Aralen
Mefloquine	Lariam
Pyrvinium pamoate	Povan, Vanquin
Quinine	generic
Thiabendazole	Mintezol
Antipsychotic agents	
Chlorpromazine*	Ormazine, Thorazine; Chlorprom [CAN], Chlorpromanyl [CAN], Largactil [CAN]
Fluphenazine	Permitil, Prolixin; Apo-Fluphenazine [CAN], Moditen HCl [CAN]
Haloperidol	Haldol
Perphenazine	Trilafon; Apo-Perphenazine [CAN]
Prochlorperazine*	Compazine; Stemetil [CAN]
Risperidone	Risperdal
Thioridazine	Mellaril; Novo-Ridazine [CAN]
Thiothixene	Navane
Trifluoperazine	Stelazine; Novo-Flurazine [CAN], Salazine [CAN]
Triflupromazine	Vesprin
Cardiovascular drugs	
ACE inhibitors:	
captopril	Capoten
enalapril	Vasotec
fosinopril	Monopril
moexipril	Univasc
quinapril	Accupril
ramipril	Altace
Amiodarone*	Cardarone
Diltiazem	Cardizem; Nu-Diltiaz [CAN]
Disopyramide	Norpace; Rythmodan [CAN]
Losartan	Cozaar
Lovastatin	Mevacor
Nifedipine	Adalat, Procardia; Apo-Nifed [CAN], Novo-Nifedin [CAN]
Pravastatin	Pravachol
Quinidine	Cardioquin, Quinaglute, Quinalan, Quinidex, Quinora; Cin-Quin [CAN], Novoquinidine [CAN]
Simvastatin	Zocar
Sotalol	Betapace; Sotacor [CAN]
Diuretics	
Acetazolamide	Diamox; Acetazolam [CAN], Novo-Zolamide [CAN]
Amiloride	Midamor
Bendroflumethoiazide	Naturetin
Benzthiazide	Exna
Chlorothiazide*	Diurigen, Diuril

[CAN] indicates a drug available only in Canada.
* indicates an agent with which reactions occur more frequently.

Continued on next page

Drugs That Cause Photosensitivity (cont.)

Generic name	Brand name
Diuretics (cont.)	
Furosemide*	Lasix; Novosemide [CAN], Uritol [CAN]
Hydrochlorothiazide*	Esidrix, HydroDIURIL, Oretic; Apo-Hydro [CAN], Diuchlor [CAN], Neo-Codema [CAN], Urozide [CAN]
Hydroflumethiazide	Diucardin, Saluron
Methyclothiazide	Aquatensen, Enduron; Duretic [CAN]
Metolazone	Mykrox, Zaroxolyn
Polythiazide	Renese
Triamterene	Dyrenium
Trichlormethiazide	Metahydrin, Naqua
Hypoglycemic agents	
Acetohexamide	Dymelor; Dimelor [CAN]
Chlorpropamide	Diabinese; Apo-Chlorpropamide [CAN], Novo-Propamide [CAN]
Glimepiride	Amaryl
Glipizide	Glucotrol
Glyburide	DiaBeta, Micronase; Euglucon [CAN], Gen-Glybe [CAN]
Tolazamide	Tolinase
Tolbutamide	Orinase; Mobenol [CAN]
Nonsteroidal anti-inflammatory agents	
Diflusinal	Dolobid; Apo-Diflusinal [CAN], Novo-Diflusinal [CAN]
Etodolac	Lodine
Ibuprofen	Motrin, Rufen; Novo-Profen [CAN]
Indomethacin	Indocin; Indocid [CAN], Novo-Methacin [CAN], Nu-Indo [CAN]
Ketoprofen	Orudis; Apo-Keto [CAN]; Rhodis [CAN]
Nabumetone	Relafen
Naproxen	Naprosyn; Naxen [CAN], Novo-Naproxen [CAN], NuNaprox [CAN]
Oxaprozin	Daypro
Phenylbutazone	Butazolidin, Cotylbutazone; Apo-Phenylbutazone [CAN]
Piroxicam*	Feldene; Novo-Piroxicam [CAN], Nu-Pirox [CAN]
Sulindac	Clinoril; Novo-Sundac [CAN]
Sunscreens	
Aminobenzoic acid (PABA)*	PABA-405 Solar Cream
Avobenzone	Photoplex, Shade UVA Guard
Benzophenones*	Bain de Soleil, Solbar
Cinnamates	Bull Frog, Coppertone
Homosalate	Coppertone, Tropical Blend
Menthyl anthranilate	Hawaiian Tropic, Neutrogena
Oxybenzone	Eclipse, PreSun, Shade
PABA esters*	PreSun, Tropical Blend

[CAN] indicates a drug available only in Canada.
* indicates an agent with which reactions occur more frequently.

Continued on next page

Drugs That Cause Photosensitivity (cont.)

Generic name	Brand name
	Miscellaneous drugs
Acitretin*	Soriatane
Amantadine	Symmetrel; Endantadine [CAN], PMS-Amantadine [CAN]
Benzocaine	Lagol; Endocaine [CAN]
Benzoyl peroxide	Clearasil, Oxy-10, PanOxyl-AQ; Acetoxyl [CAN], Oxyderm [CAN]
Carbamazepine	Epitol, Tegretol; Apo-Carbamazepine [CAN], Mazepine [CAN]
Chlordiazepoxide	Librium, Mitran, Reposans-10; Corax [CAN], Novo-Poxide [CAN], Solium [CAN]
Coal tar	Tegrin, Zetar
Estazolam	ProSom
Felbamate	Felbatol
Gabapentin	Neurontin
Gold sodium thiomalate	Myochrysine, Ridaura
Hexachlorophene	pHisoHex, pHisoScrub, Septisol
Interferon β-1b	Betaseron
Isotretinoin	Accutane; Isotrex [CAN]
Masoprocol†	Actinex
Olsalazine	Dipentum
Oral contraceptives	Enorid, Ortho-Novum, Ovral
Perfume oils*: bergamot, cedar, citron, lavender, musk, sandalwood	various cosmetic, food and fragrance products
Selegiline	Deprenyl, Eldepryl; Apo-Selegiline [CAN], Novo-Selegiline [CAN]
Tretinoin (topical)*	Avita, Retin-A, Vitamin A Acid; Retisol A [CAN], Stieva-A [CAN]
Zolpidem	Ambien

[CAN] indicates a drug available only in Canada.
* indicates an agent with which reactions occur more frequently.
† This drug is used to treat solar keratoses; patients should avoid sun exposure.

Appendix N.

Herbs and Dietary Supplements

Adriane Fugh-Berman, M.D.

Herbs and Dental Health

Many drugs used in dentistry have their origins in the plant world, including lidocaine and novacaine, derived from the coca plant *(Erythroxylum coca)*; opioids, derived from the poppy *(Papaver somniferum)*; and several antibiotics derived from fungi, including penicillin from *Penicillium notatum* and cephalosporins from a marine fungus *(Cephalosporium acremonium)*. Clove oil, which contains eugenol, is the essential oil of *Eugenia caryophyllus*.[1] In fact, the best-selling herbal products in the United States may well be oral hygiene products, which rely heavily on essential oils (or their components), including eucalyptol, derived from eucalyptus *(E. globulus)*; thymol, derived from thyme *(Thymus vulgaris)*; menthol, derived from peppermint *(Mentha piperita)*; and sanguinarine, derived from bloodroot *(Sanguinaria canadensis)*.

Chewing sticks, used in African and Southern Asian communities, are oral hygiene products made from a variety of plants; in countries that use them, caries rates are low.[1] Several genera of plants, including *Camellia*, have a high fluoride content; the chewing stick with the highest fluoride content is from a plant related to persimmon *(Diospyros tricolor)*. *Fagara zanthoxyloides* and *Massularia acuminata* reduce both acid production and bacterial growth. Extracts from *Rhus natalensis* and *Euclea divinorum*, used in Kenya as chewing sticks, inhibited the proteolytic activity of *Bacteroides gingivalis, B. intermedius*

and *Treponema denticola*.[2]

Commercial toothpastes have been made from neem *(Azadirachta indica)* and arak *(Salvadora persica*, one of several plants called "toothbrush tree"). Powdered plants used in abrasive dentrifices include root of sweet flag *(Acorus calamus)*, gum-resin of myrrh *(Commiphora myrrha)*, root of yellow dock *(Rumex crispus)*, stem of the toothbrush tree *(Gouania lupuloides)* and the ashes of European grape *(Vitis vinifera)* branches.[1]

The sugar substitute xylitol, birch sugar, is as sweet as sucrose; sorbitol, another sugar alcohol, is 60% as sweet as sucrose but is used more often than xylitol because it is less expensive and easier to formulate into products. Both stimulate saliva production; xylitol is not fermented by oral microbes, while sorbitol is very slowly fermented. An analysis of published double-blind trials using sorbitol and xylitol products (usually in the form of chewing gums administered 3-5 times daily) found that xylitol was superior to sorbitol in two longer, secondary dentition trials but not in two primary dentition trials.[3]

Adverse Effects of Herbs

Bleeding

A number of herbs can increase the risk of bleeding, especially when combined with anticoagulants. Both ginkgo *(G. biloba)* and garlic *(Allium sativum)* have been associated with bleeding episodes alone or in combination with anticoagulants. Other herbs associated with increased anticoagulant effect when combined with warfarin include dong quai *(Angelica sinensis)*, danshen *(Salvia miltiorrhiza)* and papaya *(Carica papaya)*.[4]

Cancer and Precancerous Conditions

Betel nut *(Areca catechu)*, a masticant with mild stimulatory effects, has been linked to oral and esophageal cancers.[5] Oral squamous cell carcinoma usually occurs in parts of the mouth directly contacted by betel quid (primarily in the midbuccal mucosa and the lateral borders of the tongue). Betel use also causes oral submucous fibrositis, a precancerous condition characterized by atrophy and dysplasia of the mucosal epithelium, and often accompanied by mucosal leukoplakia and loss of lingual papillae.[6] The addition of tobacco clearly increases carcinogenic risk.[5] The addition of lime may increase the generation of reactive oxygen species; oral squamous cell cancers were noted to correspond to the site of lime application in 77% of 169 cases in Papua New Guinea.[7]

Although betel traditionally is thought of as beneficial to the teeth and gums, it is difficult to assess its possible benefits because of the high rate of tooth decay and periodontal disease in populations that chew betel. Some evidence suggests that chewing betel helps to prevent dental caries, possibly via mechanical cleansing or altering salivary pH. It also is possible that the darkened layer on the teeth forms a barrier to cariogenic agents.[6]

Betel stains the saliva a reddish color and can stain the teeth, gingiva and oral mucosa red or black. Another stimulatory masticant, khat *(Catha edulis)*, also can stain teeth, as well as cause caries, thickened oropharyngeal mucosa and dependence.[8]

Vitamins and Minerals

Nutrition is important in craniofacial and oral tissue development.[9] Prolonged vitamin A deficiency during tooth development can result in enamel hypoplasia. Deficiencies of Vitamin D or phosphorus can cause incomplete calcification of teeth. Deficiency of calcium, vitamin D, magnesium or copper can cause defects in alveolar bone. Iodine deficiency can delay the eruption of both primary and secondary teeth and can cause malocclusion.

Many nutritional deficiencies are manifested first in the oral cavity. Glossitis can occur from multiple nutritional deficiencies (vitamin E appears to be particularly important in papillary health). Angular cheilosis can be caused by too little vitamin B_2 (riboflavin), B_3 (niacin), B_6 (pyridoxine) B_{12} (cobalamin), folic acid or iron. Burning mouth syndrome may be the result of deficiency of vitamin B complex, protein or iron.[9]

Vitamin C deficiency causes impaired wound healing, inflamed gingiva and swollen interdental papillae. Too little calcium can cause increased tooth mobility and premature loss; too little magnesium or vitamin A can cause gingival hypertrophy. Deficiency of vitamin A also increases the risk of candidiasis and can cause desquamation of oral mucosa, leukoplakia and xerostomia. Either too much or too little vitamin A can impair healing. Zinc deficiency can cause distortions of taste and smell, delayed wound healing, atrophic oral mucosa, xerostomia and increased susceptibility to periodontal disease.[9]

Colloidal silver, which has a long history as an antibacterial agent, has made a comeback in health food stores as a "natural" antibiotic. Silver can deposit in the skin or mucosa, causing argyria, a gray-blue permanent discoloration. Argyria often manifests first in the mouth, causing a slate-blue or silver line in the gingiva.

Clinical Trials of Herbs and Dietary Supplements for Treatment of Dental Conditions

Aphthous Ulcers

A component of *Aloe vera* gel, acemannan, has been suggested to be effective in treating aphthous stomatitis.[10] A double-blind randomized trial of 60 patients with a history of recurrent aphthae assigned patients to groups using either acemannan hydrogel or an over-the-counter product as an active control. Lesions treated with acemannan hydrogel healed in 5.89 days, while those treated with the active control healed in 7.8 days. Freeze-dried acemannan hydrogel appeared to be equivalent to acemannan hydrogel in an open-label arm of this trial.

Caries and Oral Microbial Growth
Licorice
Licorice (*Glycyrrhiza glabra*) and glycyrrhizin both inhibit bacterial adherence. In the presence of sucrose, glycyrrhizin did not affect growth of the cariogenic *Streptococcus mutans* but did reduce plaque formation; inhibition was almost complete at concentrations of .5-1% glycyrrhizin or 5-10% licorice.[11]

Cranberry
A high–molecular-weight constituent of cranberry (*Vaccinium macrocarpon*) juice reversed the coaggregation of 58% of 84 coaggregating bacterial pairs tested.[12] This effect was strongest when at least one species was a gram-negative anaerobe; thus, it may alter subgingival microflora. Most cranberry juice, however, contains large amounts of sugar.

Propolis
Propolis, or "bee glue," is an adhesive, resinous substance used by honeybees in building and sealing a hive. A double-blind study comparing a propolis-containing mouthwash with a positive control (chlorhexidine) and a negative control found that the chlorhexidine mouthrinse was best; there was no significant difference between the propolis-containing mouthrinse and the negative control.[13] Another study tested propolis and honey against oral bacteria in 10 volunteers (an in vitro study was also done).[14] Propolis demonstrated an antibacterial effect on oral streptococci, both in vitro and clinically, by reducing salivary bacterial counts.[14]

Calcium
A calcium-fortified chewing gum ameliorated the cariogenic effects of sucrose more than a conventional gum, as measured by increased pH, calcium and phosphate concentrations in plaque fluid and saliva.[15]

Oral Candidiasis
Tea tree oil
In a small open pilot trial, researchers tested tea tree (*Melaleuca alternifolia*) oral solution for refractory oral candidiasis in AIDS patients.[16] Thirteen patients with oral candidiasis that was clinically refractory to fluconazole swished and expelled 15 milliliters of a melaleuca-containing commercial mouthwash (concentration not specified) four times a day. Weekly evaluations of signs and symptoms as well as quantitative yeast cultures were performed. Of the 12 patients who were evaluated at four weeks, two were cured, six improved, four had no response and one patient was worse. (One is unaccounted for in the published study.) Mycological response was seen in 9 of 12 patients evaluated at four weeks.

Cinnamon
An uncontrolled trial of three HIV-positive subjects with oral candidiasis found that three of five improved after receiving an oral cinnamon (*Cinnamomum* species) preparation for a week.[17]

Oral Leukoplakia
A placebo-controlled trial of 87 tobacco chewers with oral leukoplakia tested 1 gram daily of a blue-green alga, *Spirulina fusiformis*, against placebo for 12 months.[18] Complete regression of lesions was noted in 20 of 44 (45%) subjects in the Spirulina-treated group, vs. 3 of 43 (7%) subjects in the placebo group. No effect was seen in those with ulcerated or nodular lesions. Within one year of discontinuing use of *Spirulina fusiformis*, 9 of 20 subjects experienced complete regression of lesions. No toxicity was noted. These results could be explained by *Spirulina*'s high vitamin A content, but, interestingly, no increase in serum concentrations of retinol or beta carotene were seen.

Oral Mucositis

Chamomile

An uncontrolled trial in cancer patients indicated that chamomile mouthwash might prevent or treat stomatitis, but a double-blind, placebo-controlled trial did not find a benefit. In a study of 164 patients entering their first cycle of 5-fluorouracil (5FU)-based chemotherapy, the patients were randomized into either a group using chamomile mouthwash three times daily for two weeks or a group using placebo on the same schedule. All patients also received oral cryotherapy for 30 minutes with each dose of 5-FU.[19] Physicians scored stomatitis severity on a scale from 1 to 4; patients also completed self-assessment scores using the same scale. Daily mean mucositis scores did not differ between the chamomile group and the placebo group. No toxicity was noted.

Vitamin E

A randomized double-blind study of 18 patients receiving chemotherapy tested vitamin E against placebo oil for treatment of oral mucositis. After five days of topical application (one mL of 400 milligrams/mL vitamin E oil twice daily), six of nine patients had complete resolution of lesions; only one of nine subjects in the placebo group had complete resolution.[20]

In a large trial examining the effect of vitamin E and beta carotene on cancer and cardiovascular disease, a substudy of 409 male cigarette smokers found that gingival bleeding on probing was more common in those with a high prevalence of dental plaque who received vitamin E (alpha-tocopherol 50 mg).[21] Aspirin alone (in varying doses) did not increase bleeding significantly, but the combination of aspirin with vitamin E was most likely to increase the risk of gingival bleeding.

However, a study designed to address the question of whether vitamin E increased the risk of bleeding found no effect of all-rac-alpha-tocopherol (in doses of 60, 200 or 800 IU

for four months) on increased bleeding time in 88 healthy subjects older than 65 years of age.[22]

Periodontal Disease

Sanguinaria

A number of trials of sanguinaria (S. canadensis) oral rinses and toothpaste for periodontal disease have been published, and sanguinaria-containing products are sold commonly. Most trials of these products are methodologically flawed; even the most recent trials are rarely double-blind.[23] Results from trials of sanguinaria are mixed. Although there is little to indicate that sanguinaria-containing products are effective in severe disease, it is possible that these products are beneficial in milder cases or as an adjunctive treatment.

Coenzyme Q10

Coenzyme Q10, involved in electron transport in mitochondria, has been claimed to have a beneficial effect on periodontal disease. Apparently two controlled clinical trials have been performed, but according to a review and critique of the literature on coenzyme Q10,[24] both are methodologically deficient. The first study, conducted with 18 patients, provided only vague assessments of clinical improvement rather than reproducible measurements.[25] A larger double-blind study of 56 patients compared placebo with coenzyme Q10 (60 mg/day for 12 w).[26] No difference was seen in gingival redness, bleeding or pus discharge, but a significant improvement in tooth mobility was noted at 4 and 12 weeks. Probing depth scores also were noted to be improved at 12 weeks, compared with baseline measurements. However, Watts'[24] critique noted that the periodontal health of both the treated group and the placebo group improved over baseline; there apparently was not a significant difference between the treated group and the control group. This critique also pointed out that none of the reports regarding coenzyme Q10 and periodontal disease was published in the periodontal literature.

Xerostomia

Yohimbine, an α_2 antagonist used to treat impotence, has been tested for its effect on salivary secretion in 11 healthy volunteers and in volunteers treated with tricyclic antidepressants.[27] A regimen of yohimbine 4 mg tid for three w did not affect resting salivary secretion levels (tested at baseline and weekly thereafter) in either group; acute administration, however, significantly increased salivary volume within 1 h in both groups.

Conclusion

Herbs and dietary supplements are used commonly by the general public and may have both beneficial and adverse effects relevant to dentistry. (The table shows adverse effects—those described above as well as others[4,9,28-31]—of herbs and dietary supplements.) Nutritional deficiencies can manifest first in the mouth; stained gingiva can indicate the use of betel, khat or silver; garlic, ginkgo, danshen and other herbs can increase bleeding after an invasive procedure. Therefore, it is worthwhile to include questions about the use of herbs and dietary supplements in the patient's health history, and to be aware of possible adverse effects or interactions. Several herbs may hold promise in dental treatment and should be researched further.

Adverse Effects of Dietary Supplements

Supplement	Common use(s)	Adverse effects/interactions
Aloe (*A. vera*)	Burns, skin/mucosal irritation	Diarrhea from anthraquinones in leaf (not gel)[28]
Betel nut (*Areca catechu*)	Masticatory stimulant	Oral leukoplakia; oral cancer; stained teeth and gingiva; bronchoconstriction; can interact with the antipsychotics flupenthixol and fluphenazine, causing bradykinesia, jaw tremor, rigidity[28]
Chaparral (*Larrea tridentata*)	Cancer	Hepatotoxicity[29]
Coltsfoot (*Tussilago farfara*)	Cough	Hepatotoxicity[4]
Comfrey (*Symphytum officinale*)	Ulcers, wound healing	Hepatotoxicity[4]
Danshen (*Salvia miltiorrhiza*)	Cardiovascular disease	Potentiates warfarin[4]
Dong quai (*Angelica sinensis*)	Gynecologic conditions	Potentiates warfarin[28]
Ephedra (*E. sinica*)	Respiratory conditions, weight loss	Hypertension, cardiac dysrhythmias, anxiety; can potentiate sympathomimetic drugs[4]
Feverfew (*Tanacetum parthenium*)	Migraine	Aphthous ulcers[4]
Garlic (*Allium sativum*)	Cardiovascular health	Anticoagulant effects; may potentiate warfarin[28]; topical garlic poultices may cause the appearance of a chemical burn[30]

Continued on next page

Adverse Effects of Dietary Supplements (cont.)

Supplement	Common use(s)	Adverse effects/interactions
Germander (*Teucrium chamaedrys*)	Weight control	Hepatotoxicity[29]
Ginkgo (*G. biloba*)	Memory, circulatory problems	Anticoagulant effects; potentiates warfarin and aspirin[28]
Khat (*Catha edulis*)	Masticatory stimulant	Caries, stained teeth, thickened oropharyngeal mucosa, psychosis, dependence[31]
Licorice (*Glycyrrhiza glabra*)	Oral or gastrointestinal ulcers, inflammation	Hypokalemia, hypertension, edema; may potentiate glucocorticoids[4]
Saint John's wort (*Hypericum perforatum*)	Depression	Decreases levels of warfarin, cyclosporine, digoxin, oral contraceptives; increases serotonergic effects when combined with sertraline, trazodone or nefazodone[28]
Silver	Antibiotic	Argyria (slate-blue or silver line in the gingiva)
Vitamin A	Acne	Excessive vitamin A can cause hepatotoxicity and delay wound healing; in early pregnancy, excess can cause severe craniofacial and oral clefts and other birth defects[9]
Vitamin D	Osteoporosis	Excessive vitamin D can cause pulp calcification and enamel hypoplasia[9]

Editor's note: Because herbs and dietary supplements are not regulated as drugs by the U.S. Food and Drug Administration, claims regarding their therapeutic benefit should not be accepted without support from extensive, well-controlled studies published in peer-reviewed journals. Only a limited number of controlled clinical trials have been conducted with these agents; more are needed. However, in light of these agents' potential adverse effects as discussed here, the practitioner should include information about use of these agents in each patient's health history.

1. Lewis WH, Elvin-Lewis PF. Medical botany: plants affecting man's health. New York: Wiley; 1977.
2. Homer KA, Manji F, Beighton D. Inhibition of protease activities of periodontopathic bacteria by extracts of plants used in Kenya as chewing sticks (mswaki). Arch Oral Biol 1990;35:421-4.
3. Gales MA, Nguyen T-M. Sorbitol compared with xylitol in prevention of dental caries. Ann Pharmacother 2000;34:98-100.
4. Fugh-Berman A. Clinical trials of herbs. Primary Care 1997;24:889-903.
5. Morton JF. Widespread tannin intake via stimulants and masticatories, especially guarana, kola nut, betel vine, and accessories. In Hemingway RW, Laks PE, eds. Plant polyphenols. New York: Plenum Press; 1992:739-65.
6. Norton SA. Betel: consumption and consequences. J Am Acad Dermatol 1998;38(1):81-8.

7. Thomas SJ, MacLenna R. Slaked lime and betel nut cancer in Papua New Guinea. Lancet 1992;340:577-8.

8. D'Arcy PF. Adverse reactions and interactions with herbal medicines. Adverse Drug React Toxicol Rev 1991;10;189-208.

9. Depaola DP, Faine MP, Palmer CA. Nutrition in relation to dental medicine. In Shils ME, Olson JA, Shike M, Ross AC, eds. Modern nutrition in health and disease. 9th ed. Baltimore: Williams and Wilkins; 1999:1099-1124.

10. Plemons JM, Rees TD Binnie WH, et al. Evaluation of acemannan in the treatment of recurrent aphthous stomatitis. Wounds 1994;6(2):40-5.

11. Segal R, Pisanti S, Wormser R, et al. Anticariogenic activity of licorice and glycyrrhizin inhibition of in vitro plaque formation by *Streptococcus mutans*. J Pharm Sci 1985;74(1):79-81.

12. Weiss EI, Lev-Dor R, Kashamn Y, et al. Inhibiting interspecies coaggregation of plaque bacteria with a cranberry juice constituent. JADA 1998;129:1719-23.

13. Murray MC, Worthington HV, Blinkhorn AS. A study to investigate the effect of a propolis-containing mouthrinse on the inhibition of de novo plaque formation. J Clin Periodontol 1997;24:796-8.

14. Steinberg D, Kaine G, Gedalia J. Antibacterial effect of propolis and honey on oral bacteria. Am J Dent 1996;9(6):236-9.

15. Vogel GL, Zhang Z, Carey CM, et al. Composition of plaque and saliva following a sucrose challenge and use of an alpha-tricalcium-phosphate-containing chewing gum. J Dent Res 1998;77(3):518-24.

16. Jandourek A, Vaishapayan JK, Vazquez JA. Efficacy of melaleuca oral solution for the treatment of fluconazole refractory oral candidiasis in AIDS patients. AIDS 1998;12:1033-7.

17. Quale JM, Landman D, Zaman MM, et al. In vitro activity of *Cinnamomum zeylanicum* against azole resistant and sensitive *Candida* species and a pilot study of cinnamon for oral candidiasis. Am J Chin Med 1996;24(2):103-9.

18. Mathew B, Sankaranarayanan R, Nair PP, et al. Evaluation of chemoprevention of oral cancer with *Spirulina fusiformis*. Nutr Cancer 1995;24(2):197-202.

19. Fidler P, Loprinzi CL, O'Fallon JR, et al. Prospective evaluation of a chamomile mouthwash for prevention of 5-FU-induced oral mucositis. Cancer 1996;77:522-5.

20. Wadleigh RG, Redman RS, Graham ML, et al. Vitamin E in the treatment of chemotherapy-induced mucositis. Am J Med 1992;92:481-4.

21. Liede KE, Haukka JK, Saxen LM, Heinonen OP. Increased tendency towards gingival bleeding caused by joint effect of α-tocopherol supplementation and acetylsalicylic acid. Ann Med 1998;30:542-6.

22. Meydani SN, Meydani M, Blumberg JB, et al. Assessment of the safety of supplementation with different amounts of vitamin E in healthy older adults. Am J Clin Nutr 1998;68:311-8.

23. Fugh-Berman A. 5-minute clinical consult for herbs and dietary supplements. Philadelphia: Lippincott, Williams and Wilkins. In press.

24. Watts TLP. Coenzyme Q10 and periodontal treatment: is there any beneficial effect? Br Dent J 1995;178:209-13.

25. Wilkinson EG, Arnold RM, Folkers K. Bioenergetics in clinical medicine. VI. Adjunctive treatment of periodontal disease with coenzyme Q10. Res Commun Chem Pathol Pharmacol 1976;14:715-9.

26. Iwamoto Y, Watanabe T, Okamoto H, et al. Clinical effect of coenzyme Q10 on periodontal disease. In Folkers K, Yamamura Y, eds. Biomedical and clinical aspects of coenzyme Q. Vol. 3. New York: Elsevier Science Publishers; 1981:109-19.

27. Bagheri H, Schmitt L. Berlan M, Montastruc JL. Effect of 3 weeks' treatment with yohimbine on salivary secretion in healthy volunteers and in depressed patients treated with tricyclic antidepressants. Br J Clin Pharmacol 1992;34:555-8.

28. Fugh-Berman A. Herb-drug interactions. Lancet 2000;355:134-8.

29. Ernst E. Harmless herbs? A review of the recent literature. Am J Med 1998;104:170-8.

30. Garty BZ. Garlic burns. Pediatrics 1993;91(3):658-9.

31. D'Arcy PF. Adverse reactions and interactions with herbal medicines. Adverse Drug React Toxicol Rev 1991;10:189-208.

Index

This index has been alphabetized strictly according to letter, disregarding punctuation and spaces between words. Page numbers followed by the letter "t" designate tabular information; page numbers followed by the letter "f" designate figures. *See also* cross-references indicate related topics or more detailed breakdowns under synonyms if a wide page range is given. Indications related to dental practice, such as **Pain,** or **Bleeding, control of,** are in boldface type. The ★ symbol indicates a product bearing the ADA Seal of Acceptance. Brand names, which often are listed in the book as examples only, are indexed where specifically mentioned; please refer to the generic drug for additional information.

α-adrenergic receptor agonists, 258–259
Alpha-Baclofen (baclofen), 370t
Alpha-Baclofen [CAN] (baclofen), 461t
α-β adrenergic antagonists, 319, 321t
Alphacaine (lidocaine hydrochloride), 3t
Alphacaine with Epinephrine (lidocaine hydrochloride/epinephrine), 3t
Alpha-Dent ★ (OTC fluoride), 237t
Alphatrex (betamethasone diproprionate), 128t
Alprazol (alprazolam), 378t, 396t
Alprazolam, 22t, 378t, 396t, 518t, 526t
Altace (ramipril), 326t, 502t, 539t
Alteplase, recombinant, 415t
Altered consciousness, 295–297
Altered host resistance (microflora imbalance), 496, 500–502t
Alternagel (aluminum salts), 350t
Alternative therapies, 626–632, 630–631t
Alu-Cap (aluminum salts), 350t
Aludrox (magnesium salts/aluminum salts), 350t
Aluminum chloride, 114, 115t, 116t
    gingival retraction cord with, 116t, 118t
Aluminum Hydroxide Gel (aluminum salts), 350t
Aluminum potassium sulfate, 114, 115t, 116t
Aluminum salts, 350t
Aluminum sulfate, 114, 115t, 116t
    gingival retraction cord with, 117t
Alupent (metaproterenol sulfate), 337t
Alurate (aprobarbital), 35t
Alu-Tab (aluminum salts), 350t
Alzheimer's-type dementia, drugs used in, 360–364, 361–363t
Amantadine, 367t
Ambemonium, 365
Ambien (zolpidem), 28t, 396t
Amcinonide, 127t
Amcort (triamcinolone), 124t
Amen (medroxyprogesterone), 431t
Amerge (naratriptan), 371t
Americaine (benzocaine aerosol), 12t
Americaine Anesthetic Lubricant (benzocaine gel), 12t
American Academy of Orthopaedic Surgeons (AAOS). See **Antibiotic prophylaxis, for dental patients with total joint replacement**
American Dental Association (ADA). See **Antibiotic prophylaxis, for bacterial endocarditis; Antibiotic prophylaxis, for dental patients with total joint replacement; Chemical dependency; Nitrous oxide; Whitening**
American Heart Association (AHA). See **Antibiotic prophylaxis, for bacterial endocarditis**
American Society of Anesthesiologists (ASA). See **Anesthesia**
A-methaPred (methylprednisolone), 123t
Amicar (aminocaproic acid), 107t, 413t
Amidate (etomidate), 57t
Amide forms of local anesthetics, 1, 7, 7t
Amiloride, 317t, 524t
Amiloride + hydrochlorothiazide, 318t
Aminocaproic acid, 107t, 109, 112t, 113, 412, 413t
Aminoglycosides, 500t

Aminophylline, 166t, 338t
Amiodarone, 5t, 311t, 505t, 526t
Amitriptyline, 6t, 14t, 384t, 504t, 519t, 526t
Amitriptyline/perphenazine, 519t, 523t, 526t
Amlexanox, 184t, 439t
Ammonia, aromatic and spirits of, 262, 273t, 287t
Ammonium compound, quaternary, surface disinfectants, 557t
Amnesia, induction of, 454
Amobarbital, 35t, 512t, 526t, 562t
Amoxapine, 384t, 514t, 520t, 526t
Amoxicillin, 138t, 140t, 503t, 526t
    in renal or hepatic impairment, 474t
Amoxicillin/clavulanic acid, 138t, 140t, 475t, 526t
Amoxil (amoxicillin), 474t, 526t
Amphetamines, 509t
    drug interactions, 14t, 90t
    as drugs of abuse, 562t, 564t, 567t
Amphojel (aluminum salts), 350t
Amphotericin B, 133t, 175t, 180t, 507t, 526t
Ampicillin, 138t, 140t, 516t, 526t
    in renal or hepatic impairment, 474t
Amrinone, 508t, 526t
Amytal (amobarbital), 35t, 512t, 526t, 562t
Anabolic steroids, as drugs of abuse, 562–563t
Anacin (aspirin), 479t, 527t
Anacobin (cyanocobalamin), 414t
Anadrol-50 (oxymetholone), 562t
Anafranil (clomipramine), 384t
Anagrelide, 499t, 526t
Ana-Guard (epinephrine 1:1,000), 265t
Analgesics, 77–103, 258. See also **Pain** and specific drugs and drug types
    nonopioid, 91–103
        adverse effects, precautions and contraindications, 99–100, 102–103t
        dosage and prescribing information, 91–94, 95–99t, 99
        drug interactions, 101t
    opioid, 67–68, 77–91
        accepted indications, 77–78
        adverse effects, precautions and contraindications, 92t
        dosages and prescribing information, 79–90t, 90–91
        drug interactions, 90–91t
Anaphylaxis, 144t, 265t, 266t, 272t, 301–302
Anaprox (naproxen), 98t, 478t, 500t, 525t, 536t
Anaprox DS (naproxen sodium), 98t, 478t
Anaspaz (hyoscyamine), 519t, 533t
Anbesol (benzocaine gel), 12t
Anbesol [CAN] (benzocaine with phenol solution), 12t
Anbocaine (benzocaine gel), 12t
Ancalixir (phenobarbitol), 361t
Andro 100 (testosterone), 422t
Andro-Cyp 100 (testosterone), 422t
Androgens, 420–421, 422t, 434–435t, 436–437t
Android-F (fluoxymesterone), 422t
Android-10 (methyltestosterone), 422t
Andro L.A. 100 and 200 (testosterone), 422t
Andryl 200 (testosterone), 422t
Anectine (succinylcholine chloride), 70t, 73, 74t, 75t, 76

Anectine Chloride (succinylcholine), 456t
Anergan (promethazine), 354t
Anesthesia. See also Anesthetics; **Sedation and anxiety control;** Sedatives
    American Society of Anesthesiologists (ASA), classification for, 20
    general: principles and background, 54–55
    mucosal topical, 11
    pulpal, 2
Anesthetic mouthrinse, 214t
Anesthetics. See also **Anesthesia; Sedation and anxiety control;** Sedatives
    as drugs of abuse, 564t
    general, 54–68
        adverse effects, precautions and contraindications, 62–63t, 63, 64–65t
        cross-sensitivities, 61t
        dosage and prescribing information, 56–59t
        drug interactions, 5t, 6t, 14t, 55, 60–70t
        inhalation, 62–63t, 65–66, 66t
        injectable, 64–65t, 66t, 66–68, 67t
        neuromuscular blocking agents used with, 68–76, 69–70t, 71–72t. See also Neuromuscular blocking agents and specific agents
        pharmacology/pharmacokinetics, 65–68, 66t, 67t
    local, 1–16
        in connective tissue/oral mucosal disorders, 440t
        dosage calculations for, 613t
        drug interactions, 71t
        injectable, 1–10, 3–4t, 6t, 7t
        overdose, 302–303
        topical, 10t, 10–16, 12–14t, 15t
        vasoconstrictor/adrenergic blocker interactions, 319
Anexsia (hydrocodone combination), 81t, 82t
Angina pectoris, 267t, 303–304. See also **Medical emergencies in dental practice; Myocardial infarction**
Angioedema, 266t, 496, 502–503t
Angiotensin-converting-enzyme inhibitors. See ACE inhibitors and specific drugs
Angiotensin II receptor antagonists, 325–326, 326t, 502t
Anhydron (cyclothiazide), 317t
Anisindione, 409t, 499t, 527t
Anistreplase, 415t
Anolar DH5 (hydrocodone combination), 81t
Anorex (phendimetrazine), 505t, 518t, 538t
Anorexiants, 505t, 518t
Ansaid (flurbiprofen), 97t, 513t, 532t
Antacids, 349, 350t, 486t
    drug interactions, 133t, 154t, 166t, 176, 177t, 185t, 202t
Antiacne agents, 516t, 518t
Antianemic agents, 406, 407–408t, 416–419t. See also Nutritional supplements

Barrier Dental Sealant (desensitizing sealant), 244t

Barrier protection, 545, 552t
  gloves and glove liners, 550–551t
  masks, eyewear and clothing, 552t

Baycol (cerivastatin), 329t

Bayer Aspirin (aspirin), 479t, 527t

Bayer Select Ibuprofen (ibuprofen), 97t

Beclo-forte [CAN] (beclomethasone dipropionate, inhalant), 130t

Beclomethasone dipropionate, 130t, 336t, 501t, 527t

Beclovent (beclomethasone dipropionate), 130t, 336t

Beconase (beclomethasone dipropionate), 501t, 527t

Becotide (beclomethasone dipropionate), 527t

Bedoz (cyanocobalamin), 414t

Beepen-VK (penicillin V potassium), 479t

Belladonna alkaloids, 519t, 527t
  cross-sensitivities, 202t

Bellergal (belladonna alkaloids), 519t, 527t

Benadryl (diphenhydramine), 266t, 396t, 439t, 521t, 531t
  in parkinsonism, 366t

Benazepril, 502t, 527t

Bendroflumethiazide, 317t, 515t, 527t

Benicide (2.5% acidic) liquid sterilant, 555t

Benicide Plus (3.4% alkaline) liquid sterilant, 555t

Bentyl (dicyclomine), 519t, 530t

Benzepril, 326t

Benzocaine, 10–16, 12t

Benzodent ★ (benzocaine ointment), 12t

Benzodiazepine antagonist: flumazenil, 31–32, 32t, 33t, 261, 263t, 279t, 282t, 291t, 460t, 464, 471t

Benzodiazepine overdose, 279t

Benzodiazepines, 18–21, 22–28t, 29t, 30t, 31, 378–379t, 459, 463–464, 567t. *See also specific drugs*
  adverse effects, precautions and contraindications, 30t, 463–464, 465, 469–470t, 471t
  dosage and prescribing information, 22–28t, 460t
  drug interactions, 5t, 29t, 44t, 176
  as drugs of abuse, 562t
  as sleep aids, 396t

Benzoxazole, 388t

Benzphetamine, 505t, 527t

Benzquinamide, 354t

Benzthiazide, 317t

Benztropine mesylate, 366t, 522t, 527t

Bepadin (bepridil), 324t

Bepridil, 324t

β-adrenergic agonists, 335
  as bronchodilators, 337t

β-adrenergic antagonists (beta-blockers), 5t, 6t, 14t, 207t, 259, 270–271t, 285t, 319, 508t. *See also specific drugs*
  cardioselective, 320–321t
  drug interactions, 5t, 6t, 14t, 133t, 207t
  nonselective, 320t

Betadine Solution (1% available iodine), 191t

Betadine Surgical Scrub (iodophor, 1% available iodine), 189t

β-lactam antibiotics, 137–145. *See also* Cephalosporins; Penicillins

Betalol (metoprolol), 321t

Betamethasone, 124t, 502t, 527t

Betamethasone diprorionate, 128t augmented, 128t, 129t

Betamethasone Sodium Phosphate, 124t

Betamethasone valerate, 126t, 128t

Betapace (sotalol), 311t, 320t

Betapen-VK (penicillin V potassium), 479t

Betatrex (betamethasone valerate), 126t, 128t

Beta-Val (betamethasone valerate), 126t

Betaxolol, 320t, 508t, 527t

Bethanechol, 515t, 527t

Betnelan [CAN] (betamethasone), 124t, 502t

BiArrest-2 (water-based dual phenolic surface disinfectant), 557t

Biaxin (clarithromycin), 506t, 529t

Bib holders, 549t

Bibs, chain-free, 549t

Bicilllin L-A (penicillin G), 479t

BiCNU (carmustine), 517t, 528t

Bicoprofen (hydrocodone combination), 82t

Biocide (iodophor surface disinfectant), 557t

Biohazard bags, 558t

Biohazard communication, 558t

Biologic agents, antineoplastic, 482, 485t, 491t

Biological monitoring, 556t

BioSonic Enzymatic Ultrasonic Cleaner, 553t

BioSonic (nonenzymatic solutions), 553t

Biozyme (enzymatic solution), 553t

Biperiden, 366t, 522t, 528t

Bipolar disorder (manic-depressive disorder), 386–387

Birex_{se} (water-based dual phenolic surface disinfectant), 557t

Bismatrol Extra Strength (bismuth subsalicylate), 345t

Bismuth subsalicylate, 345t

Bisoprolol, 321t, 508t, 528t

Bisulphan, 517t

Bite block, 549t

Bitolterol, 337t

Black hairy tongue (coated tongue), 497, 503–504t

Blanex (chlorzoxazone), 461t

Bleaching, 254–255. *See also* **Tooth discoloration**
  external, 250–256, 252t, 253t, 254t
  internal, 250–251, 252t

Bleaching agents, 250–256
  adverse effects, precautions and contraindications, 254t
  American Dental Association Statement on the Safety of Home-Use Tooth-Whitening Products, 256
  dentist-dispensed home, 253t
  interactions with other substances, 254t
  professionally applied external, 252t
  professionally applied internal, 252t
  types of tooth discoloration, 251t

Bleeding, as side effect of chemotherapy, 488

Bleeding, control of, 105, 106–108t, 109–110, 111–112t. *See also* Hemostatics

Blenoxane (bleomycin), 484t, 507t, 528t

Bleomycin, 484t, 490t, 492t, 507t, 528t

Blocadren (timolol), 320t, 508t, 541t

Blood pressure
  elevated. *See* Antihypertensives; Hypertension
  maintenance of, 272t

Bonding agents, desensitizing, 243–244t, 246

Bonine (meclizine), 352t

Bontril PM (phendimetrazine), 505t

Bosworth Vigilance (enzymatic solution), 553t

Breast feeding. *See* Lactation

Brethaire (terbutaline), 337t

Brethine (terbutaline), 337t

Bretylate (bretylium tosylate), 311t

Bretylium tosylate, 260, 263t, 276–278t, 281t, 288t, 311t, 508t, 528t

Bretylol (bretylium tosylate), 276, 311t, 508t, 528t

Brevibloc (esmolol), 270–271t, 321t

Brevicon (ethinyl estradiol/norethindrone), 428t, 504t, 518t, 531t

Brevital (methohexital Na), 58t

BrianCare Antimicrobial Skin Cleanser (chlorhexidine gluconate 4%), 189t

Bricanyl (terbutaline), 337t

Brietal (methohexital Na [CAN]), 58t

Bromazepam, 378t, 396t

Bromazepam [CAN], 22t

Bromides, 70t, 72t, 75t

Bromocriptine, 148t, 367t

Brompheniramine, 521t, 528t

Bronalide [CAN] (flunisolide), 336t

Bronchodilators, 263t, 264t, 523t. *See also* Asthma drugs *and specific drugs*
  albuterol, 261–262, 263t, 264t, 281t, 283t
  β-adrenergic agonists, 337t

Bronchospasm, 264t, 265t, 299–300. *See also* Asthma drugs; Bronchodilators

Bronkaid Mist (epinephrine combination), 337t

Bronkodyl (theophylline, theophylline sodium glycinate), 338t

Bronkometer (isoetharine HCl/isoetharine mesylate), 337t

Bronkosol (isoetharine HCl/isoetharine mesylate), 337t

Bronolide [CAN] (flunisolide), 130t

Brooks Sodium Fluoride Toothpaste ★, 227t

Bruxism, 377

Buckley's Formo Cresol ★ (formocresol), 193t

Bucladin-5 (buclizine), 352t

Buclizine, 352t

Budesonide, 130t, 336t

Bufferin (aspirin), 527t

Bumethanide, 316t

Bumex (bumethanide), 316t

Bupivacaine, 2

Bupivacaine hydrochloride with epinephrine, 3t

Bupropion SR, 382t, 572t, 576, 580

Buscopan [CAN] (scopolamine butylbromide), 201t

Busodium (butabarbital), 36t

BuSpar (buspirone), 379t

Buspirone, 379t

Busulphan, 528t

Butabarbital, 36t

Butalan (butabarbital), 36t
Butalbital, codeine with, 80t
Butazolidin (phenylbutazone), 509t, 510t, 515t, 525t, 538t
Butazolidin [CAN] (phenylbutazone), 98t
Butinal with codeine, 80t
Butisol (butabarbital), 36t
Butler Fluoride Foam, 236t
Butler Fluoride Foam (2% neutral sodium fluoride), 236t
Butler Fluoride Prophylaxis Paste (2% fluoride prophylaxis paste), 236t
Butorphanol, 43t, 86t
Butyrophenones, 388t
    as antiemetics, 353t

Cafergot (ergotamine tartrate and caffeine), 371t
Caffeine
    codeine with, 80t
    drug interactions, 166t
Caffree Anti-Stain Fluoride Toothpaste, 224t
Calan (verapamil), 278t, 324t, 511t, 542t
Calcilean (heparin), 409t
Calciparine (heparin), 409t
Calcium, in cardiac applications, 261
Calcium channel blockers, 323–324, 324t, 508t–509t, 511t, 516t, 521t–522t. See also specific drugs
Calcium channel blocker toxicity, 278t
Calcium chloride, 263t
Calcium hydroxide (Ca[OH]2), 194t
Calcium hydroxide powder ★ (generic), 193t
Calcium salts (calcium chloride), 278t, 282t, 289t
    as antacid, 350t
Calculus prevention, 223t, 288. See also Dentifrices
Camalox (calcium salts), 350t
Camphorated parachlorophenol USP ★, 195t
Canadian schedules for controlled substances, 592–593t
Cancer drugs, 481–493. See also Antineoplastic drugs
Cancer pain, 77
Candesartan, 326t
Candidiasis, 131,173, 488. See also Antifungal agents; Fungal infection prophylaxis; Infection; Infection/infection prophylaxis
Cannabinoids, as antiemetics, 353t
Cannabis, 562–563t
Cantil (mepenzolate bromide), 350t
Capoten (captopril), 326t, 502t, 508t, 511t, 513t, 516t, 521t, 528t
Captopril, 326t, 502t, 508t, 511t, 513t, 516t, 521t, 528t
Carafate (sucralfate), 351t
Carbamazepine, 361t, 387t, 393t, 506t, 510t, 519t, 528t
    drug interactions, 39t, 90t, 148t
    in renal or hepatic impairment, 474t
Carbamide peroxide, 252t
44% Carbamide Peroxide (assisted bleach), 252t
Carbenicillin indanyl, 139t, 140t
Carbidopa/levodopa, 367t, 522t, 528t
Carbocaine ★ (mepivacaine hydrochloride), 3t

Carbocaine with Neo-Cobefrin ★ (mepivacaine hydrochloride with levonordefrin), 3t
Carbolith (lithium), 387t
Carbolith [CAN] (lithium), 507t
Carbonic anhydrase inhibitors, 508t
Carboplatin, 484t, 517t, 528t
Cardene (nicardipine), 324t
Cardiac arrest, 278t
Cardiac arrhythmias. See Antidysrhythmics; Dysrhythmias
Cardilate (erythrityl tetranitrate), 315t
Cardiovascular drugs, 267t, 309–333. See also specific drugs and drug classes
    acting on renin-angiotensin system, 324–325326–327t
    adrenergic blocking agents, 319–322, 320–322t
    adverse effects, 330–333t
    antianginal agents, 314, 315t
    antidysrhythmics, 310–312
    antihypertensives, 90t, 259, 263t, 267t, 270–271t, 284t, 314–315. See also Diuretics
        centrally acting, 325, 327t
        drug interactions, 5t, 44t, 60t, 101t
    calcium channel blockers, 323–324, 324t
    cardiac glycosides, 6t, 14t, 71t, 133t, 148t, 154t, 176, 313, 313t
    cholesterol-lowering agents, 328–329, 329t
    diuretics, 315–316, 316–318t
    dosage and prescribing information, 310–311t
    neuronal blocking or depleting agents, 327, 328t
    vasodilators
        direct-acting, 322t, 322–323
        for erectile dysfunction, 323, 323t
Cardizem (diltiazem), 324t, 508t, 511t, 530t
Cardoquin (quinidine), 310t
Cardura (doxazocin), 521t, 531t
Care-4 ★ (acidulated phosphate fluoride gel), 236t
Caries prevention
    dentifrices, 221–229
    fluorides
        systemic, 231–234
        topical, 235–241
    mouthrinses, 211–221
Carisprodol and combinations, 461t, 466, 467–468t, 471t
Carmustine, 517t, 528t
Carteolol, 320t, 508t
Cartol (carteolol), 320t, 508t
Cartrol (bisoprolol), 528t
Cataflam (diclofenac potassium), 96t, 499t, 530t
Catapres (clonidine), 327t, 515t, 521t, 529t
Catecholamines, endogenous, 260, 263t, 265t
CaviCide (alcohol-based quaternary ammonium compound disinfectant), 557t
Ceclor (cefaclor), 475t, 500t, 528t
CeeNU (lomustine), 534t
Cefaclor, 139t, 141t, 475t, 500t, 528t
    in renal or hepatic impairment, 475t
Cefadroxil, 139t, 141t
Cefamandol, 506t, 528t
Cefixime, 139t, 142t

Cefuroxime, 139t, 142t
Celebrex (celecoxib), 98t
Celecoxib, 98t
Celestone (betamethasone), 124t, 502t, 527t
Celexa (citalopram), 383t
Cellulose
    oxidized, 105, 106t, 109, 110, 111t
    oxidized regenerated, 106t, 109, 110, 111t
Celonin (methsuximide), 363t
Cel-U-Jec (betamethasone), 124t
Centrally acting antihypertensives, 325, 327t
Centrax (prazepam), 28t, 379t, 519t, 538t
Cephadrine, 139t, 142t
Cephalexin, 139t, 142t, 475t
    in renal or hepatic impairment, 475t
Cephalosporins, 137–145, 138–139t, 140–142t, 143t, 144t, 500t. See also specific drugs
Cerivastatin, 329t
Cesamet (nabilone), 353t
Cetacaine ★ (benzocaine with butamben and tetracaine hydrochloride), 13t
Charcoal, 39t
Chateau Fluoride Toothpaste ★, 227t
Chelating agents, 516t, 537t
Chemical dependency. See also Substance abuse
    American Dental Association policy statement on (Res. 64H-1987), 559
Chemical indicators, 555t
Chemical vapor sterilizer, 555t
Chemotherapeutic agents, 481–493. See also Antineoplastic agents
Chemotherapy, antiemetics with, 353t
Chest pain, 303–305. See also Myocardial infarction
Chewing gum, fluoridated, 232
Children. See Pediatric patients
Chloral hydrate, 48, 49t, 50t, 475t, 484t
    adverse effects, precautions and contraindications, 50t
    dosage and prescribing information, 49t
    drug interactions, 49t
    as drug of abuse, 562t
    in renal or hepatic impairment, 475t
Chloral hydrate, generic [CAN], 49t
Chloramphenicol, 511t, 528t
    drug interactions, 528t
Chloraseptic (benzocaine), 12t
Chlorazepate, 23t, 378t
Chlordiazepoxide, 22t, 378t, 459, 460t, 463, 475t, 518t, 528t
    in renal or hepatic impairment, 475t
Chlordiazepoxide/clindinium, 519t, 528t
Chlorhexidine gluconate (CHG), 188, 189t, 509t, 528t
Chlorine-based surface disinfectants, 557t
Chlorofon-F (chlorzoxazone), 461t
Chloromycetin (chloramphenicol), 511t, 528t
Chloro-Pro 10 (chlorpheniramine), 266t
Chloroquine, 484t
Chlorostat Antimicrobial Skin Cleanser ★ (chlorhexidine gluconate 2%), 189t
Chlorothiazide, 317t, 515t, 524t, 529t
Chlorox (sodium hypochlorite, NaOCl), 194t
Chlorpheniramine, 258, 263t, 266t, 281t, 284t, 521t, 529t

MetriCare Surgical Hand Scrub (chlorhexidine gluconate 4%), 189t
MetriGuard (alcohol-based quaternary ammonium compound disinfectant), 557t
MetriTest (glutaraldehyde concentration monitor), 556t
Metronidazole, 40t, 160–164, 161t, 162t, 163t, 347t, 477t, 506t, 536t
  in renal or hepatic impairment, 477t
Metubine Iodide (metocurine iodide), 69t, 75t
Mevacor (lovastatin), 329t
Mexate (methotrexate), 485t
Mexiletine, 5t, 505t, 520t, 536t
Mexitil (mexiletine), 505t, 520t, 536t
Mezoridazine, 514t
Micardis (telmisartan), 326t
Microbial resistance, 605
Microfibrillar collagen hemostat, 106t, 109, 111t, 113
Microflora imbalance, 496, 500–502t
Micronase (glyburide), 430t
Micronor (norethindrone), 431t
Micro prime (methacrylate polymer desensitizer), 244t
MicroStat 2 (sodium bromide/chlorine disinfectant), 557t
Midamor (amiloride), 317t, 524t
Midazolam, 26–27t, 269t, 281t, 285t, 459, 460t, 463, 464, 503t, 505t
Midmark steam autoclave, 554t
Midol (ibuprofen), 97t
Midrin (isomethepene mucate, dichlorophenazone, acetominophen), 371t
Miflex (chlorzoxazone), 461t
Migraine headache, drugs used in, 370–372, 371
Milk of Magnesia (magnesium salts/aluminum salts), 350t
Milontin (pensuximide), 363t
Miltown (meprobamate), 53t, 519t, 535t
Miltown [CAN] (meprobamate), 53t
Minestrin 1/20 (norethindrone acetate/ethinyl estradiol), 429t
Mini-Ovral (levonorgestrel/ethinyl estradiol), 428t
Minipress (prazosin), 321t, 522t, 538t
Minocin (minocycline), 153t, 477t, 516t, 536t
Minocycline, 153t, 477t, 516t, 536t
  in renal or hepatic impairment, 477t
Minocycline hydrochloride gel, 153t, 156–157
Minoxidil, 322t
Miradon (anisindione), 409t, 499t, 527t
Mirapex (pramipexole), 522t, 538t
Mirtazapine, 382t
Misoprostol, 351t
Mitomycin-C, 486t
Mitran (chlordiazepoxide), 460t
Mivacron (mivacurium chloride), 69t, 75t
Mivacurium chloride, 69t, 75t
Mixed connective-tissue disease (MCTD), 442
Mizoral (ketoconazole), 477t, 503t
Moban (molindone), 390t, 523t, 536t
Mobenol [CAN] (tolbutamide), 501t
Modecate (flubenazine), 391t
ModiCon (norethindrone/ethinyl estradiol), 428t

Moditen (flubenazine), 391t
Moduratic (amiloride/hydrochlorothiazide), 318t
Moexipril, 326t, 502t, 536t
Mogadan [CAN] (nitrazepam), 27t, 396t
Moi-Stir, Moi-Stir Swabsticks (saliva substitute), 209t
Molindone, 390t, 523t, 536t
Mol-Iron (ferrous sulfate), 408t
Mometasone furoate, 127t
Monitan (acebutalol), 320t
Monitoring, biological, 556t
Monoamine oxidase (MAO) inhibitors, 14t, 40t, 44t, 91t, 439t
Monoclonal antibodies, antineoplastic, 485t
Monodox (doxycycline monohydrate), 153t, 476t
Monopril (fosinopril), 326t, 502t, 532t
Morieizine (moricizine), 536t
Morlutate (norethindrone), 431t
Morphine, 43t, 88–89t, 524t, 536t, 564t
  in renal or hepatic impairment, 478t
Morphine Extra-Forte [CAN] (morphine sulfate injection), 43t, 89t, 268t, 275t
Morphine HP (morphine [CAN]), 43t, 89t, 268t, 275t
Morphine sulfate, 258, 263t, 268t, 275t, 281t, 284t
Motrin (ibuprofen), 97t, 476t, 499t, 513t, 517t, 525t, 533t
MouthKote (saliva substitute), 209t
MouthKote Toothpaste, 227t
Mouthrinses, 211–221
  adverse effects, precautions and contraindications, 219t
  anesthetic, 214t
  antitartar, 214t
  chlorhexidine, 213, 214t, 219t
  cosmetic, 214t, 219t
  dosage and prescribing information, 214–218t
  essential oils, 215–216t, 219t, 220
  fluorides, 215t, 219t, 220
  for halitosis, 216–217t, 219t, 220
  oxygenating, 216t, 219t, 220
  prebrushing, 217t, 219t, 220
  preprocedure antimicrobial, 548t
  sanguinarine and other herbal agents, 217t, 219t, 220
Movement disorders, 498, 514t
M-Prednisol-40, -80 (methylprednisolone), 123t
MS Contin (morphine), 478t, 524t, 536t
MSIR (morphine sulfate), 89t
MSIR [CAN] (morphine sulfate), 89t
MS/L (morphine sulfate), 89t
MS/S (morphine sulfate suppository), 89t
Mucosal and skin antiseptics, 190–192.
  See also under Antiseptics
Mucositis, as side effect of chemotherapy, 487
Mucous membrane pemphigoid, 449
Muscarinic receptor antagonists, 524t
Muscle relaxants. See Neuromuscular blocking agents; Skeletal muscle relaxants; Spasmolytics
Muscle relaxation. See Neuromuscular blocking agents; Skeletal muscle relaxants; Spasmolytics
Mus-Lac (chlorzoxazone), 461t

Myasthenia gravis, drugs used in, 360–364, 361–363t
Mycelex (clotrimazole), 174t
Mycogen (nystatin with triamcinolone), 175t
Mycolog II (nystatin with triamcinolone), 175t
Mycostatin (nystatin), 175t
Myco-Triacet (nystatin with triamcinolone), 175t
Myelo [CAN] (clotrimazole), 174t
My First Colgate Anti-Cavity Fluoride Toothpaste ★, 227t
Myidone (primidone), 362t
Mykrox (metolazone), 318t
Mylanta (calcium salts), 350t
Mylanta (magnesium salts/aluminum salts), 350t
Mylanta Soothing Lozenges (calcium salts), 350t
Myleran (busulphan), 517t, 528t
Myocardial infarction, 265t, 268t, 275t, 277t, 278t, 304–305
Myochrysine (gold sodium methylate), 439t, 516t, 532t
Myrosemide (furosemide), 316t
Mysoline (primidone), 362t, 512t, 538t
Mytelase Caplets (ambemonium), 365t
Mytrex (nystatin with triamcinolone), 175t

Nabilone, 353t
Nabumetone, 96t
Nadolol, 6t, 14t, 320t, 508t, 522t, 536t. See also ß-adrenergic antagonists
  in parkinsonism, 368t
Nadopen-V [CAN] (penicillin VK), 503t
Nadostine [CAN] (nystatin), 175t
Nafcillin, 139t, 141t
NaF rinse ★ (prescription fluoride), 236t
NaF rinse Acidulated ★ (OTC fluoride), 237t
NaF rinse Neutral ★ (OTC fluoride), 237t
Nalbuphine, 43t
Nalfon (fenoprofen), 97t, 525t, 532t
Naloxone (opioid [narcotic] antagonist), 45–47t, 46t, 90, 261, 280t, 292t
  adverse effects, precautions and contraindications, 46t
  dosage and prescribing information, 46–47t
  drug interactions, 46t
  in renal or hepatic impairment, 478t
Naltrexone, 90
Nandrolone, 422t, 562t
Naprosyn (naproxen), 98t, 478t, 500t, 525t, 536t
Naproxen, 98t, 485t, 500t, 525t, 536t
  in renal or hepatic impairment, 478t
Napthylalkanone, 95–96t
Naqua (trichloromethiazide), 318t
Naratriptan, 371t
Narcan ★ (naloxone), 47t, 280t
Narcotics. See also Opioids
  as drugs of abuse, 564–565t
Nardil (phenelzine), 383t, 520t, 538t
Nasalcrom (OTC) (cromolyn sodium), 509t, 515t, 530t
Nasalide (flunisolide solution), 501t, 532t
Nasocort (triamcinolone), 501t
Naturetin (bendroflumethiazide), 317t, 515t, 527t

muth subsalicylate), 345t

Pepto Diarrheal Control (loperamide), 345t

Peractin (cyproheptadine), 521t, 530t

Percocet ★ (oxydocone combination), 82t

Percodan ★ (oxydocone combination), 83t

Percodan-Demi ★ (oxydocone combination), 83t

Perfecta 3/15 Extra Strength (home bleaching agent), 253t

Perfect Care (chlorhexidine gluconate 0.75%), 189t

Perfect Choice ★ (acidulated phosphate fluoride gel), 236t

Perfect Choice ★ (OTC fluoride), 237t

Perfect White (hydrogen peroxide 35% power bleaching agent), 252t

Pergolide, 368t

Pericyazine, 391t

Peridex ★ (chlorhexidine), 509t, 528t, 548t

Peridol [CAN] (haloperidol), 388t

Peridres (zinc oxide-eugenol), 195t

Perio-Care Periodontal Dressing ★ (zinc oxide), 195t

Periochek (OTC fluoride), 237t

PerioChip (chlorhexidine chip), 220

Periodontal therapy, 153t, 195–196t, 220, 237t, 548t

Periodontal dressings, 195–196t

Periodontitis, refractory, 151–152, 151t

PerioGard, 548t

Perio-Putty (zinc oxide), 195t

Periostat (doxycycline hyclate), 153t

Permapen (penicillin G), 479t

Permax (pergolide), 368t

Permitil (flubenazine), 391t

Peroxide. See Carbamide peroxide; Hydrogen peroxide

Perphenazine, 391t, 512t, 514t, 538t

Perrigo Fluoride Toothpaste ★, 227t

Persantine (dipyridamole), 413t, 499t, 509t, 531t

Pertofrane (desipramine), 385t, 520t, 530t

Peyote, 562t

Pfizerpen (penicillin G), 537t

Phenacemide, 363t

Phenalzine, 538t

Phencyclidine, 562t, 568t

Phendimetrazine, 505t, 518t, 538t

Phenelzine, 383t, 520t

Phenergan (promethazine), 521t, 539t
  as antiemetic, 354t

Phenobarbital, 37t, 484t, 510t, 512t, 538t
  as anticonvulsant, 361t
  drug interactions, 162t
  in renal or hepatic impairment, 479t

Phenol, benzocaine with, 12t

Phenolic compounds, 192, 194t, 196t

Phenolic surface disinfectants
  alcohol-based, 557t
  water-based, 557t

Phenothiazines, 44t, 391–392t, 484t
  as antiemetics, 354t, 357t

Phenoxybenzamine, 6t, 321t

Phenoxymethyl-penicillin (Penicillin V), 139t

Phentermine, 505t, 518t, 538t

Phentolamine, 321t

Phenurone (phenacemide), 363t

Phenylacetic acids, 96

Phenylbutazone, 40t, 98t, 485t, 509t, 510t, 515t, 525t, 538t

Phenylpropanolamine/chlorpheniramine, 524t, 538t

Phenytex (phenytoin), 311t, 362t

Phenytoin, 133t, 162t, 311t, 362t, 484t, 510t, 511t, 538t. See also Anticonvulsants

Phetylureum (phenacemide), 363t

Phos-Flur ★ (prescription fluoride), 236t

Phosphajel (aluminum salts), 350t

Photosensitivity, 155
  drugs causing, 621–625t

Phytonadione (vitamin K₁), 107t, 110, 112t, 113t

Pilocarpine, 206t, 206–207, 207t

Pimozide, 148t, 390t, 523t, 538t

Pindolol, 320t, 508t, 538t

Pipecuronium bromide, 70t, 75t

Pirbuterol acetate, 337t

Pirenzepine [CAN], 350t

Piroxicam, 96t, 500t, 525t, 538t

Pirportal L4 (pripothiazine), 391t

Plak Smacker ★ (OTC fluoride), 237t

Plaquenil, 439t

Plaque reduction
  dentifrices, 221–229, 225t
  mouthrinses, 211–221

Platelet disorders, 104–105

Platinol (cisplatin), 484t

Plavix (clopidogrel), 499t, 529t

Plendil (felodipine), 511t, 532t

PMS-Acetinominophen with Codeine [CAN], 79t

PMS-Baclofen [CAN] (baclofen), 461t

PMS-Benztropine [CAN] (benztropine), 366t

PMS-Chloral Hydrate [CAN] (chloral hydrate), 49t

PMS-Clonazepam [CAN] (clonazepam), 378t

PMS-Diazepam [CAN] (diazepam oral solution), 24t, 396t

PMS-Ferrous Sulfate [CAN] (ferrous sulfate), 408t

PMS Hydromorphone [CAN] (hydromorphone), 87t

PMS-Methylphenidate [CAN] (methylphenidate), 395t

PMS-Piroxicam [CAN] (piroxicam), 96t

Polocaine ★ (mepivacaine hydrochloride), 3t

Polocaine with Levonordefrin ★ (mepivacaine hydrochloride with levonordefrin), 3t

Polyflex (chlorzoxazone), 461t

Polygesic (hydrocodone combination), 81t

Polymyositis, 442

Polythiazide, 318t

Pondimin (fenfluramine), 518t, 532t

Ponstan (mefenamic acid), 95t

Ponstan [CAN] (mefenamic acid), 500t

Ponstel (mefenamic acid), 95t, 500t, 535t

Porter Sterilizer (steam autoclave), 554t

Potassium aluminum sulfate, gingival retraction cord with, 117t, 118t

Potassium chloride, 202t

Potassium-depleting drugs, 72t

Potassium supplements, drug interactions, 101t

Powergel (bleaching agent), 252t

Poxi (chlordiazepoxide), 378t

Pragmin (dalteparin), 499t

Pramipexole, 522t, 538t

Pravachol (pravastatin), 329t

Pravastatin, 329t

Prazepam, 28t, 379t, 519t, 538t

Prazosin, 6t, 321t, 522t, 538t

Prebrushing mouthrinses, 217t, 219t, 220

Precise QTB (alcohol-based quaternary ammonium compound disinfectant), 557t

Precleaning solutions, 553t

Predalone-50 (prednisolone), 123t

Predcor-50 (prednisolone), 123t

Predicon-M (prednisone), 347t

Prednicen-M (prednisone), 122t

Prednisolone, 123t

Prednisol TBA (prednisolone), 123t

Prednisone, 122t
  as antineoplastic, 486t, 491t, 493t
  in Crohn's disease/ulcerative colitis, 347t

Pregnancy. See also Lactation; Teratogenicity
  agents affecting fetus and nursing infant, 594t, 594–595t, 595t
  analgesics in
    nonopioid, 94
    opioid, 85
  anesthetics in
    general, 61
    local, 14
  antibiotics in, 143–144, 149, 155, 158–159, 162–163, 165–166, 170
  anticholinergic drugs in, 199
  antifungal agents in, 178
  cancer chemotherapy in, 488
  caution information list for, 594–595t
  drugs contraindicated in, 462
  glucocorticoids in, 131
  neuromuscular blocking agents in, 73
  nicotine replacement systems in, 576, 580
  pilocarpine in, 206
  sedation in, 21, 31, 34, 42, 46, 50, 52
  spasmolytics in, 467
  U.S. Food and Drug Administration Classifications, 593t

Pregnancy risk factors. See also Teratogenicity
  thalidomide, 441t, 445t, 452, 453

Premarin (conjugated estrogen), 423t

Prenatal fluoride administration, 232

Prenisolone Tebutate (prednisolone), 123t

Prepulsid [CAN] (cisapride), 348t

Prescriptions
  abbreviations used in, 620t
  sample, 617–620t

Pressurized sprays, hazards of, 15

Pres-Tab (glyburide), 430t

Prevent Tartar Prevention Toothpaste with Fluoride, 223t

PreviDent ★ (prescription fluoride), 236t

PreviDent Gel (prescription fluoride), 236t

PreviDent 5000 Plus (prescription fluoride), 236t

Price Chopper Fluoride Toothpaste ★, 227t

Prilocaine Forte ★ (prilocaine

drug dosing in, 474–479t
Renedil (felopidine), 324t
Renese (polythiazide), 318t
Renin-angiotensin system, drugs acting on, 324–325, 326–327t. *See also* Diuretics
Renoquid (sulfacytine), 510t, 540t
ReoPro (abciximab), 499t, 526t
Requip (ropinirole), 522t, 539t
Rescudose (morphine), 89t, 478t
Reserfia (reserpine), 328t
Reserpine, 6t, 14t, 328t, 522t, 539t
Respiratory depression, nonopioid-induced, 272t
Respiratory distress, 265t, 268t, 299–300
Respiratory drugs, 334–343. *See also* Asthma drugs *and specific drugs and drug types*
adverse effects, 340–341t, 341t
American Society of Anesthesiologists (ASA) Classification of Asthma, 335t
bronchodilators, 338t, 339–340
evolving therapies, 339t, 340–342
inhibitors of chemical mediators/anti-inflammatory drugs, 335–339, 336t
precautions and contraindications, 342t
Respiratory stimulants, 262, 272t
Responsans-10 (chlordiazepoxide), 460t
Restore Ultrasonic Cleaner (nonenzymatic cleaning solution), 553t
Restoril (temazepam), 28t, 396t, 480t, 525t, 540t
Retinoids, 445t, 451–452, 453, 516t, 518t
as antineoplastics, 485t, 491t, 493t
in connective tissue/oral mucosal disorders, 440t
Retraction cords. *See* Gingival retraction cords
Retrax (gingival retraction cord, plain), 116t
Retreat (gingival retraction cord with aluminum chloride), 116t, 118
Rheumatoid arthritis, 439t, 441–442
Rhodis [CAN] (ketoprofen), 499t
Rhodis-EC (ketoprofen extended release), 97t
Rhotrimine (trimipramine), 385t
Rhythmol (propafenone), 505t, 539t
Rid-A-Pain Dental (benzocaine gel), 12t
Ridaura (auranofin), 503t, 505t, 516t, 527t
Rifampin, 40t, 133t, 176, 177t
Riopan (magnesium salts/aluminum salts), 350t
Risperdal (risperidone), 388t, 514t, 523t, 539t
Risperidone, 388t, 514t, 523t, 539t
Ritalin (methylphenidate), 395t
Ritonavir, 178t
Rituxan (antineoplastic monoclonal antibody), 485t
Rituximab, 485t
Rivotril (clonazepam), 378t
Rizatriptan, 371t, 525t, 539t
RMS Inserts (morphine sulfate suppository), 89t
Robalate (calcium salts), 350t
Robamol (methocarbamol), 462t
Robaxin (methocarbamol), 462t
Robinul (glycopyrrolate), 200t
Robinul Forte (glycopyrrolate), 200t

Robitet (tetracycline), 503t, 540t
Rocuronium bromide, 70t, 75t
Roferon-A (interferon alfa), 184t
Romazicon (benzodiazepine antagonist: flumazenil), 31–32, 32t, 33t, 261, 263t, 279t, 282t, 460t
Root canal medications, 192–193, 193–195t. *See also* **Endodontic therapy**
Ropinirole, 522t, 539t
Roxanol (morphine), 89t, 478t
Roxicet (oxydocone combination), 82t, 83t
Roxicodone (oxycodone HCl oral solution), 89t
Roxilox (oxycodone combination), 83t
Roxiprin (oxycodone combination), 83t
Rubber dams, 548t
Rubion (cyanocobalamin), 414t
Rubramin (cyanocobalamin), 414t
Rufen (ibuprofen), 97t, 476t, 499t, 513t, 525t, 533t
Rust inhibitors, 553t
Rynacrom [CAN] (nedocromil sodium), 336t

Safety suction, 548t
Safety syringes, 558t
Salagen (pilocarpine), 206t, 207t, 208t
Salazopyrin [CAN] (sulfasalazine), 347t
Salicylates, 97t, 485t. *See also* Aspirin; Nonsteroidal anti-inflammatory drugs (NSAIDs)
Saliva ejector tips, 549t
Salivart ★ (saliva substitute), 209t
Salivary gland involvement, 498, 515t
Saliva Substitute ★, 209t
Saliva substitutes, 208–210, 209t
Salivation, augmentation of, 208–210, 209t
Salivation, inhibition of. *See also* Anticholinergic drugs
by anticholinergic drugs, 198–199, 200–205t, 269t
by cholinergic drug: pilocarpine, 206t, 206–207t, 207t
Salix (saliva substitute), 209t
Salmeterol, 337t
Salsalate, 99t
Sal-Tropine ★ (atropine), 200t, 269t
Saluron (hydrofluromethiazide), 317t
Sample prescriptions, 617–620t
Sana Prep Solution (0.75% available iodine), 191t
Sana-Scrub Surgical Scrub (iodophor, 0.75% available iodine), 189t
Sandimmune (cyclosporin A), 440t, 502t, 511t, 530t
SaniSept (0.3% triclosan), 189t
SaniTex Plus (alcohol-based quaternary ammonium compound disinfectant), 557t
Sanorex (mazindol), 505t, 535t
Sansert (methysergide maleate), 371t
Saquinavir, 178t
Sav-On Fluoride Toothpaste ★, 227t
Scandonest ★ (mepivacaine hydrochloride), 3t
Scandonest with Levonordefrin ★ (mepivacaine hydrochloride with levonordefrin), 3t
Schein dry heat sterilizer, 554t
Schein Home Care (OTC fluoride), 237t
Scleroderma, 442, 443

Scopace (scopalamine hydrobromide), 201t
Scopolamine, 540t
as antiemetic, 352t
Scopolamine butylbromide [CAN], 201t
Scopolamine hydrobromide, 201t
Scrub-Stat IV Antimicrobial Solution ★ (chlorhexidine gluconate 4%), 189t
Sealants, desensitizing, 244t, 246
Secobarbital, 38t, 510t, 512t, 540t
Secobarbital/amobarbital, 38t
Seconal (secobarbital), 38t, 510t, 512t, 540t
Sectral (acebutolol), 320t, 508t, 526t
Security Holding Solution (enzymatic solution), 553t
Sedation and anxiety control, 17, 21, 34, 50, 53, 454–458. *See also specific drugs and drug classes*
administration routes, 18–20
barbiturates, 33–34, 35–38t, 39–40t, 41
benzodiazepine antagonist: flumazenil, 31–32, 32t, 33t, 261, 263t, 279t, 282t, 291t, 460t, 464, 471t
benzodiazepines, 18–21, 22–28t, 29t, 30t, 31
chloral hydrate, 48, 49t, 50t
ethchlorvynol, 50–52, 51t
meprobamate, 52, 53t
opioid (narcotic) antagonist: naloxone, 45–47, 46t, 90, 261, 280t, 292t
opioids, 41–42, 43t, 44t, 45t
principles and background, 17f, 17–18
thalidomide in, 441t, 445t, 452, 453
Sedatives
in connective tissue/oral mucosal disorders, 441t
as drugs of abuse, 562t
systemic effects, 525t
Seizures, emergency management of, 269t, 297–299
Selective serotonin reuptake inhibitors (SSRIs), 383–384t, 525t
as antiemetic, 354t
Selegiline, 368t
Senoquid (sulfacytine), 513t
Sensitivity reduction. *See* **Dentifrices; Desensitization**
Sensitivity-reduction dentifrices, 225–226t
Sensodyne Cool Gel Toothpaste, 225t
Sensodyne Extra Whitening, 224t, 225t
Sensodyne Fresh Mint Toothpaste, 226t
Sensodyne Original, 226t
Sensodyne Sealant [CAN] (ferric oxalate desensitizing agent), 244t
Sensodyne Tartar Control Plus Whitening, 223t, 224t, 226t
Sensodyne Toothpaste for Sensitive Teeth and Cavity Protection with Baking Soda, 226t
SensoGard Canker Sore Relief (benzocaine gel), 12t
Septanest [CAN] (articaine hydrochloride with epinephrine), 3t
Septisol Solution (0.25% triclosan), 189t
Serax (oxazepam), 28t, 379t, 478t, 519t, 537t
Serentil (mesoridazine), 391t, 512t, 514t, 535t
Serevent (salmeterol), 337t
Seroquel (quetiapine), 389t, 523t, 539t
Serpalan (reserpine), 328t

Super-Dent ★ (benzocaine gel), 12t
Super-Dent ★ (OTC fluoride), 237t
Superinfection, 144t
Superoxol with sodium perborate ★ (bleaching agent), 252t
Supeudol [CAN] (oxycodone HCl suppositories), 89t
Supeudol [CAN] (oxycodone HCl tablets), 89t
Supracaine [CAN] (lidocaine aerosol), 13t
Suprane (desflurane), 56t
Surface asepsis, 546–547, 557t
Surface aseptic covers, 557t
Surface disinfectants, 557t
Surgicel Absorbable Hemostat ★ (oxidized regenerated cellulose), 106t
Surgicel Nu-Knit Absorbable Hemostat (oxidized regenerated cellulose), 106t
Surmontil (trimipramine), 385t
Sus-Phrine/Sus-Phrine parenteral (epinephrine combination), 337t
Swan Sodium Fluoride Toothpaste ★, 227t
Symmetrel (amantadine), 367t
Sympathomimetics. *See also specific drugs*
  drug interactions, 14t
Synacort (hydrocortisone), 126t
Synalar (fluocinolone acetonide), 126t, 127t
Synalgos DC (dihydrocodeine bitartrate with aspirin and caffeine), 80–81t
Syn-Chlonazepam [CAN] (clonazepam), 23t, 39t
Syncope, 295–297
Synflex (naproxen sodium), 98t
Synkayvite (menadiol sodium diphosphate vitamin K₄), 108t
Syn-Nadolol [CAN] (nadolol), 320t
Synphasic (norethindrone/ethinyl estradiol), 428t
Syn-Pindolol [CAN] (pindolol), 320t
Synthroid (levothyroxine), 432t
Syringes, safety, 558t
Systemic agents, oral manifestations of, 496–542. *See also* Oral manifestations of systemic agents
Systemic disease-related oral morbidity, 119–135
Systemic fluorides, 231–234. *See also under* Fluorides

Tabarine [CAN] (tubocurarine chloride), 70t, 75t
Tac-3 (triamcinolone), 124t
Tac-40 (triamcinolone), 124t
TACE (chlortrianisene), 423t
Tachycardia, 270t, 271t. *See also* Antidysrhythmics; **Dysrhythmias**
  paroxysmal supraventricular, 278t
Tacrine, 503t, 515t, 540t
Tacrium (atracurium besylate), 69t, 75t
Tagamet (cimetidine), 351t
Talacen (pentazocine combination), 83t
Talwin (pentazocine), 43t, 479t, 525t, 537t
Tambocor (flecainide), 311t, 505t, 532t
Tamone (tamoxifen), 486t
Tamoxifen, 486t, 491t, 493t, 501t, 540t
Tapazole (methimazole), 435t, 507t, 535t
Taractan (chlorprothixene), 512t, 514t, 529t
Tardive dyskinesia, 381, 498, 514t
Tartar Control Listerine ★, 214t

Tasmar (tolcapone), 522t, 541t
Taste disturbance (dysgeusia), 487, 497, 505–509t
Tavist (clemastine), 521t, 529t
Taxanes, 491t, 493t
Taxol (paclitaxel), 486t
Taxotere (docutaxel), 486t
T-Cypionate (testosterone), 422t
Tecnal-C1/2 or C1/4 [CAN] (codeine with aspirin, caffeine, and butalbital), 80t
Tegretol (carbamazepine), 361t, 387t, 474t, 506t, 510t, 519t, 528t
Tegretol Chewtabs [CAN] (carbamazepine), 387t, 393t
Teladar (betamethasone diproprionate), 128t
Teledyne Water-Pik Prophylaxis Paste (2% fluoride prophylaxis paste), 236t
Telmisartan, 326t
Temazepam, 28t, 396t, 525t, 540t
  in renal or hepatic impairment, 480t
Temovate (clobetasol propionate), 129t
Temporomandibular joint dysfunction, 93
Tenex (guanfacine), 327t
Tenormin (atenolol), 320t, 508t, 527t
Tenuate (diethylpropion), 505t, 518t, 530t
Tepanil (diethylpropion), 518t, 530t
Teratogen, thalidomide as, 441t, 445t, 452, 453
Teratogenicity, 594–595t
Terazosin, 321t, 522t, 540t
Terbutaline, 337t
Terfluzine (trifluoperazine), 392t
Testa-C (testosterone), 422t
Testamone 100 (testosterone), 422t
Testaqua (testosterone), 422t
Testex (testosterone), 422t
Testoderm (testosterone), 422t
Testoject (testosterone), 422t
Testone L.A. 200 (testosterone), 422t
Testosterone, 422t
  as drug of abuse, 562t
Testred (methyltestosterone), 422t
Testred Cypionate (testosterone), 422t
Testrin P.A. (methyltestosterone), 422t
Tetracaine [CAN], 11–16, 13, 13t
Tetracycline/ethylene/vinyl acetate copolymer fiber, 153t, 156–157
Tetracyclines, 151t, 151–155, 153t, 154t, 156t, 500t, 503t, 506t, 510t, 540t
  in renal or hepatic impairment, 480t
Tetracylic antidepressants, 384t
Tetracyn (tetracycline), 480t
Tetrahydrocannabinol (cannibis), 562t
Teveten (eprosartan), 326t
T-Gesic (hydrocodone combination), 81t
Thalidomide, 441t, 445t, 452, 453
Thalitone (chlorathalidone), 317t
Thalomide (thalidomide), 441t, 452, 453
THC (cannibis), 562t
Theo-24 (theophylline), 338t
Theoclear (theophylline/theophylline sodium glycinate), 338t
Theodur Sprinkle (theophylline/theophylline sodium glycinate), 338t
Theolair (theophylline/theophylline sodium glycinate), 338t
Theophyllines, 29t, 40t, 148t, 166t, 338t, 485t
Theospan-SR (theophylline/theophylline sodium glycinate), 338t
Theostat (theophylline/theophylline sodi-

um glycinate), 338t
Theovent (theophylline/theophylline sodium glycinate), 338t
Theraflur ★ (prescription fluoride), 236t
Thiazide diuretics, 316–317t, 515t. *See also* Diuretics *and specific drugs*
Thiethylperazine, 354t
Thioidazine, 523t
Thiopental, in renal or hepatic impairment, 480t
Thiopental Na, 59t
Thiopentone (thiopental IV), 480t
Thiopropazate, 392t
Thioproperazine, 392t
Thioridazine, 6t, 392t, 512t, 514t, 540t
Thiosulfil Forte (sulfamethizole), 510t, 513t, 540t
Thiothixene, 393t, 514t, 523t, 541t
Thioxanthenes, 393t
Thorazine (chlorpromazine), 391t, 512t, 514t, 523t, 529t
  as antiemetic, 354t
Thor-prom (chlorpromazine), 391t
Thrombin, 107t, 108t, 110, 112t, 114
Thrombinar (thrombin), 108t
Thrombin-JMI (thrombin), 108t
Thrombogen (thrombin), 108t
Thrombolytic agents, 414–415, 415t
Thrombostat (thrombin), 108t
Thyrar (thyroid), 432t
Thyroglobulin, 432t
Thyroid hormones, 6t, 14t, 60t, 425, 432t, 434–435t, 436–437t
Thyroid Strong (thyroid), 432t
Thyrolar (liotrix), 432t
Tiagabine, 362t
Ticlid (ticlopidine), 413t, 499t, 541t
Ticlopidine, 413t, 499t, 541t
Tigan (trimethobenzamide), 354t
Tilade (nedocromil sodium), 336t
Timolol, 320t, 508t, 541t
Tindal (acetophenazine), 391t, 514t, 526t
Tipramine (imipramine), 385t
Tips
  evacuation, 549t
  saliva ejector, 549t
Tissue contraction, 114–115
Tissue plasminogen activator, recombinant (rt-PA), 415t
Tizanidine, 369t
Tobacco, drug interactions, 91t, 254t
Tobacco-use cessation, 569–581
  adverse effects, precautions and contraindications, 577–579t, 580
  general drug information, 572–573t
  transdermal patches, dosage information, 575t
Tocainide, 5t, 311t, 511t, 520t, 541t
Tofranil (imipramine), 385t, 520t, 533t
Tolamide (tolazamide), 430t
Tolazamide, 430t, 501t, 541t
Tolbutamide, 430t, 501t, 506t, 511t, 541t
Tolcapone, 522t, 541t
Tolectin (tolmetin), 96t, 500t, 541t
Tolinase (tolazamide), 430t, 501t, 541t
Tolmetin, 500t, 541t
Tol-Tab (tolazamide), 430t
Tolterodine, 524t, 541t
Tometin sodium, 96t
Tom's Natural Baking Soda Toothpaste with Fluoride, 227t